Also by Jeanne Lowe

URBAN RENEWAL IN FLUX: THE NEW YORK CITY VIEW

MAN AND THE MODERN CITY (*co-editor*)

CITIES IN A RACE ▪ WITH TIME

Jeanne R. Lowe ■ ■ ■

CITIES IN

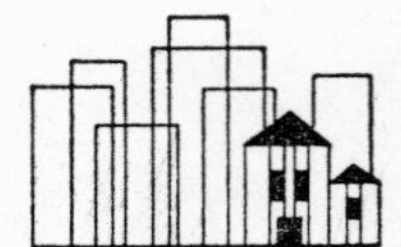

RANDOM HOUSE : New York

A RACE . . . WITH TIME

Progress and Poverty in America's Renewing Cities

TO MY FATHER

FIRST PRINTING

 Published in New York by Random House, Inc., and simultaneously in Toronto, Canada, by Random House of Canada Limited.
Library of Congress Catalog Card Number: 66–21478
Manufactured in the United States of America
by Vail-Ballou Press, Binghamton, New York.
Design by Leon Bolognese

Acknowledgments

This book would not have been possible without the interest and cooperation of hundreds of people, as well as many organizations and agencies, who over the years gave generously of their time, knowledge and resources, to my great benefit. From the inception of the idea for doing a book, through the many stages of research, writing and revisions, to the final tasks of editing and fact checking, I am grateful for the indispensable outside assistance and encouragement which accompanied its development. My debts are too numerous for complete or adequate mention. But I welcome this opportunity to record publicly my thanks and appreciation to those, among the many, who made particularly significant contributions.

My primary debt is to the several organizations whose support made it possible for me to undertake this work, most importantly the Avalon Foundation, whose generous grant enabled me to examine the subject at length, in depth and extensively at first hand. I am also indebted to the National Municipal League, which kindly afforded me office space and research facilities during the first year, and to the MacDowell Colony, where two long periods of residence provided the freedom of concentration necessary to commit a first draft to paper.

For their invaluable interest and professional support at critical stages in the book's evolution, I also wish to express my permanent personal gratitude to J. R. Cominsky, Andrew Heiskell, James E. Lash, Leo Molinaro, John P. Robin and Ordway Tead. Special thanks go to Eric Larrabee for editorial encouragement of my *Harper's* article, "Lee of New Haven," which turned out to be the germ of this book, and to Carey McWilliams, who got the book started with his suggestion that I write one and gave important initial help in this direction.

For their essential contributions to content, I am especially and doubly indebted to a number of people. These men and women, most of them central actors and movers in the events related in the book, not only shared unstintingly with me the fruit of their crucial experiences, aims, knowledge and insights during numerous interviews over the years. They also kindly undertook the time-consuming and important task of reviewing for accuracy of fact and interpretation of events portions of the manuscript for which they were major sources, and of making suggestions for corrections and clarification of points.

For this invaluable help, I wish to express my deep enduring thanks to John A. Bailey, James G. Banks, Edmund N. Bacon, Mary Small Carlson, Senator Joseph S. Clark, Gerald E. Finley, Walter S. Fried, Harold Grabino, John Grove, Howard Hallman, Theodore Hazlett Jr., Mary Hommann, Nathaniel S. Keith, Mayor Richard C. Lee, Edward J. Logue, William L. Rafsky, John P. Robin, Rep. James H. Scheuer, John R. Searles Jr., Chloethiel Woodard Smith, Roger L. Stevens, Mitchell Sviridoff, H. Ralph Taylor. William L. Slayton, another major source, was particularly generous in reviewing a considerable portion of the manuscript for substance. They all helped immeasurably; the errors, viewpoints and conclusions are mine.

To many other important sources who also allowed me to draw heavily on their first-hand knowledge, expertise and special resources in developing the substance of the book, I should like to express my great appreciation and thanks:

Gustave G. Amsterdam, Norris Andrews, L. Thomas Appleby,

Thomas Barringer, Harry G. Batten, George Bennett, Edwin C. Berry, Grace Bliss, Seon Pierre Bonan, Samuel R. Brooks, Karl S. Brown, Alice Brophy, William Cassella, Dennis Clark, Henry Cohen, Fern Colborn, Albert M. Cole, Edgardo Contini, Charles A. Cronheim, James Cunningham, Leonard Czarniecki, J. Clarence Davies Jr., William Day, former Mayor Richardson Dilworth, Cushing Dolbeare, Richard Dowdy, G. Franklin Edwards, Lester Eisner Jr., Paul Ertel.

Mario Fantini, W. H. Ferry, James Felt, Graham Finney, Ben Fischer, Margaret Fisher, James W. Follin, Carl Freese, Henry Fialkin, Marc Fried, Dorothy Gazzola, Walter Giesey, Richard Graves, Thomas H. Green, Albert M. Greenfield, Eunice and George Grier, Victor Gruen, Charles Grutzner, George Hallett, Gus Harvey, Ernest Henderson, Roger Herz, Herman Hillman, Perry Holmes, Charles J. Horan, William Howell, Stanley Isaacs (now deceased), Reginald Johnson, Fred Kramer.

James Lanigan, David L. Lawrence, former Governor but now deceased, Frances Levenson, Aaron Levine, Margaret Madden, Howard Mantel, Park Martin, Marie McGuire, Jack Meltzer, Anna S. Miller, Robert B. Mitchell, John Mitchell, Leo Molinaro, Dorothy S. Montgomery, Don Moore, Ralph Morhard, William O'Dwyer, former Mayor but now deceased, Frank O'Brion, John O'Shea, Robert B. Pease, Walter Phillips, Jan Puckett, Chester Rapkin, Samuel Ratensky, Ann M. Robert, Ira S. Robbins, Arthur Row, Robert H. Ryan.

Henry Saltzman, Marion Sameth, Wallace Sayre, Charles Shannon, Roger Shafer, Howard Stewart, Stephen G. Thompson, Charles Twyman, Arthur Van Buskirk, David Wallace, Walter E. Washington, Isadore Wexler, William L. C. Wheaton, William Wilcox, Louis Winnick, Elizabeth Wright, Paul Ylvisaker, Carrie Young, Joseph Zimmerman.

I am very grateful to Robert C. Doty, Robert Heilbroner and John H. Nixon for their critical reading of portions of the manuscript and for many beneficial suggestions for both form and content. My warmest thanks go also to Margaret L. Kaplan, who kindly labored over portions of the manuscript and made many valuable editorial contributions.

The book also benefited greatly from the substantive contributions of a number of other people who were good enough to read individual chapters and added their important knowledge to the detailed correction of fact and suggestions for content. For their help in this regard, I wish to express my appreciation to David B.

Carlson, Robert Dormer, Sylvan Kamm, John Maylott, Alan Rabinowitz, Roger Starr, Arthur Singer, Donald C. Wagner and G. Harold Welch.

The staff and resources of numerous public and private libraries aided significantly at many stages. I particularly wish to express my appreciation to Audrey Davies, head librarian of the Institute for Public Administration, for making important materials available to me, and for her sympathetic understanding of the need for re-researching.

For extensive, indispensable research assistance and enthusiasm, and for acting as a valued sounding board during the book's development, I am deeply grateful to Betty Ann Pudney. Linda Davis, Judith Greenfield and Elizabeth R. Hepner added much through their diligent research help, and Joseph W. Freeman kindly aided me in the preparation of the bibliography. I also wish to note particularly my thanks to Hugh Mields for his important cooperation and contributions.

My acknowledgments would not be complete without an expression of my appreciation for the many meaningful contributions of my editors, Jason Epstein and Alice E. Mayhew. In their interest, enthusiasm and patience, they went far beyond their obligations; through their sound criticisms and suggestions, they improved immeasurably the contents and clarity of the entire book.

Finally, to old friends and new, I wish to convey heartfelt thanks for the faith, help and understanding which meant so much during the long years of this work.

Contents

1. THE DEAD HAND OF THE PAST 3

■ *Urban Reconstruction: The Early Leaders*

2. THE MAN WHO GOT THINGS DONE FOR NEW YORK ✦ Robert Moses Tackles Slum Clearance 45

3. THE NEW COALITION ✦ Pittsburgh's Action Formula Saves a City 110

4. THE FRUSTRATING BUSINESS OF REBUILDING ✦ Redevelopment of Southwest Washington 164

■ *Emerging Social Problems*

5. "WHAT ABOUT THE PEOPLE?" ✦ Relocation from Southwest Washington 203

6. WHO LIVES WHERE ✦ Urban Housing and Discrimination 232

7. THE END OF THE LINE ✦ Race and Poverty in Cities 278

■ *More Comprehensive Approaches*

8. SURVIVAL THROUGH PLANNING ✦ Philadelphia's Style 313

9. WHAT URBAN RENEWAL CAN AND CANNOT DO ✦ New Haven Goes the Whole Route 405

■ *The Urban Landscape*

10. LOOKING BACKWARD AND AHEAD ✦ The Demands and Dilemmas of Being Urban in America 555

BIBLIOGRAPHY 579

INDEX 591

CITIES IN A RACE ▪ WITH TIME

1

THE DEAD HAND OF THE PAST ■

As almost every American knows, our cities are in serious trouble.

More and more the local problems of cities have become the major domestic problems of the nation and a challenge to national policies as well. For an ever greater portion of our rapidly expanding population—nearly three out of every four Americans—and of our economic activities, too, are concentrated in metropolitan regions. Our urban centers must function better if the country is to prosper and our people to live well. In the next two decades, of the expected 50,000,000 more people who will be living in America, four out of five will live in cities. As President John F. Kennedy stated in 1963, in his historic proposal for a Cabinet-level urban affairs department, "We will neglect our cities at our peril, for in neglecting them we neglect the nation."

But what can we do? And what must be done? We look either for ready, clear-cut cures or for handy villains. But there are none. We have only begun to face the extraordinarily complicated job of making our cities fit to live in and work in. The answers must come, as have the problems, from a bewildering number of sources. The problems themselves are open-ended, interacting and hard to identify. Some are rooted deep in the past; many originate far beyond the locus of the city where they have settled and must be dealt with, and in activities which seem unrelated to cities.

There is not only the visible mess we have inherited—vast areas built up in earlier eras—hastily, thoughtlessly, tastelessly, greedily constructed, or, even if once satisfactory, badly maintained over the years. Recently this neglect has been aggravated and urban obsolescence accelerated by enormous technological, social and economic changes which have been taking place at an unimagined pace in industry, on farms and in patterns of living.

Rising family incomes, expectations and living standards have made old central cities, and even some close-in suburbs, less acceptable to the large part of the population that has residential alternatives available. New methods of production and transportation make the city's form less workable. Its traditional basic functions are sucked away by shifts in population and changes in the organization of our economy, and new functions must be accommodated or created. Its facilities and services cannot meet the needs of untrained rural migrants who have little choice but to live in central cities. The problems of centuries-old racial discrimination, now concentrated in these urban cores, demand immediate solution. We must run to stand still.

But the private forces that built up our cities are commonly incapable alone of remolding them for new needs; government intervention and massive public spending are also required. However, our public institutions, too, are inadequate. Local government machinery and agencies have lagged far behind the current needs of cities and their citizens and new national trends.

Several other factors add to our confusion and to the complexity of this unaccustomed work of urban improvement: Even as we try to develop the *ways* to deal with accumulated urban decay and the recent societal changes which impinge on our cities, we must simultaneously define the *ends* of this recently recognized responsibility. Further, although the activity is peculiarly local, broad assistance (and even some prodding) is required from the federal government, as is action from the state legislatures, most of which are not attuned to urban needs. Moreover, this public activity calls for the closest participation of private forces which are often unprepared for, or reluctant to involve themselves in, such a risky partnership.

Yet a growing number of cities, assisted by federal programs and funds and new local leadership, have made important starts in this new direction. My purpose in this book is to report on some of the most noteworthy of these local beginnings during the past two decades, in a context that will relate their separate efforts and give meaning to the steadily expanding nationwide effort that is yet to come. Through their pioneering labors each, as we shall see, has added to our understanding of the tools which we have been using or will need as well as of the dimensions of the urban problem.

I have taken the case history approach to the subject of our cities for several reasons. First is the underlying belief that one can learn from the past and from others' experience. But beyond that, case histories seem to illustrate best the unique nature of the process in which we have become engaged. They indicate, better than do generalizations, the steadily growing number of people from various fields who must become actively involved—directly or indirectly—in setting urban goals and in finding the means to achieve them; they also exemplify the new roles to be played by leading local public actors and bodies. The cases also illustrate the kinds of forces, pressures and conflicts from inside as well as beyond a particular community with which those involved may have to contend. Many people must participate, and in achieving greater understanding one gains the first key to constructive involvement.

These case histories will show how and why local actions take shape; how, in the process of using the new tools, these pacesetting communities have by necessity developed new techniques and patterns of cooperative endeavor; how unexpected obstacles arise and are overcome—or at least are recognized. They also point up how strongly a local approach is ruled by each community's particular structure, style and past development. For cities and neighborhoods are not alike—as we well know.

At the same time, these local efforts and programs clearly reveal the need for cooperative federalism. They demonstrate that cities are not autonomous creatures which can shape their destinies alone. Rather, they are often buffeted by forces that they do not remotely comprehend, but to which they must nonetheless respond; and cities must look to outside help in order to realize local goals.

I have chosen the particular case histories in this book because each has been or still is influential as a pattern-setter and front-runner whose example has been studied and followed by other communities across the country. Each illustrates particularly well one or more of the several important elements in our new civic-business-public enterprise, even though some of these elements have been at least temporarily put aside. Indeed, we can learn from the inadequacies of these approaches, too.

To a large extent, the separate stories of these urban pioneers are presented chronologically and delineate stages in this new national effort. Taken together, however, they are both complementary and cumulative. With various modifications, the problems they encountered, the mistakes they made, the lessons they learned, the new tides they faced, the new tacks taken and approaches developed in response, have been or are repeated in city after city. Each program was regarded as the most advanced, hopeful or progressive at one point during these two decades; some have continued to be. But each encountered limitations or new problems and challenges as it moved ahead. Thus, by following these separate stories, the reader will gain greater understanding of the new terrain.

To act, often in the face of the unknown and unmapped, often bogged down by the heavy baggage of the past, but to try to learn and do better, is what the cities and people in this book have done—some with more sensitivity, imagination and apparent success than others. Only time will tell whether even the most "successful" have actually succeeded.

For in such a rapidly moving era as ours, observation shows that solutions tend to become outdated; in fact, in an urban society the solution of a problem in one area commonly creates new problems elsewhere. Thus this book does not pretend to offer solutions. There are, however, higher purposes and goals for cities and the nation to set and better ways of working toward them. We need courage to try and perhaps to be wrong. Hopefully, the stories of these cities will also suggest the local, business and national climates needed to let us do the best we can. America will become what its cities become, and this requires that the most inventive brains and talents work at this task, in and out of government, at all levels.

For, as we can readily surmise and shall soon see, the struggle of today's cities goes far deeper than improving their physical environment and social programs—though both are necessary—or even developing new instruments or forms. The real challenge we face goes to the very bedrock of our civilization: can our democracy innovate sufficiently to make a technically advanced urban society work well for man as well as for machine?

Americans have developed cities poorly in the past and have reacted to urban problems only in crisis. Even recent efforts at renewal and development leave much to be desired. Generally lacking community goals and positive standards as well as national or even state urban policies to guide us, and hobbled by outmoded ideology and dogmas, we have too often mistaken means for ends and repeated the errors of the past.

But now as we accelerate the job of making cities—old or new—more fit and as we pay the costly consequences of our careless past, it would profit us to inquire, first, where did we go wrong and why? The ability to do better in the future lies partly in comprehending the many-layered past on which we must build or rebuild.

PHASE ONE: EARLY IDEALS VERSUS ACTUAL PRACTICES

Many of America's urban problems began with the founding of this nation and with the schizophrenia that has dominated our thinking about cities since. The United States was conceived as a rural country, yet it became urban more rapidly than any other nation in history. Our country's founders failed to provide for this irreversible occurrence. We made our material progress at the expense of desirable communities.

The federal system was intended to govern widely scattered agricultural people living on the edge of a vast wilderness; the

Constitution established the respective roles of state and national governments. Cities were so few and unimportant that they were not even considered in the federal scheme. Rather they were left, by default, to the separate states, to be established as needed for the administration of their local affairs. The familiar problem of rurally dominated state and federal legislatures governing a steadily urbanizing nation was thus built into law—and it is one of the greatest problems we have faced since.

Add to this ill-suited legislative heritage our early national ideals as enunciated by Thomas Jefferson and intoned by an astonishing variety of Americans in following generations: that our democracy would endure and our government remain virtuous as long as we remained a nation of self-sufficient yeoman farmers, each manufacturing for his own needs; that such a nation could be perpetuated as long as there was open land—then unmeasured and apparently limitless; and that in such a society of rural freeholders, that government was best which governed least.

Jefferson's dislike of strong central government and bureaucracy was based on the oppression he had seen accompanying these forms in autocratic Europe. His dislike of cities—which was to become a strong American credo—emanated from his fear that propertyless workers could be too easily led by demagogues, as in the French Revolution. "Let our workshops remain in Europe," he advised our country. He also warned, "When we get piled up on one another in large cities, as in Europe, we shall become corrupted, as in Europe, and go to eating one another."

But a basic conflict between these ideals and the realities of our society was built in at the start. A democracy where opportunity was open to all was inevitably acquisitive and commercial, and destined to be urban, for cities are the seat of commerce. And it was here that the wisdom of the founding fathers failed them and us: they did not reckon with the tendency toward urbanization of the richly endowed new nation, nor did they consider the kinds of public controls, intergovernment relations, and community viewpoint that are required when people live and work close together in cities.

Yet even before the mid-nineteenth century, the great phenomenon of the United States—one more remarked upon then by European visitors than by American observers—was the rapid rate at which the new country was spawning cities in the wilderness, and this well before the great surge of urbanization which would accompany the technology of steam and mass production.

This early city-building was closely tied to the great American pastime of land speculation—another evil that Jefferson did not foresee, and one which began in his own times with the disposition of the public domain. The underfed national treasury was far more interested in obtaining the most revenues from the land than in using it properly; as most freeholders lacked cash to buy farms in the newly available western territories, the government sold millions of acres (which it had already divided up wholesale in gridiron patterns) to land companies that were organized for the specific purpose of reselling the land at a retail profit. Thus another conflict was built into our urban growth.

These absentee landowners early discovered that town lots—which were usually sold at auction by their agents in the big eastern cities—could be disposed of far more easily and profitably than farm acreage. Because land was one of the readiest sources of new wealth (thought not in the Jeffersonian sense of mixing one's labor with the soil), "town-planting" and booming quickly became enterprises in which almost anyone could and did engage. In the full flood of Jacksonian democracy, paper cities were laid out over forests, on sandhills and on open prairies. Scarcely a river mouth lacked a prospective town scheme—or penniless squatters trying to prove up claims. This was the first phase of city-building in the United States. It led to some very sloppy but enduring practices.

New American cities were private real estate speculations, designed to be populous beyond any foreseeable demand. The primary goal of their promoters, who were generally the "town fathers" as well, was to get rich quick from selling the land. Few of these ambitiously conceived, unsettled cities, however, had a real government. Their quick exploitation was more important to the principals than the community amenities—the public squares, churches and opera houses—that were drawn in on paper. In fact, the chief purpose of these plans, with uniform, numbered lots laid out by surveyors' rulers in the familiar easy gridiron, was to facilitate lot sales—often to absentee purchasers and speculators who never saw their holdings.

People never knew whether the town in which they had invested their savings might boom into another Chicago, thanks to natural forces or a sudden new development like the Erie Canal, or disappear into wilderness scrub. Why encourage spending on improvement? If one town scheme failed, one could try again elsewhere. Transportation arteries—turnpikes and canals as well as rivers—were regarded not so much as a way to serve or help shape these communities, but as a means to bring in more settlers and thus boom land values. Vastly inflated prices and then shattering collapses that had national economic repercussions were frequent in these speculative cities.

Such a tradition of new city development in the young United States persisted well into the twentieth century. But although they were commercial, careless, unfinished, at least these cities were open and not mean places. And where a land promotion succeeded or a river harbor thrived, a certain local pride, pleasing architecture and community style promised to develop.

PHASE TWO: STEAM AND RAIL CENTERS

But before our half-formed cities had had time to mellow and learn to govern themselves, the second, decisive phase of American city growth came with the end of the Civil War, which precipitated the long-delayed industrial revolution. For in spite of Jefferson, our factories could not remain in Europe. And now as cities grew from one decade to the next by the hundreds of thousands, everything happened at once.

Again we were unprepared—this time for the enormous centralizing forces of rail and steam, the brutalizing effects of unrestrained technology, and the basic human needs of the millions of ignorant European peasants whom we encouraged to emigrate so they might tend our machines and lay our rails. Nonetheless, it was in these few late-nineteenth-century decades, when the country coalesced into manufacturing centers and laissez-faire commercialism flourished in its cruelest form, that America's urban mold was set. Municipalities handed over their land and resources to private profit and exploitation, and our cities became the abused by-product of national industrial development.

Railroad tracks cut right through the middle of cities, often right on Main Street. They pre-empted beautiful river banks and lake fronts, and consumed acres of centrally located land with their switching yards and freight depots. Their grimy barn-like depots sprawled in the heart of the ugly, growing business cores. Their locomotives, as they chugged back and forth across town, cast soot over people and buildings. Office structures were dark and unadorned. No public gardens humanized the cities' centers.

In all the great cities, the industries that were making some men rich cast a blighting pall. The low-hanging cloud of coal smoke, the stench of stockyards, the slick of oil, the refuse of industry fouled the air and polluted the waters. The belching chimneys of the huge new mills dominated the urban landscape. Their smoke killed the beautiful shade trees on streets, stained once-bright brick and frame buildings. In public squares and backyards, grass and flowers withered. Even in fine residential neighborhoods, noisy factories gave owners little choice but to move away.

More than ever, growth was an urban end in itself. All across the country cities vied with one another for the greatest gains in population, since a big pool of cheap labor would attract new factories and in turn bring business to local stores and revenues to municipal coffers. The current urban philosophy was aptly summarized in 1871 by a spokesman for the Milwaukee Chamber of Commerce, one of the popular new local organizations being founded by merchants, bankers and realtors to organize their city's overtures to outside industry. "Commerce can make a city," he declared, "but manufacturing alone can make it great."

The first desperate need of the swelling flow of new immigrant workers was for housing—as cheap as possible and within walking distance of work. But having encouraged them to come to work in Chicago, Milwaukee or Cleveland, the factory owners and rail magnates and chambers of commerce let the newcomers find shelter for themselves. Supplying housing thus became the enterprise of a new breed of businessman—the slum landlords.

First these operators chopped up the interiors of deserted mansions into tiny one- or two-room apartments for whole families, and also rented unheated cellars and stables to the roofless poor.

Then they devised a more systematic form of housing America's new urban proletariat—the tenement, into whose cramped, insanitary and airless quarters families were squeezed at extortionate rents.

Space soon disappeared. Every available piece of land—rear lots, vacant side lots, even public squares—was covered by private enterprise with still more buildings. Tenements sprang up on block after full block, from front line to rear, and cheek by jowl with factories. In these close-packed tenement districts, districts which soon became known as slums, city services were minimal, sewerage systems primitive, the terror of disease ever-present. But because demand for worker housing always outstripped supply in these swollen cities, ingenious operators were able to pack still more people into already bursting tenements and to charge still higher rents for even less space. Families took in roomers to help pay the higher tariff, and the crowding grew worse.

Slums became a highly profitable form of real estate investment, with annual expected returns of 20 to 30 per cent. And as it became apparent that city land could be sweated even more intensively, the speculative value of these properties continued to rise. Since most of the slum dwellers were foreign-born, people generally assumed, and said, that slum conditions were caused by immigrants.

THE POWERFUL: LOCAL FAMILIES, POLITICAL "BOSSES" AND WASHINGTON

America's cities came to confirm the worst predictions of its anti-urban prophets, and nothing seemed capable of stemming this course. The idea of restricting private enterprise and its use of property went counter to the strong currents of the day. Besides, the powerful people were all profiting from the existing mode of city development.

The old prominent commercial families were the principal slum owners, having retained title to their inner-city land and properties when they moved out. Cities' new leading citizens, the industrial and rail magnates, were interested in national prizes and markets, not in the cities their enterprise was building. Their

Calvinist heritage equated prosperity with virtue, and poverty with lack of effort; and in fact, both the magnates and the nation's economy prospered mightily. Civic responsibility was not part of their credo. Such favors as they required of local government could be obtained easily from legislators and bosses who were in their pay. Occasionally a civic-minded citizen would cry out against his community's handing its best natural assets over to the railroads. But cities were so dependent on rail for their economic health that such protests were naturally ignored.

The main local privilege-seekers and corrupters, those who sought and won municipal franchises and contracts to perform profitable public tasks in these burgeoning cities—to provide lighting, gas and public transportation, to dig sewers and pave streets—and behind them local bankers and lawyers, formed rings with the politicians to share in the apparently unending municipal bounty. It was generally accepted in America then, as now, that private enterprise could do things better than government. Indeed, the untrained party faithful whom the Jacksonian spoils system had placed in City Hall were completely overwhelmed by the sudden new public needs. With the publicly admired tactics of business as their example, and the invocation of free enterprise as their license, local so-called leaders in business and government began devouring their cities.

Taxpayers had to pay prices for municipal services that were vastly inflated by the boodling and grafting of these rings, and had to do without many services that were not profitable to someone. But in spite of flagrant corruption, scandals and public squalor, the unholy alliance of city government and local business interests was perpetuated by the voters. For the bosses and aldermen, many foreign-born themselves, served the mass of exploited, helpless workers so well—providing them with a form of social security and unemployment relief in return for their votes—that the voters continually re-elected the machine men. If state governments reined in their municipal wards, it was generally so the legislators might obtain a larger share of the local prizes.

What of Washington? The national trend to cities was clear by the 1890 census. And this urban move was not just from foreign shores, but also from American small towns and farms. Manufacture had already migrated from streams and cottages to stream centers, and as agricultural productivity tripled with the use of new tools, farmers' sons were free to strike out from the dreary dull land for the new job opportunities in cities.

One might argue that the federal government believed it was benefiting cities with the substantial stimulants it provided to private industry. Traditionally the national scene was divided by our government into agricultural and industrial spheres, not rural and urban, and cities were certainly growing with industry. But although federal aids to agriculture promoted the general welfare of the rural population, the assistance to manufacture tended to benefit the favored few out of all proportion to the mass of city dwellers, and to the detriment of desirable community development. There simply was no city sense in the government. Nor, if there had been, would federal interference in local affairs have been acceptable in the country's philosophy.

In the one area where Washington could have wielded direct and powerful local control over land use and urbanization, in its disposition of the public domain, it had been derelict from the start. Then, starting in the 1850's, it had actually encouraged a repetition of all the early evils, on a far grander scale, with its transportation policy: chartered railroad companies were given huge portions of the nation's open land and the resources below as an inducement to lay tracks across the vast empty West.

Since serving these underpopulated stretches promised the rail companies no ready profit, and since most of them even lacked the capital to build the tracks, they first tried to make money from the free gift of land. Again town-making—to boom land values—was the principal order of business. Through their placement of rail depots, they used their exceptional position to create or to break cities.

Town lots in railroad-developed cities, among them Omaha and Duluth, were advertised for mail-order sale in eastern newspapers, with promises of great speculative gains. Meanwhile, along the tracks' advancing front, town planting and booming was reduced to a wholesale, point-of-purchase system. Inevitably wild land trading and speculative price increases accompanied announcement of a new division point. But several months later, when the depot was pulled up and moved on to create another temporary rail town further on, the land bubble would burst and another ghost town would dot the plains.

The few towns in the Far West, among them San Francisco and Los Angeles, the latter a sleepy Spanish town of 7,000, were forced by the predatory rail companies to float large bond issues, to hand over terminal and harbor rights, free rights of way, acres of valuable land for depots—in fact, to pay for what the government charter charged the company to do. For towns, the fate of being "off the tracks" was far worse, however. Most tiny settlements had visions of becoming a thriving rail metropolis.

"Must they be permitted to ruin the towns and enhance their own lots?" demanded Senator Harlan, a lone voice of protest in Washington's "Millionaires' Club," the name then given to the Senate. He was ignored. Most senators and congressmen were getting rich on railroad land and securities.

The city in America came to be regarded as an economic necessity—the place to make one's living or a fortune, not to live the good life. Successive evacuation of inner-city neighborhoods by more prosperous citizens for somewhat greener, quieter and more healthful settlements a little further out—typically land promotions of the burgeoning streetcar or traction companies—became a commonplace of the American urban scene. So, too, did the crowding into these deserted older districts by the growing poor, as slum operators took over and converted absentee-owned properties. Immigration of peasants from backward or oppressive Eastern and Southern European nations continued unabated.

The price of building the nation's industrial plant and transportation grid without providing for the inevitable urban side-effects and needs was high—and would prove higher yet. From now on, the discouraging and often futile struggle would be to remove from cities the dead hand of the past.

PHASE THREE: A SURGE OF REFORM

In fact, hard on the heels of these excesses there came a new phase in American city development, the short-lived but historic surge of municipal reform. By the turn of the twentieth century, organized efforts on the part of the growing urban middle class to reform city governments, to beautify cities, to improve workers' housing and to uncrowd tenements, even to "settle" with the poor, were widespread. These separate movements are now as important for what their oversimplified "solutions" failed to accomplish as for what they initiated. Both sides of the coin left their imprint, even on the present.

City planning was launched by the "City Beautiful" forces, its particular form dramatized by the beaux-arts style Columbian Exposition of Chicago in 1893. As a result, some overdue amenities adorned cities—classic monuments and museums, tree-lined boulevards, and circles to soften the harsh gridiron. But this movement, promoted mainly by commercial clubs and architects, failed to broaden its concern to urban social problems, such as housing; nor, with the exception of Chicago, did the plans consider transportation. Improvements were often carried out at excessive public expense and with scandalous profiteering—Chicago being the prime example. In most cities, the costly "frills and furbelows" did not get beyond the planners' expensive bound volumes due to lack of mass support, adequate public powers and funds. Thus city planning was triply discredited at its birth and languished for a generation, reviving only briefly during that time as the handmaiden of private land speculation.

The housing reformers were successful, in some one hundred cities, in achieving passage of codes that applied cities' police powers to the enforcement of higher building standards in new tenements or to the improvement of existing slum housing. Yet the codes failed to make a significant dent in the slum problem. Both new and repaired tenements were soon overcrowded, as poorly paid workers could ill afford the higher rents for improved housing. In fact, the demand for urban shelter continued to exceed the supply, and wages never advanced as rapidly as rents. (Low labor costs were a major selling point of local chambers of commerce to new industry.)

Nor did the tenement house reformers recognize that the necessary corollary of reducing over-occupancy, the most elusive slum condition, was to increase the supply of decent city housing at rents low enough for the worker. A few millionaire philanthropists produced such projects by accepting a limited return on their investment, but more pillars of local society were interested in the handsome income they derived from slums.

Most politicians were singularly uninterested in the enforcement of housing occupancy codes or other statutes which would reduce the number of voters in their district. The main advantage they could see in these new laws was helping a landlord subvert them for a payoff. Corruption of the new building departments was soon notorious. Nor could the settlement house workers, as good as their intentions were, cope with the most urgent needs of their slum neighborhoods. Although they could run free kindergartens and concerts and successfully press for legislation to end sweatshops, they could not provide people with jobs or pay their rents, as could the politicians.

The "good government" people, the other main urban reform force, were remarkably successful, too, in passing laws—for example, laws designed to activate the average voter and thus eliminate machine control of local government by simplifying electoral procedures. Yet they failed in their ultimate objectives, mainly because they were more concerned with the mechanics than the purposes of city government; they naïvely ignored the economic and legal roots of municipal corruption and the machine's perpetuation.

Moreover, the most powerful businessmen were either uninterested in reform or opposed to it. Those local leaders who did back reform or pressed, later on, for the adoption of businesslike methods of scientific management and efficiency in public affairs too often saw these improvements not as avenues to serving city dwellers better, but as ways of reducing the cost of local government and thus cutting their own taxes. But since the mass of voters needed more government spending, not less, to provide them with services, such middle-class "good government" proposals had little popular appeal, and the new laws soon proved relatively ineffective in curbing machines. The bosses were shrewd. They soon learned that "respectable" mayors would both appease the reformers and front for the machine. As a result, disillusion with government reform, too, became commonplace.

Basically, the city reformers still mistrusted urban government. They saw it at best as a regulator, not as a leading co-participant.

They still believed that the profit motive alone, mildly curbed by the police power, was sufficient for most civic jobs. It was the rare reformer who attempted to change causes or the underlying system by removing the special law-given private privileges which encouraged leaders to milk their community instead of developing it. And such reformers were given short shrift by the odd but effective state alliance of rural representatives, big city business and rail interests that controlled the legislatures from which municipal powers derived, or by the conservative courts.

Municipal corruption did become less flagrant as the twentieth century advanced. But this was in good part because municipal prizes had become far less rewarding. The major offenders, the traction companies, were already shaky from over-capitalization and decades of speculative building. Now, as the automobile began to scatter their customers beyond the radius of a profitable run (often streetcar rails had been laid only in hope of attracting new residents to their land rather than to serve existing customers), they were going into receivership and were trying to sell back their municipal franchises.

Meanwhile, the new revenues to be collected from the vehicles owned by an auto-borne, metropolitanizing population were placed beyond the grasp of the still-suspect municipal politicians, as well as the limited geographic reach of city governments. Such revenues were put in the hands of the state or of the versatile new state-created, limited-purpose corporations known as public authorities, which gained popularity in the 1920's with business leaders and political scientists. States even appropriated receipts from the gas tax. Cities were left with the non-revenue-producing or loss operations. They had to provide traffic control facilities and police, maintain heavily used streets and sacrifice curb space for parking. But they had an inadequate property tax base to pay for these and other emerging needs.

Not until the depression would city dwellers begin to feel the almost revolutionary benefits of the federal income tax, an advanced measure which had been enacted back in 1912 with little fanfare because few realized its potential. Then, in the 1930's, the New Deal provisions for welfare assistance, unemployment insurance and social security further undermined the old style of municipal politics by reducing the dependence of many poor city voters on the charity of the local machines. But this is getting ahead of our story.

Performance of municipal tasks was already becoming professionalized, as were many private occupations, and thus many political faithfuls were ineligible for the public payroll. But equally important, the urban electorate was far more educated and thus less easily led. Indeed, probably the most effective turn-of-the-century social reform emerged largely in response to American business' need for more skilled and educated workers as its operations became more complex and office work grew. That reform was the establishment of tuition-free high schools and laws of compulsory attendance. Paralleling these trends, the urban middle class—white-collar workers, bank clerks, salesmen, corporation executives—doubled and redoubled.

NEW GROWTH, NEW BLIGHT AND ZONING

What finally weakened these intense drives to embellish and reform cities were World War I, prosperity and technological advances. Along with the latter came major new forms of urban development and another layer of troubles.

As structural steel came into use, city centers shot upward. Skyscrapers housed the multiplying office functions, and a new phenomenon appeared—luxury elevator apartments for the non-suburban well-to-do. Meanwhile, the mass-produced motor car spread most of the new middle class outward. These trends were accompanied by intense speculation and insidious new blight.

Market prices of downtown properties rose continually, based largely on the more dense and profitable *future* use of land which seemed promised by skyscraper and apartment house construction, rather than on the actual value or current income of these properties. The financing behind many of these high-rise structures was also thin and speculative, as was the general prosperity—which time would soon reveal.

But realtors (and evidently bankers) could see no end to the increase in city land values. "There must always be a business center, and it can collect what the traffic will bear . . . ," stated the authors of an investment primer, *City Growth and Values*, published in the mid-1920's and endorsed in its introduction by the National Association of Real Estate Boards. City assessors went along with the bull real estate market. They pegged property valuations at these high levels, hypothetical as they were, to boost the local tax base.

Beyond the cities' fringes, land speculators bought up thousands of acres of inexpensive farm land which city workers could now reach easily by automobile; they cut them up into gridiron pattern subdivisions that were as over-optimistic and unsettled as the paper towns of the 1830's had been. Outside Chicago, enough land was subdivided in one year to house the projected metropolitan population for 1960. One town of 9,000 boasted sufficient vacant lots for a city of 190,000. Credit was easy, and lending institutions did a land-office business; they let new homeowners put themselves into debt over their ears and take out expensive second mortgages to cover the short terms of their first home loan. Less well-off lot purchasers merely put up hand-built shacks. The better new subdivisions were complete residential developments—incorporating improved street design and, commonly, restrictive covenants—in exclusive suburbs separated jurisdictionally from the central cities to which their golf-playing residents commuted.

Much of the extravagant municipal over-bonding of the decade was designed to lure these new satellites into central cities with the promise of needed public facilities and services, or perhaps to help a politically favored private subdivider. Meanwhile, between the prosperous auto suburbs and downtown business districts, recently elegant residential avenues were turned into fume-filled motor thoroughfares, dotted with gas stations and decorated with billboards. Traffic jams at rush hours began to be ominous.

The one public planning control that really took hold at this time was zoning. But this promising new tool, instead of protecting cities from the rampant commercialism of the day, became its servant—with the help of city-powered bodies. It was common for the boards that administered a local zoning code to use it for placating or promoting special business and property interests, and to preserve or create new and often false land values, rather than to regulate and direct building practices and land uses with zoning for the benefit of the whole community.

One of the worst abuses perpetrated with this new instrument was over-zoning—a term applied by planners in the 1930's to describe the irresponsible and widespread practice in the 1920's of designating far more land or space for a future, more profitable use than could possibly be employed by a community in the foreseeable future.

New York's pioneer zoning ordinance of 1916 set the example. Its residential zoning allowance, if filled, would have permitted 55,000,000 people to be crowded legally into the city's five boroughs. Many cities zoned up to 600 per cent more land for commercial use than was currently thus used. Such a "higher" use meant that when and if increased demand for office or retail space warranted the change from residential use, the land owners would receive a greater return on their property, and the city would receive more taxes. Zoning and planning boards were apparently undeterred by the fact that, since cities' business centers were shooting up and not out, such a designated change would probably not occur for another five or six centuries. Meanwhile they planted the seeds of future blight throughout the hearts of cities.

Architecturally, zoning changed—and then in effect froze—downtown building shapes into look-alike forms as each owner strove to gain maximum use and income from his land under the new restrictions. And there were inevitably epidemics of overbuilding under old laws as developers tried to get new buildings "under the line" before new zoning regulations took effect.

Cities further damaged themselves with zoning in efforts to placate industry. Older residential neighborhoods that had some factories were zoned completely for such a use. The result of such designations, here as in over-zoned commercial areas, were bank blackouts on home mortgages and loans in those neighborhoods. Also, residential property was neglected by owner-investors who could see little profit in maintaining a building which might soon be replaced by a new and more profitable land use.

Predictably, politicians found in this new municipal code one more device for winning constituents' gratitude. Zoning boards of appeal were kept busy granting variances to the official ordinances, to help favored interests.

Even at best, zoning was a negative control. It might designate the limits to which private enterprise could build, and it did prevent some gross over-building. But it could not force private enterprise to build where there was not the hope of reasonable profits. Indeed, the tall new luxury apartment houses often looked down on neighboring decaying slum buildings—whose owners were waiting for a "higher," more intense use of the land. Zoning could neither cope with the invasion of cities by automobiles, nor alter poor land uses inherited from the past. Cities needed much stronger powers and more public tools than the climate of the day would allow.

THE NEW DEAL: A NEW ERA FOR CITIES BEGINS

The climate changed markedly—and far sooner than one could have anticipated—as the shaky urban house of cards suddenly collapsed along with the private economy. The great depression presented, almost accidentally, the breakthrough situation that allowed radical new instruments of cooperative urban reconstruction to develop and a new era for American cities to begin.

The start of this new era was a confused one, however, both in programs and in philosophy. This was so because the development during the 1930's of some of the most important current tools, principally government-assisted or subsidized housing and slum clearance programs, was bound up with the failures and recovery of the private economy, rather than with a specific concern for the problems of cities. Indeed, a big part of the urban problem we have inherited from the past is the *ad hoc* mixture of legislative measures and agencies which have been accumulating since depression days; these need to be related and reoriented to the problems of today's cities and their residents. The evolution of these tools was nearly as pragmatic as the urban centers they have been employed to help renew—and this fact is very germane to the current struggles. Yet, without the depression we might not have even such instruments.

The crash brought to an abrupt end the long era of governmental localism and the unquestioned primacy of private development, out of sheer necessity. Cities were broke. Many, unable to amortize bonds floated so extravagantly in recent days, and suffering from speculative developments, faced bankruptcy. Local revenues had shriveled up almost overnight as real estate values plummeted from artificial heights to hundred-year lows. People out of work could not pay bank loans or taxes; 1,000,000 homeowners were in default. Owners demolished buildings in the recently booming downtowns to avoid taxes. New construction came to a halt.

Cities were forced to cut back essential services and abandon others. But one service which they could not slough off and which grew increasingly burdensome was poor-relief, a traditional local responsibility. Private charity had already proved incapable of feeding the steadily increasing number of unemployed and their families. Cities built up by private industries now attempted to compensate for the latter's failure as factories across the country shut down.

For the first time in the country's history city populations fell, as those who could returned to small towns and farms. Even slums thinned out. But bread lines continued to grow as more men lost their jobs. Limited local resources were stretched thinner. Toledo, Ohio cut municipal food allotments to 2.14 cents a person per day. Its despairing Mayor voiced a widely held new belief: "We of the cities have done our best, but we have failed miserably."

States, however, were not in a much better position. Only the federal government, with its unlimited borrowing power and its ability to act and tax nationally, could deal with this "local" problem. As the new national administration in Washington stepped into the void, not only localism but also the days of little government came to an end.

Government was no longer just a big policeman, restraining private excesses. It now had a positive role and a major responsibility to act where others had failed in order to revive the economy. Men had to be put back to work and money put into circulation.

It was a time of fact-gathering and searching for causes and cures. A new spirit of experimentation and community endeavor emerged. Many programs never before acceptable in America were suddenly put into practice by government as temporary work-relief measures. Direct dealings were initiated between Washington and municipal governments. Cities, with few exceptions, were willing to accept any federal aid. (Washington even paid municipal salaries so that basic local services such as fire and police could be continued.) In the process, the new national leadership and federal funds led cities into accepting responsibilities they had long ignored. This new cooperative federalism and some of the new joint activities became permanent national programs.

SLUM CLEARANCE AND PUBLIC HOUSING

Government-financed slum clearance for low-rent public housing was one of these measures—the first radical instrument obtained by cities to deal with their long-standing, seemingly insoluble problems of slums and decent dwellings for low-income families. This pioneer program also proved to be the pathbreaker for the development of other major urban tools of today.

By the late 1920's the housing reformers had become convinced that restraining police power alone would never eliminate slums, and that government must employ other fundamental, more positive powers—especially eminent domain and public funds—to acquire and demolish slum buildings, as was being done in some European countries, and to finance construction of government-owned and operated low-cost housing for poor slum dwellers.

Such a public undertaking was, of course, regarded by many as socialistic and un-American, and under ordinary circumstances would have been resisted. But housing groups found the opportunity to press for a trial of this bold new approach as one of the many multi-purpose experimental projects carried out under the Works Progress Administration.

In just a few years, acres of generations-old city tenements were knocked down, and government-paid workers had put up clean and airy projects that housed many thousands of families.

But the constitutionality of the federal government's use of eminent domain to put up housing for low-income families had been challenged by the courts in 1935, and slum clearance for housing was not proving to be as quick a pump-primer as other public works. It might have fallen by the wayside, along with other less effective WPA emergency employment programs, had not cities been required to gather some facts about their slum areas as a prerequisite to obtaining federal housing projects.

The findings of the local surveys of the mid-1930's made slum clearance and public housing a cause for persons other than just the socially concerned or the new public housing officials. By measuring the slum problem in terms of the dollar cost of these conditions to city government, as well as by indices of physical decay and accompanying social ills in slum areas, the surveys established slum clearance as an issue understandable and compelling to city officials and some local businessmen, as well as to the federal government.

Surveys in one city after another showed that populous slum neighborhoods required disproportionate municipal outlays for fire and police protection, crime prevention, health and other public services, compared to the low revenues their deteriorated properties paid the city, and to the relative costs of other neighborhoods. Cities' slums, it seemed, were being subsidized by the rest of their taxpayers, especially by the central business district which paid the highest taxes. It appeared that clearing these areas would relieve cities' (and downtown business interests') fiscal straits, lighten the general local tax burden, and wipe out the social ills which slums harbored.*

The key legal issue in public housing revolved around the use of eminent domain. This local power had previously been applied to projects which were for use by the general public. The low-rent projects, however, would be available only to people with certain minimum incomes. But the case made by the slum surveys was sufficiently strong to validate the public-benefit concept in localities exercising eminent domain to wipe out such costly disease and crime-producing areas and to put up on these sites low-cost housing (the two phases being tied together in practice and by the early court decisions) for those whom the private market could not serve decently. In state after state, enabling legislation allowing localities to undertake this new activity was passed and was cleared by the courts.

* Time would reveal that the cause-effect relationship which was drawn by the depression-time slum surveys between the bad physical environment of slums and their social ills and costs was tenuous. By the late 1950's, this slum syllogism would contribute to a growing disillusionment about public housing.

Facts were also gathered for the first time about the condition of the nation's shelter and pointed the way to public housing and slum clearance becoming a permanent federal aid program. These surveys, also conducted as a relief project, found that one third of the nation's housing was substandard, and that the one third of the nation who were poor were generally the occupants of these dwelling units. Slums, so long considered a local, city problem were clearly a threat to the general welfare. (Many were in rural areas, too.)

With the newly liberal Congress that was elected in 1936 and the Supreme Court's broadened definition, in 1937, of the federal responsibility for the public welfare, the way appeared clear and the purpose justified for using federally collected income taxes to help financially disabled cities to eliminate this omnipresent evil.

The Housing Act of 1937, the first permanent government subsidy program for housing in the nation's history, made this new federal concern explicit. In the Act's preamble, Congress declared that the shortage of decent dwellings for families whose incomes were so low that private industry could not meet their needs was "injurious to . . . the nation," and that the provision of housing for this group was a federal responsibility. It also declared the elimination of slums to be a national goal.*

This new public endeavor was to be a cooperative effort—carried out by localities with federal financial aid and regulation. Washington would give or lend to municipal housing authorities, at low government interest rates, up to 90 per cent of the capital costs of clearing a slum and developing a project for low-income families (they were no longer called "the poor"). Once these housing projects were in operation, however, they would have to be self-sustaining and pay, out of rents received from tenants, the costs of their operation and of the services received from the city, the latter sum to be paid in lieu of taxes. (Interestingly, this sum was generally greater than revenues collected by cities from the former slum properties.)

* A slum was defined in the 1937 Act as "any area where dwellings predominate which, by reasons of dilapidation, over-crowding, faulty arrangement or design, lack of ventilation, light or sanitation facilities, or a combination of these factors are detrimental to safety, health and morals."

The rent was determined by a family's size and ability to pay. Generally this amount did not exceed one fifth of the income. Once the family could afford private housing, however, it would have to leave the project and make way for other needier families.

The 1937 Act was a giant step forward. "For the first time in a hundred years the slums of America ceased growing and began to shrink," Nathan Straus, first administrator of the United States Housing Agency, exulted several years later. By 1941, public housing projects already sheltered some 200,000 people.

But it was becoming apparent that the big new program provided only a limited answer. For one thing, the public subsidy was tied to slum housing elimination, rather than to the production of enough decent low-cost housing to eliminate the market for and private profit from slums. Had city slums not started to empty out during the depression years, and had the real estate industry not been prostrate then, perhaps even this bill might not have passed. Once the private economy picked up, the shelter industry's opposition to the public housing program intensified. (Even so, the 1937 Act had compromised with real estate interests by leaving a profitable "20 per cent gap" between the incomes of families eligible for low-rent public housing and incomes needed to afford decent private rentals.) Moreover, due to the Act's strictures and its failure to insist on desirable city planning as a prerequisite, new government-subsidized housing was being built in many places where dwellings should not have been built originally. Equally important, it was obvious that cities could not be rebuilt with just public housing.

URBAN REDEVELOPMENT: PRIVATE SPONSORSHIP AND GOVERNMENT WRITE-DOWN

By the late 1930's the need of cities for broader, more flexible powers of land acquisition and re-use concerned a number of rather disparate groups.

Business interests, particularly downtown property owners and realtors, wanted a clearance and rebuilding program that would be on a more "economic" basis—that would allow private entrepreneurs to participate as developers; permit re-uses other than public housing, especially in centrally located former slum areas; and let cities reap the higher tax returns which private developments promised. Equally important, these interests had come to accept the fact that in order to assemble land for feasible rebuilding, local government's power of eminent domain would be required to eliminate hold-out prices.

Meanwhile, means for rehabilitating deteriorated city housing were being explored by architects and planners and by opponents of government-subsidized slum clearance and housing. The most popular proposals were for private, voluntary fix-up of slum properties by the owners of buildings within a designated area. Special loans to help owners to carry out the work were also suggested. These proposals were actually tested in very few places, however, and where they had been tried, such lack of interest and action was displayed by those whose cooperation was most needed—the banks, insurance companies and other key lending institutions, who seemed only to care about the highest rate of return from a property on which they held a mortgage—that it became evident that force would be required. But whether even public force would achieve significant, area-wide housing rehabilitation was questionable, since the ownership pattern in such districts was riddled with faulty titles and absentee or deceased owners. Planners believed that it would make more sense to clear poorly built residential areas instead of trying to fix them up. So these varying groups came to believe that rebuilding, preceded by the use of eminent domain, was necessary to cut the ties of slum ownership.

Government itself had also begun to do some broader thinking about cities and their needs. The main federal agency to address itself to urban matters was the National Resources Planning Committee. Its overall task was to provide a framework for the federal government's enlarged role in the economic life of the country. Having studied the farm plight thoroughly, the planning body then brought together the country's leading city planners, economists and local government experts to undertake the first official inquiry into the problems of the urban community in the United States.

A major point made in the landmark, but sadly neglected, 1937 publication of the Urbanism Committee, *Our Cities—Their Role in the National Economy*, was that the mess in American cities was much more than a housing problem. It stated that tumble-down industrial districts, deteriorated central business areas, old structures made obsolete by new technology—all these and other poor, inappropriate or outmoded land uses of the past —undermined urban vitality, as did residential slums, and must be altered. Devices for changing such obsolete urban land uses and for guiding their improvement were among the many far-sighted proposals in the report.

The concepts forwarded by these variously oriented groups soon found common ground under the name of urban redevelopment, which was to become the second of the important new tools cities would have for rebuilding. The redevelopment formula, as generally understood, was to use eminent domain to acquire and clear slum or blighted land which would be sold to private enterprise for rebuilding under public controls. Redevelopment had gained sufficient currency by 1943 for eleven states to have passed the necessary enabling legislation. The courts, in general approving it, viewed the public purpose or benefit of such city rebuilding as similar to that of public housing—the elimination of slums and the prevention of slum conditions which breed crime, disease and other social ills—and offered little opposition.

But there was very little action under these state laws alone. They did not recognize the other apparently major obstacle to urban redevelopment: the high and generally inflated value of slum land. It appeared that unless these costs were reduced, not only would redevelopment not take place; worse yet, if it did, it would lead to a repetition of the very land crowding and high residential densities which had plagued cities from the past; for developers would have to absorb this cost and would try to make their usual expected profit.

How to overcome this problem in order to achieve desirable urban rebuilding became the concern of two Federal Reserve economists, Alvin Hansen and Guy Greer, who developed and set forth, in a monograph issued in 1941, the seminal concept of a government "write-down" on slum land. This was the program of federal loans and grants to cities for urban redevelopment which emerged as Title I of the Housing Act of 1949. Since this write-down has been the cause of considerable public confusion and misunderstanding, it would be useful to look at the reasoning behind it.

Hansen and Greer proposed that in publicly designated blighted areas the government should absorb the difference in price between acquiring the built-up slum and that of the cleared land, priced at its real earning power when rebuilt; and this deflated but realistic cost would be made the price of the cleared land when it was sold to the private developer. His rebuilding of the site would be controlled by federally approved city plans for its re-use.

The economists recognized that this redevelopment write-down from current to real market value might be regarded as a bail-out of the owners of slum properties and the lending institutions that held the mortgages. But they maintained that this was not the issue, that the social and economic mess in American cities was the fault of so many public and private groups—indeed, of society as a whole—that society should pay the price of cleaning it up. The write-down would be, as Greer put it, a "down-payment on a new start for cities," to let them rebuild better than in the past.

The economists maintained that federal assistance to cities for the broad-scale land re-use program they envisioned was not only appropriate, but also essential. For one thing, cities were so heavily in debt that they could not assume the full cost of land purchase and property clearance, either by floating bonds or by direct allocations from local revenues. Further, as had been made clear by the Urbanism Committee in *Our Cities*, more than half of the nation's population now lived in cities that were also the seat of the nation's productive output. Thus a majority of the nation was affected by these detrimental and widespread conditions, and the very welfare of the country's economy was at stake.

Hansen and Greer also went beyond a new urban land use program. They, like the Urbanism Committee, proposed creation of a new federal agency to administer this program, one with the same relation to the urban economy that the Department of Agriculture had to the rural economy. They also urged that the proposed new federal aids be given on a metropolitan basis, and that local plans include housing and transportation plans as a prerequisite.

But such advanced proposals for redevelopment, federal aid to cities, a national urban agency, and even national resources planning, fell by the wayside as the country moved from recovery and social pioneering into World War II and a new congressional conservatism.

SENATOR TAFT'S VERSION: THE HOUSING ACT OF 1949

When urban redevelopment did receive serious consideration by Congress, it was under the aegis of a postwar employment subcommittee on housing headed by Senator Robert A. Taft of Ohio. Taft was the chief architect of Title I of the Housing Act of 1949, and his narrow construction of the new federal urban aid program, as incorporated in the Housing Act, proved to be one of the big stumbling blocks to redevelopment.

Although basically a conservative, Taft had a deep conviction that government was responsible in three areas of public welfare: health, education and housing. He was, curiously enough, one of public housing's most ardent advocates and believed there was a clear constitutional precedent, under the New Deal-broadened general welfare clause, for an additional federal subsidy to help cities eliminate and redevelop slum and blighted areas with privately built housing. But he did not agree that the federal government was responsible for helping cities rebuild their economic base or readjust poor urban land uses with the proposed "write-down," as planners and some business groups were arguing it should. The Senator conceived of redevelopment basically as a supplement to the earlier slum clearance and low-income housing program, designed to encourage private participation in rebuilding with housing priced for middle-income familes.

Debate over whether federally aided redevelopment was to be used as a housing or a city rebuilding program was intense in the Taft Committee hearings, as it was later between various federal agencies that wanted to administer it. Finally the issue had to go to the White House for resolution. Unfortunately, the complex measure received little public attention; everyone was too busy adjusting to peace. But it was clear that housing had the political leverage.

Thus, when urban redevelopment became a two-thirds federal aid program in Title I of the Housing Act of 1949, the law specified that use of the new government funds for helping cities reduce land costs in designated project areas was to be limited to deteriorated or deteriorating areas that were "predominantly residential" in their original use or would be in their re-use.

Under the write-down formula of this new cooperative undertaking, the federal government would absorb two thirds the net project cost.* The city's one-third contribution could be made either in cash or in an equivalent worth of such new public facilities as were needed to realize the redevelopment plan.

Like public housing, urban redevelopment was a compromise, with built-in conflicts. The new Division of Slum Clearance and Urban Redevelopment was placed under the Housing and Home Finance Agency, a new federal umbrella which encompassed other federal housing and slum clearance programs. Although federal aid for city rebuilding has been greatly broadened in scope since 1949, and an urban department now exists, the public still mistakenly regards redevelopment and its later outgrowths as a housing program.

Indeed, as if to confuse both public and program further, Con-

* The net project cost was the difference between what a city had to pay for acquiring slum or blighted properties, clearing the site and providing the necessary service facilities and street changes for the area when rebuilt, and the smaller amount recovered by the city from selling the cleared land to a private redeveloper.

The resale price was to be determined by independent appraisers on the basis of the official re-use plan, which was to guide the rebuilding. (The original purchase price was determined by the usual appraisal methods for city real estate, and could be appealed in court if the owner felt a condemnation award was too low.)

To be eligible for federal redevelopment aid, a project site had to be a "slum area or a blighted, deteriorated or deteriorating area."

A designated Title I area had to receive the approval of a city's planning commission and its top legislative body, generally the city council. The latter body had to approve acquisition of property in the project area, following public hearings on it, before federal grants were advanced. A new federal administrative agency, the Division of Slum Clearance and Urban Redevelopment disbursed the funds and had to give its approval at a number of points along the way.

gress introduced urban redevelopment in the very statute—the Housing Act of 1949—where, for the first time, it declared a National Housing Policy: "the realization as soon as feasible of the goal of a decent home and a suitable living environment for every American family." Redevelopment would, of course, be a necessary instrument in the achievement of this ambitious general housing goal, as well as in carrying out the specific intent of Congress, stated in the 1949 Act, that "private enterprise should be encouraged to serve as large a part of the total needs as it can."

The trouble was that Congress failed to provide adequate housing tools to accompany private redevelopment. Accepting the recognition by the Housing Act of 1937 that the private market could not serve low-income families decently, Congress did make a major new authorization of 810,000 more low-rental units. (This action served as the lightning rod for most public controversy over the 1949 Act.) But the legislators evidently expected that by combining the lowered land costs in redevelopment sites with the somewhat lower rentals required by the Federal Housing Administration, Title I sponsors could produce housing for the great number of moderate-income and low middle-income families in cities.

This premise, and the ambiguous FHA itself, were to present major drawbacks, as will be seen in the case histories. The Federal Housing Administration was another of the multi-purpose, depression-born housing agencies that became permanent. It was to stimulate private housing construction and thus create jobs by unlocking the country's private lending coffers, which had been shut to building since the 1929 real estate collapse. FHA's novel approach to this task was to offer government guarantees on private loans made for single-family and multi-unit housing.

The government insurance device proved so popular, both with the shelter industry it was intended to revive and with home purchasers—banks were required by FHA to offer terms more liberal than conventional loans as a prerequisite to its guarantees—that it was continued. Not until 1949, however, did Congress try to join the powerful and remarkably independent FHA (its administrator was appointed by the President, not by the administrator of the overall Housing and Home Finance Agency under which it had been placed) in city rebuilding efforts. What happened to this new partnership is an important aspect of cities' struggles to rebuild.

A NEW AND BROADER APPROACH: URBAN RENEWAL

Redevelopment proved doggedly slow in getting started, in spite of the apparently attractive opportunity that Title I presented to private enterprise and cities themselves. Cities were technically ill-prepared or politically afraid; investors were leery. The local ramifications of the new private-public partnership and the re-use of city land went far beyond even the most advanced thinking about redevelopment.

The pertinent fact here is that by 1954, few municipalities had been able to take a redevelopment project beyond its initial planning stage. Then Congress added a new, far broader, more flexible and exacting orientation to cities' federal aid and encouragement to city improvement. This was urban renewal. The enactment of urban renewal as an expansion of Title I, coming so hard on the heels of the scarcely tried redevelopment program, caused even greater public confusion. Most people used the two terms interchangeably, an error which was compounded by the fact that projects originating under the 1954 Act would demand an even longer lead time before cities could move them into execution. Such projects were to present still other problems not envisioned by the lawmakers.

Today the phrase "urban renewal" has come to be used as the encompassing term for all official conservation, rehabilitation and rebuilding efforts in cities. But the philosophy behind this third major approach to urban physical decay and the more selective diversified tools prescribed under urban renewal were developed mainly in response to what had been recognized in the early 1950's as a great urban problem: the accelerating deterioration of many older but still livable city homes and neighborhoods.

The magnitude of this trend was disclosed in the findings of the 1950 census. It revealed how much urban shelter, nationally, had suffered during the preceding decade of wartime rent control, doubling-up of defense workers, little property maintenance and virtually no new construction. In addition to 5,000,000 slum dwellings that were beyond salvaging, the census found that 15,000,000 homes required major repairs and another 20,000,000 were deteriorating and needed conservation treatment if they were not to become slums.

This alarming situation became the chief concern of a citizens' advisory committee on housing policies appointed by President Eisenhower in 1953. The committee proposed, after long study, a nationwide effort of neighborhood conservation and urban housing rehabilitation, supported by federal aid, and aimed at protecting the nation's $500,000,000,000 investment in its existing housing supply. Redevelopment was not to be abandoned. The committee and Congress recognized that in unlivable slum areas, area-wide clearance was a necessary precursor to rebuilding. Spot clearance would also be needed in sections of renewal or conservation areas. But urban renewal's primary, original aim was to save and rehabilitate neighborhoods, not to clear them.

The 1954 Act's new formula called back into use some old familiar tools, most notably municipal housing codes, but provided for their application in a different context; the goal was to gain practical rehabilitation of deteriorating homes in slipping but decent and salvagable neighborhoods, rather than to fix up slums. (Indeed, efforts to use code enforcement, promoted this time mostly by home builders and realtors as an alternative to public housing, had once again proved this tool's inefficacy in improving real slum areas—as the widely heralded and briefly successful "Baltimore Plan" revealed. The failure of that effort provided valuable lessons for the President's Advisory Committee.)

Under the renewal formula, property owners were offered the carrot of an improved neighborhood environment brought about through new public actions and investments, as an accompaniment to the stick of code enforcement. The hope was to win real property improvement, above the minimum standards enforceable under housing codes. The federal government would pay two thirds of a city's costs in designated project areas for clearing limited areas of blight and decay, and for providing the new community facilities—schools, playgrounds, off-street parking and other public improvements—which a renewal neighborhood might need to meet contemporary living standards. Since securing a bank loan for private property improvement in such declining areas was commonly impossible, Congress also authorized the Federal Housing Administration to issue special mortgage insurance to lenders so that they would help finance the property repairs required of owners by code enforcement in renewal areas.

A new citywide slum-prevention effort emanating from City Hall was intrinsic to the 1954 Act's approach. As part of the 1953 studies, the President's Advisory Committee had sent a team around the country to study such local efforts. They reported that growing slum conditions were the product of neglect, not only by owners and tenants, but also by local officials.

In fact, the investigators found most municipal governments derelict in using their present powers to halt slums and blight. Comparatively few cities had developed adequate housing codes, and these were generally not effectively enforced. Zoning laws had been so riddled with variances that many were worthless and legally unenforceable. Few cities had comprehensive plans for the use of land or to guide capital spending on the construction and improvement of public facilities. The surveyors reported that the deterioration of older neighborhoods and the departure from them of middle-income residents were actually encouraged by the failure of city governments to modernize and maintain facilities (a failure partly enforced, however, by shortages of materials and personnel during the World War II years).

Along with the new federal aids available to localities under the Housing Act of 1954, the federal government also put a broad new set of requirements on cities—that of developing communitywide plans of action to combat slums and blight. This "Workable Program" would have to be submitted annually by the Mayor and give evidence of local progress in developing this plan in order to qualify for any federal housing assistance.*

The federal government's widening concern for city revitaliza-

* The seven elements of the Workable Program, as defined administratively, also included adequate, effectively enforced codes and ordinances; a comprehensive plan for community development; and analysis of blighted areas to determine their appropriate treatment—clearance, rehabilitation or conservation; adequate administrative organization; adequate financing; a program for housing displaced families, and citizen participation in renewal plans.

tion was also demonstrated in the 1954 Act's "10 per cent exception" clause, which allowed that proportion of Title I aid to be used in projects which did not qualify under the "predominantly residential" limits of the 1949 Act. In addition, for the first time, federal grants were made to localities for planning—although only to communities of 25,000 and under and to metropolitan areas.

NEW TIDES

These expanded government aids to cities came none too soon. The question was: were they sufficient for the problems? Neighborhood renewal, although a necessary complement to redevelopment's bulldozing, was, in its conception, a finger-in-the-dike measure. It had been forwarded first in Chicago and was adopted as state law by Illinois in 1953, as the local planners' and businessmen's answer to a situation that Chicago had been experiencing more severely than most other old urban centers. This was the accelerating flight of middle-income families to the suburbs at the same time that lower-income families were migrating from rural areas to cities. These population shifts were accompanied by the overcrowding of homes and facilities in older neighborhoods, the spread of blight and the decline of property values—the same old familiar pattern, but on a far vaster scale, with physical decline now concentrated in the central city and growth mostly in the new suburbs.

Reporting on local findings from the 1950 census, the Chicago Planning Commission had warned that fifty-six square miles of that city's middle-aged, close-in neighborhoods were deteriorating so quickly that they would become slums and the city would face bankruptcy, unless preventive measures were soon taken. The Commission calculated that such action would be far cheaper than ultimate clearance.

Figures extrapolated from Lake Meadows, the city's first redevelopment project, showed that $200,000,000 in public funds would be required for each square mile cleared. On the other hand, it was estimated that neighborhood conservation, a technique devised by University of Chicago planners, would, if applied in time, entail only an estimated $60,000,000 in public outlays and would forestall the expensive and traumatic alternative of more and more clearance.

This new approach appealed particularly to the city's downtown retailers and leading real estate investors who were feeling the pinch of their customers' flight to the suburbs and the decline in city property values. Hoping that neighborhood improvement measures plus code enforcement could draw back the fleeing middle class (and hold off the newcomers), as well as shore up property values, they lobbied the conservation plan into Illinois state law and were influential in making conservation the chief thrust of the 1954 Federal Urban Renewal Program.

By the mid-1950's the threat to many cities' commercial-retail centers was becoming omnipresent; vehicular traffic strangled downtown areas, and branches of big department stores started to follow the new suburbanites—the sons and grandsons of the immigrants and their bumper postwar crop of children—out of the cities. In the new suburbs there soon sprawled shopping centers as big in retail space as many an old downtown's, and with some of its former specialty shops, plus adequate free parking space, which was easy to provide on cheap former farm land.

Meanwhile, trucks and highways were freeing industry from dependence on the old urban rail centers. With this, many manufacturers, who needed to move from lofts and change their operations to modern one-story production methods in order to remain competitive (and hoping, in some cases, also to reduce their property taxes), left central cities for cheap open land on the metropolitan fringes. Services and offices followed. Branches of industry began moving to, or expanding in, new consumer markets in the exploding new regions—the sun states and the West—or sought cheaper labor in the South. These regional shifts and booming new urban areas were accelerated by the defense, space and electronics industries. These required good weather conditions, and their hard-to-get technical personnel sought "the good life." Again the free market moved faster than local government's ability to cope with these new forces; and thus the spreading metropolis developed new urban problems at the same time that these forces assailed urban cares.

Tremendous business pressures built up for a federally aided highway construction program to accommodate the vehicular population of the United States which, by the 1950's, almost equaled the nation's human population of 1900. But the federal government still showed no concern in its transportation policy for the special requirements of cities. Although the new $27,000,000,000 Interstate Highway Bill passed by Congress in 1956 did, for the first time, make provision for urban highways, this state-administered gift threatened to be more of a burden than a blessing and would often add to cities' struggles. No provisions were made for urban mass transportation, although railroads were cutting back commuter services, and transit companies continued to drop unprofitable runs while more and more suburban and city dwellers switched to space-consuming automobiles and demanded still more highways.

The torrent of rural newcomers to the hard-pressed urban centers was also unabated as the 1950's advanced. There were hillbillies from the Appalachian Mountains, Indians from reservations, Mexicans, Puerto Ricans—all leaving subsistence living and slipping employment in backward areas and on increasingly mechanized farms. Most of all there were the Negroes, pushed off farms by new agricultural techniques or leaving the fading plantation South for greater rights and job opportunities in cities. By the mid-1950's, Negroes were moving north and west of the Mason-Dixon line at the rate of 175,000 a year. Between 1940 and 1957, some 3,000,000 had emigrated to urban centers—not just to Chicago, New York and Washington, but also to Des Moines, San Jose, Rochester, New Haven and other smaller cities. They were also converging in southern cities. These newcomers presented some unexpected challenges to the city rebuilders and renewers, and with the emergence of the civil rights struggle have forced a restructuring of some methods as well as a redefinition or re-examination of ends.

So now we come to our main story: that of pioneering cities and individuals who have been using this assortment of government tools locally and inventing new techniques, programs and patterns of cooperative action as they try to undo the sorry past, deal with the complex present and plan for the uncertain future.

We start with significant and influential early, but limited, approaches to reconstruction; see how these programs became embroiled with emerging social issues; and then move on to more comprehensive programs which include the conservation of the good in cities as well as institutional, human and economic development.

Each case history is related in terms of the signal contribution which a particular community, project or effort has made along one or several lines to the practice of city renewal and development and to our growing understanding of its nature and dimensions. Not all cases are followed in detail to the present; for although they have generally continued to advance and broaden their line of attack, their subsequent contributions and lessons are not as distinctive nor instructive.*

Inevitably I have had to omit many worthwhile plans and programs, even in the communities I have focused on, and I have treated some vital problem areas passingly or not at all. One book cannot begin to tell everything. On the other hand, I have followed in depth the experiences of several cities and have given them what may seem to be a disproportionate share of attention. This is because their far-reaching innovations and influential approaches to problem areas illustrate unusually well the nature of and the inevitable interrelationships in the urban scene.

My approach is not that of a professional planner, an architectural critic, or an expert in a particular field. Rather it is that of a "generalist"—an interested and increasingly concerned reporter and observer. I have tried to see how certain conditions arise and how programs take shape; how leaders conceive and try to effect them; how people react to them; and how the programs actually turn out. Few people qualify as experts in the overall urban field, and one of my hopes is that this book will help the diverse specialists and participants in the urban scene better perceive their relationships to one another and to the process in which they are mutually engaged.

The approach of the book came initially from my own manner of involvement in the urban scene, as public information officer ten years ago for ACTION Inc., then a new national organization concerned with citizen participation in urban betterment.†

* Cutoff date for research was August, 1966.

† In 1966, ACTION merged with the American Civic and Planning Association to form Urban America, Inc.

This work took me to many cities that were just starting such programs, and brought me into contact with officials and professionals who were running these programs, advising local leaders and shaping new government policies. I also came to know a number of business, civic and neighborhood leaders who were engaged in the new activity of urban renewal.

I was impressed by the eagerness of many local leaders to know more about the experiences of other cities in order to meet their own problems. Laymen also wanted to know "what it's all about." I was struck then and in subsequent years as a writer in the urban field by the lack of common information and a comprehensive view among the many different people from various backgrounds and fields who are concerned with urban improvement. It seemed that a book reporting on local programs, problems and achievements could help answer some of these needs, and also chronicle an important new chapter in the country's history. A grant from the Avalon Foundation allowed me to pursue the subject in much greater depth and with the perspective of years—as efforts have advanced, new forces have emerged, and cities and programs have changed directions as they faced new and unexpected circumstances.

During the decade in which I have gathered my material, I have seen that our cities struggle with powerful and impersonal economic, technological and demographic changes—forces which must be much better understood than now. They labor under great social and fiscal burdens, and try to avail themselves of funds bureaucratically administered from afar. But as a rule, it is individuals, individuals alone or in organizations in each community, who can use these new tools and government funds. They must react to the trends, grasp problems, set goals and create new physical or institutional forms. Individuals at all levels must innovate and commit themselves, and take political, personal or financial risks, to achieve new community goals.

Thus, above all this is a story of people—of people with different motives and responsibilities and varied contributions. Using imperfect but gradually improving tools in an imperfect and rapidly changing world, they have learned from working at the task, from one another, from the "experts" and the grass roots, and sometimes from their own mistakes, as they have sought answers to and have acted on many of the great unsolved problems of urban life today. They have made an important beginning in this new phase of our country's development—the gradual maturing of the United States into an urban nation.

Urban Reconstruction: The Early Leaders

2

THE MAN WHO GOT THINGS DONE FOR NEW YORK ■ Robert Moses Tackles Slum Clearance

New York is the run-away city, always inventing new and inadequate governmental forms to solve increasingly vexing problems.

It was the first city in the country to establish metropolitan government in 1898 by joining four neighboring counties with the core city to create the five boroughs of Greater New York. Tammany Hall celebrated this governmental advance with one of its most spectacular binges of corruption. Before long, there was a new charter and a new reform Mayor. Soon even the recently enlarged metropolis of 3,500,000 was overwhelmed—by the immigrants from Eastern Europe who poured in, further filling its already bursting slums, and by the metropolitan explosion that commuter rails, electricity and the automobile facilitated.

Today, the country's largest city and its financial-cultural capital—its "corporate bazaar"—finds itself the core of a three-state, twenty-two-county region of 17,400,000 that houses one tenth of the nation. The Mayor of New York holds the second most important elective office in the United States. But not one Mayor has advanced beyond the post in nearly a century. City Hall has been described as "a badly organized management center for a huge set of public services." The task of running this city of almost 8,000,000 and finding the money to finance its services and facilities would sap the strength of any mortal. To ease the executive burden the charter now provides for a Deputy Mayor and a Deputy Mayor-City Administrator, and there is an army of 270,000 municipal employees which is large enough to repopulate Wichita, Kansas. But someone must resolve the conflicting demands of all the contending forces, within and outside government. Usually the office of Mayor consumes the man.

An old city has new needs, and extra energy is needed to advance this disorganized complexity. But how can funds be spared from growing service needs and an overwhelming debt service? Benefits demanded by one group must be taken from another, unless one can turn to Albany, Washington, or to a special-purpose revenue-raising authority. Even so, when something is built in New York, as a rule something old must be torn down and people moved from businesses and homes.

New York—at least the core of Manhattan and the city's outer reaches—builds and rebuilds with a unique private dynamism; building is a multibillion-dollar business. The main trouble is that the end product is generally more dense, more irritating and less human, and requires more public services and facilities. Between these extremes of old and new stretch neglected "gray areas," left to slowly decay.

Is New York an example of our urban future? Its magnitude alone is staggering. Squeezed into the 320 square miles of the five-borough city is a population equal to that of the fourteen smallest states and twice as large as the country's second city, Chicago. In Manhattan's closest-packed slums, people exist at densities of over 1,000 to a city block. After a century of leading the nation in new housing programs, the whole city has more slum dwellers than most U.S. cities have people. No wonder New York has been called "the square of the urban problem."

Who can grasp New York's diversity and scale; who can discipline the city's dynamism? Is it possible to meet private business' enormous demands and simultaneously serve the public's growing welfare needs? Can any man overcome the bureaucratic inertia both of official procedures and of the more than 250,000 merit-employed, generally underpaid civil servants? The rules that were set up to prevent the municipal spoils system and to protect the public have seemed to smother progress.

Only one Mayor in recent decades, Fiorello La Guardia, was able to take the reins and humanize the city's administration as well. He was also believed to have solved New York's financial problems. Informed hindsight suggests, however, that "the Little Flower" had time to ride fire engines and read the comics on the radio during his two depression-time terms because Washington was paying over a third of the city's bills and financing the fine new and refurbished facilities to which he could point with pride. (In fact, his successor found the city in 1946 saddled with facilities that were unbearably costly to maintain and physically run-down due to wartime neglect.)

Moreover, La Guardia relied to a large extent, as did his three immediate successors, on a unique public servant. One man in the city had the combination of personality, prestige and ability and, already by the mid-1930's, the unique constellation of public powers, that could provide the persistence and extra thrust.

THE PARADOX OF MOSES AND TITLE I

For the generation to come, the story of public building in New York City would be largely the story of that one man—Robert Moses, the superman who got big things built for the super city. He towered over New York and its region. And since for many years New York was almost the only city that progressed physically, Moses personified for the rest of the country those qualities needed to build for American cities.

Yet the legacy of Moses the Master Builder is filled with paradox. No one else in American history produced so much for local public improvement and urban reconstruction—about $5,000,-

000,000 worth by 1960. But no single person contributed more through his works and his methods to New York City's problems—the remote, fractionalized local government; the unplanned private overgrowth; the traffic congestion; the inhumanity and citizen discontents; the real estate "project" approach to community building; and the abdication of political and business leadership.

New York City's billion-dollar, federally aided urban redevelopment program under Title I of the Housing Act of 1949 is integral to the Moses paradox, for Moses, as chairman of the Mayor's Committee for Slum Clearance from 1948 to 1960, directed New York's program. Urban redevelopment differed from slum clearance for public housing in a number of notable ways. This new legislation was government's first attempt to attract private investment to city rebuilding. The new federal funds were to be used for clearing not only outright slums, but also areas that were "deteriorated or deteriorating." The land was to be sold for rebuilding, generally to private sponsors and at a reduced cost that would make it economically feasible for them to develop the cleared site according to an officially approved plan. Housing was to be the predominant re-use of the land, but other uses were permitted by law; rentals were not subsidized.

To achieve such urban land changes and to facilitate rebuilding to desirable standards, a new system of loans and grants was initiated under Title I. The federal government would absorb two thirds of the public cost of acquiring eligible areas, of clearing the project site, and of reducing the price of the land to an appraised value based on the re-use plan. Cities would pay the other third of the project cost, either with cash or supporting public facilities. The formula was highly complex, even in its statutory conception.

Moses created in New York the biggest Title I program in the country—one with more results by 1960 than all other cities combined. New York by then had fifteen federally assisted redevelopment projects in execution: three were already complete, seven were over half rebuilt, five were contracted for and undergoing clearance. Twenty-four more were in various stages of planning. None was bogged down because it lacked private sponsors—the most common stumbling block in other cities.

From dilapidated areas on the edges of Brooklyn to densely packed, unheated and unsanitary nineteenth-century "Old Law" tenement * districts in the Lower East Side and Harlem, 314 acres of such blighted land and deteriorating housing were cleared and being redeveloped privately. North of Columbia University, for example, 972 units of airy high-rise cooperative apartments widely separated by grass and trees replaced old walk-ups which had covered almost entire blocks. South of Washington Square, two modern residential apartment houses with 2,004 dwelling units had taken the place of a cramped old loft and manufacturing district. In all, about 28,500 privately financed apartment dwelling units were completed and occupied, in construction, or being planned.

A number of Title I projects transformed sections of Manhattan's eroded mid-West Side. At the southwest corner of Central Park, facing Columbus Circle, a $22,000,000 exhibition hall, office tower and apartment buildings replaced a mixture of Old Law tenements, shabby rooming houses, and commercial structures. On eighteen blocks northwest of Broadway, stretching toward the Hudson River, the Lincoln Square project was to include the Lincoln Center for the Performing Arts and other new cultural and institutional facilities and housing. Elsewhere, hospitals and universities were also being helped to remove adjacent blight and to expand.

In any other city, a fraction of these changes would be regarded as a triumph. Moreover, the financially pressed City of New York enjoyed a net annual gain in tax revenues of $5,000,000 from increases in building and land values attained through

* Approximately 82,000 such dwellings were built between 1867, when the first "Old Law" governing tenement house construction was passed, and 1901, when it was revised. These five- and six-story walk-up units extended from sixty to ninety feet back on the city's twenty-five- by one-hundred-feet lots and covered the whole width. A ten-foot rear gap was required by law. Narrow airshafts down the middle supplied all the ventilation most of the rooms in these railroad flats received; sunshine was unknown. In 1901, three quarters of the city's population, some 2,500,000 people, lived in such dwellings, which also lacked inside plumbing, hot water, private toilets and bathrooms. Today, 40,000 of these buildings still stand, housing 1,000,000 people in 350,000 apartments. The "New Law" tenements built under the 1901 law were not a great deal better. Some of both types have been improved internally with sanitary facilities in recent years.

the first ten Title I projects. These new funds were sufficient to pay off the entire local public cost of clearance and land write-down in six years—and then could be used for other of the city's many needs. Federal redevelopment officials pointed to New York as proof that the unprecedented new public-private partnership for rebuilding American cities' slum areas was successful.

But in mounting the nation's biggest and fastest-moving Title I redevelopment program, Moses had also launched the most controversial, civically disliked and scandal-tainted program in the country. As one of the leading architectural journals expressed it: "The nation's biggest program is the biggest mess." Furthermore, by the end of the 1950's, 1,000,000 New Yorkers —just as many as at the start of Title I activity—still lived in slums. Moses, whose works had for decades brought acclaim to the elected officials he had served, now was a grave political liability to New York's Mayor.

Perhaps the sponsorship scandals, citizen outcries and abuses of dislocated persons that accompanied Title I activity in New York were a concomitant of redevelopment progress. The New York program aroused suspicion about federally aided urban redevelopment in general. Moses said later, "Slum clearance is the most unpleasant thing I ever was in and the only one I've got out of that I was glad I got out of."

When he stepped outside public works (parks, bridges and parkways) and applied his efficient, limited-goals approach to New York's century-old war against slums, even Moses stumbled and fell. Perhaps Moses was not the man for the job. Yet, when Title I was launched, he was looked to locally and nationally as the one person who could make the complex formula work. After he retired from redevelopment in 1960, talented and well-intentioned men tried and appeared to accomplish little. Before long, even some of his critics wished Moses, or someone with his assets, would come back and get New York moving.

Other cities devised more palatable, less simplistic approaches and institutions for advancing redevelopment locally and avoided scandal and citizen outrage. But then none has had to contend with a city like New York. And without Moses and his visible results, it was feared that Congressional aid to the slow-starting Title I program might have been cut off.

New York, like Moses, is atypical, but vastly influential. No man's name and no city's record are more closely associated with the tone and opening phase of the portentous new federally aided program for rebuilding American cities. While almost every other city was still drawing up Title I project applications and plans, New York City under Moses had new buildings above ground. Unfortunately, the roar against Moses' bulldozer and Title I abuses, and public confusion compounded by haphazard reporting of the program, diverted attention from the lessons to be drawn.

REFORMER TO PRACTITIONER

To understand what happened when Moses headed New York's redevelopment program, it is important to see Title I as just one more of the many interrelated responsibilities he carried in a legendary career of building for New York.

In 1937, before Moses had reached fifty, his most celebrated local works already included Jones Beach on Long Island, six sandy miles of public ocean front with accompanying play areas and parking lots dredged from sand spits and the sea: the spectacular Triborough Bridge, connecting three of New York's boroughs for travel by cars and trucks; refurbished Central Park and its new zoo; and the West Side improvement—a complex of highways, bridge and park areas—along the Hudson River. There were also hundreds of new smaller parks, playgrounds and sports facilities in or near the city; miles of landscaped parkways encircling the boroughs; and other parks throughout the state. He was also working round the clock to make the swampy garbage dump that was Flushing Meadows fit for the 1939 World's Fair buildings.

As celebrated as his works, and virtually inseparable from their realization, was Moses' style—his arrogant manner, his reputation for honesty and efficiency, his artillery of statistics and his outspoken pronouncements, as well as his deliberate use of invective against opponents, even those in high offices. Stories about the audacious, sometimes ruthless, means he used to get things built, and built on time, were picked up by the press and subsequently relished by the public. Some became local folklore.* He was also credited for projects that he had not built, such as Manhattan's East River Drive and the Queens Midtown Tunnel. Moreover, those who pointed out the inaccuracy of such statements were accused of being Moses detractors. Frank Lloyd Wright, not one to hand out verbal bouquets, declared, "New York should be given outright to Robert Moses."

In fact, elected officials had been giving him chunks of the city for years. It was rarely necessary for him to relinquish one public job to take on others. Temporary assignments became permanent. By 1948, at sixty, he held seven major public appointive positions (one of them dating back to 1922) and seemed to fulfill them all with ease. He was the Chairman of the New York State Council of Parks (his oldest continuing job); then Chairman of the Long Island State Parks Commission; Chairman of Jones Beach; President of the Bethpage Authority; Commissioner of the New York City Parks Department; City Construction Coordinator; and Chairman of the Triborough Bridge and Tunnel Authority.

Chairmanship of the Mayor's Slum Clearance Committee was merely his eighth post. Moses had long ago developed the technique of putting together a small team of loyal, efficient technicians, administrators and private contractors. He would establish the operation's aims and then let his team follow through. Often, he used his staff people on several different jobs. Even the lines between his different public positions and projects were fuzzy and were probably kept so to allow him to unofficially coordinate many separate projects, even some over which he had no jurisdiction.

In each job, he added significantly to the undernourished public estate and to his own prestige. Furthermore—and this was a

* It is related that Moses borrowed $20,000 from his mother to pay for the completion, on schedule, of a causeway at Jones Beach which he had promised local officials would open on a certain date. Another classic is the story that he asked Governor Alfred E. Smith for $25,000,000 more in state funds to complete a state parks project after the Governor had struggled to win an earlier request for an unprecedented $30,000,000 from the unsympathetic legislature. "If I told you how much it would cost the state," Moses is said to have explained, "you'd never have approved it." The tactics he employed to acquire from opposing townspeople the vast acreage he wanted for Jones Beach caused one local paper's editor to call him a "dictator."

keystone in the Moses legend, and in his increasing power—he received pay for only one of his positions, that of City Parks Commissioner.* In the Parks job he had replaced, on his own insistence, five commissioners, who among them received $68,000 annually in political sinecures, and took it all on for only $10,000 a year.† Moses, son of a well-to-do former New Haven, Connecticut merchant, had means which were purportedly sufficient for him to serve the public with relatively little or no financial compensation.

His public image was that of the apolitical builder. But Moses was neither an architect nor an engineer by training. He was a master of local government administration and politics, who gained knowledge of how to apply these skills to public building in a long, fruitful apprenticeship.

Moses is said to have determined on a public service career as a child. Public life during his youth was dominated by Teddy Roosevelt, whose patrician, vigorous style ("Damn the law. I want the canal built!") and early career in municipal reform influenced Robert's natural bent. Six-foot Moses was also an athlete, an outdoorsman and a conservationist. Captain of his swimming team at Yale, a gifted writer, a brilliant debater and student at Yale and later at Oxford University, he was not, however, known for his diplomacy.

While completing his Ph.D. in government at Columbia, he volunteered in 1913 to work for a new business-backed, municipal reform bureau. This group was trying to train public administrators to serve in local government in place of party hacks, and to install efficient, "scientific" methods of management in New York and other city governments. Moses learned his way around City Hall, and by 1918 was appointed by newly elected Governor Alfred E. Smith as unpaid director of a commission to revise the state constitution.

Drafting laws for Tammany's Smith and influencing legislators in Albany changed Moses from a reformer to a political realist

* A special state law was passed ruling that New York City's Park Commissioner shall not "be ineligible to hold any other unsalaried office filled by the Mayor."

† Subsequently this was raised to $25,000. Later he also received $10,000 for the additional job of Chairman of the State Power Authority, which he assumed in 1954.

and practitioner, one who was more concerned with the actual processes of government than legal, procedural improvements.

Smith was the first in a long list of New York Governors and then Mayors (ranging from old-line Democrats through the insurgent Republican) who found that Moses could conceive and finish in time for the next election visible and often visionary monuments to their term in office. Moses never won elective office, but through appointive jobs he built up for himself a supra-elective power.* This power was a key in his Title I story.

Under Governor Smith in the early 1920's, when the automobile age was just blossoming, he initiated an unparalleled network of parks and motor parkways for New York State. As a rule, he not only initiated the idea for these works; he also devised an agency to construct and administer them; drafted the necessary state legislation; convinced the Governor with the help of an impressive illustrated brochure that contained specific financing plans and results of engineering studies. Usually, he was put in charge of building the multimillion-dollar projects. (Moses evidently saw that if he served without pay, it was not difficult to gain public appointment.) First Smith named him head of the State Council of Parks, an advisory umbrella agency which Moses invented; once there, Moses was able to appoint himself to other parks and parkways jobs. He became Smith's Secretary of State, his speech writer, and coordinator of all the state's public improvements, with vast power to direct expenditures to localities.

By 1930, when Jones Beach opened, his widely reported and successful fights against millionaire Long Island estate owners, parochial townspeople, speculative subdividers, and parsimonious upstate legislators to build this Riviera for New York City's middle class had established him not only as a builder but also as a fighter for the people and the public interest.

CITY PARKS AND BRIDGES: ON THE SIDE OF THE ANGELS

In America it was unique for a man of Moses' extraordinary talents and drive to spend his life in local public service. If some-

* In his one attempt, as the Republican candidate for Governor of New York in 1934, he won the largest defeat to date in the state's history.

one other than Franklin Roosevelt had been elected President in 1932, Moses might then have moved on to Washington. But years before, as State Parks Chairman, he had prevented FDR, who was head of a parkway commission near Hyde Park, from creating a sinecure by putting his political secretary, Louis Howe, on the Commission's payroll. Relations between the two since had been barely civil. Moses was also outspokenly anti-New Deal. Nonetheless, the New Deal and its spending for recovery allowed Moses' talents to flower in the city.

In Washington, Moses might have been just another brilliant administrator-planner. In New York, he was Triton among the municipal minnows. New York, like other American cities, had long suffered from a vacuum of talent, drive and funds to execute public building projects. Tangible achievements had generally been accompanied by municipal graft. But in November 1933, the voters of New York had once again thrown the Tammany machine out of City Hall, and unprecedented federal funds were becoming available for cities with plans to spend them. Moses was considered by the fusion reformers for their mayoralty candidate but was turned down because of his close association with Al Smith; however, he supported their nominee, Fiorello La Guardia. The Mayor-elect soon offered Moses any job he wanted. Moses had already sent La Guardia a detailed memorandum of projects to be undertaken by the city (at the time of the election, he was Chairman of the State Emergency Public Works Commission in addition to his other jobs), and he soon accepted several city posts, starting with one in the shabby, graft-ridden municipal parks system.

In a few years, by using 69,000 federally paid relief workers and millions in federal works funds, Moses quadrupled the number of parks, completing 1,800 proposed parks, recreation and parkways projects in the five boroughs, and had become an irremovable force in the city.

The parks position served Moses as a base of operations from which to forward other projects. There were many things that needed to be done for New York City, and Moses supplied certain missing ingredients. On the opening in 1936 of the Henry Hudson Bridge and Parkway, the most impressive and complex of his city works to date, Moses, who had directed the project as

Parks Commissioner, explained in a special commemorative brochure: "Every scheme [for improving New York] has been thought of before. . . . If we make any claim, it is that we have had the gumption to translate plan into reality. . . . The first appropriation for plans for the Henry Hudson Bridge was made in 1904." The big job, he found, was to coordinate the different government agencies—federal, state and municipal, as well as the river holdings of the New York Central Railroad—and the funds from various sources that were involved.

While still in Albany Moses had given a push to another ambitious city project, the Triborough Bridge. The proposal to connect Manhattan, Queens and the Bronx across the East River's widest point was first forwarded in 1918, and had been started in 1929, financed by municipal bonds, when the crash came. Municipal credit was soon useless.

A state-created instrument, the semi-autonomous public benefit corporation—known also as the authority—was a versatile device which Moses had used in the 1920's when the authority concept was still new and he could not win state appropriations for his projects. He got enabling legislation passed to allow an authority to build the bridge, and arranged for a $35,000,000 loan from the WPA. Then, as Moses put it, Tammany bogged down. When La Guardia became Mayor, however, he appointed Moses to the post of chief executive of the Triborough Bridge Authority to expedite the project, which now could also benefit from public works funds which became available under the Democrats.

This appointment secured Moses' extraordinary local position. President Roosevelt was outraged to have his old adversary directing this federally financed behemoth; he exerted indirect but intense behind-the-scenes pressures on La Guardia, culminating in a secret threat to withhold all federal works funds unless Moses were removed from the Triborough Authority. Moses, learning from the Mayor of the peril to his big new project, let the story leak out and said that if he were forced to resign, he would also drop the city parks job.

PWA Administrator Harold Ickes, the man in the middle, wrote in his diary, "By making a martyr of [Moses] we are only serving to build him up." Indeed, the public and press let out such a roar that the President was forced to back down. But when the $45,000,000 complex of soaring bridges, intricate approaches, river-level parks and a sports stadium was completed in mid-1936 (on schedule, in spite of the temporary withholding of federal works funds), Roosevelt, who was running for reelection, participated in the ribbon-cutting ceremony. That year La Guardia appointed Moses chairman of the Authority's three-man board.

New York City's five boroughs are divided by some fifty miles of inland waterways. By the early 1930's only a few bridges provided convenient vehicular transportation between the boroughs. To compensate for this deficit and stitch the city together for interborough driving, Moses formed and headed other authorities (sometimes serving ex officio as Parks Commissioner on a one-man authority), and created a series of new toll-collecting bridges. Approaches and limited-access routes usually extended far into the boroughs (Moses' interpretation of his laws was lenient), and a recreational development was often part of the facilities. The supporting roads and peripheral play areas were maintained by the city, while the toll-collecting bridges remained in Authority control.

Both traffic and revenues exceeded expectations. Beyond the Triborough Bridge, Queens and Long Island were mushrooming. Beyond the Henry Hudson Bridge—a toll-collecting extension of the Henry Hudson Parkway that spanned the Harlem River between Manhattan and the Bronx—suburban Westchester County sent still more commuters to the business hub of New York. The Authority and its facilities expanded rapidly. By 1946, when Mayor O'Dwyer consolidated with Triborough the City's financially strapped tunnels,* giving the expanded Authority responsibility for operating and building all intra-city toll-collecting bridges and tunnels, its combined facilities were collecting some

* The Queens Midtown Tunnel was built without Moses, largely because of the Roosevelt–Ickes quarrel. Intended to open for the 1939 World's Fair, it was completed instead two years later, shortly before World War II, and did not get sufficient traffic during the war to pay off its bonds. The Brooklyn–Battery Tunnel was held up by the war and completed by the Triborough Authority.

$10,000,000 annually from 50,000,000 motorists, and had revenues to spare.* (That same year, O'Dwyer doubled the local sales tax in an effort to meet the city's transit deficit without raising the subway fare.)

These public works attracted to Moses powerful constituencies, ranging from the Army Corps of Engineers (which has rights over navigable waterways), to motorists' and trucking associations, to the citizens' Park Association (whose president was married to the publisher of *The New York Times*). Borough Presidents, who were responsible for public works in their boroughs and could share credit publicly with Moses for the works he created, were also kindly disposed.†

Not surprisingly, the city's financial and business community displayed toward Moses a deference rarely granted a public official. Government subsidies were increasing in the 1930's, and municipal bonds were rated low. However, Moses' authorities were, as he liked to point out, "businesslike." They paid their bond-holders on time and earned extra revenues with which to finance other multimillion-dollar, revenue-producing facilities without, in Moses' words, "tapping the public till or involving government credit." Wall Street, at first reluctant to fully underwrite his proposed early projects,‡ not only floated the Tri-

* The Triborough was the first intra-city toll bridge in the country. During its first year, some 11,000,000 motorists deposited $2,845,000 in tolls; these revenues were collected not by the city but by the Authority, which operated the bridge and had to pay off the construction loan. The Triborough Bridge was intended to be self-liquidating. But with state legislative permission, the Authority could refinance and issue new, larger bonds to be sold in the general market in order to finance still other facilities. By this means, the excess toll revenues collected by the Authority were pledged to retire the new bonds. The Verrazano Bridge over the Narrows was financed this way.

† When the Henry Hudson Bridge opened, the Borough President of the Bronx stated, "Commissioner Moses, permit me to congratulate you on this achievement. With your customary genius, you have prosecuted in an unusually short period of time the accomplishment of this great public improvement and the people of the Bronx are truly grateful. Your aid in preparing the legislative program is especially appreciated."

‡ The private bond-holders who had bought the $3,000,000 to finance one deck of the Henry Hudson Bridge in 1934 hadn't thought there would be enough traffic for two tiers. But Moses had built it strongly enough for the second deck. Indeed, in 1938, when the New York Parkway Authority, successor to the Henry Hudson and Marine Parkway authorities, floated a new bond issue, the former was carrying two-and-a-half times its expected load. "Practically all the investment bankers in New York City showed a lively

borough bonds (which were coming out in the hundreds of millions by the 1950's), but also bought them.

For favored firms, there was a tremendous amount of private business to be done with the prosperous Triborough Authority. Its millions in toll revenues and its growing cash reserves had to be deposited in banks which could use the funds for temporary investments. Lawyers were needed in every phase of the operation, from consulting on new bond flotations to handling suits brought by users. Insurance had to be written, from the high-risk, high-premium collapse contracts covering the hazardous construction stage to workmen's compensation and replacement carried on each costly facility. There were contracts to be let for engineering, materials and construction on each element of these complex structures, and for demolition work on approaches and paving of access roads. Bidding was not required to be competitive. Nor was a pre-audit necessary. The books of the Authority were closed to the public.

Businessmen also admired Moses' "miracles of engineering." *Fortune*, the magazine of business, wrote in 1938 that, "Judged by his works, Robert Moses is a great and good man . . . 'on the side of the angels.' "

THE "PLANNING REDS"

A city pays a price for such a modern-day Ramses. New York, like other cities, was accustomed to building for its public needs by fits and starts, commonly in response to special pressures, without scheduling, establishing priorities, balancing its overall needs or considering its fiscal resources. Planning, when it existed in cities, had been largely ceremonial, with no statutory teeth aside from zoning,* and with little or no budget or technical staff. Meanwhile, there was, until the depression, continual runaway, speculative, private building; such building required sup-

interest in the bonds," read the Authority's report. The Triborough's great success made funds available for other bridge and parkway building programs. In 1940, the facilities and separate authorities were consolidated and refinanced to make cash available for still more multimillion-dollar improvements.

* New York's zoning ordinance had not been thoroughly revised since its passage in 1916.

porting public facilities, such as roads, sewers, water and schools, and more public services, such as fire and police protection and traffic controls.

The establishment of a strong and semi-independent Planning Commission under New York's celebrated new charter of 1938 was hailed as a great victory for city planning and served as an inspiration for other cities. The formal stature given to the new Commission by the charter was unparalleled in the United States. Seven paid commissioners were to run and control it; the terms of six, including the full-time chairman, were arranged to free the Commission from political control by any four-year, one-term Mayor. Some planners viewed the Commission as virtually a fourth power of government. It was to direct New York's growth and its public-works spending through two new devices: a master plan for land use and a six-year capital budget and annual program to guide the building of public facilities and effectuate the plan. Zoning would be under the aegis of this policy-making Commission, which would have a full-time Department of Planning staff to carry out necessary technical studies.

La Guardia, the first Mayor to preside under the new charter, offered the planning chairmanship to Moses. Moses consulted the charter drafters to learn how they construed the new agency's role and power, since accepting the position would have required him to resign from the parks and the bridge authorities. "One said it was the steering wheel; another . . . the brakes . . . all agreed it was not the engine nor the carburetor," he recounted. Emerging from an era where planning was believed to have failed to execute projects largely for lack of funds, Moses, a pragmatist and activist, evidently felt that he would be trading the substance for the shadow. He turned down the job.

"As soon as we were in office," one of the original planning commissioners recalls, "Moses had his expediters at our door to tell us what stages various operations were in. They had resolutions in hand for projects needing the Board of Estimate's action, and when the Board passed that resolution, his men would come back with another to forward the project to the next stage." Moses himself took the planning commissioners on tours of his works in progress.

Before a new project of his came up for the planning body's approval, Moses would mail out an illustrated promotional brochure, so official in appearance and seemingly complete in detail —with even the schedule for construction—that it was hard for the Commission to question his plan, much less turn it down.

Moses' pungent, acid-tipped pen and his tireless mimeograph machine provided extra guidance and prodding for his commissioners and other officials. It might require most of the morning to read Moses' advisories, but they could not be ignored. Copies of Moses' mail were sent to a wide list that was believed to include top city officials as well as the press. Once Moses' charges that his opponents were "enemies of progress," "mud-slingers" or "crack-pots"—some of his more familiar, everyday epithets—had appeared in the papers, it was difficult for the inexperienced planning commissioners to stand in the way.

But Rexford Tugwell, the man who became Planning Chairman in March 1938, took the charter seriously. Tugwell, an early Roosevelt brain-truster and a former economics professor, held liberal beliefs that were controversial even for the New Deal. As Federal Resettlement Administrator, he had carried out imaginative programs of rural land re-use and new-town development, and he was a strong, though disappointed, advocate of greater national planning. In New York, he drafted the first stages of the master plan mandated by the charter.

Among the major proposals for shaping the future New York developed under Chairman Tugwell's aegis by 1940 were land-use controls that would restrict building coverage, and provisions for greater amenities, including new open spaces in neighborhoods —a system of "green-belts."

Moses' formative years in government were spent during the earlier "efficiency" era; his politics and utterances, if not his practices, reflected a conservative bias from those days. Until the 1938 charter, Moses had been free to select his projects and sites and, as long as he could find the necessary funds, carry them out. The public sector was so neglected that anything he built—especially with federal work-relief funds or fees from vehicles rather than with city taxes or credit—seemed a big improvement for the city. Although he always maintained that he worked for limited objectives, many people, himself included, had come to regard

Moses as the city's and the region's master planner *—even though he professed to despise the term.

The emerging master plan for New York City not only threatened Moses' general freedom. The charter responsibilities of the Planning Commission also trespassed on his special preserves—parks, bridges, playgrounds and roads, and Tugwell's "socialistic" doctrines were anathema to him.

Moses opened fire to destroy the master plan. The tenor of his campaign of vilification was captured in this pronouncement which appeared in the papers: "It reflects the program of socialistic, planned economy whose aim is to reconstruct the entire city and with it our economic and political systems. [The people] would rather have Tammany back, with all its evils, than be in the hands of the Planning Reds."

La Guardia himself was no planning enthusiast; nor, despite his vocal campaign support, was the pragmatic Mayor a defender of the charter in practice.† La Guardia maintained to Tugwell that he knew what the city needed better than did the planning body. In fact, the very independence from the Mayor of the potentially powerful Planning Commission (which had seemed such a triumph to the reform-minded 1938 charter writers) alienated the support of the top elected official which city planning needed to be effective. Thus the charter helped vitiate the planning role. Instead of serving as a guide for city growth, planning became a malleable tool in the hands of the Board of

* In July 1941, writing in a Triborough Authority publication, Moses stated that its function "is not merely to build and maintain certain water crossings within the city but to solve metropolitan arterial and recreational problems. [In order to provide unified execution] the expedient was adopted here of having one person hold at the same time several city and state authority positions, so that he could act as a sort of coordinator and liaison officer between the various agencies responsible for parts of the work. This lot has fallen to me. The Triborough Authority has provided the warp on the metropolitan loom. . . ."

† At first La Guardia had even refused to give his appointee Tugwell—who has conjectured that La Guardia never read the planning chapter of the 1938 charter—the information about city funds. The planners required this to prepare the capital budget and six-year program for scheduling public works called for in the charter. He had also turned down the Chairman's request for an adequate budget to staff the Commission, and, to Tugwell's horror, requested zoning variances for his political friends.

Estimate, that strange and highly influential institution which is part of the unique New York story.

Public hearings on the master plan were postponed from month to month as Moses and the real estate interests fought it. In August 1941, Tugwell resigned to accept the Governorship of the Commonwealth of Puerto Rico. In January 1942, La Guardia appointed Parks Commissioner Moses to the Planning Commission, in spite of what seemed a public conflict of interest,* and he granted Moses special permission to be represented at meetings by a deputy.

Early in 1942, the battle between the Planning Commissioner-in-absentia and the "long-haired planners" was won by Moses. "TUGWELL PLANNING FOR CITY JUNKED," the headline in *The New York Times* announced. "Board Votes to Discard Maps After 18 Months Spent Preparing Them; Green Belts to Beautify All Residential Areas Now Dead, Says Moses."

Denied operating funds and the Mayor's support, and cut down by one of its own commissioners, the planning agency for years did little except record other departments' "master plans" and projects on the city map and patch up the threadbare 1916 zoning ordinance.

Moses may well have planted the seeds of his eventual Title I debacle by helping to decimate planning. Because the city lacked a comprehensive development plan and firm program for its public works, the most powerful contender for city funds could generally win approval from the Board of Estimate which, by its power of veto over the Planning Commission and other bodies, controlled land use and spending. The absence of a generally agreed-upon public concept of where the city was to go or not to go made it easy for Moses to go anywhere—and he often did. Ultimately, however, lack of a disciplined framework for the selection of redevelopment sites, of positive criteria for land reuse, and of an officially accepted community guide for determining the needs of the city made his huge, disruptive, narrowly construed and politically tainted Title I program indefensible.

* The appointment was challenged in court by the Citizens' Union, which saw a conflict of interest in the Parks Commissioner passing on his own projects as Planning Commissioner, but the courts found nothing wrong: Moses received no salary in his new post.

URBAN REDEVELOPMENT BEGINS

In 1948, it no doubt seemed natural for Mayor William O'Dwyer to put the emerging federally aided urban redevelopment program under the wide wing of his City Construction Coordinator. O'Dwyer's first official act in 1946 had been to create the unprecedented and originally temporary Coordinator post so that Moses could expedite the building of community facilities and housing. By the Mayor's statute, the Coordinator was given charge of all state and federal construction funds coming to the city.

O'Dwyer, a Tammany man who rose to prominence in the role of crime-busting district attorney, had little experience in running a big city. But it was obvious to him that New York faced a tremendous building backlog. Although Republican Moses had opposed him in the general election, he seemed to be the only man capable of handling this big job.

Even before O'Dwyer's term, Moses was busy planning for postwar public works, including housing. As La Guardia's representative, he had been directly responsible for initiating and pushing through the first privately financed, publicly assisted slum clearance and redevelopment project in the country. That was Stuyvesant Town, a $110,000,000 project built by the Metropolitan Life Insurance Company on eighteen blocks of the old "Gas House" district bordering on the Lower East Side of Manhattan. The private redevelopment was made possible by the state's 1943 Redevelopment Companies' Act (as amended by Moses), which allowed a municipality to use eminent domain in assembling slum land for sale to a private rebuilder, as well as to grant tax abatement to the sponsor in order to lower rentals,* the rent charges being subject to city approval. The huge Stuyvesant Town housing project opened in 1949, thanks in good part to Moses' cutting through layers of red tape and postwar federal material priorities; the project provided homes for 26,000 veterans and their families at a modest $17-a-room rate.

Stuyvesant Town was regarded as a Moses coup—or a disaster. About 200,000 letters of application were received for its 8,755

* Profits were limited by law to 6 per cent.

housing units, and waiting lists were always long. But planners and architectural critics judged this development harshly. It nearly tripled densities from the original 3,000 dwelling units in the demolished low-rise housing—and reducing congestion in close-packed Manhattan was a planners' goal. (No write-down of the land cost was yet available, and the sponsor had had to absorb the difference and still try to make his state-limited low profit.) They also objected to the "institutional" appearance of the thirty-five high-rise apartment houses with their look-alike cost-cutting design. They criticized the poor site planning and the failure to provide adequate community facilities, such as an elementary school, in the neighborhood.

Civil rights groups, then timid, opposed the sponsor's "whites only" rental policy, which was maintained in this municipally assisted project with the open support of Moses and the Board of Estimate. Metropolitan Life's president had firmly announced that "Whites and Negroes don't mix." Another similar redevelopment known as Riverton was being put up by his insurance company in Harlem, to house 8,500 Negroes at similar rentals.*

Moses was not originally a housing man, and he had opposed public housing at first because it depended on government subsidy. But when it became apparent that this was to be a large-scale, permanently funded program, he moved in on it, first through his Parks Commissioner position and then unofficially through La Guardia's appointment of Moses' men to the New York Public Housing Authority. In 1945, he had also ridiculed urban redevelopment—"this long-hair planning of ripping up cities and doing them over"—at a Senate hearing on postwar economic policy and planning. But he had a penchant for locating government construction funds available to the city, and when it appeared that Title I was to become federal law (his Yale classmate, now Senator Robert A. Taft, had consulted him about the emerging legislation), Moses laid the ground to administer the anticipated local share.

A year before Title I was passed by Congress, Moses had put through Albany a bill that would enable New York City to accept its full share of funds. (No state could receive more than 10

* A subsequent New York State law made discriminatory renting practices in publicly assisted housing illegal.

per cent of the original $1,500,000,000 federal appropriations available for redevelopment.*) This bill also made the city itself, rather than an authority, the local public agency for receiving the funds, with the Board of Estimate in charge. Moses was able to add to his roster this non-salaried job as Chairman of the *ad hoc* New York Mayor's Committee on Slum Clearance.

By December 1948, the Slum Clearance Committee was operative and the chairman began sounding out sponsors. He presented a first report to the Mayor and Board of Estimate the day before the President's signature made the Housing Act of 1949 into law.

Presenting new programs or proposed legislation in simple, persuasive language to those whose support was necessary was another Moses talent. In this preliminary report he made the complex Title I program sound as simple as buying blue-chip bonds. The object of the new federally assisted slum clearance program, the report stated, was "to select slum sites suitable for private investment." Winning private backing for his public projects was also one of Moses' strengths. (He once defined government's role: "It not only keeps order; it paves the way for private profit and risks.") He had persuaded Metropolitan Life to sponsor Stuyvesant Town, and he, like the authors of the federal redevelopment legislation, expected such institutional sponsors—which had already built a number of moderate-rental, limited-dividend housing developments on open land in New York with public aid—to be the main sponsors in cleared slum areas, as well.

Sponsorship prospects were bright in late 1949. Moses reported to the Board of Estimate and Mayor that several life insurance companies, the Marshall Field Foundation, New York University and other "responsible financial groups" had expressed interest in specific sites. But no sponsors were signed up six months later, when the Slum Clearance Committee presented its second report in January of 1950. "For various reasons, those representing large reservoirs of private capital in banks, insurance companies, real estate and building enterprises have been hesitant to take a lively interest in slum clearance," Chairman Moses wrote. "The field is new, untried and experimental. The procedure is necessarily cumbersome. The timetable must be slow, and is complicated by

* This figure is now 12½ per cent.

difficulties of moving people and businesses . . . no wholesale reconstruction will be brought about overnight by this method."

The reasons for the unexpected disinterest and withdrawal of institutional investors as sponsors of housing projects in general, and redevelopment in particular, and for the slow subsequent entry of other private investors, are so complex and so basic to the course of Title I that they will be treated separately in Chapter 4.

The federal aid program for cities had been drafted with the basic assumption that the high cost of assembling slum land and demolishing the buildings was the only major deterrent to the participation of private enterprise in urban rebuilding, and that once this was eliminated private investment would follow easily. This was not true during the early years.

The few cities outside New York that cleared slum sites with the new federal funds and then found themselves without buyers waited uncomfortably, often for years, until the situation changed. But Moses did not brook delays. Characterizing himself as a public servant, he once said, "We've taken our oaths of office, and we're supposed to do certain things. Our only claim to distinction is the fact that we do them." He had long ago found that if he could not gain all he wanted at a project's inception, it was usually possible to realize his ambitious developments piecemeal.

To get Title I moving in New York and to attract private sponsors, it seemed the city itself would have to take extra steps. Thus, Slum Clearance Chairman Moses proposed that the Board of Estimate should publicly solicit offers from private developers for the slum sites, the minimum project size to be twelve acres. He suggested that the Board should specifically call attention to the inducements of redevelopment to private capital, inducements which he helped make more attractive than the Title I legislation itself.

The slums and deteriorating areas of New York City were vast. In Manhattan alone, some 7,000 acres had been found blighted by the 1940 census and were mapped as suitable for redevelopment by the City Planning Commission. The choice of sites was extensive, from well-located areas on midtown's periphery to the depths of Harlem and remotest Brooklyn. Before long, New

York newspapers announced that the city was looking for Title I sponsors.

THE NEW YORK METHOD

Not since the building of the railroads in the West a full century before had the United States government devised a program aimed specifically, as was Title I of the Housing Act of 1949, at involving private enterprise in a peacetime public purpose. But Congress recognized the great abuses of both public powers and private rights that were potentially inherent in redevelopment. A project would usually entail public acquisition of hundreds of separate parcels of land, either by negotiation or condemnation; displacement of thousands of residents and businesses; and the resale of the land to a private rebuilder for the "fair value" appropriate to its re-use—a price considerably lower than acquisition cost. It therefore called for certain local responsibilities, public hearings and legislative approval before the property was acquired, in order to avert abuses. The new federal slum clearance agency that administered the program added a series of reviews and approvals to make sure that the federal money was being spent according to the law. States and municipalities also had laws governing redevelopment and the disposition of public land.

Congress believed that local determinations should play an important part. It required that the redevelopment plan conform to the general plan for a locality's development, and relied on the locality to select the sponsor and to determine the blight findings that made a project area eligible. But the program was so new that many exigencies were not considered.

Moses was accustomed to writing his own laws (he had drafted the state statute governing Title I proceedings) and to circumventing rules and procedures that threatened to block progress. The disinterest of the usual private investors was only one obstacle to getting rapid results in Title I. The federal agency, with its rules and processing, was more like a time-wasting regulative body rather than a disbursing agency. It was also clear that redevelopment could become enmeshed in local political and bureaucratic drags. To avoid these delays, the Slum Clearance Committee established unique procedures for New York City almost every step of the way.

The federal officials were eager for action, and not anticipating the unfortunate consequences of Moses' unusual, although not illegal, approach, supported him for some years. His desire to launch and expedite a large-scale urban redevelopment program in the country's biggest city seemed to justify the exceptions. He claimed to be under pressure to produce results, and in 1950–51 he initiated eight Title I projects. The means he devised for advancing these and subsequent ones became known as the "New York method."

Most unusual and most abused, among the several distinctive elements in this unique method, was the immediate transfer of an uncleared Title I site to a sponsor on his signing the contract with the city to buy and rebuild the land. Other cities first demolished the slums and cleared the site before delivering Title I land to a sponsor. In New York, although the sponsor paid the city only the reduced price at which the land was valued after clearance, by virtue of the quick turnover, he became the owner of the existing property complete with occupied slum buildings. Thus he became in effect a slum landlord until he had relocated the residents and demolished the buildings.

The quick turnover seemed designed primarily to placate local politicians, as well as some top elected city officials. The sponsor would pay real estate taxes during the clearance period, and the city would not have its borrowing ceiling reduced through taking costly property off the tax rolls during the clearance process. Such a matter was particularly important to the powerful City Comptroller who, with the Mayor and City Council President, was one of the three most important members of the Board of Estimate. Other cities forewent taxes during that period—and did not attempt such large-scale programs.*

The quick turnover also shifted from the city to the private sponsor the touchy and onerous task of uprooting families from their homes and of clearing buildings—not just slum dwellings, but also the shops and institutions that were part of the neigh-

* Under a subsequent amendment to the Housing Act of 1949, real estate taxes can be charged against gross project costs until the site is cleared, and two thirds of this loss is absorbed by the federal government under Title I.

borhood. The city's Bureau of Real Estate was to supervise the professional relocation agencies which the sponsors hired.

Other cities assumed the responsibility for relocating families into standard housing. Various explanations have been given for New York's avoidance of this part of the job. Moses purportedly told the federal officials that the Board of Estimate would never support redevelopment if the city was responsible for relocation. His slum clearance director later explained that "Every office holder would be subject to pressures from tenants and property owners to hold off." Thus, Title I, far more radical than other public actions that alter existing living and property patterns, might have been similarly bottled up in the conservative Board of Estimate "for further study." The Slum Clearance Committee ignored the fact that a number of reliable real estate developers shunned New York projects because the city gave them this relocation responsibility.

Other cities first designated a Title I site, made plans for its rebuilding, acquired the property—after the necessary public hearings and legislative approvals, and then looked for a sponsor.

This procedure consumed a great deal of time, and there was no guarantee of a sponsor at its end. New York combined the process of site selection and re-use planning, doing this privately in cooperation with a pre-selected but unannounced sponsor. This was not illegal (until 1959, when Congressman John V. Lindsay sponsored a law prohibiting such undisclosed dealings), but it was suspicious. In a number of instances, it later became known, sponsors proposed project sites and the Slum Clearance Committee accommodated them with a Title I designation.

Moses insisted that he would not put a Title I site up for bidding, much less have the city acquire a site, unless one private sponsor had already agreed to buy and rebuild the project area. His recognition that a project had to be saleable, and that investors were generally reluctant to speculate much time and money on the possibility of sponsoring such risky projects, was important; in time, negotiated sales came to be accepted by the federal agency. Indeed, the problem of Title I land disposition in many cities, where slum sites that were selected by planning bodies and met all the federal requirements sat cleared and unsold for years, haunted not only localities but also the federal administrators. But the particular manner in which New York selected sites, negotiated and in effect shut out competitors made its system eventually unacceptable.

Projects did not become public knowledge until they had to go through the two public hearings required by state and federal law.* But by then, the site (and its sponsorship) was virtually a *fait accompli*. Public notice was given of the hearings that the Board of Estimate was required to hold, but this notice was placed in an obscure journal with a circulation of several thousand, *The City Record,* which is published primarily for people who do business with the city. The federal administrators claimed that this procedure was not in the spirit of the law's intent.

Around the time of the hearings, the Committee would issue an elaborate brochure about the project. These publications covered everything from extensive statistics on surveys made for blight designation, to the availability of housing units on the site and elsewhere for family relocation, and the redevelopment plan, with sketches of the new structures, the expected "moderate" rents and even the anticipated profits for the sponsor. As a rule the pre-designated sponsor's name was not mentioned, although a statement was included that "a bid had been received from a reliable builder." Everything appeared official and final, except for the sponsorship.

Other cities promoted their projects to potential sponsors widely and well in advance of putting the land up for sale. They placed advertisements in local as well as New York newspapers, including *The Wall Street Journal,* which invited interested sponsors to write for details. The New York Slum Clearance Committee met the municipal code requirement that all public property be sold at public auction, with public notice given fifteen days in advance. But the announcement of the auction, placed in *The City Record,* was hardly designed to stimulate

* State law required that the Planning Commission approve, following a public hearing, findings that the project area was substandard and insanitary, and thus eligible for redevelopment. The Board of Estimate, as the governing body of the city, had to approve the project before property acquisition and the issuing of federal grants, and this only after a public hearing.

competitive bidding—especially since investors who might sponsor a Title I project were unlikely to read this publication. The brochures themselves were also hard to obtain.

It should have been possible for a competitor to outbid the Committee's pre-designated sponsor at the auction. But practically speaking, it was too late. Since outsiders were given virtually no time to study the feasibility of the novel and costly redevelopment undertakings (a pre-designated sponsor usually had at least six months), it was almost impossible for them to make an intelligent bid.

The lure of acquiring a large tract of ordinarily inflated, built-up city land at a price reduced to its fair value when cleared had been deemed sufficient to attract private investment into urban redevelopment when Title I was conceived. But even with the write-down there were many risks to a developer, and profits were uncertain. To sweeten the enterprise for potential sponsors, New York did more than negotiate the sale price privately. The city contract specifically allowed Title I sponsors to earn an unusual 10 per cent risk fee, to be taken out of the rents they collected from the site tenants after paying operating expenses on the old buildings. This fee was purportedly a return for the responsibility they accepted of operating a slum (and incurring such expenses as making repairs on building violations); the fee was to be put back into the project, to build up the equity the sponsors needed for rebuilding. Contracts generally called for the rebuilding phase to commence after four years. The contracts also guaranteed that if the sponsors defaulted, the city would return to them any profit it might realize from the project's resale—a clause in direct violation of the federal law.

THE SLUM CLEARANCE COMMITTEE

The operation of the Slum Clearance Committee was also unique. The billion-dollar Title I program was run like one more of Moses' free-wheeling authorities. It was as removed as possible from citizen scrutiny, public approval and attack, and also from the ponderous municipal bureaucracy which such a big operation would ordinarily entail in New York. Since it did not even exist as a bookkeeping unit, the Committee was not subject to audit. Only five staff men, including Moses' Triborough director who doubled as the unsalaried head, plus five clerical workers, ran the vast New York City Title I program. At first some of them were merely loaned to the Committee from city departments, but in time, the two top men worked directly on the Triborough's far more generous payroll.

The offices of the Slum Clearance Committee were at Randall's Island, the headquarters of the Triborough Authority, about seven miles up the East River from City Hall. Since the Committee's telephone number was not listed in the Manhattan directory along with other city agencies, reaching it by telephone was difficult.

The voluminous technical and planning work required during the course of a redevelopment project, from the initial findings required to establish project eligibility to the detailed plans for rebuilding, were contracted out to selected private firms by the Committee; the Triborough Authority operated in a similar manner.

The City Planning Commission had little advance knowledge of projects. It was brought in only when its approval was required by local law, and this just before the Board of Estimate's hearings; it could do little but go along with project selection and plans. During the early years of Title I in New York, Moses' supporters dominated the Commission. (As one 1952 Title I project announcement baldly put it, "It is anticipated that the Planning Commission, three of whose members are members of the Slum Clearance Committee, will approve acquisition of the land at its meeting this afternoon.") New York had no long-range master plan to guide Title I, but only a map of blighted areas designated by the Planning Commission, from which the Slum Clearance Committee was to select its sites.

In other cities, lay boards of leading citizens headed Title I agencies. New York's Slum Clearance Committee did not even have a citizens' advisory committee to consult. For many years all of its members were public officials * —men whose cooperation

* The original members included: City Comptroller, Chairman of the City Housing Authority, Corporation Counsel, Chief Engineer of the Board of Estimate, and City Construction Coordinator.

was particularly needed to expedite projects through the city machinery.

The Committee's infrequent meetings, generally held at the Triborough's headquarters on Randall's Island, were hardly deliberative sessions. Called at the Chairman's pleasure, for late morning, the Committee met five times in 1952, four in 1956. One member described the preliminary executive session as "You'd listen to Moses for forty-five minutes." There followed an "open" session—open to the Committee's invited guests—other city officials, consultants, would-be sponsors. Press representatives had to wait in the hall; sometimes they were locked out. Subsequently, they might be given some news.

Official business rarely took up more than two hours, and by 1 P.M. the Committee and its guests could retire to the Triborough's panoramic dining room to enjoy a delicious buffet luncheon prepared by the Authority's kitchen and served by its uniformed staff. Moses' efficient methods recognized that the way to a man's good will was often through his stomach.

THE MANHATTANTOWN PROJECT

The severe problems of Moses' early Title I projects cast a long, dark shadow over the entire redevelopment program.

Most notorious of the several projects that failed under the New York method was Manhattantown, located on the decaying West Side of Central Park. Manhattantown's six blocks of rat-infested, mostly Old Law tenements, inhabited by some 3,600 people, had been turned over to the sponsoring corporation in August 1952; the sponsors were to complete family relocation and property demolition by October 1954. They were credited $1,000,000 on the sale price of $4,500,000 by the city to cover expenses for these two activities.

But at the end of two years, it was apparent that little headway had been made in clearing the slums which the city had sold to the sponsors, and that most buildings were still inhabited. Some of the more scandalous side-effects of this inaction did not become public knowledge until early in the fall of 1954, when a Senate subcommittee investigating certain Federal Housing Administration insurance programs conducted hearings in New York.

Manhattantown, Inc. had applied for, though it had not received, an FHA commitment, and the Senate subcommittee invited the firm's secretary, Samuel Caspert, and others involved in the project, to appear before them. They were curious to know "whether the attractiveness of the operation that these people had been engaged in hasn't perhaps delayed the construction. . ."

Cross-examination brought out details of what a federal government audit of the records had documented: that Manhattantown's slums had yielded nearly $650,000 that was drawn out of the operation by various stockholders, syndicate partners, relatives and friends. This sum exceeded by far the return allowed in their contract on their cash investment, which was only $1,100,000, most of it borrowed. The sponsors were required by contract ultimately to pay a total of $3,150,000 by the end of four years. This sum, plus the $1,000,000 credit, was the appraised value of the land when cleared for rebuilding. But they had actually acquired a $15,385,784 revenue-producing property, the higher sum being the acquisition cost paid by the city for the site in its uncleared state, one that had changed little.

Among the special sources of income drawn from the slum (and which were not required to be put into the project as equity) were salaries paid to some of Manhattantown's forty-two owners and their relatives and friends for services allegedly performed in connection with the property's maintenance and which yielded $221,637. They also set up several separate companies that extracted further profits from the property. The most novel of these was a corporation headed by Caspert's son-in-law, and owned by some of the other principals. It bought the tenements' stoves and refrigerators from Manhattantown, Inc.; leased them back to Manhattantown; and then sold them back after a year at the original purchase price. This brought in an additional $115,320.

Caspert's testimony raised some question about the interests of the project's architect, who was a stockholder in Manhattantown and a top partner in the firm that handled almost all the architectural work for Moses' Title I sponsors as well as for the Slum

Clearance Committee.* Caspert was accompanied by Manhattantown's lawyer, Democratic Presidential advisor Samuel Rosenman, a friend of Moses and sometime lawyer for the Triborough Authority. His legal firm had an eight-year contract with Manhattantown, Inc. to receive $250,000 in fees.

Not until mid-1959, when the Citizens' Union investigated the Slum Clearance Committee, did the press and the public begin to learn of the close ties not only between Manhattantown's sponsors, but also some other Title I speculators in New York, and top city or party officials, as high as the Borough President of Manhattan. Caspert, it was disclosed, was president of his West Side Democratic Club and had gone to his district leader to express an interest in sponsoring a Title I project in their neighborhood. He, in turn, was introduced to Moses' men through the Congressman for Caspert's area, Franklin D. Roosevelt, Jr. Many members of the original Manhattantown group had become stockholders in three more Title I projects, but their identities were lost among the large number of people involved.

At the time of the 1959 revelations, building groups asserted that Title I had been a "closed club." Indeed, it seemed not only wise, but also necessary, to hire certain consulting firms to do project work, including legal, architectural and banking services, if one wanted to win a sponsorship. Some firms' names showed up regularly on each brochure. But no one who wanted to do business with the city protested publicly, much less admitted that there might be a system. Most firms just never tried for sponsorship.

At the time of the 1954 Senate hearings, Chairman Moses attributed Manhattantown's rebuilding delays to the reluctance of the Federal Housing Administration to issue mortgage insurance in the former slum areas. It was not until 1955 that the FHA did issue its first urban renewal commitment. The FHA's unexpected failure to support urban rebuilding with government mortgage guarantees caused almost the entire program to stand still for years, as we shall see in Chapter 4.

* The federal urban renewal commissioner claimed that working for both sponsor and public agency should be prohibited to prevent a conflict of interest. Moses maintained that in this manner he got the "best talent . . . at nominal fees," and he continued this practice.

But Moses had gone ahead on the assumption that the banks, the insurance companies * and FHA would come through. Only a handful of Title I sponsors could obtain financing and rebuild in New York without the backing of FHA's insurance. There were two types of projects. The first were the cooperatives sponsored by and for unions or institutions which had been given municipal tax abatement; the state's Redevelopment Companies Act allowed this to limited- or nonprofit companies to reduce cooperators' carrying charges. The second type included several projects in exceptionally desirable locations, such as Columbus Circle and Washington Square South, which had been able to secure conventional mortgages. But these had rebuilt at such high rentals (the Slum Clearance Committee in the Columbus Circle brochure called them "proper rental fees for the neighborhood") that although their developments were fully tax-paying and the city received from them many times the taxes previously paid by properties in the project area, they became by the late 1950's ammunition for the mounting public opposition to Title I.

In 1954, within a few days after the Manhattantown revelations, the city seemed to have forgotten about what it had just read. Title I was sullied in the public eye, but New Yorkers have an almost infinite capacity to absorb shock, novelty, even scandal, and to continue business as usual. The Manhattantown sponsors were not even forced to give up their project; nor were the other syndicates, composed of some of its stockholders, prohibited from sponsoring and milking several other similar Title I sites. Two years later, the Manhattantown slums were finally razed, but rebuilding had not yet commenced—despite FHA's offer of mortgage insurance. Two other cleared New York projects were similarly lacking new apartments.

"PEOPLE ALWAYS STAND IN THE WAY . . ."

"People always stand in the way of progress," Moses believed. He was accustomed to organized opposition, but he believed the

* Metropolitan Life did not need to obtain an outside mortgage to build Stuyvesant Town; it had sufficient reserve cash to underwrite its own development.

time allowed it should be limited. He was also used to mowing down opponents and obstacles to his projects, and then receiving adulation—even from former opponents *—for the completed work. He disposed verbally of one of urban rebuilding's greatest traumas with his dictum, "You cannot rebuild a city without moving people. You cannot make an omelet without breaking eggs."

Redevelopment's ingredients, however, were far different from public parks, arterial parkways or bridge approaches. First of all, large numbers of people had to be moved from the densely crowded slum areas. Also, poor people don't know how or where to find another place to live. Because many of their families are larger than average, and the largest group of slum dwellers in New York are non-white or Puerto Rican, their chances of finding another home are still more limited.

Further, there was a vast difference in most people's eyes between the exercise of eminent domain for a public facility and its use to acquire a slum area for resale at a marked-down price to a private sponsor. Few people understood the function of the government write-down of the land cost, much less the concept of the public benefit in clearance for redevelopment, whether the re-use was public or private—although the concept was validated by almost every state's highest courts and ultimately the U.S. Supreme Court in 1954.† Nor did Moses use his great verbal skills to explain these matters. This lack of understanding increased public mistrust.

Here was another part of the Moses paradox. In 1942, before venturing into redevelopment, he had written in a critical essay

* The *Herald Tribune,* which had sided with the Long Islanders in their fight against Moses' Jones Beach project, editorialized, after the popular facility was in operation, "There is . . . nothing of its kind as fine as Jones Beach anywhere."

† The elimination of a slum or the prevention of blight through an area's rebuilding has been consistently upheld as promoting the public welfare and thus as justifying the acquisition and clearance of a slum or blighted area, for public housing *or* private rebuilding, after payment of just compensation to property owners. In earlier days, many states had adopted a test of public use ("use by the public") for the exercise of eminent domain. But this was abandoned as the concept of the public welfare broadened. Several state courts specifically noted that whether a private interest benefited from rebuilding was immaterial; the public taking and clearance of blighted land was the test. The Supreme Court, in 1954, went still further: it ruled that the public welfare may actually be enhanced by private redevelopment.

on Paris' late-nineteenth-century master rebuilder, Baron Eugene Haussmann (a man to whom he was often compared and with whom he identified), "No great program of municipal reconstruction can rest upon any other basis than that of informed majority public opinion, and the majority has to be substantial. Haussmann knew what the public ought to want, but did not concern himself with educating public opinion and building up the support which would allow him to finish his work." Once in power himself, Moses apparently forgot the lesson—or he changed his mind. The Committee's policy seemed to be: the less the public knows, the better.

The first notice received by New Yorkers living or conducting business on a site designated for Title I clearance under Moses was generally a story in the newspapers.

The residents panicked. Committees were formed. "Watch a Sneak Play. Come to City Hall," was the message circulated by the residents' committee of one such Title I area. Busloads of protesting citizens would arrive for the public hearings. "Our Neighborhood Is Not a Slum," read the placards carried before City Hall at the time of one hearing. Some residents were also stirred up in the early days by left-wing demagogues. "TENANTS AT CITY HALL PROTEST MOSES' MASS EVICTION PROJECT," read a *Daily Worker* headline.

Hearings on these projects appeared on the Board of Estimate's crowded agenda in a routine manner, as just one more of hundreds of matters which this body had to consider at its biweekly sessions. Moses was not on hand after the first few projects, and there was no formal presentation by a Committee spokesman. Evidently, the project brochures, which also carried a general report on Title I progress to date, were supposed to convince those select people—especially the Board of Estimate—who received them. Moses has stated his belief that the average person lacks the ability to visualize projects involving dramatic land-use changes. His staff director would answer questions raised by the Board of Estimate.

It is important to understand the unusual character and tradition of this municipal body, a hybrid "upper house" which combines executive and legislative functions; it shares the former with the Mayor and the latter with City Council. Although chaired by the Mayor, the voting majority of the Board of Estimate can be composed—when combined with the votes of the Comptroller or the City Council President—of four of the five Borough Presidents. Not only did each "B. P." represent a separate constituency; his nomination was dominated by the party leadership in his borough, and they in turn had at their disposal extensive patronage with which to repay favors. Thus, linkage between the dominant political party and the Borough Presidents was intimate.

According to custom in the Board of Estimate, before a project could proceed in any borough, it would need the informal advance approval of the Borough President involved. This would be given or withheld at the Board's closed executive sessions, where no minutes were kept. The Board's regular biweekly open sessions were attended by citizens and reporters, but the Board, operating in its "cult of unanimity," rarely presented anything but a united front. The Mayor was commonly a prisoner of this tradition.

People could and did protest at Board of Estimate hearings, and a Borough President might speak out in defense of his constituents. When pressures grew too intense, the Board, rather than reject a project, would lay it over "for further study." But in the case of Title I, if the needed approval were delayed too long, New York might lose the millions of federal Title I funds earmarked for the city, which created special urgency. To obtain a prompt and favorable decision Moses could also use his great power from his other positions—as City Construction Coordinator, Parks Commissioner, arterial highway expediter and Triborough Authority Chairman—to hold up, withdraw or give as reward the roads and other public works projects Borough Presidents might want in their area. His political bargaining position as a non-elective local official was extraordinary.

Public confusion and antagonism were intensified by the Slum Clearance Committee's apparently arbitrary selection of project sites around town, its frequent changes in boundary lines, and, some held, inadequate criteria for determining the extent of blight and thus an area's eligibility.

One of the most misunderstood and most bitterly contested of the early projects was Washington Square South. This site was a light manufacturing loft district—considerably old, increasingly obsolete and deteriorating—where, nonetheless, 1,100 firms employing 15,000 workers conducted their businesses. The federal program did not at that time provide financial assistance to displaced businesses, nor did the city have any plans for their alternate locations. Employers and employees, fearing the loss of their businesses and jobs, descended on City Hall.

The Washington Square South Committee insisted that Title I was intended to clear residential slums, not commercial or manufacturing areas, and that the project was thus illegal. Like most New Yorkers they understood redevelopment to be exclusively a housing program. This was not so, but no one in authority had made it clear to them. The federal regulations then called for all project areas to be "predominantly residential," either in their previous state or in their redevelopment; Washington Square South met this requirement because housing was to be built on the site. The group failed to get satisfaction in New York and carried the fight to Washington. It was not until 1955 that a Congressional subcommittee on small business made officially clear to them that their protests were out of order. By that time, two new apartment buildings which met the "predominantly residential" requirements of the original Title I law were already rising. However, the small units, high rents and monolithic style were so unrelated to the surrounding neighborhood, and to the community's wish for family-size apartments, that the apartments provoked further protest from the Greenwich Villagers.*

But the most widely criticized aspect of Moses' Title I program was the touchy problem of family relocation.

In spite of the alleged supervision of sponsors by a city agency, then the Bureau of Real Estate, the conscience of each sponsoring group seemed to be the actual guide to its relocation performance. Again, the responsible institutions and sponsors—like Morningside Heights, Inc. at Columbia and the United Housing Foundation, which was carrying out the Corlears Hook coopera-

* After 1965 the final site plan was changed to include two dormitories for married New York University students and faculty and one middle-income-housing building for the public.

tive project for the sponsoring I.L.G.W.U.—handled this sensitive task well. But the sloppy, abusive way in which several of the more speculative sponsors, especially the syndicated corporations, treated their tenants blackened the whole program.

Federal law required localities to relocate families displaced by the Title I program into "decent, safe and sanitary housing within their means." But the federal agency accepted the word of the local public agencies as to what actually happened to the families.

It was extremely difficult in New York to obtain reliable information. The Slum Clearance Committee brochures appeared to account for every contingency. They even specified the percentage of dislocatees who could be expected to find new homes in the "moderate rental" apartments to be built in the Title I area, and carried a letter from the Chairman of New York City's Housing Authority assuring enough low-rental units. But, as the City-Wide Council for Better Housing, one of the many groups organized specifically to fight the Title I program, claimed, these were "a jumble of meaningless figures thrown together for public relations."

As experience in New York and elsewhere would show, very few Title I projects rehoused dislocatees. Even if such persons could afford the redevelopment's rents, which was unusual, most had long since moved elsewhere. Moreover, to have housing vacancies available, and to move in dislocatees, even into low-rent housing, were two very different matters. To further complicate the problem, the New York City agency that was responsible for supervising the private relocation agents who were employed by the sponsors turned out to be one more of New York's scandal-ridden, building-related agencies.

Between 1953 and 1956, at least six different public and civic agencies—the federal Housing and Home Finance Agency, the New York City Administrator's office, the City Planning Commission, the Community Service Society, the Women's City Club and the Mayor's Committee on Housing—were investigating relocation practices and making proposals, which were ignored, for their improvement.

Even the City Planning Commission issued two opinions in its

1954 report. The minority stated that "practically no effort had been made to inspect the rehousing conditions of relocatees," and warned about the inadequacy of the available housing supply. The majority report, which bore the name of Commissioner-in-absentia Moses, found that the job was being handled well and the future would present no problems. ("No wonder the radicals would like to get hold of tenant relocation," Moses wrote in an appended statement, dismissing the minority's insistence that much more publicly assisted housing needed to be built.)

Other cities handled relocation themselves, and the moving costs might be charged to project cost, under the federal financing formula. New York sponsors were charged only the value of the cleared land, but had to relocate tenants themselves. It was stated that they would absorb the cost of moving their site tenants into decent housing, but their contracts did not bind them to do so. Only some of the sponsors actually paid moving expenses as provided.

In Manhattantown, according to a study by the Women's City Club, 82 per cent of the tenants received neither moving nor rehousing assistance or payments. Many residents had been handed eviction notices without court orders. Others were merely "relocated" to remaining buildings on the site (thus continuing the sponsor's income *), although the buildings had no heat, hot water or basic maintenance, and in spite of the fact that such renting was against city laws.

Often site families were not informed by the sponsor or the city of their rehousing rights under federal law. A policy of "stimulating independent relocation" to speed site clearance was urged in several Slum Clearance Committee brochures. According to elder statesman Stanley Isaacs, the chairman of the subcommittee on relocation of the Mayor's Committee on Housing, and former Borough President of Manhattan, tenants were "hounded out like cattle" at the Godfrey Nurse–North Harlem site, another notorious project where several thousand of the city's most disadvantaged citizens lived. Moses told Isaacs, who

* As demolition of buildings on the site advanced, the sponsor's profits decreased.

was the sole Republican Councilman and the only elected official in the city speaking out against such abuses, "In ten years, you'll be grateful you've got the project."

THE "GOO-GOO'S" AND THE BIG GUNS

Default of local leadership was another price that New York paid for Moses. New York's leaders, both public and private, had become flaccid from years of letting Moses do things for them and their city.

Mayors, from La Guardia on, continually let him take on new jobs and acquire greater power. William O'Dwyer, who left the city and Mayor's office under something of a cloud in 1950, virtually turned over New York's development to Moses during his few years at City Hall. It was O'Dwyer who created the City Construction Coordinator job; empowered the toll-collecting Triborough Bridge Authority to take over the tunnels and build all other intra-city vehicular connections; and established the unusual Slum Clearance Committee.

But it was during the administration of O'Dwyer's successor, Vincent Impellitteri, a Democrat and former City Council President, that the dreary history of Title I in New York was made. Elected, with Moses' backing, during one of the New York Democrats' periodic intra-party splits, "Impy" seemed relieved, once in office, to let anyone who would share his heavy burdens of office. He was eager to obtain the regular Democrats' backing for his renomination to the Mayoralty, and so gave jobs and favors to many who could help him in this. His try for renomination was unsuccessful, but the worst damage had been done in the Title I program and in the city by 1954 when the machine's choice, forty-three-year-old Robert Wagner, Jr., came to City Hall, and inherited Moses.

Wagner, who had been chairman of the City Planning Commission and then Manhattan Borough President, seemed unwilling to concern himself with the criticisms and mounting civic resistance to the program directed by his Slum Clearance Committee. He reappointed Moses to his various city jobs. His attitude toward many problems seemed to be that if you waited long enough, they would go away or somehow resolve themselves.

He also seemed to avoid the great new responsibilities put on Mayors by the "Workable Program" the year he entered the job.

Along with the broadened scope of urban renewal, the federal government in 1954 required that a city's chief executive submit annually his city's Workable Program for community development. This called for evidence of progress in various municipal activities concerned with renewal and slum prevention, and required citizen participation in developing local renewal plans.

As proof of this participation Mayor Wagner listed dozens of citizen groups that were actively interested in the city's housing and urban renewal programs. But his report "neglected to state that all the groups listed were opposed to the city's program," observed Walter Fried, until 1960 director of the regional office of the Housing and Home Finance Agency, through which the New York report was transmitted to Washington.

Moses regarded the Mayor as "Junior" and had contempt for the "Goo-Goo's," the civic organizations concerned with good government, city planning and better housing in New York. They had often found fault with him, an unforgivable sin. Relatively few businessmen of leadership stature—of which New York had an unequaled number—served on these organization's boards, another debilitating element in New York which Moses helped perpetuate. There was no other citywide top power organization concerned primarily with the development of their city.*

When Wagner had been running for office, Nathan Straus, Jr., a close friend of his father and the first administrator of the federal public housing program, suggested that an association of qualified citizen leaders, appointed by the Mayor, be formed to bring the best brains and private leadership of the city to study its problems and to advise the chief executive. The Mayor approved the proposal "enthusiastically," according to Straus' memoirs, and the Mayor's Advisory Council was born on January 1, 1954, when Wagner took office. Straus, a wealthy civic leader, was its head, and many business and civic luminaries, such as Frank Abrams, former President of the Standard Oil Company, who served as its vice-chairman, David Rockefeller, a top executive of R. H. Macy and Co., and others became members of the

* The New York Regional Plan Association concerns itself, as its name indicates, with the overall New York region.

Council's executive committee. They took their appointment seriously, and formed subcommittees which initiated studies in different major areas of municipal concern.

Before long, however, the Mayor's Advisory Council shriveled up. Old-time political leaders opposed the committee's "intervention," wrote Straus. Committee studies, an early one calling for basic fiscal reforms, were ignored by City Hall. The Housing subcommittee never got a chairman. Abrams was the first to resign. Others followed. Some who stayed on regarded it nonetheless as "a waste of time." Within several years, the Council slipped out of existence.

This was to be the fate of many of the honorific Mayor's committees appointed during the Wagner era. The Mayor's Committee on Housing, also created in 1954, was critical of Moses, was ignored by Wagner, and soon withered away.

However, individual Title I projects enjoyed the active, outspoken support of some of New York's most respected, powerful business figures. Moses was helping make land available to build things they, or the expanding private organizations and institutions they headed or supported—hospitals, universities, cultural and business promotional groups—wanted. In his usual style, he marshaled their support to squelch the enemies of progress. Department store owner Bernard Gimbel was chairman of the New York Convention and Visitors' Bureau which had long been handicapped by the city's lack of an adequate exhibition hall. Moses' Triborough Authority, in a remarkable departure from bridges and tunnels, decided to use some of its reserve funds to erect and operate such a structure as sponsor of a Title I project facing onto Columbus Circle. Originally a site for a new Metropolitan Opera Hall was also to be included.

Most of the city's civic and artistic organizations asked that public hearings be postponed until they had time to study the Coliseum project. The Citizens' Housing and Planning Council considered the site planning poor; *Art News* magazine called the structure to be erected at this focal point of the city "tragical." Moses told the "arty" critics that public officials have no right to experiment architecturally on a big scale. The businessmen who wanted the hall apparently agreed, and Gimbel issued a statement underlining its importance. Protests of the Real Estate

Board about tax concessions to be given to the Coliseum hall were ignored also. The tax-exempt opera hall was eliminated due to Moses' ultimate veto. Several high-rise apartments met the federal "predominantly residential" requirements.

Residents of the projected NYU-Bellevue redevelopment, north of Bellevue Hospital and the University's medical school complex in the East 30's of Manhattan, were also girding for battle. Bernard Baruch sent a telegram to the Board of Estimate on the importance of this Title I project, which was to clear the blighted area of Old Law tenements and mixed commercial areas surrounding the medical center and provide housing for its nurses and technicians. The project went through; sponsorship was awarded to what turned out to be another Manhattantown-type syndicate.

What to do with the Metropolitan Opera? Before long, New Yorkers and the rest of the country learned about the city's sixteenth and most ambitious Title I slum clearance project to date, an eighteen-block odd-shaped site called Lincoln Square, which was to contain the Lincoln Center for the Performing Arts on eleven of its acres. The Center would include not only the Opera, which had been seeking a new home for decades, but also the Philharmonic Symphony, whose 57th Street hall then appeared destined for a private speculator's axe, the Juilliard School of Music, several new theaters for ballet and drama, a music library, and a park for open-air concerts. Some 6,500 people and 800 businesses would have to move for the huge redevelopment. The project would also provide Fordham University, a major Catholic institution, with a midtown campus for its graduate schools, and put up new housing further west toward the Hudson. The stellar board of the new multimillion-dollar performing arts center was headed by John D. Rockefeller III, who had a particular interest in the opera, and promotion of the cultural advantages of this unusual concentration of major institutions was intense.

Further north, in the Columbia University religious and educational complex, David Rockefeller headed Morningside Heights, Inc., a nonprofit organization that was sponsoring another Title I project. This one, between the University and Harlem, would clear encroaching slums for new moderate-cost cooperative housing, Mr. Rockefeller was also leading a private body planning for the redevelopment of Lower Manhattan, where the Chase Manhattan Bank, which he headed, was to build its huge new headquarters. Land for that structure was privately acquired, but the Downtown-Lower Manhattan Association was also urging Title I help to clear some blighted nearby areas for new housing.

The city's two powerful apparel unions, the International Ladies Garment Workers Union and the Amalgamated, the former the very backbone of the Liberal Party, were sponsoring huge cooperative housing projects on city-cleared sites, and would benefit from municipal tax abatement. The equally powerful building trades were busily employed, and so were many contracting and building materials' supply firms.

In 1955, Wagner named to the Mayor's Slum Clearance Committee its first "public" member, Thomas J. Shanahan, President of the Federation Bank and Trust Company. Businessman Shanahan, who was at the time unsalaried Vice-Chairman of the city's five-member Housing Authority, might have been regarded as a leading citizen. He was also chairman for many years of Cardinal Spellman's Committee for the Laity, and even helped raise money for Jewish philanthropies. But Shanahan was probably best known municipally as Tammany Hall's number-one fund raiser and was a familiar figure to building and real estate interests, particularly around campaign time. Until the demise of the Slum Clearance Committee in 1960, he served as its Vice-Chairman, and project sponsorship had to be cleared through him.*

In 1957, Moses brought in tycoon William Zeckendorf, the first figure of stature in real estate development to sponsor a project in the city's federally aided program. Although Zeckendorf had been busily seeking—and sometimes getting—major Title I project sponsorships in so many other cities that professionals had nicknamed him "Mr. Redevelopment," he could not get a New York project. Now Moses offered Zeckendorf the fully taxpaying apartment house development site at prestigious Lincoln Square, which several other reputable developers had

* He resigned from the Housing Authority's board in 1957, but Moses convinced the Mayor to let him remain on the Title I committee.

turned down. They didn't like the relocation burden and certain other aspects of the New York method. Also, the area, adjoining the railroad tracks along the Hudson River, appeared dubious.

Zeckendorf, who once explained his operations with the words, "I make grapefruits out of lemons," officially received the award in due course. Meanwhile, he bought up the vacant Manhattantown project which the city had put into receivership, paid the sponsors' $1,326,725 in back city taxes, took on the original architect (although he had his own staff of urban designers) and made two original stockholders his partners in what became known as Park West Village. Zeckendorf also acquired the stock of the NYU–Bellevue project, whose sponsors had not rebuilt and were near default. Renamed Kips Bay, the area was now to be developed not for the medical center but with $62-a-room housing which was expected to find a ready market among the rapidly increasing members of the nearby United Nations. After Zeckendorf's participation, some of the city's more conservative developers began to take a second look at Title I.

"WHEN WILL THEY LEARN?"

The New York press did not help the public to understand Title I. Several afternoon papers were frequently critical of Moses, and the exposés that they occasionally ran gave off more heat than light. The city's biggest circulation paper, the tabloid morning *Daily News,* relished Moses. The Republican *Herald Tribune* treated him as untouchable.

In the *Times,* city news in general was neglected compared to space given to foreign news and Washington features. Although housing is generally considered the city's major problem, this beat had a notoriously high staff turnover. Coverage of the big and controversial local Title I program was episodic; new projects were generally reported at face value. Reporters who suggested more intensive digging were informed by the City Desk that the *Times* was "a newspaper of record," not of inquiry.

On its editorial pages, however, one could count on glowing tributes to Moses, while the paper's Sunday magazine was most hospitable to Moses' brilliant, if rather incoherent, critiques of long-haired planners and other of his favorite whipping boys.

Evidently, the editor found Moses' copy better than thoughtful articles about city planning and redevelopment.

But regardless of their papers' slant or style, city reporters soon learned that if they wished to obtain any information from the Slum Clearance Committee, it was unwise to write critically about that body and its projects, or even to ask the Chairman questions. Moses did not like "snoopers." He did not hesitate to use what favors or pressures he could to try to make reporters and editors withhold stories or write favorably about him.

While such a situation prevailed in the sovereign city of New York, the federal housing agency, although it was paying two thirds the public cost of this huge local program, was put in a difficult position. It could take the extreme step of withholding funds from the city when Moses flouted laws or took short cuts, or when the city plainly failed to perform under the Workable Program. But if New York and Moses did not continue to show results, the federal administrators feared for the future of the whole Title I program.

Was it worth jumping into the hornet's nest of Moses' retribution in order to try to make him follow rules? James Follin, Eisenhower's first urban renewal administrator, tried. When an office tower that had not been submitted to the federal agency as part of the Columbus Circle project plans was being built next to the Coliseum exhibition hall, Follin insisted that the sponsoring Triborough Authority pay the higher price for the land which such a use entailed (and thus reduced the government land write-down). Eventually Moses gave in—but not until, as Follin recalled, "he tore me to pieces across the front pages." Yet even Follin, an engineer by training, was ambivalent about Moses. "No man in history has ever done so much for the city, and you hate to throw impediments in front of that kind of public servant," he commented.

The sloppy relocation practices of some sponsors, as well as the city's failure to enforce maximum legal occupancy standards, apparently spread slum conditions around the very areas into which the government had been pouring millions to eliminate such conditions. This drew increasing federal agency criticism—without results.

Finally, the nation's top housing official, Albert M. Cole, administrator of the Housing and Home Finance Agency, decided to curb the troublesome Mr. Moses and change New York's unique system. The straw that broke Cole's back was what he and the agency's real estate analysts regarded as a deficient (too low) appraisal of the land re-use cost at Lincoln Square, an unprecedented project which entailed huge sums of federal write-down money. The government was subsidizing not only the cultural center but also a religious institution—Fordham University—by selling them land at far less than the fair value * which an alternative profit-making use would pay for that site. Moses refused to consider reappraisal; it was to him a time-wasting process that would "scuttle" the whole project. But behind Cole's quarrel with New York was also his concern about several Title I projects that had not been rebuilt and in which, under the New York method, sponsors had been allowed to milk the property and re-rent slums instead of rehousing tenants. (Slum Clearance Committee brochures blandly stated that "responsible sponsors" were relocating tenants and demolishing buildings.)

Administrator Cole could find no support for his original behind-the-scenes attack, however, either in White House circles or among New York's top groups. He then decided to lower the boom publicly. Cole announced in July 1957 that unless Moses changed his methods and complied with the federal agency, he would cut New York off from all federal housing funds—public, Title I and FHA insurance.

The next day, Moses insisted—with Wagner's backing—on New York's "unique" status. "No Mayor or Board of Estimate of

* The Title I statute requires that the land be conveyed at its "fair value" for the uses provided in the redevelopment plan, as determined by the locality and approved by the federal agency. The local public agency also recommends the re-use value on the basis of two independent appraisals, and this is either confirmed or adjusted by the Urban Renewal Administration.

Emphasis in the administrative interpretation of fair value has changed since the start of the program. In the early days, the land sale was regarded as a real estate transaction; both the federal agency and cities sought the largest dollar return from the land sale and the largest local tax return from the redevelopment. Since the 1954 Housing Act, there has been an increasing emphasis on civic and social objectives, as well.

In practice, appraising Title I land according to the usual market test is difficult, since there are not the usual willing buyer and seller, and because there are so many unusual land uses, Lincoln Center being a case in point. Where there is no comparable use, the appraiser should take into account the next highest use and value the land on that basis.

this city would approve any Title I project that required the city to relocate tenants and demolish buildings before offering the site at auction to private developers," Moses declared.

Several mornings later the *Times,* in an editorial headed "The 'Unique' Bob Moses," challenged the top federal housing official. Recalling President Roosevelt's unsuccessful attempt to force Moses out of the Triborough Authority by withholding works funds, it asked, "When will they learn? New York isn't going to drop Moses as long as he's willing to work for it . . . that is the way we will travel farthest fastest for the public good." (Soon thereafter, the Sunday real estate section featured a front-page roundup headed, "City Leads Nation with Title I Projects.")

Mayor Wagner, who could boast the biggest Title I program, declared, "I have every confidence in Bob Moses."

THE RICH AND THE POOR

Behind the scenes, New York quietly began to pick up the loose ends of its contracts in order to avoid delays and abuses. But the city retained its basic method and approach. It concentrated on the razing of Title I sites, in spite of the 1954 Housing Act's call to conserve cities' deteriorating homes and neighborhoods, and it continued to let sponsors handle relocation.

Moses' scorn for rehabilitation was well known. "Critics build nothing . . . . They think we should . . . fix up with rubberbands, Scotch tape and violations." Others could rehabilitate; he would stick to clearance for rebuilding.

But it seemed by the late 1950's that Moses' approach was compounding rather than reducing New York's housing problem; it was tearing down slums in project areas and crowding displaced people into new slums.

However, in blaming Title I for new slum areas, the public drew erroneous generalizations from limited first-hand observation and newspaper reporting, and from the relatively few bad projects. City Planning Commission figures showed that while about 21,500 families had been displaced by the federally aided redevelopment projects, twice that number had been dislocated by other public programs, among them low-cost housing, highways and new school buildings. Clearance for the latter facilities did not draw the same kind of ire, although the areas were often similar to Title I sites in population composition, and although they lacked comprehensive requirements for the satisfactory re-housing of displacees.

Two other concurrent factors had a still greater impact on the overall shelter situation than did public displacements during the period when large-scale Title I clearance was beginning: New York City was experiencing the tightest housing market in the country, as well as the greatest immigration of low-income families in half a century.

In 1950 the city's housing shortage was at an all-time peak. It was short 430,000 units, which included 280,000 in its current stock that were deteriorated and required rehabilitation or clearance, and another 100,000 that were badly overcrowded. The vacancy rate in standard housing was only 1.2 per cent. This was approximately 3 per cent less than normal in other cities, and was considered by some housing experts to be insufficient to accommodate the relocation load. Knowledgeable people questioned whether slum clearance should not be prohibited entirely. Some critics and citizen organizations urged the city to build only on open land, in order to increase its total housing supply rather than to continue eliminating it. They argued that if there were enough housing, there would be no market for slums.

During the 1950's, Puerto Ricans and Negroes of generally low income poured into the crowded city, while 1,000,000 middle-class white families departed. By 1960, there were 750,000 more members of rapidly reproducing minority groups in New York than in 1950. Many newcomers moved into the deteriorating areas in and around projects scheduled for (or in the process of) clearance; others moved into neighborhoods that would soon be designated for Title I. Aggravating the shelter situation was the fact that discrimination in the private market was largely unchecked.*

Unscrupulous landlords squeezed the newcomers into one-room apartments in illegally converted brownstones or rooming houses and into legally converted furnished "hotel" rooms. Since

* The city passed an open-housing law in 1957, to make discrimination illegal in multiple units. But the law operated on a complaint basis, and few newcomers knew what their rights were, much less how to obtain them.

the city's archaic zoning ordinance did not adequately control residential density, it had been possible to crowd any number of persons into a given floor space in these old buildings. By the time this loophole was legally plugged, most of the damage was done.

Wartime rent control, still in effect due to public pressures, acted as an incentive for owners to convert rent-controlled apartments into more profitable uses, and discouraged property maintenance. Municipal taxing practices penalized rehabilitation by raising the levy on improved properties and made slum landlordism even more attractive.* The city's housing and health codes made substandard housing statutorily illegal. But to enforce these laws (as called for by the 1954 Housing Act) was not only administratively difficult, due to the multiplicity of municipal agencies involved; it was also politically inexpedient and impractical.

What was the Mayor to do? Decant a quarter of a million poor families into Central Park? Public housing could not possibly be built fast enough to shelter them. One out of every eighteen New Yorkers—a group equal to the population of Buffalo—already lived in subsidized low-rent projects, and the huge public housing program was running into heavy local weather.

New York, at least Manhattan, was becoming more and more the city of the rich and the poor. Virtually no new structures were being built privately in that central borough for under $50-a-room rentals. After the Third Avenue elevated train tracks came down in 1956, the Upper East Side of Manhattan had mushroomed into a speculative builders' paradise. Jerry-built, $75-to-$120-a-room apartment houses were rising in the place of old "railroad" flats and displacing the former moderate-income residents. Title I appeared to accelerate the trend elsewhere. Many people questioned the expenditure of public money to knock down old low-rent housing just because it was rated substandard by Moses and the Slum Clearance Committee, when more luxury housing was put up in its place. The new apartments at the Coliseum Title I project near Columbus Circle were renting for

* The city had a statute aimed to encourage tenement rehabilitation through the granting of tax abatement for a nine-year period on the improvements. But very few owners or investors found it economically practical, despite this incentive, to fix up these old structures.

$55 and more a room. At Washington Square Village, the development built on the site of the old loft factory district whose clearance had been so bitterly contested, one-bedroom penthouses rented for $375 a month.

Actually, many more units of moderate-cost housing were built in New York Title I sites than the publicized high-rental projects. In some apartment buildings that received FHA mortgage insurance, rents were held down between $35 and $45 a room. The nonprofit cooperatives which benefited from partial tax abatement under the state's Redevelopment Companies Law offered apartments with monthly carrying charges as low as $17 to $25 a room. Still, dwellers in Title I developments came to be labeled "rich people living in poor people's houses."

It meant nothing to most New Yorkers that the high-rent, fully taxable projects were helping to pay off a much larger share of the public cost incurred in clearing slums than were the abated projects. High-rent housing was also building up the taxable real estate of the city much more substantially. Most New Yorkers are renters, but few seem aware that in paying their rent they are paying municipal taxes.

The public demand for middle-income housing grew, especially as the migration of middle-income white families to the suburbs continued. "Middle-income housing" became a political rallying call, an inevitable plank in many candidates' platforms, although there was wide latitude in their definition of middle income. (Individual difficulty in affording Manhattan's high rentals in the new buildings seemed to be the main measuring stick.)

Rehabilitation was also sure to win applause, although its supporters seemed ignorant of the fact that rehabilitation, like clearance, brought with it substantial displacement of lower-income families. To denounce Moses and his bulldozer virtually guaranteed a favorable audience. Title I or urban renewal came to be blamed for more and more that was wrong with New York.

Complicating matters was the fact that the city's conservative Comptroller, Lawrence Gerosa, administered a new state and city program for encouraging construction of middle-income housing through low-interest loans and partial tax abatement to limited profit or nonprofit sponsors. Although this was not generally known, Gerosa would not allow use of the Mitchell-Lama middle-income housing program,* or public housing, in conjunction with urban renewal; he considered this an undesirable "double subsidy."

As the 1950's drew to a close, conflicts, charges and counter-claims for the efficacy of various renewal tools in solving the city's manifold housing headaches filled the air, and appeared to be paralyzing administrative efforts. Opponents of bulldozing looked hopefully to a pilot urban renewal project on the mid-West Side; Moses had reluctantly let this come in for Title I funds, although it was carried out under the aegis of a separate board headed by the new and independent Planning Commission Chairman, James Felt. This decaying twenty-block area was to be the first in the city to try out the combination of spot clearance, rehabilitation, and installation of new public facilities which the Housing Act of 1954 had proposed as the remedy for declining city areas.

But no one was setting citywide priorities for the use of Title I funds. Nor was the program receiving a public review. With public and private actions tearing down old housing for new housing and facilities, and poor newcomers crowding into the steadily diminishing but sound older stock, the city's slum problem stood in 1960 just about where it had been ten years before, and little hope for improvement was in sight.

MOSES MOVES ON

Even Moses sounded disenchanted with slum clearance for redevelopment by the late 1950's. But Moses did not give up. He let his staff carry on while he headed still another billion-dollar public works job at Niagara Falls, the New York State Power Authority. He was tilting with the Tuscarora Indians, who balked at having to sell part of their reservation to the Authority to make way for a storage reservoir.† Then, late in the spring of

* See Chapter 6 for a description of the Mitchell-Lama program.

† They finally sold the disputed 1,231 acres for a higher price—$3,000,000—than the Authority's original offer of $2,500,000.

1959, revelations of some highly questionable practices under the Mayor's Committee on Slum Clearance brought Moses back to the city.

The Citizens' Union, an organization that former Mayor O'Dwyer once described as a part of the "I hate Moses club," sent a public letter that spring to each of the Committee's members, asking for an explanation of how Title I sponsors had been selected and projects awarded in the first four sites. Two new officials, Planning Chairman Felt and J. Clarence Davies, Jr., head of the Department of Real Estate (the city agency which had recently replaced the scandal-shot Bureau) now sat on the Slum Clearance Committee. They were not rubber stamps for the Chairman. Moses, although he did not provide the information sought by the citizen group, found it impossible to deny them permission to dig it out for themselves. The Committee's closed files were opened to Citizens' Union's counsel, and reporters went along.

Tales of favoritism in project awards and contracts for technical services, as well as apparent conflicts of interest, or at least ethical wrong-doing, soon filled the city's newspapers. Now the names of past sponsors of the sour projects became public for the first time, as did the unsavory background of some sponsors who had received the Committee's tentative approval for future projects.

Vice-Chairman Shanahan was at the center of the scandal. His Federation Bank was responsible for investigating the financial abilities of Title I sponsors, and for approving those who were to be designated. To many it looked as if Shanahan's bank benefited from the program and cut politicians in on Title I, but Moses defended using the bank's services as saving the Committee money.

Most dubious of the future project sponsors approved by Shanahan's bank was a well-known slum landlord, Sidney Ungar, who had served in 1957 as campaign manager for Hulan Jack, Democratic Borough President of Manhattan. Ungar had proposed to the Slum Clearance Committee a Title I project adjacent to slum properties he owned. He had offered to demonstrate his financial ability, the papers revealed, by placing a $700,000 "good faith" deposit with the Federation Bank.

The following year, when Borough President Jack was forced to resign for accepting a bribe from would-be sponsor Ungar, it was revealed that Moses had approved the Ungar project on Jack's "earnest" recommendation. But in 1959, New York's Deputy Mayor Paul O'Keefe, after a hasty investigation ordered by Wagner, found Shanahan to be not guilty of a conflict of interest; therefore, he was not removed from the Slum Clearance Committee. It was next revealed that Shanahan's bank had also approved a former business associate of Frank Costello, a mobster reputed to have great power in Tammany Hall.

The papers were filled with stories in late June, and some people were demanding Moses' removal. The weekend that the exposés reached their peak, however, Mayor Wagner was playing golf with Shanahan. He announced that both Moses and Shanahan would stay, but that he would "pull the reins on Bob." Now the Vice-Chairman would share his responsibilities for sponsor selection with Felt and Davies. Wagner also added three new "public" members to the Slum Clearance Committee. *The New York Times* editorially welcomed the "good news . . . that Mr. Moses—hard to live with, but impossible to live without—will still be in there pitching."

Still the scandals refused to disappear and the critics were not satisfied. They insisted Title I needed more than a "scratch committee."

Wagner now ordered an independent management study of the city's many housing and renewal activities in order to devise a new administrative body. Fortunately, it was not necessary to attempt to fit Moses into the proposed three-member Housing and Redevelopment Board. By the time the study and recommendations were issued, Congress had selected New York for the 1964 World's Fair and Moses was offered the $100,000-a-year job as its president. He resigned most of his city jobs, but not the Triborough Authority. Despite the scandal about Title I, over a thousand New York notables from business, civic, government and political circles attended a swank black-tie, $100-a-plate testimonial dinner in Moses' honor held by the Greater New York Planning Council; this organization, with its office at the Coliseum, seemed to have come into existence just for this purpose.

THE WISHES OF THE PEOPLE

Moses had moved into a vacuum in New York and he left one behind. For a long time he had diverted responsibility from where it now came to rest—with the Mayor and his own appointed, not inherited, officials.

Authoritarian methods of rebuilding had proved unpalatable; New York would now try democracy. Wagner appointed as Chairman of the new Housing and Redevelopment Board, J. Clarence Davies, who seemed the embodiment of virtues sought by good citizens. A former chairman of the Greater New York Fund and of the New York Citizens' Housing and Planning Council, he was also on the board of Bronx settlements and hospitals, and a critic of Moses. A former realtor, Davies had recently gained government experience as the head, for the previous several years, of the new Department of Real Estate.

On taking his new office, Chairman Davies announced that the Board would carry out a five-year program for building 15,000 units of middle-income housing a year, using the Mitchell-Lama program, which was now administered by the Housing and Redevelopment Board. An advantage of this program, indeed part of Davies' announced goal, was that the plan could be used not only on Title I sites but also on open land; thus it could avoid housing demolition and tenant displacement to the greatest possible extent.

Moses had said to Davies about slum clearance, "It's not like high school civics, is it?" Indeed, the Board members were hardly at their desks when they discovered that "the people" had special interests, as did private developers. They found that the citizen groups believed their interests—which also required public assistance to reduce the cost of housing and acquire sites—were superior to the motives of the developers.

Representatives of churches, political clubs and neighborhood groups flocked to the Board with proposals for taking half a block of property here, a few blocks there, for some tax-abated middle-income housing. A group from Greenwich Village proposed tearing down blocks of factories to the south for an assisted cooperative. They defended that site because it would require no family dislocation. An Upper East Side group, led by the representative of a settlement house, insisted that the city should put an end to the building of all private luxury apartments there and just allow small public housing buildings or tax-abated middle-income housing. (The recent building boom, by changing the East Side's character, had displaced much of the settlement's old clientele.)

Such government assistance on $100-a-square-foot East Side land would equal an annual direct subsidy to each "middle-income" family of about $250, according to Davies' estimate; it would entail a direct loss in tax revenues to the city of $100,000 on just one block, not to overlook a decrease in the city's borrowing limit. He believed that "A city can run into financial suicide via slum clearance unless areas are improved to pay what they're capable of bearing." This stance began to make some citizen groups—to whom the Mayor listened—suspect Davies.

When the Board tried to obtain sites on vacant land in Republican, homeowning Queens or bucolic Staten Island, the two boroughs with most of New York's remaining open land, their Borough Presidents balked. They maintained that their constituents objected to subsidizing middle-income tenants and to high-rise projects; much of the underlying opposition there was believed to come from the fact that city-assisted projects would be open by law to non-white tenants. No one on the new Board, however, had the power to move the Borough Presidents. Density controls in the city's new 1960 zoning ordinance also excluded middle-income multiple units from using some vacant land. In several instances the City Planning Commission ruled that a desired site was too well located for subsidized housing. The Housing and Redevelopment Board had to accept odd chunks of land, mostly in the Bronx, located and brought to them by private builders who wanted public assistance so they could achieve lower rents.

The *Times* criticized the Board at the end of its first year for moving slowly and having nothing to show above ground. Chairman Davies replied that it took time to follow the federal laws and rules and listen to the people. For just one Title I project, which the Slum Clearance Committee had initiated but whose plans were not final when the new Board took over, he had spent hundreds of hours meeting with eighteen different neighborhood groups, seeing some as many as five times, to discuss their wishes for the area's re-use. However, no two groups could agree on the kinds and combinations of housing (public, middle income, fully taxpaying, rehabilitated) that they wanted.

Then, the first renewal project initiated by the Housing and Redevelopment Board was killed by what Moses had been able to slough off: organized resident opposition. This project, located in a section between Greenwich Village proper and the Hudson River known as West Village, also felt the full backlash of citizen mistrust which Moses and his program had exacerbated—even though both had left the Title I scene.

Ironically, the new Board believed that the West Village project was just what the people of that community wanted. Many families in the Village were being displaced by new private luxury apartments and deconverted, previously rent-controlled older buildings that were ripe for speculative re-use. Delegations of Villagers had been seeking the Board's help to put up new middle-income apartments for the displacees. Because of the high cost of construction in New York, as well as of land in Greenwich Village, various government aids—the special low-cost loans, partial tax abatement and the write-down of cleared land possible under urban renewal—would be necessary.

To find a suitable renewal site, the Board members themselves had trudged through the entire Village.* The fourteen-block area in the West Village seemed ideal. The cost of removing the space-consuming overhead tracks of an unused rail spur that blighted the surroundings could be paid for under renewal, and new housing could be built in its place. Still more land could be made available without family dislocation through removal of an old post office. Many of the existing old tenements needed rehabilitation, and this could be fostered by renewal. Another potential change was to alter street patterns, to divert through-traffic, especially the trucks garaged along the river. Many children lived in the area, and the trailer trucks now had to drive over the sidewalks where children played in order to pass through the narrow streets.

* The vice-chairman, Robert C. Weaver, was appointed Federal Housing and Home Finance Administrator in 1961, and named Secretary of the new Department of Housing and Urban Development in 1965.

Not only did the new Board propose rehabilitation and ways to minimize tenant dislocation and rehouse families on the site. Unlike the old Slum Clearance Committee, it had submitted the project proposal to the Planning Commission at this initial stage, and had received informal approval. The Board had also announced its intention to request a federal survey and planning grant—a way of giving advance announcement of the public hearing. Once received, the grant would allow the Board's staff to make a more thorough study and detailed plans for the area, in cooperation with the West Village residents, before the area was definitely designated for renewal.

However, the Board had neglected at this early stage to consult the people who lived in the specific project area.

Before twenty-four hours had passed, a Committee to Save the West Village had been whipped together by architectural critic Jane Jacobs, a homeowner there who was completing a book that was extremely critical of government-aided housing and redevelopment.* Her Committee insisted it did not want high-rise projects in its low-rise neighborhood. It was certain that the plans —although no official plans had been made—were all wrong. The Committee would not give the Housing and Redevelopment Board a hearing. At one meeting held to explain the tentative plan to the community, city officials were shouted down as they tried to speak.

Bitter accusations of secret agreements between builders and the Board attended the West Village Committee's unrelenting campaign to stop the project before it began. The Board of Estimate's packed hearings, which were held after many months of delay, lasted until four in the morning, with relays of new opposition coming in to fill the ranks; these hearings were climaxed with libelous charges that Planning Chairman Felt and Housing Board Chairman Davies stood to profit personally from the renewal project. The matter was referred back by the Board of Estimate "for further study."

The Committee's campaign became a national issue in syndicated columns and magazines. The *Saturday Evening Post* ran an editorial headed "Urban Renewal Can Make An End to a City's

* Jane Jacobs, *The Death and Life of Great American Cities,* Random House, 1961.

Charming Historic Sites," although "charming" was hardly an appropriate adjective for most of the area.

By now not even the Mayor of New York would look at the area, or even review the evidence. Fighting for his political future in September 1961, in a close Democratic primary, Wagner announced on the eve of the party vote that he had asked the Planning Commission to drop the West Village project and to study the entire Village instead. Evidently, one of his bitter appointees commented, the Mayor felt that if the people screamed, they were right. But he did not question who was screaming or why.

That summer the West Villagers spoke in several voices which did not jibe with the Committee's main themes. One attitude expressed in interviews by residents was plain mistrust of the city. Housing Board Chairman Davies was almost unknown; so was the difference between renewal's selective approach with its emphasis on rehabilitation and Moses' blanket bulldozing. Residents found it hard to believe that all their homes would not be demolished and that tenants who had to move would be relocated by the Housing Board in the new middle-income housing to be built on the former site of the tracks and old post office. It had never happened this way before.

There was also another, subtler theme. A rosy-cheeked, pregnant, thirty-year-old housewife, one of the Irish who so long dominated the West Village before the overspill of Village "bohemians" started moving in, articulated it most clearly. "I don't want those projects here. If you get them, you'll get colored and Puerto Rican and Spanish-speaking people, like they got on the Lower East Side. I wouldn't want to live down the hall from one of them Negroes, especially if you have kids. That's why a lot of people don't like the plan." The newspapers, however, did not dig into this project to learn what was behind the opposition.

RUNNING TO STAND STILL

After its West Village fiasco, the Board consulted residents of possible Title I sites first. But conflicting opinions, special interests, opposition to newcomers and insistence by newcomers on their right to be rehoused in the area persisted. Davies resigned in 1962 and returned to private business. A civil servant, a lawyer with political ambitions, was appointed in his place, and before long became the city's Housing and Development Coordinator.

More new policies and programs were adopted. One of these put an end to luxury apartment houses in urban renewal sites. Only middle-income tax-abated housing with a $30-a-room ceiling and public housing units would be built in Title I projects. Relocation became a city responsibility; a separate department was created to handle it, and the city made a commitment to rehouse residents on-site to the greatest extent possible. A Citizens' Advisory Committee * was appointed to consult with the Housing and Redevelopment Board, and local citizen councils were organized in each renewal area to work out preliminary plans with the city.

The staff of the Housing and Redevelopment Board grew to several hundred (mostly civil service) employees, occupying two floors and heavy with project planners and community relations personnel. There was a notable improvement in the concept and design of new projects. As new housing tools became available and the Board's willingness to consider the people's wishes became known, local groups even came to the city to request that their area be designated for urban renewal.

But the more the city tried to please the people, the slower execution of the program became, and the more government subsidy was required. In fact, so much time was spent listening to the people and trying to make plans acceptable to diverse community and citywide groups that it was hard to advance projects. The city agency had to deal not only with the officially recognized local renewal councils; self-appointed spokesmen for various communities and independent citizen committees also would spring up in project areas. Often the latter developed plans which, they maintained, more truly represented what the community desired, and the newspapers were quick to pick up the

* The citywide Citizens' Advisory Committee is composed of representatives of settlement houses; civic agencies—the Women's City Club, Citizens' Housing and Planning Council, Community Service Society; the National Association for the Advancement of Colored People and other Negro, Puerto Rican and civil rights groups; the Ford Foundation; and banking and business groups.

protests of any articulate critic. Citizen groups also put forth various new social goals which they felt renewal should achieve: balanced neighborhoods, community preservation, integration or deghettoization—by using the new variety of housing tools and subsidies, including rehabilitation. But few, including the city officials, were willing to admit that these goals could not coexist within one project area, or perhaps were impossible to realize.

Efforts to provide permanent on-site housing for socially troubled low-income families displaced from slum homes in renewal areas also slowed down execution. Meanwhile, the agency designated so many areas for renewal that federal funds and city staff were inadequate to advance projects beyond preliminary studies. Local residents who had engaged in initial planning steps became disillusioned when their project was stuck for several years in the "pipeline" to Washington awaiting funds. Even the Citizens' Advisory Committee could not understand why things took so long.

Nor was the ambitious middle-income housing program a panacea. Problems of available land, mortgage money and marketability cut production to one third of the 15,000 annual volume hoped for in 1960. Democratic planning and attempts to please the public also delayed construction and thus increased eventual costs. Subsidies given in land price, low-cost loans and tax abatement were eaten up in rising costs of labor, materials, maintenance and operating costs. To maintain a $30 ceiling became more and more difficult. One Commissioner frankly admitted, "We're running to stand still." One third of the city's families could afford only rents at or under public housing levels.

In the fall of 1965, the voters of New York elected another reform Mayor, Republican-Liberal candidate John V. Lindsay. He appointed a task force of experts from other cities to take a fresh look at the city's renewal problems and to write a new prescription.* Their analysis suggested that in spite of all the tools and resources that were being employed, New York's approach to a slum problem of such magnitude was like bailing out the ocean

* Main proposals: a new super-administration for planning, housing and developments to include planning department, public housing, rehabilitation and codes; decentralized administrative units; concentration of physical and social renewal and housing resources on the city's three major slum-ghetto areas.

with a teaspoon. It seemed that only billions in federal aid could help New York City begin to get hold of the problem—the huge submerged slum communities of Bedford-Stuyvesant, Harlem and the South Bronx.

THE PRODUCTS OF MOSES

Here, before looking at the approaches of other cities, we might ask: Did Moses' end products justify the means? Given his great powers, and in spite of the limitations of his tools, could he not have done better?

Moses, in 1960, felt that he had done his job: he had put "an active program into execution under the Federal Housing Act of 1949," as he stated in his letter of resignation to the Mayor.

His literal Title I program did, indeed, give concrete form to the limitations and emphasis of the original Act; it reflected the bias toward material and fiscal values that was part of the Act's approach to urban slums as well as of the country's climate in the 1950's. But it was not possible to approach urban redevelopment as a mathematical formula or real estate operation. That thousands of slum dwellings were cleared, and that more privately financed housing and a stronger tax base were produced through Title I in New York than elsewhere, did not create public acceptance of the new instrument. In Manhattan, the principal scene of Title I activity under Moses, as well as of the growing citizen revolt against him and redevelopment, wrecking balls and building cranes were at work everywhere. At the same time, new slums were formed before the old slums were cleared.

It was in Manhattan, the city's heartland, that everyone—rich, poor and middle income—seemed determined to live, whether or not they could afford it. And it was here that developers most wanted to build. On that tight little island were nearly half the assessable values the city could tax to meet its meteorically rising budget and use to bond for new publicly assisted facilities and housing within state-imposed debt limits. There, too, were the greatest potential land values that could be captured or maximized through private or publicly aided redevelopment. Much could have been done in Manhattan to stimulate and guide rebuilding using local urban renewal powers without federal assistance—if there had been plans. (The City Construction Coordinator might have tried to elevate the level of public architecture.)

The vast stretches of increasingly blighted Brooklyn, close-in Queens and the South Bronx—the homes of Manhattan displacees as well as poor newcomers *—were almost completely ignored under Moses. Private sponsors, even labor unions and philanthropic organizations, were not interested in projects there when locations in Manhattan, where most Old Law tenements stood, qualified for Title I designation.†

But Moses was loathe to stop and evaluate. Custodial in his attitude toward the city, although he lacked the public's mandate, and determined to realize his limited objectives, he carried his various schemes for the city under his different public hats and hardly let anyone else have a peek.

To a good extent, it was possible for Moses to accomplish as much rebuilding as he did with Title I because national trends were working in his favor. The country's economy, its executive concentration and new managerial structure, even jet transportation and the population's new age distribution all nourished New York. More than anything else, the local commercial boom and its ramifications set New York apart from the rest of American cities in the 1950's. While other downtowns were dying, some 40,000,000 square feet of new office space, much of it housing national corporate headquarters,‡ were shooting up in New York's hub, the throbbing section south of Central Park to the Battery. Along with the new headquarters came new executive suites, advertising agencies and law firms, and all the other special services, amenities and white-collar jobs that accompany such top-level corporate concentrations. (New York also had more renewal and housing tools, such as tax abatement, than any other city.)

Simultaneously, the demand for new luxury apartments and expensive converted units was created by the increasing number

* In Brooklyn alone 500,000 white people left, and that many lower-income Puerto Ricans and Negroes moved in during the 1950's.

† Even Mitchell-Lama middle-income housing at $23 a room was hard to market, the Housing and Redevelopment Board discovered, if it was located out along Bruckner Boulevard in the Bronx, instead of in Manhattan.

‡ More than 135 of the largest industrial corporations in America had their headquarters in New York by the mid-1960's.

of couples over forty-five years old who were moving in from suburban homes now that their children were grown, and by young adults from across the country who were drawn by the new jobs and opportunities.

But most of the billions that were being spent in private rebuilding and rehabilitation compounded the congestion of Manhattan. There was no coordinated transportation and land-use plan to funnel all these activities in order to create a more livable city.

Given the circumstances working in favor of New York, it becomes clear that rebuilding action, especially at central Manhattan high rents, was not a defensible goal of publicly assisted redevelopment. The institutional, unimaginative apartment developments stamped out for Title I sites by "efficient" architects were not a notable aesthetic advance; some were hard to distinguish from New York's public housing projects. Even the best seemed to rupture the fabric of the city.

The squat Coliseum Hall, which should have been—and so easily could have been—an outstanding amenity on the southwest corner of Central Park, was instead an unfortunate monument to Moses' get-it-done style. At Lincoln Center, the opera-symphony-theater complex had considerable promise, but the overall project lacked significant urban design and visual integration with its immediate surroundings and more distant points. On the west, the gigantic apartment house slabs would wall off the spectacular sunsets of the Hudson River and Palisades, while on the eastern side the project was surgically cut off by Broadway's speeding traffic. And it was not clear that New York's cultural institutions would perform better as a result of their proximity to one another. Rather, there was some concern on the part of critics about cultural sclerosis.

MEN TO RUN PROGRAMS

As city agencies took on more responsibility for new housing and renewal functions and related social programs, New York began running into a major municipal roadblock: This was a critical shortage of skilled manpower required to staff and carry out increasingly complex city government operations. The Brookings

Institution, reporting on a 1963 survey, stated that in New York, one out of every five budgeted positions was vacant, primarily because of two factors: a pay scale not competitive with private industry, and a poor image of city government. The difficulty of getting qualified people to take high administrative jobs at low pay was compounded by the high cost of living in New York; attempts to raise municipal salaries in order to compete for talent were met by objections from the news media, and other economy-conscious groups who were not as much interested in program execution as in saving money.

Can a city today attract the talents needed to meet the demands of the new programs? Mediocrity at the technical-managerial level and lack of effective leadership at the top are major urban problems of today.

Moses had some answers, or perhaps expedients, in his task-force approach. But governmental responsibility must accompany opportunity for individual innovation and the satisfaction of project execution. And some of the incentive and rewards of local government service have to be non-pecuniary. Ultimately, the Mayor must provide the overall drive—searching out, attracting to the city and then holding in its employ able public servants and administrators; he must give them and their programs high purpose and political backing. There are many hopeful signs that this is taking place in New York, and that the city will profit from the talents and programs developed in other, more civically advanced cities.

As the number of poor, undereducated and ill-housed people who cannot meet their own basic living requirements or function adequately as workers and citizens grows, and as the city becomes more of a developmental and service agency, the need for capable people in government becomes increasingly urgent.

New York's powerful business leaders, whose concerns are national rather than local, will probably continue to remain remote from city affairs as long as they do not feel the adrenalin kick of economic fear which has coalesced the power structure in other cities into the cause of civic betterment. For a long time, New York could ignore its poverty because the center of the city was booming. But the growing sickness—the multiplication of less able citizens paralleled by the loss of low-skill jobs—will also effect those who toil at the top in the nation's corporate bazaar.

3

THE NEW COALITION ■ Pittsburgh's Action Formula Saves a City

During the immediate postwar era, the city that stood out to many as the symbol of hope for urban reconstruction was Pittsburgh.

Indeed, no city appeared more changed on first impression. The dramatic physical transformation that had taken place there since the late 1940's was already apparent out in Allegheny County, as one arrived at the region's new portal—huge, marble-columned Greater Pittsburgh Airport, opened in 1953, with giant runways designed to handle transoceanic jets. From there, one motored toward the heart of downtown for seventeen nonstop miles over a new multilaned arterial expressway, past unscarred, green countryside atypical of Pittsburgh. Not until the exit from the costliest link in this modern new approachway—Fort Pitt

Tunnel—blasted through a rocky Pittsburgh hillside, did one suddenly view the much-photographed, celebrated panorama of the "new Pittsburgh" unfolding miles off into the horizon, instead of obscured, as before, even at the nearby tip of the Point.

Smog, the traditional, gritty trademark of the Steel Capital, was gone. So were many other remainders of the past. Within the city's triangular heart, rising back from the forks of the Ohio River's two great tributaries, the Allegheny and Monongahela, the changes were most evident.

At the Point, where the rivers come together, there was a green public park instead of the grimy, flood-battered industrial blight of warehouses, overhead rail freight trestles and tracks which in the late nineteenth century came to disfigure the site of Pittsburgh's birthplace. There, the shores of the cleaned-up rivers were now lined with pedestrian walks instead of ugly freight barges and old wooden wharves. In summertime, concerts were held at this new public river-side.

Just behind Point State Park, on land that had been similarly blighted, a skyscraper galaxy of colored metal and glass towers—some office buildings already complete and others on the way, apartment houses and a hotel in advanced planning—was being built in or designed for a park-like setting. These were the building blocks of the "new Pittsburgh." Even the dense older commercial core of the Golden Triangle was opened to the sky with a new public square on a cleared block of land. Next to it several more new office towers rose. By the mid-1950's, when other cities were just waking up to the extent of downtown decay, one quarter of Pittsburgh's business district was in the process of being rebuilt. The Golden Triangle, its older buildings steam-blasted clean of soot, had become a reasonable description of the city center's exceptional corporate-financial concentration, as well as an accurate name for its tax-paying ability.

Still further back, just beyond the Triangle, all the century-old slum tenements were gone from the Lower Hill. In their places would rise the huge steel dome of a new civic arena, first structure in what some Pittsburgh leaders optimistically expect to be their city's "new Acropolis." A museum, theater and other cultural facilities were also planned. Renewal projects completed or under way in Pittsburgh and its environs included university and industrial expansion, neighborhood rehabilitation, new housing developments and industrial research parks. These did not have so visible and dramatic an impact, however, as the prospect from the Point.

From there, the environment seemed so transformed it was hard to believe that this was Pittsburgh, the city that just a few years before had been so sunk in dirt and decay. One needed to know the city as it had been to appreciate fully the extent of change. Street and office lights used to burn all day when river vapors rose and held the region's soft coal smoke in suspension over the city, casting a midnight gloom of smog throughout the day. Smog would turn office workers' collars gray by noon; coughing and colds were an unhealthy commonplace in Pittsburgh. Even in the suburbs, housewives had to wash curtains weekly to cleanse them of soot. Airline pilots had a particular dread of landing at the Pittsburgh field, with its "ceiling of black ink."

Pittsburgh, the eighth largest city in the country, with a population just over two thirds of a million, seat of Allegheny County and center of a region of 2,500,000, seemed to hide in shame. Until the late 1940's, no new construction had taken place in its oppressively drab downtown for nearly two decades. Forty per cent of the business district was blighted or vacant. This commercial stagnation was reflected in the steady downward slide since the early 1930's of the Triangle's assessed valuations of some $18,000,000 a year. The drop was felt severely by public agencies and was reflected in their services. Real estate was the preponderant source of local revenues; the Triangle yielded not only one quarter of all such municipal funds, but provided the base for Allegheny County's taxes and those of the school district as well.

Pittsburgh had never spent adequately on public facilities, much less on amenities. But by the mid-1940's the extra municipal belt-tightening of the depression and war years showed up in city streets filled with potholes, obsolete school buildings, the few badly maintained playgrounds, narrow, rusty iron bridges spanning the rivers. Because of the city's unusual topography, downtown was a natural bottleneck for the ever-increasing vehicular traffic that had to cross these bridges and travel the narrow old downtown streets to get from one part of the city to another.

The threat of river floods, still not under control, also cast a pall on downtown Pittsburgh, discouraging new building or renovation.

More ominous, although masked by the immediate prosperity from post-World War II orders, was the fact that Pittsburgh's great industrial plant was wearing out, and various new trends militated against its replacement there. Some old mills, overworked during the war, were marked for abandonment, and Big Steel was planning to build production facilities near new national markets in the growing areas of the West and South, instead of expanding in the Pittsburgh region. Another participant in the growing exodus, the Aluminum Corporation of America, a Pittsburgh-based giant, was moving two of its local manufacturing divisions to the Midwest. Westinghouse Electric Corporation, also a prime Pittsburgh concern, had already regionalized much of its consumer production before the war. Now it was planning to move two Pittsburgh plants to other cities. Even some of the big glass mills, founded a century earlier in Pittsburgh, were moving closer to consumer-oriented automobile markets.

Not only were market locational factors working against the old Steel Capital; changed technology had reduced the demand and market for bituminous coal—once Pittsburgh's biggest drawing card for steel manufacture. Would the steel industry modernize its huge old plants (the newest of them built in 1911) or withdraw?

Another part of the economic problem was that the big corporations with headquarters in Pittsburgh were not able to attract the executive and managerial talent they needed. Some companies were talking of moving their administrative staffs to cleaner, more livable cities. Many of the community's most capable young men and women did not return to their home town after the war. The lack of recreation facilities and of housing were chief among their reasons. The supply of decent homes in the middle-income range in Pittsburgh was actually far below the national average; over 40 per cent of the dwelling units in the area were rated substandard and overcrowded.

That Pittsburgh was ill had been evident for a number of years before the war. But the efforts made to save Pittsburgh—to get rid of smog, improve housing, do something about downtown and its traffic, even to preserve the historic Blockhouse at the Point by creating a park—were picayune, piecemeal, stymied by quarrels among opposing special interest groups and lacking in real power. The decay was also in the city's top leadership. In the past, business had attempted to stem the tide by rigging rail freight rates. But those who had the biggest financial and political stake in the survival of the city and the region had not been sufficiently concerned or alarmed to improve Pittsburgh.

THE PITTSBURGH FORMULA

Pittsburghers soon came to refer matter-of-factly to their city's postwar spurt of improvement and rebuilding as the Renaissance. National magazines were also impressed by the striking visible changes in downtown Pittsburgh's appearance and its air, as well as by the new style of civic action. They seized upon the city as the best available answer to the revival of blighted urban areas. During the dozen postwar years, Pittsburgh became a mecca for elected officials, businessmen and planners from other cities who had become concerned enough about urban revitalization to look for useful examples. Delegations from several hundred American cities, as well as from abroad, visited Pittsburgh to study the city's bold and wide-ranging use of redevelopment and other new instruments for urban improvement which it had devised—to see the new city center that was being built on the old.

Businessmen were particularly impressed by the mathematics of Pittsburgh's widely publicized commercial and industrial redevelopment projects. The public subsidy and government outlays were very low compared to the new private investments these generated, and substantial new tax revenues were created as an important by-product.* The new program for urban improvement made economic sense to the visitors, and the fact that the projects had been carried out by the locality, without federal aid also had great appeal. Politicians were especially impressed by the

* According to Pittsburgh calculations, in the first eight redevelopment projects $197,500,000 of private money was spent and a $175,000,000 increase in taxable values realized, while the per capita cost to each citizen was $1.40 per annum.

way physical improvements moved forward so expeditiously in Pittsburgh.

Behind the rebuilding results was an equally publicized new civic action formula which the Pittsburghers had devised and which seemed to be the key to ending the stagnation that was laying hold of more and more old cities.

The Pittsburgh formula seemed simple enough: first, bring together the top industrial-business leaders of the community in an organization to support a general program for overall community improvement; second, establish a cooperative working relationship between them and the political and government leaders to advance specific projects.

Actually, the formula was almost without precedent for American cities.* Businessmen were prone to pronounce that municipal affairs should be apolitical, though in practice they had displayed their knowledge of the need for local political governmental cooperation to achieve corporate needs. The quasi-municipal organizations that they had sponsored were generally not designed to forward programs and projects benefiting the community as a whole or its residents. Instead, these groups helped promote the city to outside industry or protect local business interests and to trim public spending to the "efficient" minimum. Some businessmen backed regional planning organizations, but these private bodies wanted power. Up to now, the businessmen had lacked a device or even a desire for constructive civic development action. Mayors were regarded by the private powers as little more than city housekeepers; they sought re-election by doing favors for "little people" and publicly eschewed a coalition with the top businessmen who bank-rolled their campaigns through party contributions.

The Allegheny Conference on Community Development was new: a civic action organization whose members were the top local business and industrial leaders; the extraordinarily open coalition of Democratic Mayor David Lawrence with Republican banker Richard Mellon and top members of the Conference, working together for a better city, became celebrated. The civic

* Probably the one notable exception was the Chicago commercial and political leaders' backing of the Burnham city plan of 1910, and their promotion of it to the public—a lesson lost on most cities, and an example soon discredited by the notorious grafting attendant to the plan's execution.

agency and coalition furnished dozens of other cities with an example and workable pattern that could be applied in varying ways. The combination of organized power and politically opposed forces for the new common goal was particularly praised. Pittsburgh introduced a new style of doing things for American cities, not only among business leaders but also among politicians. Lawrence, thrusting aside City Hall politics for a risky community improvement program, emerged as a civic statesman, was returned to the Mayoralty by increasingly larger votes and went on to be governor.

The Pittsburgh approach was, in a number of ways, a notable advance over New York under Robert Moses; it was as unlike New York in style as it was in thrust. The program was not based on the abilities of one extraordinary administrator-builder. Pittsburgh's civic innovation reflected the top power that exists in many American cities, power that could be extremely helpful for urban improvement when made operative. Granted, power was far more tightly held in Pittsburgh than other cities and therefore could be brought into play more quickly and effectively. Further, the efforts of the Pittsburghers had more meaning for their city's future than did New York's.

What is not generally understood, although it is basic to the success of their action formula, is *how* the coalition used its power to make the formula work. Indeed, a basic error made by many visiting delegations that tried to adapt the Pittsburgh formula was that they copied outward forms and not the less apparent, and far more important, substance of effective action.

Still—and this would prove to be as much a part of Pittsburgh's lesson as its new formula—the accomplishments of the Pittsburgh coalition clearly suggest the limitations to what top local public and private power working together can achieve when they are confronted by continuing rapid mid-twentieth-century change. Pittsburgh's illness goes much deeper than the original prescription could cure.

By 1960, there were 70,000 fewer young adults, the base of the working population, in Allegheny County than in 1950—a 29 per cent drop. The city's total population fell by 9 per cent, from 676,000 to some 604,000. This was the fourth highest central city decline during that decade in the nation, and this in spite of its Renaissance. And at the same time, sixty-five plants and 35,000 jobs were lost, while almost no new industry came in. Those which remained sharply reduced employment by adopting automated production processes; steel was far below capacity. Meanwhile, the inventory of deteriorated housing was changed only slightly.

Does Pittsburgh have the potential for genuine urban revitalization? Can a great and humane city be grafted onto the physical ruins, the human scar tissue and the communal indifference—its legacy from the unrestrained industrial era? And can a region whose economy is overburdened with the hardware, and the extreme specialization of nineteenth-century basic industry, respond adequately to community challenges? A few original participants in the Renaissance, along with some new leaders, have been striving to find new, more adequate answers. Others have passed on, grown old, or run out of steam, and this may ultimately be beneficial.

If, from the perspective of the mid-1960's, Pittsburgh's Renaissance seems superficial or narrow when compared to the full dimensions of the job that still confronts the city, it is in part because we have all learned much more since then. Also, the nature of the problem has been changing. But we should not forget that what Pittsburgh accomplished in the early days was herculean in light not only of its own heritage but also that of urban America generally. Pittsburgh by now might well be a ghost mill town had the coalition not formed and acted.

If we tend to take Pittsburgh's original formula for granted, or disparage it as limited and simplistic, we should not forget the nature of such an innovation in the postwar decade, nor its subsequent influence on other cities' leaders. It is important to realize that the new coalition Pittsburgh evolved, and the power alliance that was formed, provided other troubled American cities with at least a starting point for a new civic tradition. Most cities have not yet gone so far.

STEEL, MILLIONAIRES AND UNREMITTING TOIL

There is a certain justice that Pittsburgh, which thrust the nation from the Jeffersonian age into the urban-industrial era, gave rise to a new civic approach to urban rebuilding. For Pittsburgh was the most palpable example of the devastation wrought on American cities by rapid industrialization which disregarded human life, community welfare or urban amenity.

Singularly blessed by nature in its location, topography and unparalleled access to raw materials then necessary for basic industry—iron ore, natural gas and bituminous coal—Pittsburgh was singularly abused by its exploitative industrialists. These curiously religious, hard-driving Presbyterians regarded the local gifts of nature and the extraordinarily fortunate circumstance of timing as given to them by God; this allowed them to take without giving back.

The city, situated at the great pre-rail river gateway to the West, started as a colonial trading post and fort. By the Civil War it was a diversified manufacturing town of small producers and skilled laborers that served the steadily increasing flow of migrants going West. Thus at the very time America was changing manufacturing methods to steam and large-scale mass production, Pittsburgh was exceptionally able to convert to new methods and produce for new needs. (The city was practically sitting on top of the best coking coal in the country, the element whose proximity most determined the location of plants for smelting iron and making steel by the new blast furnace process.) It also found itself at the center of the nation's population and enjoyed unusual natural advantages which facilitated distribution of its products. Moreover, it was uniquely equipped among cities to provide for and profit from the Union Army's needs.

Pittsburgh's industrial entrepreneurs threw their genius, energy and wartime-acquired capital into obtaining the costly new equipment necessary to manufacture coke, steel and iron ore. Soon their mills were producing these indispensable ingredients required by America's factories and railroads. By 1888, the region's sixteen steel works produced two thirds of the country's crucible steel and one fourth of all its rolled iron, as well as one seventh of the world's supply. Instead of its earlier diversification, over 60 per cent of its manufacturing employment was now in metals alone. In that period of intense concentration and functional specialization, Pittsburgh was the prime example of the age.

Meanwhile, the local landscape and atmosphere were being

devastated. The huge steel works sprawled along the flatlands of the river banks, pouring industrial sewage into their waters, slag into the green valleys and heavy coal smoke into the air. The new methods of mass production no longer relied on the city's skilled Scotch, Irish and German. Rather, these workers were becoming a costly nuisance. As the heavier branches of metal-working grew, and required the cheapest possible labor, the big industrialists began to import from East Europe illiterate immigrants whose main qualifications were strength, endurance and a willingness to accept low pay, long hours and the subhuman working conditions in infernally hot and noisy factories. Such docile, unlettered blue-collar immigrants became the main body of Pittsburgh's and Allegheny County's population.

Their lives were mean and drab. Living quarters were commonly thrown up close by the mills, clustered at the foot of the plants like peasant hovels near a feudal palace. Other mill workers lived in tenements. Few had time or resources for anything beyond work and survival, and a nip on payday. The poverty and insecurity of their lives were intensified by the violent cyclical ups and downs of the heavy industry and mines. Layoffs and unemployment were common. No accident compensation or worker relief was provided, though one Carnegie mill was so dangerous it was called "the slaughterhouse." When workers protested conditions at the great Homestead plant by going on strike, the Governor of Pennsylvania sent 8,000 national guardsmen to subdue and, if necessary, shoot the rebels.

In this Pittsburgh of the late nineteenth century was forged America's sudden industrial eminence, many of the country's giant combines and its great new fortunes. These rapid developments were capped, in 1901, with the formation of U.S. Steel, the first billion-dollar corporation.

What then occurred among the principal beneficiaries of this colossal merger was typical of what had been happening to industrial ownership in Pittsburgh for some time. No sooner had the forty new "Carnegie millionaires" turned their shares into convertible securities than most took themselves and their stocks away from the source of their wealth. They built showy palaces in New York and Newport, and flaunted in Europe and Florida the wealth they continued to siphon off from the region. The decision-making base for steel also moved away—to New York and the Morgan Bank.

Behind remained "The Workshop of the World," "The Forge of the Universe," "The Iron City"—as some people referred to this urban distillation of late-nineteenth-century America.

Few visited this dingy capital of a black country except those who came to do business. But outside curiosity about Pittsburgh began to grow as the city sprouted steel and millionaires and as interest in social problems developed in the nation. A team of surveyors was dispatched there in 1908 by the new Russell Sage Foundation to find out whether this exceptional concentration of wealth had been of social benefit. In the eight-volume *Pittsburgh Survey* they reported: "Certainly no community before in America or in Europe has ever had such a surplus and never before has a great community applied what it had so meagerly to the rational purposes of life."

Managers ran the giant plants in place of the vanished barons; but the twelve-hour day, seven-day week continued. "The general law of the city is protracted, unremitting toil" for both labor and management, the survey found. The moralistic and materialistic tone that prevailed in the Calvinist city not only made work a way of life, but distorted it into a religion. Strikers, the survey reported, were considered "guilty of a certain impiety [which] might embarrass the momentum of a great business administration." As factory managers held down workers' pay, the shareholders' dividends skyrocketed.

The social surveyors saw a city moving ahead economically while its elite remained unconcerned about the contrast between unequaled industrial prosperity and an almost unbelievable neglect of life, health and physical vigor. Pittsburgh was characterized by absentee landlordism as well as absentee capitalism. Just a few minutes' walk from the massive office skyscrapers which were rising in the Triangle to house the growing sales and office activities of the flourishing giant industries were festering slums. The biggest (absentee) tenement owner became, by a quirk, the city's biggest philanthropist; she bestowed her unoccupied estate, Schenley Park, on the city after a civic leader visited her abroad. In the 1890's Andrew Carnegie, Pittsburgh's leading absentee capitalist, and one of the few who put anything back into the region, gave the city a generous shot of culture—a concert hall, museum and art institute. But wealthy resident Pittsburghers continued to display a negative attitude toward culture and other amenities of life. Artists born there left; and hardly any middle-class public was fostered by the big, basic industrial combines. These provided all their own services and had little need for white-collar skills.

A brace of Republican bosses ran the city—built its bridges, paved its streets, and contracted for street railways and other public facilities for their own personal enrichment at the heavy expense of the citizens. The ring which ran Pittsburgh was tied to the state ring, which in turn worked with the Pennsylvania Railroad, whose heavy embrace spread everywhere—from giving free passes to sympathetic rural legislators to special freight rates for industry in favored localities (Pittsburgh being top among these).

Lincoln Steffens, another visitor drawn to study this urban phenomenon, found Pittsburgh in 1903 "a growing town too busy for self-government." Most industrialists' interest in local affairs was limited to taking care of their own corporate needs, which they could do more easily by dealing with the Republican bosses than with the elected representatives in city council. Local merchants and the small professional class naturally deferred to this elite on whom and on whose style of self-government they were dependent.

Early twentieth-century improvement drives—governmental reform, city planning—had a vogue, but nothing seemed capable of altering the city's physical or social mold. As it "prospered," Pittsburgh continued to grow without plan or community-mindedness. Its steep slopes were covered helter-skelter with cheap frame houses that were reachable only by a long climb up rickety wooden staircases from the streets below. Factories expanded into attractive residential neighborhoods and drove the residents to the suburbs. Choking coal smog was pervasive, and the decaying wreckage from the late railroad wars cluttered up the city's gateway at the Point.

THE MELLON EMPIRE

One of the few powerful families that evidently could stomach the environmental horrors, and in fact stayed and even profited mightily by them, became the financial kingpin of the city. This family, curiously unknown outside Pittsburgh, was the Mellons. Their dynasty, fortune and first bank, T. Mellon and Sons, were founded by Judge Thomas Mellon (who arrived there with ninety-nine cents by foot from Poverty Point, his home town twenty-one miles away) in the early nineteenth century. By the end of that century, the Mellons had made many millions out of the demand for Pittsburgh's produce, and had bought out smaller local tycoons who preferred to take their millions and escape the smoke and grime. Economic booms and busts of the early 1900's further increased their fortunes, as the Mellons' new Union Trust foreclosed on the weaker of the companies that they helped finance.

Andrew Mellon, Thomas' son and successor, and the guiding force behind the Mellons' extraordinary growth to billionaires in the early 1900's, apparently had as much dislike for his fellows as he had disregard for the common laborer, and was rarely seen even by his peers in their clubs. The fact that his wife and children went more and more often to Europe without him did not seem to disturb the financial genius who lived in increasing isolation in his gloomy castle on Forbes Street and quietly directed his vast empire from his bank office. Little of this family story was chronicled or publicized; even the fact that Andrew's wife divorced him was kept secret. The local press was well ordered, and the Mellons owned a good share of the papers' underlying mortgages.

Much of the family's spectacular rise to huge fortune and local industrial control came through lending venture capital to young manufacturers with promising new products and a need to expand. Not only had the Mellon bank helped finance Henry Frick, the Pennsylvania and other railroads, and steel companies. It also backed and came to partially own or control the Gulf Oil Corporation of America; the Koppers Corporation, a large manufacturer of coke by-products; Pittsburgh Plate Glass; Pittsburgh Consolidation Coal, largest in the country; and Westinghouse Electric Corporation. It was natural for some to be centered in Pittsburgh, where certain manufacturing resources were to be found. But the availability of financing there was also crucial, and the Mellons liked to have their companies near the bank. In effect they demanded, as an extra price for their backing, that all their companies be headquartered in Pittsburgh. This factor was to have great significance for the city's post-World War II Renaissance.

Equally important, Andrew Mellon came to exert extraordinary control over local politics. Originally, the state's Republican bosses paid regular visits to him and he, in return for their sympathetic actions on such matters as keeping a low tax rate for Pennsylvania manufacturers, supported their candidates generously. But during the 1910's these bosses died, and Mellon acted to put the anarchic party back in line—and to keep taxes on industry low.

One key to the Mellons' growing political influence, then and later, was that Andrew placed his companies' heads in key party roles—including even chairmanship of the Republican State Committee, which he gave to a nephew who was president of Gulf Oil. Mellon personally headed the Allegheny County Republican Committee until he went to Washington.* In this way, the Mellons served not only as the behind-the-scenes powers and financial mainstays of the dominant machine in the Pittsburgh region and much of Pennsylvania, but also as the party's political front—and as a prime target for the frustrated Democrats.

During the 1920's growing property values from the office building boom in the Triangle were not tapped to help improve the average Pittsburgher's living conditions. Instead, municipal neglect increased, and so did slums. This was documented by the Pittsburgh Housing Association, a small civic organization that was formed by a handful of social reformers and university professors. Its first annual report, published in 1928, remarked on the littered streets, wrecked houses and overflowing garbage cans, even on the edges of parks and better residential areas. It stated that "in summer, 'odors of the middle ages' [had] led a recent immigrant to say she didn't like 'the smell of America.'"

* At sixty-five, with his wife having left him and his close friend Henry Frick dead, Andrew evidently came to desire public recognition more than just making more money. He was by now one of the richest men in America, and after he, virtually alone, wiped out the national Republican party's deficit of $1,600,000 following Harding's campaign, he was appointed in 1921 as Secretary of the Treasury of the United States, although his name was as little known to the new President as to the country at large.

The big industrialists and bankers who had not fled the region now lived in exclusive suburbs, or as far as fifty miles away by motor car in fox-hunting Ligonier. But the city had not lost interest for visiting journalists. R. L. Duffus, in a scathing article entitled "Is Pittsburgh Civilized?" published by *Harper's* in 1930, described the city as a "glorified and incongruously pious mining camp." He reported that the "city's masters . . . the little group of Scotch Presbyterians who regard themselves as having been elected by Providence to be . . . and who are, in fact, its masters," still retained control, and regarded labor as "just another raw material, to be bought as cheaply as possible."

To these opinion makers, he wrote, "culture or anything else which does not produce dividends [was] superfluous." (According to the author, there was not even a decent nightclub in town.) "What have the rulers of the city done with the civilizing power that is so abundantly theirs?" he demanded. "Pittsburgh has the wealth to buy a high degree of civilization. It remains on the whole barbaric."

A TIME FOR SELF-EXAMINATION

The depression shook Pittsburgh's arrogant prosperity to its roots, and the New Deal ripped in two the area's traditional business-political hegemony. By 1936, the local Democratic party, using the Mellons and the low-tax Pennsylvania Manufacturing Association (which the bankers supported) as their whipping boys, had completely captured control of the city and the county government—both for the first time since the Civil War. Also, for the first time since the 1860's, the steel industry faltered seriously.

Although those in business power would not acknowledge it until the 1950's, Pittsburgh's national steel supremacy had started to peak off even before World War I. Total manufacturing employment had begun to slip behind the national growth rate by the turn of the century, when Pittsburgh had seemed most booming. In the dark days of the early 1930's both the huge steel mills and the region's cavernous coal mines were shut down for weeks on end not only for lack of orders, but also by labor union strikes, carried out bitterly but this time successfully under the protection of new federal legislation.

Downtown Pittsburgh stagnated then, too. On St. Patrick's Day of 1936 the center of the Steel Capital was literally on the verge of drowning, as the river waters, rising twenty-one feet above flood level, poured in over the main downtown streets, taking days to recede, and causing many millions in property damages and losses. No force could hold back the rivers then; nor did any liaison exist to draw the separate parts of the ailing city together for regenerative action.

These changed times gave pause to some of the community's business leaders as they gathered to commiserate in their gloomy downtown Duquesne Club, or out at the Rolling Rock Country Club. Some of these men were part of a new generation of industrialists who had inherited control of Pittsburgh industry from the aging or deceased barons. One of them—in fact, top among them—was Richard King Mellon, nephew of the recently departed Andrew. Richard, a modest, earnest and retiring man, had recently, at the age of thirty-eight, become head of the by now $3,000,000,000 Mellon empire, which his cousin Paul, Andrew's artistically inclined son, had declined.

R. K. Mellon now sat on the boards of over twenty corporations, some of the nation's greatest, and the mainstays of Pittsburgh's economy. In addition, the Mellon Bank and Trust Company was first in assets in Pittsburgh and fifth largest in the country. Whatever happened in Pittsburgh deeply affected the Mellon family's fortune. Little in Pittsburgh could move without them.

Along with his immense business responsibilities, the new ruler of the Mellon empire accepted a civic job in 1941, as president of the Pittsburgh Regional Planning Association. Richard's father, quite a different cut of man from his brother Andrew, had helped to organize this privately financed planning body in 1918. But the achievements of the agency, which had become almost dormant, were so insignificant that most Pittsburgh businessmen had long since lost interest in it or in planning.

Just a few years before Mellon became president of the organization, however, a new staff director from outside, with new, vital ideas, had been brought in to run it. Wallace K. Richards, a former roving correspondent in Europe and an art critic, was fresh from service in several New Deal agencies where he had planned new communities and developed conservation programs. For Pittsburgh, Richards became the sand in the oyster, the new personality who would develop the germ of the "new" city.

Richards concluded that Pittsburgh needed an umbrella civic organization composed of the top interests in the city—those whose investments depended on its future. Such a body could help overcome the jealousies, clashing special interests and pettiness which had thwarted so many community improvement projects in the past, and could develop and forward needed new programs as well.

Richards' ideas interested Mellon. But soon Pearl Harbor came and Mellon left the city for government service. The proposed new organization, like many New Deal-inspired schemes, seemed destined not to see daylight.

TO SAVE PITTSBURGH

But for Richard Mellon, as for many other Pittsburghers who went off to service, World War II offered sharp and disturbing new perspectives. Returning home on leave, they found the city they had accepted before unbearably drab and grimy. Its air was even worse now, clogged with the choking smog of war-busy mills. One story relates that Mellon's wife told him she did not want to come back to live in Pittsburgh. Another, that she had declared her home to be wherever Richard lived—"But couldn't you do something about the smoke?"

It was becoming apparent to the city's top private citizen that unless something were done to improve Pittsburgh, it would gradually be abandoned, and the Mellon fortune would be jeopardized. It was clear that the war prosperity was only temporary.

Early in 1943, Mellon called together in Washington a small group of his advisors and intimates, Richards among them, to discuss what could be done to save Pittsburgh. Specifically, they were to find ways to keep industry there and to encourage new concerns to move offices or locate plants there.

Now that the economic base that had produced their fortunes was in grave danger, Pittsburgh's tight group of business leaders began to concern themselves with using their power not just to milk the city, but to improve it. At this time Wallace Richards' community organization proposal took hold.

Soon after this meeting, the top industrialists, as well as leaders of labor, civic organizations and local educational institutions received invitations to a luncheon to help establish a new civic agency, the Allegheny Conference on Post-war Planning. They were informed that its field of action (for it was to be concerned with action, not—in spite of its title—just planning) was to be not only the city but also the region.

The Allegheny Conference had no precedents, and the new organization got off to a vague, academic start. Studies of the area's wide-ranging ills and possible cures—from flood control to housing and redevelopment—seemed to be the principal action. "At the end of eleven months," the Conference minutes read, ". . . we have eleven committees." Inertia and disillusion threatened.

A strategy for action was needed. This was supplied initially by Park Martin, a shrewd and hard-headed former country engineer, who in February 1945, became the full-time paid executive director of the renamed Allegheny Conference on Community Development. Martin, who previously had been the elected (Republican) Burgess of a suburban township (a position similar to Mayor), as well as staff director of the official Allegheny County Planning Commission, understood community politics as well as technical planning. Originally he had been chairman of the Conference's Steering Committee. Now he set about activating the civic organization.

One of Martin's new rules was that only heads of the corporations and institutions that were Conference members would attend executive board meetings and sit on subcommittees. Their deputies could not substitute for them. Further, instead of committees doing the Conference studies, these would be carried out by a full-time technically qualified staff which would report to and advise the members. The members would then determine action. Such a staffed operation would require a budget of $355,000 for the first three years, Martin estimated. The Conference members were taken aback, but they accepted his advice, and the necessary funds were raised.

Martin recognized that the Conference's single biggest contribution probably would be in giving the necessary "power" backing to advance community projects. He also believed that one of its greatest strengths would be in having a comprehensive program; if all the projects fit together, he reasoned, it would be easier to defend and push any single one of them.

In order to earn the indispensable confidence and support of the top private business leaders, Martin also recognized that the Conference had to show visible results, and soon. The city and county had had six master plans since 1906—all of them pigeonholed, largely for lack of funds.

Thus he decided on two other rules: a project would not be undertaken unless some body, public or private, had first agreed to put up the money to pay for its execution; and execution of key projects would be given precedence over making long-range plans.

But regional planning agency director Wallace Richards also served as secretary of the board of the Allegheny Conference and thus helped to coordinate the new action agency with the older planning body; in this dual capacity he did much of the planning. Conference Director Martin also consulted with Richards on priorities. One need was the alleviation of traffic downtown, especially if new corporate offices were to be built there. Richards and Martin agreed that it was necessary to build new arterial expressways with connecting bridges; these would divert through-traffic around the constricted business district and ease the way of those headed there. The abatement of smoke was also essential for new downtown growth and to improve the general environment—and had to be accomplished at the earliest possible date.

These projects would require the expenditure of vast sums of as yet unallocated public money, and the exercise of tough governmental power. Just to get the costly initial leg of the expressways built would first require a large shift in state allocations to the region. To build a modern expressway over Pittsburgh's rough and rocky terrain would cost an estimated minimum of $5,000,000 a mile. But since Pittsburgh and Allegheny County had turned Democratic, the Republicans who controlled both the legislature and the state purse strings had displayed a niggardly attitude toward the region's needs, and had only spent $2 to $3,000,000 annually on all of the area's state-financed public facilities. Even without taking into consideration Pittsburgh's new needs, this allocation was inequitable. Local motorists paid the state twice that sum in vehicle registrations and gasoline taxes alone.

To change these allocations just for the expressways would require political pressures on, and action by, state bodies. It began to be increasingly evident that state action would also be required in a number of other areas to achieve many local improvements desired by the Conference and long overdue.

The problem was how to get action, even by local government. Pittsburgh's Democratic Mayor Cornelius Scully had as little liaison with the Republican administration or legislature in Harrisburg as the Allegheny Conference had with the local Democrats at City Hall. In fact, Mayor Scully had stayed at a leery arm's length from the new Mellon-backed body. Meanwhile the chairman of the Conference, then a university president, told Park Martin that he would have nothing to do with "any damn politician," Republican or Democratic. Yet Martin knew that political backing was the *sine qua non* of success. The Conference could plan, promote, coordinate or help persuade, but it lacked the government power required to create agencies and public funds to execute projects. Martin also knew that Richard Mellon, who was the main source of Republican campaign funds in Allegheny County, had an immense capacity for influencing state action.

Any member of Pittsburgh's top power, it is said, would listen to any other, sooner than to a professional. Martin, no doubt, was a notable exception. But the return to Pittsburgh in the summer of 1945 of Mellon's legal counsel, Arthur Van Buskirk, provided the support necessary to implement the Conference director's approach to getting results. Van Buskirk, originally a Philadelphian, now had an additional role in Pittsburgh: that of overseeing the Mellon family's varied financial and civic interests. In this new capacity, he moved into the Republican County Committee as chairman of its finance committee. He became

Mellon's representative on the Allegheny Conference (Mellon himself was not a member), where he took on chairmanship of the subcommittee assigned to make the historic site of prerevolutionary Fort Duquesne into a public park.

To nonresidents, and even to many who live there, Point State Park may have seemed a frill, a green bow on a still rotten package. But to many civic-minded Pittsburghers, the historic site had great symbolic significance, and it was a terrible eyesore at the city's projected new approach. For decades, plans for the park had been repeatedly frustrated, mainly for lack of funds. Execution of this centrally located project would indicate that something *could* be done to improve Pittsburgh.

Moreover, as the Conference's highway plans began to take shape, it became evident that since some new routes would enter the city over bridges near the Point, to give vehicles ready access to downtown, the two facilities should be integrated and proceed simultaneously. But the price of executing these initial projects was high. To build the Penn-Lincoln Expressway would require, Conference technicians estimated, an initial $57,000,000 (ultimately, with inflation and rises in construction costs, the twenty-mile artery came to over $200,000,000); and to reclaim the land at the Point for the park would cost another $4,000,000.

Arthur Van Buskirk went to Pennsylvania's Republican Governor Edward Martin and told him that when Allegheny County received its fair share of state funds for highways, the park and other purposes, the community's business leaders would have more money for the party.

The Conference, a tax-exempt organization, claimed nonpartisanship. Nonetheless, when Governor Martin informed its leaders that he would support them and assure funds for the expressway and park by executive order, they asked him to announce the projected and unprecedented plans for state spending on Pittsburgh in late October, hoping this would help the Republican candidate for Mayor in the city's forthcoming elections.

However, the ground was cut from under them by the opposition's nominee, Democratic state "boss" and County Committee Chairman, David L. Lawrence, who openly declared that he was delighted that the state was at last going to do something for

Pittsburgh. Furthermore, Lawrence announced, in a statement that made front-page headlines and dumbfounded the leaders of the Conference that, if elected Mayor, he would work to support their program.

THE COALITION FORMS

What a surprise this stand was can be appreciated by the fact that Lawrence, a career Democrat from the age of fourteen, and the party's County Chairman since thirty-three, had been brought up in the "hate Mellon" tradition. Lawrence had become the most powerful political figure in the Pittsburgh region and in Pennsylvania Democratic politics in the 1930's by delivering the county, then the city and state to the Democrats. A State Committeeman as well, he had become known as a "king-maker" in the national party by swinging the necessary convention votes to Franklin D. Roosevelt for the presidential nomination when Alfred E. Smith appeared to have turned too conservative for Lawrence.

Even the Mayoral candidacy of Lawrence was a surprise. He had never before run for public office and, aside from brief public service as Secretary of State of the Commonwealth in 1934, he had always stuck to what his aides euphemistically called political management, supporting himself with a prosperous insurance business. But in mid-1945, ailing Mayor Scully was to retire, and the Democratic leaders in Pittsburgh could not agree on a new candidate.

The one thing an entrenched professional politician tries to avoid is a debilitating primary fight. It is said that Lawrence let the party persuade him to run even though he felt that a boss seeking elective office might prove a liability.

Another seeming deterrent to his accepting the nomination was that to be Mayor of Pittsburgh offered so little honor. Pittsburgh was the butt of endless jokes—a "city of apologies," as one local put it. To assume this office appeared a step down for Lawrence.* But guided by shrewd and progressive advisors, Lawrence

* When Lawrence told New York's Mayor La Guardia that he was running for Mayor of Pittsburgh, the peppery "Little Flower" shot back, "You're a damn fool."

decided to run on a new kind of mayoralty platform—one that would elevate both the office and the city. What Pittsburgh needed at City Hall, he declared, was political leadership, not just housekeeping or management. To create a different image of himself, and to gather specific ideas for the necessary improvement of his community, he visited several cities where rebuilding programs were already under way. His itinerary included New York City, where he met some of Robert Moses' builder-planners. One of them inquired whether Lawrence knew Wallace Richards, the regional planner, and suggested they get acquainted.

As soon as Lawrence returned to Pittsburgh, he phoned Richards. Lawrence was immediately impressed and excited by Richards' vision of a rejuvenated Pittsburgh. "Wally could dream up things we staid Pittsburghers couldn't see," he recalled. As a result of this meeting, Lawrence determined to work with the Conference, if he were elected—in spite of its heavily Republican sponsorship.

When the region's leading political power publicly backed the businessmen-planners' program, he gave it a prominence that it had lacked before. His campaign pledge and subsequent support of the program in office would also provide essential, hitherto missing, muscle. It was out of this decision that the new Pittsburgh formula began to take shape.

Lawrence was elected, but by a very slim margin, and his attention the first year in office was claimed largely by local problems of postwar readjustment in the area. Prominent among them was a rash of strikes against various industries and city agencies, which he proved successful at mediating. But it did not seem that his fine campaign pledges for improving the region would soon be realized.

Behind the scenes, during that time, however, the foundations were laid for the new compact between Pittsburgh's key political and business powers. Arthur Van Buskirk and Allegheny Conference director Park Martin set up a series of quiet little luncheons for them in the Mellons' dining room. Present were what Van Buskirk called "the handful of men in the city, county and state who could say 'Yes' and 'No' " to the emerging program. They were Democrats Mayor Lawrence and Allegheny County Commissioner John Kane, then also Democratic leader in the county; Richard Mellon and Van Buskirk; Republican Attorney General of the state James Duff who would soon—with Mellon's help—become Governor; and the staff directors and planners of the two key community agencies, Park Martin and Wallace Richards.

By sitting down together in this manner, these decision-makers could discuss and decide in an hour's time what programs to push and how to pay for them. They could also iron out conflicts which they, as political opponents, might ordinarily have. All believed that this program was, and of necessity must be, nonpartisan; they were determined not to let it become a political football, recognizing that the cooperation of opposing parties was essential to their wide-ranging, interrelated plans.

But even local two-party support and gubernatorial backing were not enough. For some of the most decisive first steps would have to be taken in the state legislature when it met in its next biennial session in Harrisburg in 1947. Local governments in Pennsylvania had to ask the state body for a ridiculous number of special local powers before they could act. The broad gaps that existed in the rights granted to Pittsburgh by the state would preclude much of the revitalization program unless these could be removed by legislative action. Thus, the Conference staff carefully drew up, with legal counsel, the laws they wanted passed in Harrisburg the following year.

It was during this period, also, that Van Buskirk went to Mayor Lawrence and proposed that the city establish a redevelopment agency that could exercise eminent domain for redevelopment under the new state law, and that he appoint to its board leading citizens, naming himself, Lawrence, as the chairman.

This unorthodox suggestion momentarily nonplussed the Mayor. "I'd be laughed out of town if I appointed myself," he replied. Evidently, the Mayor had not yet fully grasped the basis of urban rebuilding—the essential collaboration of political and business leaders. In fact, he thought that the banks, the insurance companies and other private investors that Pittsburgh needed for its redevelopment would be frightened off by his own political stamp. And he knew that he, personally, and even in his elected role, lacked the entree to the moneymen. He believed the business leaders were needed for this. Further, he was concerned that if a Democratic administration were to take private property for redevelopment, local business people would label the program "socialistic" and state Republicans would block the needed new legislation. To make such a radical program acceptable in Pittsburgh, according to his experience, the Mellon stamp was necessary. Thus, Van Buskirk seemed the logical person to chair the new agency.

But Van Buskirk reasoned differently: "If we condemned people's properties, it was better for the Mayor with his popular following to be responsible, rather than someone with the Mellon or U.S. Steel nameplate." He urged the Mayor to take on the position, promising to seek the support of the Chamber of Commerce and the newspapers. And as part of the buildup, the Conference passed a resolution, duly publicized, requesting the Mayor to appoint himself.

Lawrence worked out his end of the quandary by naming Van Buskirk vice-chairman. The other members of the new Pittsburgh Urban Redevelopment Authority, whose appointment he announced in November 1946, were Lester Perry, retiring president of Carnegie-Illinois, U.S. Steel's largest operating company; Edgar J. Kaufmann, president of the city's leading department store and a civic leader; and Democratic Councilman William A. Stewart. The bipartisan top political and private power composition of the Redevelopment Authority—actually Democrats formed a minority—indicated publicly, for the first time, the nature of the new coalition of business and government which was to push the Renaissance programs.

SMOKE CONTROL

The first time that the new coalition applied its combined strength was in seeking the abatement of coal smoke. This long-needed action cut to the very heart of the city's economy and folkways.

Pittsburgh's soft coal fueled the giant blast furnaces of its steel mills, stoked the engines of the essential freight rail carriers, warmed the homes of its workers and gave direct employment to thousands of men. Local custom had it that smoke was good for you, a line propagated by the Mellon Institute for many years. Smoke was a sign of prosperity: the mills—and the people, too—were working. A little dirt, it was held, never hurt anyone.

But Pittsburgh was choking to death on its coal smoke. Smog was costing residents alone an estimated $10,000,000 a year directly—in ferociously high bills for cleaning clothes and household furnishings, medical expenses, lost work days for colds and sinus infections, ruined store merchandise. Smog was also keeping from the community untold millions of dollars in new capital investment, in real estate and industry. It certainly made Pittsburgh an unattractive location. Yet the city had lived with the smog—and with anti-smoke committees and even ordinances—for generations.*

During his Mayoralty campaign Lawrence—in spite of warnings by some advisors that it would be political suicide—had pledged to put into effect the abatement ordinance which the City Council had finally passed in 1941, but then had had to shelve after Pearl Harbor. He was convinced that Pittsburgh must immediately get rid of coal smoke if it were to survive. And he knew that householders forced to comply with the ordinance would ultimately be able to save money in heating, cleaning and medical bills by using the more efficient (though initially more expensive) low-volatile fuels or converters that would be necessary under the bill. But it was difficult to convince them of this. To complicate matters politically, the ordinance called for homeowners to comply sooner than industry, which would have to order and to install elaborate and costly new equipment, which the Mellon Institute now helped develop.

As October 1, 1946, the date for home enforcement of smog abatement, drew close, pressures to soften his stand were brought upon the Mayor from almost every side—from steel workers who feared loss of their jobs if industry decided to move away from the area rather than comply; from coal miners whose future already was shaky; from Democratic businessmen who were soft coal suppliers; from homeowners and landlords who would have to pay for converters or new gas heating systems. There were also

* The town's Burgess proposed a smoke control ordinance for the first time in 1804. In the 1890's, a native wrote that "soot, grime and black dirt covered everything. Every cleanly Pittsburgher learned not to touch his face."

problems of assuring an ample supply of alternate fuels, but the Conference staff and members helped overcome the shortage.

Then, in an effort to force indefinite postponement of smog control, the local coal interests threatened to boycott Pittsburgh industry. Here Richard Mellon (briefed by Conference members) moved in to use his power as a director of Consolidation Coal, the biggest of the fuel suppliers, to make them withdraw their threat.

Still the railroads were able legally to ignore the ordinance and thus sabotage its effectiveness, as they could fire up their engines out in the county without violating the city law. To get their compliance, as well as that of the county mills which produced much of the coal smoke, would require a state law.

Thus, one piece of the "Pittsburgh package" of enabling legislation drafted by the Conference to implement its programs, and to be presented for action at Harrisburg in the winter of 1947, was a bill for smoke control in the county.

This was potentially the most explosive of the nine laws the Pittsburghers sought, but several others were also sure to encounter fierce opposition. The Pittsburgh real estate board was already pressuring the legislature to reject two other bills—one that would allow the city to create a Public Parking Authority, the first agency of its kind in the country; the other, indispensable to the city's first redevelopment project, to permit insurance companies to invest in real estate in Pennsylvania, an enterprise not then permitted.*

Pittsburgh's informal steering committee shrewdly reduced opposition. For example, they commissioned outside experts to study the proposal for the Parking Authority; then worked to gain joint public backing locally for the measure from six separate civic and business organizations which might have caused trouble. Van Buskirk briefed the Governor on the package and expressed Mr. Mellon's desire for his cooperation. Caucuses were

* Less controversial measures in the package were a bill to set up a countywide refuse disposal system and charge communities fees for the service; a bill to let the county create a Transit and Traffic Commission to study mass transportation; another to let Pittsburgh create a Department of Parks; one to let both Pittsburgh and its suburbs broaden their tax base beyond real estate; and a bill to make the state liable for condemnations in building limited access highways.

held for legislative members of each political party in the region by their leaders.

Then, almost on the eve of the biennial session, a dinner was held for *all* state senators and assemblymen from Pittsburgh and Allegheny County—both Democrats and Republicans—to explain the benefits of the various measures in the package to the region and their constituents, and to try to secure bipartisan support at Harrisburg. At this unprecedented gathering, some Republican legislators complained that the proposed municipal parking garages would compete with private initiative and put "the little guy" out of business. Another voiced concern that the Democrats would get all the credit for the legislation. Mayor Lawrence told him, "If you want to help me politically, oppose the bills. The Governor will sign them anyway." The region's delegation went to Harrisburg united in support of the package.

There the Pittsburghers would have to win over the Republican representatives from rural areas around the state; these had no interest in cities' problems but, due to misapportionment, dominated the legislature. The operators of the Philadelphia parking lots were also organizing to do battle, employing state senators as their lawyers.

The fight to pass the laws in Harrisburg was led by Democrat Joseph Barr,* Pittsburgh Senate minority leader. Mayor Lawrence was also there, in the background, to help him. Lawrence well knew from his days as the Commonwealth's Secretary of State which legislator was on whose payroll and who controlled and could deliver votes from certain counties. No holds were barred in trying to win legislators—or in locating the people who could move them.

Still the most formidable adversary was not an elected official, but the Pennsylvania Railroad. The Pennsy was so powerful in state politics that its Harrisburg lobbyist was known as the "fifty-first Senator." If the county smoke ban passed, the line would have to spend many millions to convert to Diesel equipment. To line up legislators against the proposed new extended anti-smoke ordinance, or in favor of a clause to exempt the line from it, the railroad hired another full-time lobbyist.

When the Pennsylvania announced its stand—that railroads

* Barr succeeded Lawrence as Mayor in 1959.

should be exempt from the enforcement of smoke control—the fighting editor of the Pittsburgh *Press,* Ed Leach, ran a front-page, boldface editorial headed "A Hell of a Way to Run a Railroad."

But such headlines were not enough to make the Pennsylvania back down. Conference leaders told Mellon that probably only he had the power to get the measure off dead center. Mellon was a director of the railroad company and one of its principal stockholders. He let its top management know that if the line failed to comply, or continued to block the new law, the companies he controlled would probably switch their freight haulage to other, competitive lines. Other customers of the railroad company took similar stands.

In a matter of days, the smoke control bill passed through the legislature, unamended. Soon the Pennsylvania line started replacing its old engines with Diesel equipment. Major local industries, now convinced that there would be no retreat, began to spend hundreds of thousands of dollars to make their plants smokeless. Only two minor bills in the package failed to pass.

Though not foreseen in 1946–47, several years after the fight to win the Pennsylvania Railroad's compliance, Diesel equipment began to be used generally by railroads instead of old-fashioned coal-eating engines. But the psychological effect of the Pittsburghers' victory over the Pennsylvania line was of enormous import for their subsequent enforcement of smog control and the execution of other programs. It showed they meant business. Furthermore, Pittsburgh railroads "Dieselized" much sooner than those in the rest of the country.

REDEVELOPMENT PLANS

In the meantime, thanks to Governor Martin's 1945 executive order, Point State Park was getting under way, and with it important related projects.

Over the years, as Pittsburgh had moved back from the river front and its periodic floods, the site of its prerevolutionary heritage had become almost buried in a jumble of unused railroad tracks, freight warehouses, decrepit rooming houses, and the iron railroad bridges that entered the city at its very tip. Most of the historic buildings had been destroyed. After the 1936 river deluge, Army engineers had initiated a series of dams to end such floods. But mothers who wanted to take their children to see the Block House, the only structure that survived from Fort Pitt, had to pick their way through the blight, always on the lookout for drunks and vagrants.

Point Park would probably be little frequented unless the rambling sheds, rail overpasses and huge obsolete buildings of the Wabash line which cluttered the area between the projected park site at the Point and the downtown Triangle could be removed as well.

The statutory power to remove these obstacles was contained in the state's redevelopment law, which had just passed the legislature in 1945. Pennsylvania's enabling legislation was exceptionally broad in its definition of the blight conditions which could be eliminated with the use of eminent domain.* But there was not as yet a federal land "write-down," and the prohibitive cost of acquiring the land for redevelopment, in view of the "good" buildings which also stood in the twenty-three-acre tract, cast grave doubt on the economic feasibility of the area's private redevelopment. In the spring of 1946, however, a fire that raged through it fortuitously caused some $8,000,000 in property losses there; it provided, in effect, the needed reduction in the public cost of acquiring the property for redevelopment.

Now a developer had to be found. A conference delegation, led by Van Buskirk and including Thomas J. Parkinson, president of the railroad which then owned the old Wabash facilities, set off for New York. The big insurance companies, which had their headquarters in Manhattan and many millions of dollars to invest, seemed the most likely prospects. Metropolitan Life was already sponsoring Stuyvesant Town, the first publicly assisted redevelopment in the country, and was their logical first prospect. But that Manhattan housing project proved too demanding for the company to take on another at that time.

Railroad president Parkinson had another idea. The next call they made dramatically illustrated the importance of the partici-

* This law, part of Governor Martin's postwar planning program, passed unopposed because, some surmise, the state legislators did not grasp the extraordinary powers they were granting cities.

pation of local business leaders. The president of the Equitable Life Assurance Society was a personal friend of Parkinson, and Pittsburgh was one of Equitable's chief insurance markets. They got to see the president promptly. Pittsburgh's smoggy atmosphere made it unappealing to a real estate investor. But after the delegation informed the Society's president of plans for early smoke abatement, he proved receptive to the general idea of sponsorship.

The Pittsburghers proposed that the insurance firm construct high-rise housing on the redevelopment site—to bring people back downtown to live. But the Society rejected the area as unsuitable for housing, since it was isolated from schools and shops. Their real estate advisor, Robert Dowling, thought it should be used instead for new offices. Commercial re-use had never been tried in the still very green history of urban redevelopment, but the proposal was legal under state law, and the Conference delegation did not object. A subsequent market study gave substance to the real estate consultant's hunch: he found that there was a great unrealized and scarcely recognized need for larger and more prestigious modern commercial space among the city's big corporations whose headquarters had become scattered around downtown as the companies' office functions had grown.

With Mayor Lawrence as chairman of the Redevelopment Authority, the prospective developer would have the needed assurance of full political backing and governmental cooperation for this huge risk-filled undertaking. At the same time, the composition of the powerful bipartisan board of the Authority promised that execution would not be caught up in partisan politics or grafting.

After Equitable's participation in redevelopment had been legalized by the state legislature in 1947, plans and negotiations advanced for Gateway Center—the name chosen for the office complex that was to rise behind Point State Park in honor of its location at the historic pioneer's gateway to the West. To expedite the program, the Mayor placed his right-hand man, then his executive secretary, John P. Robin, in the position of staff director of the new Redevelopment Authority. Local business concerns raised $150,000 to finance the new agency's initial staff operation.

Gateway Center's design conception was a striking departure from usual, piecemeal commercial developments, with their dense land coverage calculated to extract the maximum return from every foot of buildable real estate.* The first-stage plans called for three twenty-story office structures which would cover only a third of the given plot of land. They would be placed in a garden setting, separated by lawns and walkways, landscaped with trees, hedges and fountains, and lined with benches. These were all non-income-producing amenities which Equitable, as the developer, would have to maintain and support. Underground there would be a variety of rent-paying restaurants of different price ranges; these could be reached from the outside walks by stairways or from the building interiors by elevator. There was also a garage system tied in to the new expressways. The underground development part of the total design plans proposed by Dowling alarmed Equitable, as the top executives were familiar with Pittsburgh's famous floods at the Point. But Dowling pointed out that with the completion of the anti-flood dam network, the floods would probably never recur.

Equitable also agreed to pay Pittsburgh the full current value of the site—then some $12,000,000 with all of the standing structures, plus a $1,000,000 extra "toll charge" to the Redevelopment Authority for the privilege of using the public power of eminent domain. (This has been used since to pay staff and administrative costs.) But the developer held that the Redevelopment Authority must assure them of twenty-year leases on 60 per cent of the 1,000,000 square feet of new office space planned for the first stage of Gateway Center. Such a guarantee was the minimum usually required to obtain a mortgage commitment on office buildings.

Yet, in spite of the local market revealed by the studies, securing such long-term leases in the redevelopment site at this stage would not be easy. Rents in the projected modern, air-condi-

* The only precedent was New York's Rockefeller Center, where all the land had been owned by one family prior to its development for an office complex separated by promenades and a sunken plaza with skating rink and restaurants. Ironically, it was Equitable's construction of its block-covering downtown Manhattan headquarters, back in 1910, which, by robbing surrounding properties of air, light and values, precipitated New York's original 1916 zoning ordinance.

tioned offices would have to be 25 to 100 per cent higher than those charged in structures built several decades or more ago, and already depreciated. A much larger obstacle in the eyes of potential tenants was that Gateway Center, far from offering an impressive location which warranted these higher rents, was at the far edge of the established Pittsburgh business center, in a famous blighted area.

It was whispered that the project would never be carried out. Why should U.S. Steel's Lester Perry, one member of the Redevelopment Authority, or Arthur Van Buskirk, its vice-chairman, help further it? U.S. Steel, with the Mellon Bank, and the Aluminum Company of America had recently announced plans for two huge and potentially competitive office skyscrapers in the heart of the Triangle.

Another member of the Authority was Edgar J. Kaufmann, whose store's chief local competitor, Joseph Horne, was located at the lower end of the Triangle practically across the street from Gateway Center. Kaufmann's top executives, fearing that the project would take customers away from their store, which was in the Triangle's heart, urged their president to stop the development. But their arguments were futile.

On the contrary, the connections of the coalition's and Authority's business members were used, and they proved the indispensable key to lining up the major tenants for Gateway Center. Van Buskirk led the members of the Authority in the search. Richard Mellon asked the officers of the Pittsburgh corporations which he either owned or controlled to move their company's offices into the new Center as an act of "civic responsibility." In fact, they were being asked to sign long-term leases for space in buildings which were not only not yet designed, but which were also to be erected on land not yet acquired. It was furthermore an unprecedented public undertaking whose very legality was then being tested—of necessity—in the courts by a taxpayer's suit brought by the Authority to clear the law.

Not unexpectedly, owners of some of the older office structures that would be almost emptied by companies moving to Gateway Center fought the project bitterly. The president of Pittsburgh Plate Glass, whose company was a prime tenant of the old Grant Building, had said his company would take a whole building in the new area. The owners of the Grant Building, in a desperate attempt to prevent the company's departure, sent photographs to the directors of Equitable Life in New York showing Pittsburgh shrouded in smog and the site of Gateway Center inundated by the flood waters of 1936.

Organized real estate interests also opposed the project. Some testified against Gateway Center at the required public hearings, but the big opposition from that quarter had been effectively reduced by the Authority's retention of several leading realtors as property acquisition agents. The redevelopment received the needed local legislative approval, and the only legal obstacle to putting the project into execution was the pending settlement of the taxpayer's suit.

Meantime, Lawrence faced the approaching mayoralty election.

The controversial programs for rebuilding and improving Pittsburgh which the Mayor had been forwarding were piling up, but there was little to show as yet. His opponents within the Democratic party had already accused him of "selling out" to and "sleeping with" the Mellons when he had, as he had promised in his 1945 campaign, helped expedite the Conference's program. His liaison with the banker-industrialists was a radical departure from the partisan, bitterly class-conscious denunciations of these business powers which had been the local Democrats' oratorical mainstay for decades. Now, in 1949, Lawrence's enthusiastic support of Mellon Square added fuel to the fire that was being built up against him by some elements in his party.

The idea for the block-large downtown public plaza is said to have occurred to Richard Mellon one day as he looked down from his office window on the assorted ugly roofs and tiny parking lots that covered a particularly drab block of Pittsburgh's congested downtown. Possibly Wallace Richards helped plant the seed, but Mellon was struck now by the contrast with San Francisco's Union Square, with its greenery, walks and benches over a subterranean garage in the business center. Plans for the new Mellon-U.S. Steel Building were also being formed, and the idea of creating an attractive open setting for the new skyscraper was a factor.

But the city of Pittsburgh plainly could not afford, fiscally or politically, to pay the large cost of downtown property acquisition and clearance to create the square. Only the Mellons could underwrite development of such a plaza. They quietly offered to donate the necessary money to the city—$4,000,000—and Lawrence, who knew that part of that centrally located block had already been earmarked by the Parking Authority for a public garage, agreed, in return for the gift, to use the city's power of eminent domain to acquire park land (and thus prevent present owners from asking hold-out prices) for the new public downtown plaza. He also committed the city to pay for the park's annual maintenance.

When this plan became public, the real estate board immediately charged that the proposed square would be one more drain on the city's fiscal resources, removing still more blue-ribbon property from the tax rolls and burdening the taxpayers with the extra cost of its upkeep. Point Park was another new land use on formerly tax-paying land that was also non-taxable now. It was also pointed out that an underground garage cost more to construct than a surface garage.

At the same time, a Democratic rival of Lawrence's capitalized on the public costs of this latest improvement project in an attempt to unseat him as Mayor in the party's primary. Running as the champion of the "Little Joes"—the homeowners who were complaining that industry was being given a number of years to comply with the smoke ordinance while they had had to convert almost immediately—he charged that the people were being hurt by the high costs of fuel conversion. He further charged that Lawrence was too concerned with "middle-class matters" such as smoke control and downtown parks, and that he was too friendly with the Mellon interests.

But on the Democratic primary day, a record turnout gave the Mayor 77,000 votes against his challenger's 50,000. In the November general election, Lawrence went on to win by a 56,000 plurality—a record for a Pittsburgh Mayor, in marked contrast to his slim 14,000 margin in 1945. It appeared that his stands had won the public's mandate.

RESULTS BEGIN TO SHOW

Late that year, the Pennsylvania Supreme Court decided the taxpayer's suit challenging the legality of Gateway Center in favor of the Redevelopment Authority, and the way at last appeared clear for drawing up a formal contract with Equitable. Then, unexpectedly, the litigant appealed the state court's decision to the United States Supreme Court.

By now, however, nine of the city's largest corporations—Pittsburgh Plate Glass, People's Gas, Westinghouse Electric, Jones and Laughlin among them—had found that they needed larger, more efficient quarters to centralize their administrative operations and had signed agreements to move their offices to Gateway Center. If the new buildings were not ready for occupancy several years hence, when the companies' old leases expired, the firms might be homeless.

Equitable, weighing the high cost of waiting (construction and total development costs keep rising) against what seemed the comparatively minor risk that the high court might decide against the redevelopment, signed a contract with the Pittsburgh Redevelopment Authority in February of 1950. It agreed to undertake the project and bound itself to be financially responsible for all property damages if the decision of the Pennsylvania court should be reversed. To prepare against owners' claims in that event, the Authority photographed every building that was to be torn down and took measurements of each, to provide irrefutable evidence of just what was being demolished. It also hired a large staff to help business tenants on the site of the project find suitable new quarters. Clearance proceeded rapidly, and by July 1 the foundations for the first three office buildings had been laid. (It turned out that the U.S. Supreme Court refused even to hear the case.)

As smoke abatement took effect, the air cleared over Pittsburgh and revealed intolerably dark and dirty building façades. The Conference organized a committee to get owners to scrub and sandblast the city's smoke-stained skyscrapers; altogether about $3,000,000 was spent for this long-needed cosmetic treatment. Meanwhile, office workers and shoppers found they could now wear lighter-colored clothes when they came downtown. Fashionable women even wore white gloves. And in the neighborhoods, for the first time in years, householders applied fresh coats of paint to homes and planted grass and flowers in yards which they could now enjoy.

The new instrument for re-using city land was also being put to work in other parts of the city. The most important redevelopment project after Gateway Center was one for the steel firm of Jones and Laughlin. Its need for space had grown with automated processing, and it now sought this new public help in order to enlarge its facilities. The alternative, the company indicated, was that it might well have to move out of Pittsburgh. The loss of J. and L., which was a major Pittsburgh employer and the second largest taxpayer in the city, was obviously something to be avoided, and the proposed redevelopment, although for the immediate benefit of one firm, was clearly in the public's interest.

The steel firm desired to join up and expand its two South Side plants by acquiring, with the aid of eminent domain, the thirty-two-acre strip of blighted land which now separated them. This site was partially occupied by run-down worker housing built in the nineteenth century, which should never have been built there in the first place. It was still occupied by 235 families, many of whom owned their homes.

Mayor Lawrence asked fellow Democrat Philip Murray, president of the United Steelworkers, to explain to the residents and property owners, many of whom worked for J. and L., the importance of this holding operation—if J. and L. stayed, so would their jobs.

The steel firm paid the city $1,000,000, the full value for the land and buildings, and the homeowners in turn received from the city full assessed compensation for their properties. They were also assisted in finding other homes, not a major problem. The basis for opposition evaporated and the project moved forward.

As a result of this industrial redevelopment project, Jones and Laughlin installed eleven new open-hearth furnaces, worth $70,000,000, on the reclaimed land, and the city gained $10,000,000 in new taxable values. The steel firm subsequently undertook, with redevelopment assistance, some more expansions and added another $10,000,000 to the tax base.

At the same time, two of the city's landlocked universities, Pitt and Duquesne, also needed to expand, and requested help. Pittsburgh's power structure hoped to attract new industrial research laboratories and thus plants to the region by enlarging and improving their local universities' medical and scientific, as well as general facilities. The Authority obliged by clearing a blighted block out in Oakland for a $6,000,000 extension to the Children's Hospital at Pitt; another ten acres for Pitt's School of Public Health (where the Salk anti-polio vaccine was subsequently discovered); and thirty-six acres for athletic facilities. Like Pittsburgh's previous redevelopment projects, none of these received a public financial subsidy; but only—and significantly—the use of eminent domain to acquire land for re-use at a fair market price.

By 1953, the first, $50,000,000 section of Gateway Center—three office towers—was open and occupied and Equitable was making plans for additional buildings called for in the official plans on the rest of the land it was committed to rebuild.*

Mellon Square, too, was now a reality— a landscaped public plaza with figured marble pavement and fountains and benches occupied by office workers at lunchtime. Across the street, on one of its sides, rose U.S. Steel-Mellon's forty-one-story, $28,500,000 new tower home, while on another side there was Alcoa's elegant thirty-story, $10,000,000 new headquarters. Far from suffering from Gateway Center, Kaufmann's Department Store, on the block next to Mellon Square, had built an $11,000,000 extension and increased its space by 50 per cent.

What had these publicly aided, private redevelopments and expansions and the other Renaissance projects meant to Pittsburgh in tax terms? An analysis of the effects was released in 1953 by the local office of the Pennsylvania Economy League; this privately financed municipal research agency was established by big business in the 1930's to study and influence the provision of the best possible government services for the lowest possible costs.

* The original plan, calling for eleven cruciform office structures, was considerably modified by Equitable after the first three buildings remained at only 70 per cent occupancy—just the "break-even" point—for several years. "There was not anything like the demand for space to fill the rest of the buildings. It's not a big city," John H. Muller, Senior Vice-President of the insurance firm, stated. "The thing about Pittsburgh is that its appetite exceeds its digestion. We were stuck with it."

The solution, Equitable found, was to diversify the development with complementary buildings—a hotel, the state office building, the Bell Telephone Building, and an apartment house. Ten years passed before the Society's returns from Gateway Center were satisfactory. "At the time we didn't realize what we know now—that it's a long-range proposition."

This report, entitled "Debits and Credits," revealed that Point State Park and the related highways had cost the city $5,287,265 in ratables removed from the tax rolls. However, Gateway Center, even with its limited land coverage, had already added double that sum in new assessables—four to five times the previous valuations in the entire old blighted area. Further, the city's outlays for servicing that decayed rabbit warren had been sharply reduced and thus released public revenues for other needs. The state's huge park and parkway outlays were not mentioned, although these were essential supporting facilities.

Mellon Square had cost $2,459,740 in taxable property, but this loss for the new open-space downtown was more than offset by taxable gains of $17,457,185 from the adjacent new office towers and the additions to Kaufmann's. Part of the department store's expansion was offset, of course, by the $1,931,385 lost for the Parking Authority's four new downtown garages—which were built to help shoppers park conveniently. But without these new parking facilities, it was held, retail decentralization, still a big problem, would have been worse.

Meanwhile, those concerned about the untenanting of office space formerly held by the major Pittsburgh corporations which had moved to Gateway learned from the report that much old but still serviceable space had been taken up by smaller professional firms, labor union administrative staffs and government agencies—all of which were expanding personnel and operations in Pittsburgh as they were elsewhere at this time. They required more room, but could not afford new office building rentals. To house all the new civic agencies together, the Redevelopment agency purchased J. and L.'s old office building on Ross Street.

But new buildings were going up in other parts of the Golden Triangle as well, among them two new apartment-hotels. These structures would have been inconceivable for any one either to construct or occupy before the air had been made breathable.

That fall, Lawrence was re-elected again by an even larger plurality.

SLUM CLEARANCE

Yet in spite of all the visible, taxable redevelopment, the city's slums still festered, virtually untouched by the Renaissance.

Some of the oldest and worst slums spread like a dark blot down the side of the Hill, overlooking the "new" Pittsburgh. It was obvious that this area must be cleared and redeveloped, too. Conference leaders also realized that this project would probably require the public subsidy now available to cities under the new federal Title I program, in order to reduce the land cost for suitable re-use.

In fact, in spite of their statements about the Jeffersonian, local nature of the Renaissance, the Pittsburghers were quite Hamiltonian in availing themselves of federal and state help for the city, and planner Wallace Richards kept them informed on the proposed Title I program before its passage. In 1950, the year after enactment of the new program, a hundred acres of the Lower Hill were earmarked for such government-assisted redevelopment. About $28,000,000 of public money, two thirds of it federal, was pledged to its execution.

Yet it was not until 1955 that clearance of that miserable slum began. A good part of this long delay between designation and the commencement of clearance was caused by legal complications. But in fact, none of Pittsburgh's top power had pushed to get rid of their city's worst slum area first.

The thrust of the Renaisssance thus far—as contrasted with other early redevelopment projects elsewhere—had been economic rebuilding. Mayor Lawrence was convinced that unless the city's commercial and industrial base were saved, the city government would soon be bankrupt. Under his administration, $10,-000,000 in municipal funds were committed to help carry out the public share of projects which would eventually return more tax funds, save or add jobs, and help stabilize the local economy. He believed the city could not undertake more at that time. Pittsburgh's fiscal problems were already so severe that in 1954 Lawrence had put through a politically unpopular one per cent sales tax in order to gain extra revenue.

But equally important to the timetable of the Lower Hill's redevelopment, in Pittsburgh style, the community's decision-makers had first to agree on the best uses for the strategically located, century-old slum area before it was cleared for rebuilding.

How the re-use evolved is illustrative of the way Pittsburgh operated. As the city fathers and civic agency directors and planners catalogued the community's resources and needs, it became apparent that lack of an adequate municipal auditorium had cost Pittsburgh dozens of conventions (and the millions of dollars in business they bring to local hotels and merchants). Sports events such as track meets and prize fights took place in an ancient car barn, the city's excuse for an athletic stadium. Still another of the inadequately quartered semi-public activities scattered around the city was the new Civic Light Opera. Summer rains washed away the popular company's open-air performances in Schenley Park far too often. Other cultural events took place in Oakland, which was a fifteen-minute drive from downtown and poorly served by public transportation. The city also lacked a large central place for community gatherings.

An ingenious solution for housing many of these events together was first put forth by a Democratic City Councilman who had promoted the Civic Opera. He proposed an auditorium with a push-button roof that would open it on clear summer evenings and close it tight on rainy or winter nights. There had never been a structure like it, however, in Pittsburgh or anywhere else, and his idea had been greeted as "crazy." But the president of the Mellon-controlled Koppers Company, then ex-General Brehon Somervell, studied the plan and said the retractable roof was feasible from an engineering viewpoint. Plans for the unique multi-purpose civic auditorium could then move ahead; and it was deemed desirable to place it on the Lower Hill, in the redevelopment area.

The Conference helped establish a new city-county authority to sponsor what was to be a $20,000,000, 14,000-capacity auditorium. It also proposed an adjoining cultural complex on the Lower Hill which would include a symphony hall, an art museum and a legitimate theater. The Economy League studied the fiscal implications of the redevelopment and found that a 900-unit luxury-type housing development, which was planned for ten acres of the Lower Hill project area, would more than offset the loss in taxable values of present revenues from the fifty-five slum acres which would be removed from the rolls for the tax-free civic complex.

Everything seemed to be moving ahead in Pittsburgh's usual Renaissance style. But even as the solution to the Lower Hill's re-use was put into motion, the coalition encountered a new, more complex, and more serious matter.

The Lower Hill was the first Renaissance project to entail mass displacement of families. About 8,000 of the city's poorest and most disadvantaged citizens had lived there. One price of the long delay between the slum's designation for redevelopment and its clearance was that many of these families had left the area on their own in search of other housing, and had crowded into the middle and Upper Hill or the few other neighborhoods which accepted Negroes and offered low rentals. But even after relocation became a legal public responsibility with the start of property acquisition by the Redevelopment Authority, rehousing was still a multiple problem. Probably most serious was the fact that of the majority of relocatees, half were so poor that they were eligible on the basis of income for public housing; yet less than half wanted to move into the city's low-rent projects. In fact, however, there were too few of these units to accommodate all those who qualified. Like other cities, Pittsburgh had not reckoned with the challenges of family relocation.

And, as in other cities, many of the Title I area's former residents overflowed into other parts of the city at the same time that migration from the South was swelling the local Negro population. Most people in Pittsburgh were not aware of the size of the new inmigration to their city and wrongly assumed that all the changes were caused by redevelopment. Slum clearance began to be known as "slum moving." Pressures started to mount within the City Council against the program.

But the Lower Hill was only the first of the city's residential slums that were earmarked for clearance and redevelopment. Pittsburgh desperately needed to allow its old industrial plants to expand their production facilities. It also had to attract new industries in order to diversify its steel-heavy economic base, which was so sensitive to recessions in the national economy. Industrial redevelopment—making more land available for plants, as had been done for Jones and Laughlin—seemed to be a key to industrial growth and the salvation of the area's economy. Indeed, in such a built-up, hemmed-in city as Pittsburgh—and in Allegheny County, too—virtually the only way to get reasonably priced new land was to redevelop blighted sites.

In 1955, a new agency, the Regional Industrial Development Corporation, was established to promote these economic goals, and the RIDC asked the Planning Commission to report to it on potential industrial sites in 1956. Many of the areas it pinpointed were the narrow strips of old mill-side homes built when workers had had to live close to factories, for lack of transportation and money. Although these residences were now fifty to a hundred years old and in disrepair, they were, as at the J. and L. Southside site, still inhabited. In fact, the situation prevailed throughout Allegheny County's mill towns where redevelopment for industry had taken place. Dislocation from them had only exacerbated the Pittsburgh housing situation, as dislocatees had had to move into the city proper to find homes because the middle- and upper-income suburbs were so exclusive.

The implications of the industrial sites report for housing and relocation disturbed civic lawyer Theodore Hazlett, Jr. As full-time legal counsel to the Redevelopment Authority, the Allegheny Conference and several other of the key community improvement agencies, Hazlett had an exceptional overview of the various Renaissance programs as well as access to the top policy-makers and Pittsburgh movers. He asked the Planning Commission to calculate the number and incomes of families who might be displaced were the full industrial redevelopment program outlined in the report carried out.

THE HOUSING BOTTLENECK

Hazlett brought the Commission's data to a small private luncheon given by Richard Mellon soon thereafter for the executive vice-president of ACTION, Inc.*—a national private council for better cities on whose board Mellon served. The ACTION official was in Pittsburgh from New York to address the annual meeting of the Pittsburgh Housing Association. It was almost as a courtesy that the Mellon lieutenant who arranged the luncheon also invited the top officers of the small housing organization.

But this impromptu gathering was significant. As an official of the Housing Association said later, it was "the first time in the

* Now merged into Urban America, Inc.

history of Pittsburgh that housing and power were together." At this luncheon, too, Richard Mellon, a Ligonier resident and commuter, was confronted for the first time with the unpleasant truth about the housing situation in the city where the Mellons made their money.

Housing improvement had been an item on Allegheny Conference agendas since the early days of the eleven committees, but in the subsequent years it had always been postponed or shelved. It was not a matter that was susceptible to ready solutions by using the new Pittsburgh action formula, and the Conference, as one of its board members stated privately, "didn't go into areas where it couldn't succeed."

The city of Pittsburgh believed it was doing its part through publicly assisted low-rent public housing. Although the local Authority's program was one of the best in the country (it had built on difficult hillside sites that private entrepreneurs did not consider economically feasible), its 7,000 units were obviously a token. During the 1930's, government surveys had found that one quarter of the city's dwelling units were substandard and required clearance; but little had been done about them since.

During the luncheon, Hazlett disclosed the figures he had received from the Planning Commission. These showed that 18,000 families would have to move for industrial redevelopment. Interestingly, only 30 per cent of those in the first two areas had incomes low enough to qualify for public housing. But, as some of Mellon's other luncheon guests pointed out, these dislocatees as well as the rest, who were in the lower-middle-income range, would have to move into slums or probably would create new slums by overcrowding, unless the supply of decent, moderate-priced housing were increased.

Mellon was shocked. He recognized that these facts would scare off the companies he and others were endeavoring to attract to the Pittsburgh area. The coalition's favorite new program was clashing with the other major unsolved community headache—housing—and unless they were tackled together, the Renaissance might grind to a halt.

The condition of Pittsburgh's housing could no longer be ignored. At Mellon's suggestion, the Conference asked the Economy League to carry out a study of the city's housing problem—

"to tell them," a Housing Association officer subsequently remarked with irony, "what we knew all along."

But the Economy League did not cushion the harsh realities in its report to the Conference in 1957. "Present renewal activities are not keeping pace with the rate of the deterioration," the report began, "and indications are that a serious shortage of housing exists for minority, aged and lower-middle income groups." One quarter of the city's and county's entire housing supply—150,000 units—were substandard, it continued, and slums were spreading ten times as quickly as blighted housing was being demolished. If this trend continued, it warned, the economic effects would be severe, and "the task of attracting critically needed industry will become more difficult if the spread of blight is not reversed."

The Economy League recommended that Pittsburgh undertake a much larger, coordinated and comprehensive housing program—one that would conserve and rehabilitate homes, or clear areas and help rebuild as necessary, and also assist in overcoming the obstacles to what it called "normal" private and community efforts for housing improvement. For such an enlarged effort, the housing industry, government agencies and top civic leadership must join together, the report stated. It added, however, that this was not likely to take place except under "the accepted and respected community leadership" of the Conference. This was a euphemism for Mellon.

Mellon, however, did not favor having the Conference take on this proposed housing program. He preferred to add business leadership to the Housing Association board, or to form a separate organization with it. The officers of the small, liberal citizen organization feared, as one put it, that this suggested merging of "the power" with their group might lose sight of "the people." But, they reasoned, perhaps under the Mellon-Conference aegis, housing improvement in Pittsburgh could command the money and influence it had always lacked.

What evolved was a new civic organization—ACTION-Housing, Inc. (The Allegheny Council to Improve Our Neighborhoods) into which the Housing Association was merged. Both camps were represented on the new agency's board. Mellon's assistant was named chairman; its vice-chairman was an executive of the Steelworkers union who had been a president of the Housing Association; and the top executive of a local foundation which had, years before, sponsored some well-designed moderate-cost housing was made president.

One of ACTION-Housing's first objectives was to increase the almost nonexistent supply of new homes for what it called "the forgotten third"—families with incomes from $4000 to $7000 who were just above public housing income limits. This group appeared to create the chief relocation problem. To start cracking this bottleneck, the new agency planned to set up a $2,000,000 revolving fund, raised from private sources, which would, by furnishing low-cost intermediate equity capital to private builders, help reduce the high cost of financing housing construction, and thus housing itself. Initially, this fund would be used to help develop one of the last open sites in Pittsburgh, on one of its hilly terrains, East Hills. There ACTION-Housing hoped to demonstrate that with good planning and production innovations as well as building trades unions' cooperation, housing (the industry which economists say the industrial revolution forgot) could be produced at significantly lower cost to the consumer, without a sacrifice in livability.

Another major job was to provide staff and technical assistance to citizen groups and institutions in various run-down areas which were starting to ask for neighborhood renewal and which needed help to organize and make plans.

That the downtown business power was starting to turn its resources to housing and neighborhood improvement seemed the most hopeful aspect of the Renaissance at the beginning of the 1960's. But even as this occurred, their latest civic agency encountered some tough social issues—among them housing integration, changing neighborhoods and the city's growing number of low-income, unskilled and unemployable Negroes—that could not be resolved or treated as rapidly as putting up some new buildings downtown.

These new problems revealed not only a certain myopia on the part of the private leaders in their approach to such matters; industry did not prove eager to innovate in order to reduce the cost of housing. The problems indicated the need for city government to shed its technical mediocrity (most of the Renaissance was carried out through authorities or private agencies) if Pittsburgh was to renew its residential neighborhoods and become more livable.

But these emerging human issues were among the omnipresent growing urban problems that hardly a city had yet attacked, certainly not with programs commensurate to the task.

THE CONTRIBUTIONS AND LIMITATIONS OF THE COALITION

Each city has its own ingrained style and traditions, its special strengths and weaknesses. When it responds to the challenges of urban decay and regeneration, it does so in its own way. Some regard Pittsburgh's approach as undemocratic, too tightly controlled, and too little concerned with the average citizen and his living conditions. But, with their Mayor as the leading coparticipant in the coalition, the public could always resort to the polls in order to express its dissatisfaction.

In a larger sense, however, the major elements in the original Renaissance suggest how other communities may use their potential to deal with certain of their vital problems. Pittsburgh demonstrates both the need for, and the limitations of, the coalition approach.

Some corporate executives in Pittsburgh (granted they were preponderantly Mellon men) gave as much time to civic development affairs as to their company duties, providing talents and powers no city or even a well-funded nonprofit agency could hire. But it was *men*, not formal organizations, and mostly two men and the power they wielded, delegated or allowed to be directed that got things done. And the open cooperation of Mellon-Lawrence did much to make it respectable for business and government leaders of opposing parties in other cities to act openly and in concert for city rebuilding.

Behind the leaders were the key staff men, including, originally, planner Richards, the politically astute Conference director Park Martin, and Van Buskirk. The directors of this and other Renaissance agencies were paid salaries much larger than City Councils usually vote, but which must be paid to make local public service competitive and sufficiently attractive to high-caliber public servants. They moved with a flexibility uncharacteristic of government, and developed, forwarded and coordinated the new programs; these were the men who, as former Conference director Martin put it, "move the kings and queens around."

Time and again the usefulness of this coordinated, well-staffed partnership between top public and private power was demonstrated in advancing the cause of the city against the pressures of organized special interests and selfish business concerns and in moving the state government to grant new local powers and funds. Each recognized the other's importance. Democrat Lawrence knew that he needed not only the consensus and backing of top Republican business locally, but also its outside connections, in order to redevelop the city's misused land, to shore up its fading economy (and revenues) and to eliminate crippling smog. The business leaders were well aware they needed Lawrence because of the public powers and funds he controlled as Mayor and Redevelopment Agency Chairman; they needed his backing as the elected local leader who was ultimately responsible to the people.

Essentially, the two groups joined in response to a crisis: The city which had given them their separate powers was seriously threatened by shifts in the national economy and changes in technology, threats which were compounded by the accumulation of urban industrial blight.

But as the city moved on into a new stage, the Pittsburgh coalition began to show severe limitations, even in the economic area which had seemed to be its great strength. Its inability to cope effectively with the basic economic disorders of the region as well as the omnipresent challenges of social change became increasingly evident.

Pittsburgh's big, early successes in urban revitalization were achieved in good part by taking the cream off the top of commercial-industrial revitalization and effecting the dramatic reform of smog abatement. Moreover, the Renaissance occurred at a singular moment of converging forces in the city's history, as had its earlier swift industrial rise. In the mid-1940's the business generation was new and political control split, but nonetheless the power, both public and private, was tightly and personally held, as it had been at the start of the century. Although the coalition that formed in the postwar years was willing to pioneer in the use of new powers, the basis for change was rooted in the city's old mold.

The spectacular downtown building boom capitalized on the latent needs of the long-established Pittsburgh-headquartered (and mostly Mellon-controlled) giant firms for larger and better office space—which was part of a national corporate trend in this period. To have expanded so was no mean achievement. Subsequently, the city was able to attract other regional offices that would no doubt have bypassed the former "Smoky City" if the local leaders and corporations had not taken the initiative. By the late 1950's, Pittsburgh was surpassed only by New York and Chicago as a headquarters center, and this might not have happened without the airport, highways and parking facilities, as well. Still, the rate of central-city office employment had leveled off then, as did the flurry of research and development expansion. But the mid-1960's saw a great new spurt. The Pennsylvania Railroad announced plans for a 148-acre office-park redevelopment between the Golden Triangle and the Allegheny River, with the backing of Richard Mellon, a member of its board. U.S. Steel was shifting headquarters of its divisions in other cities to Pittsburgh, which was to be increasingly its decision-making center.

With the center-city office boom, however, auto congestion increased downtown, and in rush periods it took half an hour to drive eight miles from the suburbs. The arterial highways and the big, once-radical public garage program were palliatives of limited value. The costly twenty-mile Penn-Lincoln Expressway was a mere scratch in an enormous regional transportation problem.* New answers were needed.

As the national recession of 1959–60 shook the steel industry, the region of the "Comeback City," with 9 per cent of its working population unemployed, was officially declared a depressed area by the federal government. It was once again evident that Pittsburgh was basically the steel capital, and that the overly-

* The Keystone Shortway, built as part of the federally assisted interstate highway system, would bypass Pittsburgh by seventy-seven miles, leaving it "off the highway" until a connecting link was built in 1986.

specialized, nineteenth-century industrial bulwark was too heavily dependent on cyclical trends in the national economy.

In a new phase of deeper critical self-examination, Pittsburgh undertook major studies of its economic base, mass transportation and the impact of urban renewal to get the facts about what was wrong, and what should be done.

THE MORE IT CHANGES

The reports from the various studies challenged the community to a new set of long-term efforts and presented the prospect of huge, probably permanent, subsidies with the immediate returns less promising than from commercial-industrial redevelopment.

"In terms of its economic base, the area is little better off than it was twenty years ago," according to the policy statement of the economic study (issued in January, 1964), "when, at the end of World War II, the outlook for Pittsburgh was at best uncertain."

The Renaissance had made Pittsburgh a "better, cleaner and more productive city. [But] the region continues to suffer from chronic unemployment; the population reflects sizable outmigration in the 20 to 29 age group; and the prospects of new growth are uncertain."

While steel had spent close to a billion dollars to modernize existing plants and increase productivity, its manpower needs were progressively reduced. Between 1947 and 1960, the economic study reported, there was a 26.7 per cent drop in workers required per unit of output. During that same period, the aggregate employment in twelve out of sixteen of the basic local industries—mainly metals and glass—suffered a net decline of 76,617 jobs. Further, Pittsburgh had missed opportunities in some of the newer growth industries, such as electronics and aerospace. "Unless it organizes to reverse this trend, [the area] faces the prospect of relative, if not absolute, decline."

The small group of top men who had dragged Pittsburgh out of the murk of smog and central-city decay were now twenty years older; many of them, like Van Buskirk and Park Martin, retired; others, like Richards, were dead. Of course new, talented Renaissance agency directors had come in, but Richard King Mellon was fast approaching the 65-year retirement age that he set for his companies' executives, and he had no successors with the same emotional commitment to the city, and the power to improve it. A big question is: how much longer will the momentum continue? The Allegheny Conference had become a promotional agency, with membership a status symbol, and some observers worry that the new generation of top management is far more interested in corporate profits and dividends than in the Pittsburgh region. The early action formula threatened to get rusty.

Some economists believed part of the problem of diversifying industry was the lack in Pittsburgh of private venture capital and local encouragement of young new industry. Accumulated wealth tends to become conservative and fiduciary; and small Pittsburgh businessmen have an inferiority complex when it comes to the top private power. The service industries, booming everywhere, are too small a part of the local base in Pittsburgh—again due to the predominance of big industry. The nonprofit, Pittsburgh-centered Regional Industrial Development Corporation of Southwestern Pennsylvania has had to seek out and finance promising new industry. The research and development companies are too closely tied to the ferrous field.

The findings of the Urban Renewal Impact Study, issued by ACTION-Housing, were grim. "Despite all that has been achieved in so short a time, Allegheny County faces, in 1963, a deepening crisis"; the study called for new and far broader efforts.

Significantly, this report exposed the extent of the community's social problems and called for a far greater investment—this time in people—to keep Pittsburgh modern and economically healthy, as well as to compensate for past neglect of local human resources and housing. Some 40,000 new jobs would have to be found annually to keep people from leaving and the economy from stagnating, it stated. To attain these new jobs by attracting new growth industries, Pittsburgh required a vastly improved educational system and retraining programs to upgrade labor. Unless the legislature removed present restrictions on school district taxing, or loosened its own purse strings, the fiscally squeezed city's old school system would soon find itself in crisis.

In the public transportation field, the Pittsburgh power groups were extremely slow to accept the facts about the chaotic assortment of some thirty-three privately owned bus and trolley lines that "served" the city. A 1959 study of the situation advised that the lines be coordinated and improved through public acquisition and a substantial investment in new equipment, plus an annual subsidy to run the merged system. Not until 1964 did the Port Authority exercise its five-year-old powers to acquire the first of the private lines. According to knowledgeable people, acquisition of private lines and permanent local subsidy of transit went against the top power's grain (it would be the first Renaissance project to do so), and they did not grasp the relation of a sound metropolitan circulatory system to the region's well-being.

But the need to serve the "new Pittsburgh" better—to transport office workers in the business district efficiently—began to outweigh objections. The Port Authority ordered a feasibility study of a new, rapid transit system which might start operation in 1973. Anticipating a new, multibillion-dollar market nationally in urban mass transportation, several Pittsburgh companies began preparing for it. Richard Mellon announced in 1966 a $300,000 gift to establish a Transportation Research Institute at Carnegie Tech. (The institute expected to have an annual budget of $1,000,000 from federal, state and private grants.) Westinghouse actively promoted the computer-controlled aluminum "Skybus" it had developed with federal grants and was demonstrating on a two-mile elevated test track. U.S. Steel and Alcoa were also developing equipment for what might become a major local growth industry in the 1970's.

In the shelter field, however, the Pittsburghers were not yet willing to consider public means for reducing shelter costs for the "forgotten third." New York, with its municipal tax abatement and low-interest government loans, was able to do much more, proportionately, than did ACTION-Housing. The necessary enabling legislation was said to be politically impossible.

The leaders also did not use their vast wealth to further the city's civilizing role. "Florence without Lorenzo," one outspoken advocate of a local cultural renaissance characterized Pittsburgh.

True, the city government did establish the first municipal educational television station in the country; the Pittsburgh Playhouse initiated a repertory company; and the Mellon foundations were starting to give to the city—with many millions for the arts, schools, ACTION-Housing and scientific research at the universities. But few other sources of wealth joined. Raising money for the arts and music was an uphill struggle.

Schools, so long ignored by the Renaissance, began to respond at the end of the 1950's. A Citizens' Committee on Schools formed in 1963, and in 1965, citizens and some power joined in pushing the state legislature to give more assistance to urban areas.

During the early 1960's, the area saw a continued outmigration in its prime-age labor force. (A special census in 1965 found that the metropolitan area had experienced an absolute decline in population in the past five years—the first time this has happened in the country's history.) Then in the mid-1960's, a national boom in "hard goods"—automobiles, business machinery, construction, highways, and military equipment—demanded steel and other metals. Plants were running at 90 per cent of capacity, and the Pittsburgh region, with half its jobs in steel and an unemployment rate below the national low average in 1966, needed skilled workers. For the moment, the region was riding high.

Can the downtown Renaissance be called a success in terms of people? Certainly working downtown is much pleasanter, as is visiting and shopping—if the customers come. But Pittsburgh residents do not dawdle downtown, or come back down there after work and on weekends. Despite the golden Hilton Hotel at Gateway Center and the civic arena's telescoping roof, there is little to attract or hold people there. (There is still not a decent night-club in town.) Having so long lacked a middle-class market for good restaurants, book stores, retail and other specialty shops and services, downtown has not developed these attractions. The center of the city, although cleared of nineteenth-century blight and sprouting twentieth-century high-rise offices, is still deeply set in the old pattern and class split.

As one of the key staff men of the Renaissance expressed it, "You can build a whole new city with bricks and mortar, but you can't change people much. The people here don't know how to relax and play. They just know how to produce."

There are, however, some signs of promising change. (Not the least of these are the downtown sitting places—at Mellon Square and Gateway Center, where there is even an outdoor cafe.) The downtown office boom, the new industrial research laboratories and the expansion of the universities have begun to create a new professional-technical group and an enlarged intellectual community. This may result in a more active middle-class polity and consumer public than big basic industry has created. There has been talk at the universities, where there are new centers for urban studies, about forming a citizens' housing and planning council that is not under the Mellons.

These forces will have to work hard to change the city's image. "The world's biggest company town" is how the wife of one U.S. Steel executive from New York described Pittsburgh. He, like many management people, refused to go to Pittsburgh, though he had to forfeit substantial company benefits. "Ethnic and religious labels are on everything. When you come to look for a house, you are told what suburb you should live in, what clubs to belong to, what families your children shouldn't play with. You can't lose yourself in the community as you can in New York." Another perceptive resident who works with the steel companies observes, "The working people have no sense of progress. Perhaps they have just accepted the idea that they won't get ahead."

Pittsburgh is still a town of a few big movers and the mass of little people who are used to having things done for them. Yet the Renaissance—although it was basically the old-style coalition at work—wielded its joint powers for nobler ends than in the past, and furnished other, less rigidly structured cities with a pattern of action on which to start building a new civic tradition.

4

THE FRUSTRATING BUSINESS OF REBUILDING

■ Redevelopment of Southwest Washington

To the layman, residential redevelopment is mysterious and heavy with suspicions of big-deal operators making a killing at the expense of taxpayers and dislocated slum dwellers. When he sees rising over slum sites apartment houses with rentals priced far beyond the pocketbook of not only the former residents but even the average city dweller, he assumes that the sponsors are making exorbitant and illegal profits, especially because he knows the land cost has been reduced.

The purpose of the government "write-down" on slum land is probably the best-kept open secret in the country. Almost everyone believes, incorrectly, that the reduced resale price is a subsidy to the private entrepreneur and his "luxury" developments; the more suspicious are sure it is a give-away. Few seem to be aware that the public subsidy is to the community, to pay for eliminating slum structures and to deflate land costs to fair market values so that former slum sites may be put back into use at good development standards, and necessary new service facilities be built. Nor does the public generally realize the extensive controls exerted by local and federal government agencies over the sponsor.

If at first redevelopment seems a jackpot, the market place negates this supposition. The comparatively small number of redevelopers have yet to buy yachts. In fact, those who have been making profits even comparable to low-yield "safe" investments can be counted on the fingers of one hand. Some have given up their unprofitable projects by either defaulting or selling out to an investor who needs a tax loss. And most builders, realtors and investors have avoided this venture.

Yet some unusual investors do continue to bid for and sponsor Title I projects. The experience of the initial developer in what is today the outstanding showcase for residential redevelopment in the country, Southwest Washington, will be related here. His story illuminates the unique role of the private sponsor, and the misunderstood matter of building privately financed housing on government-cleared slum sites.

The redevelopment formula is based on the not uncommon American practice of using government power and resources to encourage private participation in an activity where immediate profits are not apparent, but where a public need must be met. Indeed, if fallow slum and blighted areas of central cities had been sufficiently attractive to private investors alone, government intervention to encourage rebuilding would not have been necessary. The alternative—complete government financing and building—neither sits well with the American public, nor appears feasible from the viewpoint of the national or local economy.

Economists have generally agreed that to revitalize central cities and finance their renewal, private investment on a much larger scale than the public share is essential. This was part of the concept written into the Housing Act of 1949, which introduced

Title I redevelopment. Its preamble specified that ". . . (1) private enterprise shall be encouraged to serve as large a part of the total needs as it can; (2) governmental assistance shall be utilized where feasible to enable private enterprise to serve as large a part of the total need as it can . . ."

What has remained subjective and fraught with conflicting views is the question of how much government assistance or incentive is necessary to attract private investors to redevelopment areas, how much regulation is required to protect the public interest, and to what use should their land be put. These questions are particularly susceptible to public scrutiny when they involve a social commodity like housing.

When urban redevelopment became a federal aid program in 1949, it was assumed that the government deflation in land cost, plus its use of eminent domain, would be sufficient to attract private investors to Title I rebuilding. But it soon became clear that to change the character of a blighted neighborhood and permanently eliminate the slum, a project that would encompass an extensive area was necessary—and such an undertaking demanded a great deal of cash on the part of the sponsor-builder. As it turned out, the insurance companies were virtually the only investors with sufficient money ready and available for a relatively low return.

Several of them had undertaken mammoth residential redevelopments with rents aimed at the middle-income market; most notable of these were Metropolitan Life's Stuyvesant Town in Manhattan, and New York Life's Lake Meadows project in Chicago, both initiated under earlier state laws.

But just as cities generally were being stimulated by the new federal loans and grants under Title I, the life insurance companies began to withdraw from direct sponsorship. In fact, several sold their developments, and none have entered as direct investors since 1952.

The disquieting lack of interest was partly caused by the battle for investment capital, a factor Congress had not considered. At the end of World War II, interest rates were at a record low, and earnings from apartment projects were satisfactory to the insurance companies compared with alternative investment possibilities. But as money conditions changed, the net yield on such housing developments fell below even that of government bonds. Yields were lowest of all on projects like Stuyvesant Town, where the rents were set by local government, and the sponsor's return was limited in exchange for municipal tax abatement, as provided under New York State's redevelopment law.

But life insurance companies have obligations to millions of policy holders and must be assured a safe return on their investment. Further, their company images are important, and they are reluctant to become engaged in any kind of public controversy. It had appeared during the 1940's that by building housing, insurance companies would meet a widespread social need and create a safe investment, as well as a desirable public image.

However, the role of landlord in a redevelopment project plunged insurance companies into front-page disputes and the touchy issue of housing integration while failing to assure them their expected annual return. Further, they found themselves frozen into positions from which they could not easily pull out. The deathblow to direct investment by Metropolitan Life, the giant in the housing field, came in 1952 when New York's Board of Estimate, submitting to pressures from Stuyvesant Town's tenants, broke its contractual agreement with the company by rejecting its application for legitimate increases in rents to cover rising operating costs.

Thereafter, it proved more remunerative, and far less troublesome, for insurance companies to take a mortgage position instead of investing directly.

THE ROLE OF THE FHA

With the withdrawal of institutional investors, the obvious question was: How could the non-institutional investor be encouraged to sponsor residential redevelopment? His attitude toward urban real estate—rental housing, in particular—had been negative since the precipitous collapse of the inflated real estate market of the 1920's. Instead of regarding city real estate in the traditional American manner, as a safe long-term investment providing a reliable annual income, investors had come to look for a very rapid return of cash put into this highly illiquid and risky form of property.

In his nationwide study of *Rental Housing* in 1958, economist Louis Winnick found that unless a non-institutional investor could foresee an annual return of 15 to 20 per cent, compared to the insurance companies' 6 per cent, he would not be attracted to rental housing. Because the opportunities for such a high return from new rental projects were limited, Winnick wrote, the amount produced had been cut sharply. The exceptions were where very high debt financing could be obtained, or where the risk was shifted to government's shoulders.

This situation pointed to a much larger role for the Federal Housing Administration in cities. The history and character of the FHA, the most powerful and ambiguous of the depression-born government housing agencies, has been an integral part of the redevelopment investment problem.

When the FHA was created in 1934, its main function was to administer a new invention—government mortgage insurance. This device was conceived as a means of stimulating the production of housing, both single-family units and multiple units. FHA did not lend or give money; it underwrote the traditional risk of the suddenly reluctant private lending institutions by pledging the unlimited credit of the federal government to back up their mortgages and thus insure their loans. Should a mortgagee default on an FHA-insured loan, the federal agency would compensate the insured bank.

FHA also tried to reduce the cost of housing for consumers and thus stimulate demand by requiring that the loans it insured offer much more liberal credit terms than those on a conventional mortgage. Then the home purchaser or equity investor would have to put up less cash initially and would have a substantially longer repayment period.

This premise proved to be remarkably effective. By the 1940's, a considerable segment of the revived housing industry had become dependent on government insurance. But the stimulus of federal credit was restricted largely to suburban single-family home developments. In fact, FHA's liberal home purchase terms accelerated all the other factors working in favor of the suburbs:

low-cost accessible land, growing families' apparent preference for this style of living, and the many tax advantages of homeowning.

With the end of World War II, there came still more generous governmental boosts to the home purchaser—the Veterans Administration's no-equity insurance and direct loan programs for returning G.I.'s. These federal aids, coupled with wartime savings and stimulated by the baby boom that started in the late 1940's, resulted by 1956, in 30,000,000 Americans—or 56 per cent of the country—owning homes, compared to 16,000,000 in 1945.

Thus the builder or investor was able to operate with ease and assurance in the country or the suburbs. But when he turned to the central city, he found land costs relatively high and often inflated, if sites were available at all. The city environment was drab and cramped. Public facilities had deteriorated as a result of the depression years and wartime neglect. Schools were old. There were inadequate playgrounds for the mushroom crop of youngsters, and growing traffic made residential side streets dangerous and noisy. Nor was there much profitable consumer demand in cities. Furthermore, there was little financial incentive—in fact there was major risk—in putting up investment housing in the midst of such spreading deterioration.

The FHA did not, with one notable exception, particularly encourage central-city building. Its less generous rental housing terms displayed a mistrust of building investors born of the unhappy 1920's. And its attitude toward blighted city areas was just like that of a mortgage banker; these were not economically sound areas for housing investment. Builders could not get FHA loans in many parts of the inner city.

The Title I legislation of 1949 aimed at overcoming many of these negative factors. By helping to clear large enough areas, absorbing clearance costs and deflating the land price to fair market value, it hoped to make rebuilding attractive and economically sound. But, as the first few years of the new program showed, the legislative assumption that former slum land, when cleared and offered for sale at fair market value, would be as marketable as other types of land was wrong. The banks still would not issue mortgages in former slum areas, and the FHA, as conservative as the private banker, still maintained its *cordon sanitaire,* apparently unconvinced that redevelopment could change the character of an area sufficiently to make a long-term loan economically sound.

This financing impasse was largely responsible for the lack of rebuilding under Title I during the program's early years. Recognizing this, Congress in 1954 legislated a special assistance program for FHA, one to insure housing in urban renewal areas, known as Section 220. The most significant difference between "220" and other programs was that Congress directed FHA to drop its "economic soundness" requirements for urban renewal areas. It was directed to consider what such an area would be like after it was rebuilt according to official city plans, and to underwrite the private risks of redevelopment. It also called for loans on 90 per cent of value, terms much more generous than the two-thirds or three-quarters loans generally available from banks.

When these provisions still did not sufficiently attract investors, Congress further liberalized FHA's urban renewal terms. It called for loans on 90 per cent of replacement cost, instead of value, and reduced the sponsor's cash requirements still more. Now the sponsor could include as part of his 10 per cent equity the FHA allowance for builder's profit and risk, thus making it possible, on the books, for him to go in with about 3 per cent cash equity, including the 2 per cent working capital required by FHA on its estimate of total project cost. Thus, he could sponsor for as little as one per cent in cash.

This gave the sponsor what is known as "maximum leverage" on his cash outlay, and offered just about the most attractive housing investment terms available anywhere.

Still there was no rush to redevelopment. For one thing, few builders were long-term investors and, in spite of the relatively small cash requirements in the revised Section 220 program, most Title I projects by their very size and nature still necessitated immobilizing a substantial amount of money for a long period. Builders were also put off by other factors: the long and uncertain incubation period; the many layers of government they had to deal with; the intricate, voluminous and ever-changing rules of the game, as written by the various agencies that are joint participants (though not necessarily enthusiastic partners) in city rebuilding.

Finally, the FHA, which should have been the big risk-taker, turned out to be an extremely conservative agency. It had just been through a grueling Congressional investigation centering on its Section 608, a rental housing program mandated by Congress in 1947 to overcome the city housing shortage. Under "608" no cash investment was required of a builder, and FHA had promoted the program to builders as virtually guaranteed to return more than the cost of the mortgage. It had been remarkably successful in terms of housing volume—470,000 dwelling units were built or scheduled by the time the program ended in 1951.

But the first time FHA pushed rental housing with "608," it got burned. In 1954, when Congress learned of the windfall profits made by many "608" builders, Senator Homer Capehart launched his headline-making probe, bringing many builders and FHA insuring officers into an uncomfortable national spotlight. FHA suddenly put cash requirements on past projects, gray-listed nonconforming builders, and purged itself of many local insuring officers who had been following its administrative orders. It also required cost certification on future projects.

The Capehart investigation literally paralyzed the industry as well as FHA, leaving the agency loath to take any kind of chances, and making most builders unable or reluctant to participate in future government rental housing programs. This was the unpromising climate that faced the new Section 220 mortgage insurance program.

Even without this unexpected complication, redevelopment does not lend itself to the conventional wisdom of real estate investment, which holds that the way to make money is see someone else make a profit and imitate him. In fact, redevelopment contradicts this canon. Nor does the program have its own firm set of rules, even after a decade and a half of experience. The redeveloper must be an innovator. Each project appears to have its own eccentricities and, in spite of the attraction of FHA insurance, the initial cash risk in project sponsorship must still be made by the private builder or investor.

The program was summarized by one of the country's most

knowledgeable mortgage bankers back in 1958: "Redevelopment is a fine opportunity for profits served on a silver platter. [But] the platter has a tight lid and is surrounded by mousetraps."

Comparatively few entrepreneurs were willing to brave the mousetraps for the potentially large but still uncertain future profits. Redevelopment had to rely largely on a handful of off-beat, long-term promoters who were motivated by more than just profits to front-run the course. Several of them have been responsible for the new residential community rising in the Southwest Washington, the first area in the District of Columbia designated for Title I of the Housing Act of 1949.

REHOUSING VERSUS REDEVELOPMENT

Southwest Washington, a 550-acre triangle of land whose apex is the Capitol itself and whose base is the Potomac River, was one of the country's worst slum areas in 1953. By the end of 1965, the redeveloped site was emerging as an attractive, racially integrated community of 5,700 residents, among them Congressmen and Senators, living in new private high-rise apartments and townhouses, with new shops, five new churches, a legitimate theater, new school and motor hotel. When complete, the new Southwest will have 18,000 residents (5,000 of them already in public housing), and over 20,000 office workers just in new government and private buildings. Southwest is a product of mixed capitalism and the most complicated federal grant-in-aid program in the country.

This history sheds much light on the profit-consuming gap that exists between legislative theory and the actual practice of redevelopment, and on the risk-taking role of the private investor-developer. The experiences of James H. Scheuer as sponsor of seventy-six-acre Area B, first redevelopment tract in the new Southwest, illustrate the problems and processes involved and are no doubt related to the high price of pioneering. But what he experienced and what he produced raise the question: Can you realize social objectives along with a profitable real estate development?

Plans for rebuilding Southwest had been the subject of widespread local debate in the early 1950's. Should the area be rebuilt to house its present residents, or higher-income groups who would bring a greater tax return to the District? John Nolen, then director of the National Capital Planning Commission, argued that Southwest was "ideal for low-income families working in the terminal, the railroads, the markets. These people must live somewhere." The commission drew up plans late in 1951 which preserved the basic character of the area.

Then in 1952 the Redevelopment Land Agency of the District, the official local body in charge of the new program, retained two of the capital's outstanding architects, Mrs. Chloethiel Woodard Smith, a progressive and creative young woman, and Louis Justement, one of the city's better known practitioners, to make a comprehensive plan for Southwest. Their proposal called for dramatically changing and upgrading the superbly located area for its highest possible use.

Southwest was one of the oldest and most central parts of the federal city planned by L'Enfant. General Washington had urged his friends to buy homes there, and it became the residential locale for some of the city's most prominent leaders. But the unsanitary James Creek, which became virtually an open sewer, the nearby malarial marshes and the tracks of the Pennsylvania Railroad discouraged proper development and isolated the area from the rest of the city. By 1860, Southwest was known as "the Island."

But Mrs. Smith and Justement pointed out in their 1953 plan that these basic undesirable features, particularly the character of the swamps and drainage canal, no longer existed. In rebuilding, the train tracks that cut off Southwest from the rest of the city could be crossed by overpasses. The food and fish markets could be removed from the decaying waterfront, and the Potomac's shore redeveloped as another attraction of the area.

When the detailed Smith-Justement plan was published it was pilloried by many leading voices in the capital as too extravagant. District bankers said "no one" would live in Southwest. Local builders saw the area as suitable only for cheap walk-ups for Negroes. An unspoken, though well-recognized, cause for opposition on the part of several important business organizations was their desire to contain Negroes, who formed the majority of Southwest's residents, within the area instead of spreading them to other parts of the city.

Then in February 1954, William Zeckendorf, the well-known investor-developer and center-city enthusiast, came to Washington with illustrated brochures, press releases and sketches. His scale model (unveiled before Congress, top businessmen and the press) for a master redevelopment of the whole area would, he stated, give the city "the cosmopolitan atmosphere of a great world capital" that it now lacked.

One aim of the Zeckendorf plan was to establish Southwest as one of the most desirable residential areas in the city. He also proposed "L'Enfant Plaza"—a complex of cultural, recreational and commercial facilities as well as government buildings grouped around a traffic-free pedestrian mall. This, he said, would be to Washington "what the Champs Élysées is to Paris or the Piazza San Marco to Venice." He conjured up a setting for sidewalk cafés, fountains, theaters, skating rinks, dining and dancing spots, and a delightful new waterfront.

The plan strongly resembled the Smith-Justement proposal, both in philosophy and in particulars. It even included the important overpass to obliterate the railroad tracks and the Tenth Street Mall, which would provide an imposing gateway and direct connection between the reborn area and the rest of the city. But Zeckendorf had the money—or thought he knew where he could get it—to make the dream come true.*

The Washington *Post*, whose publisher had been responsible for Zeckendorf's firm undertaking the master plan, hailed the proposal as "the most ambitious city rebuilding project ever attempted in America," and one which Zeckendorf "is eager to undertake as a guide to other cities faced with the problem of the flight to the suburbs." Other local groups, which had been pressing for bolder and more imaginative planning than the present compromise between rehousing and upgrading, were enthusiastic.

Within a month, a memorandum of understanding was drawn

* To swing his audacious deals, Zeckendorf would borrow money at extortionate rates ("I'd rather be alive at 18 per cent than dead at the prime rate," he stated), and got into continual financial jams which delayed or complicated many of his projects. These finally put his firm in bankruptcy in 1965.

up between the District Redevelopment Land Agency and Webb and Knapp, signifying the firm's intent to carry out at least 50 per cent of the 440-acre Area C redevelopment if all the problems now standing in the way could be ironed out. Most important was gaining the cooperation and coordination of various government agencies whose buildings would be part of the proposed new complex.

AREA B SPONSORSHIP

Zeckendorf's Washington agreement provided a striking national stimulus to redevelopment. Letters from other cities whose programs were stalled for lack of local builder-investor interest began to pour into his office. He became the prototype of a small but ambitious group of national developers who began to make whirlwind trips across the country, talking up redevelopment from platforms, stirring up local interest and rescuing idle Title I projects.

Among them was James H. Scheuer of New York. Scheuer is the son of a Manhattan real estate investor who made millions by purchasing luxury apartment houses—among them block-large London Terrace—at distress prices during the bottom of the depression, and by building up his equity through good management and improvement of facilities. Before joining the family business in 1952, Scheuer had earned graduate degrees in business administration and law and worked for federal government agencies in Washington. Long active in the New York Citizens Housing and Planning Council, of which he became president in 1958, and a politically ambitious Democrat,* he had studied new housing legislation and developed advanced social and design ideas about residential developments. His successful racial integration of two state-assisted housing developments owned by his family firm had already won him recognition by the National Urban League.

Scheuer first became interested in Washington's renewal program early in 1955 when John R. Searles, Jr., then executive director of the Redevelopment Land Agency, invited him to discuss housing rehabilitation work which the Housing Act of 1954

* Scheuer was elected to Congress from a district in the Bronx in 1964.

encouraged. Scheuer's visit was inconclusive, but had included a tour of Southwest B, which was under contract for redevelopment to a Norfolk, Virginia building firm.

Then Scheuer received an unexpected long-distance call from Searles. The redevelopment director wanted to know whether the New York realtor would be interested in bidding for sponsorship of Area B. The current sponsors, then under investigation by the Capehart Committee for several "608" projects, were withdrawing.

Fearing this might occur, Searles had already sounded out the other original 1953 bidders. None was interested. A new cost certification element in FHA insurance discouraged some. Even Zeckendorf refused. He believed that no investment in Southwest would be sound until renewal of all the vast slum area was assured. The papers announced the sponsors' withdrawal in blazing headlines the evening of Searles' call to New York.

Here was the nightmare situation that haunted redevelopment directors across the country—cleared land and no buyer. In Detroit and Baltimore unsold Title I sites lay vacant, subjecting agency heads to official censure, public jibes and private humiliation. Searles was determined that this should not occur in Washington, where the eyes of Congress and the nation were fixed on the rebuilding of the notorious "slums in the shadow of the nation's Capitol."

Scheuer was interested in sponsorship of Area B for a number of reasons. Through his government work, he was familiar with Washington. The city, with its continual flow of government workers who prefer to rent rather than buy, was "depression-proof" and seemed an excellent market for the 1,020 units of rental housing called for in the redevelopment plan. The location was another major attraction; it was only 500 yards from the Capitol and within walking distance of a large complex of existing and projected government buildings. It seemed obvious that one day it would be a prestige area. He also liked the proposed mixture of different building types and rent levels. There were to be elevator apartments as well as row houses and garden apartments for families, one third of them to rent for a maximum of $17 a room in order to assure a socially desirable mixture of income groups.

The concept of redevelopment intrigued Scheuer. As he saw it, the government was assembling large tracts of centrally located city acreage which he as a private businessman could not possibly acquire unaided, and was cutting the price to a value that made rebuilding the land at highest planning standards economically feasible for him. Further, the city would hold the land he had contracted to rebuild free of interest and real estate taxes until he was ready for construction, and would build and pay for the new streets, sewers and other public facilities that a private development would need.

Webb and Knapp's memorandum of understanding for rebuilding the large tract of adjoining land made investment in Southwest seem reasonably safe and attractive. Not to be overlooked was the glamour—Scheuer preferred to call it the "challenge"—of being a rebuilder of the century-old slum in the Capitol's shadow, with members of Congress observing the results. Southwest also offered Scheuer an opportunity to put into practice on an impressive scale some of his advanced concepts about the design of urban neighborhoods and their racial integration.

The deciding factor was the financial incentive offered by FHA's Section 220. Scheuer recognized that the FHA placed a ceiling on the rentals he could charge as well as the initial returns he could receive,* and supervised operation closely. However, under this special urban renewal program, his cash equity in the initial $5,930,000 apartment house would have to be only $325,000—the maximum leverage under Section 220. With few vacancies it should be possible to get a cash return of close to $90,000 a year—or about 30 per cent—on the first 402-unit apartment house, with his equity back in three or four years. This compared very favorably with the terms most residential real estate investors required then. Once his equity in the project had increased to one third of replacement value, he could pay off the FHA mortgage and refinance it conventionally, thus freeing his development of the agency's rent restrictions and payment of its one half per cent premium charge.

* Section 220 rents were figured to allow the sponsor a 7.25 per cent return at 93 per cent occupancy. Once debt service and the FHA's premium were paid off, he was left with a .5 per cent return at that vacancy rate. Should there be fewer vacancies, his profits could go up substantially, and this was what Scheuer hoped for.

The income tax provisions were also important. Fast depreciation allowances offered on real estate investment under 1954 amendments to the Internal Revenue Code virtually eliminated the need to pay corporate taxes on the project's income during the first five to seven years. These allowances could also be used to offset profits made from other corporations held in common ownership. Furthermore, if he sold the project he need pay a capital gains tax of only 25 per cent on the profits.

This was Scheuer's estimation in 1955. Yet five years after Searles' call, in 1960, Scheuer and his partner had only one building up and renting in Southwest; far from making any profit, they had yet to earn their equity back. They had invested three times the original anticipated sum and were putting in $15,000 a month more just to keep that building going. With a vacancy rate of 25 per cent (they could only start making money when vacancies reached 7 per cent) it would take fifteen years to get their cash back even if the building were soon to reach full occupancy. One could make a similar profit from government bonds. To compound their problems, a Congressional committee had ordered an investigation into the unbelievable slowness of rebuilding Southwest. Theirs was the only new structure in the whole area, and the redevelopment agency had threatened Scheuer and his partner with forfeiture of the rest of their project unless they proceeded with its completion. Looking back on his early optimism, Scheuer observed, "I was naive about the problems." What had gone wrong?

THE GOVERNMENT GAUNTLETS

Scheuer's first problem was the time and expense involved in winning the sponsorship. After Scheuer's interest in Area B leaked out in the newspapers, two local bidders suddenly appeared, and a competition loomed. Unable to associate himself with a local builder or real estate investor (all but his two competitors regarded Southwest as an impractical proposition) Scheuer decided to associate himself with a well-known outside figure. He approached Roger L. Stevens of New York, nationally known realty trader-operator and theatrical producer, who was then chairman of the Democratic Party's Finance Committee.

Stevens became Scheuer's equal partner in the First National Redevelopment Corporation, which retained architect Chloethiel Smith to design their project design bid.

The land price was not to be subject to a competition because, in what was then a somewhat unusual arrangement, the price was to be set by the Federal Housing Administration. All three bidders appeared to have more than sufficient cash reserves, an important qualification. But those of Stevens and Scheuer seemed unlimited, which persuaded some members of the board of the Redevelopment Land Agency in their favor. On the other hand, neither had ever put up a building. Each of the prospective sponsors also had influential outside pressures exerted on their behalf.

The board split its vote. Two were in favor of the New York development team, two for a Washington builder. The fifth, undecided member, was a Negro. There was no clause in the sponsor's contract for renting the dwellings they were to build on an open-occupancy basis; in fact, since Washington was basically a Southern city, the issue had not arisen. But Scheuer and Stevens got word to this member that they planned to integrate their project. In October 1955, their firm was announced as the new sponsor of Washington's first redevelopment project.

Between this designation and the eventual signing of the contract, however, they had to run an initial delaying gauntlet of government agencies. One issue was the leasehold on the $3,000,000 worth of land. Instead of purchasing the land outright, they proposed to rent it, with an option to buy. Although not uncommon in real estate, this was the first such arrangement in urban renewal and it had to satisfy the requirements of three different public agencies—the District redevelopment agency, the federal Urban Renewal Administration and the Federal Housing Administration. But this was only one problem.

Eight months passed. Much of the delay was due to disputes about the land cost between administrations within the Housing and Home Finance Agency. The Federal Housing Administration wanted to lower the price in order to reduce rentals and thus lessen the agency's mortgage insurance risk. The Urban Renewal Administration wanted a higher price so that the federal subsidy on the write-down could be reduced. It still did not approve, but did not stand in the way when, on July 2, 1956, about fifteen months after Searles' call to Scheuer, the sponsors signed the fifty-page official land disposition contract with the redevelopment agency.

Now Mrs. Smith could begin preparing the detailed site plan. She first had to make a major revision to accommodate Webb and Knapp's still embryonic plans for Area C. Originally, Area B was to include a neighborhood grocery and convenience shops, which are not generally money-makers for a developer. Zeckendorf proposed that Stevens and Scheuer drop these facilities and let him consolidate them in a community shopping center to serve all Southwest. This center would be close to Capitol Park Apartments, the name they had given their development; Scheuer and Stevens agreed to the change on the premise, and promise, that Webb and Knapp's town center would be in operation by the time their first dwellings were ready for occupancy. The necessary approval was given by the planning commission and redevelopment agency.

The most crucial pre-construction step for the sponsors was the submission of plans to the Federal Housing Administration for the agency's necessary "test of feasibility" to get a mortgage commitment. Yet even before Mrs. Smith's plans could go to the FHA's local insuring office, they had to be approved by four other government agencies—the District government, the Redevelopment Land Agency, the National Capital Planning Commission and the District's Fine Arts Commission. In addition, her advanced design proposal had to run another, special government gauntlet of six District departments because her plan appeared to conflict with an assortment of local regulations.

Many of the obstacles encountered explain why the sponsors of most public *or* private developments avoid architects who will design anything different, and why we end up with such commonplace repetitious structures in cities. When one tries to do something different and better, one runs into trouble.

The sponsors and Mrs. Smith were determined to produce an outstanding development. Scheuer reasoned it would take something special to attract people back from the suburbs or other parts of town, especially to live in a former slum area. As a long-term real estate investor, not a speculative builder, he also wanted to create a project in advance of the market, so that

Capitol Park would hold tenants over the long pull as newer buildings came up in the District and consumer standards inevitably rose. The Redevelopment Land Agency was also striving for excellence, for a development with unusual distinction, to give flair to the area. In fact, the sponsor's design proposal had helped win the contract for them.

But the challenge was more than architectural. A total new environment had to be created for this new residential community. The first eight-story apartment house was to be on stilts. Its large lobby would be completely glass-enclosed and would give an unobstructed view of a park-like area behind the building. At one end of the lobby there was to be a large metal screen sculpture executed by sculptor Harry Bertoia. At the far end of the lawn and landscaped walks in back of the apartment house, there were to be a large lily pond and a sheltered barbecue pit; tables and chairs under umbrellas were to be near it. Animal statues for the children would be on one lawn, and a large tile mosaic by Leo Leonni would decorate the wall behind the reflecting pool. The entire area would be attractively lit for evening use. Fortunately, the redevelopment agency had preserved the trees of old Southwest when the slum buildings were cleared. The sponsors planned to plant more full-grown trees to create an air of permanence. Eventually, their part of the development would be completed by about eighty townhouses at the far end, and several more apartment buildings close by.

Conflicts between the old and new caused some of the problems in carrying out this design. The District zoning law, for instance, controlled densities on a single-lot, block basis, following the old-fashioned gridiron street arrangement. Architect Smith argued that these limitations had no relevance to the large-scale planning possible under redevelopment, where densities were based on an overall coverage of the project area. Eventually, the District Planning Commission agreed to conform to Mrs. Smith's plan.

Another obstacle was that five different sets of legal specifications for "light and air" had to be considered and reconciled. The Federal Housing Administration had one set under its Minimum Property Requirements; the District redevelopment agency had another, as did several city departments. Another problem was locating underground sewer lines in this pre-Civil War area. No District bureau had the necessary information. Yet until Mrs. Smith knew where sewer connections could be made, she could not start placing buildings. She finally convinced the redevelopment agency to make a survey for her. There was also the urgent matter of a new elevated expressway that would cut through the area close to the first apartment house. The Highway Department's plans called for the road to be so high that it would block the view from the bottom three floors.

District regulations proved more and more exasperating. One bureau wanted to make sure that the opening in the lattice work on the outside walls of the apartment house would not be big enough to admit the District's ever-present starlings. The Department of Health, afraid of mosquito-breeding pools, would not approve the lily pond unless the developers agreed to stock it with a special kind of mosquito-eating fish. Restrictions on building heights threatened to force a choice between constructing the ground floor on stilts and building one less floor of rooms than was allowed by law and the official plan.

THE TEST OF FEASIBILITY

Seven months and some $200,000 in cash for architectural, legal and other consultants' fees were necessary to clear local hurdles for just the one building. Finally, in February 1957, the plan for Capitol Park Apartments One was ready to go to the Federal Housing Administration's local office for a test of feasibility for a preliminary commitment.

Another costly six months later, the FHA office decided to give Stevens and Scheuer a mortgage commitment. But this was only on 82 per cent instead of the full 90 per cent of replacement cost allowed in the Congressional statute governing Section 220. Thomas Barringer, chief of the District's FHA insuring office, claimed, "You're lucky if you come close to 90 per cent." The agency's decision would have forced the sponsors to triple their cash investment if they accepted it. They could also withdraw from the redevelopment project completely, as their leasehold contract provided that they need not proceed if FHA did not issue the full commitment. But as Scheuer and Stevens had already invested several hundred thousand dollars in the preliminary stages, they were reluctant to adopt this course. Instead, they and their team of consultants determined to push for the full 90 per cent loan.

There then began the lengthy negotiations. To appreciate this ritual, one must realize that the goals of the redevelopment investor and the FHA are, potentially, in conflict from beginning to end. The investor wants the maximum commitment from FHA, which, in turn, wants the most possible cash from the investor. The government agency is very sensitive to the risk element in former slum areas, and, remembering the "608" investigations, was very leery of builders with little cash equity. The officers in its local insuring offices worry about possible foreclosures on government-insured properties and want to minimize their record of defaults.

There is also the difficulty of accurately predicting the success of such atypical developments. As former HHFA administrator Norman Mason observed, "The [urban renewal] program requires a willingness to take a chance. But [FHA's] whole background is built on getting the facts and making large percentage loans based on the facts . . . Who knows if Southwest Washington will develop into a delightful housing area that will support rents of $200 a month or only into an area where low income families will live?"

Contrasted with the sponsors, the FHA appeared to be thinking about the past instead of the future. Southwest had been a low-income, predominantly Negro slum. The chief underwriter in the FHA's District office was opposed to the sponsors' plans for integrating the new housing. The office's philosophy, apparently, was that if the project were low rent, it should be Negro; if higher rent, all white. Furthermore, the design the sponsors were proposing was probably the most advanced concept that had ever crossed their desk. A Congressman is less likely to investigate a bureaucrat who errs on the side of conservatism than one who unsuccessfully takes a risk encouraged by Congressional statute.

In fact, the directives given by the "220" statute were skeletal and subject to great administrative discretion. Briefly, Congress sets the mortgage that can be allowed per room, but the FHA's seventy-six local insuring offices decide in each case what project costs are attributable to dwelling use, i.e. "income-producing," and therefore can be allowed under the statutory per room mortgage limits. In this limited and often subjective area, the developer, his architect and lawyers jockey with the FHA for the most favorable commitment. "Ideally," Thomas Barringer explained, "the dwelling units should cost the statutory limit and the income from them should be sufficient to support the mortgage on it. But this doesn't often happen." Thus it is usually the income required to cover the annual debt service—another of the four alternative methods the agency uses for determining mortgages—that ultimately controls FHA's computations.

The debt service provides the main answer to the question so many people raise about Title I housing: Why, even with the write-down on the land cost and FHA mortgage insurance, has urban redevelopment generally produced close to luxury rather than middle-income rentals? The debt service, particularly the interest rate which is its chief determinant, is the cause. The latter accounts for at least 50 per cent, often more, of the developer's rental changes. Consequently, of the five elements determining rents—land, construction costs, real estate taxes, operating expenses and debt service—interest has the most powerful leverage on what the renter pays.* As the FHA only insures, but does not issue mortgages, the agency's terms should meet the market rate of interest if its commitments are to obtain the necessary private permanent financing. Again, Congress was unsophisticated in its housing economics.

The housing agency's main concern was whether the insured project would have enough income left after paying real estate

* A one percentage point reduction in the interest rate from 5½ to 4½ can reduce the monthly charge in a typical two-bedroom apartment carrying a $15,000 mortgage by $12.50, or by $150 a year.

The other powerful lever is local real estate taxes. But because most cities look to redevelopment to increase taxable values, and because tax abatement is not legal in some states, this tool is used infrequently. Construction costs, double since World War II, differ little between public housing and luxury units. Operating costs have also risen steadily. Experts differ on the importance of land cost, but the general rule of thumb is 10 per cent of development cost. Very high land cost can cause rents to rise. But the redevelopment write-down aims to reduce it to fair market value within the limits of the plan. Thus while the first parcel of land in Area B cost about half as much per square foot as comparable land in other parts of the city, the sponsor could build only half as many units on it.

taxes and operating expenses to pay off the mortgage. If not, the project might end up in the FHA's lap. Integral to this concern is what rentals FHA believes a project can command. On the basis of this determination, the sponsor decides whether he wishes to build. His investment can be increased radically if the FHA differs with him by only $6 on rentals, at present interest rates.

WHAT IS ECONOMIC SOUNDNESS?

Not only was the FHA pessimistic about renting Southwest to a middle- and upper-middle-income white market; it did not believe that the $100,000 worth of art, amenities and landscaping called for by the overall Smith plan would help Capitol Park Apartments command sufficiently greater rentals to support the full mortgage requested by the sponsors. In the agency's jargon, these additions were not income-producing and thus not "attributable to dwelling use" on the basic unit of room counts. They could not be covered in the commitment. Mrs. Smith's design was, in fact, the most costly proposal to cross their desk, not in the basic construction costs, but in the environmental extras. In spite of Congress, the agency clung to its own ideas of economic soundness, which meant to cut costs and keep design extras to the minimum, to reduce the amortization and make sure it was paid.

Both the sponsors and architects thought such a philosophy ironic. The purpose of the write-down and the unusual restrictions on land coverage imposed by the redevelopment plan—then they could only build on 20 per cent of the land—was to let the sponsors produce a project that would enhance the community, not only through its openness, but also through attractive treatment of the generous amount of space between the buildings. Most apartment houses in the District could cover 60 per cent of the land, and thus builders had to spend very little for landscaping and environmental design. In Southwest, with its large open spaces, if the developers added the exterior amenities they would, it seemed, be penalized. FHA evidently expected them to pay for them out of their pocket. If FHA's approach were followed, the program would encourage ordinary and uninviting developments —plots of grass, concrete and parking lots between isolated, look-alike buildings, instead of new beauty in design and a livable, humanized outdoors.

The impasse was broken and the amenities were saved largely by Mrs. Smith's skill at the essential art of "juggling the room count"—getting more rooms out of the same floor space, and thus more mortgage money based on Congress' dollar limits per room. An architect dealing with the FHA must know how to get the maximum from these room limits, originally imposed in 1938 to keep builders from putting up too many luxury units; the restrictions worked, however, to make apartments rabbit warrens and encouraged chopping up spacious areas into needless but mortgage-producing cubicles.*

The reflecting pool was brought into coverage by the mortgage commitment after the plan was revised to place one of the supporting columns of the "income-producing" pavillion in the water. FHA rationalized the 4¼ per cent fee that Stevens and Scheuer were paying architect Smith—this is the standard professional fee, instead of the usual 1½ to 2 per cent that builders pay "FHA architects" who pull stereotyped, untroublesome plans out of the drawer—by taking into account her part in supervising the overall project construction. Unanticipated savings during construction restored funds which the sponsors put into the Bertoia screen. Mrs. Smith had saved the glass lobby and the full number of floors by persuading local officials that the ground floor was really a "no-story."

Commenting somewhat bitterly about such design by regulation, she said: "Why should we try to do something better? To get some publicity and be a hero? All you do is tie up your time and money. You have to be nutty to bother with all this."

By April 1958, FHA had issued what seemed to the sponsors a "nearly perfect" commitment of 89.8 per cent on Capitol Park Apartments One, and ground was broken for construction. But timing is all-important in rental housing. During the years of negotiations and planning, construction costs had risen 6 per cent and interest rates increased from 4¼ to 5¼ per cent. These had to be reflected in a $10 rise in monthly rents, which now came to $42 a room—$100 for efficiency apartments up to $210 for two-

* The law was revised in 1964 to simultaneously correct misuse of the artificial room count and encourage better building design.

bedroom units. Also, a tight money market had developed and discouraged lenders from FHA loans. The combined prestige of the president of the Federal City Council, an organization of District business leaders, and one of the country's top mortgage bankers was necessary to persuade the John Hancock Life Insurance Company to take Capitol Park One and make the first private commitment for housing in an urban renewal area in the country.

THE LONESOME ROSE

The first apartment house was at last ready for occupancy in June 1959. The seventy-two tenants who moved into the building —only 18 per cent of its capacity—were greeted with flowers and champagne. At the ground-breaking ceremony in 1958, the minister who gave the benediction had said, "The desert shall rejoice and blossom as the rose." And indeed, Capitol Park Apartments One was a lonesome rose blooming in the slum desert.

Across the street still stood the decrepit row houses of Area C, some now occupied by vagrants. Muggings and knifings were so common that police had to patrol the neighborhood constantly. Eighty per cent of the apartment units were efficiencies or flexible one-and-a-half-room apartments, designed in large part to meet the demands of single women who worked in nearby government buildings. But young women were afraid to come home at night. There was not even decent public transportation to the area.

Also, there was no place "where a white girl could shop" within a mile, not even a grocery. Webb and Knapp had yet to build the indispensable Town Center. Why the delay? Webb and Knapp spokesmen stated that the Redevelopment Land Agency had difficulty getting the land ready for them and did not deliver it until January 1960, when their firm commenced building. This is the official explanation. But other informed sources believed that if Webb and Knapp had been ready with cash to build before then, it could have successfully pressed for delivery of the land.

Whatever the reason for the delay it vitiated a basic, though commonly violated, assumption of any renewal plan: that all principals will perform on schedule. The lack of shopping facilities and apartment houses to help upgrade the surrounding area and make it more livable was estimated by Scheuer to have cost Capitol Park One half a year's rent-roll. (He was also convinced that Webb and Knapp had delayed because they wished to see how his apartment house fared before building their own.)

Meanwhile, Stevens and Scheuer had to spend $10,000 to convert a basement area originally intended for recreational uses into a convenience grocery store, for which they received $1-a-month rental. They also had to pay $2,000 more in legal fees because a variance from the District zoning ordinance was required to allow a store in a residential building.

Another extra, heavy expense was for advertising. To attract tenants, it was necessary to promote not only Capitol Park One but all of Southwest, and to try to alter community opinion. This ultimately involved an $89,000 promotional campaign, not covered by FHA insurance. (In other parts of the city, $15,000 was the estimated average spent on advertising a new building.)

Fortunately, many potential renters were out-of-town government workers who were unaware of the stigma attached to Southwest. But it did not help to have a cab driver tell a girl who gave him the address of Capitol Park Apartments, "I wouldn't rent there for anything. It's just a slum." Extra rental agents were required to talk with prospective tenants, and had to be hired for a longer than normal period.

Had it not been for the park-like landscaping, which allowed tenants to stroll on the grounds evenings and weekends, and to bring suppers outside to the tables during Washington's long summer, probably fewer people would have lived, or stayed, at Capitol Park One. Although tenants had the option to break their leases, none did.

Meanwhile, unexpected competition from other, established parts of the city had developed during the years of pre-construction delay. The District was scheduled to adopt a new zoning ordinance in 1958. As its enforcement would make present apartment house sites less attractive economically to owners because of greater limits on density and land coverage, there was the usual race to build and get in under the line. The general rental market also started to boom after the loosening of money late in 1958.

New elevator buildings appeared on well-known avenues around town, pretty well saturating the market. In March 1960, vacancies for efficiency units in the whole city stood at the low of 1.28 per cent; at Capitol Park One they were 13.83.

PROMISE INTO PRACTICE

Add to these problems Scheuer's publicized promise that Capitol Park Apartments would be racially integrated. The Washington *Post* had even run a story quoting Scheuer's iconoclastic testimony in New York City, where he supported that city's proposed open-occupancy housing statute, first of its kind in the country.

During the first few weeks after Capitol Park One opened, Negroes comprised the large proportion of Sunday visitors. Many were former Southwest residents who came to see what had been built in their old neighborhood, not to rent. The renting agents, Shannon and Luchs, were frantic. Their firm was the only real estate management company in Washington that would handle the redevelopment project, but even they lacked experience in integrated housing. This was the first private apartment building in the District of Columbia to be rented on an open-occupancy basis.

The sponsors had planned their integration program in consultation with the District's leading Negro civic spokesman and with one of the nation's foremost authorities on minority housing, also a Negro. The consultants had agreed that the project would first have to be established as desirable to the white community if integration were to be achieved. It seemed to them that 75 per cent occupancy should be reached before non-white tenants were accepted.

Well-qualified Negroes applied and agreed—after management frankly explained its position—to stay on the waiting list. Then, when the building was only 50 per cent occupied, the integration issue was forced by the application of a white man who was married to a Negro. The couple had a critical housing problem, having been ejected from an apartment house owned by the District's leading builder when management learned the woman was the man's wife, not his maid. The couple's lawyer, Joseph L.

Rauh, former head of the liberal Americans for Democratic Action, suggested that they apply to Capitol Park Apartments. Both had doctorates and were eminently suitable tenants. They were accepted on the waiting list, and when renting continued to go slowly, they, like others, were asked to postpone their move-in date a month.

Now Capitol Park Apartments was caught in the cross-currents between the liberal white and middle-class Negro communities. The couple's lawyer informed the developers that if his clients were not admitted at a specific date, they would stage a sleep-out in front of the building. Negro leaders, fearing there would be a strongly negative reaction to integrated housing in Washington if people drew the conclusion that open occupancy would lead to mixed marriage, begged the sponsors to wait before admitting them. Rauh threatened court action. He had no legal grounds, but Scheuer and Stevens wanted to avoid such unfavorable publicity. They settled the matter by paying the difference in rent for a furnished apartment hotel unit for the couple for several months; when other Negroes moved into Capitol Park One, the couple would not be as conspicuous.

Actually, there was no land-office business from Negro applicants. Rents were too high for most, and those who could afford them generally preferred to buy. To them, renting had a stigma —especially renting in a former Negro slum. Owning a house, however, was a status symbol. Many beautiful homes in the District were becoming available to non-whites. No doubt some prospective Negro tenants were also discouraged by the icy shoulder of several of Shannon and Luchs' representatives. One rental agent had to be fired after he was rude to the future dean of Howard University—who was just looking. Salesmen were trained on future plans and the integration policy and the atmosphere improved. Still, to get the several dozen Negro tenants in the first apartment house, it was necessary to ask Negro organizations to send applicants. A few who did not qualify on credit grounds were accepted. In 1965, 11.9 per cent of the tenants in Southwest's private housing were Negro; in public housing, 95 per cent were Negro.

Renting was so slow that the developers had to add $150,000 to keep the building in operation, and FHA made concessions to them on amortization so they could lower the rents. Meanwhile, Capitol Park One had to pay the District $45,000 annually in real estate taxes, nearly six times the amount paid by the old slum properties. This sum is based on the value of the building, not its income.

Late in 1959 the general slowness of Southwest's rebuilding—Capitol Park One was the only new building in the renewal area—caused a Congressman to introduce a bill to halt all other Title I projects in the District until this initial area was 50 per cent completed. The bill was killed, but Congress ordered a study of the causes of delay. The heat was now on agency director Searles. He showed his fist by sending an open letter to Scheuer and Stevens in January 1960, warning that if they did not proceed with the townhouses behind Capitol Park Apartments One, they would have to forfeit the entire development.

In April 1958, the FHA had issued a commitment for the townhouses, but the terms were even less satisfactory to the sponsors—only 70 per cent of cost. The sponsors did not negotiate, but waited for Congress' anticipated liberalization of the mortgages allowed per room. This came through in September 1959. Then FHA became as reluctant as the sponsors. Neither wanted these houses, the first private buildings in the new Southwest intended for families with children, to be built until Webb and Knapp's shopping center was ready. Unlike government girls who could shop on their way home from work, mothers with children and without the family car could not conveniently go out of the neighborhood.

The new elementary public school which was to be situated across the street from Capitol Park One would not be open until September 1960. The school itself was a ticklish problem, one taken on several years before by Webb and Knapp's project director. The school would be open in advance of most of the new private housing in the area. If it were operated as a neighborhood school, it would be attended entirely by children from the low-income housing project that was opened in 1959 by the National Capital Housing Authority adjacent to the renewal area, with an almost entirely Negro tenancy. This would tend to discourage white middle-class families from moving to Southwest. The Webb and Knapp representative put the problem bluntly to the

District's Superintendent of Schools, Carl Hansen. For some time, Hansen had been thinking of trying out a new grade-school curriculum emphasizing basic instruction in the three R's. He decided to initiate it at Southwest's new Amidon School and to allow any family in the city which would transport its children to the school to enroll them.

THE PROBLEMS OF TIME AND TIMING

Not until November 1960, when Webb and Knapp's first two apartment houses were up and renting, the shopping center in operation, and the new school open, did Capitol Park Apartments One reach a low enough vacancy rate to make a profit. In 1961, the first eighty-one townhouses opened. But these rented slowly, with only sixty occupied the first year. By 1963, two more of Capitol Park's apartment houses were open. These rented much faster, though vacancy rates were at first too high for profit.

That summer, construction of the fourth and final apartment house was started. Scheuer felt that his original premises were sound—that in the long run Capitol Park would be a profitable venture. For less than $2,000,000 invested, he would have half interest in a 1,750-unit, $31,000,000 development whose value could be expected to appreciate considerably in a rising economy. "But," he added wryly, "as John Maynard Keynes once wrote, 'In the long run, we are all dead.' "

For Roger Stevens, ten years older than Scheuer and less enthusiastic about long-term real estate investment or redevelopment,* five years with no money back from the project had been long enough. In the fall of 1960, although Capitol Park One was about to get out of the red, he was delighted to get back his original cash investment, plus $100,000, from this "short-run financial catastrophe." Scheuer, digging even deeper into his own reserves, bought Stevens out of the first building.

Stevens sold his position in the remainder of the project to a New York building and investment firm, HRH Construction Company, which became Scheuer's equal partner in Southwest.

* Stevens was finding himself more and more deeply committed financially in another complicated redevelopment project in New Haven, Connecticut, as we shall see in Chapter 9.

Indeed, it had appeared that Stevens and Scheuer would have a difficult time providing the large additional sums required to complete the rest of their project, as was being demanded by the Redevelopment Land Agency. HRH could provide the cash required at the start of construction and build up a substantial equity in the development by putting in its profits as the builder.

In retrospect, Scheuer felt that the problems involved, largely, time and timing. "I never dreamed how long it would take with government red tape, and how much time it would require to get acceptance of a new community in a former slum area." Compared to clearing the physical slum, removal of an area's reputation is a longer and more difficult task. Many people still regarded Southwest as a Negro slum, and the remaining vestiges of decay—acres of barren ground and the old waterfront, whose rehabilitation was some time off—made the area less desirable than other parts of town. Even by late 1965 Southwest was still far from the promised new community. Several major government offices and L'Enfant Plaza, which were expected to provide the walk-to-work market for the new housing, were not yet built. The new restaurants, marina and other attractions along the Potomac were also still to come. Although Capitol Park's buildings were close to 97 per cent filled by that date (compared to the average of 94.5 per cent for all of Southwest), its full potential was felt to be still several years off.

Several national developments which had taken place since Capitol Park was begun had adversely affected the relative appeal of apartments in the Southwest redevelopment project. With a loosening of mortgage money, a rise in suburban land costs and the changes in the age composition of the country which manifested themselves by the early 1960's—fewer growing middle-income white families, relatively more older couples, and more young single adults or childless young couples—the shelter industry greatly increased production of rental housing in both cities and suburbs. Washington D.C. was one of the urban centers that particularly benefited from this national trend. But with so many apartment houses springing up in the District, why should one choose to rent in a former slum site? Southwest's advanced, attractive design and amenities plus its convenient location proved to be its major competitive strengths.

A LEARNING EXPERIENCE

The unexpected problems, frustrations and delays which Scheuer's Washington project encountered show why, in spite of the layman's suspicions, urban redevelopment is neither a quick nor an easy way to make money.

A deep-pocketed, patient sponsor and a persistent, imaginative architect are essential to produce an outstanding, effective large-scale development on the site of a former slum. Indeed, the sponsor of such a project had better have other means of supporting himself while waiting for profits from his investment. In fact, Capitol Park One was the first and only project of six in which Scheuer participated as a sponsor that he entered as a major cash investor. After this venture he assumed only the early entrepreneurial or risk-taking role; he supplied the time and money required to win sponsorship and bring a project to the point of construction, complete with a satisfactory FHA commitment, and his partners supplied the major cash difference.*

His pioneer venture provided a learning experience for many of its principals. FHA's Washington office no longer held back on insuring amenities. Thomas Barringer was sure that without them, Capitol Park and Southwest would have failed. He even issued a commitment to cover an (integrated) swimming pool in the two final buildings of Scheuer's development.

Projects like Capitol Park helped the new administration of the Housing and Home Finance Agency since 1961 persuade even many of the old hands at the Federal Housing Administra-

* Commonly, Scheuer's outlay for architectural and legal fees plus overhead amounted to several hundred thousand dollars, which could be charged to project cost *if* it went through. Yet his partners—builders or investors who for various reasons, tax angles high among them, went into redevelopment with him and put up the far more substantial cash required for construction—considered his initial risk to be worth at least 50 per cent of multimillion-dollar projects. Once a project was in operation, however, Scheuer assumed half the risk of operating losses should the buildings not rent soon, as in the case of Capitol Park One.

Special federal income tax angles helped Scheuer retrieve most of his equity from the original part of that project. In 1961 he sold the first section to an investor who could use the early depreciation allowances on his own income tax, and who gave Scheuer an option to buy back in four to eleven and a half years.

tion to take a more optimistic look at redevelopment projects in issuing commitments. The FHA initiated a provision allowing one per cent of project cost for "non-income producing" works of art, and local insuring offices have taken a less negative attitude toward landscaping. The FHA even began giving awards for well-designed projects.

The example of successful integration in the new Southwest's first building was followed by other developers in the project area, and in 1962, the District's Redevelopment Land Agency made open-rental policies a legal requirement in their sponsors' contracts. The following year, a Presidential order made non-discriminatory rental or sales of all FHA-insured or government-assisted housing a federal requirement. (This, of course, was not attributable to the Southwest project, but rather to national pressures from civil rights and housing groups.) The real estate firm of Shannon and Luchs began, as a result of its experience in Southwest, to work quietly with the local Urban League in an effort to integrate the many apartment houses that the company manages in Washington, even though these had not benefited from any government assistance. Frank Luchs, the concern's president, was also trying to use his position as head of the Washington Real Estate Board to persuade fellow realtors to follow his firm's example.

An important modification in project design also was made as the result of experience. Scheuer came to believe that he and Stevens had made a major early error in giving up their apartment houses' neighborhood shops, even after Webb and Knapp's shopping center was in operation. Tenants at Capitol Park missed city-type convenience stores, not only for purchasing household items and services, but also as informal meeting places where they could get to know their neighbors. The sponsors applied to the Redevelopment Land Agency and were granted permission to add the type of stores and service shops the residents expected in the apartment buildings.

The Amidon School, now famous, provided an important lesson for city rebuilders. Like other District schools, it was integrated by law. Although attendance was about three quarters non-white, with many students from the nearby public housing project, the school's excellent basic educational program attracted middle-class families, both white and non-white, to the new Southwest.

There is little doubt that Southwest should have been rebuilt much more rapidly to allow it to compete more effectively with the residential alternatives available to Washingtonians, and to make it more attractive for tenants already there. But so many different agencies and principals were engaged in the rebuilding process that it was virtually impossible to phase every piece of the huge project on schedule. This problem was exaggerated by lack of executive coordination in the District government and its redevelopment machinery. A city development administrator (or Moses-type expediter) to help move the publicly approved plan through and over local red tape could have reduced the lead time prior to construction and allowed the other components of the project to move along faster.

Still, someone had to be first, to rebuild in the midst of the old slum rubble and dust, and deal with the unexpected obstacles to a new redevelopment project. Better financing mechanisms, assistance from federal agencies, and tax breaks from local government could have nursed along the original sponsor during the early period of such a large long-term undertaking.

This came to be recognized by the FHA and by Congress, which passed a law providing for a flexible amortization rate, whereby if a sponsor has an operating deficit, his debt service could be reduced by half a percentage point, which gave him considerable leverage. Furthermore, he was allowed to make up for his earlier operating losses—if and when he had enough current income to cover these losses—by asking FHA to rewrite his mortgage.

But the District, like other cities which have looked to redevelopment to increase their tax base, would not adjust its local real estate tax policies to help a project that was in trouble during its early years. FHA spokesmen contend that local assessment practices must be more realistic if cities want such projects. They suggest a program of tax escalation on Title I projects in the early days before the projects begin to make money, or a policy of taxing buildings on the basis of the income they produce, not their replacement cost. Local tax policies appear to be one of the most critical and negative factors in the determination of what housing gets built in cities and what the rents will be. But most localities are prevented by state law from taxing policies such as proposed by FHA, and assessors are usually independently elected officials —which makes such a revision doubly hard.

But it must be recognized that a big part of the problem in renting at Capitol Park, and in Webb and Knapp's apartments as well, was that private enterprise could only produce quite high-cost housing, even with FHA's Section 220, and the market for such rentals is relatively thin. The fact that it was not possible for a private developer to build the $17-a-room garden apartments originally called for in Area B (subsidized public housing rents for the same amount) caused the redevelopment agency in 1959 to drop this unrealistic ceiling from the sponsor's agreement. More townhouses, which appeal to city families, were substituted, and a denser, more urban, land coverage allowed than in the original plan.

One way to achieve the larger market for housing in cities at a somewhat lower cost was revealed in the experience of the third private redeveloper in Southwest Washington. The happy experience of this sponsor, a subsidiary of the Reynolds Metals Company, also pointed up the fortunate position of the sponsor who comes in after the pioneering phase is over.

In 1962, Reynolds Metals Development Corporation put up 530 units of cooperative apartments and townhouses. Co-ops save the consumer at least 15 per cent of shelter cost annually, primarily because his down payment on his home serves as equity. They also offer him income tax benefits similar to those enjoyed by homeowners. Almost all of Reynolds' units were sold before construction was even complete, some to former renters in Capitol Park who had since married. In mid-1963, while the rental units in Southwest were only 90 per cent filled, the cooperatives were all sold. Reynolds was in and out of the entire project in three years. The firm did not object to paying the full tax on its profits from the sales instead of the lower long-term capital gains tax which most developers prefer. It could make extensive use of aluminum in the housing it constructed there; the redevelopment site was a widely publicized showcase area for residential use of its product. There were also certain special income tax advantages which can accrue to a large company with diversified interests.

Reynolds was the first of several major national industrial and investment companies which began in the early 1960's to sponsor or acquire big Title I projects—for some of the very reasons that such projects have been unattractive to builders or promoters with limited funds or requiring early profits. In addition to Reynolds, there is the Aluminum Corporation of America, which acquired most of Webb and Knapp's projects and is sponsoring ten across the country; Gulf Oil Corporation; and the General Electric Company. Wall Street firms have also begun putting equity capital into city redevelopment.

Such big companies can charge losses from an urban renewal project during its early, red-ink years against their current profits in other areas of activity, and they are attracted by long-term investments. One spokesman estimated that the cash drain on his company would be only half of that for a developer who has no other business.

On the other hand, opportunities for small developers and builders to participate in renewal projects have multiplied in the past few years in big and small cities as smaller parcels of land have been cleared and disposed of in rehabilitation and conservation areas, and as new kinds of special government-assisted housing programs for moderate-income families have come into existence. Some of these programs will be discussed in Chapter 6.

FHA AND THE PURPOSES OF REDEVELOPMENT

Meanwhile, we must ask whether the FHA, as now constituted, has not outlived its original machinery, at least so far as the housing needs of cities are concerned.

Although the agency administration has come a long way in its stance toward urban renewal and multiple dwellings, and has encouraged excellence in project design through awards, local insuring offices too often take a dim view of city housing and apartment buildings compared to suburban houses. But we must remember that FHA's primary means for encouraging development still remains that of insuring the lender against loss. However, the residential industry was sufficiently flourishing by 1963 so that less than 20 per cent of the housing built nationally relied on government mortgage insurance, and a pittance of this was being used in cities.

To reduce the consumer's cost of housing, the Federal Housing Administration has only been able to chip away at the extras through such devices as longer-term loans. It has been unable to get at the big basic factors that make housing so expensive: the interest rate; city real estate taxes; and construction costs, which have doubled since World War II, rising even faster than the general consumer price index.

In order to lower rentals or housing costs in order to let renewal serve a much broader market, government financing tools beyond the Title I land write-down, FHA's mortgage insurance program, and cooperative housing are required. Much more direct government assistance or even subsidy is necessary, as we will see in Chapter 6 on housing.

Finally, we come to the question of the purposes of residential redevelopment. This new program originated with a negative approach. Its public purposes, as accepted by the courts, were to eliminate slums and to prevent new ones from forming. The positive aspect, the goal of urban rebuilding, has not been so clearly focused.

Different locations have a different logic of development in their re-use through renewal, and most are not susceptible to such up-grading. Furthermore, the current social climate and the Department of Housing and Urban Development do not encourage use of government funds for a luxury development. But even in considering publicly assisted housing developments to be built for lower-income levels, it seems appropriate to hark back to no less an authority than the Supreme Court and its historic *Berman* v. *Parker* ruling; this 1954 case decided on the legality of the redevelopment of Southwest Washington. The Court, acting as the District of Columbia's Court of Appeals, was only ruling on a local matter. Its opinion on this case is still the definitive statement.

In unanimously upholding the public taking of the slum property and the private rebuilding of the land, the Court not only declared that "the public end may be as well or better served through an agency of private enterprise than through an agency of government." It also went beyond the legally accepted purpose of slum prevention in justifying the public interest in area-wide clearance of the slum area for rebuilding according to the community plan:

"The concept of the public welfare is broad and inclusive . . . ," the Court stated. "The values it represents are spiritual as well as physical, aesthetic as well as monetary. It is within the power of the legislature to determine that the community should be beautiful as well as healthy, spacious as well as clean, well-balanced as well as carefully patrolled . . .

"If those who govern the District of Columbia decide that the Nation's Capital should be beautiful as well as sanitary, nothing in the Fifth Amendment stands in the way."

Those who governed the District decided that Southwest should be beautiful. The private sponsors who invested their money and skills in its redevelopment helped the city realize not only aesthetic and monetary values—when finished the area will return to the District eight times the taxes of the old slum—but also spiritual or civic values, in the relations between people in an integrated community. (These human values, as we shall see, also guided family relocation in that project.) Southwest provides irrefutable evidence that urban redevelopment, if done well and on a large scale, can work without compromising many different, potentially conflicting values. It also shows that all the goals desired in urban rebuilding cannot be realized simultaneously.

Still, there will not be other redevelopments of this type in Washington for some time. This is not because no other slum areas require clearance and rebuilding. But in the District, as in other big cities, the increasing numbers of poor Negroes, the many obstacles to dislocating them from slums and housing them decently, and the need to save good neighborhoods from becoming slums, have forced this kind of redevelopment from center stage to the wings. Moreover, the controlled staging of integration in government-assisted housing goes against the present temper of the civil rights drive, not to mention government orders, even though such an approach may be necessary for achieving integration in many cities.

Emerging Social Problems

5

"WHAT ABOUT THE PEOPLE?" ■ Relocation from Southwest Washington

The early major approaches to urban reconstruction revealed much about the possibilities of improving cities physically as well as some of the instruments for doing so. They also indicated that in the urban complex, "solutions" themselves, such as slum clearance, inevitably bring to the surface problems, or even create new ones, which cannot be ignored. They demonstrated that as one goes further in renewing cities—in removing the obsolete structures—different problems interact and the dimensions of the problems broaden. Part of the value of these early renewal efforts is that they did reveal to the localities much of what else is needed and involved.

Of all the interwoven and open-ended challenges of city renewal, none is more inexorable, unavoidable and baffling than the social problems of slum dwellers, or what has come to be called the "human" side of urban renewal. In terms of making public policy, much of the challenge is to determine what the human problems actually are. The past few years have seen many new definitions, as well as prescriptions and programs for their cure.

It is useful to approach this multi-faceted urban issue from a relatively limited, yet highly significant and continuing aspect—relocation of families from a slum area to be renewed under Title I. More than anything else, this activity has forced into the public arena the problems of "the people," and has, at its best, stimulated a hopeful and helpful response.

When the urban redevelopment legislation was being considered by Congress in the spring of 1949, the Senate chamber rang for weeks with reports of the shameful conditions that festered in the nation's slums. One day, several Senators, among them Paul Douglas of Illinois and Homer Ferguson of Indiana, decided to take time from the discussions to see how some neighbors actually lived in the century-old slum of Southwest Washington, only several blocks away.

They strolled along broad, tree-shaded streets lined with deceptively picturesque two-story brick row houses, in which families of six and eight slept in a single room and paid rents as low as $12 a month. The back alleys, littered with rotting garbage, broken bottles and rusting tin cans, were hidden from their view at first. The Senators poked into the yard of one alley house on F Street and found a crippled man lying on a bare bedspring. In the two dim rooms this elderly man rented, his son and daughter-in-law and their nine children also lived. When they entered, the Senators saw the bare exposed beams of the walls; the plaster that once covered them lay in large chunks on the dirt floor. The smoke of an oil lamp had blackened the ceiling. A squalling infant, child of the oldest (husbandless) granddaughter, lay on the soiled covers of one of the beds.

Senator Douglas, leader of the expedition, gagged on the foul smell and bolted for the back door. In the yard, flies swarmed around the privy which the family shared with neighboring alley dwellers. Only last winter, the policeman on the beat casually informed them, a man had frozen to death in a similar outhouse.

"Aren't there any health laws?" demanded Senator Ferguson. "Surely we don't permit this kind of thing!"

The police officer said that eviction notices were served by the Health Department, but were seldom enforced. "Where would these people go?"

What happened to the people? That is probably the question most frequently raised about urban renewal. And relocation, in spite of the legislative provisions in Title I of the Housing Act of 1949, was for many years a relatively neglected and frequently, although often not fairly, criticized phase of the national program.

By coincidence, the relocation of the 7,000 families in Southwest Washington—the area visited by the Senators and later cleared and redeveloped—was the most successful undertaking to date of its kind in the country, in striking contrast to many other cities' efforts. There, the local officials in charge of the program tried, for the first time, to catalogue the actual problems in moving all the people from a slum site into standard housing; they then tried to face these problems, instead of sweeping the tough cases under the rug. During this period of public agency responsibility for slum dwellers, they were able to show that those on the lowest end of the economic scale and even further up can be helped to improve not only their housing but also their general lot. Moreover, the efforts of the relocation staff proved that other local public and private agencies and the community at large will respond to and help ease the trauma of moving—if the officials in charge communicate the people's needs to the city and mobilize outside community resources.

For nearly a decade, the director of relocation for the District of Columbia's Redevelopment Land Agency until 1961, James G. Banks, stood in the forefront of a small but growing group of local officials who saw relocation in larger terms than the statutory rehousing requirements of the National Housing Act. "When a city starts comprehensive urban renewal," Banks warned the District, "the human problems it avoids solving in one project area will crop up in the next section it decides to clear."

This is no small matter. Since 1949, Title I projects have dislocated some 194,000 families. During the next decade, urban renewal and other scheduled public improvement projects are expected to dislocate annually another 60,000 to 70,000 families, most of them poor and living in slum and blighted areas.

RELOCATION REQUIREMENTS AND PRACTICES

With Title I of the National Housing Act of 1949, Congress took a notable step forward in fixing responsibility on communities for the rehousing of residents displaced by this new government slum clearance program. Specifically the law required that, as a prerequisite to receiving the federal loans and grants for urban redevelopment, a locality show that "there are or are being provided in the [project] area or in others not generally less desirable . . . decent, safe and sanitary dwellings" within the means of the displaced families and conveniently located to their places of work. While Congress, in 1949, did not accompany this statutory requirement with provisions for moving expenses, the federal administrative agency allowed paying these out of project funds (of which the federal government paid two thirds) if the local agency could show that these costs were necessary to carry out the project; that is, if a family could not move otherwise. In 1956, Congress specifically authorized moving expenses as part of the project cost and set a ceiling of $100 per family. This amount was subsequently raised to $200 per family,* but many families do not use up even the original sum; their possessions are so meager.

The purpose of the relocation statute and financial assistance was to assure that families would not be moved from one slum to another, and that Title I would result in good housing for former slum dwellers as well as desirable use of the old slum land.

By contrast, until 1964, public housing, which also clears slums, had no comparable rehousing responsibility. Local au-

* In 1964, Congress also authorized up to $500 in rent payments for the first year, where a family had to spend more than 20 per cent of its income on housing.

thorities were only mandated by Congress to concern themselves with the housing of those slum families they had uprooted who were eligible by virtue of low income for their projects. However, the authorities were not required to accept in their units dislocated poor families who did not meet many other non-income eligibility requirements. The interstate highway program, which has displaced at least as many city slum dwellers as urban renewal, had no legal responsibility at all for family relocation until 1962; however, its requirements are still less specific.

Unfortunately, for many years even Title I's higher relocation requirements were often sloughed off by local officials as an odious technicality; the people were to be gotten out of the way so that the local agency could get the federal money and start clearance. It became uncomfortably apparent, however, that while proper relocation required an adequate housing supply at suitable rents—which was not always available—satisfactory rehousing was also more than a shelter problem. Many local agency officials exhibited little understanding of or concern for complicating "social" problems. They were under pressure from their city's business and government leaders to reach the "brick and mortar" stage so that higher taxes could be realized from new buildings on the former slum land. There was a tendency, as one federal housing official put it, to "give the families a few dollars and tell them to get lost."

Federally assisted redevelopment began in cities at the time of the lingering postwar housing shortage, and coincided as well with the new migration. The fact that slums slated for Title I clearance were crowded with people who could not easily find another place to live was of secondary importance. The rationalization was that the larger city tax revenues would eventually filter down in services for the poor. In the battle for central city space, real estate values usually won over human values.

Some communities seemed to regard redevelopment as a way of dispersing their city's mounting number of Negroes. By 1964, some 63 per cent of the families relocated from Title I areas were non-white, so it is not surprising that slum clearance came to be labeled "Negro clearance," and urban renewal as "Negro removal," and a target for civil rights groups. The fact that residents were often the last to be brought into project plans, and then only to be told they would have to move soon, fostered the bitterness with which many people came to regard urban redevelopment. The result of such relocation practices was often to spread slum conditions.

Embarrassed by poor relocation results, some redevelopment agencies blamed the federal government for not providing, either in its legislation or appropriations, for the exigencies of the "social disorganization" of slum dwellers. Local officials often felt it was not the job of the redevelopment or housing agency to remake portions of society while removing old buildings and putting suitable new ones in their place. Indeed, as one recent official of the federal administration observed, "The biggest problem we have is the attitude of local officials and leaders. They've always considered the people in the slums as the city's cross, and thought them unimportant in the city's over-all plans."

Most people have incorrectly assumed that public housing would provide shelter for the displaced poor. But in fact, although over half of the dislocated families have been eligible, as of June 1966, on the basis of low income, only 21.4 per cent actually moved into the projects.

The complex reasons for this discrepancy will be explored in later pages; they can be summarized here under the heading of "resistance" to public housing, and the "social problems" that slum clearance disgorges. Actually, many localities did not even build the public housing units required for their urban renewal dislocation load.

Some socially concerned local citizen groups blamed urban renewal itself for causing and not curing these social problems, and even called for a halt to the program. They were reluctant to recognize that urban renewal had exposed, and finally forced into the area of public responsibility, some unpleasant and unavoidable aspects of urban and American life that had festered unseen and unchallenged for generations.

The issue of equity was further complicated by the designation for redevelopment of some deteriorating but well-located inner-city neighborhoods; these were not rock-bottom physical or social slums, but they had been passed over by recent private development. Such blighted areas, by virtue of their proximity to the center of the city, gave themselves to upgrading through Title I, typically with high-rental housing; the federal renewal agency encouraged this with administrative rulings for the "highest and best use" appraisal of Title I land. Redevelopment of such areas was frequent before neighborhood conservation and rehabilitation became more common in the urban renewal program, and the federal agency required more suitable treatment for such areas.

One such widely publicized project was in Boston's predominantly Italian West End neighborhood. Sociologist Herbert Gans, who lived in the old area for eight months, found that the area was socially healthy. Although structures were outwardly deteriorated and substandard, they served the important purpose of providing inexpensive private housing that satisfied their low-income residents. "Under present conditions," he wrote in a statement challenging the project's basic legality as well as its ethical validity and wisdom, "the redevelopment of American cities is economically feasible because of the hidden subsidies provided by residents of the areas."

As for the federal officials, until the Kennedy administration, they seemed far more worried about rebuilding and tended to go along with what one government housing veteran has described as "the very nice statistical documents" submitted by local agencies about their relocation plans and accomplishments. Indeed, although Title I in its first dozen years dislocated 400,000 people, and presumably relocated most of them satisfactorily,* this phase of the program rated only a dozen lines among the tens of thousands in the Housing and Home Finance Agency's annual reports. The fate of the dislocatees seemed to depend too often on the conscience of local officials.

With practice, localities learned how to relocate more success-

* Local public agency reports on relocation results as of March 1960, compiled by the Urban Renewal Administration, showed that 70 per cent of the families on the agencies' workload had been satisfactorily located. (However, in the same year, the New York State Advisory Committee on Civil Rights to the U.S. Commission called relocation reports submitted to and approved by the Urban Renewal Administration as "mostly fictional, illusory and unrealistic" in relation to minority groups' rehousing.)

During 1964, the Bureau of the Census conducted a nationwide survey of 132 cities involved in urban renewal and found that 94 per cent of all the site families had been relocated into standard housing. The percentage for non-white families was 91 per cent.

fully, and in the past few years they have been forced to do so. The government's emphasis has changed considerably, due in good part to the new administration, rising social pressures and application of useful experience. Some of the new national patterns were developed in Washington's relocation program under James Banks, who became the first Assistant Commissioner for Tenant Relocation and Community Relations of the federal Urban Renewal Administration in 1961. Banks was appointed to this newly created post as a result of his outstanding job in the District of Columbia, particularly in Southwest Washington. This project was praised by successive top federal housing officials as the best relocation program in the country, both for its efficiency and its humanity; even local citizen "watch-dog" agencies acclaimed it.

AN UNEXPECTED SUCCESS

Back in 1951, however, when the eighteen-block Area B section of Southwest, the District's pioneer Title I project, was scheduled for redevelopment, the relocation task had seemed hopeless. "This was the worst area in the city," John R. Searles, Jr., then director of the Redevelopment Land Agency, said. "People didn't think there could be any improvement in the families moving out. We were sure eighty percent would land up in another slum."

However, of the 1,049 families that were living in Area B when the agency acquired the properties and assumed responsibility for the residents, only forty-nine families, or 5 per cent, moved to another slum; about that same number disappeared and thus went unaccounted. All the rest moved to better homes: 441 to low-rent housing, 515 to decent private shelter. Not one person had to be evicted for unwillingness to move. Furthermore, the families moved to all parts of the city and the transition was accomplished on schedule.

After the entire Southwest area had been cleared, the Washington Housing Association—a citizen group whose members included many who were skeptical about the human benefits of redevelopment—studied the whereabouts of the displacees. According to their report, the "overwhelming number" of the

23,950 former Southwest residents who accepted the redevelopment agency's assistance had improved their housing considerably. Even one particularly severe critic of the "inhuman side" of urban renewal, a priest who had studied city planning, found to his surprise that most of the 200 former Southwest families whom he surveyed felt they were better off than before.

For over half a century, congressional committees, housing reformers and delegations of shocked citizens had poked into the notorious slums. Southwest's deterioration started after the Civil War and the coming of the railroad. The isolated area served as the receiving center for freed slaves and for foreign workers. First they lived in temporary shacks, then in tiny alley dwellings crowded behind once-spacious older residential squares. Alleys were sometimes built within alleys. By 1892, when Congress passed a law prohibiting such dwellings, the damage was done.

Owners of front houses had already been moving out. Alley families who could move into front houses did so, and sometimes they moved away. Southwest was left more and more to absentee landlords. In the hidden alley communities, crime grew; houses of prostitution, numbers players and "smoke joints" attached themselves to the backwash. The swarms of children were familiar scenery to visitors entering the District of Columbia on train tracks that cut along this vast blighted area. The world was acquainted with it by the famous photograph, published in the Washington *Post* and then circulated by the Communists during the 1930's, showing American children in Southwest playing next to an open backyard privy. But the decrepit houses and back alleys rotted still further as more poor Negro families migrated from the South and found cheap shelter there. During the 1940's, while living standards in Washington and the nation rose, Southwest grew steadily worse. The city had long since written off the area.

When the matter of designating slum areas for redevelopment under the new federal Housing Act's Title I came up, over 75 per cent of Area B homes were dilapidated and lacked inside running water; more than 50 per cent were without gas and electricity; 43 per cent had outside toilets. Social indices of slums, such as crime and disease rates, were also high.

With urban redevelopment, the District of Columbia had not

only to clear this physical slum and rebuild it, but also to face the problems of the people.

Redevelopment Land Agency director John Searles recognized the critical and delicate nature of the relocation phase. Supported by his chairman, he tried to find the best person to handle the job, and then gave him free rein and full cooperation.

Jim Banks was the Assistant Supervisor for Tenant Relations at the National Capital Housing Authority. A modest, outwardly calm though intense person, he had already distinguished himself in six years of working with low-income project families for his unusual sensitivity to the problems of disadvantaged and inarticulate people, for his skill at handling complex human relations, and for his genuine respect for another person's point of view. A Negro, he had the deep respect of fellow workers, white and non-white.

At the time Searles brought Banks to the Redevelopment Land Agency there were virtually no precedents for the relocation job; the federal guides were sketchy. The District of Columbia was extremely fortunate in not suffering from the postwar housing shortage that plagued cities during redevelopment's early days. As white families moved to new homes in the suburbs, decent private housing in Washington was opening in many areas formerly closed to Negroes, who comprised 97.5 per cent of Area B's families. Moreover, the Board of Directors of the National Capital Housing Authority had passed a unanimous resolution to give priority to dislocatees in the low-rent projects and expected to build enough units to accommodate the eligible families from "B".

Banks defined his job as that of "helping families take advantage of the opportunities coming their way." Thus, he first needed a staff which understood low-income people and had faith in their potential to improve themselves.

One of the slum dweller's most critical handicaps is his low self-esteem. Banks knew that government action had frequently reinforced this feeling of inferiority. He told his four relocation technicians, none of whom were trained social workers, that their primary responsibility was to treat the residents with respect. Instead of just filling out forms, they were to encourage the dislocatees to tell their problems, and to listen to them carefully. Each person was to feel that the agency worker was his friend, and his welfare the chief concern. The staff was to provide little courtesies to minimize the inevitable hardships of moving.

A year before the great exodus was to start, Searles and Banks conducted a series of town-hall-style meetings in Southwest to answer residents' questions, describe rebuilding plans and explain what kind of moving help would be available. Simple brochures outlining procedures were distributed, and neighborhood leaders were helped to form a representative citizen committee. Ministers were briefed so they could inform their congregations.

Recognizing that there would be many problems which his staff alone could not handle, Banks set up a citywide advisory committee composed of more than a dozen public and private social agencies. During the first year of relocation, to prepare the receiving communities for the Southwest residents, he also made over one hundred talks before civic associations, luncheon clubs, church groups and neighborhood organizations throughout Washington. The message Banks conveyed to the community at large was the same one he gave to his staff: "Everybody wants to be somebody. With a little help, people can be better."

ANATOMY OF A SLUM

Three months before dislocation began, in the summer of 1953, Banks and his staff carried out a unique house-to-house "problem" survey. They wanted to learn each family's composition and income, its special housing needs, the situations that might prevent a successful move, and the worries. They also urged residents not to move until relocation help was available.

In spite of the advance publicity and meetings, many residents had not yet been reached. People greeted the government agents who came to interview them with hostility and slammed the door in their faces. Often the workers had to return two or three times to gather the desired information.

When the data were finally pieced together, it appeared that uprooting Southwest's residents would be like opening Pandora's box. Among the 1,176 families surveyed, there were 109 husbandless families, including 70 unmarried mothers, 154 illegitimate children, 31 common-law marriages and 43 adulterous family relationships. These situations, although tolerated in the slum, might be major obstacles to obtaining decent housing in other neighborhoods.

The survey also revealed that over 60 per cent of the families had incomes under $3,000 a year—below the level of poverty; of these, 487 earned less than $2,000 a year and 134 had no visible means of support. The large families—with as many as eleven children—presented the most difficult rehousing problem. The survey statistics, which carefully matched the size of a family to its income, showed that this group often could not even afford public housing's low rents. Families of two and three generations that had been living together would have to be split up into separate households to fit into uncrowded, standard quarters. Public housing accepts only nuclear families—parents and their children—not the extended family typical of lower-class groups. There were also about 300 older single people, many of them sick and disabled. Single people were not yet the agency's responsibility, according to federal law. But Banks felt that the agency could not ignore them.

In some clearance areas, mobility is high. The survey revealed the unusual, unexpected stability of people's residence in Southwest. Though only 12.6 per cent owned their homes, over half had lived there for twenty years or more, 18 per cent all their lives. Some families traced their residency back for generations. For many, redevelopment would mean destruction of a neighborhood where they had friends, deep roots and a sense of belonging.

Banks decided to start relocation in Dixon's Court—the largest and most densely populated alley in all Washington, an area noted for drunken brawls, prostitution and murders. Policemen patrolled the spot in pairs for their own safety. "I figured," Banks recalled, "that we would find every conceivable kind of problem there."

Surprisingly, the first and major problem turned out to be persuading families to forsake their wretched hovels. (The worst characters had left, by and large, before official relocation began.) They were reluctant to leave familiar surroundings and friends; afraid to move from the protective, accepting slum. Part of their fear was based on ignorance of the rest of the city. Many had been locked in Southwest for so long that they regarded other neighborhoods as foreign. Lacking knowledge of housing alternatives, they could see no advantage in moving. If some had once aspired to something better, they had abandoned the hope after repeated rebuffs. Many defended the slum.

Public housing was unusually well accepted in the District of Columbia, and the waiting lists were long. Yet the promise of a low-rent project apartment failed to budge some eligible Dixon's Court families. Mary White,* her husband and seven children were shoe-horned into a two-bedroom alley house that had no heat, electricity or hot water. They shared the backyard privy and faucet with neighbors.

Apartments for such large families are particularly hard to get. But when the relocation worker told Mrs. White that there was a four-bedroom apartment for her family in a project in Northeast, she said she'd like to think about it. Banks later found her with eyes red from weeping. It took several hours to fathom the cause of the tears. She had been born in Southwest and lived in Dixon's Court since childhood. She didn't know anyone "way out there" in Northeast.

Banks' policy was to let reluctant families remain until they became enthusiastic about the move, and to proceed meanwhile with other, readier families. Several months later Mrs. White came to the relocation office in the project area, looking sheepish. "It's just as bad here as there. All my friends are gone," she said. "You might as well move me, too." Mary White came back to visit the staff a number of times, her eyes glowing with happiness. She had found friends of hers living in the Northeast project, she said, and exclaimed, "I don't know how I could have done it without you!"

Relocation was particularly hard for the elderly. Matilda Rains and her cousin Augusta Simms, both in their seventies, lived in a rented two-story front house that was falling apart under them. Yet this had been Mrs. Rains' home for sixty years. Each time the agency offered them a one-story new apartment in a low-rent project, they tearfully but firmly rejected it—even though climbing the stairs at home was a trial. Finally Banks took the bewildered old ladies under his wing.

* The names used are fictitious.

He drove them around the neighborhood of still another project, showed them the churches, shops and other facilities, the pleasant view they would have from the sunny ground-floor apartment that had been offered them. When they complained about the icebox, he found them a new refrigerator. At last they accepted the inevitable and volunteered to move. Later, they cheerfully admitted, "We were just existing in that house."

False rumors about public housing's restrictions (many of these coming from families that had been evicted from public housing)—rumors that visitors were forbidden, that one could not own a radio, that lights must be turned off at a certain hour, and that the manager could walk into one's apartment with his own key at any time—had to be dispelled. Frequently, relocation workers took families by car to see a project and its neighborhood, to allay their objections and hesitation.

Still some held back because the Authority regulations or project layouts did preclude keeping a dog or some prized possession. One family valued its dining room suite more than decent housing. Another couple had recently acquired a handsome $365 gas range they had read about in magazines for years. They preferred to pay double the rent they could afford rather than give up this symbol of middle-class status. Banks encouraged the staff to help such families pool rentals with a relative or friend so they could have enough money among them for a decent private home.

Unlike most Dixon's Court families, Marcus Brown, a pensioner, and his sister, a domestic worker, kept their three-room house immaculate. But they were accustomed to Southwest's low rents. They rejected a $37-a-month public housing unit, utilities included, as too expensive. Why spend more than the $15 a month they had paid for twenty years? They had to be educated to the economy of the outside world, as well as the actual high cost of their own present arrangements. The relocation workers showed them that with the daily extra cash outlays they now made for fuel—two bundles of wood at twenty-five cents each, a bag of coal for fifty cents, half a gallon of oil for lighting and cooking for fourteen cents—their total shelter expense was actually $61 a month.

The Jeffersons were at another extreme. Between the husband's and wife's jobs they earned $6,000 a year. They could have left long ago. Their daughter, who attended high school out of the area, was ashamed to bring friends home. But the family had lived in Southwest since the grandfather's day, and all the father's cronies were there. With the redevelopment agency's help, they obtained a mortgage on a comfortable row house in Northwest. Once moved in, they maintained, "This is where we belonged all along."

Many families were too dirty for public housing. Poverty and ignorance had driven the Jones', rural Southern migrants, into their decrepit $20-a-month alley dwelling. Mr. Jones was a day laborer, Mrs. Jones a good-natured but slovenly woman. She recognized Dixon Court's bad influence on her four children, but she no longer tried to change things. Although she had lived in the District for twelve years she had not heard of public housing. Months of patient counselling and almost daily visits by a relocation worker were necessary before they could move to a low-rent project. The family became model tenants. The boys had a vegetable garden in back and Mrs. Jones kept her neat and comfortable five-room apartment with pride. "I've always wanted to live better," she asserted, "but I never had anything to do about it."

Some remarkable changes in attitudes took place as a result of relocation. A woman who had relied on public assistance to support her ten children when living in Dixon's Court found a job as a hospital orderly almost as soon as she learned they could move into a five-bedroom project apartment. A mother of five who deserted her children for days at a time when she lived in the alley joined the PTA when she moved to a better neighborhood. "When you accomplish one thing, the light dawns and other things become possible," Banks observed.

BEFORE THEY COULD MOVE

Fired with Banks' enthusiasm and example as well as their own interest, the staff frequently worked nights and weekends without extra pay. Sometimes they stayed after hours just to share their experiences.

At one such session, Banks learned about the Madisons—

another low-income family that refused to accept public housing. When Banks visited their home, a harassed Mrs. Madison poured out a long tale of family troubles. Her husband had just lost his job. There was never enough money to clothe the children decently. Her oldest daughter, an ungainly twelve-year-old who was disfigured by a chronic skin rash and suffered schoolmates' ridicule, had attempted suicide. But it took several more visits to discover the reason for their resistance: the father felt that his family was not good enough for public housing.

Before the Madison file was closed, the staff had referred the daughter to a mental health clinic, provided the family with decent clothing and furniture for their new home, found the father employment and built his self-esteem to the point where he would risk the move. Several years later the Madison family still lived in their project apartment and the daughter had enrolled at Vocational High to become a beautician.

The Agency maintained a family-need file to keep track of each specific social, physical or economic problem that prevented a family from moving to decent housing. When needs were met, a family was transferred to a progress file.

It soon became apparent that lack of furniture was the biggest single obstacle to satisfactory rehousing. One third of all families in "B" did not have beds, chairs and other basic pieces. Many had lived in rooming houses all their lives. The possessions of others were so dirty and decrepit they were best abandoned. Yet many families were so poor that they had barely enough money to feed and clothe themselves, much less to buy the home furnishings required by both public and private landlords.

To meet this emergency, Banks turned to the Salvation Army and Good Will Industries. When their furniture supply ran out, he appealed to the community at large. He invited Martha Strayer, a sympathetic reporter who had been covering redevelopment for the Washington *Daily News*, to visit some of the needy families. When her story appeared one quiet afternoon in August, two extra girls had to be put on the Redevelopment Agency switchboard and kept there for a week to write down the names and addresses of all the people who called. Storage soon became the problem, and donors were asked to hold the furniture until a family was to move. In all, twenty truckloads were gathered and about 200 homes were furnished. Banks reinterpreted official moving regulations to cover trips to the suburbs to pick up a bed or mattress. When the first supply ran out, other Washington newspapers helped and radio and television stations gave the furniture drive free publicity. The community's response remained generous. No family was prevented from moving for lack of furniture. Some married children were able at last to set up housekeeping away from their parents. The Washington Council of Churches subsequently assumed the responsibility for furniture.

One of the major changes necessary before moving was to formalize living arrangements. Public housing accepts only "natural," i.e. legal, family units. Some middle-aged couples who lived together as common-law husband and wife for years decided to legalize their relationship when decent housing came their way. A husband who had deserted his wife and children for another woman resumed his place as head of the family when offered a furnished home in a project.

Helen Jackson was thirteen years old and in the fifth grade when she had her first illegitimate child. When relocation worker Perry Holmes came to see her mother about moving, the pretty girl was seventeen, the mother of two, still unwed, and pregnant again. Her boyfriend, a nineteen-year-old house painter, was the father of all the children and helped support them with his $40-a-week salary. Holmes inquired why they didn't get married. Helen explained, "He can't afford it." Holmes told them, "You should get married, for the sake of yourselves and your children. That's the way we do things in America." He spent many evenings with them working out a budget that would allow them to live on the boy's income in a low-rent project.

When they finally agreed to marry, Holmes drove them to Maryland, so they could wed without the restrictions of the District. He also brought their parents along to give the necessary personal consent to the under-age couple's union.

Soon after Helen moved to the housing project—her honeymoon home furnished through donations and marriage license hanging on the living room wall—a worker from Planned Parenthood came by to invite her to the nearby clinic. Several years later, Helen's third child was two years old and another was not expected. She still regarded the transition from the slum as a miracle. "I'm so glad to have a house, I don't know what to do. It's the first house I ever had."

Inability to pay even public housing rentals was another big problem. In Southwest, unemployable men could eke out a few dollars for day-to-day survival by collecting and peddling junk and scrounging scraps of food from the nearby fish wharves and wholesale produce market. Semi-disabled men made a living with pushcarts. The temporarily unemployed could look to neighbors for a meal or a loan of fifty cents for bread and milk. With redevelopment, such marginal living would be difficult, if not impossible.

Before these residents could move into "decent, safe and sanitary" homes, a stable source of income had to be found for them. Jobs had to be located for able-bodied but untrained men. This was difficult, since no vocational retraining was available then, but the staff did find work for them. The old and disabled had to be put on public assistance. Many had not known they were eligible for this government help; not all were eager to take advantage of it. Some had to be reminded week after week before they would apply for assistance; many failed to keep appointments.

Often the apparent resistance to accepting help had its roots in past contacts with government or social agencies. Some had previously failed to secure needed assistance, had not been treated with sufficient respect, or had been kept waiting in line for hours. They did not want to submit again to such demeaning treatment.

As in other cities, relocation in Washington turned out to be a source of embarrassment to many public and private social and welfare agencies, which operated on the premise that the needy will seek out help, even though their offices were often miles from the slum neighborhoods. Many Southwest families were completely unknown to them. At first, citywide agencies were reluctant to get deeply involved with relocation. But even the neighborhood houses of Southwest seemed more interested in helping families to exist in the slum than to better themselves by moving.

Another obstacle to obtaining government aid were the preliminaries, among them the forms that had to be filled out by some who were illiterate. The relocation staff had to help old people get birth certificates and other proofs of age in order to establish eligibility for old-age assistance, or arrange for the physical examinations which were necessary before they could apply for public aid on the basis of infirmity. But many had no way of even getting to clinics; often the staff took them in their cars. People who had been lying in Southwest with a neglected heart condition, malnutrition or diabetes were brought to clinics by the workers for long overdue treatment. Abandoned children were placed in foster homes.

Interest in the families' readjustments was crucial. If a group of people had been helping one another in Southwest, the workers tried to get them moved into the same housing project. They would find baby sitters in new neighborhoods for working mothers. Project managers were informed about social agencies on which the relocatees had been relying. More than one mushrooming young family which knew nothing about modern birth control was tactfully referred to Planned Parenthood so they would not rapidly outgrow their new home. Tracking down and bringing to court fathers of illegitimate children in order to get financial support for their offspring was often necessary.

Two workers on Banks' staff devoted their full time to finding private housing, through the Real Estate Board, agents and other sources, but the entire staff combed the daily newspapers for listings. Each dwelling unit was visited before a family was referred there. Part of the job was to change unfavorable stereotypes which realtors and owners of multiple dwellings had about Southwest families.

A particularly difficult relocation problem was presented by the homeowner whose property, long since paid for, was worth only a few thousand dollars according to appraisers' estimates, but who could not purchase another home for such low compensation. It was equally hard for those who had paid an inflated price for deteriorating property. For these families the staff tried to find a two-family house where they could legally rent out an apartment and thus earn the needed extra income to pay off the mortgage.

Helping the many small businesses that were forced to move

was not the legal responsibility of the agency* But Banks asked the Washington Real Estate Board to provide the agency with information on new commercial locations. About forty-four businesses shifted operations, many expanding in more desirable areas. Thirty-three went out of business. Although this was against the will of some, a number of the older store owners were relieved to have the government purchase otherwise unsalable properties so they could retire. A middle-aged grocery store owner who had labored fourteen hours a day, seven days a week for the last eighteen years, took a job with a baked goods company; he could now follow a normal schedule for the same income, spending nights and weekends with his family.

The only person Banks relocated to another slum was an elderly white woman whose interest in life was sustained by the secondhand clothing business she ran in her apartment. The old lady steadfastly declined her son's offer to move in with his family and accept his support. But she could only stay in business in a marginal neighborhood. Banks found her another spot in Area C and fervently hoped she would retire before demolition got underway there. She did.

EDUCATION OF A PUBLIC ADMINISTRATOR

No doubt to many public officials, the compassionate regard for human problems that characterized Washington's relocation program seemed too time-consuming. But Banks, although a religious man, is no do-gooder. He was convinced, as a seasoned and objective veteran of many years' work in government housing and social welfare, that human compassion is an essential ingredient in a total program which "really spells growth."

His relocation record showed that sympathy, plus a large measure of ingenuity, guidance and patience on the staff's part, were probably more efficient and less costly than a strictly real estate or give-them-money-and-get-lost approach to rehousing slum dwellers. His service cost only $85 per family in staff time and moving expenses, compared, for instance, to $200 in Chicago, or to New

* Only in 1956 were moving expenses for businesses allowed. Originally the ceiling was $2,000; in 1962 the maximum became $25,000. Now it covers full cost if the locality agrees.

York City where hundreds of dollars are paid for moving bonuses and finders' fees.

Self-help and responsibility for one's fellow man were basic tenets in Barry Farms, the tract of hilly farm land in Southeast Washington where Jim Banks was born and raised. Barry Farms was a segregated, Negro community, but white visitors frequented the Banks' home. "If you work hard and behave decently," his father, a government supervisor, preached, "nothing will stop you."

At Howard University, Jim studied with the prominent, plain-spoken Negro sociologist E. Franklin Frazier, who discerned in the tall, serious-minded student an exceptional knack for grasping broad social issues. Frazier attracted him to housing and human relations. On graduation, Banks enrolled in the University's School of Social Work, where his first field assignment was in the public assistance division of the District Department of Welfare. Here he gradually came to understand that welfare recipients needed more than financial aid to become self-reliant.

Next he was assigned to the National Capital Housing Authority. There Banks came under another profound influence—the executive director John Ihlder, pioneer slum fighter and public houser, whose repeated question, "What about the people?" was famous. Ihlder set the tradition by which the National Capital Housing Authority took problem families and worked with them so they might improve and eventually "graduate" to private housing.

The Housing Authority offered Banks a full-time, civil service job as a tenant interviewer, and he accepted. Subsequently, the Urban League gave Banks a fellowship to complete his Social Work degree at the University of Pittsburgh.

Banks worked directly with slum families for the first time in Pittsburgh. "I learned then," he said, "the deep sense of loyalty and generosity among slum dwellers that doesn't exist elsewhere, and that social acceptance and friends are often more important than solid walls and plumbing." Back at the Housing Authority in Washington, he applied these insights to a new job as tenant counselor. When Schotts Alley was to be cleared for the new Senate office building, Banks was chosen to direct family relocation from this notorious slum. He was so successful that when the Redevelopment Land Agency was looking for the right man to handle Southwest, Banks' boss urged his appointment to the job.

How much the community appreciated the relocation results in Area B was shown in 1955, when the District League of Women Voters named Banks to receive its Citation Award for the outstanding service made to Washington that year. According to a long-time federal housing official, "Banks saved the conscience of the city."

UNSOLVED PROBLEMS

Although relocation from Area B seemed successful, Banks was too aware of situations left unsolved to be fully satisfied. As a result of the first area, he and his staff, as well as other agencies in the District, knew more about the problems and wanted to apply their knowledge to the next, much larger, task of relocating the 4,000 families in Southwest Area C. They saw particularly the need for developing coordinated inter-agency programs to meet the special needs of the estimated 15 per cent of Southwest's "multi-problem" families— so they would not continue to slip through the cracks in referrals from one specialized agency to another when they moved.

One particularly severe hardship case that publicly dramatized this need was Stella Saunders and her family, whom the relocation staff first found in Area B. There the seventy-four-year-old woman, her twenty-seven-year-old epileptic daughter and unkempt seven-year-old grandson lived like animals in an incredibly filthy two-room apartment. They slept in the clothes they wore during the day; they ate from the cooking pot with their fingers. The child had never attended school and could barely talk. The family's only income derived from a tiny pension left to Mrs. Saunders by her late husband. They warded off starvation with food scraps salvaged from the wharves and wholesale market.

Banks called on the Salvation Army to prepare them for public housing and transferred the Saunders' to a refurbished house in the project area, where they could be taught basic housekeeping.

Mrs. Saunders, on walking into the house with its electric lights, running water and bathroom, thought she had "died and gone to heaven." Their old clothes were burned and clean garments donated by the Washington Housing Association. The relocation worker got public assistance for the old woman and brought the boy to the attention of child welfare. Within a month, the Saunders' were prepared to move into a housing project.

Local newspapers wrote about their metamorphosis and often cited the Saunders' as an example of how people can be taught to live better. But after two years, Stella Saunders left public housing for a one-room rathole in Area C. Tears were in her eyes as she told the newspaper reporter who investigated the story about her sorrow and disgust at returning to the slums. But she had no choice. A reduction in her public assistance allowance had reduced her income to the point where she was paying over half of it for shelter and owed $62.40 in back rent,* and did not have enough left for food. At least in Southwest the family did not have to go hungry: they could eat scraps and still have $20 a month for rent.

To meet special problems such as these and to generally improve relocation techniques, Banks, in cooperation with the District Health and Welfare Council, proposed to the federal Urban Renewal Administration a two-pronged experimental Demonstration Project. Carried out in Washington over twenty months from 1958 to late 1960, this $289,000 study-action program was the first socially oriented research effort supported by the Housing and Home Finance Agency.† (A Washington foundation gave the required local one-third contribution.)

The project's primary aim was to reach, well in advance of moving, people with serious health or social problems that might prevent their satisfactory rehousing, or which might even be in-

* Relief recipients were required to pay full rent in public housing, to eliminate a double public subsidy and to enable the housing project, which must pay its operating costs out of rents, to remain solvent.

† In 1965, the Urban Renewal Administration officially ruled that the cost of diagnosing human problems in urban renewal areas and of enlisting and coordinating local health and welfare services to meet these problems would be paid out of federal funds allocated to renewal projects. The services themselves were not federally assisted, however.

tensified by moving. It was decided to give intensive casework to 198 specially selected multi-problem families living in Area C, and to follow a set of similar problem families as a control to measure the difference in improvement between those treated and those not. Five trained social workers, whose caseloads were reduced from an average of 200 to forty, plus a community relations organizer, a public-health nurse, a staff director and a clerical worker, concentrated their efforts for nearly two years on these families. The cooperation of some one hundred public and private agencies was also enlisted and their resources made available, as needed, for these and other parts of the program.

At the same time, the project tried to help normal families to choose better housing and adjust to new neighborhoods when they moved. Useful techniques from Area B were augmented by other community education programs and were offered to the 1,500 families remaining in Area C. For example, at small evening meetings on "Planning Your Move," realtors and FHA men advised prospective homeowners on how to buy a house and make a good purchase contract. Renters were told what to look for. Families eligible for public housing were taken on regular bus tours to see projects in different parts of the city so they might choose where to live. Project managers talked with them and answered questions. Former Southwest residents who had made successful moves came to tell about their own experiences, and staff directors from various civic agencies spoke on a volunteer basis, to assure them of their groups' concern.

In another community relations effort, workers were assigned to three different public housing projects where many Southwest people were to move. The aims were to help families adjust, assure that the public facilities and services they needed were available, and encourage relocatees once there to participate in community activities. At each project a "demonstration home," which showed techniques of furnishing and homemaking, also served as a welcome center for newcomers. The Urban League cooperated in a special six-month effort to overcome the antipathy of one midde-income neighborhood to a housing project. Despite the limited time, it was possible to bring the project residents and rest of the community together in a concerted improvement program.

LEARNING SELF-HELP

The Demonstration Project also tried to turn the period of waiting for official relocation assistance into a constructive experience by involving the residents more actively in their own destiny and in improving their environment.

A community that is being dismantled, such as a redevelopment area, can be deeply demoralizing to families waiting to move. Vagrants and vandalism become common in empty or partially demolished buildings. Just when the people most need support, local institutions pull out and the city seems to turn its back. But slum residents are not used to organizing to demand things for themselves. So the Demonstration staff helped them to form an Area C Citizens' Committee. Initially this proved useful just in letting residents air out their problems and worries. But tangible results of their organized complaints included increased police protection in the area and instruction given in rodent control.

This phase of the program was so obviously successful that in the next redevelopment site, Northeast 1, the District's Redevelopment Land Agency decided to start citizen organization much earlier and to make it more intensive. With staff help, block leaders were chosen to organize each street, and block groups met regularly in homes with a relocation worker to discuss community problems and possible solutions to them.

The people's unfamiliarity with self-help was touchingly revealed by one young woman who, when asked if she would volunteer for a project, replied, "I'll volunteer if you pay me." But the residents' success at turning an empty warehouse into a fully staffed recreation center to keep children from playing in abandoned houses—a project pushed through by the Relocation Advisory Council—revealed what could be done and created new self-confidence.

In fact, the center was better than any the underprivileged area had had before, and prompted one shy mother of five to comment, "Now I'll speak out and ask for things in my new neighborhood." Another member of the residents' organization said, "We never knew so many people cared for us."

Banks believed that this community organization program was the most effective part of the Demonstration project. Many people, he pointed out, tasted success for the first time in their lives, and went on to ask for other kinds of services and instructions. "When people begin to find solutions to their own problems, they have greater movement."

The Relocation Advisory Council also proved useful to District renewal officials in gaining community-wide acceptance of their program. Members of this representative body met monthly with the staff to keep abreast of relocation activities. As a consequence of their first-hand knowledge and contacts with many sections of the community, they could counteract false rumors or accusations against relocation and urban renewal.

The fact that a number of city agencies were continuing the reoriented social programs started under the relocation Demonstration Project was considered the greatest proof of success of the community organization effort, according to the official evaluation published in 1964. The Board of Education, for instance, still offered its new homemaking course at one public housing project, and the District's Department of Welfare was one of several that finally decentralized its services, putting workers into projects where its clients, relocated families and others, lived.

The biggest payoff from the community education endeavor, however, was judged to be in the demonstration families' selection of better housing, particularly the large number of eligible families that moved into public housing—the main type of standard housing that most could afford. In all, 82 per cent of the relocated families lived in standard homes now, compared to 25 per cent in Southwest, and 86 per cent stated that they liked their new homes better than Southwest. Greatest satisfaction was expressed by those who moved into public housing—61 per cent of the demonstration families chose public housing compared to 49 per cent of the control families. (Once there, however, the demonstration families did not keep house better or pay rent more regularly than did control families, which suggested that the Housing Authority still had a lot of work to do.)

For the future relocatees, meeting together in informal neighborhood discussion groups—whether it was to learn about homemaking, housing choices or urban renewal and the process of relocation—had an especially beneficial side effect. Even where there was no satisfactory answer to immediate problems, participating in the discussions and having the chance to verbalize their worries allayed fears and helped ease the shock of having to move.

TOO LITTLE, TOO LATE

For the "multi-problem" families, however, improvement was only of a limited nature, despite the intensive casework they received, and least so among the one third that had severe disabling habits or conditions to begin with. About 9 per cent of such families actually grew worse.

The deep-seated problems of these families prevented radical improvement during the relatively short period of service. In six out of every ten families receiving intensive casework, there was no real "family"; four out of ten with children were one-parent households. Forty-five per cent were chronically ill. Eight out of ten were Negro and had to face all the additional handicaps placed on them by society. The median schooling of the adults was five years. But the most prevalent problem was financial. Nine out of ten had incomes so low as to be eligible only for public housing, and four out of ten of these relied entirely on public assistance.

Finding a steady job for men with little schooling, a strong body and no skills was very difficult. Alcoholism was also common and hard to cure. Before one father could be persuaded to reduce his drinking enough to find steady work and raise his income, a total of 292 contacts, including twenty-nine office interviews, 108 home visits and the use of twenty-three community resources over fourteen months' time was necessary. But as G. Franklin Edwards, the Howard University sociologist who supervised the Demonstration, pointed out: "A community cannot afford such a reduced social work case load to get these results."

Even so, eight and a half months' average intensive work was a short time to deal with problems that had been evolving over fifteen, twenty or even forty years. When relocation from a slum is about to begin, it is already too late to deal with most basic problems of slum dwellers.

What will happen to the hundreds of thousands of slum families who will be dislocated in the next decade as the result of government programs? The innovations and beneficial results in Southwest Washington offered hope for achieving the improved housing and community participation of many. However, they also revealed the limitations of even a good relocation program (abetted by a strong dose of social work) and thus exposed some of the built-in, current limitations to city revitalization.

Southwest was not Washington's only slum; nor, of course, were the District's social problems confined to that area and its residents. Rather, problems were multiplying as the numbers of poor, untrained, disorganized Negro families in the District of Columbia mushroomed and overcrowded older houses and other neighborhoods.

Nor could even a good, socially sensitive relocation program continue for long unless a new supply of housing within the means of displaced families became available. In the District of Columbia, by the end of the 1950's, the supply of moderate-rental private housing was shrinking very quickly as various public improvement programs uprooted more and more families and reduced the supply of shelter and the market that could only pay low rents continued to grow. In fact, by the mid-1960's, Washington was one of the tightest private housing markets in the country.

The National Capital Housing Authority had already encountered serious problems in meeting its self-imposed responsibility for family rehousing. It could not build even the units originally programmed for urban renewal dislocatees because of the acute shortage of suitable building sites for new projects, much less make an appreciable dent in its waiting list. This list averaged 6,000 applicants by 1965, and the waiting time for large families with priority due to displacement by public action was four years or more. For families without such priority, the waiting time was "beyond a reasonable estimate."

In response to this increasingly critical situation, the Authority turned to a supplemental experimental device—buying or leasing existing private dwelling units for sublease to large low-income families. Even so, the fiscal solvency of the Authority's projects was endangered because so many of its tenants were at the bottom of the economic ladder; those waiting to get in were similarly deprived. To pay for the extra social services occupants required, the Authority had to stretch its operating funds. (These extras were not financed by the federal public housing subsidy.) In 1962, the Board was reluctantly forced to raise both its minimum and maximum income ceilings for applicants, just to balance its budget, although this ran contrary to the Authority's social purpose and the recognized family needs in the District.

Meanwhile Assistant Renewal Commissioner Banks, given the opportunity to devise programs for dealing with the underlying causes of the social problems that relocation almost inevitably comes across too late, in 1963 became director of the United Planning Organization, a new District of Columbia agency created to deal with these pressing matters on a citywide basis.

6

WHO LIVES WHERE ■ Urban Housing and Discrimination

Sooner or later, one must get to the root question of where and how people live, and whether there is enough housing to meet their needs.

It bears stating that urban renewal—although part of the Housing Act of 1949—has not been, and is not of itself, a housing program. From the time that Title I began until June 1965, 311,197 dwelling units were demolished on urban renewal project sites and only 166,288 were built or are planned in their place.* Moreover, 35 per cent of all Title I funds now go to predominantly nonresidential projects. Rehabilitation and code enforcement, while they improve the housing stock that remains, tend to further reduce the net supply available to present tenants.

* These official figures include only committed land in Title I projects.

Add to such official renewal efforts other concurrent public improvement programs: highways often cut a path through cities' deteriorated areas; private activities—clearance for office buildings, parking lots, plant expansion—rip out housing but do not replace it. The total decrease in living space is formidable. Officials estimate that each year, nationally, as many as 300,000 dwelling units are demolished for all such purposes. Further, private demolition activities outweigh all public programs in volume, three to one.

In this total picture, urban renewal is relatively insignificant—although it has received the lion's share of blame by the public for destroying and not replacing low-income housing. Yet, because of its legal relocation requirements, the renewal program must concern itself with an adequate standard local housing supply, priced within reach of the dislocated, and it must compete with many others for such suitable vacancies as exist.

There has been much talk on the national level about the amount of new units that must be created annually in order to house adequately the 13,400,000 households living in substandard or overcrowded dwellings (as of the most recent national census); to keep up with the needs of the country's expanding population; and to retire obsolete housing. The consensus is that some 2,000,000 dwelling units must be produced a year, as compared to the average annual production during the past few years of only 1,500,000.

There is a vagueness, however, about what kind of housing should be produced for whom, at what cost, and where; how much government and private enterprise should or can be expected to do; and what localities can and might do to make up this deficit. We lack the machinery to make sure that enough housing exists to meet the needs of various unserved or underserved groups, especially at middle- and lower-income levels. The federal housing programs are a congeries of devices put together since 1934 to meet special needs (not all of them housing) and to accommodate special interests, pressures and ideologies. The special assistance programs that have been added since 1961 still do not implement the idealistic national housing policy enunciated in the preamble to the Housing Act of 1949—"a decent home and a suitable living environment for every American family."

Primarily, we have relied on the profit motive offered by private enterprise, with some cushioning by the Federal Housing Administration. This has not proved to be a reliable mechanism for generating adequate housing, especially for moderate- and low-income city families. We have an annual production gap of 500,000 dwelling units, and between 1950 and 1960 the number of substandard units in use in cities decreased by only 10 per cent. (While many slum buildings were demolished, other housing deteriorated.)

The point is that special-assistance housing is produced not nationally, but locally, where the lack of machinery becomes strikingly clear. Few states have housing agencies or programs. Cities just have pieces of programs vested in separate empires. One of these, the urban renewal agency (which may or may not be an independent authority), has the responsibility for tearing down obsolete buildings or encouraging their rehabilitation, and for getting private investors or owners to build on a specified site or to repair—hopefully with the cooperation of the FHA and local banks—according to official plans.

The public housing authority, another local but independently constituted body, also clears slums. It, however, has direct government financing available to build or rehabilitate low-rent housing. Federal law requires that priority be given in these low-rent projects to people eligible by income who have been displaced by urban renewal and by public housing itself. But this requirement does not insure the dislocatees' admission. It does not guarantee that the units will be built and ready when families are to be dislocated several years hence, or even that the units will be of the right size to accommodate those displaced.

Of the 126,632 families on the urban renewal relocation workload since Title I began who were eligible for public housing, only one third have been rehoused in low-rent units. (Only a handful of renewal sites have been used for public housing, though during the past few years the numbers planned have been on the rise.) Gaining construction of new city housing specifically priced for middle-income families who earned too much for admission to low-income projects but not enough to afford decent private housing was almost impossible until passage of the Housing Act of 1961.*

Yet even public housing, for reasons we shall explore, fails to serve its market. By 1966, all the units built since the program began could house only 605,000 families, or 2,290,000 people, but some 11,000,000 urban families had incomes below the median maximum admission limits of public housing.

The Federal Housing Administration is the only national public agency which has the means for encouraging the production of housing for the middle-income market in cities. But it is constituted to serve the private builder, not the public, and FHA and the urban renewal agency have often been on opposite sides of the fence. Moreover, cities do not have agencies specifically set up to program the FHA aids, a gap which urban renewal agencies are only beginning to fill as new housing assistance is legislated.

THE FILTER PROCESS AND DISCRIMINATORY PRACTICES

Central cities usually have to rely on what is known in the housing field as the filter process to create vacancies in standard housing for families of lower incomes.

Filter process describes the way in which the normal housing market should work. According to the theory, as new housing is built, families who can afford to pay more vacate older units which then become available to families of a somewhat lower income who are on their way up the economic ladder and who in turn move out of still less desirable quarters. The oldest and worst housing will then be taken off the market voluntarily by its owners since there is no longer a demand for it and it should no longer be profitable, as rents are reduced to the level of new

* Until the 1961 Act, the only tool available for such middle-income families was the now discarded Section 221, under which FHA offered insurance for private builders who put up minimal relocation housing in ordinarily questionable sites. So few builders were interested in this unprofitable housing that it produced only 5,342 multiple-family units and 21,988 home units—most of the latter were rehabilitated, not new, and, due to the problems of timing, very few were actually occupied by displaced families. The 1961 Act also eased admission of those with incomes slightly in excess of the public housing limits.

tenants' pocketbooks. The filter process does work, but only to a point.

First, not enough new housing is being built, especially for moderate- and low-income families, to create the full supply upon which the filter theory is predicated and the voluntary retirement of dilapidated or obsolete housing depends.

Secondly, where vacancies exist, families too often cannot afford the rentals at legal occupancy standards. Many must pay far more than one quarter of their income for shelter. Owners, in order to accommodate the new market and still squeeze their usual annual return from properties which have probably been depreciated several times, will divide larger living units into smaller ones. They convert old single-family homes into multiple-family use, allow more people to live in an apartment than should according to the law, or lease space in structures which should be torn down. Landlords also cut costs by reducing maintenance on such buildings.

They may thus solve the immediate shelter problem of the families, and even do so legally if a city's code specifications are not too exacting or systematically enforced. Such practices, however, prolong the life of unfit housing, create newly overcrowded housing (not to overlook the schools and neighborhoods which serve them) and spread the blight and decay which comprehensive urban renewal is supposed to eliminate.

A closely related and increasingly significant reason for the failure of the filter process is that the private housing market does not work freely for the growing non-white portion of the urban population. Instead, it excludes this sector from a substantial part of the housing supply and then exploits their situation.

The effect of discriminatory practices by the real estate, home building and mortgage lending industries was authoritatively studied and documented for the first time during the late 1950's and early 1960's by two sets of nationwide investigations—one conducted under the auspices of the Ford Foundation-sponsored Commission on Race and Housing, the other by the United States Commission on Civil Rights.* Although they found

* *Report of the U.S. Commission on Civil Rights* 1959 and *1961 Commission on Civil Rights Report, Book 4: Housing,* Superintendent of Doc-

differences between regions and among some cities, and although the studies for the Commission on Race and Housing were undertaken prior to the 1960 census, the situation has remained so unchanged (the census corroborated the general findings) for the vast majority of non-whites—who have since grown in number in cities—and it is sufficiently similar in cities across the country that the basic facts should concern anyone who is interested in the future of American cities.

The studies found that the typical non-white family receives less for its rental dollar than the white family, whatever its income level or social position. And since the large majority of non-white families are renters, the ramifications are serious. They must pay a higher proportion of family income, as much as 50 per cent more, to obtain smaller, inferior accommodations* and are forced into significantly more overcrowding. Three times as many Negroes live in structurally substandard housing, in inferior neighborhoods, and overcrowding is four times more common than among white families.

Generally the quality of housing occupied by non-white families has improved markedly since 1950—as has that of white families. But the big gap separating the standard of accommodations occupied by the two groups has remained substantially unchanged. (A 1963 report on *Our Non-White Population and Its Housing* published by the Housing and Home Finance Agency revealed that the number of overcrowded white families decreased by 200,000 while the number of overcrowded units occupied by non-white families during the 1950's increased from nearly 1,000,000 to 1,300,000, even though the total proportion decreased.)

Because Negroes can often get more for their housing dollar as homeowners than as renters, they purchase at much lower incomes than do whites. But this impulse to homeownership is

uments, Government Printing Office, Washington D.C. The major studies prepared for the Commission on Race and Housing and the Commission's final report, *Residence and Race*, were published by the University of California Press, 1960.

* The lowest-income centers, who form the bulk of urban non-whites, commonly have to pay a much larger percentage of their income for shelter than do whites of similar economic status. It is not uncommon for big city landlords to charge and obtain a bonus for allowing non-whites to rent their substandard accommodations.

exploited by realtors who capitalize on the fear they have inculcated in white property owners about minority groups' allegedly depressing effect on property values. By engaging in "block-busting," the realtor scares white families into selling their homes at panic prices by bringing a Negro family into a street. He then exploits the pent-up demand of Negroes for decent homes in better neighborhoods by selling them houses he has acquired at deflated values at inflated prices. Mark-ups by block-busters as high as 112 per cent were revealed in hearings conducted in 1962 by the New York City Commission on Human Relations.

But the lending institutions really determine who lives where, because they hold the key to financing home purchase. The U.S. Commission on Civil Rights found that banks operated "on the premise that only a homogeneous neighborhood can offer an economically sound investment," and banks thus would withhold mortgages for a "first purchase" by a Negro in a white neighborhood. Once a neighborhood began to change, however, the Commission found that the banks would do "everything they can to expedite" the trend, including withholding mortgages from prospective white purchasers in those areas. Moreover, even when a Negro was fully qualified as a credit risk, lenders might charge him a higher discount on his loan or not issue one at all.

Such practices perpetuate the fear of white families that when a Negro family moves into their neighborhood, the area will inevitably become predominantly non-white. Professor William Grigsby of the University of Pennsylvania's Institute for Urban Studies has pointed out: "It is the pattern of market segregation which itself causes the inundation that whites observe and fear. In other words, since only a few areas are available to the expanding non-white population, when a new section 'opens up,' non-white demand tends to focus at this point of limited supply. In such a situation, a quick transformation from white to Negro occupancy frequently occurs."

The suburban "white noose" is another major reason the normal market process does not work. Housing is a metropolitan commodity and almost all new housing since the war has been put up in the suburbs. But scarcely any of it has been sold to non-whites. It is held that the tract developers, who put up most new housing, fear the effect that an open-sales policy would have upon their white customers.

Suburban pressures have discouraged new interracial housing tracts. A builder who endeavors to put through such a development against the opposition of local property owners finds that town and village governments can employ a host of subterfuges —large-lot zoning, the withholding of building permits, failure to install necessary water and sewer lines, even condemnation of a proposed building site for a park or other public use—without excluding him directly. Also, his usual sources of financing may dry up. At the same time, suburban realtors, like those in cities, refuse to show homes to Negro house hunters unless these are in "changed" areas.

Even new homes built privately with government mortgage guarantees or insured loans have not served the Negro market in proportion to its size. Only one per cent of the government-insured homes constructed since World War II was purchased by non-whites, although Negroes comprised 10 per cent of the population. Generally, this one per cent was located in segregated developments, or substandard locations to which white families did not have to resort. In addition, most suburban housing was and is priced beyond the Negro market; this is a matter to which we shall return.

For many years, the Federal Housing Administration itself contributed to these patterns of residential segregation. It actually recommended restrictive covenants until the Supreme Court outlawed them in 1948, and before 1949, its underwriting manual, which governs insuring practices, warned against "adverse influences from lower-class infiltration and inharmonious racial groups." Although the FHA officially changed its policies, during the big postwar suburban building boom the home building industry still acted on the former basis and the federal agency did little to police them; thus the FHA allowed the suburbs to become more lily-white, and deprived the growing number of potential Negro home purchasers of the attractive terms of supposedly color-blind government insurance.

As white families left the drab older sections of cities for new and better homes in the suburbs, Negro families moved into these areas. In effect, these Negro families made possible the departure of the white families and the volume of new construction in suburbs to be sustained, although they could not benefit from it directly. The growing Negro middle class has, in fact, been denied a status symbol of major significance in the American way of life.

The metropolitan schism that has developed as a result can be seen at its extreme in the Washington D.C. area, which has a total of 2,000,000 people. The District of Columbia itself, with a population of 764,000, is 54 per cent Negro; the suburbs, with more people than the metropolitan area, is 93 per cent white.

The effect of all these forces on the Negro's housing has been that the neighborhood where he may buy is usually older and lower in value, as is his home, which is thus a poorer lending risk. His down payment must be larger in proportion to what he buys, his repayment period is shorter, and interest charges are often higher. Refusal by banks to lend in some older or changing neighborhoods has frequently forced minority home purchasers to resort to loan sharks who charge outrageous terms, and to buy on insecure contract sales that do not give the owner title to a property until it is fully paid for. If he defaults one payment, he loses the house and his whole investment. Moreover, the non-white has less money left to spend on the higher cost of maintaining such an older property.

So lending, building, realty and even government practices have increased segregation and perpetuated the stereotypes of the Negroes as poor homeowners and neighbors who have a depressing effect on property values. They also have encouraged the deterioration of properties and neighborhoods to the detriment of entire communities, and furthered the segregated use of schools and other public facilities.

Yet the findings of a landmark study, *Property Values and Race,* undertaken for the Commission on Race and Housing refuted the time-honored myth about racial intrusion deflating property values. This ten-year study of twenty middle-aged neighborhoods in seven cities, carried out by Luigi Laurenti and published in 1960, was the first to isolate the effect on the price of homes of non-white entry into a formerly white neighborhood. Laurenti's authoritative work concluded that minority purchasers, far from depressing values, tended to stabilize or even to raise them.

His research has since been corroborated by other studies, the most extensive being a ten-city survey of the *Midwestern Minority Housing Market* for the Advance Mortgage Corporation. Its 1963 report stated: "Property values in neighborhoods in racial transition generally held their own or rose above the neighboring norm, thus refuting a long-held stereotype." Price declines occurred in contiguous white neighborhoods which had been "written off by one market and not yet entered by another."

CHANGING TIMES AND NEW LAWS

All this suggests that it is essential to fight such blind discrimination if cities are to be renewed, civil rights to be achieved and the metropolitan schism to be ended.

It is difficult to draw a clear line between the pernicious discriminatory practices described and the actual, alleged or exaggerated fears and prejudices of white families. But it appears that the attitudes and practices of white families, at least those in the suburbs, may be changing more rapidly than those of the shelter industry.

National polls over the past decade show a steady increase (to more than 50 per cent) in the white people who say they would not object or leave if a Negro family moved next door. No doubt, events of the early 1960's—the civil rights marches, the sit-ins, Birmingham, the Federal Civil Rights Law of 1964—contributed significantly to a new feeling that integration is inevitable, and created a sense of guilt in those who would discriminate—or at least admit they would.

What is particularly interesting and relevant is that a 1966 poll by the Louis Harris organization found upper-income and suburban whites to be far more liberal in their attitudes toward Negroes than the poor and less educated whites in cities. Perhaps this is so because, as *Newsweek* magazine commented, they are "farthest removed from the struggle." The Harris poll found that a 54 per cent majority in the cities would object to having a Negro move next door. The jeers, curses and bottles hurled at open-housing demonstrations led by the Reverend Dr. Martin Luther King through all-white, working-class neighborhoods in Chicago in the summer of 1966 were attributed by King largely to unfounded fears in lower-income enclaves that Negroes create slums and threaten their jobs.

On the other hand, a concurrent report on integration progress in metropolitan Kansas City, Kansas by the *Kansas City Star* found that, in the four years since 1962, Negro families of modest incomes had moved into twenty-six working-class white neighborhoods which were broadly dispersed throughout the city and neighboring county at some distance from the central city ghetto. The paper found that in most cases "little hostility has been expressed," there was little evidence of panic selling, property values remained stable and whites continued to buy. Virtually all of the newcomers matched, and in some cases exceeded, their white neighbors in income and education. Negroes comprise one tenth the population of metropolitan Kansas City.

One of the most impressive manifestations of the new atmosphere has been the mushrooming of local fair housing councils. The main purpose of these voluntary organizations is to help Negroes move into white neighborhoods, metropolitan and suburban, by locating for them homes outside ghetto areas which they would not be able to find if they relied on realtors' services. In 1959 there were only eighteen such committees; in early 1964 they numbered 400; by the end of 1965 there were over 1,000 in metropolitan areas across the country. (The Greater Kansas City Council on Religion and Race conducted a door-to-door canvas and received signed pledges from 14,000 people, along with a dollar from each; this paid for a three-and-a-half-page testimonial for fair housing published in the *Star* and carrying all of their names. The effort was believed to be the first in the country in which supporters' names were published, and perhaps it helps explain the area's good record of integration.)

The more favorable social tide is also supported by the growing body of laws and enforcement powers that make metropolitan housing available legally on an open-market basis. In 1962, when the President's executive order barring discriminatory practices in all federally aided housing went into effect, it supplemented similar laws that already existed in many northern and western cities and states. By December 1965, seventeen states and twenty-eight cities had laws against discrimination in the sale or lease of existing and new non-assisted *private* units; some laws even covered single-family houses in new tract development.

A particularly significant early application of such a statewide law took place in Levittown, New Jersey, after the courts ordered Levitt and Son, the builders, to abide by the state's open-occupancy law which governs sale or rental of ten or more contiguous houses. About thirty or forty non-white families purchased homes, and the merchant builders continued to construct and sell new homes in as profitable an operation as before.

A number of cities and even states have also tried to use the power of local government to curb block-busters by threatening to revoke their real estate licenses. Among these localities are Baltimore, Buffalo, Detroit, San Francisco, and suburban Shaker Heights, Ohio, outside Cleveland. The states include Connecticut, New York, Pennsylvania and Ohio, with Illinois most recent on the list.

A White House-sponsored bill which would, for the first time, have prohibited discrimination in the sale or rental of private, non-assisted housing failed; not enough Senators voted to end filibuster on the measure, thus killing hopes for passage. That a comprehensive open-housing ordinance should long ago have been made a federal administrative requirement in cities' "Workable Programs of Community Development"—at least just as much as building, zoning and housing codes—seems obvious, since housing discrimination is known to lead to overcrowding, inadequate property maintenance and new slum formation.

But recent experience in the area of housing indicates that we have put too much faith in the prohibitory power of laws. A great deal must be done, from the federal level on down, to make fair-housing laws effective. Experts generally believe that these laws must be accompanied by professionally staffed agencies, adequate budgets, active educational programs for both whites and non-whites, and aggressive enforcement machinery that does not rely solely on complaints. Ideally, the laws and programs should be effective on a metropolitan basis and, where federal programs are involved, the federal government should help pay the administrative cost. These conditions, unfortunately, do not coexist in any area.

One can only guess at how a federal fair-housing law might be implemented. The National Committee Against Discrimination in Housing found that after four years, the long-awaited President's 1962 executive order had "scarcely made a dent on segregation." The order was not retroactive, and thus it affected only that small portion of all housing built with federal assistance since 1962. Further, there was practically no budget, staff or enforcement machinery in the body set up to administer the order, and each federal housing agency was left to police its own programs—with widely varying results. The Urban Renewal Administration was particularly conscientious. It withheld funds from California renewal projects which were not yet in loan and grant contracts after passage there in 1964 of Proposition 14,* a measure by which the voters not only repealed the state's fair-housing laws, but also prohibited localities from passing ordinances making discrimination illegal.

Even without the force of laws, however, the number of new suburban developments marketed on an interracial basis continues to grow. Conservative forces may be strong as in California, where a two-to-one vote passed Proposition 14. But Eichler Homes, one of California's most active and prosperous tract builders, continued to sell to anyone who wished to buy, without concern for racial quotas, even in some of the very communities whose residents contributed most to the passage of Proposition 14.

The Advance Mortgage Corporation found that in midwestern cities a new attitude was emerging among institutional lenders as a result of their "mounting and generally favorable experience with non-white borrowers," and that restrictions on financing for Negro purchasers in white neighborhoods had diminished. But, as the report stated, the lenders had "grown more interested in serving the non-white market as the volume of white loans has dwindled in cities." The survey also found that "the Negro popu-

* In 1966 California's Supreme Court found Proposition 14 unconstitutional. Real estate interests are appealing the decision to the United States Supreme Court.

lation of almost every midwestern city is more concentrated than before, and the integration that did take place was by default of the white market. . . ." *

What most of the reports on increased Negro dispersion in cities do not say, however, is that the white population that remains in or next to areas that are becoming racially integrated is generally older, with grown children.

URBAN RENEWAL AND INCOME RESTRAINTS

Where does urban renewal fit into this picture? A number of the earlier Title I redevelopment projects replaced generations-old slum ghettos with developments that offered the best values in private rental housing marketed without discrimination. As a result, these have been outstanding showcases for integrated living in central cities. The value of this achievement depends on a person's class and perspective. (We will come to the newer neighborhood conservation projects later in this chapter.)

In 1950, when part of the decaying "Black Belt" on Chicago's South Side was being cleared for redevelopment, the action was met with demonstrations and cries against racial discrimination. Yet a decade later, white and Negro families lived next door to each other in Lake Meadows and Prairie Shores, the first and second new housing developments in the area, and even had cocktails and dinner together in the project's new community center.

In fact, the first group of buildings in Lake Meadows were tenanted primarily by Negroes; yet the sponsor of Prairie Shores found no resistance on the part of white families moving into his apartments, although they knew the housing was to be racially integrated, and that Lake Meadows was predominantly Negro in occupancy. No doubt the fact that Prairie Shores' sponsor, Fred Kramer, a well-known mortgage banker and civic leader, resided in the development himself and personally showed apartments to prospective tenants, was an important contributing factor. So was

* FHA states that its big current business is in refinancing housing in cities; thus central-city Negroes may enjoy government's equal terms. (New house construction generally has declined.)

the proximity of Michael Reese Hospital, with its built-in market of white nurses and doctors. (Again, the number of families with school-age children was limited.) Kramer's rent schedule of $30 a room—achieved by bringing in equity partners who were willing to accept a reasonably moderate return on their money, acquiring the land for fifty cents an acre, and winning the city's cooperation on taxation—made Prairie Shores the best new rental value in town. The attractive layouts of the apartments and the conveniences serving them helped to make the development desirable for white families with wider housing alternatives.

In fact, Kramer's apartments were an excellent demonstration of the common denominators in housing developments successfully integrated from the start that were found by Eunice and George Grier; their analysis, *Privately Developed Interracial Housing,* was another study carried out for the Commission on Race and Housing. The best way of insuring white demand for residence and ownership in an integrated community, the study showed, was to create a development outstandingly attractive in appearance, location and facilities and excellent in value.

Yet, despite its central location and unusual open-occupancy policy in the "most segregated" city in the country, Prairie Shores was far from overwhelmed by Negro applicants, even though virtually no new private housing was available for them elsewhere in the metropolitan area. The developer said that he had to go out of his way to find non-white tenants to achieve even a 20 per cent ratio. He attributed the limited demand primarily to lack of income on the part of Chicago's Negro population. The original portion of Lake Meadows seemed to have absorbed the bulk of the non-white market for rental housing in the $30-to-$35 a-room range. Here, as in other urban renewal projects built without special government financial assistance to lower housing costs (and also in suburban developments), the high price of new housing itself placed a ceiling on the degree of integration.*

* A Chicago human relations leader asserts that the Negro market for such rents is greater than the units available and that "occupancy controls" are used to maintain balance. But he does not dispute that where the metropolitan housing market is not open, a developer who wants meaningful integration must make special efforts to keep substantial white occupancy. The fact is sophisticated civil rights groups believe it important for Chicago to have a showcase for integration.

The "thinness" of the non-white market for both new sales and rental housing throughout the country has been reported by builders and lenders. Economics is one of, if not *the,* major barriers. In fact, the report on the *Midwest Minority Housing Market* found that "the spread between white and non-white incomes remains so great, they would have to be treated as distinct markets even if no other limiting factors existed."

When the Griers undertook their study in the late 1950's, they found that "if all new private housing were open to Negroes, only a few would take advantage of it"—about 5 per cent. "And only a slight and statistically unimportant degree of integration would result." The Advance Mortgage Corporation's survey of midwestern cities revealed that under 5 per cent of the homes bought by Negroes were new.

Since the time of these surveys, there has been an increase in the number of Negro families in the middle-income bracket, and it is estimated that since those surveys the number of Negroes in the new home market has doubled. (A minimum income of $7,000 a year is considered necessary to purchase a new home on the most favorable terms. By 1964, 12.7 of the non-white urban families were in that category, although various circumstances precluded all from actually being in the market.)

But the Griers point out that the overall situation has not changed significantly. While there is a great proportionate increase at the upper levels, there is "no real narrowing of the gap between white and Negro in the new home market." (The median income of the non-farm *white* family in 1964 was $7,045 —$3,000 more than that of the non-white, and much of the latter was attributable to multiple wage earners in a family.)

This is a matter of particular importance to integration; experience shows that it is much easier to establish a new integrated neighborhood or development than to prevent transition to segregation in an old neighborhood.

But fair-housing committees have found that, in spite of the recent "spectacular rise" in Negro homeownership, more homes in established white neighborhoods are available to Negro purchasers than there are applicants. Part of this surprisingly weak demand is due to the high cost of the housing. But it is also attributable to the reluctance of many Negroes to be "pioneers"

—to subject their family to rebuffs, insults and even physical violence in potentially hostile neighborhoods, and to the human desire to live near family and friends. Karl and Alma Taeuber point out in *Negroes in Cities* (1965) that "it seems impossible to separate coercive and voluntary components of racial segregation." Evidently personal factors have outweighed a desire on the part of many Negroes to escape segregated living; this underlines the need for programs to encourage and inform, within both ghetto areas and white communities.

"Minor gains must be measured against tremendous losses": the situation was thus described by the 1965 Fair Housing Conference.* Although there is more movement into mixed or previously white communities, and although the number of new interracial city and suburban developments grows, segregation is growing faster, and Negro concentration in central cities is steadily increasing.

The magnitude of the trend can be seen in an estimate of what would be necessary to reverse it in Washington D.C. made by George Schermer,† a national expert in the human relations field.

In the Washington metropolitan area, he reported non-white families have been increasing at the rate of 6,000 annually, and the ratio is accelerating so quickly that between 1960 and 1980 it will average 8,800 a year. But no more than 100 non-whites a year are finding houses on a truly integrated basis throughout the metropolitan area.

Schermer found that if the area were to simply freeze ghettos at their present size and integrate only the additional families, it would be necessary to accommodate 8,800 non-white families annually in suburban areas. But if the District of Columbia were to reestablish a fifty-fifty racial balance by the year 2000, some 12,000 non-white families would have to be accommodated in the suburbs every year for the next thirty-five years; 4,000 white families annually would have to be attracted into the District.

"Of course, the numbers bit is only part of it," Schermer

* Held by the National Committee Against Discrimination in Housing and the Phelps Stokes Fund Inc.

† In a report made for a 1966 conference held by the National Committee Against Discrimination in Housing.

added. "There must [also] be equalization of buying power, restructuring of community and service facilities in suburban areas to meet the needs of low and moderate income families, and the revitalization of central city areas to attract middle class families."

The 1965 Fair Housing Conference, believing that the fair-housing movement had failed to make more of an impact largely because of its "middle-class nature," decided that first priority must be given to "a sharp increase in the supply of low- and middle-income housing located especially in areas which are predominantly white." The National Committee Against Discrimination in Housing began working in 1966 with local anti-poverty groups to encourage low-income Negroes to move out of ghettos.

But since private industry produces almost nothing for families with incomes under $7,000—and about 87 per cent of the urban Negro families fit into that category—publicly assisted housing is required.

More than prohibitory laws are needed, and financial assistance from government is required if the pattern of growing central city ghettos is to be reversed or even reduced. But the big problem, after getting the necessary housing programs, is how to put them to use in the larger metropolitan area.

NEW HOUSING TOOLS AND GOVERNMENT ASSISTANCE

A major step in filling the cost gap between housing produced by the private market and public housing was taken by Congress in 1961 with a new FHA program, Section 221(d)3, more familiarly known as (d)3. This was the first federal housing program specifically created to encourage private construction of rental or cooperative housing priced for the low-middle-income market, within or outside of urban renewal areas.

Although it was not legislated specifically for the non-white market, (d)3 housing has inevitably met that market's needs to a much greater extent than had earlier FHA programs like 220. Moreover, with the signing of the President's order in 1962 banning discrimination in federally assisted housing, units built under this program were all to be marketed on an open-occupancy basis.

Section 221(d)3 lowers the cost of housing by making the below-market interest rate the government pays—which varies from 3 to 4 per cent—available to finance construction, with sponsorship restricted to non-profit or limited-profit corporations and cooperatives. The program does not require private financing beyond the small 2 per cent cash equity required from the sponsor. Congress authorized the Federal National Mortgage Association* to buy all the (d)3 permanent mortgages. The program thus reduces the single largest item in shelter cost, the debt service, by as much as one third, and it results in monthly savings to the tenant or cooperator of between $15 and $25 an apartment. Occupancy is limited by law to moderate-income families.

In the first four years of the program, 45,000 units of (d)3 housing were contracted for—a marked improvement over earlier FHA special-assistance programs. For a number of urban renewal projects initiated under higher-rental programs such as 220, it made the difference between success and failure.† In many renewal neighborhoods, it would be impossible to build for the

* The Federal National Mortgage Association (FNMA) is an instrument of the federal government intended to provide a "secondary" mortgage market for government-insured or guaranteed programs. Under Congressional mandate, it may also buy mortgages for such housing in urban renewal areas or for other specific types of housing designated by Congress or deemed to be in the public interest by the President where the private mortgage market does not fill the need.

† One such early project, Park Town in Cincinnati, provides an interesting case. When originally marketed by its sponsor, the Reynolds Metals Company, as a cooperative at full market interest rates, only 20 per cent of the units were sold. One reason for such poor sales was the relatively undesirable location. But after (d)3 was enacted and the sponsor shifted the project to this lower-cost financing, sales in the project rapidly went up to 80 per cent of occupancy.

The change in financing also brought about a market shift in the racial composition of the tenancy. Park Town had been marketed on an open-occupancy basis from the start, but the higher-cost 220 housing was 40 per cent white, and the lower-cost (d)3 housing 16 per cent. The portion of whites has not gone over 20 per cent since.

The change in racial composition was believed to be due in good part to the low-income ceilings Congress imposed on (d)3 housing. Granted the project remained integrated, but many more Negro families were now eligible than before. Conversely many of the original white tenants were now excluded. And Negro families, having fewer housing choices available to them than white families, were far more likely to move in there.

market without (d)3. In fiscal 1966 applications were made for 30,000 new units, and the Housing Department estimated there would be 45,000 in fiscal 1967.

Still, (d)3 presents certain difficulties. One of these is finding qualified sponsors. Church groups, settlement houses, foundations and other groups which typically sponsor such non-profit housing lack the necessary skills for developing and managing such real estate undertakings, and the FHA does not have the staff to compensate for this lack. Local offices drag processing; they worry about defaults and Congress. In some cities, the local urban renewal agency helps guide these new housing sponsors. A national technical advisory service on the local level for this so-called "third force" in housing is also being offered through Urban America, Inc., a private non-profit urban improvement group.

One problem, the rising federal interest rate, was met in 1965 when Congress pegged the rate for this program at a flat 3 per cent. Another constriction, the need for a locality to have a "workable program," makes it presently impossible to build (d)3 housing in many suburbs. Other limits are the funds that Congress makes available to FNMA and the low per-unit construction costs; family income ceilings fixed by Congress make it difficult to use 221(d)3 in metropolitan areas with high construction, land and living costs.

In such high-cost areas, some abatement of the real estate tax in conjunction with (d)3 housing is necessary to build housing priced low enough for the low-middle-income market. In fact, localities could all do much more by using two potent local tools, real estate tax abatement and low-interest government loans, without federal aid. It would, however, require enabling action by their state legislatures.

New York, since 1955, has had the outstanding example of this type of locally assisted middle-income housing under its Mitchell-Lama or Limited Profit Housing Companies program. Under this act, the city or state can make low-interest, long-term loans of up to fifty years' duration to sponsors of limited-profit housing. Cities are also allowed to grant abatement of real estate taxes on up to 50 per cent of the assessed valuation of the property prior to its improvement for a thirty-year period. The ceiling on rents or carrying charges is set by official policies at $30 a room.* Some 30,000 Mitchell-Lama units have been built in New York City. As the cost of construction continues to outpace the rise in the cost of living and in the incomes of certain groups, such kinds of local assistance appear to be necessary in order to provide the middle third—the teachers, civil servants, nurses, policemen and bus drivers—with standard shelter.

But these public aids should be used judiciously, in the context of desired goals, and with a recognition of comparative yields and benefits. When potentially high-yield land is pre-empted for tax-abated housing, as has happened on some Manhattan sites, it might be cheaper and more efficient to raise municipal salaries or to provide families with direct housing assistance.

Moreover, experience with Mitchell-Lama has not proved that housing priced specifically for the middle-income market can, of itself, hold in the city the average white or non-white middle-class family with several children—nor can it bring them back from the suburbs. In neighborhoods where public schools are poor, these publicly assisted middle-income apartments generally do not attract families with children, and many of the larger apartments remain vacant. Families with two or three children who could afford the down payment on a cooperative seem to prefer to spend a little more and buy a house, generally in the suburbs, where public schools are better.

A study of the non-white market for Mitchell-Lama cooperatives in New York City found that only 36 per cent of the families could afford the monthly carrying charges and the initial down payment, or the similarly modest rents charged in such city- and state-aided housing. Only 5 per cent could afford non-aided new private apartments. The rest, in order to have standard homes, would have to accept low-rent public housing.

Nationally, although the majority of white families in metropolitan areas have the income and freedom to buy or rent standard housing within their means, non-white urban families are not only restricted in choice, but half have incomes of $4,000 or

* Every 10 per cent cut in taxes is reflected in savings of about $1.15 to $1.30 per room, or about $5.75 to $6.50 per two bedroom apartment. When in 1966, the city's borrowing rate was forced about 5 per cent due to municipal fiscal problems, charges in Mitchell-Lama projects were forced several dollars above the $30 ceiling.

less. Moreover, 44 per cent of the Negroes in cities live in substandard housing, compared to 13 per cent of the whites. Of the families displaced by urban renewal, 59 per cent of the non-white families (who comprise the majority) have been eligible by income for public housing.

Given these circumstances, and the fact that Negroes must spend more for less housing, it is hardly surprising that half of all the residents in public housing today are Negro. Yet there are far more poor white people than there are poor Negroes in cities. And here we run into the basic dilemma that has hounded city rebuilders in recent years: *who wants public housing?*

LOST ILLUSION OF THE 30's

The great public housing movement came tumbling down during the affluent 1950's with a drawn-out whimper. This was not because the need for it had disappeared. In some big cities by the end of the decade, waiting lists equaled the number of units occupied. Rather, it was because the program had become very unpopular in certain strategic quarters. Even some of its most stalwart friends, boosters and spokesmen for potential beneficiaries had deserted or were now among its outspoken critics.

Congress itself helped shrink the program from the generous six-year authorization of 810,000 units made with the Housing Act of 1949; it put low-rent housing on an uncertain annual basis during the Eisenhower administration, with from 20,000 to 45,000 units a year. When the Kennedy administration came in in 1961, public housing amounted to only one per cent, instead of the 10 per cent of new homes built each year, as Senator Taft had hoped when shaping the 1949 Act; and 100,000 units of the originally authorized units remained untouched. A certain hardening of the arteries also appeared to have taken place in the local housing authorities. They were unable to use up even their reduced authorizations from Washington.

Though from 1961 to 1965 there was an increase in the volume of public housing units contracted for, the large majority of these—90,944 out of the total 128,746—were special units for the elderly. These filled an important, previously unmet need, but the program did not confront the problem of housing the most needy: poor families with children in the big cities. Of the rest of the units, about 40 per cent of the public housing starts were in cities under 50,000. Some big cities, Baltimore, Cleveland, Detroit and Boston, did not even begin public housing construction between 1962 and 1964. What had gone wrong with the great social program?

During the agonizing reappraisal which began in the late 1950's, one of the first persons to commit herself publicly was Catherine Bauer Wooster, a leading advocate of public housing during its salad days. Miss Bauer, who had been the first research director of the United States Housing Authority, blamed the large-scale community design of public housing projects for a good part of the trouble.

"We embraced too whole-heartedly functionalist and collectivist architectural theories that tended to ignore subtler esthetic values and basic social needs," she wrote. Like others, Miss Bauer was particularly critical of the "public housing skyscrapers," which put occupants into "a highly organized bee-hive of community life for which most American families have no desire and no aptitude. . . . There is no room in such schemes for individual deviation, for personal initiative and responsibility, for outdoor freedom and privacy . . . [and] small-scale business enterprise."

Architectural critic Jane Jacobs came to professional prominence at this time by opposing slum clearance itself. She contended that the disruption of neighborhood life, the removal of institutions and the replacement of dense low-rise slums with public housing super-blocks were responsible for the leaderlessness, isolation and lack of safety in low-income projects. Compared to the "safe" city street, she maintained, all those "dull" open spaces invited criminality.

Elizabeth Wood, former executive director of the Chicago Housing Authority, singled out the increasing number of "hard core" problem families in a 1957 report to the New York Citizens' Housing and Planning Council on the problems of public housing. She wrote: "There is juvenile delinquency, prostitution and crime. The presence of problem families [is] evidenced by the deteriorated appearance of buildings and grounds and . . . excessive maintenance costs. But a more serious result of their presence is that public housing is getting a bad reputation; it is being stigmatized as a bad place to live by normal low-income families. . . ."

In 1958, Pulitzer Prize-winning *New York Times* reporter Harrison Salisbury delved into New York's public housing. "I never imagined that I could find the equivalent of Moscow's newly built slums in the United States," he wrote. But in Brooklyn's mammoth Fort Greene Houses, "a massive barracks for the destitute," and other low-rent projects, he found ". . . the same shoddy shiftlessness, the broken windows, the missing light bulbs, the plaster cracking from the walls, the pilfered hardware, the cold, drafty corridors, the doors on sagging hinges, the ragged plaintive women, the playgrounds that are seas of muddy clay, planned absence of art, beauty and taste . . . human cesspools worse than those of yesterday."

How could public housing have fallen so low in less than two decades? What ever happened to those nice poor families who lived so effectively when they moved from slums into public housing projects? Tenants' listlessness, apathy and withdrawal were now a common complaint.

Another public housing veteran, Mrs. Marie McGuire, who was Commissioner of the Federal Public Housing Administration * in the difficult period of the early 1960's, pointed out that "If it hadn't been for the population shifts after the war, we wouldn't have had the problems." Mrs. McGuire, a San Antonian and the first PHA Commissioner to have previously directed a local housing authority, explained: "Before the war, we had a wider range of low incomes. Then came the change in the economy and rising incomes. It was easier to buy homes through VA and FHA. Fifty percent of the units used to be occupied by young couples.

"Public housing was never started to take care of just welfare or the lowest income families. . . . [However] 50 percent of the public housing tenants nationally are on welfare. Public housing is looked on as a resource by the social agencies which are trying to improve the housing of slum people; as a place to put welfare families; as a place where health agencies can put slum families to relieve them of contagion. But the agencies

* Now part of new Housing Assistance Administration.

don't stand by after to give them direct face-to-face adjustment help. Nobody is responsible for the newcomers. So families go to public housing at densities they've never had before and are expected to have responsibility for their neighbors and property. On the West Coast, the housing authorities are overwhelmed by their vandalism and poor maintenance.

"Something we must remember is that crime and juvenile delinquency are brought to the public's attention by public housing. In a public development it's visible, and the manager has a responsibility for correcting the misdemeanor or for property destruction.

"But where do we get the funds to provide the necessary services in order to give a family the full benefit of adjusting to its new environment?"

WHO?

What seems to have been glossed over by many appraisers of public housing is that when the program was making its public record of achievement in the late 1930's and the early 1940's, the program did not, by and large, reach the lower socioeconomic class. During the depression years the ill-housed and low-income families were not necessarily lower-class families. Tenants in the PWA projects were mostly skilled laborers and the lower-income segment of clerical and white-collar workers. The communal projects seemed to work very well for the middle-class but low-income family and for the upwardly mobile lower class (as well as for veterans going to college on the GI Bill).

Those who had pointed with pride to formerly disturbed slum dwellers whose social habits were allegedly improved or whose problems were reduced by moving to public housing, underestimated the influence of public housing management, newly available services and other important non-shelter variables. It seems likely that the improvement resulted from a combination of factors: among them a decent, uncrowded home; a responsible landlord; new attention from health and social agencies; and many years of hard work by management.

Finally, one cannot underestimate the importance of new opportunities and motivations that low-income families derived from the different and better jobs becoming available nationally in the post-depression and early postwar years. Given a financial lift by the expanding economy and union wage demands, elevated from working to middle class by the changes taking place within the private economy, the ill-housed "worthy" poor of the depression, or their children, became part of the postwar middle-income bulge and headed for the suburbs. Soon they were organizing PTA's, Cub Scouts, hobby clubs, coffee klatches and improvement associations in the new developments. "When people move from . . . the city to the . . . suburb, their participation and associational life increases deeply," Max Lerner wrote in *America as a Civilization* (1957), using phrases strikingly similar to the early public housing chronicles of the transition from slum to housing project.

But people can also be found participating busily in the beehive, high-rise, middle-income cooperative housing developments in New York City. The difference in behavior appears to stem from class and cultural factors rather than from residential environment and its design.

In cities, meanwhile, portions of the neglected lower class, along with many urban newcomers, have been uprooted from slums and moved to projects designed by and largely for the middle class; they have brought with them very different family patterns, values and needs.

We have only begun to study the orientations and values attached to place of residence, environment and neighbors by working- and lower-class families. These new insights call for a reconsideration of slum clearance criteria, the design of housing for low-income families, the criteria and methods of tenant selection in public housing, and the kinds of personnel needed in projects.

Some directors are bothered because so many of today's poor are not like the old public housing tenants. Some have even blamed urban renewal and other public improvement programs for foisting on the projects all those large, socially troubled, often apathetic and increasingly non-white families, who, left on their own, would probably not have applied for admission and who also scare off "normal" low-income families.

Is public housing intended to house the needy, or to create

"healthy" communities? Can it do both? Two different schools of thought emerged. The first, and more pervasive, is obsessed by the poor image of public housing. This group has wanted to reconstitute projects into socially "normal," racially integrated communities with a "better cross-section" of low-income families, more white families, and a minimum of problem families, the "rotten apples" that spoil a project.* They have blamed income ceilings for depriving projects of leaders; they contend that these limits rob families of the initiative to earn more money because, it is said, they will then have to pay more rent, and when their earnings reach a certain level, move out. Ceilings are also unnatural and stigmatizing, it is suggested, and they make the public housing project, in the words of the National Federation of Settlement Houses and Neighborhood Centers, into "the modern symbol of the poor-house."

This group advocated that tenants whose incomes rise be allowed to remain and pay full economic rent; they could eventually buy their project apartment or house. Smaller units in scattered sites, or rehabilitated housing are proposed as an alternative to projects. These would be preferably outside of slum-ghetto areas. Some preferred to give rent supplements or direct subsidies so the needy can live in standard, privately owned housing. The goal seems to have been well summarized by one big city planning director: make public housing "invisible."

The second, less prevalent school was exemplified by the National Capital Housing Authority. It accepted early the reloca-

* The New York City Housing Authority in 1961 developed a list of social eligibility requirements for applicants as a way of keeping out undesirables and potential troublemakers. In this policy, eight "clear and present dangers" to other tenants are cited as making a family ineligible for admission. These include "grossly unacceptable housekeeping," and a "record of unreasonable disturbance or destruction of property." In addition, twenty-one conditions indicative of "potential problem" families are to be considered before a final decision on admission is made. These include "irregular work history," "two or more separations of husband and wife in the past five years," "out-of-wedlock children," "lack of parental control" and "retardation of any family member."

Recently, pressures from civic groups and City Hall have forced a reexamination of these policies. The Housing Authority applied to the Office of Economic Opportunity for a $1,100,000 grant to pay for extra caseworkers, teachers and other personnel to work with problem families in urban renewal areas so they can qualify for public housing.

tion challenge of urban renewal, and programmed all its units to facilitate the end of slums in the District. The Authority believed, as the NCHA's former director James Ring had stated, that the uprooted and disorganized families were "more acutely in need of public housing's services than other families who have taken the initiative and are eager to break away from the slums." The Washington public housing officials tried to marshal all possible community resources to meet such tenants' immediate needs and then help them graduate to the private housing market. As far back as 1954, the annual report of the National Capital Housing Authority stated that "Public housing would not be performing its job if it retained in tenancy [over-income families] in preference to low-income families who are waiting for a chance to live in decent housing."

Yet even in Washington, by the early 1960's, it was evident that the conventional approach was not keeping pace with the pressing needs of large low-income families. If some dent were to be made in just the long list of displaced families which had been waiting for admission to public housing—some for ten and twelve years—supplementary housing resources would have to be found beyond the usual projects.

Washington, like other cities, was running into two practical obstacles. One was trying to construct large enough apartments for big low-income families within the cost limits set by the Public Housing Administration. The other was finding sites on which to build.

WHERE?

This immediate question of where low-rent housing is to be located raises problems that have accelerated and have been most responsible for the slowdown in recent years. In exploring the location question, one can also begin to pick out separate threads from the tangled skein, and see why new kinds of approaches had to be legislated in the Housing and Urban Development Act of 1965.

Social insights, sensitivity to human values, and planning considerations usually got lost in the crosscurrent of community attitudes, group pressures, the economics of slum clearance for public housing sites, community finances and, finally, the rapidly changing social environment of the country at large. There have been, and are, many dissonant voices.

Nothing illustrates this discord better than the attitudes within the Negro community. During the 1930's, when discrimination was still interpreted as denial, public housing won a special place with non-white Americans by working for a policy of racial equity. That one third of all units were specifically built for Negroes, and provided many with their first adequate shelter, was regarded as a major advance in public policies.

But with the growing postwar emphasis on civil rights, integration and status, Negroes became uncertain and divided, even after many northern city projects were desegregated by local law and some authorities became officially "color-blind" in accepting applicants. Ironically, the battle for the racial integration of public housing, which was won in many northern and borderline cities by the early 1950's after many years' struggle, was an empty victory.

At first, the integrated projects were shining demonstrations of successful interracial living, and showed that favorable attitudes on the part of previously prejudiced white people came about as a result of having as neighbors Negroes of similar or superior status.*

But as these non-segregated projects became increasingly non-white, and as the type of tenants changed, it became difficult to persuade white residents to stay, or to apply. (An accelerating factor unique to New York City was the continuation of wartime rent control. For the low-income white families who had lived in Old Law tenements for years, these controlled apartments were less expensive than public housing. They were evidently satisfactory for their needs, although considered obsolete by modern standards. But Negro and Puerto Rican newcomers of similar income could escape the rent gougers only in public housing.)

The acting U.S. Commissioner of Public Housing, in his testimony to Congress in 1960, attributed the large gaps between

* "I see they're just as human as we are. They have nice apartments, they keep their children clean, and they're friendly," said one woman who had cried for three weeks before coming to the low-rent project because she didn't want to live next to Negroes, a 1951 study on *Interracial Housing* reported.

requests for units from local housing authorities and the actual needs to the requirements in many communities that projects be racially integrated. And this is still regarded as the reason that more units are not being built—except for senior citizen housing. The elderly have no school-age children.

Meanwhile, the conflict between the drive for racial integration verbalized by members of the small but growing middle and upper class who do not need public housing themselves, and the acute needs of the much faster-growing mass of relatively inarticulate low-income urban Negroes who commonly cannot afford a decent place outside of public housing, has divided the Negro—and almost paralyzed public housing itself.

Describing this status-welfare dilemma of the leadership in his four-city study of *Negro Politics*, James Q. Wilson reported that "a growing number of them feel that public housing—which for political reasons can only be built in Negro areas—is perpetuating segregation, and is becoming stigmatized as 'Negro housing' characterized by unattractive, high-rise buildings concentrated on a few sites."

In Los Angeles, where housing densities are low and distances great, Wilson found that Negro leaders did not oppose the construction of low-rent, garden-type units that would be located some distance from their own middle- and upper-class neighborhoods, although still in *de facto* segregated districts. On the other hand, in Chicago and New York, where the Negro ghetto is economically and socially heterogeneous and dense, and where housing projects are high-rise, the leaders felt threatened by the nearby, low-rent, highly visible units, and thus opposed them.

Not so Negro politicians. Negro civic leaders have charged that they have wanted the low-income projects in their constituencies because poor people are more easily led. Yet the politicians appear to know their constituents' preferences. Records in various communities with an open-occupancy policy show that eligible Negroes choose to live in projects within or near a Negro district. But the politicians have not resolved their dilemma, which is to get the desired new public housing without simultaneously clearing away crowded slum housing—and with it many of their supporters. Thus the stance of Negro politicians has also been ambivalent. (Congressman Adam Clayton Powell declared political warfare against Averell Harriman when he was Governor of New York State over one state-aided project which would have cleared a densely crowded slum of 8,000 people while providing only 1,200 new units. Powell charged that the project was "designed to destroy Negro residents in Harlem.")

Another common set of reasons for opposing the building of low-rent projects in ghetto areas, put forth by civil rights spokesmen, is that these projects ensure segregation, inferior schools, low-quality stores, and poor municipal services.

But when public housing authorities have tried to locate projects, large or small, on vacant land outside ghettos (whether to increase the total supply of shelter for low-income families or to promote integration), they have run into opposition of nearby residents, mostly middle-class white homeowners, whose protests are supported by their local political representatives and heeded by city fathers. These factors watered down or ran to the ground more than one well-conceived public housing program during the 1950's, notably in Chicago and Philadelphia.

EXCLUSIONISM, ECONOMICS AND ESTHETICS

Such exclusionism, compounded by the increasing shortage of open land in central cities, has forced local authorities to rely more and more on the clearance of congested slum areas to obtain sites, or not to build at all.

Experience in public housing management has shown that it is easier to handle social problems in row houses or projects of limited size. Keeping down gross densities in projects was a major goal of public housing from its inception.

But the necessity for the authorities to use slum land, and consequently to absorb the high cost of slum clearance into project development,* or to make the most use of limited open

* The write-down which permits Title I sites to be rebuilt at desirable densities is not available to public housing unless it is built in renewal areas. The low-rent housing project must absorb the entire cost of acquiring and demolishing slum property. In order to spread the high initial acquisition cost within the limits set by Congress for per-unit development costs—it has been found that acquisition costs average $2,285 per unit in a former slum area compared to $589 in a non-slum area—the low-income project usually must be built high-rise.

land, combined with ever-rising construction costs, resulted in the proliferation of the high-rise project—a gross caricature of the community unit of the 1930's. It provided more decent low-rent dwelling units and gave tenants more light, air and living space per dwelling unit than in the slum. But it also put large families into unfamiliar elevator buildings at densities they had never experienced. The supervision of children became more of a problem, housing management became more difficult, and social problems more disruptive, while the project, the "modern symbol of the poor-house," became more visible than ever to the rest of the community.

Large-scale projects built on former slum land have many additional "hidden" costs, the first being a social one—the enormous disruption of the former residents and their communities. Then, many more personnel are needed. Elaborate police protection is required to patrol the grounds of a publicly owned facility in the middle of a slum. High-rise buildings need more managerial and supervisory staff per capita. These costs must be paid out of tenants' rent. This is particularly important because operating expenses in public housing are not subsidized; they are financed out of rent receipts. The higher these costs, the fewer really low-income families can be housed.

The one city that for many years moved ahead, largely undeterred by the implications of these trends, was New York City, where Construction Coordinator Robert Moses' leadership gave the local program much of its thrust. As a result, New York built enough public housing to relocate the city of Buffalo, and in the process contributed disproportionately to the bad national image of public housing. But politicians could boast that they had helped the poor without offending homeowners and taxpayers.

Public housing also suffers from an esthetic dilemma. Architects who have been frustrated in attempts to improve the bleak and institutional design of public housing tend to blame government red tape, the low fees and rigid standards imposed by the Low Rent Housing Manual, and bureaucratic resistance to anything that looks attractive. However, Public Housing Commissioner Marie McGuire, who has done much to improve project design, pointed out: "If, in the interest of economy—and in my judgment false economy—we build conventional box-type apartments, we arouse the esthetic ire of the community. But when we build architecturally attractive dwellings, we are told we are squandering the taxpayer's money."

Design has been most institutional and most out of context with its surroundings where there has been the most, and thus the most conspicuous, public housing—in big cities. An inverse ratio appears to exist between quantity and quality of appearance. (Use of the same building design over and over again was encouraged in New York as a cost-saving device and created that city's barracks-like projects.)

In small communities or in western cities, where densities are lower and cost factors and political pressures milder—and where most public housing has been built—there are small-scale projects with neighborhood orientation. Even in larger cities, as in Pittsburgh or Philadelphia, where the executive director had a sense of mission, the housing authority and local architects joined to overcome inhibiting government regulations; low-rent housing in these areas displayed considerable ingenuity, sensitivity to neighborhood and site, and amenity of design, suggesting that the fault has not been entirely with federal laws, or with realtor and community harassment. However, much less housing got built.

Still, even New York's level of project design has improved considerably under new progressive leadership since the 1958 local reorganization. The Housing Authority has shown unusual initiative in obtaining private foundation financing of attractive facilities, such as plazas, which the federal formula does not finance. This seems to support a veteran federal administrator's claim that "the Achilles heel of the program has been the boy from City Hall who is given the job on the basis of party loyalty rather than ability."

What little empirical evidence there is about consumer preferences, however, suggests that project design affronts certain middle-class observers more than the low-income tenants. In a nine-city survey carried out by the federal public housing agency to learn why tenants voluntarily move from low-rent projects, "nothing was so often praised as the structural quality and general attractiveness of the projects." What bothered the respondents most of all about the physical quality and environment was the surrounding slum neighborhood—which remained unchanged.

MORE NEW TOOLS AND NEW DILEMMAS

The Housing and Urban Development Act of 1965 presented an assortment of alternative means for housing the urban poor and, hopefully, for overcoming the many obstacles that have recently blocked public housing's traditional approach. The three major programs are all designed to avoid monster projects and sharp distinctions between public and private housing by making use of existing privately owned structures or newly built private housing for low-income families.

One new provision enables local housing authorities to either lease or purchase, and rehabilitate, private structures under somewhat shorter terms than public housing's usual forty years for new buildings, and to rent these units to low-income families under the usual formula. Another provision allows authorities to contract for the use of up to 10 per cent of the apartments in private buildings on one-to-three-year renewable leases; the tenants may be selected by the owners, who are required by contract to bring buildings up to code standards. Tenant charges and rentals are on the same basis as in conventional public housing.

The most unorthodox approach is the rent supplement program, which departs entirely from the public landlord and project approach. The supplements make it possible for low-income families to live in privately owned, FHA-assisted middle-income housing built by nonprofit or limited-profit sponsors using the (d)3 program, but at full market interest rate. The Federal Housing Administration pays the difference between 25 per cent of the tenants' incomes and the economic rents required in such housing. The law also authorized that the traditional projects be continued along with these new experimental programs.*

* Other new federal housing aids which are not part of the public housing program but will help low-income owners improve their housing include: direct grants of up to $1,500 for rehabilitation to families with incomes under $3,000 in urban renewal areas, and 100 per cent loans for rehabilitated housing owned by families with somewhat higher incomes.

With such a variety of publicly assisted programs for both low- and middle-income families, it should be possible not only to move ahead with the task of housing the urban poor, but also to avoid the many objections raised to both public housing and urban renewal. Perhaps the new social end results, which people are coming to expect of renewal, may be realized along with physical improvements.

Among the principal objections raised are mass dislocation of the poor (often non-white) and destruction of communities; ghettoization by income and segregation by color. The main new social goals are planned renewal with the participation of the residents; community preservation and on-site rehousing of dislocatees; elimination of ghettos and integration of communities; economically and socially heterogeneous neighborhoods. (According to proponents of the latter view, socioeconomic distance can be bridged through residential proximity, middle-class patterns transmitted to the lower class through neighborhood interaction; ghettos, low incomes and prejudices can thus be eliminated. Talk about renewal in terms other than diversity, not merely of building types but also of racial and economic groups, has come to be regarded here as heretical and undemocratic.)

One cannot challenge the validity of these goals, taken separately. But it soon becomes obvious that realization of one goal may be detrimental or antithetical to others. Dilemmas and conflicts inevitably arise, not just between physical and fiscal versus social goals, but also among the social objectives, and hard choices must be made, both by residents and by public officials. Once we have accepted this fact, certain questions arise. Whose objectives are more representative and valid? Who will benefit? If social goals become predominant, how many of the poor will get decent housing, and how soon will cities be renewed? The fact is that people of good will are not in agreement on how to proceed.

There are, for example, strong differences between the views of proponents of desegregation and ghetto dispersion through public actions, and the practices and apparent desires of many who live in so-called Negro ghettos.

At a national conference on programs for "breaking up the ghetto" held in the spring of 1966 by the National Committee

Against Discrimination in Housing in cooperation with the federal Office of Economic Opportunity, the sharp disagreement expressed by some members of the audience was a shock to the sponsors. One California representative stated that it is unpopular in the Negro community to move into a white area, and that dispersion is called "political castration." A San Franciscan said of her community, Hunter's Point, "Some want to stay and some want to go. We know what we want—decent facilities. But we don't know how to get the money to get them." This viewpoint was echoed by the anti-poverty program director from Los Angeles. "People in Watts aren't clamoring to get out," he said. "They want more buses, quality housing and the freedom to get out, if they want." A New Orleans representative pointed out that in his city, there had always been racial dispersion, but "on a master and servant basis, not among equals. Aren't we confusing race and culture?" he asked. The dilemma several speakers raised was: do we have to strengthen the ghetto before we can displace it?

There is deep confusion, even within civil rights ranks, about urban renewal. Title I projects that entail massive clearance and family dislocation in Negro slums have been criticized as "Negro removal." Yet integrationists condemn the newer kinds of projects which instead emphasize housing rehabilitation and improvement of Negro neighborhoods; they call this "embalming a ghetto." If one were to heed these critics, urban renewal could not win on racial grounds.

There is as yet limited experience with conservation-types of renewal in Negro communities. The Washington Park project, located in Boston's area of heaviest Negro concentration, Roxbury, was the first of this kind in that city. Social surveyors from Brandeis University were so surprised by the limited desire to move out on the part of middle-income Negro families who were faced with the alternative by renewal that they returned six months later to check on earlier findings. (Trained Negro social workers carried out all the interviews.)

"We began the study in the belief that Roxbury's Negroes would rush to embrace any opportunity to escape their relatively segregated and declining neighborhood," said the report on the Brandeis study. "Integration is in the air, and the longed-for appears at last to have become possible." But only 4 per cent of the fifty families with incomes over $5,000—those financially able—actually moved away into predominantly white communities, in spite of the fact that there was plenty of housing in the $10,000 to $12,000 range for sale without discrimination in white neighborhoods with better schools in and around Boston; furthermore, a metropolitan Fair Housing Committee was active, and public agencies were interested in helping these families. Very little effort to house-hunt outside the area was even made, although a much larger percentage of the Negroes had originally expressed an interest in moving out.

A number of reasons were cited for the surprising lack of mobility: the central location of their neighborhood, near to places of work and to downtown; the good public transportation facilities; the unusually low cost of housing in Washington Park—only 12 per cent of their income (moving would have required spending much more); the feelings of comfort with people of their own skin color and the desire to be near friends and institutions; the fear of being subjected to humiliation and discrimination in new homes. Virtually all the families had favorable feelings toward urban renewal. They felt confident that the Boston Redevelopment Authority's program would make their community a more satisfactory place to live. This feeling was reinforced as renewal planning advanced, as they had the opportunity to participate in decisions for bettering their environment, and as official steps were taken to improve the local schools and to get bank loans for home improvement at reasonable rates.

These factors caused the social surveyors to speculate on the dilemmas presented by "success" in renewal. The middle-income "respectable" Negro families would, it seemed, make the best pioneers for integration, yet renewal appeared to be curtailing their mobility and discouraging integration. On the other hand, the report pointed out, "the middle income families, few though they may be, provide models of family life and bring cultural values and a degree of stability to the community." They also gave leadership to local institutions and voluntary organizations. Their outward movement would thus deprive the community of socializing agents and models, leaving Washington Park "a pocket of the poverty-stricken."

The study concluded that "another strategy is required if integration is to be accomplished": Washington Park must be made so attractive that white families will move in.

CHICAGO'S HYDE PARK—KENWOOD

In Chicago's physically deteriorating Hyde Park–Kenwood area, one of the country's earliest and largest Title I conservation projects, the main renewal goal was to improve and thus maintain the only racially integrated community in "the most segregated" city. This required some very difficult choices.

Hyde Park–Kenwood is an area of one square mile and 75,000 people bordering Lake Michigan, located between the black belt to the south of center city and the University of Chicago. An attractive, well-located and once fashionable community, with a strong liberal tradition and a high percentage of homeownership, its residents included many professional people and a large number of the city's civic leaders.

In 1948, when the Supreme Court ruled that restrictive covenants were unenforceable, the community did not fight as Negro families spilled over into it from the bursting ghetto next door. The variety of housing in the area offered suitable dwellings for many income levels and family types. Negro professionals and businessmen bought substantial homes alongside white neighbors, who welcomed them. But as block-busters crowded low-income non-whites into the area's big old-fashioned mansions, and converted apartment houses into one-room slums, block by block, many white families fled. Schools became crowded with pupils from lower cultural backgrounds, and many whites were scared away by the crime wave that was sweeping the district. By the time that renewal planning began in the mid-1950's, over one third of the area's population was non-white, and it was generally predicted that in ten years Hyde Park–Kenwood—like other changing Chicago neighborhoods—would be a slum.

The rape of a faculty wife in 1949 precipitated the formation of a citizen organization, the Hyde Park—Kenwood Community

Conference, which soon achieved national renown and a membership of 4,000. They early set their goal: "to establish and maintain a stable inter-racial community of high standards." They recognized that their community had been deteriorating physically for many years due to zoning variances, the wartime housing squeeze, inadequate city services, and postwar illegal overcrowding. They also recognized that their community could be neither interracial nor stable unless community standards and facilities were made to be competitive with those in the suburbs to which white middle-class families were fleeing.

The Conference requested designation for Title I aid, and the University retained a planner to devise the renewal proposal. Over a two-year period, the plan, which laid heavy emphasis on enhanced livability and institutional expansion to stabilize the area, was hammered out—with some 400 meetings among the planner and Conference committees, block groups, neighborhood hearings, and after endless soul-searching.

At best the plan was a compromise, and no one was really happy. In order to achieve the enhanced livability and facilities —enlarged playgrounds and schools, better traffic patterns, densities reduced to prewar levels, and expansion of the community's various institutions—20 per cent of the dwelling units would have to be cleared. Some were standard homes occupied by white families, including faculty members. But the vast majority of homes were substandard, and 60 per cent were occupied by Negroes, most of whom were too poor to afford any standard shelter except low-rent public housing.

Originally, the Conference pressed for 600 units of public housing, some to be small, scattered projects and others rehabilitated. (An eighty-four-unit project for the elderly was already scheduled by the Housing Authority.) But as the city's mortgage market began warning that the private millions necessary to construct 2,000 units of new housing called for in the plan (and to rehabilitate many deteriorated buildings) would not be forthcoming with so much public housing nearby, even the Conference watered down its demands to 120 units. (After the clearance called for in the plan, one quarter of the families in the community would still be low income.) The final plan submitted to the city by the area's Mayor-appointed Community Conservation Council—which included representatives of business, residents, institutions in the area, and white and Negro members—proposed only sixty low-rent units.

No protest came from the comparatively well-off Negro residents of Hyde Park–Kenwood. (The lower-income residents, white and non-white, rarely attended neighborhood meetings or participated in planning.) As one Negro civic leader declared, "I think we should take the same position as the white people. It's a class position, really. . . . You can't create a homogeneous community out of heterogeneous elements."

Some non-white homeowners felt that *they* had the most to lose if Hyde Park–Kenwood followed the course of racial turnover of other Chicago neighborhoods. As one expressed it to a white neighbor in Kenwood (which by 1960 was so successfully integrated that residents held a formal ball for one hundred couples of both races), "You have some place to go. We haven't. If you leave, city services and police protection will go down. Will the schools stay as good?"

The uncomfortable conclusion was that to maintain stable racial integration, the number of low-income Negro families in public housing would have to be very limited. Former Hyde Parkers Elaine May and Mike Nichols, appearing at a Conference benefit, quipped, "Here's to Hyde Park–Kenwood, where Negro and white stand shoulder to shoulder against the poor."

NEW YORK'S WEST SIDE RENEWAL PROJECT

Rehousing of dislocated residents on site was the largest new goal of New York City's renewal program, as expressed in the West Side Urban Renewal project, another of the country's early major conservation programs, and the first of its type to be carried out in New York.

Actually, the goals for this project, as set forth in a 1958 Planning Commission report, made it sound as though the city, in this one eroded area, planned to make up for all the sins of the Moses slum clearance approach, with its huge displacements, total clearance and generally high redevelopment rentals. The renewed twenty-block area would provide a variety of building types and income levels—low-income public, middle-income, luxury, and rehabilitated; dislocation and clearance would be minimized, and as many displaced residents as possible rehoused on site; occupancy would be reduced but the same density maintained; there would be rehabilitation where possible; full community participation in project planning was assured; and the general area was to be upgraded.

Four years later, little had happened except for planning and further deterioration. Part of the delay was attributable to the size of the project area and the complexity of the undertaking, which entailed many "firsts" for New York. But the biggest delay was trying to devise a politically acceptable plan.

The issue centered on the amount of the different kinds of housing to be provided at various income levels. Some 8,000 new units were to be built on the different limited-clearance sites. But it soon became evident that even limited clearance plus rehabilitation of overcrowded, deteriorated housing would entail huge displacements—some 10,500 of the area's 17,500 families. Moreover, 79 per cent of the families to be displaced (40 per cent were Puerto Rican, 10 per cent Negro, most of the rest, Irish families living in Old Law tenements) had incomes so low that they could be rehoused in the area only if considerably more than the 1,000 units of public housing called for in the original plan were provided.

A Catholic priest who became a self-appointed spokesman for the displaced opposed demolition of the Old Law tenements, as called for in the plan in order to upgrade the area with well-planned modern apartments. He suggested that the whole renewal area should be turned into public housing for displacees. The city-appointed committee proposed raising the amount of low-rent units to 1,600.

The housing committee of the local reform Democratic club proposed the principle of "maximum dispersion" of both economic and ethnic groups in order to make the renewal area a "model integrated community." Under this, 2,650 public housing units were to be scheduled, some in projects, some in rehabilitated brownstones, and others "skewed" in the middle-income housing projects (on a basis similar to the federal rent supplement plan). Such dispersion would, said their proposal, "break down barriers between various socio-economic groups and increase upward mobility among the lower socio-economic groups," as well as increase their leadership potential.

The unexpected, instructive, and perhaps tragic split at the public hearings on the final plan in 1962 was between the representatives of the Negro and the Puerto Rican constituents. A spokesman for the Puerto Ricans denounced the balanced community concept as a way "to get rid of Negroes, Puerto Ricans and other low-income families in the area." The Housing Secretary of the NAACP, however, said that to relocate every low-income family within the West Side renewal area would "give municipal sanction to containment and encourage the development of a community characterized by racial and economic imbalance." He expressed satisfaction with the proposal by the official citizen renewal committee to provide 1,600 units.

The politicians won. Mayor Wagner announced that the amended final plan would include 2,500 units of public housing.

If it all got built—and now, four years later, parts of the plan are in jeopardy—it would probably confirm above all else the tolerance for heterogeneity of middle-income families when they live in a choice Manhattan location at bargain tax-abated shelter costs and do not send their children to public school.

Even during the planning period, population shifts were so high that public schools had 100 per cent turnovers in a school year. Keeping relocation figures current to the satisfaction of the Urban Renewal Administration was nearly impossible. The fact is that the West Side was a staging area for all income levels, and in 1957, seven out of ten families there had not lived there in 1950, the big change being to more Puerto Rican residents.

During the mid-1950's the area had been a dumping ground for families dislocated from nearby Title I projects, such as the notorious Manhattantown project to the north. The Welfare Department, unable to place its growing number of destitute problem families in public housing, resorted to side-street brownstone apartments converted into small units by profiteering slumlords. By 1958, when project planning began, 11 per cent of the area's residents were on relief. Narcotics and prostitution were on the rise, and thefts by addicts were high. Drunkards and unemployed men filled side streets and idled on corners; brawls and knifings were common.

Staff people from the Housing and Redevelopment Board recall that "People looked at us as slightly mad when we said 'You can stay in your neighborhood.' The concept didn't mean anything to most of the dislocatees." As the project advanced, thousands left of their own accord, lacking any desire to stay and preserve their community. Those left behind were the least able.

Before long, the problems of the remaining people who had to be relocated loomed so large that the Housing and Redevelopment Board commissioned a special study by Greenleigh Associates to explore the project's social feasibility. Many of the poor people were even ineligible for public housing because of their social problems and extreme poverty. (The Department of Relocation finally prevailed on the Housing Authority to let the former's social work staff make a joint evaluation of such families to see whether some might not be found eligible. As a result, by the spring of 1966, seventy-one had moved into low-rent housing on the site.) Meanwhile, the HRB's social workers were questioning how they could build links between the different income levels in the renewed community.

"We've always had the poor on the West Side—but no interaction with the middle class," a knowledgeable official pointed out. "They have different values and use different facilities. Even the children segregate themselves by third grade. I think we're romanticizing democracy. It's much more difficult to integrate income groups than racial groups." But even the low-income Irish did not mix with the newcomers, the Puerto Ricans and Negroes.

An impressive body of evidence casts strong doubt on the social efficacy of the balanced neighborhood. Studies of planned and unplanned neighborhoods with various economic levels and racial compositions, both in the United States and in Great Britain, show that heterogeneity of class within a community actually increases stratification. Those of higher status draw together; the less able tend to withdraw.

There is also some question whether the balanced neighborhood meets the residential needs of low-income tenants. Recent studies have begun to investigate the orientation of the lower and working classes to living space and neighborhood; such studies indicate that these differ so markedly from middle-class concepts that the balanced city neighborhood, as a means of providing equal residential satisfaction for all groups, may be, as a spokesman for a team of researchers in Boston stated, "an impossibility." (The Planning Commission's original report on the West Side renewal project noted: "The newcomer finds that other New Yorkers disapprove of his use of the outdoors as an extension of his home.") This philosophy has the earmarks of the settlement house in reverse: the poor are brought in to settle among the better-off.

Nor, it would appear, does the model integrated community bring about meaningful racial interaction. Davis McEntire, author of the final report of the Commission on Race and Housing, called this approach "an unfortunate confusion." Discussing hopes for desegregation in the final chapter of *Race and Residence,* McEntire wrote, "Mingling of lower-class minority individuals with middle-class whites is very likely to increase the racial antagonism of the whites. . . ."

The final test is whether private investors will put up non-assisted housing in the area. As this book goes to press, the city is stuck with four vacant sites earmarked for fully taxpaying housing. But new private non-assisted, high-rise housing costs a minimum of $50 a room, and investors don't think people will pay such high rents to live in a "slum." If the sites were to be turned over to more middle-income housing, the city would have to take a tax loss on the already heavily subsidized project.

One wonders whether there are not more direct and less labored ways of realizing the balancers' ambitious social goals. Even the Housing Authority may be robbing Peter to pay Paul on the West Side—choosing the "deserving poor" to live in the middle-income projects and other public housing in that area, in an endeavor to demonstrate that low-income families can be integrated into a middle-class neighborhood. (The West Side politicians, too, indicated that they would press for informal screenings and racial percentages to keep out problem families and attain racial integration in the projects.)

If this approach is carried over into the new scattered public housing programs, where the cream of the eligible families will be selected to live in better neighborhoods, the projects in lower-income neighborhoods will be more leaderless and the problem families more concentrated than before. Early experience in Philadelphia with the rehabilitated housing program found the authorities more reluctant to place such problem families in housing scattered throughout the community than they were to admit them to projects. New Haven's Demonstration Program of leasing private apartments to large families found that landlords were reluctant to rent to families with many children and objectionable social patterns. Both programs are also more costly to administer and to operate.

The new kinds of programs are certainly worthwhile, but it seems that the officials are so concerned with making public housing acceptable to a larger cross section that they have failed to educate the public about unmet needs and to the fact that the program cannot house its mass market.

Public housing's biggest problem is poverty combined with the programs' financing formula. Many tenants have no place else to live, and millions of ill-housed people are too poor to get in. The program only serves a fraction of the need.

Family incomes nationally increased 17 per cent between just 1960 and 1964; those of public housing tenants advanced only 5 per cent. Measured in real purchasing power, the incomes had only increased .05 per cent. Median incomes were only $2,335, nearly $1,700 below the median maximum for continued occupancy, although the ceiling had been raised by $1,000 over the preceding decade. Moreover, the percentage of families found ineligible to remain on the basis of increased income declined from 22 per cent in 1949 to 2 per cent in 1958, and has remained there since, while the annual move-out rate has dropped.

For local public housing authorities, the increased immobility of tenants and the relatively decreased family incomes are of serious concern. They lack the room to accommodate the growing numbers of legally eligible poor displaced by public improvements; and since they must pay projects' costs out of rent receipts, their fiscal solvency is jeopardized. But, as Secretary (then HHFA Administrator) Robert C. Weaver told Congress in 1964, "Many of those displaced by urban renewal and public

PLANS, PROJECTS and PEOPLE in America's Renewing Cities

N.Y. Housing and Redevelopment Board photo by Skyviews

©Arnold Newman

D.C. Redevelopment Land Agency

Noel Fehm

Wide World photos

Equitable Life

KEY:
- ■ COMPLETED
- ● UNDER CONTRACT
- ◒ COMPLETED PLANNING
- ⊙ ADVANCED PLANNING
- ○ 1959 PROGRAM
- • FUTURE
- ▨ CITY HALL-MUNICIPAL AREA

HUDSON RIVER
North Harlem
Morningside
Manhattantown (Park West)
Randall's Island
BRONX
Central Park
MANHATTAN
Lincoln Square
Columbus Circle-Coliseum
QUEENS
NYU-Bellevue (Kips Bay)
EAST RIVER
Washington Square South
BROOKLYN
Fort Greene
N
0 1 2mi

Map: major projects, 1959

City's program also called "biggest mess." Tainted by scandal and some sponsor abuses under unique and secretive disposition method, lacking guide of master plan, it was criticized for scattered projects, high rents, design and relocation results. Clearance of low-rent units in tight housing markets created public opposition. Moses called slum clearance "most unpleasant" job.

In first decade of federally aided urban redevelopment, New York Slum Clearance Committee Chairman Robert Moses carried out country's biggest program. More rebuilding results than rest of cities combined: fifteen privately financed Title I projects in execution; twenty-four in planning; 28,500 new dwelling units built, under construction or planned.

N.Y. World's Fair Corp.

N.Y. Housing and Redevelopment Board photo by Skyviews

Above: Art critics labeled squat Coliseum Hall (lower left), built by Moses' Triborough Authority under Title I, "tragical." Lincoln Center for Performing Arts (center) was design rarity among New York projects. *Below:* Some, like Fort Greene (center), were hard to tell from barren public housing. Harrison Salisbury called low-rent project (top left) "massive barracks" for destitute.

N.Y. Housing and Redevelopment Board photo by Skyviews

Philadelphia Redevelopment Authority

©Arnold Newman

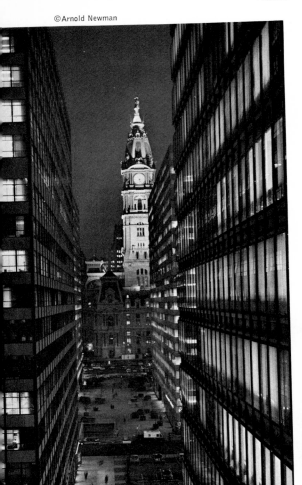

Led by two brilliant Mayors, Joseph S. Clark, Jr. and Richardson Dilworth *(below),* with organized business and civic support, and guided by distinguished planners, Philadelphia, after 1951 reform, set national patterns in urban development.

Removal of "Chinese Wall" elevated tracks *(above)* in mid-1950's freed four blocks next to City Hall for major development. Open, unified design of Penn Center with vista of City Hall *(left),* proposed by planning director Edmund Bacon *(opposite)* and fought for by top powers, set image and style of renewing city.

Wide World Photos

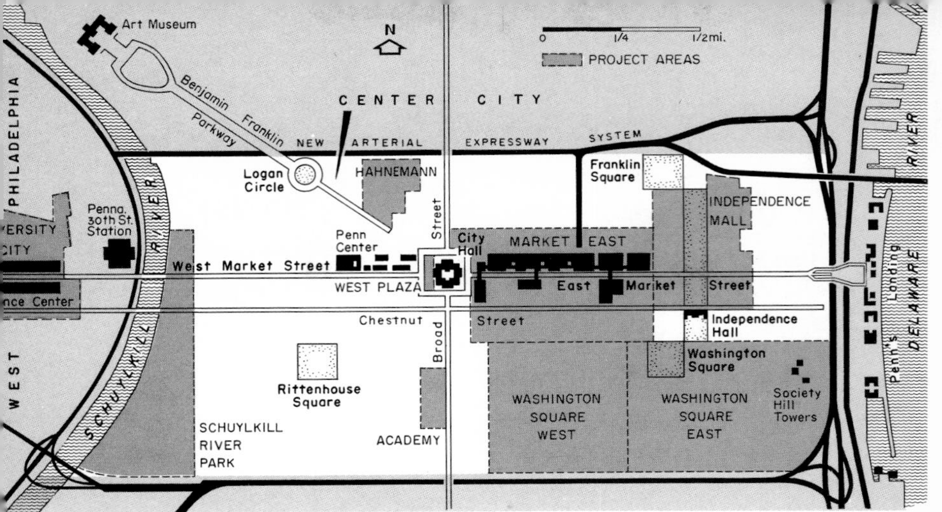

Philadelphia City Planning Commission

Above: Comprehensive city plan, tied in to transportation scheme, guides coordinated set of ambitious projects that are revitalizing residential, business and cultural life of Center City, Penn's original town. City plans also help universities expand in effort to attract research and growth industries and offset severe manufacturing decline. (Unemployment rate is double nation's.)

Below: "Gray area" renewal drags for lack of private financing. Part of first Title I project, East Poplar, still lay bare in 1965. Jobless rate in nearby slum-ghetto is 13 per cent; 54 per cent earn under $4,000; half of the young adults are dropouts.

Joseph W. Molitor for Architectural Record

Philadelphia City Planning Commission

Philadelphia Redevelopment Authority

Prestige renewal of historic Society Hill area near Independence Hall cleared insanitary 175-year-old produce market for award-winning tower apartments and townhouses and set off private restoration of hundreds of Colonial homes.

George Leavens—©Time Inc.

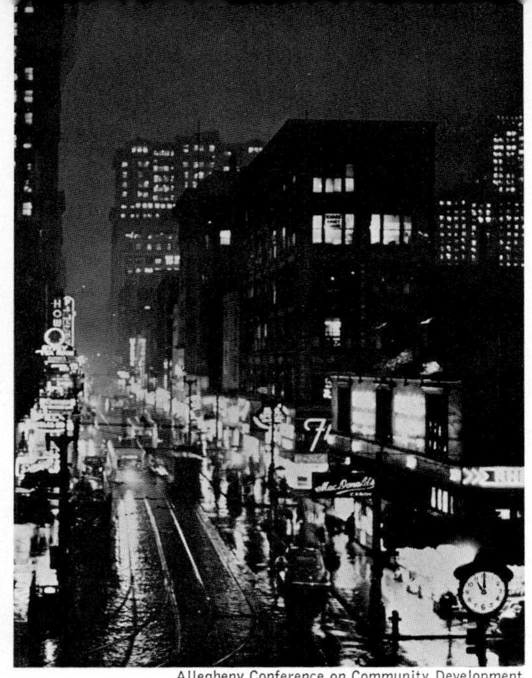

Allegheny Conference on Community Development

Pittsburgh in the mid-1940's was a sick industrial giant. Smog would shroud the city in midnight gloom, causing street lights to burn brightly at 11 A.M. *(left).* Steel mills were wearing out; major new plants located elsewhere. The environment kept away new investment and managerial talent industry needed. The historic Point *(below)*, site of Fort Duquesne, was blighted by rusty rail bridges, overhead tracks and warehouses, which worsened downtown stagnation.

Pittsburgh Photo Library–Carnegie Library of Pittsburgh

Howard Sochurek

Equitable Life

Pittsburgh Press

Margaret Bourke-White—©Time Inc.

Above: New highways and bridges eased traffic flow to Golden Triangle; Mellon Square *(right)* encouraged new office construction.

New cooperation of politically opposed top powers, Mayor David L. Lawrence *(top right, at left)* and businessmen led by billionaire Richard K. Mellon, was key from 1945 on to smog elimination and renewal. Bipartisan coalition won new local powers from state; spearheaded Gateway Center commercial redevelopment behind new Point State Park (sketch, *left,* shows final, future stage).

D.C. Redevelopment Land Agency

Left: Notorious "slum in the shadow of Capitol," cleared for redevelopment, became showcase for relocation and rebuilding. Well-located 550-acre Southwest project area is being dramatically upgraded into community of 18,000 with shops, offices, churches, theater. It is also District's first racially integrated private development.

©Ezra Stoller (ESTO)

Capitol Park One *(above* and *opposite top),* first private housing in "new Southwest," created dramatically changed environment, but paid high for pioneering. Other rebuilding lagged; government red tape delayed progress; slum reputation died hard.

Maynard Photographers

D.C. Redevelopment Land Agency

Low-rent crowded rooms in hidden alley dwellings with dirt floors, no hot water, backyard privies, garbage-littered yards were home for many of Southwest's 7,000 families. Relocation brought remarkable improvements in housing and general lot of people once written off by District. *Below:* One third moved to public housing; most into standard homes. Many received social services, health care for first time; community donated furniture. But relocation was unable to alleviate other problems of urban poor.

D.C. Redevelopment Land Agency

Wide World Photos

Housing remains most intractable city problem. In all-white Chicago neighborhood jeers and rocks are hurled at police-protected fair housing marchers. In Harlem family of six live in one overpriced, rat-infested tenement room. Many in slums are too poor for public housing.

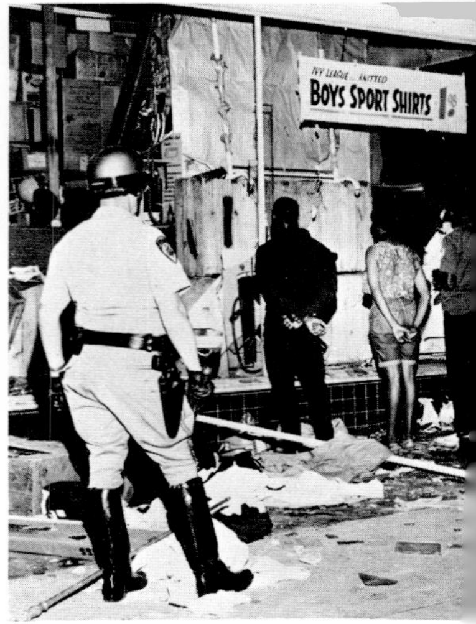

Wide World Photos

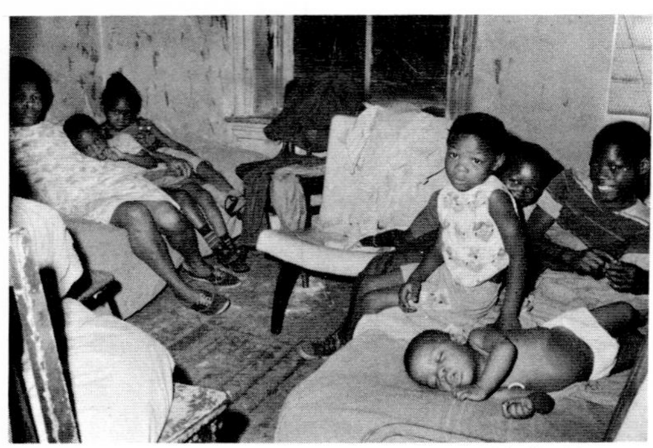

Wide World Photos

By 1960's, 73 per cent of U.S. Negroes lived in cities, the majority migrants and their children from rural South. Discrimination, disappearing jobs, inadequate education, poor schools, aggravated poor newcomers' problems, which exploded in summertime slum-ghetto riots. Three nights of uncontrolled looting and arson in Los Angeles' Watts needed state highway patrol to restore order.

Pre-kindergarten Head Start is most publicized program in government's new "war on poverty."

Reginald Jackson

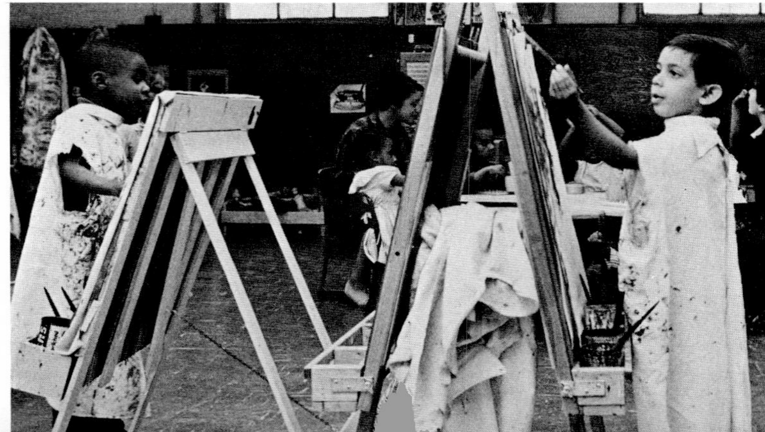

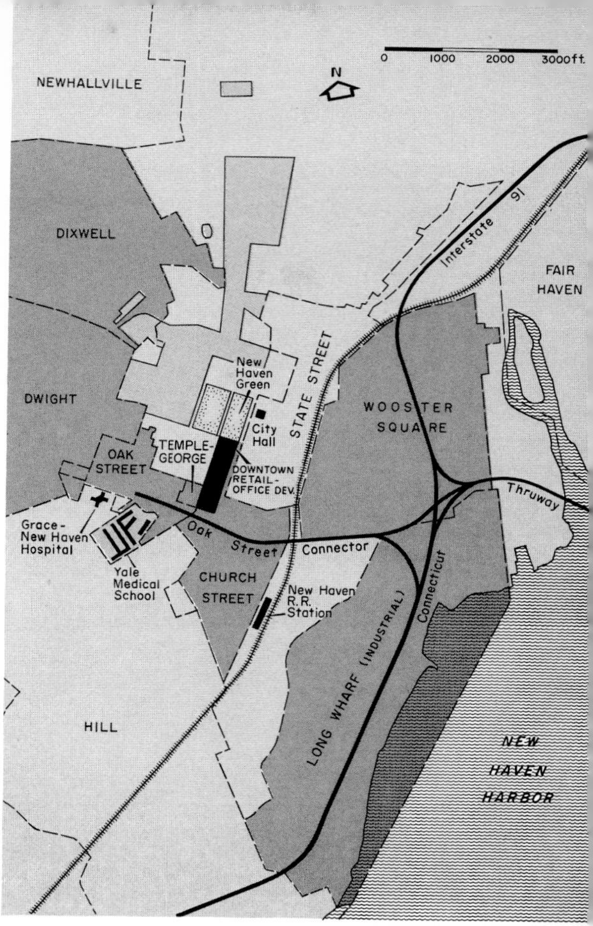

KEY:

PROJECTS IN EXECUTION

PROJECTS IN PLANNING STAGE

YALE UNIVERSITY

0 1000 2000 3000ft.

N

NEWHALLVILLE

DIXWELL

DWIGHT

Interstate 91

FAIR HAVEN

New Haven Green

City Hall

STATE STREET

WOOSTER SQUARE

OAK STREET

TEMPLE-GEORGE

DOWNTOWN RETAIL-OFFICE DEV.

Thruway

Grace-New Haven Hospital

Oak Street Connector

Yale Medical School

CHURCH STREET

New Haven R.R. Station

Connecticut

LONG WHARF (INDUSTRIAL)

HILL

NEW HAVEN HARBOR

Richard C. Lee *(below, at left),* first Mayor to make federally aided urban renewal cornerstone of his administration and political career, has carried out far-ranging modernization plan with largest per capita Title I program, and made New Haven a national model for physical and human renewal.

With $120,000,000 in federal funds and aggressive actions, Lee won private millions to rebuild and rehabilitate dying city. Local plans guide placement of new expressways for New Haven's benefit; Lee's initiative in winning Oak Street Connector traffic feeder (see dirt gash in photo below) made possible downtown revitalization. Grouping of many functions under a Development Administrator, Edward J. Logue *(below, at right),* facilitated results, set municipal pattern.

Larry Fried–PIX

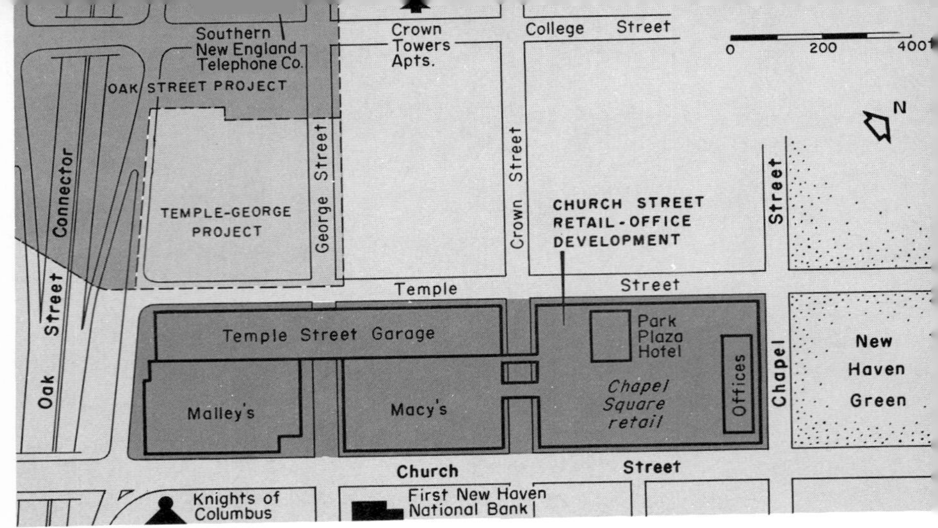

Noel Fehm

Below, left: Two-story "tax-payer" at New Haven's best corner in 1957 revealed deadening effect of traffic, overvalued land, conservative business community.

Daring Church Street redevelopment was first in country to tackle downtown decay. Project gutted three prime blocks; Oak Street Connector *(left)* tied in with expressways, doubling retail area. In 1966 site *(directly below)* had enlarged quarters for major New Haven store; new 300,000-square-foot Macy's; 14-story office building; 300-room hotel; 1,300-space garage.

New Haven Redevelopment Agency

Charles R. Schulze

New Haven Redevelopment Agency

Wooster Square neighborhood renewal cleared dangerous century-old factory lofts; built modern school-community center and apartments; transformed skid-row slums into townhouses. The owners rehabilitated hundreds of homes.

©Ezra Stoller (ESTO)

New Haven Redevelopment Agency

New Haven Redevelopment Agency

New Haven Redevelopment Agency

New Haven Redevelopment Agency

New Haven Redevelopment Agency

Noel Fehm

In New Wooster Square industrial district *(top, right)* some forty firms, like old bedding manufacturer *(top, left)* have relocated into new plants with highway access. Modern sites *(above)* on filled harbor land re-house major employers.

Inner-city youth learn skills and get jobs through Community Progress, Inc. Schools are partners in acclaimed "opportunities" programs.

Below: Yale graduate-student families live in moderate-cost integrated housing in renewed Negro neighborhood.

Charles R. Schulze

housing cannot afford to pay rents sufficient even to meet the essential costs of operating and maintaining a public housing unit. Public housing can accommodate only a limited proportion of those very poor persons. . . ." Further, the authorities are even less able to finance the supplemental health and social services required by today's public housing tenancy or would-be tenants. And fully half the families still living in all dilapidated and deteriorated housing have very low incomes, $2,200 or less.

To continue public housing as a self-supporting operation, with the "rich" poor supplementing the rent of the really poor, seems out of step with the times and the needs of cities and people.

7

THE END OF THE LINE

■ Race and Poverty in Cities

Traditionally, Americans have regarded city slums as primarily a physical problem. The federal slum clearance legislation has been written in those terms. Largely because money to get rid of urban slums was available in such programs, cities tried to eliminate their slum areas by tearing down the buildings.

During the 1950's, however, while starting to use the new government instruments of urban redevelopment and renewal, local public officials began to discover that slum elimination entailed much more than the removal of deteriorated housing and hardware—or even the substitution of low-rent dwellings. Still, most failed to acknowledge the problems that cause people to live in slums.

By the early 1960's, the changing racial-social-economic composition of central cities had magnified and vastly complicated the traditional human problems of the slums, especially in the context of a generally prospering nation. A growing portion of the city population was unable to provide for itself, and the urban community was unable or unwilling to afford that portion adequate homes and jobs in the face of changing technology and racial discrimination. Depression-born welfare and housing programs were overwhelmed; cities' fiscal resources were depleted. Northern equal-rights laws, as well as U.S. Supreme Court decisions, became empty promises as *de facto* segregation increased in core cities that were being strangled by the suburban middle-class white noose. Meanwhile, some renewal programs, caught in the crosscurrents of minority outcries of inequity and discrimination, civil rights demonstrations, the white backlash, and some apparently irreconcilable social issues, ground to a halt or radically changed direction.

The 1960 census exposed the facts about cities' changing composition. The older core cities in the North and northern central areas had lost population during the past decade, while suburbs grew. The drop varied from a little over one per cent in New York and Baltimore to 4.5 per cent in San Francisco and 10.7 per cent in Pittsburgh. The full extent of the loss was disguised, however, by the number of "new urbanites." The twelve largest cities experienced a combined net decrease in their white population of 2,000,000, but they gained 1,800,000 nonwhites. Medium-size cities, too—Rochester, Fort Wayne, San Diego—which had had few Negroes before World War II, saw their Negro populations double even as their total populations dropped. Washington D.C. became the first of America's twenty-five big cities to have a Negro majority. By the 1960's, almost as many Negroes were living in northern, borderline and western cities as in the South, and 73 per cent of all Negroes in the country lived in cities, as compared to 73 per cent on the land only half a century before.

THE WELFARE CITY

While central cities' populations fell, their budgets continued to grow, and to grow at a much faster rate than the general rise in the cost of living or the national increase in state and local spending or revenues. In the biggest cities the disproportion was worst of all.

The largest increases in expenses were for public assistance, hospitals and health services and police. More than one third of the increase in New York City's budget from $3,000,000,000 to $4,500,000,000 in the five years from 1960–1 to 1965–66 was accounted for by these three items.* Health and hospitals expenditures were up 72 per cent, to $337,920,221—and one third of the city's population, over 2,500,000, qualified for a projected free health-care program on the basis of their "moderate low income" in 1966. The Police Department accounted for another $364,120,276 in the 1965–66 budget, an increase of some $141,000,000 in the past five years; but it still lacked sufficient staff to deal with growing crime. The Welfare Department's requested allocation for 1966–67 was nearly two thirds of a billion dollars, $129,000,000, over that of the previous fiscal year.

These swelling costs were directly related to the changing population composition of central cities: more relatively young low-income families reproducing more rapidly than other metropolitan core residents; more elderly and disabled people; and the striking increase in non-white and other previously rural residents. But the latter group alone received welfare outlays far out of proportion to their percentage. In New York, where Negroes comprise only 14 per cent of the city, they accounted for 45 per cent of those on welfare. Puerto Ricans, forming 8 per cent of the population, represented 30 per cent of the welfare load. The same pattern was repeated in other cities in the early 1960's.

The single biggest growth item in public welfare was Aid to Dependent Children—ADC. (Of the 600,000 persons to be aided by the New York Welfare Department in 1966, well over half were children under eighteen.) Particularly striking—and headline making—was the proportion of illegitimate children receiving such public assistance. In Washington D.C., where ADC accounted for 71 per cent of the entire welfare caseload, 40 per cent of the children were born out of wedlock.

Unfortunately, such statistics on mushrooming welfare costs, when brought to public attention by the press and public officials, provoked outcries against alleged abuses, demagoguery,

* Making it larger than that of the State of New York.

and pressures for residency requirements and quick cures. The city manager of Newburgh, New York became a national figure (a hero to some) in the summer of 1961 with his sweeping plan for taking "bums" and "chiselers" off relief, which accounted for 12 per cent of his city's budget. Louis J. Lefkowitz, Republican candidate for Mayor of New York City that fall, proclaimed that if elected he would remove from public welfare the "wastrels" and "chiselers." National magazines ran apparently well-researched exposés of welfare abuses. The journalistic stereotype was the shiftless mother who had child after child at the public's expense to increase her relief payments rather than go to work.

The flight to the suburbs of middle- and upper-income taxpayers was directly attributed to their having to pay these mounting city expenses. These fleeing city dwellers did not realize that a third of welfare costs are borne by the state government and another third or more by the federal government. One can run —but not far.

GETTING DOWN TO CASES

Why the enormously disproportionate growth in welfare and aid to dependent children? The Board of Commissioners of Cook County, Illinois, which pays Chicago's welfare bills, was so alarmed by the skyrocketing of ADC costs during the 1950's—up from $1,400,000 to $4,400,000—that in 1960 it appointed a thirty-five-member committee of specialists, civic leaders, businessmen and educators to investigate. The committee, in turn, retained the New York firm of Greenleigh Associates Inc., nationally known consultants to health and welfare organizations. Their year-long study was the most extensive and thorough ever made of a local public welfare program in the United States.

It is interesting that the publication of the findings attracted so little national attention compared to the alleged welfare abuses. Perhaps the report, as its title *Facts, Fallacies and Future* suggests, challenged many of the popular and comforting notions about who is on ADC and why. Indeed, no more than 3 per cent in the sample of 1,000 interviewed fit the popular stereotype. Nor did the report offer any panaceas.

The typical ADC mother in Chicago was a native of Mississippi, a Negro, in her thirties. She had been in Chicago fifteen years and had three children under fifteen, all born in Illinois. Her husband had lost his job as an unskilled laborer and had deserted her.* She had had an illegitimate child since. She had waited an average of a year and four months after that before applying for ADC. Generally, she was not free to remarry, but if she was, the new husband was unable to support the child. This was her first time on ADC; she stayed on the rolls less than three years; she did not want to have more children to boost her allotment. (In fact, it only allowed twenty-one cents per meal per person.)

Most women were found to feel great guilt and resentment about having an illegitimate child, but many did not know how to prevent conception. Almost all were anxious to be self-sustaining and to return to work. However, most had no marketable skill, and many could not leave home because their children were too young to go to school.

Moreover, that illegitimacy accounted for 50 per cent of ADC was found to reflect the general growing rate of illegitimacy in Cook County. But, as the report pointed out, of the illegitimate children who were adopted—and thus who did not go on ADC—almost 98.5 per cent were white and only 1.5 per cent Negro.

In 1962 Congress amended the Social Security Act largely on the basis of some proposals in the Greenleigh Report. It provided greater federal aid for rehabilitative and preventive services for adult recipients of ADC, including financing of day-care centers for children of working mothers, more counseling and reduced workloads for caseworkers; it gave aid for an unemployed second parent to keep families together and to encourage use of parents' earnings for their children's education (books, bus fares, shoes, etc.) without cutting their relief check.

But the Social Security Act, by its nature, is supportive and could not get at the basic root of dependency found by the Greenleigh study—"the marginal level of the families" before they applied for ADC, and a history of marginal subsistence, the

* As the report pointed out, ADC laws place "a premium on the absence of the father" by not giving assistance to families with employable fathers.

end product of the social and economic effects of racial discrimination.

THE GHETTO DWELLERS

No doubt the welfare programs born in the depression dramatized certain traditional predicaments of any city newcomers' situation. The period of adjustment to complex urban life is a tension-fraught, often traumatic experience for almost all migrants, white or non-white, European, Asian, Appalachian-American, Puerto Rican or Mexican. Slum living, poverty, lack of marketable skills, low-level employment and frequent unemployment, high rates of reproduction, juvenile crime, family disorganization, ghettoization (self-imposed and socially reinforced), poor housekeeping—these have generally accompanied the first stages of life in cities, especially for rural newcomers, who comprise the majority of immigrants. But in the days of the last big urban influx, our government did not assume the burden for these problems; nor had it decided that slums were opposed to the public welfare.

Furthermore, one cannot overemphasize the special situation of the newly urban American Negro—who comprises the largest group of immigrants. He brings to the city extra-heavy baggage. He has not only the "badge of color" but also the ingrained burden of generations of cultural and economic deprivation. His move to the city makes painfully and inescapably apparent the effects of dependency and weak family organization which had their origins in slavery but were perpetuated after Reconstruction by the southern plantation system. This is the system that has shaped the mass of the "new urbanites," the people who comprise 20, 30, even 60 per cent of central cities' populations and who, during the 1970's, may be expected to increase their present number by 50 to 100 per cent.

The plantation system offered the Negro no experience with money, no incentive to save, no conception of time or progress—none of the basic experiences to prepare him for the urban money economy. Instead, it indoctrinated him to believe in his own inferiority, to be resigned, while it held him in a folk culture dominated by a spiritual, other-worldly, escapist outlook—in what sociologist E. Franklin Frazier called "the twilight of civilization."

Illegitimacy and the female-dominated household are not Negro traits. (Indeed, family instability is a characteristic by-product of male unemployment and poverty.) In the Negro's case, these traits were developed as a result of white southern culture and slavery, which deprived the Negro family of a legal base, and were perpetuated by the post-Civil War plantation system which kept the Negro male subservient, uneducated and economically insecure, usually out in the field or wandering the country looking for work, away from his family. Consequently his children were deprived of male authority and stable family life. But for the Negro man, who had almost no material possessions (he was always a tenant), his offspring were virtually the only tangible proof of his manhood, and the woman who would have him must accept this. Illegitimate children and their mothers were not rejected; instead, they were accommodated by the mothers, grandmothers and aunts who composed many lower-class southern Negro households.

But the city does not offer the mass of poor Negroes much opportunity to demonstrate the difference between what is racially and what is culturally or environmentally induced. City life tends to shatter the fragile structure of the lower-class Negro's family life and to accentuate, through differential employment opportunities, female dominance and masculine subordination. It also exposes the youngster, whose mother is probably out at work and whose father is either out of work, busy at two jobs or missing, to the worst influences of the slum.

These latest newcomers find few of the strengths of group pride in ethnic origin or the institutional supports that fortified the European immigrants. Not even the simple official process of "Americanization" which in five years is supposed to turn the foreigner into a citizen is available. The Negro's movement from one part of the country to another fails to supply that "shock of separation" which, as Oscar Handlin has written, precipitated the creation of new community organizations in cities by earlier immigrant groups. The individualized welfare services of the old city political machine have been pre-empted by impersonal government agencies, and the machine's municipal jobs for the faithful unskilled have been largely eliminated by civil service requirements or trade union restrictions. The politician does not even offer the traditional outings to the country; too often the Negro's political representative wants to keep his constituency as is.

The underworld, also, has a vested interest in preserving the minority ghetto and its hopelessness. To the despondent resident the criminal world offers "the poor man's democracy"—the chance of winning money in the numbers game. It also vends narcotics, an expensive, momentary retreat from despair, a lifetime hook that causes men to steal or kill for more and makes city streets unsafe.

The criminal world once afforded the uneducated youthful deviants in the ethnic slum illegitimate avenues to material success, but these paths are largely closed today. Crime has become as highly organized, remote and specialized as the rest of American life. Its numbers parlors are, as Richard Cloward and Lloyd Ohlin expressed it in *Delinquency and Opportunity*, like the local branch stores of a supermarket chain. The criminal hierarchy does not even provide the invisible discipline that used to hold many slum youths in line. Nor does it supply the cash that helped immigrants of earlier generations become entrepreneurs.

Even settlement houses commonly find themselves located in areas of lesser need today, because the residents whom they once served have moved away; or slum clearance and new development have altered the neighborhood. Meanwhile, vast new slum areas are neglected. Even so, settlement houses, like psychiatrically oriented social workers, are ineffective in trying to mitigate the society-induced traumas that infect the occupants of our cities' spreading black ghettos.

Meanwhile, a small group of "upper-class" Negroes, the supposed leaders and models, remain removed from and contemptuous of the masses (except for the many doctors, dentists, lawyers and businessmen who live in "golden ghettos" but enter the slum ghetto to make their living). And members of the growing middle class, who have worked their way out of the slum by dint of education and new job openings, are afraid of being dragged down by association with those still on the bottom. As the Greenleigh report noted, "upper-class Negroes are embarrassed and threatened by the public out-cry against ADC and low-income families."

This attitude, in turn, increases the alienation and frustration of the slum ghetto dweller. Speaking of the rioters at Watts in Los Angeles, a top-ranking Negro official of the federal Office of Economic Opportunity told an audience composed largely of middle-class Negroes, "Whitey isn't alone in being the object of their anger." Successful Negroes, he declared, should give the poor the benefit of their experience. But a highly placed Negro municipal employee in Los Angeles complained that he could not get other Negroes at City Hall to accompany him to the Watts area in order to persuade youngsters to get off the streets. "Why should I?" one rejoined. "I struggled for years to get out of there."

Why do middle- and upper-class Negroes fail to help their own? Primarily because the American reward system has failed to operate for them. Segregation and discrimination reinforce white stereotypes and have produced a Negro middle and upper class disproportionately small compared to the total number of Negroes, and poor compared to their white counterparts. Aside from the church, they lack the means to support their institutions. The Urban League, NAACP and CORE all rely heavily on white liberals' contributions.

His white peers have little opportunity through normal contacts and common interests to know a Negro as an individual. Practically his only civic association with white community leaders is on "interracial" committees concerned with integration or Negro rights. His isolation deprives him of the business and professional contacts and experience essential to advancing within the corporate and financial structure of American life. He does not have the extended clan that helped Europeans. Lacking entree into the American economic system, often denied credit, many Negro businessmen exploit the Negro mass as ruthlessly as do the whites. Like too many Negro doctors, lawyers, publishers and politicians, they have a vested interest in perpetuating the ghetto from which they make a living.

Ghettoization has consistently discouraged the development of a responsible elite. As Wilson wrote in *Negro Politics:* "Living in isolation from the city as a whole, . . . and desiring to differentiate himself from the [mass of disadvantaged Negroes], the middle- or upper-class Negro can see few rewards in civic leadership." Denied many of the rewards of upward mobility and the opportunity to play a serious role in American life, "the black bourgeoisie," as Frazier called them, escape into a "world of make believe," preoccupied with Negro "society" and conspicuous consumption (or else they try to earn still another Ph.D.). The Negro mass, though they may envy this elite, regards them not as models but as Uncle Toms, or as people who have been somehow "lucky in getting money"—as indeed most have been.

Who, then, is responsible for the newcomer, for easing his period of adjustment and helping him to advance?

During the late 1950's a new kind of municipal agency emerged in some cities. One of the first was Chicago's Committee on New Residents, appointed by Mayor Richard Daley as part of the city's Commission on Human Relations late in 1955 when the recent migrants' problems began to manifest themselves widely. The Committee published pamphlets and distributed thousands of simple illustrated brochures to acquaint the newcomers with the strange city and its facilities—its schools, parks, health clinics, adult educational opportunities, and even such rudimentary matters as how to use a telephone and shop at a supermarket. It organized housekeeping classes to show previously rural homemakers how to use gas stoves, incinerators and other urban novelties. It alerted other public and private agencies to the newcomers' special needs and set up field offices in "port of entry" neighborhoods.

The Committee's biggest job, however, was to find employment for the newcomers who supposedly had come in response to the siren call of industry in Chicago, traditionally a strong market for unskilled labor. The problem of finding work was twice as severe for non-white as for white newcomers.

But, as a top staff member of the Committee on New Residents commented in 1961, "In Chicago able-bodied men aren't allowed to go on relief. They assume that if you're able-bodied, you can find work. Yet there aren't jobs for the unskilled, and it's getting worse.

"In the last century, immigration was accompanied by a

demand for cheap, unskilled labor. Today, you can't push a wheelbarrow or build a railroad across the country. In this highly skilled society, we can't afford to wait for the next generation. We either train them or they'll be a drag on Chicago."

One of the Committee's early acts, in 1956, had been to arrange with the city's Dunbar Vocational High School for job-training classes for newcomers. This endeavor was reported in 1959 by Ely M. Aron, chairman of the Committee, in testimony before the Board of Education calling for a larger budget.

"It seemed perfectly obvious that we only had to make known to these new residents the superb facilities . . . you had provided for trade and vocational training. Everyone—we thought—would line up to enroll in these classes, study diligently, and become a skilled worker in possibly two or three years. We sent out thousands of flyers, used every means of communication, and the result—nil.

"Now we know better. It took us a year to learn . . . Before we can expect anyone to learn 'fine hand skills,' we must help him learn to read, understand directions, warning signals and machine dials. Today, we rejoice in the increased enrollment in the elementary school classes for adults. . . .

"It is very difficult," Aron stated, "if you're the sole head of the household, if you've moved a number of children from a rural area into a vastly complex city—it is difficult to admit that you can't read." *

THE BIG CHANGE

We used to have an acceptable rationalization for city slums. *Fortune* magazine, in a 1957 article on "The Enduring Slums," stated that they "are crowded because there are jobs to be had . . . sweepers at General Motors . . . scrap throwers at Inland Steel . . . handtruck pushers around New York's garment center." Slums were thus a sign of opportunity in cities, because newcomers are attracted to places of employment.

But these jobs have been disappearing. There is less and less heavy, unskilled and dirty work to be done—both in cities and on

* The Cook County Welfare Department established required literacy classes for such able-bodied, unemployed men.

farms. During the 1950's, agricultural and fiber production increased by 27 per cent with 27 per cent fewer workers. This trend virtually forced migration to cities, especially from the newly mechanized plantation South.

It is now known that the high rate of unemployment during the late 1950's and early 1960's was caused not only by factory automation; a sluggish economy and consumer demand were also instrumental, and behind these, conservative government fiscal policies. But the fact remains, as Dorothy K. Norman wrote in the U.S. Department of Labor's *Monthly Labor Review* in 1965: "Production requirements in industry appear to have played a hoax on the Negro, by first expanding—especially during the war years of the 1940's and early 1950's—and enticing the Negroes from the farm into industrial jobs, often far from home, and then receding, as these same jobs have become increasingly vulnerable to technological and market changes.

"Industrial employment increased in a number of cities in 1964, but the totals did not rise much above 1960 levels. And in some of the largest centers—New York and Philadelphia—the downward trend persisted, the bulletin reported.

"Limited job opportunities in major centers of Negro concentration aggravate the already difficult situation in which Negroes find themselves when looking for employment . . ."

The low-skill service jobs which untrained newcomers have traditionally filled in cities were even harder hit, relatively, by the switch to machines. For example, a great many immigrants who had never worked at any other non-farm job became elevator operators. Yet between 1957 and 1961 in New York City alone, 30,000 elevator operators' jobs were eliminated. It was anticipated that the unemployed operators could be transferred to bowling alleys. But the invention of the automatic pinsetter had eliminated thousands of these jobs as well. New mechanical cleaning processes used in many high-rise office buildings displaced still more low-skill people.

Municipal government itself, while a major growth sector for employment in recent years, has also increased use of machinery in activities that traditionally employed unskilled labor—general maintenance, street cleaning, street and road construction and administrative procedures.

The attrition in these jobs mirrors far-reaching structural shifts that have taken place in the economy since World War II. For while some jobs were disappearing, many others were being created. Between 1955 and 1965 the blue-collar work force grew only by 763,000; white-collar employment rose by 6,540,000.

Within industry itself the big shift has been from production to non-production jobs (and smaller relative pay increases for the typical factory worker). The steel industry offers an extreme but vivid picture of the shifts. Between 1950 and 1961, its blue-collar employees dropped from 503,000 to 403,000—though production rose with automated equipment, and white-collar employment in its offices and laboratories climbed from 89,000 to 117,000. In 1946 there was one white-collar worker to every nine employed in steel; there was one in four by 1963. "The time may come when it will take a ton of paper to make a ton of steel," a bulletin of the Federal Reserve Bank observed.

The many new jobs in government are also skilled or professional. This does not mean that there is not a great deal of unskilled work to be done in public service. The work merely requires public financing. The 1966 Report of the National Commission on Technology, Automation and Economic Progress enumerated six different categories of potential jobs which could produce 5,300,000 new jobs which need to be filled in order to bring public services up to levels of acceptable operation.

In manpower utilization and national wealth, the country has been moving from a goods-producing to a service economy. This fact, in combination with the exodus of manufacturing plants from the crowded old rail centers,* has profound implications for cities and their residents. Not only is there relatively less wealth in locally taxable property; fewer jobs are left in cities for the new population. To reach plants now relocated in the suburbs, but which formerly were accessible by urban public transportation, the Negro or Spanish-speaking worker who is barred from suburban residence (by income if not race) must drive many miles between home and work. Often he cannot afford to do so.

* Between 1960 and 1966 alone, New York City lost 80,000 manufacturing jobs; it is expected that it will lose 48,000 more by 1970, according to a study by the City Planning Commission.

(Meanwhile, suburban residents commute to office and professional jobs in center city.)

Since World War II, all net growth in jobs has occurred in the service sector, a 1965 study by Victor Fuchs of the National Bureau of Economic Research revealed. Moreover, Fuchs' study points out, growth within this service sector has been in jobs that make greater use of workers with higher education and relatively less use of those with only limited schooling or with physical strength. The employment increase in the field of education alone between 1950 and 1960 was found to be greater than total employment in primary metal industries in both of those years. (Most dramatic postwar advance was made by professional, technical and kindred workers. This group doubled, and by 1964 numbered 8,500,000.)

Looking ahead to the 1970's, experts foresee a continuing decline in rural manpower needs. Only 10 per cent of the nation's population will be needed to feed the country and grow fiber for it. This means continued immigration from farms and plantations, though at a somewhat slower rate than in the recent past. But the number of Negroes, Puerto Ricans and other low-income, minority residents in central cities is expected to grow and be half again as large due to the young age and high birth rate of those already there.

The number of factory jobs nationally will increase—though probably not in the old manufacturing cities, and many traditional blue-collar production jobs will be upgraded in job requirements to a white-collar or skilled level. The manufacturers remaining in cities will have less need for additional, particularly for unskilled, workers. The big proportionate increase in skilled, white-collar and professional service jobs will continue in cities (as nationally), and cities may well benefit from this trend.

The U.S. Department of Labor warned in a publication on *Manpower Needs of the 1960's* (published in 1959) that "To fill these new requirements the youth who are entering the labor market will have to have much higher skills and education." The Department's 1965 publication on *Manpower Needs in 1975* reiterated the point. It stated that "The occupational groups requiring the least educational attainment are, in general, those which are expected to show the smallest employment growth and thus provide the fewest jobs for the growing labor force. . . . The demand of employers for better trained personnel appears to be insatiable."

EDUCATION—FOR WHAT?

Yet we have been breeding a new generation that is undereducated, unemployed or unemployable—the "dropouts" who by 1965 comprised almost one third of the nation's high-school-age students. They leave school usually by tenth grade, wander the streets, form gangs and get into trouble. When this postwar generation reaches adulthood in the early 70's, when 26,000,000 young people are expected to enter the labor market, about 7,500,000 teenagers will not have completed high school. About 2,500,000 million will have failed to reach eighth grade. According to the National Urban League, "A relatively high proportion of them will be non-white." This is particularly disturbing when it is realized that 20 percent of all the new entrants into the labor force in the late 1960's will be Negro; * and if present trends continue, half of them will not have had a high school education.

The prospects for these undereducated boys and girls are not bright. The recent past shows that they have three times as high an unemployment rate as graduates. They earn $27 a week less, and the disparity increases as they grow older. Their decision to quit school before graduation means a lifetime of menial jobs with meager salaries or unemployment. Indeed, many young people who dropped out of school to go to work soon found themselves out of a job and on relief. Some have recently joined the Job Corps and other new manpower training programs. Other dropouts have been adding to the urban crime wave which, during the 1960's, has seen a rise in city juvenile delinquency double the national average.

According to recent sociological studies, juvenile deviance and crime, in disproportionate amounts among the lower classes, are caused by the society that encourages certain aspirations yet withholds the possibilities of achieving these aspirations legitimately. As Cloward and Ohlin wrote in *Delinquency and Oppor-*

* The percentage in cities will be much higher.

tunity, the cause is a discrepancy "between what lower class youth are led to want and what is actually available to them." For many young Negro males another principal cause is the early and often permanent absence of a father, as former Assistant Secretary of Labor Daniel P. Moynihan made clear in his paper on *The Negro Family*.

This combination of circumstances in ghetto areas is held to be a major cause of the recent summertime riots in Harlem, Rochester, Philadelphia, Los Angeles' Watts and other cities—circumstances to which the new government-aided anti-poverty and job training programs evidently added an extra bitter twist. The inadequately filled promise of new job opportunities and training served to exacerbate unrest in ghettos. "The Negro has gotten a much deeper sense of frustration, much deeper feelings of despair, as the gap increases between what he's actually got and what his expectations have grown to be," Dr. Philip Hauser, head of the University of Chicago's Department of Sociology, observed about the riots.

The McCone Commission, appointed by Governor Edmund Brown of California to investigate the circumstances contributing to the Watts riot, singled out inadequate schooling designed to help overcome the serious handicaps of the disadvantaged Negro child; insufficient jobs for the untrained Negro, and resentment of the police.

In a previous generation, the Italian immigrants' failure to get an education blocked their way, as they discovered too late, to economic opportunities and also led to a disproportionate rate of crime among their youth and later, among adults. For the Negro mass, moving from the twilight of civilization to cities, horizons have suddenly appeared to broaden. In cities they have achieved higher incomes and better housing conditions than in the rural South. But the newly broadened vistas of many in cities are unrealistic, considering the great obstacles.

Why should a Negro youth remain in school? Speaking primarily of the South two decades ago, the Swedish economist Gunnar Myrdal wrote in *An American Dilemma:* "Since Negroes are seldom in demand for jobs for which education is necessary, there is certainly nothing surprising in the conclusion that they, unlike whites, fail to improve their opportunities by staying in school longer." The scene has shifted more and more to northern and western city streets and their slums today.

The Negro may read in the papers about those who are succeeding. But the fact that success is news speaks for itself. What is new in today's city slum, Dr. James Conant observed in the early 1960's, is "the almost complete lack of . . . conviction" that they can ever work their way out of poverty on the part of Negro youth. "The unemployed floaters on the street are walking evidence to all youth that nothing can be accomplished by education." Conant placed a good part of the blame for the dropout problem on the discriminatory hiring practices of private companies.

Limited comfort might be derived by blaming the situation on the illiteracy and the consequent relative unemployability of the southern Negro migrant. Those who came to cities in the 1940's did have little schooling. During 1949–50 the highest migration to Chicago, for example, was of adults who had four years of education, and they subsequently bore the brunt of automation. But between 1955 and 1960, the great majority among the most mobile non-white migrants—men of twenty-five to twenty-nine years—had at least some high school training, and one fifth had a year or more of college.

Yet the percentage of unemployed Negroes during the recession of the early 1960's was two to three times as high as that of whites at *all* levels—unskilled, semiskilled and skilled. And even as the country neared "full employment" at the end of 1965, the Negro unemployment rate was still twice as high as whites, and it was even higher in the slums.* For Negro youth in 1966 it was 27 per cent, compared to 12 per cent for white youth. The President's Commission on Technology, Automation and Economic Progress warned in its 1966 report that "If non-whites continue to hold the same proportion of jobs in each occupation as in

* A special Labor Department census in March 1966 of the poorest districts in the one hundred largest cities showed the overall Negro unemployment rate to be 9.4 per cent—compared to 3.8 per cent nationally. For Negro boys it was 31 per cent. Many in the prime-working-age group were not even looking for work, and thus not technically unemployed. In some "new" ghetto areas, the West Side of Chicago and Brooklyn's Bedford-Stuyvesant, unemployment ran an estimated 25 per cent in the summer of 1966, and statistics showed a sudden national increase in Negro joblessness.

1964, the non-white unemployment rate in 1975 will be more than five times that for the labor force as a whole."

The Negro has made the least advance in the growing sector of the economy—and not always for lack of education. In 1965, the Bureau of the Census reported that "at all educational levels the Negro is less likely to be a white collar worker." According to a survey by the Census Bureau, among Negro men who had received some college training the proportion employed in lower-paid jobs was 41 per cent or twice the proportion of whites, while for male college graduates the proportion of Negroes in the lower-paid jobs was triple that of whites.

This survey stated, "Although advances have been made since 1950—the rate of progress has slowed and there remain large gaps between Negro and white achievement [even when years of schooling among Negroes are greater]. The political, economic and social issues affecting the Negro appear to arise not from lack of aspiration, but from high aspirations pressing against limited, and, in some places, declining opportunity. . . ." And fair employment laws don't help much.*

This highly demanding, specialized age affords the newcomer fewer of the jobs which he has traditionally filled and permits him a shorter period to become a self-sustaining member of the city economy. It also robs him of the realistic hope which served as an economic yeast for earlier generations.

The contrast is dramatized by the tale of a reunion, held in March 1962, of fifty men who had graduated half a century before from Brooklyn's now defunct Public School 43 in the "gray area" of Williamsburgh. "The gathering was a very satisfying experience," commented Nathan Smith, now a hardware merchant in Woodbridge, New Jersey, who initiated the reunion out of curiosity to learn how his classmates had turned out. "Not one of us failed to achieve at least modest success," he told a newspaper reporter who covered the gathering. "We were mostly immi-

* In employment, as in housing, the effectiveness of anti-discrimination laws, including the Civil Rights Act of 1964, is hampered by inadequate enforcement powers, small budgets and weak administration, a Twentieth-Century Fund report has found. Another study reveals that extraordinary efforts, including aggressive recruiting campaigns by employers, are necessary to overcome Negroes' emotional blocks and inertia. Psychological tests have also been found to keep Negroes out of jobs.

grants or children of immigrants. The only thing we had was hope and faith in the ideal of American opportunity."

The nature of that opportunity has changed. The era of the self-made, uneducated small businessman who could rise out of the slums is vanishing. He is no longer the backbone of the middle class; he is becoming part of the lower-middle class or the poor. More and more the American businessman has become an organization man; the former owner is now a manager; the clerk has been replaced by self-service. Although the current demand for new services is once again opening opportunities for small business concerns, the man who would be self-sustaining and advance on his own or in an organization must be educated.

THE PUT-OUTS

This suggests the third factor that limits the advance of the newcomers or the "culturally disadvantaged": educability. Much of this problem involves group values and cultural differences.

The lower class, whether white or non-white, differs from the middle class in its emphasis on immediate gratification and security, rather than on striving for individual status and achievement which necessitate thrift and postponement. There is practically no interest in academic education. Rather, learning is valued for immediate utility—filling out forms, applying for known civil service jobs, and so forth. Action is emphasized among the lower class; talk and reading are commonly regarded as unmasculine and are therefore eschewed.

Why should one break with one's group, become tomorrow-oriented and study hard in the expectation that doing well in school will lead to a better future? In today's slum areas, where the majority of dropouts live, many youths either see no reason to make the break or do not know how to make it.

From their earliest years, their deprived, circumscribed environment militates against the education necessary to succeed today. The family and immediate community often fail to provide the early life experiences, the sights, sounds, vocabulary and information which are necessary preschool preparations for learning; these the middle-class child receives almost automatically.

Home life is crippled. The uneducated or undereducated parent speaks to the child in monosyllables and points at objects, and may even deride efforts to learn due to his own poor experience in school, or rude treatment by the child's teachers. The harassed mother shouts "Get out of my way" to too many children. There are no books, not even nursery rhymes, in the crowded noisy room or two called home. Study, even sleeping, is often impossible. The boy in the broken home (over one quarter of the Negro children live in families headed by women) is deprived of the essential male model.

Many lower-class parents are aware of the importance of education in this society. But many lack the money and time or the necessary knowledge to help their children. They may be reluctant to meet teachers because they speak poorly or dress badly; they lack the time and organizational sophistication to join PTA activities. Further, since equal opportunities and rewards are not generally available to educated Negroes, there is a tendency to protect children against rebuffs and disappointments. This is partly a defense; often it becomes a built-in lag.

Among the strongest detrimental influences on the Negro child is his negative self-image; he senses that society views him as inferior and expects inferior performance of him. This is attested by the limitations on his father and by the family's living environment, and in effect has been reinforced by the emphasis of many old-line organization Negroes on racial integration as the key to success.

This child is behind before he starts school. One out of every three children in the school systems of our fourteen biggest cities come from such "culturally deprived" backgrounds. In the 1970's, with the lower-class population explosion, there is expected to be one such child out of every two in big cities, and one out of four in many middle-size cities.

The school world has little relevance to the child's life. Its primers are illustrated with rosy-cheeked white children playing on grassy suburban lawns; his composition assignment is to describe "A Trip I Took." He may have left home without breakfast and be too hungry to concentrate. When he is confronted with a difficult problem, he abandons it quickly with a "who cares?" attitude. Teachers, unprepared for and demoralized by these students and their attitudes, spend so much time on discipline that they have little left for actual lessons.

"One of the reasons we have such a terrific discipline problem," an experienced Negro teacher in a New York "gray area" public school pointed out, "is that the children just don't care. School is a place where they are sent. Even children who are eleven and twelve years old have no ideas of their own as to what they want to get out of school." As a result, they get only one half to one third the exposure to learning that a student usually gets. The high residential mobility of many poor families compounds the inadequacies of the child's education. When he reaches high school, the situation is completely out of hand; the street takes over, and the gang.

The burden of blame for pupils' lower achievement also rests on the attitudes of teachers—on what Dr. Kenneth Clark, in *Dark Ghetto*, called their "cultural bias." A social worker who spent many years in East Harlem, a vast depressed community of 180,000 in upper Manhattan, observed: 'Teachers come in here with stereotypes. They feel the kids can't learn. So they don't learn."

But looking behind the statistics and the signs of "cultural deprivation," one discovers that the majority of the dropouts have average intelligence, and that 20 to 25 per cent even rank as culturally superior. Recent studies indicate that the "disadvantaged" child learns differently, more slowly, and responds to different stimuli; he apparently requires different teaching techniques or programs than those generally available. His disadvantage is not so much in natural gifts as in middle-class knowhow—a lack which shows up in testing and teaching that is oriented to the middle-class culture.

Before many students drop out, they have dropped backward. Their progressive retardation may go back to third-grade level. And the boys do worse than the girls, who are more apt to have a suitable adult model in their mother, and more job opportunities at the white-collar level. Pupils who do not keep up with their grades are promoted nonetheless. By high school, the youngsters are so far behind in basic skills that many teachers find them uneducable. "The teachers call them 'drop-outs,' " a field worker for

Chicago's Committee on New Residents commented. "We call them 'put-outs.' "

As for the youngsters who move ahead at grade level, guidance counselors steer them away from jobs from which Negroes have been traditionally barred. When they cannot read well, they are shunted to vocational high schools to be trained for trades that have limited openings or are disappearing. Employers who decide to hire Negroes at higher levels or in kinds of work previously barred are not able to find enough who are qualified. College scholarships for qualified Negro students at many top institutions go begging. Attending college appears so impossible to many children from deprived communities that even preparing for it seems a fantasy. Because they live in such a separate community, Negro youths are unlikely to hear about the opportunities.

THE CITY SCHOOLS' PUBLIC

The changing nature of the urban population is dramatized by the two different school systems that exist in our metropolitan areas. These differ in budget and product as the two populations' pocketbooks and political power differ. The short-changing of cities by state legislatures compounds the fiscal disparity.

During the 1950's suburban parents put themselves and their communities into debt to build schools, raise salaries, expand curricula and improve teaching methods, to give their bumper crop of children the best education so they could get into college. Central cities also had an unexpectedly large number of pupils, but they were educating a generation of dropouts.

Dr. James Conant found that in the wealthy suburbs annual expenditures were often over $1,000 per pupil, compared to an average under $500 in slum schools; teacher pay was commensurate. (Between 1952 and 1962, nearly half the licensed teachers in New York City left the system.)

The financial issue was well put by Max Rubin, who served as chairman of the New York City Board of Education from 1961 to 1963. "Everybody wants good schools, but how far will the people go to pay for the schools?" he asked. "Politicians prefer to run on a low tax platform rather than on better schools and higher taxes. Without the priority on the part of the public, what can you expect of the school board and teachers? Until good schools become good politics, we will be struggling."

Negro organization leaders and many middle-class Negro parents have spent their energies and political leverage on integration. They have demanded that Negro children be bused into white-neighborhood schools (and the reverse), and have urged school pairing, rezoning and other expedients. They even oppose building new schools in ghettos. The Negro leaders have been reluctant to admit that the disadvantaged child (in big cities, many non-white and Spanish-speaking children test several grades below their white contemporaries) requires much more than school integration to improve his learning ability. They did not fight for the expensive special programs these children need, and they tended to ignore the uncomfortable fact that in integrated schools disadvantaged children have to attend separate classes because of their academic deficiencies.

Some significant experiments are under way on a metropolitan basis—in the Hartford, Connecticut, Boston and Los Angeles areas—to achieve greater racial balance by transferring some inner-city Negro pupils to white suburban schools. In Los Angeles the program is reported to be drawing mainly middle-class Negro children, and teachers say that poor children from Watts are upset by their exposure to Bel Air's wealth.

Perhaps the benefit of such pupil transfers is greater for the insulated suburban white children than for their Negro classmates. Associate Professor Preston Wilcox of the Columbia University School of Social Work, himself a Negro, has stated that emphasis on integration is probably harmful to the Negro child. "Psychologically, it's bad to tell a kid that he'll only make it if he sits next to a white," Wilcox comments.

In the big cities with huge and growing core ghettos, the integrationists are rapidly becoming crusaders without a feasible cause. In Philadelphia, Detroit, Chicago and New York, to cite just several big-city school systems, white pupils now form the minority, and the percentage of the white student population has been dropping a few points each year. In Washington D.C., public school enrollment in 1965 was 90 per cent Negro, compared to 85 per cent just the year before. Los Angeles was the only one of twenty-one big cities in which white enrollment did not drop that year. The trend is unlikely to level off or reverse itself, at least in the next decade.

Educational disadvantages are worsened by the unanticipated high densities in new ghetto-slum areas. Physical capacities have been overwhelmed. One old high school in East Brooklyn, built for 1,600 pupils, last year had an enrollment of 3,400, 85 per cent of them Negro and Puerto Rican. The school's wiring is so antiquated that it is not possible to use modern teaching devices to help the many students with reading problems. The need for three sessions means that some students start school by seven, eat lunch at 9:30 and are free by noon to roam the streets. Not surprisingly, the dropout rate is 40 per cent.

Middle-class Negro parents have become so dissatisfied with the quality of education in cities' public schools that a number who can afford it have also removed their children. (Unlike white families, many cannot withdraw to the suburbs.) In the District of Columbia in 1965, over 6 per cent of the Negro students were attending private or parochial schools, often at great financial sacrifice, and a surprising number were the sons and daughters of public schoolteachers.

Much of the insistence by Negroes on integration is doubtless based on a desire for quality education. (Commenting on parent attitudes, the director of an East Harlem settlement house observed, "In most neighborhoods, the teachers are cowed by the PTA. Here, the parents are cowed by the teacher.")

But a dramatic reversal seems to be coming about. In the summer of 1966, Livingston L. Wingate, director of Haryou-Act, the Harlem anti-poverty agency calling for the establishment of quality education in Negro ghettos, declared that "We must no longer pursue the myth that integrated education is equated with quality education." A poll of several ghetto areas in big cities showed that the great majority of parents are concerned with better education; only 2 per cent specifically with school integration.

A growing self-assurance and political awareness was evident among the parents of children who were to enter a new $5,000,000 air-conditioned East Harlem elementary school in the fall of 1966. At first they insisted that the school not be opened unless it were integrated or they were given control. Slowly they shifted to a demand for control, with appointment of a Negro or Puerto Rican principal, and more Negro teachers.

But the problems of inadequate funds, insufficient teachers, old overcrowded schools and outmoded curriculum still remain, and in most ghetto areas the educational situation has been steadily deteriorating.

THE BUSINESSMEN AND THE EDUCATORS

Where have the big businessmen, the "civic leaders" of cities, been in the midst of the mounting school crisis? Strangely silent. The big worry of the businessman (as opposed to the father) is that spending more on schools will increase local taxes and scare away industry. His children do not use the public schools in central cities; few even live in the cities. Only rarely have top city leaders fought for central city school improvement in recent years or pressed state legislatures to revise school aid formulas and local school district taxing powers.*

Local business, industrial and financial leaders—the men who have been working for downtown revitalization, industrial redevelopment, freeway construction, metropolitan mass transit and a "quality" urban environment in order to stop the flight of industry, the white middle class and the tax base—show a strange lack of concern about the school crisis. If the present situation is allowed to continue, it seems obvious that their city will be less able to attract desirable business concerns, and the businessmen will be less able to get qualified workers for their own companies and attract white families to their redevelopments.

For at least six years, the U.S. Department of Labor has been putting up warnings. Perhaps the businessman does not perceive the implications of the inner-city school problems for his city's economic future, nor recognize that the undereducated central-city youths are likely to cause the urban manpower crisis of the 1970's. Perhaps it is hard for them to see the economic payoff in

* One of the exceptions was Pennsylvania, led by Pittsburgh and Philadelphia and supported by Governor William Scranton. Recently, some southern states have come to spend a much higher percentage of their budgets on public education than have northern states—as part of the South's drive to attract industry from old northern cities.

education; few even recognize the economic toll of discriminatory practices.*

Yet the economists have been making a strong case for the return from investment in education, especially in post-industrial society. In 1960, University of Chicago economist Theodore W. Schultz, in his presidential address to the American Economic Association (and in a subsequent book on *The Economic Value of Education*), declared that "No small part of the low earnings of many Negroes, poor farm people and some older workers reflects the failure to have invested in their health and education . . . . We can ill afford to continue making the same mistake."

Schultz also observed that "If we were to treat education as pure investment, this result would suggest that the returns to education were relatively more attractive than those in nonhuman capital." Research has shown, he reported, that the impressive rise in real earnings per worker achieved in the past generation—the "unexplained increases" in the national income, came about "not as much through investment in capital goods, as generally assumed, but through greatly increased public and personal investment in human capital."

In 1965 the Committee for Economic Development, a national nonprofit organization of enlightened business and industrial leaders, in effect endorsed his philosophy with a policy statement on *Raising Low Incomes Through Improved Education;* they urged that all possible resources, public and private, be brought to bear on adapting the educational system to the economic system, and vice versa. A CED member, William Benton, publisher of the Encyclopaedia Britannica, observed that "although education is our largest business, our factual information about the educational system, and about how best to achieve its goals, is astonishingly inadequate for the purposes of sensible planning and decision-making."

The Ford Foundation's Great Cities School Improvement

* The President's Council of Economic Advisers found that if discrimination in employment were eliminated and the Negro potential fully realized, at least $13,000,000,000 more in purchasing power would be placed in the hands of the bottom income groups, and current annual growth would double.

Program, which in the early 1960's stimulated school systems in fourteen big cities to develop new methods and programs for teaching inner-city children, blamed the educators for public indifference. In 1963, a spokesman charged that the educators have failed to communicate the problems, and have been unwilling to evaluate the effectiveness of present methods.

"How can you expect the businessman to respond?" he asked. "He hears the Superintendent of Schools say everything is fine, and one morning he opens the paper and reads that half the students are illiterate.* He wonders what the schools have been doing with all the money they have.

"Educators have secured for themselves a unique isolation in American society. The majority of school systems have their own tax structure, are independent of City Hall and call themselves the answer to society's problems. The public goes along because Americans have an ingrained belief that education is the answer to everything. They tell the public what it should want and short-change the process of planning with the people. But because the school systems refuse to evaluate themselves, they have not documented the case for what education can do, especially in central cities, and thus it becomes increasingly difficult to sell themselves. Further, their huge unwieldy administrative structure favors the status quo and penalizes the person who tries to innovate."

WHAT KIND OF EDUCATION IS THE ANSWER?

Not all educators remained oblivious to the special problems of educating inner-city children. Many were eagerly searching for new methods "to compensate for the deficiencies which hinder the disadvantaged child from taking full advantage of the conventional education program," as a 1963 bulletin of the National Education Association summarized the new movement.

* In October 1965, the New York City Board of Education released results of standardized achievement tests given to 626,148 pupils in second through tenth grade during 1964–65. These disclosed that more than half the city's pupils were behind their counterparts throughout the country in reading and arithmetic in second through eighth grade, and that sizable numbers were two, three and four years behind in reading.

New York City led the way in 1959 with its Demonstration Guidance Program, which was widely publicized as Higher Horizons. This approach offered culturally deprived children an enriched curriculum, including special counseling, more teacher attention and outings to sites of interest and cultural facilities in the larger community. Children in the pilot program responded well, and the program appealed to the general public. The new compensatory education approach was soon followed in other cities, while the program was expanded in New York schools.

There were stirrings and changes in many big-city schools, stimulated to a large extent by the millions in matching grants from the Ford Foundation. Extra personnel were added: guidance counselors, remedial reading teachers, assistant principals, "helping" teachers, community agents from school neighborhoods to provide a liaison with the community. Remedial programs in language skills were undertaken and class sizes were reduced; new teaching techniques were used; preschool classes prepared three- and four-year olds for learning; "alienated" parents were actively involved in school activities.

But federal money was required for a national program, and the civil rights ferment, ghetto riots and mounting concern for the urban poor pressured Congress into passing the unprecedented Elementary and Secondary Education Act of 1965. Under its Title I, over $1,000,000,000 was made available in the first year alone for special programs for educationally deprived children in poverty areas. The recent compensatory education programs were predominant among those eligible for Title I.

This development seemed to be the most encouraging yet. Crisis had overcome local fear of federal control of education. In 1966 many cities began Higher Horizon-type programs, team teaching methods, remedial reading programs, talent development, and "preparation for work" programs. Some were also aided by the Office of Economic Opportunity. The most popular new program was for preschool children, Project Head Start, characterized as "the infant prodigy of the Great Society." President Johnson himself hailed it as "battle-tested."

In concluding this study of American cities facing their problems, it seemed necessary to document the achievements on the great new urban education frontier, and also to find out how much more federal and local money would be required to do a saturation job.

The results were disconcerting, but instructive. As of the summer of 1966, the returns from the new urban education programs generally show that "more of the same" does not have significant effect; that the "noticeable" improvements in pupils do not last under present circumstances; and that there are almost no measurable achievements to speak of.

What seemed particularly unsettling was that the U.S. Office of Education was loathe to admit to Congress or the public the ineffectiveness of most of its billion-dollar Title I program. (I later learned that the office *was* beginning to warn the educators.) HEW Secretary John W. Gardner told Congress in April that "Great educational strides can be made by specialized educational programs," and Commissioner of Education Harold Howe testified, "Our prior experience in several cities demonstrates that such special attention in and of itself will result in improved educational performance." Yet the Office of Education could not provide me with data from local schools that showed quantifiable results. It turned out that the legislative testimony was based on publications, several years old, of early efforts in the Ford Foundation Great Cities and New York's Higher Horizons.

These publications were, indeed, optimistic about the initial results. But the Ford Foundation could direct me to none of the Great Cities schools that had found significant differences between children in compensatory and conventional education programs when tested for specific achievements.* (Actually, these programs lacked a research component; the main concern was to get into the schools and stimulate federal action.)

Dr. Mario Fantini, formerly director of the Great Cities program in Syracuse, New York, and now a Program Associate in the Foundation's Education Program, flatly asserted that "More of the same won't have the pay-off we expect, and I doubt we'll ever have the kind of money to do the job that way. The problem

* An apparent exception has been the Banneker Schools in St. Louis, the one large-scale experiment where children are reported to be performing at grade level; but this was not one of the Ford programs and the Foundation had no evaluation of it. A part of the Banneker Schools' unusual success is believed to be the forceful personality of the principal and his use of every strategy to involve parents and students in the learning process.

with our original approach is that the schools have assumed the kids need compensation for deficiencies and that there is nothing wrong with their program. But the schools themselves are outmoded, and we have to change the process of education. There are the beginnings of a shift in this direction. But we had to start somewhere."

Pittsburgh, another of the Great Cities, has been pushing compensatory education and team teaching in slum neighborhood schools for five years and could not show measurable improvements in children's reading scores. Officials say that high pupil turnover in slum schools has made it difficult to assess the program, and the system lacks staff for more sophisticated measurements. But teachers were confident that the improved climate would eventually be reflected in achievement scores.

Coming hard on the heels of these unsettling findings, early in July a *New York Times* article reported that the city's Board of Education had quietly closed down Higher Horizons without even a press release. An independent professional evaluation of the program's first four years (grudgingly released by the Board of Education) had found virtually no measurable effect on the achievements, IQ or reading level of enrolled pupils. It was explained that budgetary limitations had made impossible the "saturation" with additional services originally envisioned. (If the original $250 per pupil had been spent on each of the 100,000 pupils involved, $250,000,000 would have been required annually; this is almost one quarter of Congress' first-year appropriation for Title I of the Education Act.) *The New York Times'* Education Editor, Fred Hechinger, called the results shown by some pupils "the triumphs of the lucky few."

But what of Head Start, the popular and battle-tested program? In most cities it had been offered only on a summertime basis, and one could not expect a great permanent effect. But New Haven, Connecticut has had the pre-kindergarten program as part of the regular school year for the past six years, and could provide no data of measurable change. "Through kindergarten, there is enormous noticeable improvement, but by second grade it's all gone," a school official stated. "The children come up against the same large classes, no extra aides, the old program and teachers."

This situation supported the findings of Dr. Martin Deutsch, a psychologist and director of the Institute for Developmental Studies at New York University, who pioneered the pre-kindergarten program; he claimed that a constant follow-up in later grades is necessary if early gains are not to be lost. It also seemed to support warnings to Congress by Education Commissioner Howe that "initial gains evaporate if special education programs are not maintained," and, "Only a comprehensive long-term program . . . can overcome [disadvantaged children's] deficiencies."

THE FLAWS IN THE SYSTEM

We should not belittle the great side-benefits of the new concern and funds—the greater involvement of parents and other potential leaders in inner-city neighborhoods, the expanded role of schools in local community life, health benefits for the children. (In the first summer of Head Start, 70 per cent of the children had their first medical and dental examination. In Tampa, Florida, twelve cases of tuberculosis and fifty of nutritional deficiencies were found.) Many schools are also getting adequate libraries for the first time.

Moreover, the limited effect of the initial attempts may well point the way to more effective action, and even compensatory education is better than what was happening before.

The lack of research-proven premises behind this billion-dollar educational program probably reflects the government's desperate need to do "something" about ghetto children as much as educators' unwillingness to evaluate themselves. HEW Secretary Gardner makes known his concern about the lack of educational research. (One city has had three research directors and no research results to show for it. One director, who recently resigned, gave an oral report to the Board of Education, but wished to keep the findings unwritten until used for his own professional publication purposes.)

Title III of the Educational Act is promising. This relatively unpublicized provision finances local "centers for change" to stimulate schools to a more innovative approach that relates research to practice. Known as PACE—Projects to Advance Creativity in

Education—Title III also encourages higher-education institutions and local cultural organizations to provide local schools with leadership, new kinds of talents and services. Another little-known program is Title IV, which encourages educational institutions and agencies on different levels to band together on a regional basis to establish "multi-institutional laboratories" for researching and developing new ideas. One recent example of university-school affiliation is New York University's "adoption" of a school in the Bedford-Stuyvesant area, assisted by Ford Foundation funds.

It is important to take note here of the three fundamental flaws in compensatory education, the "more of same" approach. These are mostly failures of society at large, not just of the educators. Indeed, much at fault is the basic American fallacy that education is a panacea. As in public housing, we have not considered all the determining variables.

The first problem is that the schools cannot remedy the deficits of home, family and slum environment. "Remember, the children only spend nine per cent of their time in school," one educator points out. A recent study by the U.S. Office of Education found that differences in the quality of a school had very little effect on the achievement scores of children who have a strong foundation for education at home. Children from disadvantaged homes benefit relatively more from a good school, but it does not fill the gap.

Secondly, much of the present school curriculum is irrelevant for inner-city children. As Dr. Conant observed in *Slums and Suburbs,* "What can words like 'freedom,' 'liberty' and 'equality of opportunity' mean to these young people? With what kind of zeal and dedication can we expect them to withstand . . . communism?" Psychologist Dr. Kenneth Clark has repeatedly pointed out that compensatory education will not work unless the content has more meaning for children from deprived homes. A hopeful step is the publication by major publishing houses of new textbooks and readers that show Negroes, Puerto Ricans and whites as a normal part of the American scene and also include the history of the Negro in America. On the question of whether what is taught in schools is relevant, one inner-city curriculum director observes, "We're finding out how bad what we've been doing is for *both* the white and Negro child. I'd dump 90 per cent of what we teach."

Dr. Fantini asserts that "Middle class children make the schools look good. They give back what's expected of them. But what's so good about middle class know-how? We're all disadvantaged educationally. One need only examine the drop-out rate in college, the performance of most citizens in the wider social arena, the apathy towards social injustice and our inability to exercise leadership to highlight the obsolescence of current education. The deeper issue is whether the educational system is equipping people to deal with the problems of society."

Finally, there is the basic problem of motivation and discrimination. How can we persuade disadvantaged students and their parents that it is worthwhile for the youngster to remain in school and study, to defer premature employment and make the necessary personal investment of time and effort on the premise that such efforts will be rewarded? (Well over half the estimated cost of higher education in the United States comes from income deferred by students.)

As Dr. Conant concluded in *Slums and Suburbs*, "To improve the work of the slum schools requires an improvement in the lives of the families who inhabit the slums, but without a drastic change in the employment opportunities for urban Negro youth relatively little can be accomplished."

Our cities, the centers of the nation's economy, are also the end of the racial line in America. In cities we must proceed simultaneously and at full speed on two parallel fronts: improving environments *and* opportunities. There is no turning back.

More Comprehensive Approaches

8

SURVIVAL THROUGH PLANNING ■ Philadelphia's Style

Of all the big cities, Philadelphia has come closest to a comprehensive approach to the complex of challenges confronting our urban centers. Philadelphia is a long way from solving its problems. Although it has made long strides in certain areas, it also displays profound weaknesses, even in spheres that were once considered among its great strengths.

But over the past two decades, Philadelphia's rational, experimental and coordinated approach has made many of the common urban problems understandable and approachable, not only for itself but also for other American cities. Substituting thought and studies for the national penchant to act first and think later, it has then set goals, devised plans, established priorities and invented programs, strategies and combinations of leadership forces.

Philadelphia's approach has an unusual number of interacting, related aspects, and this is basic to its accomplishments. Not only did that city take into account more elements earlier, starting with good municipal government and city plans; it also recognized relationships between basic elements, and these perceptions underly its planning and revitalization strategy. Renewal in Philadelphia is an instrument of city planning, and planning has been an instrument of creative political leadership. Excellence of architecture and urban design are not just planners' ends; they are civic values and are recognized by business and government leaders as creating economic opportunities which must be seized. Philadelphia was the first big city to develop a comprehensive transportation program; the projected balanced transportation system is indispensable to the city's long-range land use plans and economic health. Awareness of the negative impact slum clearance had on the city's growing Negro poor was a major factor in causing the city to reorient its renewal policies. Saving jobs and creating jobs has long been part of its planning and action programs.

Philadelphia has also shown that many sources of power and interest can be marshaled in a big, multi-centered city to help meet the new challenges. Philadelphia borrowed Pittsburgh's action formula—the indispensable combination of public and private power and purse—but in Philadelphia the combination is more intricately orchestrated and multi-layered, more democratic and diverse. The new direction was not imposed from the top; it emerged from many sources, and progress has been infused with the critical viewpoints and talents of middle-class civic leaders, university professors, urban designers, political administrators, as well as the dynamic leadership of City Hall and top business.

Perhaps more than any other big city, Philadelphia has had to rely on informed long-range plans, design excellence and aggressive action strategies for its survival. Raymond Vernon, director of the monumental Metropolitan Regional Study of New York and author of the classic study, *The Changing Economic Function of the Central City* (1959), pointed out that current technological trends, national corporate needs, and options and consumer preferences, as well as competition from its neighbors, are all against Philadelphia. New York, only ninety miles away, would continue to grow as the national office center and capture ever more of the Quaker City's office headquarters, Vernon predicted, while the nearby suburbs would continue to lure away regional offices, industry and the expanding middle class. Philadelphia would be left with vast "gray areas" where the notion of a great resurgence in middle-income housing was "chimerical," and the long-run prospect was one of declining population and declining jobs.

For this picture to change, he stated, would require "mass public intervention . . . on so large a scale as to constitute a basic departure in American public policy."

Philadelphia believes that informed long-range plans can do much to overcome adverse trends, create alternatives and channel favorable forces. The elements in its $3,700,000,000 long-range plan, published in 1960, recognize that the city must go through profound readjustments to make itself competitive in post-industrial society.

Equally important, from 1952 to 1962 it enjoyed a decade of superb leadership from City Hall and spun off a dizzying number of quasi-public corporations in which citizen leaders are engaging in the unprecedented intervention that is so necessary to the city's plans. These organizations are unconventional and daring, but they are typically Philadelphia in their conservative goal: to save what exists that is good and to build on it. They are in business in a big way, encouraging developments and backing risks that private business cannot or will not undertake by itself, and which public agencies are not equipped to handle alone. Equally important, they are providing a continuity of leadership to bridge the brilliant decade of reform and a less certain future.

Like many cities, Philadelphia has passed through several phases. Recently, it has been going through a slump. Not only is it suffering from the general economic and social problems presented by race, poverty and changing industrial technology. It is also feeling the impact of the consequent restlessness among its Negro population—witness the riots of 1964—in spite of its tradition of progressive race relations and opportunities. The times are moving faster than Philadelphia's programs, and the new executive in City Hall has not moved the city forward sufficiently to meet these challenges.

Still, there is some significant basic progress along social fronts, and if new leaders step forward to carry out new kinds of programs for renewal, as they have done in the past few decades, the city may yet realize its goals. If Philadelphia cannot again become the nation's governmental or business capital, it has a good chance of serving as the vigorous heart of a metropolitan region of 6,500,000 people by 1980, and it may advance far toward being the brain center of the eastern seaboard megalopolis. Although its economic "mix" predicts slower growth than New York's, Philadelphia expects to become more livable while New York grows bigger.

RISE AND DECLINE

The character of Philadelphia's exceptional response to the urban challenges of recent years seems to have been ordained at its birth.

Philadelphia has a heritage almost unique in American city development. It was not carelessly strewn on the wilderness and left to grow by chance; nor was it established merely to exploit natural resources or boom land values. Its founder, William Penn, was in the great Utopian tradition, and planned Philadelphia to be a great city. Before letting his deputies sail for the New World to establish his "Holy Experiment," Penn instructed them that the site selected was to be high, dry and healthy and located by rivers that were navigable for commercial vessels. He also provided them with a plan of development to ensure that the town itself would be open, green and wholesome, with five public squares situated to create four major sub-centers around a central public square.

The name he selected, Philadelphia, recorded for posterity his concept of what a community should be: the City of Brotherly Love. All settlers in his ideal community were to be assured religious tolerance and self-government, two commodities foreign to despot-ridden seventeenth-century Europe.

Penn sought out "industrious husband-men and daylaborers" as settlers, and the continued participation in the city's government of wealthy men who bought large farms across the rivers. Each was provided a town lot, as well. When Penn gave the colonists a Frame of Government (which he had rewritten twenty times), he advised that good men were even more important than good laws, and he urged them to remember that the purpose of government was not correction but "the glory of almighty God and the good of mankind."

Philadelphia was thus launched on a century of pre-eminence. People of ability from many countries came there to settle, not just to make money and move on. They gave Philadelphia a cosmopolitan character, stimulated the arts and artisan skills and encouraged diverse industrial growth. With the Schuylkill River on the city's west reaching far into the rich hinterland, and the deep Delaware on the east harboring ocean-going vessels, Philadelphia prospered mightily. By 1760 it was the largest and most cosmopolitan city in the colonies. It was natural that the Continental Congress should gather in its Statehouse, and that Philadelphia, where the Declaration of Independence was written, provide the seat of the new federal government (and of its first commercial bank).

However, the city's early pre-eminence ended. Physical deterioration was accompanied by the desertion of its elite and decay of its government. The city sank into prosperous indolence, into a municipal state worse than that of any other large American city.

But when Philadelphia's citizens became sufficiently aroused in 1951 to rebel against generations of accumulated rot, William Penn's principles re-emerged in the city's life, making the civic upheaval more than another municipal housecleaning or charter reform. As a result, old Philadelphia once again took the national lead in the arts of urban development and local government, setting patterns and standards not only for itself but also for the rest of the country. There have been some surprising weaknesses and, recently, some regrettable lapses. But innovative change has become institutionalized in the city, and many individuals and local forces have a continuing personal stake in seeing that Philadelphia meets its new problems. Despite the gloomy predictions for its economic future and the growing problems of poverty and race, Philadelphia, more than any other large city, appears to have a chance of benefiting from the present period of transition to the urban future.

Philadelphia's original decline from national pre-eminence began when the seat of the federal government was moved in 1800 to the new capital city of Washington (a city some say was laid out for speculation by politically strong Virginians). Its economic supremacy was challenged by New York, which was blessed by a naturally superior location and deep-water port and settled by more aggressive merchants; it ended with the opening of the Erie Canal. The *coup de grâce* was administered in 1836, when President Andrew Jackson abolished the national bank.

But Penn had set the city on the path of prosperity, and soon the Pennsylvania Railroad, promoted by Philadelphia's merchants as an answer to the Erie Canal, made Philadelphia a major distribution center and provided new impetus to its broad-based industrial and port development. The railroad's singular importance is attested by the perhaps apocryphal story that mothers had children end their bedtime prayers with, "Please, God, bless the Pennsy."

The railroad was also a major factor in eroding the city. In 1881 the Pennsylvania line located its Broad Street station right next to the monumental new City Hall, whose tower rose 547 feet high on the city's central square. And with the station, the company brought in, above grade, sixteen tracks all the way from the Schuylkill River—a block-wide "Chinese Wall" which cast a blighting pall over development in the western half of the city's center.

Simultaneously the rail company developed suburbs along the "main line" of its commuter service twenty-four miles to Paoli, with equally disastrous effects for the central city. Settled in these new green country towns, which are among the most beautiful suburbs in the world, Philadelphia's absentee aristocracy could commute easily to offices in the city whose politics they continued to control and whose real estate they held in trust.

From the suburbs one could remain smug about the city's colonial past, even as the dozen blocks of center city where the nation was born became silted over with dingy shops, storage lofts and deteriorated housing; suburban residents could also be content despite the growing municipal corruption and decay in the central city. The trusts they controlled found the financial returns from city slums to be particularly high, and Philadelphia still boasted the name "City of Beautiful Homes," even as drab brick row housing for factory workers spread out block after block from the core of Penn's once-green old town.

Turn-of-the-century reform movements against bad housing and machine politics had their vogue in Philadelphia, but by 1920 the Republican machine, managed by brothers who had become wealthy by feeding city garbage to their pigs, was firmly entrenched in City Hall. It evidently satisfied the men who actually ruled the city: the suburban bankers and lawyers, whose goal was a safe return for inherited wealth in trust funds; the trustees of the University of Pennsylvania; and the Pennsylvania Railroad.

Alone among big cities, Philadelphia's Republican machine survived the depression-time inroads of the Democratic party. The city's administration even turned down the New Deal's offer of $60,000,000 for federal public works. When the city's assessments plummeted, making it impossible to continue adequate city services as well as payments on its huge municipal debt from the speculative 1920's, the city's bankers bailed Philadelphia out. But they agreed to do so only on the condition that the city maintain a balanced budget. As a result, city services slipped still further, and the bankers' do-nothing control tightened.

At the end of World War II, Philadelphia was like a doughnut, a vast metropolis built up around a hollow center. At night, downtown streets were almost deserted. Only a few decent residential blocks remained around elegant Rittenhouse Square, built up a century after the colonial eastern end. The rest of the streets were being submerged in slums that now also surrounded the great universities located in the inner city, as well as the downtown hospitals. Streets were the dirtiest in the country, gas lights still flickered on many, and garbage was collected by horse-drawn carriages. Its sewage-polluted waters demanded so much chlorination to make them safe for drinking that a glass of Philadelphia water was dubbed a "chlorine cocktail."

Behind all this stood the most quiet and crudely wasteful city government in the United States. Its payroll was loaded with employees too lazy to clean even the grimy grandiose City Hall. City budgets were thrown together year by year to meet the requirements of the Republican City Committee, as expressed through the Mayor and City Council. Municipal appointments and promotions depended on a nod from ward chairmen. Political leaders often sold city jobs. But the ruling class tolerated all this. They did not live in the city, and did not have to drink its water. They just wanted to maintain the status quo.

The Quaker influence still persisted in the city's fine private schools and nearby colleges, and in religious and racial tolerance. Main Line matrons loyally came in for the Friday afternoon symphony concerts. But one could wander through the University Museum for days without seeing another person. Industry, too, fled because (it was said) of the crushing city tax burden.

THE GATHERING OF FORCES

When out-of-towners asked Richardson Dilworth, Philadelphia's second reform-era Mayor, to explain his city's dramatic resurgence, he would tell them, "What every city needs is a crisis." Philadelphia had a series of municipal scandals, and without these precipitants, it seems doubtful that the local forces which put across reform and shaped the local renaissance would have gathered. But not everyone recognizes crisis as an opportunity; not everyone has plans and ideas for taking constructive advantage of it.

For the multiple changes that have taken place since 1951 in Philadelphia to occur, many forces first had to be aroused, many people to become involved and committed, and many years to pass in this multi-centered lethargic city of 2,000,000. In fact, one key to Philadelphia's continued progress is the number of organizations and individuals who have played important parts in the revival, and the cumulative effect and onward motion provided by these different movements and personalities. The voices are not always in harmony, and progress is uneven, but each voice is strong.

The start of the "new" Philadelphia goes back to 1939, when a group of eager government reformers known as the Young Turks—recent college graduates who were struck with Roosevelt fever and sparks of municipal excitement emanating from New York's Mayor La Guardia—joined to work for charter revision. They failed to achieve this goal, and might easily have sunk into the ranks of earlier local reformers who had been disillusioned. But they were held together by a broad, long-range line of attack on their city's underlying ills proposed by the man who had originally brought them together.

Walter Phillips, a patrician Philadelphian who numbers among his ancestors four Mayors of the city (including Penn's first deputy), had gained insight into his community's basic problems by writing his college thesis on Philadelphia's fiscal plight. He suggested to the Young Turks: "Get the people interested in physical changes. Then they'll be forced to see the need for good government."

Thus was born the City Policy Committee. This group's carefully selected young membership wanted first to educate themselves on the problems facing their city—from such physical and municipal housekeeping problems as sewage disposal, housing and neighborhood improvement to issues of racial segregation and government structure. They met biweekly at a downtown restaurant to discuss their findings.

Men were also sitting around and talking in other Philadelphia luncheon clubs, even the old-time municipal reformers remaining in the Committee of 70. But the City Policy Committee was fundamentally different from the other groups. Its membership included women and Negroes; its line of inquiry was far more comprehensive; and it was an *action* group. The first goal was to strengthen city planning; next was housing improvement. The Committee would also have staff work, this to be provided by another talented young old-line Philadelphian, Edmund N. Bacon. Walter Phillips had anchored this architect-planner first by commissioning him to design his home and then by getting him appointed to the recently vacant job of managing director of the Philadelphia Housing Association, a civic organization founded in 1908.

The Young Turk organization presented its critique of the present City Planning Commission to venerable Republican Mayor Robert Lamberton (a former judge whose mayoral candidacy was responsible for frustrating the charter drive). Lamberton asked the group to draw up a plan for the Commission's reorganization. They in turn invited other groups to participate in a joint committee and received technical assistance from the local Bureau of Municipal Research.

But in December 1941, on the day that the joint committee was to present to the Mayor its proposal for a strong Planning Commission, one with statutory power, full-time staff and budget, Lamberton died of a sudden stroke.

His successor, City Council President Bernard Samuels, was a different type of Mayor. Worried about the opposition of special interests in the city to the proposed reorganization of the Planning Commission, he sat on the necessary ordinance for a year. This long delay was used by the City Policy Committee to draw in more support and make the strong new Planning Commission a community cause. By late 1942 great public interest virtually forced the City Council to pass the ordinance unanimously.

Then, to make sure that the new Commission would be well staffed, the Young Turks searched for the best man in the country to become the director of planning. Their first choice, Robert B. Mitchell, head of the urban section of the National Resources Committee, was appointed. Then, at Phillips' urging, they formed a permanent civic organization to watchdog, encourage and supplement the official activities of the new city agency. Thus was born the Citizens' Council on City Planning, a representative community organization which, along with the Philadelphia Housing Association, is among the most useful and effective bodies of its kind in the country.

AN IMAGE IS FIXED

The new Citizens' Council quickly launched its first project, Chairman Phillips' ambitious scheme for an exhibit to show Philadelphians what city planning could do. Another member of the earlier City Policy Committee, Oskar Stonorov, an architect-planner who loved the city and had a gift for visualizing abstract ideas, gave form to the exhibit's concepts. Planning Director Mitchell sold his Commission chairman, Edward Hopkinson, a financier who was one of the Republican's venerable nine old men, on the idea. Then Phillips and Hopkinson together created a blue-chip committee which raised the $400,000 needed to execute the exhibit. City Council gave $100,000, and the rest was contributed by the business community. Gimbel's Department Store housed the exhibit without charge.

The spectacular "Better Philadelphia Exhibition" was unveiled in September 1947. During the two months it was open, 400,000 men, women and children—one for each dollar expended—visited the exhibit. No doubt it was the best show in the stodgy city. The panorama was big and professional, it was exciting and fun. It was designed, according to the official brochure, "to dramatize city planning—to gain the confidence of a public made cynical by utopian futuramas and the inertia of local politicians." It employed almost every display technique and dynamic device to illustrate how many of the city's physical problems could be solved. Lights went on and off, objects moved, bells rang to call attention to changes. There were humorous cartoons, huge aerial maps, a diorama. The appalling extent of residential blight in Philadelphia was shown by a statistical display. Visitors could also walk into a life-size model of a typical nineteenth-century row house which had been rehabilitated.

To reveal how the decaying old center city would look in thirty years if proposed projects and public improvements were carried out, there was an animated fourteen-by-thirty-foot scale model of center city, with sections that flipped over one at a time to show before and after. Among the changes presented were a mall and park around Independence Hall; a series of "greenways" linking up old historic buildings for pedestrians; even a promenade along the Delaware River as originally planned by William Penn, but now also including a modern marina and recreational facilities in place of the unused ugly piers. In a matter of minutes, a whole section of the city was reborn before the spectators' eyes.

"For years Philadelphia had thought of itself as hopeless," city planning director Edmund Bacon, who helped develop many of the plans embodied in the exhibit, has recalled. "The idea that the city could be exciting was an enormous shock." Robert Mitchell commented: "The exhibit made people see the city as solvable." With it, an image was fixed in the public mind. (Eventually, the panorama was housed permanently in the city's Commercial Museum, where it is kept up to date as changes are realized.)

But the means for implementing the exhibit's idea—including the support of the politicians—were far from at hand. However, the exhibit gave "Barney" Samuels, who was up for re-election that fall, wonderful free publicity as a progressive mayor. (Democratic party workers who passed out pamphlets saying "Barney Samuels wouldn't recognize a plan if he saw one," were threatened with arrest.)

Richardson Dilworth, Samuels' Democratic opponent, carried out a sensational street-corner campaign in which he exposed corrupt practices in one city department after another and named culpable politicians. But the city was not yet ready for change. Samuels was returned to office with a 100,000 plurality.

THE PRICE OF NEGLECT

Soon after the Mayor's re-election, however, Dilworth's charges were substantiated—ironically, by a committee which Samuels had appointed to investigate the feasibility of acceding to municipal employees' demands for overdue pay increases without raising taxes. The gross malfeasances, wastes and inefficiencies which the committee found in every city department led to arrests, suicides and jailings of top city officials and, by the spring of 1948, to a Grand Jury investigation. Headlines about municipal conspiracies, scandals and embezzlements were daily newspaper fare for many weeks.

Now the leading businessmen of Philadelphia, who had tolerated municipal corruption—most of all because the local private economy appeared sound to them—were roused to take constructive action.

The impetus came from one of the less parochial and contented members of the Philadelphia WASP business elite, Harry A. Batten, the urbane, personable and tough-minded president of N. W. Ayer and Son, Inc., one of the largest advertising agencies, with headquarters in Philadelphia. In the summer of 1948, when the scandals were breaking, Batten, in California on vacation, called on business friends there with the idea of convincing them to locate an Eastern office in Philadelphia. Batten had a well-earned reputation as a persuasive salesman. But he was left without a comeback to the Californian's charge, one which has since become local legend: "Why come to Philadelphia with its stinking water and its lousy politics?"

The high price of the neglect of Philadelphia by those who depended on it for their wealth now came home to him. Back in Philadelphia, Batten discussed with several top industrial and banking executives the need for creating a better climate in order to attract new industry. This nucleus sounded out their peers around town about joining in an organized effort; and they invited Park Martin, then director of the Allegheny Conference on Community Development, to explain how Pittsburgh's top power was working together for local improvement. Appropriate fanfare accompanied the announcement on December 16, 1948, of the formation of the Greater Philadelphia Movement, another key civic organization.

The GPM was a top-power group. Its board was to be limited to thirty-five men, almost all of them presidents of home-owned corporations, men who, as Batten put it, "wouldn't have to check back with Papa" before they could act, and whose business interests would not be threatened by political activity. In general, they were WASPs—the men who control the city's banks, trusts, department stores and universities, and, by and large, run Philadelphia. But there was a sprinkling of broader representation, several Jews and Catholics, and a labor official.

Like their counterparts in Pittsburgh, the members of the Greater Philadelphia Movement were interested in general community development. But they recognized that local government improvement, starting with charter reform, had to be their first goal.

Another temporary joint citizens committee was formed by the GPM, the Young Turks and others. In 1949, the state legislature was so impressed by the Philadelphians' unprecedented show of unity that it gave them what they wanted—the right to draft their own instrument of government, instead of having it done for them by a committee appointed in Harrisburg.

A CITY WRITES ITS CHARTER

"Something comparable to the New Deal has taken place in Philadelphia," a leading member of the city's reform government observed of its genesis. "There has been a sense of fervor and a new day. A great many groups which hadn't rationalized their own thoughts in relation to each other got together—the socially concerned who wanted to get rid of slums, the Center Cityists, the silk stocking–good government forces, the civil libertarians, the home builders who saw raw land out in Northeast. All got on the bandwagon."

Much of this new civic cohesion and awareness emerged from Philadelphia's new charter. The instrument of city government was not drafted by just the small body of officially appointed Charter Commission members and their expert advisors. Virtually all the different interest groups of the city were given an unprecedented opportunity to focus their thinking on what they wanted their city to become. The Greater Philadelphia Movement was largely responsible for bringing this about. The GPM first made sure that Mayor Samuels appointed distinguished citizens, not political hacks, to the Commission, and it then went on to organize a Citizens' Charter Committee. Under the aegis of the latter body, some 500 civic groups, ranging from neighborhood organizations to citywide chapters of national organizations, were encouraged to study community problems and make suggestions, which were passed along to the official Commission. As a result, the ideas of many civically concerned groups—the advocates of strong, long-range planning; the businessmen and economy-efficiency groups; the human rights constellation of Quakers and Jews—were translated into the new instrument of local government.

The nature of the chief executive's office was a much debated question. Some liberals and old-time municipal reformers favored adopting the Council City manager plan. But the belief that a big city needed a strong elected top executive won out, and the charter's provisions recognized the important job which such a Mayor must perform. The charter stripped City Council of its administrative powers and now vested them in the Mayor. It also gave him great powers of appointment and removal, free of Council approval, so that he could hire the best professional aides and give more time to broad city problems.*

* Specifically, the charter gave the Mayor four top-level, high-salaried administrators, who, with the Mayor, were to make up his Cabinet: a managing director, to be in charge of ten service departments; a director of finance, to control budgeting, purchasing and revenue functions; a city representative-director of commerce to promote the city's commerce and industrial development as well as handle public relations and ceremonial duties; and a city solicitor.

The nonpartisan Civil Service Commission was strengthened and assured a budget to administer a merit system of employment. A strong Commission on Human Relations was given powers to subpoena and initiate investigations, making equal opportunity for all Philadelphians in effect a government mandate.

While the charter encouraged efficient spending, the Commission made known its belief that the city had not spent enough in the past to give voters the quality of municipal service they had a right to expect. There had been no guides to spending and virtually no opportunity for the public to make its voice heard except through last-minute pressures.

The charter altered this by tying together physical planning and fiscal planning on a longer-range basis. The new Planning Commission was required to prepare and make public each year its recommendations to the city administration for capital improvements, not only for the budget year but also within the framework of a six-year program, which was to be revised annually. Three members of the Mayor's cabinet were to be members of the Planning Commission and help make the policies that he would recommend to City Council, which had the final voice on city spending.

Thus the elected body responsible for spending was to be guided by the advice of the officials and body with an overview of city needs, goals and resources, and the intention to spend on specific programs would be public knowledge well in advance of the Council's decisions.*

Several vital matters remained beyond the city's control, in spite of the home rule charter. The state still determined Philadelphia's debt limits; an independent board determined assessments; and the school system was run by another independent board appointed by twenty-one local judges, an arrangement made by the state in the early part of the century to remove education from local political pressures but which also made the system slow to respond to new needs.

* This municipal arrangement would make possible an unusually constructive interaction between Philadelphia's citizen organizations and government during the decision-making process. Each year, for example, the Citizens' Council on City Planning reviews all projects proposed in the six-year Capital Program and its analysis is submitted to City Council for use in departmental and public hearings. With such public knowledge, Council is reluctant to change programs once scheduled. The charter also mandated preparation of a long-range comprehensive plan.

Public participation, public hearings and educational efforts on behalf of the charter continued right up until polling day in April of 1951. (The charter was even rewritten to make it more understandable.) An army of 34,000 got out an unprecedented 40 per cent of the voters, and the charter passed by a two-to-one vote. The document that emerged was an expression of community will and the finest big-city charter in the country.

A SHORT DISTANCE IN THE RIGHT DIRECTION

The effectiveness of Philadelphia's fine charter depended, ultimately, on the determination and ability of the city's Mayor to make it work.

The Young Turks had been fortunate in attracting to their ranks two slightly older, politically ambitious men of unusual background and rare ability. Without Joseph S. Clark, Jr. and Richardson Dilworth, the entire Philadelphia revitalization might have failed to take place.

Clark and Dilworth both came from well-to-do Republican families, graduated from Harvard and Yale respectively, and, during the 1920's, practiced corporate law in Philadelphia. During that decade, both revolted against their conservative heritage. They joined a local Democratic club and became its leading spirits. Although the two men were temperamentally different—Clark, intellectual and socially conscious; Dilworth, action-oriented, pragmatic and more political—they became good friends, and during the 1930's, managed each other's unsuccessful campaigns for City Council and State Senate.

Clark and Dilworth returned to Philadelphia after World War II with brilliant records and fresh enthusiasm both for politics and local change, but they found little welcome among the regular Democrats. Active association with the Citizens' Council on City Planning was natural for them, and would prove a very good turn for city planning and improvement in Philadelphia. Reform was so much in the air by 1947, and the Democrats so down and out, that the party sought its mayoralty candidate in the reformers' ranks. Their choice, razor-tongued Dilworth, was unsuccessful. But in 1949, with municipal scandals continuing to discredit the entrenched Republicans, sizable majorities elected Dilworth as City Treasurer and Clark as City Controller in the off-year election. For the next decade, the two men were the standard bearers for Philadelphia, and the leading local Democrats. However, the fact that they had catapulted to the top without a real reform of the party machine itself and change in the composition of City Council would prove a handicap to Philadelphia's progress once they were gone. Still, during the 1950's they were able to lay basic directions and encourage patterns of civic-city cooperation which gave continuity to programs well beyond their tenures in City Hall.

Fortuitously it was Clark's turn to run for Mayor in 1951. Dilworth ran for District Attorney and, backed by independent voter groups, the two were swept into office by substantial pluralities.

The new charter was to go into effect in January of 1952, several days after Clark took office as Mayor. Not only did he carry out his campaign pledge to implement the charter; during his extraordinary four years in City Hall he also laid the indispensable groundwork and style for his city's revitalization, and set standards for progressive administrations in other cities, as well.

A man with deep convictions and forthrightness rare in political life, Clark pondered long about the role of the Mayor of a great American city. His guiding philosophy, published in *Harper's* magazine several years after he had left City Hall, might serve as the touchstone for other elective city leaders. The bright array of professional and civic talents Philadelphia attracted and nurtured since 1951 may well be attributed to his credo.

A Mayor is not likely to succeed, Clark wrote in this essay, unless he also remembers that he is the directly elected representative of all the people in his city and that they look to him for leadership. He must stay ahead of the crowd, but not so far that he loses sight of his followers and they of him. To solve the city's problems, the Mayor requires the aid of skilled planners for the city, metropolitan area and region. They must be the best that money can buy, but "money alone is not enough to attract them." Often the Mayor must persuade them to enter public service at considerable personal loss. "He can do this only if he holds a high conception of the purpose of political leadership. Nobody can be expected to follow a mayor with clay feet. . . . A good political leader must have the ability to look ahead for the best way to the ideal future of his city [and] try to lead his community a short distance in the right direction."

The Democratic regulars watched with mounting dismay and anger as "Gentleman Joe" established the merit personnel system rather than giving them long-awaited patronage. Clark hired the best people, regardless of party, for the new top administrative posts. For administrative assistants, he appointed Ph.D.'s, and told them part of their job was "to help fight the battle for my mind." The GPM members were made close participants. He even kept on as chairman of the Planning Commission WASP financier and Republican elder statesman Edward Hopkinson, Jr. Fortunately, James Finnegan, the reform-minded Democratic City Committee chairman, had also been elected president of City Council and he was able to keep "the boys" in line during the post-election honeymoon, so that Clark could put many necessary programs into effect.

The first urgent job was to put Philadelphia's collapsing financial house in order. The new administration inherited a huge outstanding debt and a seemingly endless catalogue of overdue capital improvements. It pushed a $20,000,000 tax increase through the Council; cut bond terms form 50 to 25 years; put the city on a partial pay-as-you-go basis; and placed a lid on the annual amount appropriated for tax-supported loans. The system of interrelated fiscal planning and capital programming called for in the charter was instituted.

City Hall was thoroughly scrubbed, street-cleaning regularized, the old gas lamps replaced by electric lights. To improve neglected streets and other city facilities, a huge $150,000,000 capital program was passed. Neighborhoods long neglected soon enjoyed bright, modern playground facilities as the city inaugurated a program to bring recreation to all the people. The archaic garbage collection system was modernized; an $80,000,000 sewage collection and treatment system began. New fire stations, apparatus and training methods were installed to raise the city's fire rating from the costly classification to which underwriters had demoted it. The city also encouraged the arts. It gave money to the great, private Philadelphia Orchestra; supported free summer concerts at Robin Hood Dell; increased appropriations to the Museum of Art and the public library.

The hostile, dissatisfied Democratic regulars began to undermine Clark. He lacked enough power in the party organization to prevent them from replacing his reform-minded party chairman with an old-guard Congressman, William Green. But Clark's popular following was sufficiently great that when the regulars sabotaged the vote for an important bond issue or joined with the Republicans in an attempt to gut the charter, he was able to exert his position to win. Indeed, the best way for the Mayor to combat the drag of the machine was to give leadership for a better city.

The manner in which Clark fought for Penn Center affords a dramatic example of his concept of leadership and sets the style of cooperation between planner and political leader which has enabled Philadelphia to accomplish so much.

In 1953 the Pennsylvania Railroad finally kept its 1925 promise to vacate its little-used Broad Street station next to City Hall. Removal of the station and tracks would open up four blocks in the city's business-civic center. Edmund Bacon was now executive director of the City Planning Commission, and since the Greater Philadelphia Exhibit, he had plans for the day that the hideous "Chinese Wall" came down. His great fear was that the exceptional potential of this heartland site, the first major redevelopment downtown, would be frittered away on a piecemeal basis since the real estate was privately owned and the city had no legal control over it.

Bacon set about "injecting into the public's mind" his image of Penn Center, the name he had for the development that he visualized on the cleared site. To provide Bacon with a public platform to launch his design proposal, the Citizens' Council on City Planning and the Chamber of Commerce gave a luncheon.

By its openness, unity and beauty, Penn Center was to serve as a tangible symbol of a new kind of city. One of the projected Center's main elements was a street-level pedestrian mall extending four blocks from the suburban stations and new garages at the area's far end. This esplanade would lead the commuter visually as well as by foot toward City Hall and other center city destinations and encourage pedestrian cross-traffic as well. On the street level Bacon proposed three office buildings rising on stilts to allow uninterrupted views and maximum sunlight on the mall. Underneath the mall there would be another pedestrian concourse to the railroad station, lined with shops, restaurants, a skating rink and other places of amusement, and a sunken open central plaza with staircases between the two levels.

The citizens were receptive to the plan; the Mayor was enthusiastic. The Pennsylvania Railroad promised to study it. But soon it appeared that the company was going to make deals on separate parcels. Mayor Clark threatened the line with condemnation of the site should rebuilding plans be unacceptable to the city. He also appointed a Citizens' Advisory Committee to keep Bacon's design clearly before the developers.

When construction began in the winter of 1954, however, it appeared that the underground concourse was to be abandoned. The New York developer selected by the Pennsylvania Railroad for part of the site was refusing to provide sufficient ceiling height in the basement level of his buildings to allow for this important unifying element.

Mayor Clark, although battling for his political life against the charter gutters, threw the full weight of his office behind his planning director. Clark summoned the private developer, the railroad's real estate consultant and Bacon to his office, and delivered a lecture on the proper development of center city. A compromise was promptly worked out, and several months later the railroad announced that it would develop the entire underground concourse itself.

THE HARD GUTS OF IT

"People take pride in the 'spectaculars'—the center city rebuilding projects like Penn Center," Clark commented from the perspective of Washington after several years in the U.S. Senate. "But the hard guts of it is finding poor families a decent place to live."

Clark did not start out with a special concern for better housing; nor did the new charter centralize scattered renewal programs—slum clearance, housing, redevelopment, code enforcement. But among the people "fighting the battle for the Mayor's mind" were several who were concerned with the problems of shelter, and Clark's own experience in office had already involved him in it.

In 1948, Clark used his power as Controller to appoint two of the Public Housing Authority's five board members (the Mayor appointed two others) in order to improve that racketeer-run body. One of his appointees, Walter Phillips, was largely responsible for the Authority dropping its politics-dominated method of selecting architects and personnel, and making good design and neighborhood orientation indigenous to Philadelphia's public housing program.

When Clark became Mayor, he named as City Solicitor, Abraham Freedman, who had written Pennsylvania's redevelopment statute, served as legal counsel to the Philadelphia Housing Association, and had been a Young Turk. Freedman proposed that Clark establish the new post of Housing Coordinator, to bring into one person's hands the scattered lines of the various shelter programs, some of which were run by independent authorities, others by city agencies. Clark appointed his executive secretary, William Rafsky, a former labor union research director, to this top new city post.* He named to the board of the Redevelopment Authority another Young Turk, Dorothy S. Montgomery, an advanced, nationally recognized thinker in the field who was also managing director of the citizen housing association. Planning director Edmund Bacon was also shelter-oriented, having trained as an architect and served for a time in a public housing agency.

Influenced by its distinguished local planners and concerned citizen organizations, and enabled by the state's early and flexible redevelopment statute, Philadelphia was one of the first cities in the country to become active in programs for redevelopment, housing rehabilitation and neighborhood conservation. Not only did it pioneer significant new approaches to using the tools; many of its special concepts and experiments influenced national legislation.

In the late 1940's and 1950's, before urban renewal, the "Philadelphia approach" made that city a national favorite of planners, architects and housing reformers. Philadelphia's ap-

* The Coordinator was also made a member of the Mayor's Cabinet.

proach to slum areas combined rehabilitation of homes and small-scale clearance within single project areas; it emphasized preservation of neighborhoods and their institutions, and designed new housing to blend with the neighborhood's scale. It showed a concern for people and planning with them, mixing income groups within projects; even an awareness of the racial implications of new programs. It was a marked contrast to Robert Moses' New York formula of total clearance and high-rise building, as much in concept as in quality and quantity of results.

Philadelphia's renewal planners were also distinguished for developing concepts to guide their programs, for their ability to articulate and evaluate these. Their first operating theory was that if one worked from within the city's bad slums, clearing the worst first, the islands of good new housing would stimulate private rehabilitation in surrounding areas. Unfortunately, this theory did not work out in practice. The areas cleared were too small to change the slum environment, and the Redevelopment Authority could not get private investors to sponsor housing in such badly deteriorated neighborhoods.

At East Poplar, the city's first redevelopment venture, the city had to act as sponsor of the initial housing development, Penn Towne, using special state financing to lower rentals to the middle-income range. In spite of the lowered cost and well-designed new housing, families that could afford the rentals preferred not to live in the midst of blight. A vacancy rate of 10 to 12 per cent endangered Penn Towne's financing for many years.* Moreover, poor families dislocated from even the small clearance sites crowded into nearby houses that had been slated for voluntary rehabilitation (the problems of rehousing were far greater than anticipated). Thus, new slums were formed in the vicinity, and the cost and extent of eventual clearance rose.

In a widely studied experiment, also in the East Poplar project, the Redevelopment Authority helped the American Friends' Service Committee acquire a block of slum housing adjacent to Penn Towne which the Quakers were to help reconstruct with

* Parts of East Poplar and several other early clearance projects have still not been rebuilt for lack of publicly assisted programs designed to build housing priced for the middle and lower-middle market; there is also a high vacancy rate in reasonably priced housing out of slum areas.

cost-cutting "self-help." This was the first attempt in such cooperative rehabilitation, and photographs of the end product, with its bright, clean apartments, inner court and play area were widely reproduced and admired. The self-help techniques appealed to many, as did the fact that both Negro and white families lived in the eighty-eight-unit private project. But even though costs were reduced by the Title I write-down and by residents doing much of the rehabilitation work, rents were still too high for the original slum tenants. The public expenditure was so out of proportion to results achieved that the Redevelopment Authority and Friends abandoned plans for similar efforts.

The city also cooperated with realtor-initiated efforts to spruce up some slum blocks by closing off and cleaning back alleys and then joining the backyards with communal gardens and play areas. Here, too, the results were pleasing. Unfortunately, these bite-size projects soon reverted to their former deteriorated condition.

In still another unusual and pioneering step, the Redevelopment Authority acquired sites in the East Poplar project for the Public Housing Authority, thus reducing the project development costs. This step allowed the Authority to build low-rise housing for families displaced by slum clearance at the relatively low densities Philadelphians consider suitable for family living. If the public housing project had to absorb the full costs of slum acquisition and clearance, the inevitable alternative would have been the typical high-rise project which was so unpopular locally.

This kind of cooperative undertaking was later repeated. In fact, it appeared necessary to use redevelopment-cleared slum areas if such projects—and high-rise ghettos—were to be avoided.

Even though the city's public housing projects were legally integrated, census figures showed that the number of white families eligible by income for public housing had declined by 40 per cent between 1940 and 1950, while Negroes, who formed a steadily growing proportion of the city's population as well as of the families being dislocated by slum clearance, had increased by that amount. But City Council was increasingly unwilling to give its necessary approval to open sites for public housing, as urged by citizen groups, since such undeveloped land was located in white neighborhoods where there was heavy pressure against it by property owners. With some of these problems in mind, the Redevelopment Authority under Clark gave top priority to a project for reclamation and development of the last substantial area of open land in Philadelphia, the partly swampy 2,000-acre Eastwick area in the southwest corner of the city, which could be developed without homebuilders' opposition.

Despite these noteworthy efforts, it was obvious that slums were spreading faster than they could be cleared and that the problems of relocation added to them. People in positions of responsibility believed that many more facts were needed to assess the actual nature of the slum problem and its dimensions. Housing Coordinator Rafsky determined that a full-scale study should be undertaken, leading to the establishment of priorities and alternative approaches to the Central Urban Renewal Area —the planners' name for the inner-city district where the city's worst housing was concentrated. Mayor Clark won from City Council a $50,000 appropriation to underwrite the study. He also directed the Planning Commission to prepare the long-range comprehensive plan called for by the charter so that future developments in the city might be suitably related to one another.

At the end of his four years in City Hall, late in 1955, Clark felt far from having come to grips with Philadelphia's underlying problems. But he had run for office as a one-term-only candidate, with the understanding that Dilworth could run for Mayor next.

Clark had initiated major pioneering studies—one on urban renewal, another on urban transportation—but the facts and proposals were emerging from these studies just as his term drew to a close. His City Representative, Walter Phillips, had, as director of the city's commercial promotion, looked into the facts behind Philadelphia's slipping manufacturing base. (With unemployment running 6 to 7 per cent, the city was officially declared a "labor surplus" area.) Phillips also had some unexpected answers and a promising proposal for countering the trend. But the Mayor had not been able to push Phillips' proposal through City Council. Nor had Clark taken on the Democratic machine in that one good knock-down, drag-out fight for local control of the party which he had promised himself—for he and others feared that the machine could be the Achilles heel of the city's future progress.

But Clark had taken the city that "short distance in the right direction," and now it was Dilworth's turn to try for Mayor. In 1956, Clark took a long shot at realizing his life-long ambition of becoming a United States Senator and, despite the Eisenhower flood in Pennsylvania, he won.

It would be up to Dilworth's administration to implement the new approach and set of priorities emerging from the study of the Central Urban Renewal Area, as well as the radical solutions for dealing with the city's mounting vehicular traffic recommended by the Urban Traffic and Transportation Board appointed by Clark. The new administration, as it developed, would also have to harness the community's business power to work with the planners in order to fill in and renew the doughnut's hollow—Philadelphia's center city.

FILLING IN THE DOUGHNUT

Philadelphia had enormous untapped potential in its decaying old city, the two-mile-long rectangle between the bends in the Delaware and Schuylkill rivers which was Penn's original "green country town." The intimate scale of the old buildings and narrow streets; the handsome architect-designed eighteenth-and nineteenth-century homes now disfigured by grime, stucco and commercial use, or marred by internal misuse as lofts and rooming houses; the city's great museums, symphony, universities and other cultural institutions located there or nearby—together these held the promise of a kind of urban environment rarely possible in contemporary American cities. The neglected eastern end of the city also contained much of the United States' colonial heritage.

But only an exceptionally devoted urbanite would remain, much less settle, in the midst of the blight which had immersed much of center city. Even the elegance of the Rittenhouse Square area, last of the quadrants of Penn's original city to be built up, and the one residential neighborhood that held its own, was threatened by commercial zoning variances which were eating into the area. South of the Square, toward the Schuylkill, there was a jumble of parking lots, lumberyards and other low-grade, non-residential uses mixed in with deteriorated old town and carriage houses.

Still, a drift back to center city during the immediate postwar years was evident in that area. A remarkable house-by-house, block-by-block rehabilitation by new owners who bought and fixed up old houses was slowly pushing back blight and slums south from the Square. The new trend was encouraged by efforts of the Center City Residents' Association, which formed in 1946 to prevent further erosion of the area by non-residential zoning variances. The Association was assisted by the Zoning Alerting Services provided by the Citizens' Council on City Planning to inform subscribing members of appeals to the city for variances from official zoning. But until 1952, the city administration did nothing to support such voluntary improvement efforts.

A typical result of previous regimes' neglect was Fitler Square, a so-called park in the Rittenhouse Square neighborhood, which had become a mudhole inhabited by drunks and empty bottles. After Clark's election, his Recreation Department responded to the request of the Center City Residents' Association for the park's rehabilitation. Before long, mothers were wheeling baby carriages to this new oasis.

By 1956, the Association had 1,000 dues-paying members, and private mortgage money was available to the area for old-house restoration as well as for new home construction for the first time in decades. After the State Highway Department was persuaded by the city to place the route of its projected crosstown expressway a block further south—according to city instead of state plans—thus assuring prospective home purchasers in that strip that their fix-up efforts would not be in vain, a new wave of rehabilitation and home building activity was set off almost within weeks.

On the opposite, southeastern end of the rectangle, however, far more herculean efforts and tremendous public assistance were required to bring back the eighteenth-century city into suitable modern use.

The first breakthrough there took place in 1949, when a long struggle headed by Judge Edwin O. Lewis to get federal help in rescuing Independence Hall from the surrounding grime and honky-tonk was finally won. That year Congress authorized the National Park Service to make the Hall and its vicinity, which contained other buildings of historic significance, into a national park and shrine. The Commonwealth of Pennsylvania agreed to undertake a three-block clearance north of the Hall to provide a mall leading to the great landmark. As the rot slowly disappeared, historic houses near the mall and park began to be visible.

Next, Harry Batten, organizer of the Greater Philadelphia Movement, became concerned with the condition of Washington Square, onto which the offices of N. W. Ayer and Son, Inc. faced. The neglected Square, also a cemetery for Revolutionary soldiers, had deteriorated and now collected bums and perverts who frightened secretaries coming to and from the offices. Batten persuaded neighboring businessmen to contribute to a $250,000 fund for refurbishing the Square.

Then Batten attacked the menacing blight of Dock Street, the inefficient, obsolete and indescribably insanitary 175-year-old produce and meat market which sprawled over several blocks to the east of his office, near the Delaware River. The market was located in an area called Society Hill—so named for the Free Society of Traders which helped William Penn promote and settle the city and Commonwealth. Now the old market was a health hazard, created terrible traffic jams in the area and attracted undesirables.

Batten rallied the Greater Philadelphia Movement and other groups necessary to his new effort. Another site for the market was found on a then-disfiguring city trash dump three miles away. The U.S. Department of Agriculture agreed to prepare plans for what Batten envisioned as the world's most modern food distribution center. The GPM set up a separate nonprofit organization to build and run the new facility, and in 1956 Batten won a $17,000,000 commitment from the city to buy and prepare the land at the new location for development. This victory required the city to make a substantial revision in its capital program. (Ultimately, the new Food Distribution Center attracted $85,000,000 in private investment and paid back the city outlay with a $2,000,000 tax increase.)

Planning director Bacon clucked over these promising occurrences like a mother hen, giving pushes here and there to advance plans for reviving the Social Hill area; he first helped forward these plans in the 1947 Panorama, but they had taken shape in his mind as far back as 1932, when he wrote his architectural thesis at Cornell University on plans for Philadelphia's center city.

Since the passage of the Housing Act of 1949, the year he became planning director, Bacon had urged use of federal Title I funds to help restore colonial Philadelphia as the residential community envisioned in the exhibit. But the Redevelopment Authority, failing to find builders and bankers who would invest in such an obviously deteriorated area, did not even put the project up for bid. "Everyone thought the idea was screwy," Bacon has recalled. "Most respectable people had moved away." Yet Bacon, who lived with his family in the Rittenhouse Square area, kept stressing center city living. He also kept pushing city departments to build greenways to connect the historic old buildings as they emerged. When he found a wealthy potential old-house buyer, he would take his prospect on a tour of the colonial eastern end of the city. As the various crusades touched off sparks of interest, a few old-house buffs did buy (though not necessarily move in). But the lack of broad public powers to tie efforts together made the total effect miniscule. Moreover, the original redevelopment approach was not the right instrument for Society Hill.

In 1956, the city finally focused its powers and resources on the renewal of the old center city—for several reasons.

One motivation was the assessment of the central renewal area situation conducted by the Redevelopment Authority's planning chief with the Planning Commission. Their study led to a recommendation by the Development Coordinator (Rafsky's new title as city activities in his area broadened under Dilworth) that slum clearance be virtually shelved for the present, and that a different set of programs be initiated.

Practical economics as well as human considerations made this change appear advisable. The CURA study showed that thirty-one of the city's thirty-six most deteriorated inner-city tracts were heavily occupied by Negro families whose average incomes were under $2,000—many too poor for even the small number of public housing units. Until 1956, the city's Title I activities had been centered in this area, physically the worst and most densely populated part of the city. But until opportunities for Negroes improved, or new housing tools became available, the clearance and redevelopment of their neighborhoods would spread slum conditions and not improve housing conditions significantly. Further, the total cost of clearing the city's badly blighted neighborhoods and its 118,000 seriously substandard homes was estimated to be $1,000,000,000, a sum completely beyond the city's capacity, even with federal Title I aid. (Redevelopment, until 1957, received only an average of $900,000 cash per year plus non-cash facilities in the city's capital budget.)

The 1954 Housing Act made a more balanced kind of program possible, and the assessment of the city's varied needs made a shift to a new and broader tack advisable. Development Coordinator Rafsky proposed a new policy (formalized in a 1957 public statement under which the city would concentrate funds available for renewal—increased to $3,000,000 of capital funds in 1957—on three main areas: conserving slipping but savable neighborhoods bordering the inner-city slum district; shoring up the city's huge but slipping investment by enhancing center city as a residential and commercial area; and strengthening its economic base through industrial and institutional programs. Capital funds were reallocated accordingly.

A SURPRISING ALLY

But the final drive for official center-city action was supplied by the new chairman of the City Planning Commission, banking and realty tycoon Albert M. Greenfield.

Until Dilworth's election, Greenfield was the one powerful local business figure who had not become involved in the city's revitalization. He had owned, or brokered, at one time or another, half of Philadelphia, and had vast holdings in department stores, office buildings and hotels in downtown Philadelphia as well as other cities. He was a director of Philadelphia's Yellow Cab Company, and board chairman of the Philadelphia Transportation Company. Greenfield was also a philanthropist of broad civic interest, and as an active member of the Urban Land Institute he had exceptional knowledge of urban redevelopment. But partly because of a bitter depression-time feud he had had with the city's WASP-Republican bankers, Greenfield was not a member of that exclusive power fraternity which largely composed the board of the Greater Philadelphia Movement.

However, Greenfield was a Democratic National Committeeman and a top money raiser for the party locally, and he had generously backed Dilworth's try for City Hall. The Mayor-elect, shortly after his victory, named Greenfield as head of the Planning Commission. Bacon nearly resigned as planning director on learning of Greenfield's appointment. (Greenfield had been rejected as a developer of Penn Center because he wanted to overbuild.) But he found in his new chairman a powerful ally who would give his special genius much broader scope.

Greenfield divested himself, technically at least, of his major realty holdings. He then quickly justified his appointment by persuading the City Council (whose majority of regular Democrats were hostile to Dilworth) to increase the budget of the planning department by more than half, to over $500,000 annually. (Much of this was needed to hasten completion of the comprehensive plan and then prepare the district plan for center city.) He also persuaded City Council to raise annual tax-supported capital appropriations from $21,000,000 to $25,000,000, to allow $4,000,000 more for renewal.

Rehabilitation of old Philadelphia, an area which he, unlike Main Line Philadelphia WASPs, knew intimately from childhood, had been a special interest of Greenfield's for years. His company's holdings were concentrated in the eastern half of center city—as were those of the huge city-administered Girard Trust and other old major downtown property holders—and, like theirs, were in serious trouble. Greenfield held that if the big hotels and department stores were not to go under, and take with them the core of the city's tax base, people would have to live near and use these central facilities. Such people should be those best able to patronize the shops and the city's cultural institutions—people with incomes of $10,000 or more. The Georgian houses in the Society Hill area appeared to offer the cachet that would draw back affluent homeowning Philadelphians—if the general area improved.

But Greenfield considered the house-by-house and spot-clearance approach to reviving center-city living as impractical and unlikely to succeed. "The reason nothing is moving and nobody has bought down there," he said, "is because nobody has been given a guarantee that his investment will be protected and the climate of the whole area improved." The expanded provisions for neighborhood renewal and selective clearance under the 1954 Federal Housing Act made such a public guarantee possible, since an official plan would make sure that all necessary improvements were carried out. Greenfield believed that the entire 1,000 acres southeast of Independence Hall, an area that formed one quarter of center-city Philadelphia, should be certified for urban renewal, with an overall plan to guide and insure the revitalization.

Mayor Dilworth was enthusiastic about the ambitious proposal. His first public act in office was to issue a directive to the City Planning Department to proceed with detailed plans for the renewal of the Society Hill area, a project which became known officially as Washington Square East. Soon thereafter Dilworth announced that he was going to move to build a new $150,000 home on Washington Square.

MAKING PLANS HAPPEN

The enlarged field of public action in center city made possible the realization of a number of Bacon's ideas. Bacon was an unusual kind of executive director in American city planning, one of the few trained in urban design. Perhaps the rarity of such talents can be explained by America's manner of building cities, which has not created a demand for training in this discipline.

Bacon, although first an architect, sought out his advanced training and gained his philosophy of the city from Eero Saarinen, the great Finnish-born architect-designer, at Cranbrook Academy in Michigan. One of Saarinen's seminal concepts was that the design of the city was the relationship of form and space. He taught that "Design is not a building, but an environment. The city is the unit. You must forever extend the design." In Bacon's eye the separate parts of the city are always seen in relation to each other and as a continuum of the whole. His desire to work with what exists, and to combine old with new rather than raze and rebuild, have made him an ideal urban renewal planner. Market- and research-oriented fellow planners have viewed with skepticism his almost dogmatic belief in the power of a visual image and improved city environment to alter people's living preferences and even to affect business location decisions. In the long run, however, Bacon's embracing vision of center city and his unfaltering pursuit of its realization were indispensable to Philadelphia's renewal. But even with official renewal certification, support of the Mayor and his Commission Chairman, Bacon's planning ideas depended on many other participants for their execution.

Society Hill was the most complex and demanding project that Philadelphia had yet contemplated. It soon became apparent that fitting together the myriad, intricate elements of public and private actions and investments was beyond the scope of any existing local agency. Greenfield believed that a nonprofit leadership organization of bankers and businessmen with a stake in downtown was required. This body could interest and work with local or out-of-town investors who didn't know the city, helping them through the arduous course of renewal, and act as referee or intermediary with the city and other public agencies. If necessary it could even be the redeveloper. (The city's public agencies had a poor record of attracting private investment.) Equally important to the project's execution, such a body could outlast the current city administration and give continuity to this long-range development.

Development Coordinator Rafsky agreed that such a group would be very useful, and the Greater Philadelphia Movement endorsed the proposal. But despite its elite membership, the GPM was not the right group to take on the job. Its mode of operation was to get in and out of projects or to spin off new bodies to handle specific development jobs, as it did for the Food Distribution Center. A new organization was required to take on this long-term assignment, and to bring Greenfield and the GPM under the same tent.

Philadelphia is accustomed to old money and slow motion. Greenfield, a self-made multimillionaire then nearing seventy, had yet to leave his permanent mark on his city. Formation of the new civic body became his mission. He talked at length to every top industrialist, banker, merchant and businessman, to win personal and financial commitments. He could be lyrical about the project's significance to "this beloved city—this plot of one thousand acres that combines all that civilization has to offer." But he could get down to economic realities quickly. Retail sales on Market Street, the main shopping area, had fallen 15 per cent in the past eight years, even while the region had grown. The Society Hill project would be only the first step in a comprehensive plan. He told the banks and insurance companies that carried the mortgages on the stores and buildings in the area that they would be the long-run losers if downtown withered.

He was questioned endlessly about feasibility. Would people really live downtown? When Greenfield said yes, he was neither an urban designer putting the wish before the fact nor an economist making long-range projections based on current trends.

The Old Philadelphia Development Corporation was formed in May 1956. William Day, chairman of the First Philadelphia Bank and Trust Company, one of the city's oldest banks, was "dragged in" (as he put it) by friends to serve as the new organization's chairman. The city's elite in business and finance became members of the new privately supported ($100,000 annual budget) body whose job was to bring back the old city.

The OPDC was also important as the first new "Philadelphia kind" of organization, one which had the joint participation of top citizens and officials. Its board of directors also included the Mayor, the president of City Council and several key members of Dilworth's cabinet, as well as some civic and labor representatives and two university presidents.

Greenfield next set out to get Pittsburgh Mayor Lawrence's valued right-hand man, John P. Robin (past head of the Commonwealth's Department of Commerce), to be the OPDC's executive, offering him an annual salary of $35,000—one higher than received by any Philadelphia official. A tug of war ensued, but Greenfield won with the argument that Robin (who had directed Pittsburgh's pioneer project, Gateway Center, as executive director of the city's Redevelopment Authority) should not be denied this "unique opportunity" to make a contribution to his time. Before long the Pittsburgher was applying his native city's free-spending, do-it-now style of action to slow-moving Philadelphia's renewal timetable.

Robin had the knack of being able to coordinate, without watering down, private and public interests, and of putting together big deals without overlooking important though small details. He could also move municipal bureaucrats off dead center with such tact that few were aware he was doing it. Dilworth had Robin join the Mayor's cabinet.

His outside entrees were also useful. The Commonwealth of Pennsylvania soon allocated several millions from its general funds to advance by ten years' time the completion of Independence Mall, the spine of the huge area's rehabilitation. Another million was given by the state's Highway Department to hasten the planning along the riverfront of the projected Delaware Expressway, one leg of the projected inner-city highway loop.

The Old Philadelphia Development Corporation's official capacity was that of consultant to the Redevelopment Authority on the Washington Square East project, and its first job was to find a developer. When plans for the first 127-acre portion of the renewal area—which included the clearance site of the old market—were ready, Robin arranged for the OPDC to give a private luncheon for 200 of the city's elite and New York's William Zeckendorf, president of Webb and Knapp.

That morning Zeckendorf had toured the deteriorated area around Dock Street. Although the old market was still in operation, he saw enough of the area's potential in a few minutes to announce that he would take over the entire 127-acre private redevelopment. With Zeckendorf so interested, however, the Philadelphians (who had so recently worried about whether the project was salable) decided not to turn over the city's most hallowed ground to the first or the highest bidder. Robin began seeking out other developers. Meanwhile planning director Edmund Bacon prepared the ground rules for a new kind of competition for redevelopment sponsorship to insure the very best in design.

Both Robin and Bacon had been disappointed in the results of their first essays into large-scale redevelopment. At Penn Center, the city had saved the unifying concourse but had been unable to prevent the early developers from putting up mundane buildings.

The mediocrity of the first stage of the new development dissatisfied many Philadelphians. Robin, looking back at Pittsburgh's Gateway Center, felt that more attention should have been paid to architectural considerations at the start so that better results than the first three passable but unexciting office structures could have been achieved. The whole process was so new and complex that they had only worried about the permanent product later. (Subsequent structures in both cities' developments have been superior.)

Profiting from these experiences, Bacon and Robin determined that design excellence should be an integral part of this prestige project from its inception. The Planning Commission's new chairman (Greenfield had retired) was Holmes Perkins, dean of the School of Fine Arts at the University of Pennsylvania, and he agreed that design was important, as did the Mayor.

RARE OPPORTUNITY AND CHALLENGES

Re-creation of the Society Hill area under the control of an official urban renewal plan afforded a rare design opportunity. The project, as the planners saw it, also presented a unique set of challenges. One was how to graft parts of an exciting modern city onto the old foundation without overwhelming it; another how to preserve the historic values and enhance the intimate scale of the eighteenth-century brick row houses, the Colonial structures and narrow cobbled streets without transforming the whole area into a deadly museum.

If the renewal was successful, the area would be a major attraction for tourists and offer a contemporary residential environment of high quality that would attract and hold people of means. To accomplish both aims, it was necessary to salvage and restore as many of the colonial houses as possible, preferably by persuading present owners or new purchasers to finance historically accurate exterior renovations according to standards set by the renewal plan.

New apartment houses were to be part of the plan. The first, strategic group was to be located on the site of the old Dock Street market at the eastern end of the project, overlooking the Delaware River. As Bacon conceived the high-rise apartments, they should offer both immediate visual contrast with their surroundings and visual connection with far-off landmarks such as baroque City Hall, center city's highest point, where William Penn's statue stood watch over his city.

It was important that they not wall off the riverfront, which was to be re-created for the public as Penn's Landing, with a promenade, skating rink, restaurant, marina and marine museum, after the decaying piers and obstructing industrial structures were removed. The design solution was for three tall, slim towers instead of conventional bulky slabs, an idea originally tossed off by William Zeckendorf. New townhouses, adjacent to rehabilitated old homes, would complete the first part of the development.

To enable developers to bid for sponsorship on the basis of such a demanding concept, it was necessary to provide them with more than the usual set of re-use specifications and limitations provided in a redevelopment project—space to be provided, number of dwelling units, limitations on land coverage and density of people per acre. Consequently, the Planning Commission retained a team of consulting architects to develop a schematic three-dimensional model that set forth the design principles the bidders should aim for, and visualized the relation and scale of the proposed new structures with existing ones.

For the first time in the country, a Title I project award was to be made on the basis of the intangible and ultimately subjective criterion of "best design proposal." Five developers, four of them from out of town, accepted the exacting terms of Philadelphia's design competition; among them they spent $260,000 for five sets of proposals on the initial residential redevelopment for this $50,000,000 renewal project.

When the proposals were all submitted, the city's leading men—the full board of the Old Philadelphia Development Corporation, the members of the City Planning Commission and of the Redevelopment Authority—met at five separate three-hour sessions to weigh the merits of each design, as well as the financial position of its sponsor, in order to select the winning bidder. There were sharp disagreements and heated debates about the esthetic merits of each, especially as several proposals, including one from ten local builders, differed markedly from the official design concept. But these sessions advanced the education in and the commitment to urban esthetics of Philadelphia's political and business power.

The project area was finally divided in half and the award given to two different New York developers, one headed by Seon Pierre Bonan and the other by Zeckendorf's Webb and Knapp. Zeckendorf's architect-planner, Ieoh Ming Pei, who designed the winning towers, was given charge of the overall design. The developers agreed to the further condition, placed on them by the Redevelopment Authority, that they spend one per cent of their construction outlay on landscaping and art works.*

Aware that ultimate performance can differ from advance promises and that "practical" reasons may water down original plans, the OPDC and Redevelopment Authority appointed a Board of Design to make sure that the agreed-upon design concepts would actually be carried out.

Not surprisingly, construction costs soon mounted beyond original calculations, due to the need for additional foundation pilings. Furthermore, the towers could only accommodate eight apartments to a floor, which raised per-unit costs. (Robin commented about this: "Architects say good design is as cheap as bad design. But it isn't true.") At the end of a year Webb and Knapp announced that it would require $10 more per month in rentals than the local insuring office of the Federal Housing Administration recommended, if the project were to be "economically feasible" for the firm. But the FHA did not believe that the apartments could command the additional rentals, and it refused to give a full mortgage commitment based on returns from the larger sum.

Basic to the FHA's conservative position was the location of the new apartments. They would be very far removed from the established residential district of center city; they were also separated from the main downtown commercial area by almost a mile of unrehabilitated houses, slums and commercial blight. When the whole renewal area was much further advanced, and if well-to-do people actually came in to buy and improve the old houses, the riverfront location might become very desirable for upper-middle-income tenants. But just because the first major

* This stipulation subsequently became a part of contracts for all redevelopers on any publicly assisted Philadelphia project.

clearance and rebuilding area of Washington Square East had been dictated by the removal of Dock Street on the eastern end of the project was not sufficient economic reason for a high-rent development to be located there. (Indeed, the rent-up period for the Society Hill Towers turned out to be very slow. Hopkinson House, a non-assisted but FHA-insured high-rise slab facing Washington Square, which was built at the same time, found a market much sooner.)

Had the Philadelphia bodies involved or Webb and Knapp been willing to change to the more economical and profitable slab construction, the apartment houses could have begun a year sooner, with FHA's support. But in order to retain the original design, concessions involving each of the principals were laboriously hammered out. The local FHA office agreed to take a greater risk on its commitment after the Commissioner of the Federal Housing Administration himself stepped in. Webb and Knapp trimmed its construction costs and agreed to take less profit at the start. But as it was short of cash, the firm asked and won permission to build the townhouses first, as these required less outlay for land and construction than did the apartments. In the fall of 1961, three years after the award of the sponsor's contract, groundbreaking for the townhouses, the first new structures in Society Hill, took place.

But the delays served other goals of the Society Hill renewal. Much more private restoration of the old houses than anticipated was being carried out. Since the government was spending so many millions to give them the "best" city neighborhood, long-time residents, as well as new home purchasers, were willing to spend thousands on exterior (and often interior) renovation, following the rigid specifications laid down for historic homes by the publicly approved plan. The Redevelopment Authority retained an architect to help them comply with these requirements. Another by-product was that new buyers, among them Main Line returnees, lived alongside Polish, Italian and Negro families (relatively few) who had occupied the old city houses before renewal certification and were willing and able to renovate.

The Old Philadelphia Development Corporation had anticipated serving as rehabilitator for publicly acquired historic houses whose present owners could not or would not comply with the plan. But so many prospective purchasers indicated an interest in the first thirty-five houses that the OPDC formed a special residents' committee to help it select bidders. There was not such a rush for the $45,000 townhouses designed by Pei, however. Their extremely modern design made them a source of controversy for several years, and their availability when most of the project area was full of the dust of demolition was another drawback. But finally all were bought up, and more of the same design were built and marketed with relative ease.

The Citizens' Council on City Planning also played a significant role during the planning stages of Washington Square East. It gave public support to some of the neighborhood merchants who would have to move from shops on the ground floors of historic homes. The case was taken to City Council and the civic group won a modification of the plan which allowed commercial uses to continue during the present owner's lifetime. The public hearings also revealed to the planners that both old and new residents wanted to have shops near to their homes, instead of all in a "center" as originally proposed.

THE NEW POPULATION: SOME PROGRESS

The renewal of Society Hill for a prestige, upper-income population was an unabashedly open and highly visible bid for a return of the elite, the "taste-setters" who would, it was hoped, attract to city living others of means who had residential alternatives. The Washington Square East project was the first part of a coordinated set of efforts to revitalize center city as a place to live and work and to provide an image for the whole city's revitalization. It was also intended, in part, to offset the major postwar population shifts that were bifurcating central city and suburbs by race and economic class.

Mayor Dilworth was openly worried about the economic effect and the future implications of these outward and inward migrations. He was also forthright in expressing his belief in taking public actions to redress the situation. Commenting on this in 1958 during an interview with a magazine reporter, he stated, "The city's tax base has already been hurt. . . . Over the last thirty years, suburban income has tripled and the city income is just the same. . . . There were so many white Protestants whose incomes went up from $6,000 to $20,000 and who then got out of town to look good in the suburbs, that prosperous middle-class housing vanished."

The census showed that non-white residents in Philadelphia between 1940 and 1950 increased from 13 to 24 per cent of the city's population. This was largely a result of the migration to the city of lower-income Negroes from the South at the same time middle-class white families were moving out to the suburbs. During the 1950's the inmigration rate was falling off, while out-migration continued. But projections by the Institute of Urban Studies showed that, due to the somewhat higher birth rate of the young Negroes who formed the biggest part of Philadelphia's new population, non-whites would comprise about 30 per cent of the central city by 1970, and by 1980 the proportion might well be as high as 40 per cent.

All developers in Philadelphia's Title I project were bound by a clause in their sponsoring contract with the Redevelopment Authority to rent or sell the housing they built without discrimination. But Dilworth candidly admitted that the new housing in center-city projects was deliberately being priced out of the average Negro's income range. "We've got to get the white [leadership] back," he asserted, and to do this "We have to give the whites confidence that they can live in town without being flooded."

Despite such characteristically candid, if impolitic, statements and despite the efforts during the 1959 municipal elections of Dilworth's Republican opponent, former University of Pennsylvania president Harold Stassen, to make an issue of alleged discrimination in urban renewal projects, an estimated eight out of every ten Negroes—then one fourth of the city's electorate—voted for Dilworth's re-election.

Philadelphia during the 1950's enjoyed an outstanding reputation for opening opportunities for Negroes and peaceful progress toward integration. A number of favorable local factors were at work, including the city's long tradition of religious and racial tolerance, but the new municipal policies pursued by Clark and Dilworth under the new charter and the ingenious, sophisticated and aggressive programs developed by the city's Commission on Human Relations did much to make friends for the city and its government among the growing Negro population.

One major change initiated by the reform administration was in municipal hiring policies. In 1960, thanks to the tightly administered merit employment system instituted by the charter and generally supported by the Mayor,* 30 per cent of the city's employees were Negro, compared to a handful in 1950. Moreover, many held status jobs. At the time Clark became Mayor, there were only four Negro secretaries in municipal jobs, and there had never been a Negro sergeant on the police force. By the early 1960's there were 400 Negro secretaries and Negro staff inspectors, sergeants, lieutenants and captains on the police force. Under Dilworth, Philadelphia established the first Civilian Police Review Board in the country.

Negroes of ability from other parts of the country were also drawn to Philadelphia by the new atmosphere and opportunities. One outstanding professional "newcomer" was Yale Law School graduate A. Leon Higgenbotham, Jr., of Trenton, New Jersey, who came in 1952 to clerk for a local judge and who credited to the "Dilworth impact" the tripling of Negro lawyers since the war. At the end of his first year Higgenbotham was recommended by his employer to Dilworth, who was then District Attorney—"No ward leader had to pass on me." Soon, as an assistant district attorney, he was arguing in the trial courts, including the State Supreme Court. No Negro in that capacity had been permitted to try a case before a jury until Dilworth became Mayor. "I wouldn't have come here in 1948," Higgenbotham commented. "Now you know that a guy who has ability and works hard can move here." In 1962, Higgenbotham, who in the interim had practiced law as a partner in a center-city firm and become president of the local NAACP, was named a judge in the U.S. District Court of Eastern Pennsylvania by the President of the United States.

Housing opportunities for Negroes also improved remarkably in Philadelphia during the 1950's. The 1960 census found that the substandard units occupied by Negroes were halved during

* Dilworth, in an effort to make friends among the Democratic regulars, tried unsuccessfully to get some jobs back on patronage.

the decade; seven out of eight Negro households were living in "standard" housing, compared to two out of three in 1950; and overcrowding was substantially reduced. Moreover, Negro homeownership in Philadelphia rose from 10 per cent in 1940 to 29 per cent in 1950, and to 44 per cent in 1966, the largest increase of any city in the nation, and 85 per cent of these in 1960 were standard units.

This unusual rise was due to a combination of factors. One was the large stock of standard older housing that became available with the white exodus to new housing in the suburbs. Another was the low mean value of the large supply of row housing: 63 per cent worth less than $10,000. While a non-white buying a used home without government aid still required a substantial equity, even for Philadelphia's relatively low-cost homes, market studies showed that many Negroes had been able to do this with wartime savings and the steadier employment that Philadelphia's diversified industry afforded them.

The city's independent and strong Commission on Human Relations had the broadest powers and largest budget of any similar body in the country, thanks to the 1951 charter and the support of the reform administrations. Interestingly, Philadelphia did not try to enact a local fair-housing ordinance for many years. Dilworth frequently pointed out that the percentage of non-whites in metropolitan Philadelphia was the same as in 1920—14 per cent—but that this 14 per cent was now concentrated in the central city while the region's population had since more than doubled. Also, the Commission's knowledgeable staff knew that in housing, as in jobs, laws are negative at best. The city had had a Fair Employment Practices statute since 1948. They knew that with or without laws many more positive steps must be taken to prevent new ghettos from forming and whites from running, and to reduce self-segregation. Both the administration and the Commission felt that a city fair-housing statute would only tighten the suburban "white noose" around the city, increasing ghettoization within and exclusionism without.

Instead, Dilworth put Philadelphia's weight into a drive for a statewide anti-discrimination law, which finally cleared the legislature in 1961, after three years' struggle. Then the city passed its own law. It also pressed the state Real Estate Commission for a law under which licenses of realtors who were guilty of blockbusting tactics would be revoked.

Meanwhile, the Commission encouraged meaningful housing integration and new opportunities generally with various ingenious and bold new programs. Its staff went into white neighborhoods where "first" Negro families were moving in and helped ministers, store owners and other leaders to organize and educate local residents in order to avoid panic selling and racial turnover. It conducted an eight-neighborhood survey to learn the actual effect of racial change in ownership on property values and found that Negro home buyers had stabilized values which started to slip before they moved in. (The survey also revealed that with white demand virtually disappearing in many pre-World War I neighborhoods, Negroes were the mainstay of the Philadelphia real estate market.)

A representative of the Commission was a member of the Mayor's Urban Renewal Policy Committee, and the City Planning Commission consulted with the agency on the racial implications of the emerging comprehensive plan. In marked contrast to commissions in other cities, Philadelphia's Human Relations Commission publicly supported urban renewal, believing that it was the most effective tool for overcoming the inequities in the physical environment which have so adversely affected urban minorities. It participated in and supported the decision to make the huge Eastwick redevelopment an area for moderate-income, home-buying families rather than a ghetto for displaced low-income slum dwellers, feeling it would provide the city in general with a large-scale demonstration of sound integrated life in a new community, and help counter private real estate practices. The Commission did not favor using public housing and relocation of poor Negro families as front runners for integration.

The Commission recognized that a pioneering spirit and fortitude, plus an intimate knowledge of the real estate business, which first buyers lack, were required for a Negro home buyer moving into a new and potentially unwelcoming white neighborhood, and that as the Negro population grew, the ghetto was spreading. In 1960 it launched a program designed to actively encourage upwardly mobile Negro families to move out of ghetto areas. It prepared do-it-yourself kits containing consumer information on mortgages, housing quality, settlement costs, and even tricks of housing discrimination and distributed 600 of these to ministers, social workers, community agencies, colleges and others who were in touch with prospective non-white purchasers. In effect the kits gave the sanction of government to what had before been a wish in urging them not to be steered into ghetto areas and to buy where Negroes had not lived before.

The Commission in 1961 also mounted two separate programs to break down the barriers to employment opportunities for Negroes. One was aimed at the tokenism practiced by so many firms which hired a few Negroes as evidence that they were not violating the FEPC law, but who avoided recruiting and advertising openings where Negroes were likely to learn of them. Such practices led the Commission to send out to 17,000 Philadelphia companies six standards of fair employment practices which they must follow or face penalties, and accompanied it with a warning that the firms might be called upon to demonstrate they were "taking affirmative steps to guarantee and promote equal employment opportunities." (The Chamber of Commerce denounced this move, but the Commission was not budged.)

It prepared another do-it-yourself kit designed to encourage young Negroes to stay in school and prepare for the increasingly skilled job market of the 1960's, and to help them go out and find these jobs. The kits were distributed to community leaders, white and non-white, who could help shape the goals of minority job seekers. Its special message was that youngsters could plan what they wanted to become without worrying about being unable to get a particular job because their father or mother could not; that there was an anti-discrimination law; and that little was left for untrained and unskilled people. Significantly, the booklet enclosed on *Career Opportunities* was issued by the New York Life Insurance Company not only for minority workers but for all young people.

In the early 1960's one could observe the payoff of these new programs combined with improved physical environments in an inner-city elementary school, the Harrison school, next to the Southwest Temple area, an early redevelopment project. There, a middle-aged Negro schoolteacher, a native Philadelphian, commented, "Parents used to say 'Forget it' when a child spoke of wanting to be an airline pilot, a doctor or an engineer. Today there's a brighter concept of the future. Jobs are opening up, and the Commission on Human Relations makes people aware of the new picture. A child can go to school and plan a career.

"But we have to work extra hard to motivate them," he observed. "The frustrations of their parents and grand-parents have borne bad fruit."

The Harrison school was one of eight in Philadelphia's culturally deprived areas which were then developing special teaching techniques and community-related programs for increasing pupils' motivation, basic skills and educability under the Ford Foundation's Great Cities Program. Teachers felt that their efforts were considerably helped by the improved physical environment created in the community by the redevelopment with its new public and private housing. "Bathrooms, heat and hot running water mean a lot to those people," one teacher pointed out. "We take such conveniences for granted, but the old slums didn't have such things. And the kids had no place to study there. Now they can use the kitchen table in the housing project apartment."

GROWING GHETTOS AND POVERTY

But for every encouraging statistic and progressive program, for the few Southwest Temple redevelopment projects, the eight special schools, and the sprinkling of upper-income Negroes in fashionable Germantown or the few in status positions, there was an increasingly negative side, one documented by the 1960 census.

The growing dispersion of Negroes into white areas—up 7 per cent during the 1950's—was offset by a still larger growth in racial concentration. Eleven per cent more of the city's blocks were occupied by a majority of non-whites than during the 1940's, and 22 per cent of the blocks were predominantly Negro. While Negro homeownership increased to 44 per cent, the proportion was twenty years behind the white population (which, in 1960, enjoyed 68 per cent homeownership), and every stride toward standard housing made by the Negro was topped, as the census showed, by the still greater advances made by the whites.

Even so, the census is deceiving. It does not indicate squalid neighborhoods and substandard facilities; minimum census standards of structural soundness do not reveal the desperate overcrowding of some families; rotting houses also stand side by side with "standard" homes. Nor can a census measure the general frustration that pervades an area like North Central Philadelphia, the principal Negro district and slum, known locally as "the Jungle," where the summer riots of 1964 occurred.

The most progressive human relations program could not deal with slums and the deep economic and social problems festering there—youth crime, unemployment, below-level reading and arithmetic skills in sixth grade.

Citywide, twice as many non-whites as whites were unemployed—11 per cent, and even higher in the inner city, against 5 per cent. Non-white median income was only 71 per cent of the white's. The gap was also growing alarmingly between the small proportion of Negroes who were succeeding and the much larger bottom sector who seemed doomed to life in the "deferred clearance" areas of the inner city, the old and new "Jungles" of Philadelphia. Although 10 per cent of the families among the city's nearly 600,000 non-whites had incomes over $6,000 a year, some 200,000 were members of households who earned less than public housing's limits.

But the public housing inventory of 14,000 units met only a fraction of the need. While top local architects designed the subsidized projects, and the results showed unusual sensitivity to the desires and special life style of the poor, the quality was scarcely matched by quantity. Philadelphia had not even used up the original 20,000 units contemplated following passage of the 1949 Housing Act, and had proportionately less public housing than most other large old cities.

Nor was any group in the city pushing for an expansion of the traditional low-rent projects. Official city policy in 1957 had determined not to clear out slums with public housing. Not only would the cost have been too great, but the end result would have been socially undesirable: more segregated high-rise projects and overcrowded homes elsewhere, as long as cleared homes were inhabited by the poor.

Even the civic agency most interested in the shelter problem, the Philadelphia Housing Association, preferred no more public housing to more projects. In order to explore the alternatives, the Housing Association and Citizens' Council on City Planning set up a joint committee in 1957.

The increasing lack of suitable sites; the high cost of new construction, then some $20,000 per unit; the growing number of large poor families; the problems of relocation; and the increasing availability of older houses in the inner city, where the intense overcrowding of the postwar period was ended—all these suggested a program for the purchase and rehabilitation of existing structures by the Housing Authority for subsidized rental to low-income families. Such "used houses" could be selected on a scattered basis throughout the community, be occupied by families without the stigma attached to projects, and eventually even be purchased by the tenants as their incomes rose.

The city administration also favored such a new approach and secured the necessary approvals from local bodies and federal agencies. But in mid-1959, after the first forty of 200 row houses were bought in the Haddington neighborhood conservation area, a suit was brought by a property owner and realty boards, and the experiment stood still until the court dismissed the case in 1962. The program was then expanded to 500 homes.

In the meantime, the city was also improving the current stock in neighborhoods slated for eventual clearance by putting its housing code to work. There the code has been systematically applied to all buildings to alleviate the worst conditions and prevent further structural deterioration. City Council in 1961, prodded by the Housing Association, appropriated $250,000 (since doubled) for the Central Relocation Bureau * to pay moving expenses for families forced to vacate homes as a result of code enforcement outside Title I areas. The following year, the city also appropriated funds for little parklets, play areas and usable open sitting space on sites cleared as a result of the demolition of vacant and dangerous slum properties.

Many landlords found it cheaper to vacate a building than to continue operating a slum. When they failed to carry out work orders but did not vacate, the city could file a lien, make the

* This body handles rehousing for all Philadelphia families dislocated by public programs—another Philadelphia "first."

property repairs itself, and charge them to the owner. The boarded-up houses, and the growing vacancy rate in these neighborhoods (almost double the city's average of 6 per cent for rental housing) were among the more hopeful signs in the blighted inner city. The impressive improvement in housing revealed by the 1960 census could be attributed in part to this "slum cleansing operation." When these gray areas are cleared, as called for by the comprehensive plan, it is hoped that the costs, both in human and site acquisition terms, would be greatly reduced.

SAVINGS JOBS

The problems of the city's growing non-white population were, in part, a reflection of the deteriorating economic and jobs situation in Philadelphia, where the unemployment rate was substantially above the national average.

Like most central cities in the country's old industrial belt, Philadelphia had been losing manufacturing jobs since World War II. Between 1951 and 1956 alone, it suffered a net outmigration of seventy-four industrial firms and 9,646 jobs; remaining companies cut their payrolls by another 40,000. These facts and figures were especially ominous since 33 per cent of its working population were employed in manufacture (a rate higher than the national average of 30 per cent), and one third of the city's revenues came from the local wage tax.*

Philadelphia began, far earlier than almost any other city, to look into the causes of the manufacturing exodus and developed a program for reversing the trend. Studies undertaken for the City Commerce Director, and the City Planning Commission divulged the main reason manufacturers and industrial realtors gave for the outward move: the shortage of land and space in the city.

* The Philadelphia wage tax was put through the state legislature in 1941, over the strenuous objections of many liberals, when the bankers were trying to balance Philadelphia's budget. It has turned out to be a lifesaver. It allows the city to capture for its own maintenance and improvement the income which commuters make in the city but generally spend in the suburbs, as well as to tax residents, and relieves the pressure on revenue from real estate. One quarter of the jobs in Philadelphia are held by non-residents.

Growing firms could not acquire adjacent sites for expansion or for parking space. Old narrow streets could not handle the huge trailer trucks which delivered materials and hauled finished goods. Many companies had to change to modern automated processes and product flow to remain competitive. This necessitated shifting from old multistory lofts to one-story plants that consumed ten times as much land—often a prohibitive item in such a built-up city.

Philadelphia has the largest number of small manufacturers in the country. Eighty per cent of its 40,000 firms employ fewer than fifty people each. Many occupy century-old loft buildings, aptly described as "exhibits in an outdoor museum devoted to the birth of the industrial revolution," clinging to streams that no longer power their machines and still huddled close to rail spurs in the age of truck transportation. It was obvious that most would have to move. Yet generally they lacked the access to economic information which a large firm would secure in order to make a wise locational decision. Many could not command financing from banks to move or expand in the city, and needed special assistance to remain.

For some firms, shifts in markets or changes in transportation facilities made moving out of the city sensible. But for others—those who relied on the skilled local labor supply and whose employees used the city's public transit system, as well as those who sold contract work to each other or clustered to command special outside services—remaining in the city, although not necessarily in the same location, made sense. With economics against them, however, they took the easiest path.

The outward trend of factories was encouraged by industrial realtors who could make a quick and profitable transaction selling cheap suburban land instead of laboriously assembling parcels of land next to their clients' plant. It didn't occur to them to sell land within the city for industry.

Philadelphia's economists saw that the city commanded special resources which could help local manufacturers remain and expand. One major asset was the considerable quantity of municipally owned vacant land. At an airport, for example, the city had nearly 1,000 surplus acres of potentially prime industrial land which was not needed by airplanes since they now used long runways and two-direction strips instead of the old crisscross landings. The City Commerce Director proposed that a new non-profit corporation acquire such land, develop it into industrial districts and parks, install streets and utilities, and dispose of the property to companies. Philadelphia thus became the first city in the country to seize the opportunity of putting publicly owned land to productive use with an industrial land bank.

The Philadelphia Industrial Development Corporation, another of the multiplying Philadelphia-type corporations, went into operation in 1958, with the initial function of developing the city's land bank. This organization, like its prototypes engaged in other local development activities, was a public-private partnership venture. Its thirty-man board included leading businessmen who had a particular interest in this field, citizen leaders and key city officials, among them the Mayor. The Chamber of Commerce was an equal partner, and shared administrative overhead with the city. The chairman of Philadelphia's largest bank was PIDC's first president; the city's Development Coordinator was on its executive committee. Nationally reputed professionals in development, public administration, planning and economics were recruited to staff PIDC, and were given salaries competitive with private industry.

Although PIDC has an independence of operation that public bodies lack, it is basically an instrument of city policy, and works closely with public agencies, the other development corporations, and private property owners to further coordinated actions of mutual concern. To assemble additional land for industrial use it relies on the Redevelopment Authority, with its power of eminent domain, to acquire and if necessary clear properties. In turn, the Redevelopment Authority looks to the PIDC as its indispensable partner in carrying out Philadelphia's industrial renewal. Whether the land is built up or vacant, however, only tracts marked for industrial use by the city's long-range plan are developed by PIDC.

No public subsidies are made to the firms assisted. The land PIDC develops for industrial use is sold or leased to companies at fair market value, and each transaction generates its own financing, with payments or rentals amortizing the debt. Proceeds from the sale or lease of land finance acquisition of additional sites, and go into a revolving fund for land assembly. A special advantage that PIDC can offer to firms for financing plant development or expansion is the low-interest loans that commercial banks will make through the corporation because of its tax-exempt treasury status. Thus it can help many who would otherwise be unable to finance an economically advantageous move within the city. Firms also receive technical assistance, such as getting municipal building permits.

PIDC's chief efforts and successes have been at saving local firms and jobs, helping companies expand by relieving them of buildings which they have outgrown, reconditioning these, where practical and in accord with city land use plans, for rental or sale to more suitable users, and developing cleared or open land for new industrial locations.

The agency's executive views PIDC's main role as one of thinking ahead of business in order to make deals happen. He circulated among owners of manufacturing firms (most of whom lived in center-city apartments, as he did) to learn their problems and needs, and informed bankers that good industrial loans could be made in the city through PIDC. He showed industrial realtors, half a dozen of whom did most of the region's locational work, that it was as easy for them to transact a deal through PIDC, and still make their usual commission, as it was to move to the suburbs.

The agency's powerful board members give their own time and effort, responding to the director's request for specific assignments. The chairman of PIDC, the head of the city's largest insurance company and Mayor Dilworth even worked one New Year's Day in order to persuade the Whitman candy company, which had bought land in New Jersey, to relocate in Philadelphia instead.

Whitman, an old local firm, relied heavily on the city's pool of female labor for its profit-making, pre-holiday peak production periods, and over half of its 1,500 regular employees came to work by bus. But the firm wanted to increase its productive capacity and move from its old nine-story loft building on a cramped three-acre site in center city. The chief obstacle was the difficulty in selling its old building.*

The Redevelopment Authority acquired the old structure for

* Philadelphia has over 10,000,000 square feet of vacant similar old-loft industrial space.

$1,000,000 and turned it over to PIDC (which found a new owner who modernized and extended the structure). Meanwhile, PIDC sold Whitman thirty-six acres of land for a new 450,000 square foot, one-story automated plant with 50 per cent greater productivity in an industrial park developed on city land by PIDC. Although the shift to automatic process entailed a 10 per cent drop in employment, the remaining jobs stayed in the city.

Continuing industrial redevelopment is necessary if Philadelphia is to adjust to the changes in scale and land use required by aging plants, new technology and economic functions, and to capture potential new modern industrial locations created by the one hundred miles of new expressway and widened arterial roads called for in the long-range comprehensive plan. Indeed, without PIDC, realization of the plan, which calls for an increase in industrial acreage from 17 to 25 per cent of the city's area, would be virtually impossible, as would many of the shifts of firms required by it.

Philadelphia is fortunate in having more open land than do most old cities where it can relocate plants that threaten to leave or are forced to move by urban renewal, or accommodate new ones. At the huge Eastwick project, for example, 750 acres will be used for industry. PIDC tries to minimize the adverse effect of dislocation for public improvements by providing new sites for firms prior to the acquisition of their properties. It has been particularly helpful in moving groups of wholesalers who cluster together in inner-city sites in order to obtain contract services. Many remain in inadequate locations, often through inertia, and should move to modern sites to help themselves and to bolster the local economy and city taxes by opening up their old inner-city locations to more productive and appropriate current uses.

Removal of seventy-three Dock Street merchants from their old Society Hill market in the Washington Square East project area to the new Food Distribution Center demonstrated the value of such a publicly assisted cycle. PIDC subsequently helped meat wholesalers move into an adjacent $7,500,000 complex. The Redevelopment Authority acquired their old properties and will sell the cleared site to PIDC to develop into a merchandising district for shoe wholesalers. The latter were grouped near Independence Hall, a location now more suitable for office buildings. When soft-goods wholesalers were required to vacate their center-city quarters for urban renewal, the industrial agency helped them develop and finance a new distribution complex.

However, ten of twenty-six manufacturing firms that had to move for the Washington Square East renewal either went out of business or moved from the city. Much more needed to be done for such firms and hundreds of small businesses outside of project areas, too. Recognizing this, the city set up a special corporation to give assistance to small business.

Philadelphia voters in 1961 helped to expand and accelerate the industrial development operation by approving a $10,000,000 general obligation loan to finance a revolving industrial development fund for the acquisition and preparation of more land beyond the 1,000-acre land bank. (The city had already authorized $2,000,000 before this.) PIDC is the official advisor on its development.

By mid-1966, PIDC had carried out transactions with 289 companies, old and new to the city. As a result of transactions that helped local firms relocate or expand on site, Philadelphia had retained 29,719 jobs. (Past experience showed that without PIDC one third of them would have been lost.) Further, 14,812 new jobs had been created, one third of them from activities new to Philadelphia. The rest of the new employment came when a local company merged an outside function or expanded. PIDC's director doubts that any of this would have happened without the land and financing package the corporation provides. The city was also receiving close to $2,500,000 more annually in taxes as a result of the industrial developments.

By 1963, the precipitous decline in manufacturing employment, in which 63,000 jobs were lost over the last decade, had leveled off, partly as a result of PIDC's efforts and other conscious city policy. But the overall trend had not been reversed. Chronic unemployment persisted at 8 per cent in the city, twice the national average. Many more reasons were behind the drop in manufacturing jobs than outmoded plants, cramped sites and plant exodus.

Philadelphia reflected a national phenomenon: the leveling off of manufacture as a sector of the economy, which in turn was an indicator of the increased productivity of industry. Remaining or relocated plants in Philadelphia could produce more with fewer employees, particularly those in lower-skill production jobs. Between 1956 and 1962, although local output increased 3 per cent, employment continued to drop because productivity increased 20 per cent. Still, manufacturing in the region was not keeping up either with national growth, or with increases in specific fields. (One of Philadelphia's important industries, apparel goods, actually decreased by one per cent while this sector nationally increased 7 per cent.) This suggested a decline in the skill of the area's entrepreneurs, and the city had not attracted a representative share of the new national growth industries. There was also the growing worry whether the city was producing the skilled workers necessary to attract and hold modern plants and growth industries. Skilled workers were in such short supply that the apparel industry was importing men from Italy but 9 per cent of the labor force was unemployed.

Serious, growing manpower troubles were forecast for the 1970's by the report on Philadelphia's economic development prepared for its federally assisted Community Renewal Program,* troubles which would make the missing jobs of the 1960's seem like minor losses. The labor force in the prime-age group was growing much faster than job opportunities. Moreover, the jobs that were expected to increase would require skills, education and training, with a high school diploma a minimum for employment. But 45 per cent of the youths in the labor force had not completed high school, and the rate among the fifteen- to nineteen-year-olds was still higher. "Under-educated, inexperienced youth are a growing proportion of the labor force," the report stated, and a manpower policy was sadly needed. The city would have to not only save jobs, but also create new ones for the growing labor force; some 100,000 jobs were needed by the mid-1970's to achieve full employment but "there is no guarantee of an automatic adjustment" between jobs available and those seeking work.

There was considerable doubt whether the city could ever keep

* The Community Renewal Program, a major new grant program, was initiated in 1959 by the Housing and Home Finance Agency to help cities study and more accurately assess their renewal needs and resources, clarify community goals and develop priorities for action.

up with the scale of the industrial problems, as relocated plants showed a marked increase in their floor space requirements per employee. PIDC economists had estimated that some 200,000 acres would be needed to accommodate Philadelphia's 20,000 acres of cramped industry, but such acreage was not available. Inevitably, many firms would continue to move out in order to grow, and the city would have to search out other employers who were more intensive land users, who had a higher economic pay-off, and whose manpower could not be so easily automated.

MAXIMIZING POTENTIALS

If industry's changing requirements and the slow growth of manufacturers put Philadelphia at a competitive disadvantage for manufacture, the city did have other assets that promised much greater economic growth as the country moved ahead into the post-industrial era; such assets could be—indeed, must be—capitalized on through conscious public policy. Since completion of the Central Urban Renewal Area study in 1956, the city had been working, at an accelerating rate and increasingly sophisticated manner, to maximize those favorable, interrelated national trends.

One such trend was the shifting age distribution of the country's population, which favored increased middle-class living in the city. During the 1960's the percentage of people over forty-five in metropolitan Philadelphia, as in the country at large, was expected to increase proportionately faster than the twenty-five- to forty-five-year-old group with young children who had comprised the bulk of growth and of suburban migrants in the 1950's. These older persons, together with young single adults and the recently married whose proportion was expected to expand similarly, comprised the biggest obvious potential market for in-town residence. An expected general 25 per cent rise in incomes meant that more of these older and younger people would also be able to afford their own households. Even a certain proportion of families might be expected to live in center city as the changing national job structure led to greater professionalization of jobs and created types of work which leaned to city residence.

The city planners did not expect to reverse the trend of family living in suburbs. But they hoped to capture for Philadelphia its fair share of regional growth—some 2 per cent or 20,000 of the middle- and upper-income families who would, if offered a desirable environment, choose to live in the city rather than in the suburbs or "ex-urbs."

The advancing renewal of Society Hill as a prestige community and city government's growing commitment to reviving the core were exerting a strong pull in the 1960's. Within the Washington Square East project, developers were asking for land parcels to build more new townhouses, and by the end of 1965 there were commitments for rehabilitation of all the 700 historic homes. Outside the renewal area, a number of new apartment houses were being constructed in center city as builder-entrepreneurs anticipated the growing demand for in-town living. There was, in fact, a temporary glut of vacancies as the buildings came on the market too quickly to be absorbed.* But demand for townhouses continued strong. "Reverse block-busting" was proceeding at an accelerating pace along the southern band of center city in the area marked for residential use. From river to river individual families or builders bought up and remodeled run-down row houses on alley streets and blocks, even next door to houses marked by city inspectors "unfit for habitation." Well before the second residential renewal project, Washington Square West, was advanced into the federal survey and planning stage in 1963, builders were also putting up new townhouses for sale in that area; property values were rising despite the generally deteriorated condition.

Some home purchasers were middle-aged returnees attracted by center city's walk-to-work, theater and concert style of living. Many were young professional couples with children. Four more resident associations had formed to press for more and better schools, parking and playgrounds, the facilities and amenities whose lack has, in large measure, kept families away. The residents of the Rittenhouse Square area enjoyed a fine new $125,-

* High-rise apartments were found to appeal mostly not only to older couples whose children were grown, as has generally been assumed, but within that market to a markedly Jewish tenancy. Housing economist Chester Rapkin, who carried out housing market studies for Philadelphia and other cities, stated that "unless a city has a sufficient number of Jews, it won't have a downtown apartment revival."

000 playground. The city also advanced plans for a major park to replace the commercial blight along the Schuylkill River, to give the riverbanks to the people to enjoy and perhaps provide a springboard for further residential redevelopment.

A major obstacle to the more substantial return of middle-income families to center city, and to center city's ability to hold families as their children grew to school age, was the inadequate, overcrowded public schools and their mediocre teaching standards. A 1960 survey of center-city families indicated that while many preferred to remain there, the children's education came first, and thus many contemplated moving to the suburbs.

Back in the early 1950's the Rittenhouse Square area residents had to struggle to convince the Board of Education that there were enough children in the area to establish an elementary school.* Again, in the early 1960's, when children had grown older and still more young couples moved in, there was another long struggle for a larger elementary school and a junior high school, a fight aided this time by a school committee of the Old Philadelphia Development Corporation. But there remained the question of how to get white middle- and upper-class families to send their children to school with the many lower-class "culturally deprived" children who lived in these changing neighborhoods. The Board of Education did not take this problem on.

Enhancement of the residential environment near the central business district could markedly maximize another potential for center city, making it the dominant center of the metropolitan region.

This potential was the relative growth of services in the economy—services for consumers and business firms † as well as

* The Board maintained that the few children in this high-income area went to private school. The Residents' Association carried out a neighborhood survey on the advice of the Citizens' Council on City Planning, and found that twice as many children as the Board of Education had estimated were going to fifty-two different far-flung schools; they learned that 528 wanted to go to public school. Still the Board did not commit itself at first and only reluctantly agreed to open a school in leased space at a local "Y"—a location found by the Residents' Association.

† Consumer services occupying office space on which consumer expenditures grew most rapidly were banking, life insurance, brokers, investment, and legal services. Leading business services used by other business firms were engineering and professional consulting, legal, finance, insurance, advertising, accounting, auditing, and real estate services.

the growth in manufacturers' administrative functions, which was reflected nationally in the explosion of the office-occupying work force. During the 1950's this sector grew 30 per cent compared to the general population increase of 18.5 per cent, a trend which was expected to repeat itself in the 1970's. These kinds of firms need face-to-face contacts to conduct business; many desire prestige locations, and prosper where they are most accessible to their clients or customers—in the core.*

But Philadelphia had to make special efforts to realize the core's unique attributes. Much potential office space downtown was occupied by outdated buildings or inappropriate uses, and demand in the region was not strong enough to bring about the spontaneous private office redevelopment that was taking place in New York. Nor did Philadelphia have a national headquarters constellation of giant industries as did Pittsburgh. Most of its manufacturers were small, and the heads of the city's banks and trusts did not press for shiny modern offices. Rather, elite Philadelphians had a predilection for old buildings and old clothes. Penn Center had satisfied much of the latent market for new space.

Yet national trends showed that successful companies were doubling their office staffs every ten years, and to make sure that center city would not lose expanding local firms and regional offices of national companies to the outskirts, the city had to create prestige locations and modern office facilities. The planners hoped they might even attract the headquarters of national companies. "When New York gets impossible," one spokesman suggested optimistically, "we'll get the overflow." The offices would, in turn, increase demand for nearby residences and provide a much-needed stimulus for downtown stores.

The planners set themselves to capitalizing on the development possibilities in locations with sufficient prestige and esthetic appeal to attract major offices. The value of urban open space seemed a key in stimulating higher private development.

* That location in the business core had such economic advantages for these services and administrative functions was pointed out in 1949–50 in studies undertaken for the City Planning Commission; this fact was elaborated in more detail and on a national scale by Raymond Vernon's seminal report on the changing function of the central city.

Independence Mall was bordered by old and ugly commercial lofts, but when the Mall was still in early planning, in 1958, the Old Philadelphia Development Corporation recognized the location's potential and the area was designated for federally aided commercial redevelopment. Plans were made for a $2,800,000 municipal garage under the Mall (the cleared land served for a long time as a huge, ugly parking lot), and the state advanced the necessary funds to finish the Mall's landscaping.

Top forces in the city began seeking out likely developers. Government, whose office functions were also growing, was high on the list of possibilities. Mayor Dilworth made the first commitment when he decided to put the city's new Police Headquarters Building near the Mall. The federal General Services Administration, which was contemplating an addition to its present courthouse in Philadelphia, was persuaded by the Mayor, members of the Planning Commission and of the Old Philadelphia Corporation, as well as judges of the Federal Court, instead to construct a new courthouse and federal office building on another site bordering Independence Mall. Congress in time agreed to a proposal from Philadelphia to build a new U.S. Mint there, thus maintaining an industry traditional to Philadelphia, and providing another attraction appropriate to the historic district for the income-producing tourist trade.

Rohm and Haas, an old Philadelphia firm and one of the city's most successful enterprises, had outgrown its present office building, and was spread over several buildings near Washington Square. The firm was persuaded to give up its plan to move these to the suburbs, and to build instead on the more prestigious Mall. The firm agreed to do so if the Redevelopment Authority acquired its present properties. Top local officials and the OPDC gave high priority to carrying out this complicated transaction * in the belief that Rohm and Haas' example would exert a powerful influence on others.†

* The process required a series of approvals by the Urban Renewal Administration and City Council, as well as some one hundred meetings with representatives of the city, Old Philadelphia Development Corporation and Rohm and Haas to overcome a host of technical problems.

† A two-year national promotional campaign to attract out-of-town headquarters has not yet resulted in commitments to Independence Mall, but another office building and a motel have acquired sites.

Since the cooperative essay into urban esthetics for Society Hill, the city government has supported the Planning Commission's insistence on excellence of design, open space and amenity. First-rank architects designed the new police administration headquarters near Independence Mall and handsome Municipal Services Building, which is set back in an imposing manner on a key block immediately northwest of City Hall, creating a standard of distinction for all future office structures. Private developers in or out of Title I sites have worked with the planners on building design and site placement, and the contagion of excellence is evident in many new structures throughout center city.

Striking evidence of this official commitment was furnished in 1959, when the city learned that the Pennsylvania Railroad was ready to dispose of the remaining portion of undeveloped land in its old Broad Street station site. The railroad planned to permit construction on this plot of land, immediately next to City Hall, of a commercial structure which would block out the uninterrupted visual pedestrian link with City Hall of the Penn Center esplanade. The Mayor wanted to preserve the vista, and he and his Cabinet had pledged themselves to replace the open plaza near City Hall, which they were taking for the Municipal Services Building. Dilworth sold City Council on spending the $2,500,000 needed to buy the site from the railroad, and the planners developed a scheme for a landscaped park and sunken plaza. But they also pointed out that it would be cut off by through-traffic from Broad Street. The administration and Council decided to spend some $4,000,000 more to acquire the adjacent block to the south, get rid of several ugly old buildings (the owner of one, Albert M. Greenfield, had been complaining about his loss of city tenants for the new municipal building) and to divert Broad Street traffic, thus making the new West Plaza a two-block extension of City Hall Square.

With this Plaza, the new developments and old landmarks north and west of City Hall would blend into the cityscape. In turn, new opportunities were set off for prime commercial development of the block immediately southwest, where low-rise, cut-rate stores and service shops, rabbit-warren offices, some bars and restaurants had clustered along the old "Chinese Wall."

The city planners proposed a redevelopment so that the city could acquire and control the block's rebuilding, in order to realize the full design potential and financial increment of the site. The Parking Authority, which needed a major facility in the vicinity, was brought in as a partner, to lease the air rights to Continental Square. The expected $50,000,000 worth of new private investment on the block—two impressive bids were received from interested firms—would return more than enough to cover the annual tax loss from the West Plaza as well as the city's outlay for acquiring and developing the Plaza.

MARKET PLACE OF THE INTELLECT

Simultaneously, Philadelphia has been trying to maximize its great potential for being what Mayor Dilworth called "a market place for the intellect," and to reap the economic benefits that could accrue from its exceptional assets in this field.

Most of the city's institutions and cultural facilities—its great universities (Penn and Temple), its hospitals and medical schools, its world-renowned symphony and museum and its legitimate theaters—are located in the core; together they offer the greatest single hope for Philadelphia as a vital and prosperous heart of the future metropolis. These are the specialized facilities that the central city can best provide for a region. They are the new escalators for metropolitan economic growth, and hold out the promise that in a society of increasing leisure, rising standards and growing demand for brainpower, Philadelphia can provide the essential amenities and facilities.

But if these facilities were to keep up with population growth in the region, meet the generally accelerating demand for them, and still remain in the city, then the city would have to accommodate their expansion needs.

The boom in higher education is a case in point. Projections for the 1970's show that colleges nationally will have to accommodate double the number of students they educated in the 1950's, both because of the greater number of youths and increased demand for their products; graduate schools will have to expand similarly to keep up with the demand for brainpower.

These requirements present urban centers with problems, but also with promising potential, as education is the growth industry of the future. Higher education is one of the area's largest employers, not only of teachers and administrative personnel but also maintenance and hospital staffs. Penn students alone spend an estimated $13,000,000 on consumer products and services a year.

Philadelphia, which has 1.1 per cent of the nation's population but employs over 4 per cent of the college and university personnel in the country, is in an exceptional position. With consumer and federal expenditures for health, hospitals and medical care doubling, the city's excellent medical institutions may benefit. Universities can also provide the scientific research and laboratories to attract new growth industries and create new ones.

But expansion of tax-exempt educational institutions removes revenue-producing land from city tax rolls, and usually displaces low-income families, since these inner-city institutions commonly sit in the midst of blight. This blight, in turn, often makes institutions look outward to the suburbs for a new location. They, too, need public assistance to remain and expand in the city.

On the other hand, colleges and universities may attract faculty families and intellectuals, groups with a proclivity for in-town living, if certain of their requirements are met. Such families are also more likely to live in racially integrated or economically heterogeneous neighborhoods—although more and more fled to the suburbs as university neighborhoods deteriorated. University growth also creates many new jobs in the city and, in Philadelphia, new income which is directly taxable for the city.

Sophisticated planners are aware of these trends, but Philadelphia was the first city in the country to make expansion of its private institutions in conformance with city plans a public policy; it specifically assists them with appropriations from capital funds as well as use of the public powers of eminent domain. In turn, the resources and brains of these institutions have become working partners in Philadelphia's renewal.

Following the 1956 assessment of renewal needs and priorities, the city shifted 10 per cent of its annual budget to help the universities, cultural institutions, hospitals and medical centers improve and expand.* In some instances Title I is used to help reduce land price to fair market value (broadened provisions in the 1959 Housing Act for nonresidential aid facilitated such financial assistance); in other instances, the Redevelopment Authority merely uses its power of eminent domain to acquire blighted land and sell it at full value to the user. Pennsylvania's General State Authority has played an expanding part, by acquiring land and constructing buildings for lease to the universities. With increasing federal and state support of higher education, even more funds for expansion than could ever be raised by voluntary contributions poured in.

The first area to benefit directly from the city's new policy was West Philadelphia, where the University of Pennsylvania and Drexel Institute are located, right across the Schuylkill River from center city and a few minutes' drive to the main railroad station. West Philadelphia was becoming badly run down. Some housing had deteriorated into slums requiring clearance; illegal conversions and dilapidation were increasing. Meanwhile, old residents were leaving and faculty families lived off campus.

To reverse this situation and plan living, medical, educational and research expansion in that area, five major institutions located there joined in 1959 to form the West Philadelphia Corporation, a nonprofit coordinating and program development agency. How necessary this was can be seen by the fact that the five institutions, which in 1960 had an enrollment of 28,000, expected to have 37,000 by 1970. Penn, in September 1961, announced that it expected to spend $150,000,000 in the next fifteen years to enlarge its campus to 250 acres and its enrollment to 26,000.

Temple University, located in North Philadelphia, almost in the heart of the city's most densely crowded and deteriorated slum, had been growing at the rate of 2,000 students a year since the end of the war, when it had only 10,000 enrolled. By 1965, there were 35,000 students, and by 1975 there would be 50,000. The University was seriously considering moving to the suburbs in order to build a new expanded campus, but the city promised

* This increased to 13 per cent as the universities' funds for development grew more quickly than anticipated in the late 1950's.

help, and there were many advantages to remaining in the city for a university with a large city student body. Temple has been slow to meet the reciprocal responsibility which an urban university has toward the city, and long maintained a "castle and moat" relationship with its immediate community.* Only two faculty members are reported to live in its neighborhood.

On the other hand, what has happened in West Philadelphia since 1959 is regarded by many as a miracle. True, conditions there are not as bad as those near Temple. But instead of walling institutions off from the predominantly non-white, lower-income residents, the program developed by the West Philadelphia Corporation has opened up the institutions and their talents to the community, and simultaneously drawn back faculty families. By 1965, 25 per cent or some 1,500 of the faculty lived there compared to 6 per cent in 1959, and a total of 3,500 staff personnel are expected to be residents by 1970. The University of Pennsylvania has helped this trend by making 100 per cent loans to faculty for home purchase. The WPC encourages new home construction, nonprofit sponsorship of FHA's 221 (d)3 housing and rehabilitation; a staff member helps residents get the FHA mortgage insurance which is available in a renewal area. The 2,000 acres of West Philadelphia have been certified for renewal. But efforts to attract Negroes with means have met with little success; West Philadelphia lacks prestige in their eyes.

Although there is inevitable hostility and resentment on the part of residents who fear dislocation, efforts are made to draw them into planning and neighborhood meetings. Leo Molinaro, WPC's executive director, spends several days a week knocking on doors in the neighborhood and going to meetings of dissidents who may have to be relocated to encourage them to discuss their problems.

The unique Universities-Related Public Schools program, which has achieved a remarkable upgrading of teaching quality, student opportunity and parent involvement, has done much to create a favorable environment. While the student body in these six elementary schools and the high school is heavily Negro,

* Temple, a low-tuition university, lacks Penn's resources. But it has joined in a new nonprofit group, the North City Corporation, which is concerned with the development of North Philadelphia.

integration has been taking place as more faculty members return to the area, in turn attracting other middle-class families. Interestingly, the Negro families have provided the main energy and articulate parent body for improving the schools.

In 1960 the West Philadelphia Corporation, recognizing that highly educated families would not move into the area unless they knew their children would receive good education, but rejecting the idea of establishing a special private school as the University of Chicago had done, went to the Board of Education and offered to make resources available to the public schools in the local community. As a result, innovations and enrichment programs are under way in practically every area, benefiting directly 4,000 of the 7,000 children in school there. The programs also have indirect promise for the entire school district, since they are planned to be exportable.

The unusual Motivation Program aims to encourage tenth-grade students with potential for higher education, and to help an increasingly larger number enter college; it offers them curricular and cultural enrichment and a tutoring system using university students, and encourages active parent participation. What makes the program practical and realistic are scholarships, ranging from $100 to $2,600 a year, depending on need, which are funded by various local institutions through efforts of the Corporation. When the first group of "M" students graduated in 1965, almost three fourths were accepted in one or more colleges throughout the nation, far exceeding expectations, and none was prevented from going for lack of financing. The program has proved so successful that the 135 students who started in 1962 have increased to 500 in the fall of 1965. During the summer, another special program brings college-bound students onto the University of Pennsylvania campus so that they can gain pre-college experience. The Penn students are as involved as the young high school graduates.

THE ACCELERATOR FOR GROWTH

The most ambitious project generated by the West Philadelphia Corporation is the $50,000,000 University City Science Center, which began operations in 1964 in a reconverted industrial building and will move into a six-block-long complex of buildings on both sides of West Market in 1967.

The Center, which is sponsored by thirteen educational and medical institutions in the metropolitan area, is also Philadelphia's major bid to capture its share of the booming research and development industry, and make up for the loss of manufacturing jobs. Urban university-oriented research and development is generally believed to be the heaviest accelerator for future growth (witness the Greater Boston and San Francisco Bay areas), stimulating twelve jobs in other industries for every one of its own. The Science Center, which will employ an estimated 5,000, is expected to generate 60,000 new jobs, most of which will stay in the region.

The Center will be a complex of laboratories for industry and government use, conference and meetings rooms, computer and rapid printing facilities, with a special staff to do contract research. Major research-oriented organizations who are the first tenants include General Electric, the Institute for the Advancement of Medical Communications, and the Marketing Science Institute.

Latest of West Philadelphia's unique enterprises is the Regional Development Laboratory, an incubator for infant research ideas with special promise for regional employment. There, inventors and researchers rent professional laboratory facilities where they can develop job-producing products and services. Professional consulting services on marketing and sales and other necessary services are also made available. All patent rights and future profits belong to the investor. The International Resistance Company is cited as one local example of the "spin-off" value of such university-based research. The company, which grew out of research done by two Philadelphia college professors, employed 2,000 in 1964 and had net sales of $30,000,000. A grant has been given to the Regional Laboratory (which is sponsored jointly by the West Philadelphia Corporation and the newer South Eastern Pennsylvania Economic Development Corporation), by federal Economic Development Administration to find ways of solving the area's hard-core unemployment problems.

Philadelphia has been below average in its share of scientific brainpower, and it missed out on the federally financed space boom. However, its unusually strong medical institutions, plus industry in the drug and medical instrument field, put the area in an exceptional position to benefit from the new and growing federal research largesse in the "life sciences." The University City Science Center and institutional expansions are calculated to capitalize on the opportunities.*

The first phase of the Washington Square West urban renewal project has been designed to help the Jefferson Medical Center, located there, carry out its $41,000,000 development program for new classrooms, laboratories, student and nurse housing, a library and off-street parking. Hahnemann Hospital, another of the city's most important teaching institutions, also located in center city, is being similarly helped through renewal.

But to attract the brainpower which is essential to not only more brains but also research money, cities must provide a highly livable environment and cultural and educational amenities. Philadelphia's current plans to expand cultural and performing arts facilities, in the vicinity of the Philadelphia College of Art and the Academy of Music, should attract to the city not only suburbanites but also new talents from out of the region.

TO BRING THE CUSTOMERS BACK

The big unanswered question in the city's physical development plans for center city is: will the shoppers return to Market Street?

Even while center city was coming back as a residential locus and sprouting new offices at the rate of 500,000 square feet of space a year, the city's main retail street, directly east of City Hall, continued to decline. Not only had Market Street failed to benefit from regional growth; in the decade before 1964, department store sales suffered an absolute decline of 30 per cent, and lost thousands of jobs. The first victim of suburban competition and population spread from the city, Frank and Sedar, located

* Between 1953 and 1964, the National Institutes of Health increased their support of college and university research from $14,000,000 to $319,000,000. As the 1960's advanced, the Health, Education and Welfare Department increasingly dominated federal research grants to educational institutions. Consumer expenditures for health, hospitals and medical care are also booming.

near to the Reading Terminal on Market Street, closed in the mid-1950's. Then in 1963, Snellenburg's, one of the remaining five Market Street department stores across the street from the Reading, went out of business. The loss of customers was accompanied by an influx along the once-prosperous shopping street of seedy hole-in-the-wall shops and distress merchandise dealers. General physical deterioration made the area one of the most unattractive retail districts in the country, and gave shoppers even less desire to come downtown. The Reading line suffered large operating losses and cut back its unprofitable commuter service. The distance of the line's terminal from the major office concentrations along Broad Street to the south of City Hall and Penn Center on Market Street West was another disadvantage. As both the Reading and Pennsylvania's commuter services deteriorated, still fewer people wanted to come to center city by rail; if they came by car, they found traffic jams and inconvenient or inadequate parking space.

The Market Street East project, which went into execution in 1966, is the $250,000,000 answer, developed by Philadelphia's planners, transportation bodies and economic consultants, to restore Market Street's retailing pre-eminence in the city and region. Although it focuses on the main shopping street, which stretches between City Hall and the Independence Mall office redevelopment area, the project is expected to act as a major stimulus for all of center city. It will tie together downtown's various sub-centers, and also generate the pedestrian traffic on which a city center depends in order to work well. Because Philadelphia's planners have kept the core compact, and are making it beautiful as well, walking between destinations in center city is not only possible, but also more and more pleasant.

The Market Street East project itself is a seven-block-long structure, a multi-level shopping-office-hotel complex tied into a major underground transportation terminal and interchange. Shoppers will be able to walk by stores and restaurants along a skylighted air-conditioned mall, stroll on open-air cantilevered esplanades and cross-overs between the Market Street stores along special footbridges. People working in the 3,500,000 square feet of new office space to be constructed above the retailing level should add substantially to the customer volume.

But the entire project's feasibility—the $125,000,000 in private construction, and the new uses and revival of shopping it expects to stimulate—hinges on plans to make this critical location as accessible, pleasant and convenient as possible. The plans must increase the volume of people coming there by mass transportation from throughout the metropolitan region.

To achieve this the various means of transportation serving the general area will be coordinated and modernized. Indeed, the partial use of present mass-transit facilities was found to be a major roadblock not only to downtown's retailing health, but also to the commercial vitality of all downtown; Larry Smith and Co., nationally renowned marketing consultants, also found in their 1962 study of the plan that the proposed improvements could do much to alter the situation.

The centerpiece of the newly coordinated transportation systems under Market Street East, and the most expensive element in the project, is to be a new railroad tunnel. This structure will integrate the thirteen separate commuter runs of the Reading and Pennsylvania lines, the two railroads that serve downtown, but whose stub-end terminals are separated by a quarter of a mile. Through-runs of their trains, and several new station stops, will give the commuter or shopper a greater choice of destinations in center city without changing trains. The reconstructed underground will also provide direct connections from the trains to the Market Street subway (also scheduled for rehabilitation) to a new terminal for commuter buses and to the new 3,000-car-capacity garage which will give automobiles direct access by ramps to center city's expressway loop. Escalators will carry passengers from the transportation terminus to the upper levels. A bonus for the pedestrian shopper will be the closing to vehicular traffic of Chestnut Street, a narrow shopping thoroughfare next to East Market Street, and the installation there of a seven-block trolley line, the first to be built in this century.

This entire concept had been on the drawing boards for years, and the project itself was the keystone in the Planning Commission's 1960 plan. But in spite of the retailing decline, several years passed before the leading merchants and major downtown business interests took it up. (The OPDC, its sphere in center city extended from river to river, formed a special committee on

Market Street East in 1962.) No doubt the conservative bankers and merchants required not only proof of feasibility, but also success in other center-city projects before they would support this mammoth undertaking.

Even so, not until the passage of the federal Mass Transit Act of 1964 were the public means to finance the railroad tunnel little more than a hope. With the new legislation, however, Market Street East began moving; its target date of completion is 1976, which happens to be the 200th anniversary of the signing of the Declaration of Independence in Philadelphia.

THE TIE THAT BINDS

Philadelphia has been far more awake than most cities to opportunities for creative action because it determined in advance where it was going, perceived relationships, and then translated this information into action programs. This approach is particularly impressive in the transportation field. Indeed, had not Philadelphia started some fifteen years before Market Street East to think about its traffic problems and their implications for land use, it would have been futile even to contemplate the ambitious downtown retail redevelopment which depends on the transportation system for its success.

Most of the city's development programs and ingenious quasi-public action agencies are directed at coping with the impact on a built-up city of technological changes, and with the readjustments which these innovations require if a city is to remain viable. Major shifts in scale as well as land use are required, and in the process these often present potential dilemmas.

The ever-increasing, apparently irreversible popularity of automobile travel presents dilemmas to every urban center. How can the specialized and regional functions that belong in the core be accommodated there and made accessible to as many people in the region as possible without, in the process, sacrificing the very compactness which makes the core work so well for these activities?

Until the latter 1950's, cities seemed unaware that this traffic dilemma existed and, like Los Angeles and Detroit, were letting more and more expressways, parking lots and widened streets eat up their downtowns. There was a widely held belief that traffic experts and highway engineers could solve cities' traffic problems. Indeed, the sudden availability of billions of dollars in state and federal highway construction funds made this approach seem the only feasible one. Actually, no one had thought much about planning for downtown and its special land use functions.

The first modern plan for a city's business district to jointly consider land and transportation uses and attempt an overall solution was proposed in 1956 by Victor Gruen Associates in their plan for Fort Worth, Texas of 1980. The plan's principal concept—a vehicle-free city center in which the automobile is parked in huge garages located on the expressway-circled perimeter and the pedestrian is king—had an enormous national impact; it redirected thinking about downtowns in an estimated one hundred cities, Philadelphia among them.

But the Fort Worth plan superficially appeared to be merely an adaptation to downtown of the firm's effective shopping center designs. It was commissioned by a private utility in a city whose leaders were weak and divided, fell into a vacuum and was not carried out; its radical answer tended to be dismissed as too diagrammatic and unrealistic.*

Less understood, but basic to the logic of the Gruen firm's sweeping prescription, was the mathematics of the auto as a space consumer versus the functions of a city's core. The planners calculated future metropolitan growth and the parallel increases in vehicular trips that could be expected downtown; they found that at peak hours, four times as much land as at present would be needed for the car in 1980, and the central business district would be exploded into nothing but parking lots. Thus they proposed to eliminate all automobiles from the core in order to keep it tight.

A basic proviso to the plan went virtually unnoticed at the time, but held the key to the plan's realization, and was a major lesson for cities generally. By 1980, even with the huge, 60,000-car capacity of the perimeter garages, 50 per cent more trips to the

* A similar plan by the firm has been carried out since in Fresno, California, and includes a six-block pedestrian mall on what used to be a downtown street.

core would have to be made on mass transportation if the plan was to work. (This implied a radical change in the habits of auto-happy Texans.)

Philadelphia's Mayor Clark had early instituted panaceas for ending midtown strangulation—placing a ban on center-city curb parking, extending one-way traffic streets, building municipal garages, and appointing traffic committees to advise him. But growing congestion cost an estimated $150,000,000 annually in business slow-downs or losses and decreased land values, and train commuter service was steadily cut back.

A start had also been made on an inner-city highway loop to rim the core of the city and divert through-traffic. But, as Philadelphia's former planning director, Robert Mitchell, who had studied the relation of traffic and land use, warned, "Every major highway can be expected to generate much more driving than there was before it was built." Already, 55 per cent of the people entering and leaving the inner city did so by car, and one third of center-city ground space was devoted to streets and parking.

The lack of centralized machinery for determining transportation policy or carrying it out compounded the problem; responsibilities for different aspects of the city's circulatory system were scattered among various city agencies, independent authorities and state departments. The latest of Clark's traffic committees, aware that it, like its predecessors, had failed to accomplish much, recommended that an adequate study be undertaken, with staff and budget, and that a board composed of different major interests in the transportation field be appointed to conduct a closer examination. Clark worked closely with the leaders of the Greater Philadelphia Movement to gain support, and the Bureau of Municipal Research refined the idea. The Bureau proposed the development of a comprehensive transportation program and policy to tie together the piecemeal efforts of nineteen different city, state and federal agencies plus private companies.

Late in 1953 Mayor Clark appointed members of the Urban Traffic and Transportation Board (established by City Council) and assigned it the task of developing what no other city had yet attempted, an overall, long-range transportation program. The Board was unusual, comprising those who actually make decisions about the supply of transportation services. Heads of railroads, leaders in downtown commerce, banking, labor unions, automobile clubs and public transit, and a number of civic leaders—all those with vested and often conflicting interests—sat on the Board. Not until they reached a consensus, Clark reasoned, would it be possible to put a total strategy into effect.

Now, while other cities poured all their money into traffic-generating, core-destroying highways and downtown garages, and let mass transportation die, Philadelphia stopped and thought.

Planner Mitchell, then head of the new Institute for Urban Studies at the University of Pennsylvania, was brought back to direct the study and develop the program for the Board. Mitchell had recently completed, with Chester Rapkin, *Urban Traffic, a Function of Land Use;* this pioneer study analyzed traffic in terms of its underlying causes and generators, specifically the functions of various establishments in the urban community. The new principles laid down in it became the basis of the bold, sensitive and sophisticated interrelated land use and transportation planning that has taken place in Philadelphia since 1955, and are virtually the gospel for a new kind of metropolitan transportation planning.

The study's first tenet was that planning urban transportation is a specialized but integral part of total city planning. Further, a transportation system must be developed as a whole to serve the city's activities differentially and with maximum efficiency. The study also pointed out that it is possible to improve traffic conditions by altering land use patterns, and by removing from congested areas obsolete establishments which generate antagonistic traffic. (A basic earlier study undertaken for the Planning Commission had revealed that much of the traffic congestion in center city was caused by inappropriate goods-handling activities. Further, it predicted that with the relative growth in the economy of core-type functions and the growing distance between home and office, travel to and from the central business district, and mounting traffic jams at rush hours, could be expected.)

Finally, *Urban Traffic* posited the belief that in the dynamic urban community, where a change in any one part inevitably brings other changes, the transportation system could be used as a tool to shape better communities and regions.

The same year that Gruen's Fort Worth plan was being

readied, Philadelphia's Urban and Traffic Transportation Board presented its *Plan and Program, 1955* to Mayor Clark. Interestingly, and not coincidentally, although the Gruen firm and the Mitchell study started from different poles and with different aims—the former concentrating on the city center and the latter concerned with a transportation system for the entire city and ultimately the region—Philadelphia also found that the system's balance had first to be struck in the core, and that in order to save the core, a shift in the present habit of traveling to center city by car was also required.

In contrast to Fort Worth, Philadelphia was the product of an earlier, transit-based era and already had perhaps the finest basic network of commuter rail lines and transit in the country. But as the transportation study disclosed, although few expressways had been built in the region, public transportation was losing out to the automobile. The commuter lines, with annual deficits running to $7,000,000, were letting service decline at an accelerating rate; by the mid-1950's only 45,000 commuters used rail, compared to 75,000 in the late 1920's when population was much smaller. The privately controlled (though 60 per cent city owned) Philadelphia Transportation Company, in fiscal straits since the days of corporate pyramiding, was also cutting back on loss operations while it duplicated service offered by trains on more profitable runs.

This trend was ominous. It meant a 25 per cent increase in downtown automobile traffic by 1980. But William Penn's twenty-six-foot-wide cartways could not handle a greater flow.

The main recommendation of the Urban Traffic and Transportation Board was to achieve a balanced system of rail and highway transportation, using present systems as efficiently as possible. But its first aim, to save the central business district, required two things: the expressways circling the core to siphon off through-traffic, two thirds of which was bound elsewhere; and much greater use of more efficient mass transportation. Rail travel should be made so convenient, comfortable and inexpensive that it would be preferable to driving. The improvements entailed would, in turn, require a substantial reallocation of money. In 1956, $843,000,000 was being spent in the region on private automobile transportation and only $117,000,000 on transit systems. Although a new system of urban highways was needed, public assistance to transit and rail must be given equivalent expenditures. The Board's report also held that a regional body was necessary to develop and control transportation in the region since so many of the city's traffic problems originated outside the core.

THE "PHILADELPHIA PLAN"

Another difference between Fort Worth and Philadelphia was in the local leadership. Mayor Dilworth made the report prepared for Clark the transportation bible of his own administration. He assigned responsibility for its realization to his managing director, appointed a new board, and won City Council's approval of a regional approach.

But the surrounding counties, afraid they would be dominated by Philadelphia, abruptly rejected the idea. (They did, however, accept the basic network of highways for the city and region developed by the Philadelphia planners, and these were adopted basically by the state highway department.) Next, the Pennsylvania Railroad threatened to abandon service on its commuter runs which were so vital to the region's transportation network. It seemed the cow would get out of the barn before the door could be closed.

Discussions initiated with the Pennsylvania line proved fruitless. Dilworth's city solicitor even threatened litigation before the courts and state regulatory bodies to restrain the railroad from abandoning service. But then Congress passed the Transportation Act of 1958, which considerably eased constraints on lines wanting to discontinue train service, and bolstered the line's position. Litigation could go on for years while Philadelphia's commuter service quietly died.

The city moved from planning to emergency action, based on the recommendations of the UTTB report. Mayor Dilworth appointed a task force, and within a few months they initiated the "Philadelphia plan," the most novel, successful and influential publicly initiated scheme in the country for nursing commuter rail back to useful service. One result is that metropolitan Philadelphia has not had a single line abandoned.

The main thrust of the Philadelphia plan is to buy improved service from the railroad carriers, paying the lines for the extra runs which they cannot afford and for rides at reduced rates. A market survey indicated that more people would commute by rail if the frequency of service was increased, fares cut and the antiquated cars and tracks and Victorian stations replaced with comfortable modern facilities and equipment.

In the fall of 1958, a trial program was initiated on two Pennsylvania and Reading runs to Chestnut Hill. These were entirely within the city limits, had suffered a decline in ridership, and partly paralleled the new Schuylkill Expressway, which was to open soon. At the end of six months, "Operation Northwest" had increased ridership by 40 per cent for a total public subsidy of $160,000, and the opening of the new expressway had little effect. The experiment was then extended to two more runs of the Pennsylvania as well as the Reading. Reduced-fare connecting bus service was provided at both ends, with a special ten-cents-a-ride loop to run between the downtown stations and center city offices. Tallied results showed a 30 per cent increase in train riders and a marked reduction in downtown automobile trips. The cost to the city was $320,000, and annual savings to the commuter were $250. The subsidy plan was next extended to the northeastern section of the Reading, with even more striking results. Another market study revealed that if modern rail cars and smooth new tracks were provided, the ensuing increase in riders would be still greater. The rail companies still lost money on these commuter runs, but they were willing to continue the program.

The city was so pleased with the results that it proceeded to put the plan on a more permanent basis. In 1960, another nonprofit Philadelphia agency, the Passenger Service Improvement Corporation, was set up to administer and extend the plan, with a new Board. In October 1960, three more runs were added, and in mid-1961 the PSIC was able to report a 44 per cent increase in riders on the city-subsidized private commuter lines since the start of the plan three years before. Suburban commuters were even driving out of their way, leaving cars behind, in order to take the less expensive and more efficient rail rides. The city's annual outlay by that year was $1,500,000, which bought

6,000,000 rides that would not otherwise have been provided.

But why should all the city taxpayers subsidize rail commuters? John A. Bailey, who was moved from the post of Philadelphia's assistant managing director to director of the PSIC, pointed out that even with new expenditures under the Philadelphia plan, the city's subsidies to automobile riders were still much higher than to rail riders. In Operation Northwest, for example, the city paid only nine cents a commuter ride, while it expended nineteen cents per trip on freeways, an additional twenty-five cents daily for each car parked downtown, and $50 annually per car on its street system. Were everyone entering the central district on rail to be accommodated on freeways, the city would have to pay out sixty-three cents per person on each round trip. The Delaware Expressway, whose twenty-six miles were expected to cost $300,000,000, could carry only one tenth the number of people which existing transit, modernized and extended, could move for $175,000,000.

The direct public subsidy to automobile transportation did not even include the consumers' own expenditures for gas and oil, insurance, repairs, depreciation and parking, nor did it calculate the loss to all the city taxpayers from non-taxable highways and streets. Popular support for better commuter service was sufficiently strong in 1961 for the voters in Philadelphia to approve a $5,600,000 loan to the railroads to pay for more parking and new equipment.

But several key elements necessary to improve mass transit and to achieve the balanced system were still missing. One was purchase of the Philadelphia Transportation Company, which ran most of the city's buses, streetcars, subways and elevated lines. Philadelphia's transportation planners believed that transit should be run without profit, like other government services, but the owners and directors of the PTC were concerned about making money and paying dividends to their stockholders. The company's board (headed, ironically, by two former chairmen of the City Planning Commission, Hopkinson and Greenfield) rejected the amount offered by the city to purchase the company. Negotiations ended in a city lawsuit against the PTC.

Another gap was in the cooperation of the surrounding counties where one quarter of the people holding jobs in Philadelphia lived. Large additional sums were also needed to replace the present obsolete equipment whose maintenance was a needlessly costly drain on the carriers; to modernize or relocate stations and to supply them with sufficient nearby parking. The OTTB had called for a $100,000,000 investment in the region's mass transportation facilities. To connect the stub-end terminals of the Pennsylvania and Reading lines in center city and build the tunnel would itself require an estimated $40,000,000. But it was regarded as a public investment which would be well worth while; it promised the rail carriers savings of $2,000,000 annually, since fewer cars would be needed to provide for the same level of service, and the improved convenience would draw more rail commuters to center city.

NEW AIDS AND METROPOLITAN COOPERATION

But the city was nearing the borrowing capacity set by its own financial policy; it had already passed one major bond issue to buy 270 new subway cars for the PTC, which it was also subsidizing annually out of the expense budget for $5,500,000, in addition to the financial assistance to the railroads. The state had shown no interest in Philadelphia's transportation problems; it shortchanged the city even in highway construction funds.* Therefore, Mayor Dilworth told members of Congress in 1960, at the first hearings ever held on possible federal aid to mass transit, that it was up to the federal government to provide the balance from national revenues, since the city's transportation system was not only regional but also interstate. (Through the Delaware River Port Authority, Philadelphia was extending and improving its subway service to New Jersey.)

These Congressional hearings culminated five years of nationwide effort originated by Clark and carried forth by Dilworth to put urban mass transportation on the federal aid-to-cities list. The results dramatically showed that local studies, demonstrations and initiative can influence new national legislation to help cities help themselves.

* The pace of constructing the center city expressway loop dragged far behind schedule.

Clark believed that maximum federal aid would be necessary to realize *Plan and Program, 1955*, and tried that year to get this new item on the grants-in-aid agenda of the American Municipal Association. But few cities were then even thinking in such terms. Passage of the 1956 Highway Act, which made billions available for urban highway construction, was a tremendous setback, but Mayor Dilworth took up the mass-transit idea and promoted it energetically across the country. With other mayors, newspapers, railroad interests and civic groups, he stressed the importance of an integrated metropolitan circulatory system which could move people, not cars, quickly, conveniently, and at the lowest possible cost. By the end of 1959, stirred into action by the Transportation Act of 1958, an effective lobby of interest groups took the mass transportation package to Washington.

When Dilworth testified before Congress in 1960 as current president of the American Municipal Association, he spoke for American cities in general. But what made the great impact was his ability to cite from Philadelphia's unique mass transportation experiments and to show that federal aid allowing cities to purchase capital equipment for improved rail service would more than pay for itself; it would increase commuter rides and rail revenues and reduce the demand for costly new streets and urban expressways which government would otherwise have to build and maintain.

Congress in 1961 for the first time made a small but significant appropriation to help localities plan public transit facilities and carry out demonstration projects, and this was the foot in the door leading to the 1964 Mass Transit Act. However, Congress stipulated in the legislation that the funds were to be available only on a metropolitan basis. This provision allowed Philadelphia to bring all except one of the four recently reluctant suburban counties into the Philadelphia plan. In October of 1961 Mayor Dilworth and the commissioners of three counties signed the South Eastern Pennsylvania Transportation Compact, to extend the program beyond the city line, with costs to be shared.

Why had the counties changed their minds in five years' time? Certainly the prospect of forfeiting federal funds was a goad, and influential Republican suburbanites who had offices and civic commitments in center city added their persuasive powers. Most important, however, the rapidly urbanizing counties were developing city-size traffic jams, and the success of the Philadelphia ridership program made it seem that improving mass transit might cost them less than building more roads and installing expensive traffic systems. At least Philadelphia had the planning staff and technical expertise to help the counties find out. (John Bailey, who moved on to direct the regional compact, said, "You have to create the public. But you can't sell them on facts; you have to show them.")

The initial extensions over the city line proved so successful, and the economic effect of two strikes by the transit unions early in 1963—one in the city and the second primarily in the suburbs—were so serious, that the elected officials of the city and counties determined to make more formal governmental arrangements. Enabling legislation was submitted to the state for a body that could not only take over management of special programs but also acquire rail lines, the city and county public transportation systems, and the Delaware River Port Authority, and fuse them into one unified system; the South Eastern Pennsylvania Transportation Authority was in operation in 1964.* When the Reading line, which was suffering heavy operating losses, threatened to abandon all its commuter rail service that summer, the new Authority was able to give it emergency aid, and prevent it from the collapse which would have wrecked the whole system. When the state, led by Governor William Scranton, considered financial aid to urban mass transit in 1965, Philadelphia and its four suburban counties fought together in Harrisburg for the first time. All were committed to the idea of center city Philadelphia, and Philadelphia itself was becoming more and more aware that its economic health was interdependent with that of the metropolitan region.

To qualify for grants under the Mass Transit Act of 1964, the new regional transportation authority was required to have programs that fit reasonably well with those of the new Delaware

* The Authority device was necessary to encompass the five counties and 208 municipalities which were involved in SEPTA, and to issue bonds. The board is composed of one member appointed by the Governor of the Commonwealth, and two by each of the top elected executives of Philadelphia and the four suburban counties. Eventually, the Delaware River Port Authority is expected to be brought into SEPTA.

Valley Regional Planning Commission, successor to the Penn–Jersey Transportation study.

How this will succeed is open to conjecture. Experience with the $5,000,000 Penn–Jersey Transportation study—an ambitious project bringing together officials at four government levels in order to obtain their agreement on future transportation development in the region based on alternative modes projected by computers—revealed that while the planners were planning, basic transportation decisions had to be made; furthermore, the politicians were unable to make the abstract decisions required by the study.

WILL THE CITY BE READY?

"Sometime between now and 1980, the relative advantage of the central city and the suburb will come back into balance," William L. C. Wheaton stated in a 1959 address on metropolitan Philadelphia's future population presented to the Citizens' Council on City Planning. Wheaton, then director of the Institute for Urban Studies at the University of Pennsylvania and one of the country's foremost urban authorities, explained why he expected this to be so. During that period, the suburban areas would have to absorb a major new population explosion, and with this, the huge advantages of lower land costs and real estate taxes, accessibility and high amenity which the suburbs had enjoyed during the past thirty years would be reduced.

If the city's renewal program was massive and effective and center city's amenities were raised, Wheaton predicted that the city by 1980 could regain its popularity and be competitive. "When that time comes, will the city be ready?" Can Philadelphia by 1980 realize the goals of its long-range comprehensive plan of greater amenity and accessibility for all?

The renewal called for in the $3,700,000,000 plan—renewal taken in the broadest sense of all improvements necessary to make the whole city workable, attractive and competitive—is massive. But at the present rate of carrying out plans, Philadelphia will not be ready. That city has moved ahead more sensibly, in a more coordinated way and more comprehensively in preparing itself for the urban future than other big cities, and civic involvement there is second to none. But the pace is not fast enough, the scale in no way commensurate with the size of the city or the extent of blight. The administration has not taken adequate advantage of new federal aid programs to deal with underlying socioeconomic problems, nor has the city accepted the proposals recommended by its renewal planners.

Moreover, the public costs of carrying out the plan are far beyond any sum imagined by the planners in 1960. Getting the $3,700,000,000 for the public improvements called for in the plan was predicated on the assumption that the state and federal governments—mostly the federal—would contribute more than one third of the total. But this would have required a fundamental shift in the pattern of national spending in favor of cities, a shift that has not taken place under the New Frontier or the Great Society. In fact, the Commonwealth's new urban aid programs for higher education, open space and mass transit have advanced state assistance much faster, proportionately.

Locally, the timetable of the plan is dependent on the city's self-imposed limits on annual expenditures for tax-supported projects, a figure based on the proportion of capital expenditures to the city's gross income. At the 1960 rate of $25,000,000 annually, the total local share of $921,000,000 would not be reached until the year 2000—unless the city were to encumber itself with huge debts. The plan's completion could be accelerated to 1988, however, if the growth in personal incomes anticipated by 1980 was realized.

With one third of the city's families currently earning $3,000 or less, such calculations seem unrealistic. Moreover, it is evident that the city plan far overestimated Philadelphia's industrial potential, and the growing job gap is totally out of line with the plan, which was predicated on a total increase of at least 36,000 jobs by 1970.

It has also become clear that the city grossly underestimated how long it would take to eliminate blight and rebuild neighborhoods at the present rate of expenditure. An analysis of renewal in Philadelphia undertaken for its Community Renewal Program found that, as stated in the 1966 report to the Department of Housing and Urban Development on progress under Philadelphia's Workable Program: "Under existing levels of public financing it would take more than 100 years to complete Title I projects for all the areas needing treatment."

Center city renewal projects were moving ahead on schedule; institutional expansion was proceeding at an even faster rate than anticipated. (Projects benefiting from new public grant programs, such as the universities and mass transit, accelerated most.) The big delays came in residential renewal projects outside of center city. These were the largest Title I programs in terms of acreage and public expenditures, receiving 45 per cent of the city's annual renewal outlay. Experience in the conservation areas program, which was initiated in 1957 under the new balanced approach, suggested that Philadelphia had indulged in some wishful thinking about the cost of rehabilitating its older neighborhoods, and the CRP analysis indicated that urban renewal in the gray areas had gone about as far as it could—alone.

In 1957, it was expected that five of these older neighborhoods could be rehabilitated annually at the public cost of $500,000 each, based on a fairly low level of public treatment. As the Development Coordinator stated: "In such conservation areas, an improvement here and there may be enough to do the job . . . getting rid of a factory . . . clearing up a traffic problem . . . taking care of an isolated run-down house. . . ." Such spot clearance, plus code inspection, scattered public housing and support by aroused local leadership, were deemed sufficient to win substantial rehabilitation and halt decline. Through these programs, he expected that available funds could be spread out and used "far more effectively" than in redeveloping slum areas.

By 1965, however, the public costs in conservation areas were running between $4,000,000 and $12,000,000 per neighborhood, and the Redevelopment Authority believed that only two such projects could be undertaken annually. The first was still far from finished.

The unanticipated problems started with a cutback in federal renewal funds which delayed the program's start. Making plans with the residents took considerable time, resulted in raising their standards and expectations, and thus created demands for greater public investment in community facilities. Self-help leadership proved ineffective, partly because the population in these areas was changing. Much more city staff was required than was necessary in clearance projects, and it was obvious that continued public efforts would be required even after the renewal program was "finished" to prevent new decline. Property rehabilitation itself proceeded much more slowly than expected; there were far fewer resident owners than originally, and the pace was held back by the slowest and least cooperative owners. There were so many holdouts that the Authority had to go into extensive property acquisition, the single biggest factor in high project costs.

But the major deterrent to carrying out rehabilitation was lack of private financing. Banks were reluctant to make loans for neighborhoods which, despite urban renewal, they regarded as still on the downgrade—certainly not likely to last for the forty years assumed in the renewal treatment. And the economic validity of spending much on the row housing in these areas was questioned. As the Citizens' Council on City Planning pointed out in a 1965 critique of urban renewal in Philadelphia, the conservation approach is not effective in areas where the costs of private rehabilitation are out of scale with the resulting values of improved properties. Much larger public subsidies would be needed.

The public housing authority was the chief residential developer in the Morton project, the most advanced of the conservation neighborhoods. Tax-exempt local institutions were also helped. The effect on the tax base, according to Community Renewal Program estimates, was a 36 per cent decrease in total assessed values. (Center city projects—Washington Square, Independence Mall and Park Towne—would result in a net gain of 265 per cent and "help to balance the losses in revenue.")

The Redevelopment Authority looked hopefully to two new special assistance programs made available to homeowners in urban renewal areas by the Housing Act of 1965; this offered rehabilitation loans at 3 per cent interest, and grants of $1,500 to homeowning families with incomes below $3,000. However, the funds Congress appropriated for these two programs were limited * and had to be spread across the entire country. Even so, the city agencies were laggard in promoting use of previous special aids for building lower-cost housing, such as 221(d) 3. The Philadelphia Housing Development Corporation—a new quasi-

* Congress appropriated $100,000,000 for the loan program and $1,500,000 in grants, in the first year.

public agency established in 1964 and given $2,000,000 by City Council for a revolving fund to rehabilitate properties or stimulate construction of new ones on a limited profit or nonprofit basis—remained largely on paper.

THE NEW RENEWAL

The relatively poor results in neighborhood conservation combined with the growing restlessness and problems of the city's Negro population gave rise by the mid-1960's to a new dissent; citizen organizations and city planners at the University of Pennsylvania called for new approaches to planning and renewal.

University critics charged that the local "renaissance" was a façade which hid the city's teeming, neglected slums. It was asserted that the welfare mandate of the 1949 National Housing Policy—"a decent home and a suitable living environment for every American family"—had lost out to economic development; that physical planning had been overemphasized and human needs ignored; that urban renewal had done too little in creating jobs and better housing for the poor.

Philadelphia, more than any other city, has emphasized provision for low-rent housing in renewal areas. It provided the Housing Authority with hard-to-find sites at reduced cost, tried to avoid economic and racial ghettos by putting low-rent and middle-income units in the same project areas, and pioneered new approaches, such as the Used House program and scattered sites, to avoid stigmatizing poor families. The city's Centralized Relocation Service helped several thousand families find better homes when forced by code enforcement to move outside of Title I areas. (As a result, it pioneered new federal aids for local code enforcement.)

But if some critics felt that the volume was too low—only 14,000 units of public housing in the whole city, and 1,500 more scheduled for acquisition and rehabilitation under the Used House program*—others, the citizens' Philadelphia Housing As-

* The experimental program began working faster in 1965 after the Housing Authority set standards for private contractors to do the acquisition and rehabilitation, and then bought the houses from them instead of doing the work itself. But some experts said it would be cheaper to buy the many $4,000–$6,000 price homes on the market in "move-in" condition.

sociation foremost, felt that low-rent housing was an inadequate answer to present needs. From a massive analysis of housing problems in Philadelphia, the citizen organization concluded that the new approaches authorized by the Housing Act of 1965—even rent supplements—did not deal with the basic cause—poverty. Because the federal program requires that projects' operating costs be paid out of rents received, it was too expensive for the poor and was not reaching the really poor. The Association proposed a federal housing subsidy directly to poor families in order to close the gap between what they could pay and what standard housing cost. Philadelphia had a large supply of standard, low-value housing, but poor families had to spend too much of their income on it.

The city, itself, had also gone through an intensive analysis and rethinking of renewal, aided by the Community Renewal Program studies. These had provided an opportunity to stand back from project planning and execution and look at all aspects of the renewal problem. The inherent limitations of a strictly physical approach to renewal, and the importance of social factors became more and more obvious. A statistical profile of the city's "blue areas"—inner-city slums marked in its plan for eventual clearance and reconstruction—made the reasons appallingly clear. In these eleven square miles of the city, 377,000 families, 80 per cent of them non-white, lived at densities of 34,300 to a square mile, only 58 per cent in housing that was sound, with all facilities. Of the labor force there in 1960, 13 per cent were unemployed (the number was no doubt much higher, since statistics only classify those seeking work), 84 per cent were unskilled or semiskilled. Fifty-four per cent of the families had incomes below $4,000. School records in 1963 showed that 50 per cent of the young adults dropped out between grade 10 and graduation, and sixth graders' reading and arithmetic scores ran an average of a year behind grade.

It was obvious that these problems of poverty, unemployment, ignorance and lack of skills, which made renewal so difficult in the inner city, could not be met by just the Redevelopment Authority or a good relocation program. Here, where the human problems were greatest, the city had pushed the urban renewal formula about as far as it could go.

In view of the large public investments that had to be made to bring gray areas up to standard physically, but which left the people with many of the basic problems that led to blight, the CRP analysts decided to consider a completely new approach. Influenced by the new mission-oriented thinking of the Department of Defense, the CRP analysts—and these included not only physical planners and redevelopment administrators, but also educators, economists, sociologists, an anthropologist and welfare agency people—began asking new questions. What *kind* of public investments should be made? How much might a dollar spent on a community organizer or on job training accomplish against a dollar for brick and mortar? More important, what was the goal, and what were the problems?

Four major problem areas were defined: housing, jobs, education and mobility. The analysts then asked how Philadelphia could best attack these problems and use the various resources and programs most effectively. The result was a basic redefinition of renewal: that renewal is not an end in itself, but a means to an end, and that urban renewal, anti-poverty and other programs are just tools in the larger program, whose purpose is to improve the human condition.

How would this redefinition be put into practice? The CRP studies had not yet jelled into an official policy statement by the city at the time this book was going to press. But the three big new ideas emerging from it have been unofficially discussed, and there is some indication of their chances of adoption. The three new ideas are the "distributed" approach, the development programming process, and a program development unit in the Mayor's office.

Under the distributed approach, the entire inner city would be certified for urban renewal. Public investment in new facilities there—health centers, schools and recreation areas—would be distributed throughout the area on the basis of people's needs, instead of to meet the demands of the usual Title I project. Equally important, provision of these facilities would not be contingent upon a renewal plan achieving full compliance with code enforcement or high standards of rehabilitation. A new Title I formula would be necessary to make Philadelphia's distributed approach eligible for federal aid. But the city has several years to lobby for this; the capital programming process commits it to the old renewal policy at least until 1970.

The development programming process is a means of coordinating physical, social and economic programs in renewal areas, to guide allocation of public resources in the most effective way. With the new process, which in many ways anticipated the federal proposal for the "Demonstration Cities," * in the inner-city renewal area expenditures for services under the city's expense budget, such as for health, welfare and anti-poverty, would be considered together with capital expenditures. The technique of systems analysis would be used to evaluate the performance of services and facilities to determine which combinations give the highest relative payoff compared to investment.

Factoring in these various programs is the big challenge, and to make this possible, the CRP proposes putting into the office of the Mayor a program development unit, to provide an overview, analyze program performance and enable him to make the requisite executive decisions based on this information and the available resources.

But these sophisticated new techniques and approaches must win acceptance in the local political market place, and success depends ultimately on the ability and willingness of the elected political leaders to forward and use the planners' ideas. Philadelphia's current Mayor, James H. J. Tate, former president of the City Council, who moved into City Hall when Dilworth resigned to run for Governor in the winter of 1962, is an honest, plodding product of the Democratic machine.

"Tate tries to do the same things as Dilworth and Clark, but he doesn't know how," a distinguished former city official who served all three administrations in key positions observed. A former top member of the city planning department commented, "He wants people who are not as bright as himself around him. He doesn't know how to use people or take advice." There is much concern that Tate would not know how to use the program development unit. But City Council is not eager even to give the innovation a trial. In December 1965, Council turned down the

* See Chapter 9.

Mayor's request for funds to set up the new administrative unit; it chose more policemen instead.

"Lack of money isn't the only constraint on cities," a shrewd observer of the planning process in Philadelphia noted. "You have to have the talent that knows how to get it and spend it. We have more bright ideas here than people to implement them. The Great Society got ahead of us."

Under Tate there has been a steady outward flow of top people from City Hall, slowdowns in on-going programs, such as transit, and a reluctance to take political risks or start new programs.* The chief victim so far has been the anti-poverty program, which originated after Tate became Mayor and is integral to the new development programming approach to renewal.

Attacked by a militant and demagogic new Negro leader, lacking commitment from the white power structure, cut down by sniping city bureaucrats, Philadelphia's program (started as a Ford Foundation gray areas program) was one of the slowest to qualify for federal manpower training and economic opportunity funds, and still has relatively less money per capita. ("This wouldn't have happened under Dilworth," a veteran of this struggle commented. "Clark and Dilworth tried to make the city whole. Tate fractionates it.") As the CRP report on economic development stated, "Bits and pieces of a manpower program are scattered about the governmental landscape. No mechanism exists for preparing and carrying out a comprehensive and integrated . . . frontal attack on unemployment." Even to get the report published was a struggle. The city's most successful job training program is Opportunities Industrialization Center, started by the Reverend Leon Sullivan, who in the early 1960's led 400 local Negro ministers in consumer boycotts against discriminating companies, and then found he could not fill jobs with qualified Negroes. The significance of this effort can be appreciated when it is realized that by 1985, 50 per cent of Philadelphia's labor force is expected to be non-white.

Fortunately, there has been a major step forward since 1962 in

* On becoming Mayor, Tate pronounced acquisition of the public transportation facilities a "dead duck." According to informed sources, he felt it would be politically easier if the public blamed poor service on the PTC, not the city. The 1963 strike changed his mind.

education, a critical public area that was untouched by reform. Clark and Dilworth could take on only so many big fights, and the schools promised to be a tough one. Dilworth commented, in 1961, that the board was still back in the nineteenth century. But by the early 1960's there was a growing uneasiness and active concern that the Philadelphia public schools were not doing their job.

The businessmen in the Greater Philadelphia Movement were becoming aware that a Philadelphia high school diploma didn't mean much to employers. They were also concerned that unless the quality of the schools was improved the flight of the middle class would continue. The NAACP sued the school board for discrimination in its administrative appointments. The chairman of the Citizens' Committee for the Public Schools believed that eighty, not eight, schools needed programs like those in the Ford Foundation assisted effort. But the conservative school board was dominated by a budget-conscious business manager, and had little interest in new needs and programs. The school system was so remote from the rest of the city that the board had not participated in developing the comprehensive plan.

A Chamber of Commerce survey revealed the gap between work-force skills available and skilled jobs going begging, and industrial planners worried that without an educated labor force they could not attract desirable new companies. The dropout rate was so high that in the 1970's, over one third of the prime-age labor force would not have finished high school.

In 1961, the Greater Philadelphia Movement, urged to action by the less prestigious Citizens' Committee on the Schools, as well as by its own members, commissioned studies of the school system; these, when released in 1962, lit a time bomb under the ossified "House of Lords," as the unresponsive, remote old school board was known.* The studies spelled out the failures of the system in educating Philadelphia's youth and in encouraging citizen interest, and proposed a complete reorganization, starting with a request to the state for home rule and authority to determine school tax rates.

The reforms were achieved faster than anyone had dared hope.

* Pittsburgh, with the same original setup, has a school board that is responsive to new needs.

An Educational Home Rule Assembly lobbied in Harrisburg for fiscal home rule and Mayoral appointment of the school board and won its requests from the legislature in 1963. In May 1965, the voters of Philadelphia approved the new simplified organization and the home rule school district. The new board was to be appointed by the Mayor from a list of names submitted by a nominating panel.

The victory was crowned by former Mayor Dilworth's agreement to accept the presidency of the new Board. (He was persuaded by a close associate, John Patterson, who was a key behind-the-scenes mover in the education reform.) It was not difficult to win the agreement of Tate, whose image was then suffering from snipes that the City Council president was taking at him. Even before the new school board was to take office in December, Dilworth appointed volunteer task forces, which recommended major changes and an innovative approach that augur well for the future.

Dilworth's acceptance of this new responsibility is also a good indication of the future. Although local government seems in need of renewal, much of the top talent that has left City Hall has not left Philadelphia. Former Development Coordinator Rafsky is an unofficial member of the Mayor's cabinet and serves as chairman of the Community Renewal Program study, although he has been executive vice-president of the Old Philadelphia Development Corporation since 1962. Other former members of Clark's and Dilworth's cabinets hold top executive positions in quasi-public development organizations or teach at the universities. Edmund Bacon, almost alone among the special talents in the city, has remained as executive director of the Planning Commission.

If the city administration is not eager to take on new responsibilities, the GPM has a widening sphere of concern, and continues to spin off new development agencies, the most recent one for improvement of the city's port, which has failed to realize its great economic potential for the city.

There is, and will continue to be, the multiplicity of these strong organizations and citizen agencies, the cadre of civic elite who compose their boards and who are also training the next generation, and the enormous momentum of the multiple activities which they, together with past city administrations, have set in motion since 1952. There will also be the beacon of 1976—the 200th anniversary of the Declaration of Independence—when Philadelphia's planners, its power and perhaps even its politicians expect to show off their reborn city to world visitors as a model for urban living in America. They will have to widen their scope and speed up their pace, for in the inner city, the time is growing short.

9

WHAT URBAN RENEWAL CAN AND CANNOT DO ■ New Haven Goes the Whole Route

Richard C. Lee of New Haven is the first Mayor in the country to have made urban renewal the cornerstone of his city's administration as well as of his own political career. Under Lee, New Haven has done things that many other cities have just talked about or dabbled in.

Because New Haven is small enough to make the city comprehensible, and because the treatment applied to its common urban ills has been comprehensive, creative, and apparently more successful than in almost any other city, New Haven has come to be regarded as the best example of what federally aided urban renewal can do for stagnant older American communities. Moreover, because it has been successful in improving its physical environment, New Haven reveals what particularly well other ingredients besides physical rejuvenation are required to treat the sickness that besets older American cities.

Since 1954, when Lee took office, this 300-year-old Yankee community of 152,000 in southern New England has undertaken the largest per capita program of any city in the country. Some $120,000,000 of all Title I funds—$790 for each resident—has been given or reserved for use by New Haven.* Thirty per cent of the land, where half of the population lives, is under renewal treatment or planning; more of New Haven's future is dependent on such federal aid than any other American city. Without urban renewal, plus $100,000,000 in state † and federal highway funds, New Haven could not do much to save itself.

By late 1957, New Haven seemed to have found many ways to pump new life into a tired old city. Its worst slum, Oak Street, rotting for generations near the center of the city, had been cleared with Federal Title I aid, and private millions were pledged to rebuild it. An eleven-story $11,000,000 office building for the Telephone Company was to rise there, bringing 2,700 employees within a lunchtime stroll of downtown shops, and large new ratables to the sagging municipal purse. Nearby there would be three high-rise apartment houses, also privately financed, separated by green lawns and playgrounds for children, with room for 700 families and ample parking space. Only half the community services required by the former Oak Street slum would be needed after redevelopment; five times the taxes would return to the city.

But Oak Street was only the first step in a grand design for community renewal. Parallel to the Title I site, a pathway was being cleared for a six-lane, mile-long traffic artery, the Oak Street Connector. This was designed to pump motorists from the new Thruway coming up the harbor-side, as well as from the inland suburbs, to the city's slipping retail center for which a daring redevelopment plan had just been announced. Plans were under

* New York's record: $41.35 per capita, or a total of $319,000,000, since 1951, which is 46 per cent of the state's permissible share.

† Connecticut also splits its cities' one-third Title I contribution.

way also for renewing one quarter of the city's neighborhoods and for building new highways. Moreover, there was little opposition from people who were to be displaced.

Albert M. Cole, then HHFA Administrator, described New Haven's program as "a model for urban renewal in the cities of America." It seemed that one did not need a Moses or Mellon to get results. The backing of business and civic leaders, in the Citizens Action Commission, created by Lee, appeared wholehearted and nonpartisan, as did that of the average resident, as it was expressed at the polls. By mid-1957, Lee was being described as "the hottest piece of political real estate in Connecticut" by the Hartford *Courant*. He was considered a sure bet, if he wanted it, for the Democratic U.S. Senatorial nomination the next year.

When Lee was returned to office that fall by a plurality of 23,000 or 64.9 per cent of the voters, the largest in the history of the city or state, it seemed to other awed and envious top municipal executives that New Haven's Mayor had struck paydirt in unpromising political soil. Many small and large cities whose renewal programs were stalled began to imitate New Haven's new style. Citizen action commissions were organized by other cities. New Haven was featured by magazines and television networks. At national meetings and in Congress, mayors, businessmen, planners and elected officials heard New Haven's mayor or his lieutenants explain renewal. More and more, visitors also came to New Haven to see.

What American cities needed, it was being said, was political leaders who, like Lee, could identify themselves with urban renewal, interpret the program to the people, calculate its risks and minimize them, and carry through without sacrificing the human values or letting the overall conception be watered down. In New Haven, official spokesmen predicted that if the people stayed with the program and federal funds held out, in ten years theirs would be the first slumless city.

AGONIES OF REBIRTH

During the following years, when the daring renewal plans were being executed, unexpected traps inevitably surfaced. This confirmed some of the scepticism expressed by veterans of redevelopment and revealed both the weaknesses and special strengths of a renewal directed primarily by City Hall.

By 1961, New Haven had improved unrecognizably from a mere eight years before; and it would change for the better in many other less visible but important ways. But progress then was measured largely by the three precious blocks of downtown real estate which form the heart of New Haven's much-publicized Church Street project. These blocks had lain cleared and unrebuilt for eighteen long months. With its center looking like a bombed-out area, the city was already the butt of out-of-town visitors' jokes. "I came to New Haven and saw the ruins," quipped Billy Gaxton. The Saints and Sinners Club dubbed Lee "Mayor of the hole city."

New Haven's bankers and businessmen were not amused. The commercial core was off the tax list, and retail sales were down. Although the latter trend was due partially to the recession, plus the long-term decline in New Haven's downtown, people tended to blame it all on redevelopment, which made the heart of the city dusty and still less inviting to shoppers, in spite of the new acres of parking space. Even the high-rental Oak Street apartments were lagging; the first was filling slowly, and the second was barely under construction. Meanwhile, dislocated businessmen both downtown and in the Wooster Square neighborhood renewal project were muttering, as were residents who were being forced to move and finding that new housing within their means was not being built.

New Haven appeared to be suffering from redevelopment indigestion, as well as from unforseeable events and the almost crippling gaps in local support. The Mayor was paying the price not only of committing himself to a big, difficult program while running for election every two years, but also of personally supplying the energy and enterprise for a city which, left alone, would still have taken fifty years to roll over in bed. Perhaps he was also paying for making renewal look simple and inexpensive to the city in order to make it acceptable. "Before, it was done so smoothly, they thought you did it with mirrors," Lee observed in the summer of 1960. "It looked so easy and it didn't hurt. Now they realize there are pitfalls."

By sticking to the program through unforeseen difficulties, Mayor Lee had not capitalized on perhaps his only opportunity to go to the Senate, and he appeared to be stuck with a city grown less appreciative of his special genius. In November of 1961, Lee was re-elected to a fifth term, but only by a slim, 4,000 vote plurality, less than half the vote he expected, and a sharp contrast to 1957. Again, the drop had less to do with renewal than people assumed. In some normally Democratic wards, voters were expressing resentment against increased, but long overdue, property assessments; others were reacting against the Connecticut State Highway Department's blunt notices, sent out six weeks before elections, of plans to take property for Interstate Route 91 which slashed right through "sure" Democratic wards. Other usual supporters were telling the Mayor that he was letting New Haven get too "integrated." To the outside world, it seemed that Lee's political star was falling—and falling as a result of urban renewal.

Yet in 1965, with the federally assisted renewal program now in a far more advanced stage, Mayor Lee was re-elected by a plurality of 17,000—only 4,000 votes short of his great 1957 victory. The Church Street downtown project was nearly completed; imaginatively designed, moderate-cost housing developments were being built or were already occupied throughout the inner city; neighborhood rehabilitation was saving thousands of old homes; and industrial redevelopment was helping local firms build new plants and thus save thousands of local jobs. That fall, Robert C. Weaver, then Administrator of the federal Housing and Home Finance Agency, declared that, "New Haven is coming closest to our dream of a slumless city." The American Institute of Planners presented the city with an award for having "one of the most comprehensive, concerted and completed city planning and development programs in the country."

As the history of New Haven's renewal reveals, there are no simple and sure answers to saving cities, and even with all the government aid, many negative circumstances must be reckoned with. Nonetheless, New Haven still continues to provide the best example of how to revive a small, built-up older American city and make it more livable and workable. That city's broad and creative approach to urban renewal, combined with transportation planning and the important new programs for improving public education, combatting poverty, and expanding opportunities which New Haven pioneered in the early 1960's, may well provide what Lee has called "the answer to urban civilization in the twentieth century." And the Mayor may go down in American history for his administration's unequaled response to the total crisis of the inner city.

DECAY OF A CITY

Some people call the change in New Haven since 1954 a "revolution." If there has in fact been one, Lee pushed it through alone. There was no civic revolt against corruption and broad-based charter reform drive, as in Philadelphia; nor did the black pall of smog and migrating industry galvanize the business leaders into united action with the city government, as in Pittsburgh. In 1953, when Lee was elected Mayor, New Haven was quietly dying.

The city, seventh oldest in the nation and an outstanding example of colonial town planning, had long since outgrown and forgotten the order of its original nine squares. Only the elm-lined Green with its three churches was intact. Erosion had been eating away at New Haven for decades. Dark old loft factories hulked next to rows of homes; garish billboards topped "taxpayers" * at the choicest locations in the business district; there were pervasive strips of low-grade commercial shops. Block after block of pre-1920 frame houses, now two- and three-family homes, grown dark and shabby with the ravages of time and neglect, marked the inner core.

For generations, New Haven had been the first city of the state, both in population and wealth, reaching 162,000 in 1920. Then, seemingly in the midst of a national boom, it stopped growing. The deep-bay harbor, the source of the colony's eighteenth-century prosperity, had long since been passed over for other, better-located and deeper ports. Now the harbor was silted up and neglected. The New Haven Railroad, which had helped speed the harbor's commercial and visual decline in the

* "Taxpayers" are one- or two-story structures erected to yield just enough money to pay the land tax.

past centuries, tottered on the brink of receivership, due to mismanagement and the sudden challenge of the motor vehicle.

With changes in transportation technology, the location which once had been the city's fortune became its curse. The routes of the old wagon turnpikes that had made New Haven the trading and wholesale center of a rich agricultural region were becoming clogged with commuter traffic from its satellite suburbs. Local traffic fought for space with heavy interstate delivery trucks that inched through the city's narrow streets and bridges as they traversed the old Boston–New York Post Road along the seashore. Thundering trucks and buses also used the city's spacious elm-lined avenues as traffic arteries, making once-elegant residential sections unlivable and driving old families to the suburbs. The city's most important industry, fine, famed carriages, had gone under with the emergence of the automobile.

In the decade before the first World War, New Haven had arrived at a stage of ripe equilibrium; it was well governed, a very pleasant place to live, and apparently prosperous. But the handwriting was already on the wall, and warnings sounded. Architects Gilbert and Olmstead, retained by the new City Planning Commission, urgently recommended a program of street widening and arterial road building to prevent annihilation of the already traffic-congested downtown. But their plan "failed to catch the imagination of the municipal authorities," wrote city historian Rollin Osterweis.

The city was coming into the hands of the new ethnic politicians, who were more concerned with pleasing nationality blocs than maintaining municipal vitality. But even the city's Chamber of Commerce failed to heed a civic leader's warning in 1909 that they must make the city attractive and inviting both for residents and new manufacturers, by providing excellent schools, well-paved and lighted streets, and other civic improvements. Gripped by "a conservatism [that] threatened to develop into a vice," the Chamber could not bring itself to act. They believed New Haven was "doing pretty well."

By World War I, the age of enterprise that had pushed New Haven forward precociously to a busy manufacturing city by the Civil War, was passing. The early-nineteenth-century entrepreneurs were artisans who had by invention, skill and slow accumulation of capital built up the city's many small and diversified manufacturing firms. Their firms were now in the hands of the second- and third-generation descendants who either lacked the old zeal or the new know-how to compete with the big national corporations.

One of the most famous home industries, Winchester Repeating Arms, had a boom during World War I that concealed the city's industrial decline. Then, in 1929, it went from receivership into the hands of an out-of-town corporation. Other prosperous old firms, unable to secure sites for expansion or replacement of old loft buildings, were moving away, and with them went thousands of jobs. The depression further hastened the collapse. New Haven industry lagged behind Hartford and Bridgeport and never really recovered as fully.

By the mid-1930's, the city's cramped old manufacturing district was a graveyard of the carriage industry and its allied products, a monument to early industrialization that could not adapt to mass-production methods. Into antiquated lofts where skilled workers once produced fine products, there swarmed small and often shaky concerns, many of them apparel firms. These were absentee-owned and hired piece-goods workers whom they paid sweatshop wages.

For decades, capable and ambitious young men had been leaving New Haven for greater opportunities in New York or giant industrial enterprises in the Midwest. Now, the city's growing middle white-collar and professional class followed the Yankees out to the nearby suburbs. Some people began to feel that the business center of New Haven existed only for its dormitory satellites. In the mid-1930's some 13,000 suburbanites had business addresses downtown.

Apathy sat on the community like a pall; no crisis stirred it. John Day Jackson, who came from Hartford in 1912 to manage the evening *Register*, was publisher of the city's two remaining newspapers by 1925. He quietly built one of the great personal fortunes in Connecticut, and held a tight muzzle over New Haven's mounting troubles. Jackson's front-page editorials calling for low taxes and economy in government were a familiar feature. Mayors who ventured to spend for improvements soon heard of his displeasure. Sporadic efforts by business groups to stop the downward trend found little support.

Being Mayor of New Haven was a low-salaried part-time job and, once the "plebes"—representatives of the new ethnic population—had taken over City Hall, a position with little prestige. During the dreary 1930's, it was also a thankless job. City expenses mounted, but the tax base shrunk as the city was forced to pay for the excesses of the previous decade. Tax delinquencies and foreclosures continued late into the 1930's. Essential city services were cut to balance the budget. Potholes remained unfilled on main thoroughfares pounded over by heavy through-traffic. A number of deaths were caused by poor street lighting. Rather than invest in a sewage plant, a Mayor of that time let the city's refuse be dumped in the harbor, spoiling its waters for pleasure crafts and bathers. Three city schools were still made of wood.

Part of the city's financial crisis was caused by the sudden number of "enormous families." An estimated 22,550 of New Haven's residents in 1930 belonged to families of eight or more, and most of them were poor. From a city of homeowners, the majority were now renters; 70 per cent of the population was foreign-born or of foreign parentage. As the number of pupils increased, the amount spent by the Board of Education decreased proportionately. Many parents, laborers with little schooling, considered that finishing eighth grade, as required by the state, was all that was necessary before their children contributed full time to the family's support.

Tax assessment policies followed politics. Valuations of downtown properties were abruptly raised, and some were pegged 15 to 20 per cent over market value to maintain municipal revenues. The owners of these properties were few compared to the number who owned residential properties that were generally undervalued. Overvaluation further encouraged a wave of center-city demolitions, since taxes on expensive buildings exceeded the cost of maintenance. Land values were so high that construction of anything but "taxpayers" was discouraged. Even during the previous decade, false store fronts were the principal visible tokens of the prosperous era. The latest hotel, the Taft, built in 1912, narrowly escaped foreclosure in 1936.

The old rich were grown markedly less so. The patricians had never turned their family fortunes, which had been made in trade, to manufacturing, but had preferred to invest in canals, railroads and bank stocks and bonds. Now the remains of the early mercantile fortunes shriveled up with the heavy bank failures of 1931–32 and the bankruptcy of the railroad. For several consecutive years the Community Chest failed to meet its quota—an untoward occurrence in this traditionally philanthropic community.

By 1950, a third of all New Haven's housing was substandard, according to the census. No measure was given to the decreasing livability of neighborhoods built before the automobile age and now suffering from too many cars, no garages, too much through-traffic, old schools, and no play space. Worst of all was the Oak Street slum, a canyon of filth and hopelessness sunk between the central business district and the hill where the Grace–New Haven Hospital and Yale Medical Center sat.

On the site of a dried-up stream which had once emptied into New Haven's thriving harbor, the slum still retained its early-nineteenth-century tanneries, plus the cheap tenements that had been thrown up for successive waves of immigrants who had flooded the busy rail and manufacturing center. Oak Street served as a receiving station for each group—the "new immigration" from Europe that followed the earlier waves of Irish and Germans, and then Negroes. In time, it became a repository for the human backwash of the city, where families of six crowded in two unheated rooms and where rats terrorized the sleep of children. Five-cent bathhouses stood next to shops of penny-ante merchants. Debris piled deep in its alleys and was left to molder there.

Those who prospered had moved on to the newer neighborhoods which spread out like a giant fan, their backs to the Green and the sea. By the 1950's, the children of the new immigrants were also being drawn out to the suburbs, leaving New Haven's population older, poorer and less educated than the national average for urban residents.

Downtown, the automobiles and trucks threatened to choke off the lifeblood of the city's commercial heart. To thread through residential avenues and traffic-jammed streets to go shopping downtown was slow and nerve-wracking; to find a parking place in center city was almost impossible. But the New Haven stores did little to make the customer's struggle worthwhile, and as retail sales fell, vacancies rose alarmingly. G. Fox, the dynamic department store fifty miles away in Hartford, was said to have 12,000 New Haven charge accounts; many women looking for the latest styles took the train seventy-five miles to New York. But the downtown New Haven shops did not serve the growing lower-income population well, either. In 1952, the Gamble-Desmond Company, a major New Haven department store, had folded, leaving a gaping hole in the ground on Chapel Street. That same year, Sears-Roebuck closed its Church Street store in favor of a new $2,500,000 building in suburban Hamden's huge new shopping center. Had the chain store made the unlikely effort to remain in downtown New Haven, the difficulty and expense of assembling adjacent land would have made expansion there virtually impossible. At the "100 per cent corner" of Church and Chapel the two-story taxpayer building topped by a billboard advertising beer symbolized downtown's stagnation.

New Haven was also losing conventions to other cities. Even local organizations preferred to hold banquets at the smart new motor inns springing up on the inland Boston–New York motor parkway. Many traveling salesmen were relieved that it was no longer necessary to go into New Haven at all. There was less and less cause to spend time there.

Rising and spreading in the heart of New Haven, yet aloof in its intellectual grandeur, was the city's greatest and most enduring institution—Yale University. Visitors from around the world were drawn to the now-shabby industrial city mainly by Yale and its famed medical center. To the city's working-class majority, the University was a source of both pride and deep resentment, a focus for the anti-intellectual and anti-Yankee feelings of the ethnic groups; the omniscient "they" whom the uninformed believed controlled things.

But there was also a split between the University and the entrepreneurs. Yale was the last strong outpost of the theocracy which settled and for many generations ruled New Haven, the force which consolidated a tradition that stretched back to the colony's education-minded founder, Congregationalist minister John Davenport. To the University circles, being "in trade" was vulgar; even in the eighteenth century, the artisan-entrepreneurs were considered interlopers, and were tolerated only because their skills were necessary. Their descendants mixed like oil and water.

During the very decade when New Haven stopped growing, the University, with millions contributed by out-of-town alumni, began to expand. When Yale was founded in 1716, on the westerly edge of the Green, it sat at the city's outskirts. Two centuries later, as it began acquiring adjacent land, it seemed to be consuming the city's heart. By virtue of the eighteenth-century legislative dispensation in its charter, granted with the assumption that the community would reap its graduates' wisdom, Yale had become the largest owner of tax-exempt real estate in the city, some 800 acres valued at $50,000,000. By the mid-1930's, Yale was also the city's largest employer, with a payroll of 3,100.

During the era of good will inaugurated by Yale's President Arthur Twining Hadley in 1908, the people of New Haven were welcomed to, and enthusiastically took advantage of, concerts at Woolsey Hall, exhibits at the University art gallery, lectures and the volumes at Sterling Library. But with the new ethnic majority in the city, and with Yale's student body coming from around the world and not remaining in New Haven, these University contributions to the community were little valued. "Much that it offers does not and cannot reach directly many working people who pay taxes . . ." stated an official committee headed by the Mayor which in 1937 asked Yale to pay for the many municipal services it then received tax-free. The *Register,* irked by the quantity of real estate becoming tax-exempt, had for years been running editorials criticizing the trend. The University, strapped for operating funds, refused to pay such taxes, but countered by detailing the many ways it aided the city's economy: millions of dollars in payroll, services purchased, visitors attracted to the city, construction workers employed, retail sales to its 5,500 students and 850 faculty members and its hospital's growing services.

Yale's defense had little popular appeal. It had become fashionable to blame the University for blocking the city's growth and undermining its tax base. The University served as a convenient scapegoat to explain away the fact that New Haven was on the way down.

I. GETTING MOVING

FROM SANDLOT TO CITY HALL

"It seems," Lee once observed, "that I've been preparing for the job of Mayor all my life."

Richard Charles Lee was born in New Haven in 1916 in a cold-water flat. He attended St. Mary's Parochial School, worked before and after classes to help his family make ends meet. The story goes that a political wheel who liked to have Dick wait on him at the A & P where the boy worked after school, prophesied that one day Lee would be Mayor. He learned his way through the intricacies of local politics and administration as a reporter for the *Journal-Courier*, where he went to work at eighteen. He spent five years on the paper, first on the police and fire beat, then covering City Hall. There he also developed his skill at putting information into simple, understandable terms. Shortly after he reached voting age and enrolled in the Democratic party in 1939, a vacancy came up for the unpaid job of Alderman. Dick had attracted the attention of the woman ward leader, and received the nomination.

As a freshman legislator, he asked to be assigned to the City Planning Commission where, in 1941, he helped the Chairman push through the Commission's first budget. He left the newspaper, borrowed money to take a two-week course in community affairs at Northwestern University, and then became associate secretary of the New Haven Chamber of Commerce. As an Alderman, Lee was instrumental in hiring the brilliant French city planner, Maurice E. H. Rotival, then a professor at Yale, to draw up New Haven's master plan.

Within six months Rotival had come up with an exciting new image and statement of the daring principles on which New Haven should be rebuilt. Rotival's advice was to take advantage of the natural setting: the harbor, the hills, the central Green, the city's geographical position as a distribution and trading center.

Let visitors enter by the front door—the original harbor approach—instead of the cluttered back streets or the railroad yards. A transportation overhaul was basic to his proposal. "Fresh, healthy arteries encourage all kind of tissue to grow around them," Rotival said. Automobile transportation, he insisted, was the lifeblood of New Haven. The city must build back on itself, recentralize the fleeing business district, and use highways to bring people into the downtown center instead of passing it by. He drew great arteries which swept up along the harbor and brought traffic directly into a rebuilt business district.

The conception was brilliant—but who would build the roads, rip down the old buildings, pay the costs? Half the land along the harbor was under water. Rotival went around New Haven for months trying to sell his plan. Lee was off in the Army. The business community was highly skeptical, and the real estate interests kept building new nonconforming commercial structures further out on Whitney Avenue. The League of Women Voters was his principal supporter. In 1944, Rotival went to Algiers to join the Free French forces and De Gaulle.

Lee returned from the service in 1943 when Yale was searching for a reporter to handle its wartime news digest. The late Carl Lohmann, cultured, urbane secretary of the University, who ruled its protocol with such an iron hand that Yale was sometimes called the Holy Lohmann Empire, hired Lee for the job. Lohmann instilled in Lee a sense of New Haven's venerable history, an awareness that it was not just another old factory town, and a respect for detail. In the eleven years he worked for Yale, Lee built the one-man press operation into a five-man News Bureau that was respected by national editors as well as the professors.

Part of Lee's special talent as an urban renewal Mayor has been his ability to move freely between ideology and ethnic interests, to understand the technicians' requirements and the city's long-term interests as well as the people's needs, and to forward each with a minimum of compromise. Though he lunched with faculty friends while at Yale, he remained a regular at wakes, the Saint Patrick's Day parade and Rotary Club luncheons. He became a director of the Negro Dixwell Community Council, master of ceremonies of the Yale Bowl Pops Concert, and he continued to take an interest in the Junior Chamber of Commerce, which he had helped organize.

Lee served four terms on the Board of Aldermen, the last one as minority leader. In 1949, at the age of thirty-three, he won the party's nomination for Mayor. He conducted a high-level campaign for municipal reform and city planning, and lost by a margin of 712. Two years later, nominated again, he waged a tougher, rougher fight and missed victory by a heartbreaking two votes.

That looked like the end of politics for Lee. But there were those nagging two votes and a flattering petition signed by over 4,000 independent voters asking him to run in 1953. He was also influenced by his first campaign inside the Oak Street slum homes in 1951. "I began putting together the ethereal city planning I'd been preaching for years with the facts of life," he recalls. "I knew that Oak Street was all wrong and that something had to be done about it."

The style of politics in New Haven before Lee took office has been characterized by Yale political scientist Robert A. Dahl as one in which "scheming [was] preferred to the grand strategy, timidity to boldness, immediate gains to long-run ones, political reliability to technical competence. . . . It was difficult for any political leader to emancipate himself from the iron grip of the lower middle class outlook and values. . . ."

After his second defeat for Mayor, Lee studied about urban redevelopment, which was then a new and scarcely tried federal aid program. From professors at Yale he learned of the economic threat of slums and blight to a city. A new concept of city government was evolving in his mind, "something more forward-looking, more idealistic." Lee recognized there were risks in redevelopment. "But I thought if I could sell the program and educate the people, they could take the rich diet of change."

UNITING A CITY

United community support was the first essential. When Lee accepted his third nomination for Mayor in September 1953, he declared, "We must take the public into partnership with city government." He promised that within sixty days of taking office he would set up a representative non-partisan Citizens' Action Commission, to investigate the cause of the city's decline and find the remedies. One of the newspapers which refused Lee's ads as libelous in 1951 now ran a front-page editorial opposing his election. But Yale faculty members and volunteers from the recent Stevenson presidential campaign formed Independents for Lee. With their help, plus paid television, the support of a crusading local radio station, WAVZ, and neighborhood meetings, Lee got through to the electorate. He won with a comfortable 3,500-vote margin, supported equally by the high-income, college-graduate voters of the 30th ward and those in the "Irish" 14th.

The promised Citizens' Action Commission took nine months to form. Many conservative local leaders regarded the vast and expensive rebuilding program as "Lee's Dreams," the non-partisan commission as a political ploy. Several refused to participate. They were wary of getting tied to a Democrat, and worried by the possibility of corruption and conflict. "You're too young and inexperienced," one leader told the Mayor. The program, they thought, would never work in New Haven.

Gradually—by showing them the economic threat of decay to the city, convincing them of redevelopment's financial soundness, and finally by pure force of personality—Lee won the support of *some* of the leading businessmen. Carl Freese, a savings bank president who lived in the suburbs but made his living at Church Street and Crown, agreed to serve as chairman. Together, Lee and Freese recruited representatives of a cross section of the powerful interests in the community, from Yale's president to the president of the State CIO-AFL Council, to serve on the CAC's executive committee. Neighborhood leaders and opinion-makers were added to the Commission. The resulting 600-member organization seemed so carefully composed that, as Chairman Freese held, "If anyone throws a rock at the program, they're bound to hit one of their own."

To explain redevelopment to the citizens, Lee had the office of Maurice Rotival * prepare a thirty-panel exhibit of how New Haven would look if the master plan were carried out, and then

* Rotival returned to New Haven after modernizing Caracas, Venezuela.

displayed it at the CAC's opening luncheon in September 1954. That winter he persuaded a member of the Commission's executive committee, Patrick McGinnis, then president of the locally headquartered New Haven Railroad, to transport seventy-five members of the CAC in his private car to look over projects in Philadelphia. "The trip would have been a success if we'd never gotten off the train," one member recalled. Social workers and bankers, labor leaders and merchants who had never talked to one another before spent congenial hours in the car. Before the trip's end, they were urging each other on to greater efforts for a greater New Haven.

The CAC was supported by the private New Haven Foundation,* but was housed on the same floor as the city's redevelopment staff, with whom its own full-time director, New Havener Gordon Sweet, worked closely. The executive committee met monthly in the Mayor's chambers to review and criticize the emerging renewal program, and to let Lee know what they felt the city would accept. Although not initiators of policy, they made "citizen participation" more than a nice phrase for speeches. They lobbied through the Republican legislature in Hartford a bill establishing and financing a badly needed new Regional Market in New Haven, an integral part of the redevelopment program and long a Chamber of Commerce goal. The CAC also sponsored a nineteen-acre industrial-retail park on reclaimed city park land to house wholesalers and light industry dislocated from Oak Street.

But Lee had to take the first step alone: that was the battle for the indispensable "Oak Street Connector."

By 1953, the State Highway Department, taking advantage of filled-in land that had become available through a federal harbor-dredging program, was already bringing up along the shore line a major new limited-access expressway. This, the Connecticut Thruway, followed the 1941 Rotival plan. A Redevelopment Agency had been established in New Haven and the French planner was retained to guide its program.

Rotival's new "short approach" plan had been published dur-

* The New Haven Foundation, established in 1928, is a community trust that receives contributions and bequests from people in the New Haven area and distributes the income to community agencies.

ing the previous administration. In it, he and traffic expert Lloyd Reid had proposed a method of handling the anticipated 34,000-car stream which the new Thruway threatened to funnel daily into the already choking city streets. Their solution was the expressway-wide, below-grade Oak Street Connector, which would cut through the slum to link up with the Thruway to the East, provide limited-access exits and entrances to downtown, and tie in with another highway planned for the west of the city. They also urged that the rest of the slum be simultaneously cleared and redeveloped by means of federally aided urban redevelopment. This plan would relate land uses to the new artery to gain its full increment. But slum clearance was politically risky, and there was no assurance that the state would support New Haven's costly plan for the Connector. Lee had the foresight to make sure of the Connector before he submitted final plans for Oak Street to the Urban Renewal Administration.

In March 1954, he invited State Highway Commissioner G. Albert Hill and his engineers to New Haven to convince them to provide the additional millions of dollars necessary for building Rotival's traffic feeder. With well-marshaled facts, a coordinated presentation of community plans, and endless trips and phone calls to Hartford, Lee secured Hill's support, despite the opposition of the highway engineers who did not think it was their job to rebuild cities. In the process, Lee also found his first customer for the redevelopment land, the Southern New England Telephone Company, New Haven's largest employer, whose proposed office building was in the path of the projected Connector. He persuaded the Company to relocate in the cleared Oak Street site downtown.

By October, it was public knowledge that Lee had convinced Commissioner Hill. The state's agreement to invest $10,000,000 in New Haven plans made it clear that redevelopment was more than talk.

WAYS AND MEANS

Many officials from other cities marveled at how Lee converted the hard and risk-filled work of urban renewal into votes.

The Oak Street project required, first of all, a staff considerably larger and better paid than the one Lee inherited. He pushed through a $250,000 planning and redevelopment budget—five times the previous size; and by late 1955, he had recruited a staff of top technicians, many of whom had practical experience in other cities. Early that year Lee had appointed Edward C. Logue, his executive secretary, as his deputy for redevelopment. A graduate of Yale Law School, where he studied with Rotival and on the side organized University janitors and maids into a union, thirty-four-year-old Logue had returned for a visit in 1953.

Logue had been an aide to Connecticut's Chester Bowles in Hartford and in India, and planned to enter private law practice, probably in his native Philadelphia. He volunteered to work in Lee's third campaign, and then, after the election, accepted the post at City Hall temporarily. He has recalled, "I didn't see being secretary to a part-time Mayor in a town of 167,000 as a full-time job." Within two years he was working almost around the clock as Lee's Development Administrator, head of nearly half the city departments—planning, redevelopment, traffic and parking, and housing standards. Driven by his own desire to realize ambitious plans "to do a whole city," Logue was rewarded by the satisfactions of serving a Mayor who wanted to put good programs into effect, one who would back him all the way.

During his first year as Mayor, Lee visited every municipal installation, from elementary schools to truck-parking lots and sewage plants, and thereafter cut much of the fat off the city payrolls. The administrative changes produced a surplus of almost three quarters of a million dollars. Instead of reducing taxes, though, Lee plowed the savings back into long-overdue capital improvements and the still unfulfilled redevelopment program. Lee also took risks to raise the prestige and strengthen the independence of the office of the city's chief executive. He redecorated the Mayor's chambers in a handsome style and made the Mayoralty a full-time position, with a $10,000 salary,* and a Cadillac limousine.

Sinecures were wiped out to provide money for the new program; politicians, instead of being consulted about City Hall jobs, read of the appointment of out-of-towners in the news-

* Lee's salary is currently $25,000.

papers. But Lee did not neglect the politicians. "Dick brought us along step by step, until we thought it was our program," recalled an Alderman. Soon after he took office Lee gave them concrete improvements to point to.

He began building playgrounds in decaying residential neighborhoods, modernizing old ones with bright new equipment, remodeling and adding new rooms to turn-of-the-century school buildings. Wherever an improvement was to be undertaken, a sign appeared on the site reading "An Awakened New Haven Builds for the Future." At the opening ceremony, the Mayor, whose name was large on the sign, would be on hand along with the ward's Alderman. Nor did Lee lose any opportunity to address PTA and other neighborhood meetings, taking maps and models with him to explain redevelopment.

"How do you sell blueprints?" asked one Alderman whose ward needed, and got, a playground. "In 1955, that was all we had. The playgrounds were used like ads. You can talk all day about bond issues, but when you open a new dog shelter or a corner playground—that brings it home."

Streamlining the city's administration and simultaneously beginning to create a new city proved an almost crushing burden for Lee, landing him in the hospital three times during his second year in office and costing him a major operation for ulcers. During the 1955 election campaign he was ill, his top-priority program for rebuilding Oak Street was still unapproved in Washington, and his opponents thought they had found an issue which would cost him votes. This was the sale to Yale of the land on which two old high schools sat.

For decades the city had needed to replace its three turn-of-the-century downtown school buildings with modern ones that offered adequate modern recreational and classroom facilities and were located closer to where families lived. The University, in whose shadow they lay, was the logical purchaser, and agreed to pay the city $3,000,000 for the property instead of the appraised $1,900,000. Yet when Lee sold the schools to Yale, at a price far above real value, cries of "Sell-out" and "Little Boy Blue" still arose from Republican throats. The transaction made good newspaper copy that fall.

But a week before election day, with an assist from Republican

Senator Prescott Bush, federal approval of the $7,650,000 loan and grant for Oak Street came through; the announcement by Lee and Bush in a joint press conference from the Mayor's office made eight-column headlines.

Lee was re-elected by a margin of 20,000—the largest ever achieved by a Connecticut Mayor—and the voters also gave him a 31–2 Democratic Board of Aldermen. (Two big, new campus-like high schools were ready for use by election-time two years later, to help boost Lee's popularity.)

HIGH GEAR

The time had now come for the first public hearings on Oak Street. Here the project, and perhaps Lee's political future, would be won or lost.

In those days, there was a cartoon in the office of New Haven's Planning Department depicting the city department heads chained together in the Mayor's chambers. Lee was shown pointing his finger at them and stating, "You will all freely testify in your own words why Oak Street must go." Helped by Development Administrator Logue, the officials gathered evidence from the facts in their departmental files.

At the actual public hearing the six-foot Chief of Police, in his dress uniform, came first: "We have more than six arrests in this area every day." The Fire Chief was next: "Calls from Oak Street are 600 per cent higher than the rest of the city." The judge of the city court declared that Oak Street had prostitution on a greater scale than anywhere else in the city. Not until the very end did the planners and redevelopment staff present their case. By then, anyone opposed to redeveloping Oak Street would have been championing crime, disease, juvenile delinquency and higher taxes. Not a voice was raised in protest.

Perhaps if New Haven's newspapers had backed redevelopment editorially, as do publishers in many cities, and if Lee had less personal need for public acclaim, the Mayor would not have exerted his ingenuity to command space in the news columns. As it was, hardly an occasion was unexploited.

Even the rats, symbols of slum evil, had a press conference. When the Director of Environmental Sanitation sent a routine announcement about his rat-eradication plans to the Mayor's office, he was summoned in. "Let's find out how many rats there are, what diseases they carry, what kind of poison you're using," Lee said. When the extermination began, the fact that 10,000 rats would be killed in Oak Street made a front-page story, and their disappearance was covered like a regular news beat. The people of New Haven talked about the rats for years.

Under Lee, the Oak Street slum, so long in the backwash of the civic conscience, became a symbol of the city's new pride and hope. Lee himself was in the cab of the wrecker's truck, directing the swing of the steel ball as it shattered the first slum house in Oak Street. Official visitors always accompanied the Mayor on his daily tour of the clearance area, and were often treated to a special demolition—and a follow-up news story. Sunday afternoons, parents took their children down to see the tenements that were being demolished. But the most delicate human problem, and what many believe to be the real miracle of Oak Street—the peaceful, personalized rehousing of the 881 families—went unpublicized, and with good reason. The knowledge that they were being moved into other, better neighborhoods might stir up residents' fear and resentment.

The social agencies, which had many clients in the slum, were skeptical about the possibility of helping many of these disorganized, broken families. But no effort was spared by the city's dedicated and ingenious relocation staff to help former slum dwellers get a new start, to find a decent home for a large family or an elderly couple, to reassure the fearful. Thirty per cent went into low-rent public housing. Each private landlord who accepted an Oak Street family received a personal note of thanks from the Mayor for his important contribution to New Haven's revitalization. Often the official appreciation inspired landlords to provide a second and third unit.

The city also took on the burden of rehousing the hundreds of other Oak Street families who were being displaced for the Connector by the State Highway Department, which bore no such responsibility. To help the more than a hundred merchants, manufacturers and wholesalers of Oak Street find new space, New Haven established the first business relocation office in the country. Many, freed from obsolete, substandard facilities by the government's acquisition of their property, were able to enlarge operations in better quarters. Some moved into the CAC's industrial-commercial park. A handful of merchants eventually moved back into the project area, to the new College Plaza Shops, which the city helped them organize, build and buy on a cooperative basis. Some marginal retailers, among them the agonized operators of the Flea Market, were driven out of business. But Lee regarded such losses as the inevitable hurts which must be suffered in rebuilding a city.

By May 1957, the rats were gone from Oak Street and the slum dwellers rehoused; and as the heaps of rubbish and crumbled tenements were swept away, the major pieces of the Oak Street jigsaw puzzle were put in place. Within one week, groundbreaking ceremonies for the $11,000,000 Southern New England Telephone Company building took place and, at a dramatic public auction, three private syndicates each bid over $1,000,000 for the land on which the three high-rise apartment houses were to be built. The winner, a Boston–New York group, outbid Yale and other would-be purchasers with an incredible $1,150,000 offer—$450,000 more than the Redevelopment Agency's appraised value price. It seemed that property in downtown New Haven was beginning to mean something after all.

II. REBUILDING THE CORE

THE PLAN UNDER WRAPS

As the auctioneer's gavel was falling at the Oak Street auction, an adjoining, yet-to-be-announced project, one more than twice as large in area and cost and immeasurably more audacious in concept, was clearing federal channels. This was the unprecedented Church Street downtown redevelopment.

Rumors about private attempts to assemble land in center city had circulated for several years. But only a handful of insiders knew the particular details. Late in 1953, a local banker, G. Harold Welch, had acquired the leasehold on the narrow Gamble-Desmond site and an adjoining plot on Chapel Street facing the Green. But his efforts to augment the site were frustrated by adjacent property owners who asked unreasonably high prices; the city, which was not enthusiastic about his limited-reuse scheme, also refused his petition to close a rear alley for parking space.

The next private attempt was by a development group headed by the national real estate dealer, Roger L. Stevens, who was already involved in New Haven's redevelopment as Yale's associate in the Oak Street land negotiations. Early in 1955, during a meeting about Oak Street, Mayor Lee had revealed to Stevens tentative city plans for redeveloping the front block of Chapel Street that abutted on Church Street. Stevens counseled against redoing downtown a bit at a time. New Haven would be ruined commercially, he warned, if it did not simultaneously counteract all the negative forces. Stevens, who was then also one of the country's busiest theatrical producers, had been bringing plays to the Shubert Theatre for years, getting caught in the city's traffic jams, staying at its dreary, under-serviced main hotel, and was more uncomfortably aware than most New Haven citizens of downtown's dire need for modernization. He advised the city to tie into the Oak Street Connector project a large-scale redevelopment of at least the three under-utilized key blocks between the Green and the new traffic feeder; this site should have a new hotel, another department store, better retail shops, plenty of parking and widened access streets.

Like really big traders, Stevens worked by intuition. He looked, above all, for location and undervalued property. If full advantage were taken of the emerging highway system, he felt that New Haven's downtown could become an excellent location in several years. Stevens told the Mayor that if the city widened the access streets between the front block and the Connector, and provided sufficient parking, he would undertake on his own the commercial redevelopment of the block facing the Green.

He acquired banker Welch's lease of the Gamble-Desmond site for $400,000. But then, when owners of other properties began asking prices higher per square foot than those obtained in midtown New York's Fifth Avenue, Stevens dropped this approach in May 1956. He informed the city that he believed the only way New Haven could secure the major new downtown facilities and businesses it required was to employ its power of eminent domain to assemble the land and make it available for re-use at fair market value.

After Stevens' original discussion with the Mayor, Development Administrator Logue had extended the boundaries of a tentative Title I undertaking known as the South Central project (primarily an area of deteriorated commercial buildings between downtown proper and the railroad station) to encompass the strip of three blocks off Church Street right up to Chapel Street on the Green. He recognized that, in addition to eminent domain, federal aid in writing down the high land cost of this area would be essential to finance the project. Now Logue decided to submit the revised project for federal approval. Stevens agreed to stay as the sponsor of the commercial-retail redevelopment if the application won approval; the city promised to negotiate the land price with him without going to public bid. Logue was impressed by Stevens' success and financial standing, and by his reputation for never failing to go through with a deal. He did not worry that Stevens was not a developer. Logue had the development staff begin planning in detail the ninety-three acres of what became known as the Church Street project, and incorporated into it Stevens' big, bold ideas for the front blocks.

Opponents of Mayor Lee and Logue were to accuse them—with much justification—of carrying the Church Street project forward in secrecy. The very minimum advance interpretation was provided by the Redevelopment Agency staff, even to members of public bodies whose approvals were necessary on the federal application. This was done in order to keep the huge project under wraps until every facet seemed provided for. But the necessary local approvals to the South Central project boundaries had been given in mid-1955 by the Board of Aldermen and members of the Redevelopment Agency, and since then the property inspections required for the Title I application had been made. An alert newspaper reporter or Board member could have learned more. However, the plan was so audacious that even those who had heard something about the project did not believe it; at that stage, the pilot Oak Street redevelopment was still not accomplished.

Premature announcement of the unapproved application for this highly uncertain project could prove demoralizing to those most immediately involved—the area's shopkeepers and businessmen—especially if there were long delays. They would receive no relocation payments or assistance until property acquisition began, but their businesses and properties might be adversely affected meanwhile. Furthermore, the project might well be killed by local objections if the specific plan became known before federal approval was assured. Not only were many businesses to be dislocated, but the competitive uses to be introduced in the Stevens redevelopment would be viewed as a serious threat by existing concerns. Controversy would also hurt Lee politically.

The non-administration insiders in New Haven during those days were few but powerful. The First National Bank, which handled over 50 per cent of the city's commercial banking and owned substantial real estate within the project area, including its present office building, became involved in the project in 1956. Through the redevelopment, the First National Bank could obtain the assessed value of some $1,000,000 for the old-fashioned structure, which it had been trying to sell unsuccessfully; it could also obtain a prestige location within the project area at a reasonable cost. The bank officials had their eye on the Gamble-Desmond site facing on the Green, with more land to be added at the rear. Had the bank tried to obtain a similar location on its own, it would probably have encountered holdout prices and would have had to pay heavily.

Frank O'Brion, chairman of the Redevelopment Agency and president of a leading New Haven bank, had known about and approved of the administration's plan since mid-1956. The new CAC chairman, Lucius Rowe, president of the Southern New England Telephone Company, which was a major taxpayer and beneficiary of new growth, also enthusiastically supported the Church Street project, as did the CAC's former chairman, banker Carl Freese.

A DARING CONCEPT

So many different land uses were encompassed in the ninety-three-acre, pie-shaped $85,000,000 redevelopment project that it was not difficult for the administration to minimize the significance of the potentially explosive Stevens development during the planning stages. The project extended from the railroad station up to the Green and planned to clear some in-between residential slums which would be replaced in time by apartment houses and a commercial park. It also included the rehabilitation of four blocks of homes, and a long-needed new school for the neighboring Hill district—a facility which could be counted as part of the city's one-third contribution to the total project cost. The odd contours of the project were dictated in good part by the federal law's emphasis at the time on residential redevelopment, which has since been altered to allow substantial commercial and industrial renewal. Logue was also determined to drag as many needed municipal improvements as possible into the sharing with the federal government that the urban renewal formula makes possible.

Local public cost was always the big issue, and the administration's selling point to the boards of city agencies and the business community was the small outlay the vast project would require from New Haven. Only $500,000 in cash was necessary to meet the city's obligation. Even reconstruction of the decaying midtown sewage system, which required an expenditure of $1,140,000 that would have to be made with or without redevelopment, could be credited to the project cost as a non-cash local contribution, and thus could earn more federal renewal dollars. It was anticipated that even the city's small projected cash outlay would soon be returned through increased ratables in the finished project.*

Some $34,000,000 in new private funds were expected to be invested, which would raise tax returns from the area two and a half times. The major portion of this new investment was to be concentrated in the rebuilt core. There the private developers were to put an eighteen-story, 300-room air-conditioned hotel with banquet facilities for 1,000 people; a terrace-top restaurant overlooking the Green; a modern retail shopping development with from 450,000 to 700,000 square feet of rentable space to include a major new department store. There would also be the new $2,000,000, five-story office for the First National Bank. The

* Ultimately no cash was required of New Haven.

city itself would build public parking facilities for at least 3,000 cars in this core area and would widen the access roads to bring customers off the Connector and from other parts of the city. The New Haven Parking Authority could issue general obligation bonds against the city's faith and credit to finance construction of a $3,000,000 multilevel garage, which would also serve as part of the local non-cash contribution. The city appeared to be getting a lot for almost nothing.

But approval of the Church Street proposal by the Urban Renewal Administration had also to be obtained.

By 1955, when planning of the project started, a "10 per cent exception" clause in the federal Housing Act made some Title I money available for commercial redevelopment.* But New Haven's downtown redevelopment project was the first application of its kind in the country. It took all the persuasive powers of Logue and Redevelopment Director Ralph Taylor to convince the government that New Haven's criteria of commercial blight (underdeveloped land in the 100-per-cent block, obsolete narrow streets that could not accommodate the expected increase in traffic from the Thruway, three or more structural deficiencies in non-residential buildings) were applicable to the federal land write-down, and that the downtown redevelopment project was, in fact, in the spirit of the housing law.

What New Haven intended to do with federal aid under the Housing Act was to virtually gut the heart of its downtown—removing the crazy quilt of "taxpayers," cobblers' shops, gin mills and hundred-year-old half-empty lofts and unattractive buildings which, along with a few sound modern structures, occupied most of the block at Church and Chapel and the blighted blocks to its rear. Several hundred small businesses would have to move. Only the eight-story, 180,000-square-foot Malley's Department Store, located at one far edge of Chapel Street facing the Green, was to remain.

New Haven's Church Street redevelopment plan was the first project, either in or out of Title I, to tackle a decaying commercial center, and to do so within the framework of a coordinated land use, traffic circulation and parking plan that would allow the

* Currently 35 per cent of Title I funds are allowed for projects that are predominantly non-residential in their original use and re-use.

urban core to accommodate the vehicles so essential to a thriving central business and retail district in a city of New Haven's size.

The most daring element of the plan was the concept of recentralization, especially at a time when commercial construction in older cities was on cheaper, less-central land, or else in the suburbs. The Church Street project would counteract the commercial "ribbonization" that had been ruining residential avenues in New Haven and elsewhere; it would instead anchor the drifting business-retail center to the historic Green and civic center along Church Street, as Rotival had counseled years before.

By providing appropriate and accessible retail-commercial facilities and parking in the traditional core, the Church Street redevelopment would allow downtown New Haven to capitalize fully both on the older interior parkways and the great new forthcoming expressway system. When complete, these arteries would extend the city's potential retail market area far up and down the Connecticut coast as well as deep into the urbanizing state, doubling the possible number of downtown customers. The redevelopment would thus enable the city center to compete for what had now become its greatly diminished share of regional consumer spending; and it would do so before the emerging new highways had siphoned off even more stores and customers to the growing, wealthier suburbs.

The federal Urban Renewal Administration, which would have to provide $37,000,000 of taxpayers' money in loans and grants for the land acquisition and property demolition necessary to this city plan, deliberated many months about the Church Street application. Senator Bush's prodding in Washington helped. But central to the federal agency's final approval was Roger Stevens' commitment to sponsor the heart of the redevelopment.

LETTING THE PUBLIC IN

In New Haven, a hint of the Church Street concept had come to public attention more than two years before actual announcement of the project. At that time Development Administrator Logue impoliticly but accurately had told the CAC's Business District Committee that New Haven was "a dying city," a remark picked up by the papers. Only adequate parking, relief of traffic congestion and a new department store, he asserted, would cure the illness of its business heart. Leading businessmen denied Logue's allegations, but Mayor Lee publicly came to his aide's defense, pointing to the losses in downtown sales and the threat to New Haven of several emerging multimillion-dollar suburban shopping centers.

At several executive committee meetings, CAC members were made aware of statistics documenting the problems of New Haven's slipping business district. But not until the last days of May 1957 did the full committee, gathered for its monthly afternoon meeting in the Mayor's office, learn about the Church Street project itself. Then Chairman Rowe announced that unofficial approval had come from Washington for a federal urban renewal loan of $23,500,000 and a grant of $13,500,000 to help New Haven rebuild its downtown. Then, too, the drawings in color prepared secretly by Logue's office were finally unveiled, and the significance of the plan for New Haven spelled out. "This is the greatest thing that has happened in my whole life in New Haven," Rowe said. Detailed strategy for public introduction had been worked out by Lee, Logue and O'Brion, and each executive committee member received written "assignments" for obtaining advance support of the major interest groups which he represented. "We want to be sure it will be received with enthusiasm," Rowe noted.

In typical Lee style, not a detail was overlooked. Lack of opposition was essential for the swift execution of this project at the city's nerve center and for his own political future. First public announcement, the committee was told, would take place the following week at a Lawn Club luncheon, to which 400 invitations had been mailed that morning. On that day, several of the key CAC members had given the news to the sons of the elderly newspaper publisher Jackson. The Vestrymen of Trinity Church, another major property holder in the project area, had also been briefed. During the next few days, Mayor Lee, bankers Freese and O'Brion, and other key business, political or civic leaders would tell the rest of the twenty-seven principal property holders about this great opportunity to share in the future of New Haven, and try to bring them on the team.

The publicity build-up was in Lee's best manner. The day before the luncheon, there was a full press preview in the Mayor's office—complete with a scale model, an illustrated brochure put together by the public relations department of the Telephone Company, color renderings, kits with voluminous news releases and aerial photographs of the project area. "This," the Mayor told the reporters, "is the most important thing that will ever happen in New Haven history."

Present was the pivotal figure, sponsor Stevens, who, Mayor Lee reminded his audience, had organized the syndicate that purchased the Empire State Building for $52,000,000. Stevens, he informed them, would undertake the $18,000,000 retail, office and hotel development off Church and Chapel. If all went according to schedule, the project would be finished and in operation in three to five-and-a-half years.

Not made public—not even indicated specifically in the elaborate plans and model that were displayed—was the fact that Stevens was committed to build a major new department store as part of what was referred to publicly as the general "retail uses of the type ordinarily found in central shopping areas." The Mayor wished to avoid until after the election that autumn the public opposition which Malley's store would express, as well as the probability of a delaying lawsuit brought by the store's owners, when announcement of the new department store was made. But the interest expressed by R. H. Macy and Company in leasing or building the proposed department store, and a similar interest of the Sheraton Corporation in the projected hotel, were critical to the city's and Stevens' undertaking the project.

That evening at a special dinner for the thirty-one Democratic Aldermen, Lee let them in on the stunning news. "Dick, you'll win by 30,000 this year!" one enthusiastic Alderman called out.

The next day, a standing ovation—the greatest in his life and the greatest anyone in New Haven could remember—greeted the Mayor when he finished his speech at the Lawn Club. Roger Stevens, a man not given to unsolicited words of praise, paid tribute to the Mayor and to the city's businessmen, contrasting New Haven with other decaying New England communities. On the corner of Church and Chapel, where newsboys hawked papers with the banner headline announcement, the people of the city were visibly excited. The store owners in the project area were bewildered; they didn't know what to expect.

The *Register* grudgingly admitted "the major virtues of the project are excitingly obvious," and for once praised Lee. Next day, the Hartford *Courant* featured Lee's "challenging announcement" in its front-page lead story. "In the long run only such enthusiasm, determination and imagination . . . will check the blight and decay now ferociously attacking our cities," said its editorial column. The New Britain *Herald* declared that Church Street "staggers the imagination . . ." The Hartford *Times*, noting its own city's lagging program, wrote "We congratulate New Haven and tell ourselves—go and do likewise."

At the public hearings on Church Street, citywide support for the downtown redevelopment was impressively displayed by neighborhood and business groups, with inevitable opposition voiced by some businessmen-tenants in the project area. By early September, the Church Street project was approved by the Board of Aldermen and the final petition was on its way to Washington.

TIME, TROUBLE AND ATTORNEYS' BILLS

Then, three days later, the Bahr Corporation, owners of Savitt's store, the largest jewelry concern in the city, filed suit with the Superior Court of Connecticut. They challenged the project's constitutionality and the legality and propriety of the Redevelopment Agency's hearings.

Robert Savitt, head of Bahr's, was the one Church Street property owner whose approval the CAC had not been able to win. In fact, he had demanded a holdout price before the project became a government undertaking. Four years before, Savitt had put up a new two-story building on Church Street, on a spot now in the middle of the project area. One side of his building covered some of the land scheduled for the new hotel; its back overlay some of the projected First National Bank site; and the front of the store would be cut into by the proposed widening of Church Street.

But the Bahr Corporation held that nonetheless its new building should be integrated into the project. The company charged in its lawsuit that the public hearings had been unfair because the Redevelopment Agency was pre-committed to the plan; that the Agency had been secretly negotiating with a private developer to whom it planned to sell the land under Savitt's store for a large profit; and that the plan was "unreasonable, arbitrary, discriminatory and confiscatory" of his corporation's property because Malley's store was exempted but not Savitt's. Yet when the judge inquired whether the good faith or ulterior motives of the Agency were questioned, Savitt's lawyer denied this, and the trial judge agreed with the Redevelopment Agency that these were the only grounds for a court review. The suit was withdrawn in June 1958. Savitt's lawyer then let it be known privately that his client's main interest was the purchase price, and the city offered to settle for the highest of the three land value appraisals—$990,000 plus a good site in the redevelopment area. But this was rejected.

Condemnation procedures started on the property. When Savitt's learned that its building was to be acquired for the average appraised value of $700,000, the lawsuit was reinstituted. The court upheld the city, and Savitt appealed the case. The State Court ordered New Haven to leave the property stand until it heard the suit.

The entire project was immobilized for six months while awaiting trial. On March 17, 1959, the Supreme Court ruled that Savitt should be allowed to introduce new evidence in the lower court, as requested, although the Redevelopment Agency's good faith was still not questioned. This ruling meant the trial could open again at an uncertain future time.

It was now less than six weeks before May 1, 1959, the date the Redevelopment Agency had agreed to turn over to Stevens his land, cleared of buildings. But after the Bahr Corporation reinstituted its suit, relocation had slowed down; present tenants and owners would not move as long as Savitt remained there.

The city did not wish to risk the untold delay of another trial, and so it once more pursued a cash settlement. This time Savitt's accepted, but could obtain only $66,000 more than the original offer, since federal law limited the maximum payment to top appraised value. Only when the case was settled, on April 20, could relocation and demolition be pushed to completion.

On May 1, Stevens could legally have broken his agreement with New Haven as the land was far from clear, and he would have had good reason to do so. But if his gambling instinct had brought him to redevelopment and New Haven originally ("I got into it without thinking too carefully; I just wanted to see whether it would work . . . I never thought New Haven was such a good town"), no doubt his stubborn streak kept him there, putting more and more money into a less and less promising deal. Some of Stevens' closest advisors begged him to get out; but he had a reputation to maintain.

Even had the land been delivered on schedule, it seemed highly doubtful that Stevens–New Haven Development Corporation, the company set up by Stevens Development and three Church Street project partners—G. Harold Welch, the New Haven banker; Gilbane Building Company; and the architectural firm of John Graham Associates—could have started construction then. The major new pieces which had seemed in place in June 1957 had been dropping out, until in the spring of 1959 there was little left but the Gamble-Desmond site, the basic highway plan, the sponsor's 10 per cent deposit of $400,000 on the land, and the ninety-seven-page Land Disposition Agreement which would have to be renegotiated because the land delivery date had passed. The Stevens group agreed to renegotiate, informing the city of their firm decision to proceed. In October, shortly before election time, the sponsors paid $1,200,000 in cash for the first block of cleared land, in good part to help Lee.

But many months would yet pass before even the first retail tenant was acquired for any part of rebuilt Church Street. By the summer of 1960, the hope of reasonable profit was gone, and to the sponsors the development was just something to see through. "All I've had since Church Street is time, trouble and attorneys' bills," Stevens grumbled then. "Our group tied up two million dollars and I can never be compensated for the headaches."

THE RETAILING-FINANCING PLAN

To understand some of Stevens' and the city's subsequent troubles in rebuilding, one must first understand the basis of the Church Street concept. The redevelopment and the sponsors' financing and merchandising plans were much the same as if they were putting up a regional suburban shopping center.* The principle of shopping center development determined the steps they had to take and in fact dictated the way to get the necessary mortgage for the retail part.

The automobile trade would be delivered by the new expressways which, tied into the Connector, would form a giant interchange. Shoppers could drive into the huge multistoried garage and other parking areas directly from the Connector. The new department store would be accessible to the garage through doorways. With Malley's as another major magnet at the opposite end by the Green, the department stores were expected to generate customer traffic to feed the 50,000 additional square feet of new retail shops the sponsors contracted to build in-between.

The three blocks were to be developed as a unit, to encourage full pedestrian flow. But as the cross streets were not being closed —due largely to local pressures, not to project design considerations—unity would have to be achieved by a second-floor prome-

* In the typical regional shopping center, a developer buys a tract of inexpensive vacant land located in a rapidly growing residential area, near a highway interchange, and with acres of extra land for free parking, to draw on a wide radius of autoborne customers. With preliminary plans in hand, he proceeds to sign up his principal tenants. The banks and insurance companies who issue the permanent mortgages are concerned with the annual guaranteed income that the developer will receive from his center's tenants after he pays taxes and operating expenses, so that he can pay off the amortization and interest on their loan. To assure the necessary annual return of some 7 per cent to service the mortgage, the lender requires the developer as a rule to have 65 to 75 per cent of his total tenancy among retailers with AAA national credit rating, such as the national chains and major department stores enjoy. Without such long-term leases, the developer cannot get a conventional mortgage.

Department stores and well-known chains draw customers to a shopping center. Because they enjoy high standing with the financial community, do a low mark-up, high-volume business and spend extensively on advertising, these major chains ask and get low rentals. The department store is the kingpin. It alone can create a retail location, but it is a loss operation for the developer. His profit comes from the little retail and local specialty shops that lease space between the big advertisers, the national chains and department stores, and pay high rentals for the opportunity to draw on their customer flow. The seasoned architect places the magnets at strategically located poles to create the maximum traffic for the smaller merchants. The higher the volume of the latter, the greater will be the "overages" to the developer, and thus his profit. Church Street was being planned on these retailing and financing principles.

nade and bridge connecting department stores, hotel and specialty shops. As a retailing concept, the plan had several other weaknesses. The bank and hotel were "dead spots." Ideally, the second department store should have been on the corner of Church and Chapel, the hotel parallel to the Green at the far end, and the bank eliminated completely from the front block. But the First National had taken the prime spot on Chapel Street, next to Malley's. Temple Street, another major access street next to Malley's, should have been widened, but this was not possible as long as the old department store remained.

In spite of these flaws, Stevens believed downtown to be more desirable than a suburban location because the stores could tap the random flow of people who come to center city to work, get professional services and do municipal business, and who use public transportation as well as private cars. Furthermore, the city would supply the parking.

WHY DOWNTOWNS DIE

Downtown redevelopment cannot be equated with suburban shopping center development, however, as was made clear in January 1958, when Macy's indicated that it was no longer interested in New Haven.

In 1956, when Stevens' representative had first approached Thomas M. Green, Macy's vice-president for planning and development, Green was impressed by the unique situation opening up there. Although Macy's steered clear of such static market areas, New Haven seemed to be an exception. The central district of New Haven was notoriously under-retailed: Malley's, the principal competition, appeared so weak that Green had little doubt that Macy's, with its skill in mass merchandising, would figuratively "kill them." There also appeared to be room for a major new department store between Hartford and New York. With New Haven's redevelopment plans promising to solve downtown's traffic, parking and land cost problems and highways opening it up to the suburban market, the Church Street project seemed attractive. The terms of the lease Stevens proposed were satisfactory; now Green had to translate the initial concept into concrete realities and convince the firm's board of directors to break their standing rule.

Macy's economic studies showed some strong negative factors. There was the unusually slow growth of the New Haven metropolitan area and the drop in the central city's current population. Studies also revealed the extraordinary pulling power exerted by Hartford's G. Fox and Company on a considerable segment of the potential market area. Meanwhile, a successful developer was drawing up plans for a regional-size shopping center in Milford, fifteen minutes south of New Haven right off the Thruway, halfway between New Haven and Bridgeport. To overcome surrounding competition, a 240,000-square-foot store was deemed necessary by Macy's; but to support such a big store, Macy's would have to do a business of at least $15,000,000 a year from scratch, which was "hard at best," Green felt. This represented a tremendous increase over downtown New Haven's present department stores' sales: Malley's was doing 60 per cent that sum.

It seemed to Macy's board that the only real benefit for them in a New Haven location would be to operate in a vacuum. As long as Malley's remained, however, this did not exist. If Green could make a satisfactory deal to acquire the old New Haven concern, the directors would go against their established rule. Late in 1957, through the local bank which is one of the trustees of the Malley estate, Green made a contact with the Malley store's president and general manager.

The story of the Edward Malley Company explains some of the less obvious reasons why downtown New Haven was dying, and why its redevelopment was so difficult. It shows what happens when trusts get hold of a city's heart, and why eminent domain may be necessary to remove the dead hand of the past. Like many of downtown's problems, this one originated in the horse-and-buggy days.

Edward W. Malley, founder of the dry-goods store on the corner of Chapel and Temple Streets, died in the 1890's, leaving his property in two separate trusts,* which were to terminate upon the death of the last surviving child. The shares of stock of the department store corporation were set up in one trust, with the income

* By use of the trust device, no federal estate or inheritance tax or capital gains tax had to be paid, or has yet been paid, by the Edward Malley estate.

to be paid to his three children and their descendants. His real estate holdings, including the store itself and the land on which it was located, were placed in another separate trust.* Under a lease arrangement, the department store paid a percentage of its annual sales as ground rent to the real estate trust. The two younger children soon removed themselves to Europe. Older son Walter managed the store almost to the end of his ninety-eight years.

During the halcyon downtown days, horse trolleys and electric streetcars delivered customers to Malley's front door. When his son Wally took over, the suburban pull and automobile jams downtown were beginning to hurt. But Wally was more interested in cash reserves than in modernizing the store or downtown to meet new times. Yet many other New Haven merchants were also hanging onto old styles of business and operation, sure that downtown was dying.

In 1945, Malley's sales were only $4,000,000. Even the temporary downtown revival of the early postwar years failed to lift them beyond $5,000,000. Elevators creaked up and down its eight floors; dress fashions were behind the times. Popular brand names were not stocked. Deliveries were infrequent. There was no basement-type operation to serve the growing lower-income market.

Despite this, the Malley store continued to pay annual dividends to its beneficiaries and had accumulated a surplus of over $1,000,000. But if some of the surplus were not soon put into modernizing the dowdy store and revamping its merchandising program, the store would die. Wally insisted that it was better business to have $1,000,000 surplus, and vigorously opposed the suggestion of air-conditioning and borrowing to expand.†

Meanwhile, downtown New Haven continued to fade. Before any big suburban shopping center had been built, central business district retail sales were already slipping $7,000,000 annually. In fact, New Haven's department store sales were the lowest for any comparable metropolitan city in the country—only $54 per capita—while Hartford's were $145 and Bridgeport's $77.

* This trust, however, benefited only the two children of his second marriage.

† The directors representing the other principal beneficiaries and the New Haven bank that was trustee of half of the stock, somewhat reluctantly supported Wally. A corporate trustee is concerned about possible "surcharges" by the beneficiaries in case of "extravagance."

Without the pull of a strong department store, almost without exception, a city will have no retail district. Chain stores and specialty shops soon take themselves closer to their customers. This was happening in New Haven. The seedy look of remaining stores reflected downtown's weakness. Only jewelry sales seemed to increase. Yale's students and faculty sustained the high end of the men's clothing business. Demolition of the Gamble-Desmond store left a gaping hole on Chapel Street; Sears pulled out; and Malley's frumpy store was failing to attract the shrinking downtown market. The city administration became extremely worried that Malley's, New Haven's one remaining downtown "magnet," might also fold. If New Haven did not attract a dynamic new department store, it seemed that remaining downtown business enterprises would be sucked out to the suburbs, and with them would go taxes for schools and other municipal services. Thus there was a provision for a new department store in the Church Street plan.

A LAST RESORT

But in the few years between the redevelopment plan's inception and Macy's overture to Malley's, the latter experienced some marked changes. A strong new president and general manager, Richard Edwards, began breathing life into the decaying enterprise. The directors agreed to let him spend the $1,000,000 surplus and borrow another $1,000,000. Elevators were replaced, decorations refurbished, escalators installed, inventories and merchandise improved, deliveries stepped up. In three years, retail sales rose to $8,000,000. This, however, was only $44 per square foot of sales space compared to the $60 minimum to which a new department store looks. And it left Malley's with its sixty-nine-year-old main building, which was incapable of real modernization, a desperate parking problem, and insufficient capital or borrowing power to put up a new store.

But Edwards would not listen to Macy's proposition. He stated quite openly that here was an outside giant trying to swallow up a local store. Green could convince no one in the Malley group. Sensing that an outsider could not push through such a deal, he hoped that local bankers might make clear the advantages to

Malley's of selling out for cash or an exchange of Macy's stock. But the New Haven bankers were quarreling among themselves, apparently jealous of the First National's position on Church Street. Green next turned to Stevens, who also got nowhere; he turned to the Mayor. Lee would have nothing to do with it. Edwards was already lighting fires around town.

Macy's was busy in other directions. The firm decided not to pursue this uncertain project. Fortunately for Lee, Macy's left as quietly as it came. Still the Mayor had been promising a new department store, and Stevens was bound by the redevelopment agreement to provide such a facility. Stevens sounded out other major chains. One had a similar policy against "dying" New England cities. Another considered participation for six months, and even undertook studies. During that time the recession of 1958–59 deepened and its board decided not to commit itself, especially with Malley's in the picture.

Stevens finally commissioned a leading consulting firm on store location, Homer Hoyt Associates, to analyze the retail potential of redeveloped downtown New Haven. The findings looked excellent on paper. Hoyt found that as a result of the new highways and parking plan the market area would double and department store sales increase by $33,000,000, of which a new 240,000-square-foot store should do $20,000,000 in its second year. This would mean sales of $83 a square foot in the second year of operation, a volume unequaled except by the first suburban branch store of Detroit's giant J. L. Hudson Company at its spectacular Northland center.

According to Green, "You don't figure on this. It takes four or five years to get to $70. We estimated it would take eight to ten years in New Haven." The enlarged market area Hoyt drew reached almost to Hartford. Other department store chains also regarded New Haven as a one-department store town but did not go as far as Macy's.

In the spring of 1959 Stevens turned, as a last resort, to Malley's. He did not propose to buy out the company, but rather to lease to it a new, larger building, cheek by jowl with the 1500-car garage—the building and site that the "second" New Haven department store was to have had. In return, Stevens wanted to acquire the high-priced land that the store now occupied on

Chapel Street, facing the Green, for the new hotel's location. He was also eager to get rid of the eyesore building.

W. Ward Malley, Jr., son of the late Wally, had now succeeded to the store's presidency, and he was very interested in Stevens' proposal.

UNTANGLING PROPERTY RIGHTS

But the beneficiaries of the real estate trust had to be satisfied. Everyone, it seemed, had his price, and what the trustees of the land trust held out for came high: the equivalent of the annual income paid to it by the store—some $180,000 a year, plus a cost-of-living adjustment. If the real estate were sold outright, the amount they received would be its appraised value—about $1,650,000. But the capital gains tax would take a sizable part of this sum. If the property was condemned for redevelopment, the financial outcome for the land trust would be the same.

Use of eminent domain by the city to obtain the property would automatically cancel the ground lease that assured the beneficiaries of the real estate trust their income from the store's sales. The trustees were ready with a lawsuit and evidence that the city was not taking slums in case the city included the store within the redevelopment.

As anticipated, the city still had no intention of extending the project lines to take Malley's. The redevelopment director at the time observed that the department store was "somewhat of a sacred cow." The administration was delighted that the dowdy old structure with its mismatched annex would be eliminated from its location facing the Green, but maintained that the federal Urban Renewal Administration would never approve the sizable additional outlay entailed in acquiring Malley's. The Mayor, worried that the *Register* would howl if concessions were made to help Stevens, also maintained that condemnation was "politically unfeasible." *

The Stevens group arranged the equivalent of a land swap. The sponsors would acquire use of the store's site on Chapel

* When the Redevelopment Agency amended its land disposition agreement to allow the sponsors to carry out their unusual solution, the *Register* did object.

Street on a 102-year lease; the land trust would get the plot within the redevelopment area where the new store would be built by Stevens–New Haven. The Malley Company would rent the new building from Stevens–New Haven and guarantee the sponsors $300,000 annually, plus 3 per cent of gross sales over the store's present $10,000,000. Stevens–New Haven, under a ground lease agreement with the land trust, would, in turn, have to pay at least $180,000 annually to its beneficiaries.

This was an unprofitable arrangement for the Stevens group. They would not receive sufficient income to finance the $6,200,000 mortgage required to build the new store, much less real estate taxes, insurance and maintenance. But the sponsors were getting high-value land on the front block and anticipated that Malley's would increase sales to $20,000,000 and thus eventually pay the sum required to cover the sponsors' annual costs.

First, however, the bundle of property rights encumbering the Malley land had to be untangled and rebound. This entailed negotiations with the two trustees, their lawyers and certain other principals; gaining the approval of three different local banks representing Malley family interests; then obtaining the written consent of each of the thirty-two adult beneficiaries of the two Edward Malley trusts. The beneficiaries now included grandchildren and great grand-children living in Ireland, England, France, Spain and the United States. Months passed. The New York lawyers were busy with other deals. The old New Haven law firm representing one corporate co-trustee was not certain that such a big job could go through. Stevens was producing ten Broadway shows a year and swinging other multimillion-dollar transactions. Finally Mayor Lee called a conference in his office of the fourteen lawyers involved to find out why it was taking so long. One from New York suggested that no one was working hard enough. Stevens' lawyer agreed, and the intricate transaction began to move more rapidly.

Several absentee Malleys now turned sentimental about the location of the family business facing the Green. The founder's only surviving child, who had not lived in New Haven for nearly half a century, thought it should stay where it was. Her lawyer had to make two trips to Florida and two to France to convince her that the store should be moved back three blocks. Overseas phone calls had to be made to grand-children. Tracking down the last beneficiary took three months. Then a court ruling was required to insure the unusual arrangement against possible contest by a beneficiary or infant who would come of age during the 102-year lease period.

Finally, in August 1960, the legality was established. The sponsors could proceed with assurance to line up the chain store leases necessary to obtain the mortgage commitment for financing construction.

TIMING IN A FREE ECONOMY

But now the sponsors were hit by the rise in the interest rate from 4.2 to 6.3 per cent which had occurred since 1957. This 2 per cent increase probably meant the difference to them between profit and loss.

The appraised value of the Church Street land was very high —averaging $18.69 a square foot, compared to fifty cents in most suburban locations. This meant that the rents had to be some $1.80 more per square foot (before taxes) than suburban-center rents if the investors were to receive even a 10 per cent return on their money, much less the 15 per cent expected for such a speculative undertaking. The high land cost, appraised on the basis of the exceptionally good income that owners of downtown stores were making from high rentals on run-down, written-off properties, had originally seemed to be a selling point of Church Street to the Urban Renewal Administration, since it would reduce the federal subsidy.

But the economics of development made this excessive land cost a deficit. Stevens, too, had not fully realized the negative effect the high land price would have on leasing when he made the original agreement.

There now had to be added to the already steep rentals the 2 per cent increased interest on the annual carrying charges of the $20,000,000 mortgage—about $400,000 a year. But a department store would not absorb the cost differential and the chains did not believe they could do sufficiently more business in downtown New Haven than in suburban locations to warrant the much higher rentals. They would not give guarantees high enough to finance the development and still return a profit to the developer. "That's why downtown redevelopment is so difficult," observed Stevens. "You can't get the rents in those small cities. People can drive to shop anywhere so easily."

Meanwhile, some of the quality New Haven stores, the profit-producing but non-mortgageable potential tenants, were being signed up by new suburban centers. In the fall of 1960, Milford started renting, and Hamden Plaza, which in 1956, its first year, had sales of $33,000,000, announced plans to double space.

Stevens was also running into difficulties raising capital. He and his partners had gone into Church Street with $2,000,000, recognizing they would need $3–4,000,000 more cash in order to get a $20,000,000 construction loan. Stevens' fortune and reputation with the most conservative banks and financial institutions had been built on pushing through, and profiting from, deals generally considered impossible. But for the first time Stevens could not find others, beyond his original group, to take an equity position on his venture.

His usual sources objected to a land agreement with a public body, the restrictions on re-use for decades to come, the approvals required from government agencies before the deal could even be set. The land cost was too high; the rents too low. New Haven was not a promising town. The risks were too great for the rate of return that could be expected. Stevens was spending more time trying to raise capital than seeking prospective tenants. The best selling point he had for an equity position in Church Street seemed to be that it would provide a tax loss for someone who needed one.

The New Haven business community did not help counterbalance the unattractive economics and unforeseen problems. Lee and the dynamic forward thrust of early redevelopment had temporarily allayed the chronic pessimism which so long characterized their posture toward downtown. Now as the project's timetable dragged out, the pessimism returned. Representatives of possible out-of-town tenants heard disparaging remarks from local banks. The retail division of the Chamber of Commerce sat on its hands, although its president was on the CAC.

Yet even if Stevens had found interested chains, they could not have been signed up. A layout and definite location are necessary for a store lease, but plans were always changing. Indeed, when in August 1959 the First New Haven National Bank withdrew from Chapel Street, it seemed that the principal local developer had lost faith in the project.

It was only by indirection that the city learned of the bank's secret negotiations for a merger which, if consummated, would mean that the First New Haven would not need a new building at all. The project plan had already been changed once, when the First National had merged with the New Haven bank and needed a larger site than originally. The combined bank had then proceeded with construction preparations, initially by shoring up the foundations under Malley's next-door. Due to the Savitt suit, however, the rest of its required land could not be delivered on the promised date of February 1, 1959.

When news of the proposed second bank merger became public, the administration was upset, but Stevens was pleased. For if the bank stayed out, the redevelopers would be able to take over the entire Chapel Street frontage. Six weeks later it was learned the federal antitrust division wouldn't approve the merger and the bank dropped the reorganization scheme. Stevens, in a gesture to get the First–New Haven's good will and also keep them out of the project, offered to pay the bank's expenses to date for the Chapel Street site, thinking this would amount to $150,000. The bank said it had spent $400,000, took the money in the form of a loan due in two years, and was able to write off the investment as a business expense. With an assist from the Mayor, and the $1,500,000 paid by the government for its old office in the renewal area, plus Stevens' good-will bonus, the bank then acquired several dilapidated properties on land opposite the project area, and proceeded to build its new five-story home independently of the redevelopment.

Meanwhile, the Sheraton chain had also been hanging on a verbal agreement. And when, in the fall of 1960, Stevens could offer them a definite location—the desired Chapel Street site—for the high-rise hotel which they had been considering operating on a long-term lease, he learned that their top executives had also done some second thinking.

The profitability of downtown hotels had deteriorated markedly in the few intervening years and made the chain extremely cautious. With greater air travel and automobile rental services, many men were not staying overnight or as long as they used to on business trips, or were stopping in more conveniently located motor inns. (Even wives, it seemed, preferred motels to hotel lobbies when on family travels.) Motor inns, which cost considerably less to build per room than high-rise hotels, could charge practically the same room rates, and thus Sheraton was shifting into this field. The New Haven hotel appeared even less attractive because three motor inns recently opened in the vicinity.

The Sheraton corporation was still willing to make a lease agreement with Stevens. But the guarantee they offered him was now so limited that it would not have been sufficient for the sponsors to get a mortgage on the $6,000,000, 300-room hotel that was supposed to be built in Church Street. Nor was regular financing available elsewhere for hotels. Some cities were in effect subsidizing new downtown hotels through local bankers' lenient financing terms. This was not likely to happen in New Haven.

In 1958, the Taft Hotel—whose down-at-the-heels operation had prompted Stevens to put up a new hotel in the redevelopment site—had tried to halt the Church Street project in court. It charged "commercial cannibalism" and claimed that redevelopment was illegal if it hurt an established business. But the courts gave the argument short shrift, and Stevens–New Haven was still contractually bound to put up a new downtown hotel in the redevelopment site.

Mayor Lee, meanwhile, was becoming desperate. Since January 1960, when the last old building was cleared from Church Street, the site had remained bare due largely to the Malley negotiations. As soon as the store agreement was signed, Lee persuaded the sponsors to begin construction, even though the legality of the deal was not settled and financing was not secured.

The first necessary element was a tunnel for trucks coming off the Connector to a new delivery basement under the project area, an arrangement designed to avoid jam-ups on city streets. The tunnel entailed large out-of-pocket expenses, and no mortgageable assets. Banks only lend on improved land and income-producing property. The contractors hit water when they started digging and costly equipment was required to pump it out. The sponsor had to spend more money on heavy foundations to solidify the subsoil.

Meanwhile, Development Administrator Logue was not satisfied with the project design and felt there was not enough openness in the commercial development. He wanted a set-back at the corner of Church and Chapel and a pedestrian promenade with fountains. Stevens pointed out that this would reduce rentable store space; every inch must produce profit on $18 land, he felt. But the city agency had final approval on design in its contract with the sponsor.* Plans were redrawn and compromises were attempted between esthetics and economics.†

Profits from other ventures of Stevens Development Corporation were steadily, though reluctantly, poured into New Haven. A costly $1,500,000 loan was taken from a finance company. Stevens paid taxes on the empty land out of his own pocket several times. Before long, the development corporation's entire assets were buried in New Haven land and watery subsoil. Rather than put in more funds of their own, the sponsors halted construction in the winter of 1960–1. The project stalled for six more months.

For some time, Stevens had been saying quite openly that anyone could have the Church Street project for the sponsor's investment, minus interest and time. But he found no takers. In the fall of 1960, he privately told the Mayor that he would be glad to forfeit the $2,500,000 spent thus far and get out completely, though Stevens subsequently denied he would have done so. Lee prevailed on him to remain; Stevens observed, "I've had all the disadvantages of a political deal and none of the advantages, while I've had all the disadvantages of a private deal and none of the advantages."

The hard fact for Mayor Lee at election time in the fall of 1961 was that four years after the Church Street project's announcement the area stretched out as one huge municipal park-

* Distressed by the appearance of the bulky, unlandscaped Telephone Company building in the Oak Street project, Logue had written this clause into subsequent sponsor contracts, hoping thus to make the city's redevelopment more esthetic in the future.

† Ultimately, the city allowed the sponsors to dedicate the open spaces for the promenade to public use, so they would be relieved of taxes and maintenance on this non-income-producing portion.

ing lot. The only permanent new above-ground construction was the $6,000,000 poured-concrete, 1,200-space multi-storied municipal garage designed by the dean of architecture at Yale—at double the original estimated cost. But the only taxpaying construction was the First–New Haven Bank's new building across the street, outside the redevelopment area.

IS DOWNTOWN REDEVELOPMENT FEASIBLE?

Meanwhile, fifty miles away in the state capital, Hartford's $50,000,000, twelve-acre downtown redevelopment project, which had come to a halt in February 1960, had construction aboveground in 1961 and invited comparisons to New Haven's Church Street project.

Several crucial differences between the two were generally overlooked. The original sponsor, an out-of-town construction firm, the F. H. McGraw Company, had defaulted because it could not arrange financing. And the developer-investor that had taken over Hartford's project was the huge Travelers Insurance Companies, a locally headquartered national concern with almost unlimited funds at its disposal. Further, Hartford's Constitution Plaza was to contain primarily new office structures, with very limited retail uses. And the community itself, with its multibillion-dollar bevy of insurance companies, commercial and savings banks, the United Aircraft Company, and literally hundreds of aircraft suppliers and machine tool manufacturers, was infinitely more promising for downtown development as well as for general metropolitan growth.

Yet the millions of dollars that moved in and out of the insurance capital daily were not invested in Hartford's redevelopment at first. The Connecticut General Life Insurance Company had built its handsome new headquarters in the suburbs; other firms, put off by problems of land assembly and the inner city's drabness, also looked in that direction. An important exception was the great, hundred-year-old G. Fox and Company, now in its third generation of homeownership and family management. In 1960, while other retailers were suburbanizing, Fox, with $50,-

000,000 annual sales, was completing a $12,000,000 addition to its store, which had helped make Hartford one of the great retailing centers in the country.

The Travelers Insurance had come to see that its civic duty, as well as its self-interest, required that deterioration near its downtown national headquarters be halted through joining Citizens for Hartford, a civic organization initiated by Hartford's progressive Chamber of Commerce. (Two other local insurance companies provided the financing necessary to build a Statler-Hilton Hotel when their city needed a new hotel.)

When The Travelers rescued Constitution Plaza, little space was leased, and this to several local institutions that needed to expand. Indeed, The Travelers recognized that it would have to promote an underdeveloped market. "We're not attracted to it for investment alone," admitted Roger C. Wilkins, vice-president in charge of real estate for the insurance firm and president of its subsidiary redevelopment company, Constitution Plaza, Inc. "We wouldn't have been interested if the McGraw Company had come to The Travelers for a mortgage. If you don't have the tenants in a package to start with, it's difficult to get a loan. It's hard for an individual to go out and finance a project large enough to change the environment of downtown, as you need to do in redevelopment. You can't solve this through normal financing. We had the ability to carry it through. We don't need a mortgage."

Can downtown redevelopment by private enterprise work in small, slow-growing older cities? Edward Logue had commented, on the eve of leaving New Haven to be Boston's Redevelopment Administrator in mid-1961: "You can't rebuild downtown New Haven at a profit for many years. This is the problem all over the country. We haven't learned that private enterprise shouldn't have to take a loss on urban renewal, that it should have extra profit for extra risk."

Thus the question remained: who would take the extra risk or supply the extra incentive to attract private investment? The economic feasibility of redevelopment was supposed to be assured by eminent domain to eliminate holdout prices and by federal financial assistance to write down the land costs to fair value. In New Haven's Church Street, this was not sufficient. The appraisals did not take into account other problems. Financing of new development was the key, and the big stumbling block.

THE LOCAL LEADERS

Stevens said, in mid-1962, when his group had $6,000,000 invested in Church Street and not a penny back after five years, "If we had gone in with the $6,000,000 originally, we'd have been further along. But then it wouldn't have been an attractive investment."

Perhaps Church Street needed a body comparable to Philadelphia's nonprofit center-city development organization, the Old Philadelphia Development Corporation, to play a much greater initial role in winning local acceptance, and to take the project over the unforeseen hurdles. But the closest thing to the OPDC in New Haven, the much-heralded Citizens' Action Commission, pulled away from the administration in 1959, when the going got rough in Church Street. It set itself up as an independently constituted membership organization, reportedly so people would not continue to accuse it of being a rubber stamp for Lee.

Even had the CAC's relationship to City Hall remained unaltered, however, it seems doubtful that the group would or could have done more. The Church Street project brought out the failure of the Commission's executive committee as a body representative of community power or, as Lee once put it, as the group with "the biggest set of muscles in New Haven." But behind this failure lay the inherent weakness and conservatism of New Haven's business community. In some cities there simply is no progressive "power structure" to back redevelopment.

The CAC had created the aura of respectability and nonpartisan support Lee needed to get redevelopment into high gear in New Haven. Its members helped clear away some early local obstacles, but they could not fuel redevelopment. They lacked the power, the know-how, and the basic desire to promote ambitious, difficult plans. And they shied away from public controversy as much as did Lee. Moreover, some of the biggest muscles were pulling the other way.

Greater local public and private cooperation could have countered the high land cost and interest rise to a large degree, and speeded the project. "If a group of New Haven's leading citizens had sat down at the Qunnipiac Club, or John Day Jackson had called in five or six of the city's wealthiest men," Stevens maintained, "things might have been different. In cities where they have decent people and cooperation, they'll go ahead and do it.

"The leadership of the city is the essence of the thing. The rich people of New Haven never offered to do a thing. They even made it politically impossible to apply to the Urban Renewal Administration for a reduction in the land cost. Their attitude was do nothing but criticize—mainly because they were so anxious to beat Lee. The First National put every obstacle in my way. The first time the Chamber offered to help was in the summer of 1962.* The ultra-cautious New England-type lawyers wasted at least a year and a half. Lee was too afraid of the papers to do the really tough things—like condemn Malley's.

"But ultimately," Stevens added, "New Haven will be a city that has solved its downtown problem—which others haven't done. It's at our expense. But somebody will come out with a good investment. The project is good, and New Haven is lucky."

Compared to Hartford or Pittsburgh, New Haven has little local wealth and much absentee ownership. Several powerful local moneyed forces which could have helped were not members of the CAC. Even more important, they lacked faith in or sufficient concern for the future of the city, to back up or assist the redevelopment. They only made the "business climate" more unattractive for outsiders. The only person in New Haven to support the project for many years was G. Harold Welch, who invested $200,000 from the start.

Publisher John Day Jackson died in 1961 at the age of ninety-four, leaving a personal fortune of $61,000,000, most of it made in New Haven and relatively little invested in the city's future.

* In a 1961 report on the "Business Climate Story," climaxing an eighteen-month survey, the Chamber's Manufacturers Division stated: "In our City Administration there is too great a responsibility in the hands of a few able men. This could be potentially dangerous [and] lead to central planning of the economic future of New Haven."

Lee was the one Mayor who had not come running to the publisher. Jackson had not been consulted in advance on Church Street. To the *Register's* owners, beating Lee was apparently more important than revitalizing the city's commercial center. The paper seemed to take every opportunity to hit his administration and cast doubt on the reliability of the sponsors, the competence of the development staff, and the acumen of the Board of the Redevelopment Agency—which was headed by Republican Frank O'Brion, president of the Tradesmen's Bank—as well as on the concept of the project. Instead of digging for and publishing the facts about the extraordinarily complex undertaking, the paper wove a cover of half-truths, damaging innuendos and glaring omissions over the downtown project.*

Malley's department store and the scattered heirs of the founder went along with a good deal. For several years, it seemed, the entire redevelopment was a subsidy to the old firm, which anticipated increasing its volume by $6–$8,000,000 in several years.

New Haven did have one ace-in-the-hole, though. It was probably the major prop that made New Haven more than another played-out New England town. This, of course, was the University. Unlike a bank, Yale could lend on empty land, and would do so at 6 per cent—though probably not in Bridgeport or Hartford. Stevens began discussions with them in the fall of 1960. In June 1961, the Finance Committee of the Yale Corporation approved not a loan, but a guarantee, on a three-year bank loan of $4,500,000, which would help the sponsors complete the con-

* On the fifth anniversary of the downtown project's announcement, the *Register* published a five-part serial on "Redevelopment: On Its Back or On Its Way?" This series would, it said, give the people of New Haven a "hard look at the facts" of Church Street which a team of its reporters and editors had spent several weeks digging out. A sample of what they found: "Only the Malley company's willingness to supply its local funds and its local initiative has permitted the coming realization of this key Church Street retail installation." And J. Coy Reid, the president of the First–New Haven, stating why his bank had built out of the project area: "We decided that our best interests demanded that we cut out the wrangling [about a larger building] and do something on our own outside of redevelopment." (When asked by an outside reporter to clarify this statement, in view of the abortive Union–New Haven merger and Stevens' payment, Reid verbally shut the door with "I would rather not discuss it.")

struction of Malley's and purchase the third, highest-priced block of land, which cost $6,500,000.

Because Yale would not guarantee the full cost, Stevens still had to raise the difference on his own. This could only be obtained through another expensive loan from a finance company. Then, before the loan guarantee could be issued, legalities also had to be worked out. Inertia again set in. Not until May 1962, after eleven months, were details straightened out and the full financing available, allowing Stevens–New Haven Development to complete the Malley store, buy the third and final front block, and sign up tenants there and on the block between.

AN UNEXPECTED DEVELOPMENT

The city administration criticized Stevens for not really "pushing" Church Street, or "setting up an organization" to promote it and get tenants. The fact was that the sponsors did have a leasing office for three years; but they had no leases to offer because of the fluid state of the project. Also, Stevens was, by background and temperament, a trader and not a developer. He himself admitted that he could have been more efficient. Stevens' pace turned out to be an eventual advantage to him and the city, however. When he had a satisfactory lease worked out with a major chain store for the block between the new Malley store and the front block facing the Green, late in the winter of 1962, Mayor Lee asked him to wait. It seemed that Macy's was now taking a second look at New Haven.

Finally, in December 1962, nearly five years after the chain turned its back on Church Street, Macy's announced that it would build a three-story, 300,000-square-foot, full-line store, employing 700 people, on the middle block of the project. The store expected to be open for business September 1, 1964, and the firm's president declared that "Mayor Richard C. Lee's remarkable foresight in planning and executing [the revitalization of downtown] has been the catalyst in our decision . . ."

Why did the firm change its mind? Most important was the passage of time, which had brought with it some internal changes at Macy's, some external improvements in New Haven's downtown, and reduced risks. In New Haven, redevelopment plans were now in execution. The municipal garage was aboveground and operating in the Church Street project, and the state had scheduled construction of Route 91, the major new expressway to the north, for completion in 1964. Further, Macy's could now acquire land that was cleared and ready for construction, without waiting out the costly, uncertain delays that seem indigenous to redevelopment.

At Macy's–New York, meanwhile, there had been organizational changes. The problem of moving merchandise such a distance from the firm's headquarters, another early negative factor, had been eliminated by new systems. The division's new president, David Yunich, looked favorably on the New Haven location—*with* Malley's there. His previous experience with shopping centers had shown that two big department stores were complementary to each other and boosted business for both.

The basis on which Macy's was to come to New Haven was completely different, also. Instead of being Stevens' tenant, the firm would lease the land from the city, which had bought it back. The city would float a federally backed bond to make municipal financing, and thus an inexpensive ground lease, available to Macy's without encumbering city bonding limits. The city would also guarantee Macy's sufficient additional parking for the next forty years. Stevens–New Haven could not have given the store these extras. Had the sponsors and the department store negotiated directly, it would have been less profitable for both.

In fact, Lee himself did much of the selling of New Haven to Macy's new top management. A friend of his, who happened to be both a Yale trustee (and thus familiar with Church Street's problems) and a director of Macy's (and thus acquainted with the management changes), suggested that the Mayor go to New York for a talk with the store's executives. New corroborative information about the economic base of the New Haven area and its downtown retail market potential, which came from a federally financed community renewal study undertaken by the same firm which Macy's used for its own market studies, was also available—and helped the Mayor.

Even Stevens was delighted with the development, despite extra costs incurred while waiting. With Macy's next-door, he considered his front block to be "the best piece of real estate in the country." It could probably now command the higher rents from retailers that were required, and thus carry out that portion of the project.

To complete the terms of the redevelopment contract, and to finish the development, Stevens–New Haven did two things, both of them costly.

The front block was leased to a local builder-shopping center developer backed by British financing. The firm, Fusco-Armatruda, would erect on that site a fourteen-story office building and the officially contracted retail stores. With the proposed improvement of the land secured, Stevens was also able to borrow money (though at a high rate of interest) to repay the Yale-guaranteed loan. If the building rented well, the sponsors would have a salable property and eventually could come out even in their investment in the front block.

The final piece in the jigsaw puzzle was the hotel. To get it built, and to pay off the $1,000,000 owed to the Gilbane Construction Company for the extra costs of constructing the Malley store, the developers gave the construction firm land to the rear of the front block free, on the condition that it build a hotel there. Gilbane was able to find a multimillionaire partner, John McShain, Inc., Philadelphia builders. Their financial reserves were large enough for them to guarantee construction without the mortgage that Stevens' group would have had such difficulty in obtaining. The city agreed, as part of the deal, to construct a 300-car underground garage, to serve the hotel and offices, financed with revenue bonds whose interest Gilbane guaranteed.

These arrangements were completed in June 1964, and by the fall elections of 1965, the steel skeletons of the office building and the hotel were rising behind the New Haven Green. The three, key front blocks of the Church Street project were well on their way to completion.

THE LESSONS OF CHURCH STREET

Ultimately, the proof of Church Street will be in how well the completed project works—for the sponsors and their tenants; for the rest of downtown's merchants; for the people who come to use and enjoy downtown; and for the city as a whole.

It is too early to judge with certainty, as the project is not yet complete and open for business, and the accessory highways not yet finished. But substantial evidence already points to the revitalization of downtown New Haven as a result of the project. In the first six months of 1965, the Mayor announced in his October annual report, retail sales in the city had grown by 18 per cent over the previous year, to a total of $275,000,000; sales volume was rising for small merchants as well as the large department stores. Also, more people were shopping downtown, nearly 10 per cent of them people who lived in the area but had not shopped in New Haven before. And 40 per cent did more buying downtown than before. The Malley store itself had reached an annual sales volume of $14,000,000 ahead of target.

The renewed faith and prosperity of merchants in other downtown locations was displayed in the extensive modernization and refurbishing that they were carrying out on their own. The city was encouraging this with an extensive program of street planting, installation of modern "street furniture," signs and other public improvements to brighten up the non-redeveloped parts of downtown.

Most of the merchants who had been displaced from the Church Street project site had found satisfactory locations in the empty ground-floor stores that then dotted downtown New Haven. (Six of them had started a lawsuit against the project in 1958. But when the city offered to house them in a temporary prefabricated building right across from the redevelopment, with ample parking, they withdrew the case and waited. All had priority to space in the redevelopment, with a 10 per cent rent reduction.) Savitt's jewelry store had moved into space directly across from the project area, on Church Street.

Most relocated businesses enlarged their space, and 81 per cent increased volume in their new location, according to a survey by economists from the University of Connecticut. Many found better situations, helped by the city's relocation office. Only 9 per cent moved out of town. Owners of property in the central district found they could command higher rentals. Affected firms in New Haven and in other cities studied by the university surveyors agreed, said the report, that "forced relocation is usually a blessing in disguise."

Twenty per cent of the firms did go out of business. Some could only survive in a substandard area at submarginal rents—virtually a city subsidy. Other owners were elderly and ready to retire. Some could not gather the necessary financing to make a satisfactory move. Had the more generous business relocation provisions of the 1961 Housing Act and loans from the Small Business Administration been available then, many of the latter might have survived. Even so, in 1962, another old New Haven department store, Shartenberg's, which was not in the project area, folded up.

Retail stores have not returned from the suburbs and the "front block" rentals are still so high for the New Haven area that the signing up of stores has been very slow. But it does appear that the outward tide of retailers whose long-term leases on downtown stores are now expiring, who have a choice of where to go, is being stemmed. These are the major tenants who have taken leases on space in the new front-block building. "Before they couldn't visualize what was going to be done," developer Fusco commented. "Now they are willing to take a look at downtown." In short, people have to be shown.

As more and more elements fell into place, and the Church Street project, with highway access, widened streets and parking became a modern downtown facility instead of a blueprint, it was easier to attract new investment and sign up tenants.

The fourteen-story office building on the front block facing the Green is an interesting case in point. Although the original project plan called for some office space, nothing as ambitious as the high-rise structure with its 120,000 square feet of rentable office space had been envisioned. Furthermore, a survey carried out for Fusco's firm was pessimistic about the market. But he agreed with Stevens that there was a need for modern office space in New Haven, and his firm decided to build, even though little space was yet leased. The city went along happily.

The builders were able to start construction without having the usual percentage of leased space required for a conventional mortgage because Stevens–New Haven Development loaned them the $4,000,000 in necessary financing. The builders had to take the risk that they would be able to get tenants. At the end of 1965, the instincts of the developer and builder appeared to be confirmed. Some 65 per cent of the office space was signed up—most of the tenants were moving from second-rate space in other downtown New Haven buildings, and Fusco wished he had two more floors. The moral, he maintained, was that you cannot go by market studies, but must follow intuition.

As to the hotel, the McShain company, whose participation made it possible to move ahead, apparently had a different opinion of the New Haven location than did the Sheraton Corporation. A top executive of the construction firm stated, "We were influenced by the locality—it is a coming area with corrections made in downtown by urban renewal." McShain executives had flown over the region in the company plane to look for industry —in the hotel business today, some 80 per cent of the business comes from groups, not individuals, they stated—and they had found the metropolitan area's manufacturing activities booming. More detailed market studies were also favorable. It seemed that in spite of the motor inns and new patterns of business travel, there was a local need for a good center city hotel with banquet and parking facilities. Already, without solicitation, and some six months before the hotel was to open, they were receiving many expressions of interest from convention business.

The city of New Haven itself anticipated nearly an $11,000,000 increase in assessments from the Church Street project area—and thus substantial new tax revenues, not to overlook 700 new local jobs from Macy's alone. Beyond the Stevens project, other new construction was also scheduled, most significantly a new, twenty-eight-story headquarters building for the Knights of Columbus International, which was relocating from an old New Haven building. To the south, on the twenty-acre site of the old market area, an extensive residential development was planned.

The man whose intuition and reputation had encouraged New Haven to redevelop its core in such a big ambitious fashion, and the group that had gone along with him as sponsors of the main part of the project, were the big losers. They were in for $17,500,000—some $6,500,000 of it owed to finance companies and banks at the end of 1965, plus the $4,000,000 mortgage loan to Fusco. Stevens figured that at the very best they would lose $3,000,000, which was the extra sum paid for Malley's. They could lose as much as $7,000,000. While the store was doing well, the developers in 1965 were receiving only a one per cent return on their $6,000,000 investment in it. Their current income was about equal to the ground rent payable to the Malley estate plus local taxes, and the real estate tax of $160,000 on the new store made an already unprofitable deal even less so.

That New Haven's downtown redevelopment actually went through seems to be a commentary on Roger Stevens' unusual character. Granted that Lee and his staff deserve credit for their determination and tenacity, if Stevens had been a conventional developer or an ordinary man, he would surely have walked away from the project long ago (as his close advisors had counseled). Even with redevelopment aid, the project was not a market place transaction and could not be done through conventional financing mechanisms. Indeed, each one of the principals had received a major break along the way or, except for Stevens–New Haven Development, had not needed to resort to mortgage loans, much less finance companies. Where special financial reserves or guarantees were available, things got built.

This seems to be the main lesson of Church Street for other small old cities. So many unpredictable elements crop up, and the early stages are so risk-filled, that even with federal financial aid, eminent domain and good transportation planning, older cities' downtowns cannot be redeveloped through "normal" economic channels. Where local leaders are willing to help the developer-entrepreneur during those early stages, and take some of the risks onto themselves, they may be able to utilize the new tools for revitalizing their downtown.

III. RENEWING NEIGHBORHOODS

A ONCE-FINE NEIGHBORHOOD

A city may die without its downtown heart. But if its other parts wither, if the people do not live well, the city will still be ill. The many changes that have taken place in New Haven—the reweaving of the city's worn but still useful fabric—impressively reveal the quality of the administration's sensitive response to the citizens' needs and the imaginative local use of new tools.

In neighborhoods, too, the forces to be reckoned with and counteracted are powerful. The solutions there are more complex, demanding and time-consuming; results are not as dramatic as in slum clearance and downtown rebuilding. Development Administrator Logue, the policy maker and program developer, knew that Mayor Lee wanted the best, not only at Church and Chapel, but in the whole city. Lee's interest in neighborhood progress and Logue's own conviction that renewal must work for "the folks" were communicated to the talented staff people who went to work in the neighborhoods. Logue and his successors encouraged them to develop new approaches where existing tools proved insufficient. The continual interplay of ideas that accompanied the evolution of programs, and Logue's guide words —*Stay loose*—seem as much the key to New Haven's success as its skill at "federal grantsmanship."

Because the neighborhood improvement program involves the traditional city departments and meets people in their homes and neighborhoods, a new philosophy of local government service has evolved, and even, perhaps, a new style of municipal politics has begun. The city administration became aware of the enlarged role that local government and institutions in the central city must play for residents.

Mitchell Sviridoff, former Connecticut CIO-AFL president, who emerged in the 1960's as the key person in shaping New Haven's future, observed, "What Dick knew so well at the start—because he knew and loved the city—is that the disease which afflicts all cities today affects all organs at once, and hence cannot be isolated. He knew the attack has to be comprehensive in scope, but that even a comprehensive attack has to start somewhere."

Oak Street was the classic, rock-bottom slum that demanded redevelopment; Church Street was the obsolete downtown that was desperate for modernization. Wooster Square, the first neighborhood scheduled for renewal, not clearance, seems to have been virtually what the authors of the 1954 Housing Act had in mind when writing their new prescription for cities. The first in the country to apply all the new techniques and varied urban renewal restoratives, Wooster Square, became a model of how to keep a once-fine neighborhood from becoming a slum and give it new life.

Wooster Square, the neighborhood closest to downtown, is only a five-minute walk from Church Street. Within its bounds were diverse elements, some recognized as endangering a residential area, others giving it strength and thus making substantial rehabilitation possible. Its population was homogeneous; it had strong local institutions; most of its residences were physically sound though neglected; a large number were owner-occupied. By a miracle, the area had also retained some of the distinguishing amenities provided by the Yankee shipping captains and merchants who established this first suburb beyond the nine squares in the early nineteenth century: handsome, architect-designed mansions; the pleasant, tree-shaded "little Green"; some of the spacious townhouses built by the new industrialists and professional men; even the elegant villas, decorated with New Orleans-style grill work, that belonged to southern families who summered in this charming seaside neighborhood before the Civil War. Moreover, the move to "save Wooster Square" started with the people of the neighborhood. Led by Father Ugo Cavicchi, pastor of St. Michael's Catholic Church, blue-domed guardian of the Green, they launched a paint-up, fix-up drive in 1953 to halt population loss and housing deterioration.

But the Wooster Square area was also an industrial district. Much of its architectural legacy was hidden behind industrial grime or commercial appendages. The elegant neighborhood had started changing even before the Civil War, when manufacturers seeking locations near the city's harbor and excellent rail facilities began building factories in its eastern section. Here was the seat of New Haven's first industrialization, which made the city the Detroit of the carriage industry by 1868. That year, the J. B. Sargent Company put up its sprawling locksmith factory with big smokestacks near the recently fashionable Pavillion Hotel. Breweries, rubber plants and corset manufacturers edged further in on residential streets. The classic pattern of change ensued.

Brick tenements and flats were put up among the factories for the growing body of foreign workers, principally the southern

Italians imported by New Haven industrialists, Sargent's among them. Inevitable clashes occurred between the newcomers and the Irish and Germans who then lived in Wooster Square. But when a site facing the Square was selected for St. Michael's, the first Italian Catholic Church in Connecticut, the new ethnic character was set. A convent and parochial school, and the many activities sponsored by the church, reinforced the Italian nature of the parish community.

Some elegant Wooster Street homes sprouted store fronts with Italian names. On Grand Avenue, Italian merchants took over from Irish shopkeepers who followed their clientele to Fair Haven. Northern Italians of larger means who had come to the city earlier bought mansions at panic prices.

During the explosive Italian immigration of the 1900's, block after block was taken over by *paisanos* from villages in the province of Salerno. Most came to America to accumulate money. They worked at pick and shovel jobs, bred large families, sent their children to work early, took in boarders to pay rent, and saved constantly for two main goals. The first goal was to bring over the rest of the family and pay off their own passage. The second was to buy a house and have money for emergencies.

Other ethnic groups would rent in Wooster Square and then move on, leaving behind them, as had the Yankees, religious institutions. Protestant missions and community houses tried to "Americanize" the community, but the Italian character held firm. And in spite of continued infiltration of factories, the people would start paying for a house and improving the interior.

In 1926, the city's first zoning ordinance legalized Wooster Square's changing character by designating virtually the entire neighborhood for industrial use. The depression hastened residential and manufacturing decay. Big employers folded up or left. Banks foreclosed on owners left without jobs or sufficient income to continue payments on homes. They also placed a ban against new mortgages in the area. Many repossessed homes were sold to absentee investors who converted them into multiple units. Slum landlords chopped up others into flophouses. Some of the loveliest mansions were torn down for parking lots; a few more became funeral parlors. In homes, unemployed men set up barber shops, mechanic shops, shoeshine establishments. Wives went to work for the garment manufacturers and other marginal firms who came and went from the old industrial lofts. Wartime rent control encouraged landlords' neglect of properties. Only the institutions on the Square seemed to prevent slums from sweeping the entire community.

The mortgage ban remained after the war, virtually forcing second- and third-generation families who wanted to buy in Wooster Square to move away. Others, finding that hostility in "American" neighborhoods had faded, naturally looked elsewhere. Rents in Wooster Square were falling; vacancies were frequent; the neighborhood was shabby. The character of "Little Italy" was also disappearing. The only newcomers were Negro families and a few Puerto Ricans who began moving into the tenements in the eastern section, now a rock-bottom slum, or into the housing project which had cleared away others.

Old-timers, attached to the institutions, social clubs, the *boccia* games, would remain or return after work. Politicians also stayed with their constituents as the Italian era in New Haven government arrived in 1946 with the election of Mayor William Celentano. Low rents and the Italian pattern of family apartments in homes held some married children to the area. But through-traffic and all-day parking by downtown workers and shoppers made the streets, which were the only play area for youngsters, unsafe. The Square was taken over by the drunks who inhabited miserable, cheap furnished rooms in the brownstones on Court Street, the main pedestrian connector between the Square and center city.

The improvement drive launched by Father Cavicchi and the Neighborhood Association had little success. The committee turned to the city, but they soon learned that New Haven itself lacked the resources for a major conservation effort. The only outside help then available was for urban redevelopment, which would have wiped out most of the neighborhood instead of saving it.

The committee members became desperate when they learned that the State Highway Department planned to obliterate the Square, using the inexpensive park land as the site for a giant interchange for its relocated Route 5.* They turned to the Yale Planning School, which espoused their cause with the city planning director, then Norris Andrews, a native of New Haven. Andrews was able to convince the city and state that the highway should be placed further west, thus sparing the park and its environs and simultaneously clearing the more expensive but obsolete and dangerous factory lofts and tenement slums.

PLANNING WITH THE PEOPLE

Lee's first year in City Hall, 1954, coincided with passage of the federal urban renewal legislation which, for the first time, offered government assistance to rehabilitate and conserve deteriorating neighborhoods. Lee was familiar with the provisions and eager to use them for New Haven.

Early in 1955, the Mayor invited Father Cavicchi's committee to meet with him and the city planning staff to discuss the new act's potential. The enthusiastic committee called a neighborhood meeting. The Mayor, Development Administrator Logue and Planning Director Andrews came to explain the purpose and techniques of renewal. The committee called another meeting at which all 112 people attending voted to petition the city for Wooster Square's designation as an urban renewal area. They also voted to empower the eleven-man group organized by Cavicchi—a tailor, a retired government employee, a civil engineer, a banker, a real estate broker, two undertakers, an insurance agent and two businessmen—to act on their behalf in developing a renewal plan with the city. In May 1955, the neighborhood was officially designated by the city as a renewal area. The restoratives available to Wooster Square were just about as varied as the neighborhood's problems.

The new urban renewal approach aimed not only to halt the continuing decline which threatened to turn many older city neighborhoods like Wooster Square into slums. It also aimed to stabilize and reconstitute them as vital, attractive living areas for the next forty or fifty years, beyond the lifetime of most of the people now there. The new federal funds could be used selectively to remove elements harmful to the neighborhood, such as

* The road is now Interstate 91.

factory intrusions, to build new public facilities, create greater amenities and shift traffic patterns. Because the majority of residents in the immediate neighborhood would remain, the renewal plan would be designed in good part to satisfy them. Not only would their opposition hinder the plan's realization; without their enthusiastic cooperation, the private spending on property improvement would not take place.

Yet the matter of citizen participation and support is one of the most perplexing in urban renewal. The people cannot readily visualize the changes that can or should take place, nor do they understand the processes leading to these changes. Planners, on the other hand, often lack an understanding of the residents and their values. Community conflicts are inevitable, especially because groups with different values and needs live within the same neighborhoods. One must also question whether the self-appointed, original committee truly represent the neighborhood, or are they serving special ends? Voluntary leadership is another problem. Typically, the successful people with organizational ability have left a slipping area; the leaders of the remaining institutions may live elsewhere, and these institutions may not even serve present residents. Those who attend renewal meetings do not necessarily represent local consensus, and it is often hard for a planner or community organizer to ferret out the actual leaders recognized by a low-income or working-class community.

However, the greatest challenge is how to balance neighborhood wishes against citywide needs, and the immediate pressures of present population against desirable long-range change. Should the city put new public housing construction into a well-located neighborhood to meet the relocation needs of some displaced low-income families, or to "balance" a neighborhood? Should it leave substandard property alone if a long-time resident-owner cannot or will not improve it? Who is to decide industrial and commercial requirements of the whole city? How can people be placated whose good homes must be cleared to make way for necessary new facilities?

The original Wooster Square committee had clearly indicated what they expected from urban renewal: (1) new—but not public—housing in the neighborhood for families displaced by the new Thruway at one edge, and for the even larger numbers to be cleared by the Route 5; (2) housing code inspection and enforcement of standards to prevent further overcrowding and deterioration of dwellings; and (3) exclusion of industries to be displaced by Route 5 from resettling on land they believed should be redeveloped residentially. These three goals fitted into the city's tentative plans.

But the planners also recognized possibilities—in fact, necessities—beyond what residents saw, both for improving the neighborhood and serving the city as a whole. To take full advantage of the available federal and state aid, the project boundaries must be extended eastward, well beyond what the committee—most of them owner-residents in the section near the Square—regarded as their neighborhood, in order to encompass the obsolete and dangerous old industrial district. Little more than half of the 235-acre area designated for federal aid was suitable for rehabilitation. A major redevelopment, involving complete clearance of the eastern section where old tenements and cold-water flats intermingled with the ancient loft factories, was necessary to improve the city's economy and local employment opportunities. To accommodate displaced manufacturers and wholesalers from Wooster Square and other parts of the city, and to capitalize on the new highway, the city planned a modern industrial district on the other side of the new expressway.

A new elementary school was also needed to replace several that would or should be cleared, including the Columbus School facing the Square—a fifty-year-old, curb-hugging three-story structure already labeled obsolete in 1947. The planners envisioned the new school building also as a community center, with a library branch, swimming pool for adults and children, meeting room and other cultural and recreation facilities. A central, convenient location was thus important.

Before new housing or facilities could be built, however, a complicated series of steps had to be taken. Manufacturing firms that now stood on one proposed housing site had to be relocated; the new school-community center had to be completed before the old school could be demolished and its site could become available for still more housing; some sound structures, along with obsolete ones, would have to be demolished for the larger land area required by modern facilities. It was necessary to educate the renewal committee to the complex timing of changes and to the reality that in a built-up neighborhood, two desired uses often conflict and hard choices must be made; indeed, that they well might have to sacrifice one thing in order to gain another.

New Haven appointed a professionally trained city planner who had a background in community relations to work full-time with the Wooster Square Committee. Mary R. Small had worked for the Citizens' Council on City Planning in her native Philadelphia, and was then earning her master's degree in city planning at Yale.

During the early months, as the city worked out plans and she and the committee—now expanded to twenty-three members—grew acquainted, Miss Small dug into city archives and libraries to gather information on the origin and development of Wooster Square. Presented at their open monthly evening meetings, the history of the neighborhood she unearthed gave a new perspective to current problems, showing that the past erosion was not the fault of the current city administration or of the present residents. The history also engendered a new pride and interest in saving or restoring features of special worth. The Wooster Square story was presented to other groups around the city, complete with illustrations. It helped win support for the people who wanted to save part of the city's heritage, and acquainted other neighborhoods with the potential of renewal.

Through meetings with Mary Small, the neighborhood representatives learned what was possible through renewal, while the planners in the city agency found out what was acceptable to the Wooster Square residents. The matter of the new housing soon became a burning issue, revealing special neighborhood values and attitudes that could not be ignored.

Because so little clearance was to take place within the remaining residential section, the city planners had proposed high-rise apartments on the available land to accommodate the large number of neighborhood families whom the new highway would displace. This scheme was quickly vetoed by the committee. They preferred low-rise housing to more dwelling units. Many wanted only single-family homes. They also were opposed to any public housing, low-rent or even moderate. This strong stand reflected not only their dislike of the public landlord, but also the antagonism of the Italians to the low-income, lower-status Negro families who made up the bulk of residents in the nearby Farnum Court housing project and slum tenements. In fact, an unarticulated though major motivation behind their original drive for renewal was the changing character of the population in the eastern section.

The committee wanted new housing open to all income levels, they said, with "middle-income" predominating. Yet what was middle-income to Wooster Square residents would be considered closer to low-income elsewhere. Most of them were blue-collar workers and small businessmen making between $4,000 and $6,000 a year. Current construction costs, higher than average in New Haven, put new private housing beyond their reach. Cooperative housing, which could lower the costs somewhat, was proposed by Miss Small and won ready acceptance, especially as it would allow them in effect to own their homes.*

Considerable confusion was brought to the plea for new housing in Wooster Square by the pastor who took Father Cavicchi's place in mid-1955. The Connecticut Thruway at the neighborhood's southern edge had already removed many of St. Michael's parishioners, and Father Minchiatti unhappily saw that many more would be removed by Route 5 and the industrial redevelopment. Father Minchiatti had recently arrived from Italy and did not readily grasp the complicated new program. When the $115,000 survey and planning advance for Wooster Square came from the Urban Renewal Administration in December, he requested that "this large sum of money" be spent to build new homes for the highway displacees. He also found it difficult to understand—as did others opposing high-rise apartment houses, or even garden apartments—that one- and two-family homes would house even fewer people and, due to the high cost of clearance, be expensive. Later, when the large site on the Square was being cleared for the new school-community center, he insisted the land should be used for housing instead.

Clearing up such misunderstandings was an important function of the renewal committee. They also discussed with the renewal planner the full implications of housing code enforcement. Once Miss Small made it clear that their choice was between

* FHA's 221(d)3 housing was not yet available.

holding rents down and keeping slums, or raising the rents and saving the neighborhood (more recent government aids for rehabilitation were not available), they chose the latter. They also agreed that the home businesses in front parlors and yards should be discontinued. Plans were revised as much as possible to suit their wishes. Additions were made to the community school: the branch library would have a special Italian section, a room for older people to play cards and get together, and an open area for *boccia* players. When one of the committee members opposed part of the plan which called for his home's clearance, the group overrode him. Also overridden was a proposal by the city for an outdoor, Italian-style café on the Square, principally because Father Minchiatti did not want drinking near his church.

The latest series of tragic fires in the old carriage lofts, in January 1957, killed fifteen workers and pointed up the need to tear down these dangerous structures where many residents worked. The committee began meeting weekly to complete the plan. In spite of the desire for more housing, there was virtually no opposition to redeveloping the land east of Route 5 for industry. This was due in part to the education the committee received on the requirements of modern factories and their relation to local employment opportunities. Also, the people in that peripheral clearance area who would be displaced did not participate actively in the committee meetings. No doubt, the city's success in family relocation from Oak Street also gave the committee confidence that those to be displaced would find satisfactory new homes.

But an unexplained delay of nearly a year was added to the plan's completion by the city's attempt to buy up the Sargent Company through the Wooster Square Title I project. This involved shifts in project boundaries and reduction of much clearance desired by the committee in order to divert all possible funds to purchase the huge obsolescent plant on the area's eastern edge. The Wooster Square Committee attributed the delays to the fact that their project was the first of its kind in the country. (The revisions for Sargent's did not receive federal approval, however.)

During the planning period the committee also developed measures to make the neighborhood more livable and to prevent the deterioration which so often occurs in a renewal area between its designation and the plan's execution. They discussed and adopted in 1956, with guidance from city technicians, a new interim zoning ordinance to change the old industrial designation to residential. When a gas station operator appealed for a zoning variance, a delegation from Wooster Square testified before the zoning board for the first time and succeeded in preventing the change. When matters related to the project area came up at public hearings before city agencies, spokesmen from the neighborhood testified.

Encouraged by Mayor Lee and by Logue, the renewal planner served during those years as a contact between the neighborhood and the regular city departments, whose representatives were invited to committee meetings. The Assistant Police Chief explained his department's duties and powers and discussed ways it might help improve the neighborhood. The Liquor Control Board, after hearing about noisy taverns in the neighborhood, curbed these nuisances. Renewal would institute permanent changes in the street pattern to buffer the neighborhood from the Thruway and provide sufficient off-street parking. But in the meantime, as a result of such meetings, the traffic department instituted some temporary improvements—new signs and stop lights, two-hour parking limits, and one-way streets, to reduce all-day curb parking by workers and shoppers and to reroute trucks from the Thruway.

Residents came to see how their actions and organized expression of interest could alter problems they regarded as insoluble. The new style of politics also became evident. Several committee members who were active in Democratic or Republican party affairs admitted that the committee accomplished more for the neighborhood than they could through political influence.

When the $10,800,000 renewal plan received final federal approval, in June 1958, the committee celebrated by putting on a *fiesta,* with food and wine supplied by neighborhood merchants.

FOR REHABILITATION TO WORK

Mary Small had familiarized the residents, both at committee meetings and in block visits, with the procedures and premises of the housing rehabilitation plan; she explained how the individual's investment in home improvement should pay off as everyone on a block would be required to fix up and the city would improve facilities. Now was the time to make rehabilitation work.

According to housing economists, slipping neighborhoods like Wooster Square are characterized by under-investment in property. Regardless of where the cycle of deterioration starts, it eventually becomes a vicious circle. Landlords do not spend on adequate maintenance in a neighborhood with an uncertain future. They rent to tenants who accept poor service, peeling walls, inadequate plumbing, space heaters and out-of-date wiring—even cold-water flats—in exchange for low rents. Or they overcrowd the property to get maximum rents from slum dwellers. Individual resident owners who have extra cash are afraid of sinking their nest egg into property in a slipping area, especially if others are not making improvements. Banks, in turn, will not make loans for property improvement, or will charge double the interest to get their money back quickly, and thus encourage neglect in neighborhoods most needing extra investment. At the same time, the city slights its own facilities and lets public services slip.

The urban renewal legislation aimed to eliminate this stalemate through three principal devices. The first was public spending to clear blight and finance modern community facilities such as schools and playgrounds which enhance an area's desirability and increase property values. Such actions would, it was reasoned, restore the property owner's faith in the future of his neighborhood and stimulate private investment in rehabilitation. In fact, part of the purpose of an official renewal program—though this is never stated explicitly—is to force a change in owners' spending patterns, so they will invest a larger proportion of income in housing repair and maintenance. This requires the second governmental device. To encourage banks to provide the money needed for home improvement, Congress, in 1954, also mandated FHA to take the financing risks; it would provide government insurance on rehabilitation loans in urban renewal project areas, loans which were to be available on considerably longer and more generous terms than conventionally. These loans would be essential for the third device, systematic code enforcement, to work.

Everything being equal, neighborhood rehabilitation should be preferable to the tear-down-and-rebuild approach—less costly to the public; more palatable and even desirable to residents, shopkeepers and neighborhood institutions; and kinder to the varied texture of the city. Therefore, it should have caught on once government could remove the major recognized obstacles. But "making rehabilitation work," to borrow the tired phrase of frustrated renewal administrators, continues to be the chief embarrassment of the 1954 Housing Act. Most cities have not pushed it.

Lack of municipal enthusiasm for improvement of existing housing has been reflected in the relatively low caliber of staff and departmental drive compared to redevelopment. Forcing voters to spend on home improvement is not calculated to win politicians friends; taking them off the hook of code enforcement may do so, even if it defeats the program. Also, renewal is often at cross-purposes with older entrenched departments. But even the average city planner is often not anxious to conserve what appear to be out-of-date neighborhoods and houses.

A municipality can force some private investment through its housing code, but this is no better than the administration and political stamina behind it. Too many residents have a friend at City Hall. Even so, the code's level is usually quite low. After health and safety violations are corrected, there is still a large gap between the minimum housing standards that are legally enforceable, and basic improvement in the dwellings necessary to improve their appearance, desirability and value. Despite the often-quoted *Berman* v. *Parker* opinion of the Supreme Court, the legal standing of the public interest in beauty is not clear. The results of code enforcement have been either invisible or all too visible and ugly, with pipes showing, patchwork repairs, dreary or garish colors, and unsuitable synthetic or metal siding outside.

Moreover, few cities have code standards high enough to meet the minimum property requirements of the Federal Housing Administration, and the FHA has been reluctant to accept lower-than-new house standards. Under FHA insurance, improvements were to extend the life of the structure for at least the thirty-nine-year term of the special renewal loan. This unusually long term is questionable for many old buildings. Location of the insured structure must also be considered, and local FHA insuring offices, and banks, have not readily accepted the power of urban renewal to reverse the character of a slipping neighborhood, much less to maintain such improvement.

Even when government-insured loans are available, the complexity of filling out the endless forms—forms that are the same for a two-family house as for a multimillion-dollar property—may discourage all but the most determined individuals. Then a bank must be found that will accept the comparatively unprofitable FHA loan. Sometimes it will charge the borrower several extra points, which adds to the owner's expense and negates part of the congressional mandate. For a long time, only one bank in New Haven would ever process the loans, and that was the bank headed by the former chairman of the Redevelopment Agency.

Ultimately the question remains: will rehabilitation really add to a building's value? Many types of housing can go out of style and demand, though they may be structurally sound. Somehow, each individual property owner must be convinced that making the substantial additional investment in his home or rental property, sometimes incurring considerable debt on a free and clear property, makes good sense—either for profit, pride or pleasure. Then he must be persuaded to do it properly.

How far the landlord will go is generally determined by the additional rents he can obtain from present tenants or area residents. Should he improve his property sufficiently to attract a different, higher-income market, there is often considerable doubt whether such a resident would choose to move into the neighborhood. There is also the question whether such upgrading defeats one purpose of the program, which is to provide better housing for the present residents of the neighborhood. Also, the long term of the renewal loan, intended to reduce rehabilitation's annual cost, may be unrealistic for the building and improvements. City taxes, too, go up and penalize the rehabilitator. Finally, many absentee owners are just waiting for government to relieve them of a property they no longer want and will do only the legal minimum—under court orders.

The actual job of old-house rehabilitation is full of booby traps, not the least of these being the primitive state of the home improvement "industry." Housing economist Miles Colean has stated, "In a market economy, the test of feasibility is profitability." And the promise of potential profits from rehabilitation in low-to-moderate-income neighborhoods has not been sufficient, despite federal urban renewal, to stimulate private enterprise to provide the entrepreneurial skills necessary to make rehabilitation work on a large scale. Each item—wiring, plumbing, painting, carpentry—is handled by a specialist; the general contractor who ties them together charges an extra fee. But making accurate estimates on the cost of improvements for an old house is, at best, difficult. Thus, the contractors, generally an individualistic, high-pressure group, tend to charge what the traffic will bear. Most are not interested in small jobs such as the average old home entails, and in their desire to make some quick money, they sell all sorts of product tie-ins to the customers. Some are notorious fly-by-night operators; but even the reliable contractor is not an architect. The end product of older-home rehabilitation is often an unsuitable, unesthetic attempt to strip down and modernize, somewhat less than a neighborhood amenity or even a source of enhanced value for the property itself.

Until recently, the only impressive results have been in a few exceptionally located areas with substandard but promising housing stock of the townhouse variety, such as Washington's Georgetown, Philadelphia's Rittenhouse Square and now Washington Square East, and New York's Greenwich Village—where neighborhoods have been upgraded from near-slum to upper-income dwellings or, as in San Francisco's Jackson Square, where use was changed from residential to commercial. Most of these improvements were accomplished without federal urban renewal aid.

For rehabilitation to work on a meaningful scale in a moderate-income neighborhood, and to prolong the life of a building as well as its present occupancy at reasonable cost, it seems that the city government must supply the extra imagination, enterprise and enthusiasm (if one can judge from New Haven's success in Wooster Square, compared to that of many other cities).

Early in the development of plans to rehabilitate Wooster Square the need for many new official services became apparent. First was a talented, dedicated and inventive staff, one based in the neighborhood and good at working with the people. Again, the project director was a Philadelphia-trained city planner—one with enthusiasm for rehabilitation.

Working with Mary Hommann in the field office in Wooster Square was a full-time neighborhood representative, Theodore DeLauro, a former Alderman and insurance agency owner who once served as an interpreter for the city and was a member of Father Cavicchi's group in 1953. Development Administrator Logue was able to persuade the federal official that DeLauro's salary should be included in the project staff costs, as should that of a "rehabilitation specialist." Mary Hommann believed that the latter position encompassed separate functions, and that the field office needed one person with architectural training and another who had practical experience with construction. Logue convinced the Urban Renewal Administration to pay for the extra technician, and after seeing the remarkable results achieved in Wooster Square, the federal agency made architectural services part of the allowable costs in every neighborhood renewal project.

MATTRESS MONEY

The first person to approach property owners in each block in Wooster Square was neighborhood representative DeLauro. He literally and figuratively spoke the people's language. He was known to most, and they trusted him.

DeLauro, still a member of the renewal committee, prepared owners for visits by the housing code inspector (renamed "field inspector" to make the job more palatable). The inspector surveyed the inside and outside of each house for code violations and gave the list to the project's field office for review by its architect and construction specialist. The architect would look over the home's exterior. His suggestions for ways to enhance appearance were incorporated with the code violations requiring corrections onto a work sheet which each owner received. The architect's ideas were often not expensive and not enforceable, but they were capable of making the end product much more desirable.

If the files of the historical society revealed the home to be of special interest, the owner was supplied with facts, a photograph of the original structure when available, and details on how to make an accurate reconstruction. The majority of Wooster Square homes are ordinary frame or masonry-covered structures, but each owner still received a color rendering prepared by the staff architect, showing his property as a part of its block, and depicting how it might look if the extra suggestions (such as a pastel coat of paint) were followed. DeLauro advised on how much an owner could afford.

"People are afraid of change," James Skerritt, Yale graduate architect who served on the field staff for several years, pointed out. "You can't talk about it, but you can show how it will look after." Some owners were flattered that the city went to such trouble for them. They would even frame the water color and hang it in a prominent place, although the paint colors were not necessarily followed. Many residents would do the work themselves, or get relatives to help. A list compiled and checked out by the field staff, of general contractors who expressed a willingness to do the home improvement work was helpful for the timorous or inexperienced.

To further owners' knowledge of how to get work done and improve their taste, the Redevelopment Agency distributed free a series of four handsome illustrated booklets whose type face and layout, by themselves, set standards of excellence. One booklet on exterior design showed how bad modernization could ruin the appearance of a house and good work enhance it. Suggestions were offered for materials suitable for use on the old frame houses that predominate in New Haven. Ideas were expressed in simple language. Other booklets gave advice on how to finance home improvements, how to find and work with a contractor, and how to maintain exteriors once work was done. The field office kept a permanent exhibit of building materials and a changing gallery with photographs of rehabilitation work being done in the neighborhood.

Individualized staff assistance was available at every step. The project director would help owners get financing; she even went to the bank with them or for them and helped fill out forms. The staff told residents how to get the various city permits necessary to undertake work. Before an owner signed with a contractor,

Gene Lubocki, the staff construction expert and a former home builder, checked over the estimates. As people saw Lubocki figure out ways of doing work better and for less money—one widow with code violations amounting to a first estimate of $17,000 was helped to pare down the cost to $2,500—they sought his advice.

Lubocki also helped landlords achieve more pleasing results for less money; sometimes he worked out the entire plan. For the reconversion of one of the large mansions on the Square from a rooming house to family-size apartments, he eliminated a proposed fire escape which would have marred the building's exterior as well as the Square's appearance, and saved the owner $1,500. "There are always several ways of doing things," Lubocki observed. "The contractor figures out the easiest way for himself, but it may be more expensive for the owner. We warn them if it's too high, or too low."

No owners were pushed for the first year and a half. DeLauro made clear to the administration that the people could not be rushed. Old-timers had been content to live in shabby houses, some of them cold-water flats but all paid up. They had never made capital expenditures for adequate heating, electricity or plumbing. When rehabilitation forced them to bring their homes up to modern standards, they worried whether they would ever get their money back. Yet in the first two years of this five-year program, with work sheets issued for 228 of the 498 structures to be rehabilitated, $1,142,817 worth of improvements was under way or completed in 189 structures, with no enforcement orders necessary.

Measured against the dollar value of private investment, the staff cost of New Haven's "lead them by the hand" approach was very small: approximately $100 per structure against an average of $5,073 per structure spent by the owner. Over half this sum was for improvements beyond the city's code, which already met the FHA minimum.

Surprisingly, few of the property owners required bank loans. There were only six FHA mortgages, amounting to $144,000. Seventeen more conventional loans, totaling $136,000, were mostly for larger rental properties. The banks, their faith in Wooster Square restored, had lifted the mortgage ban.

The largest amount of financing for improvement, however,

came from "mattress money"—savings that the owners, most of them factory workers, traditionally put aside against possible lay-offs and other emergencies. The rehabilitation program came after several years of comparative prosperity and regular employment and found property owners with ample reserves which they had been reluctant to invest before. Some of the most expensive improvements, as high as $24,000 per structure, were made without borrowing.

As people saw the city fulfilling its renewal promises—tearing down rat-infested slums, removing grimy factories, forcing slum landlords to comply with official standards, and building the handsome new Conte School, with its cheerful glass-faced library overlooking the Square—and as their neighbors also complied, they were inspired to go far beyond the required minimum.

Investments appeared to be paying off. Property values were rising in Wooster Square, judged by selling and asking prices after a few years, and investors started to pick up properties. Rents did go up some 50 to 75 per cent, from an average of $40 to $75, to finance major improvements such as full bathrooms, complete wiring, hot-water and heating systems. But the income-level of the tenancy remained largely the same. The availability of modern attractive apartments made it possible for some who were considering a move to remain and live better, even though they had to spend more. It used to take two to three months to rent a vacant apartment; now there are waiting lists. Even some slum landlords responded to the promise of higher returns from an improved property.*

The staff's energy and enthusiasm never appeared to flag. Much of their drive came from the satisfaction of seeing results begin to blossom all over, from the appreciation of the residents who came to regard them as friends, and from the continued encouragement of the Development Administrator. Mayor Lee also participated, presenting each owner with a certificate when his work was completed. Lee believed there should be a properly

* It should be noted, however, that the public outlay in Wooster Square's neighborhood renewal was found to produce only two and a half times as much private investment compared to the city's redevelopment areas, where the ratio was five to seven times the governmental project cost.

staffed rehabilitation office for every 3,000 to 4,000 dwelling units in the city. "It instructs the individual in his stake in the program and the contribution he can make to the community. And it makes him see he's not a faceless image at City Hall." The administration's support also assured the neighborhood of the essential cooperation of other city departments.

OTHER PUBLIC VENTURES

But on dismal Court Street only four of the nineteen owners of the twenty-seven skid-row rooming houses agreed to comply with the renewal plan, which called for conversion of these eighty-year-old brick row houses into two-family, owner-occupied units. No doubt it was difficult for them to visualize the changes possible in these oppressively dark structures. But even the few compliant owners found it difficult to obtain financing, as New Haven banks would not lend on row houses with common walls.

Several alternatives were considered by the city. The Redevelopment Authority could force legal repairs on the structures, with the end product of such coercion uncertain; or it could condemn and clear the properties, making the site available for redevelopment with new structures. It could also use eminent domain to acquire the structures, rehabilitate them, and taking advantage of the Title I write-down, resell the houses at appraised fair value to private purchasers. There was little precedent for such a course, but it was adopted, using the field staff's expertise to design and supervise work to be done by an outside contractor. Trees were to be planted on the street and parking provided in back by the city.

Court Street's former ugly ducklings emerged from the grime of the industrial revolution as swans, their façades now light brick or pastel-tinted, with handsome, spacious apartments inside. They were so attractive that on the date of the buildings' sale, more bidders put down the required $200 deposit than there were houses to sell. Some 500 visitors came to look. Five purchasers, who were displacees, had priority. The rest included three families returning from the suburbs, professional families, one of them Negro, and Yale faculty members who wanted to live within walking distance of town and the University. The city's modest investment of $1,600 per structure * to produce these twenty-eight conveniently located two-, three-, and four-bedroom homes may have been its best expenditure to date for encouraging middle-class families to live in center city. Even this outlay soon came back in increased tax revenues. Further, the dramatic transformation encouraged other owners in the neighborhood to undertake still more and often costly improvements.

The economics of this public venture, the first of its kind in the country, made as much sense as did the handsome end products. Average acquisition price was $11,700, and an additional $18,000 was spent for rehabilitating each. Appraised resale price was $21,000. If the $8,300 difference had been spent on clearance and new buildings at present high construction costs, the result would have been minimum-priced, minimum-featured, two-story duplexes. Instead, the interior amenities offered by solidly constructed, nineteenth-century row houses—the high ceilings, handsome appointments, and fireplaces—were preserved. Equally important, an integral part of Wooster Square and the city was saved. Purchasers of the modernized two-family buildings had to make down payments of only $2,000, with thirty-year FHA mortgages; their monthly payments of $171.71, including insurance and city taxes, could be substantially defrayed by the income from the rental apartment in the building.

The city renewal staff went on to improve other small but important neighborhood features. Designer Skerritt worked with the light industry in the neighborhood to erect decorative concrete fences that would hide their parking areas instead of using conventional, see-through cyclone wiring. On little odd-size parcels of land along the deep cut of the railroad separating Wooster Square from downtown, he designed delightful parklets with tables, shade trees and sitting places for neighborhood people and workers. The Square itself was refurbished, with new trees and improved lighting so that people could enjoy it by night as well as by day. Trees were being planted by the city on blocks where private rehabilitation was completed. Sites were acquired

* The total public cost to rehabilitate the thirteen structures was $125,000, of which the city paid one sixth under the Title I formula. The state pays one third of the local net project cost.

for off-street parking by the city parking authority to give Wooster Square homes a one-to-one parking ratio. On Grand Avenue, the most dilapidated structures were cleared, and displaced businessmen from other parts of Wooster Square started putting up new structures in their places. Other spaces were saved for parking. The remaining owners, together with new merchants, spruced up store fronts with the advice of designer Skerritt, who sketched ways of making the shopping avenue appear more inviting.

No wonder New Haven's Wooster Square was being singled out by the Housing and Home Finance Agency as proof that older city neighborhoods could be given new life.

THE UNHAPPY PEOPLE

Of course, there are always the unhappy people. Some residents, accustomed to spending as little as $20 to $30 (plus heat) for a family apartment, were not easily reconciled to higher but economic rents. Among them were tenants who had to pay more for old quarters after landlords were forced by the code to install safety and sanitary devices, fire sprinklers, wash basins and adequate wiring, but no visible extras. "They make us pay more rent, but our incomes haven't gone up," grumbled tenants in one such rehabilitated three-family house in the summer of 1961. Many displayed cynicism about democratic planning. "The neighborhood meetings were rigged," asserted one homeowner who had only attended the first meeting. Yet in the next breath he added, "But renewal was needed. It's a good thing."

What stung many who spent extra on remodeling exteriors of their homes were the increased assessments. Some owners who liberally improved interiors in the past had purposely left the outsides shabby, more concerned about the tax assessor than the world's opinion. But even those who had not yet rehabilitated found assessments doubled during Lee's administration. Wooster Square valuations had been much lower than the rest of the city, 25 per cent instead of 60 per cent of value, left that way by the previous Republican city administration which was no doubt trying to favor the Italian wards. Equalization inevitably caused resentment, which showed up at election time against Lee. Some blamed the rise on all the downtown demolition. "If we'd had Church Street up, we wouldn't have had reassessment," declared one man. After the 1961 election, assessment policies were altered to encourage rather than penalize property improvement wherever possible.

Many were distressed that the promised new housing in Wooster Square was not yet built, and dislocated families were being forced to move away. Living in the suburbs seemed alien to old-timers. But others, at first heartbroken about moving away from their lifetime surroundings, became proud suburbanites and admit they could never have done it themselves.

Even the committee members found it hard to recall the complicated series of steps necessary before sites in the neighborhood would be available for new housing. Why should a bottling plant be relocated ahead of housing? Moderate-rent, well-designed garden apartments for relocatees were being built in another part of the city, but that did not interest many in Wooster Square.

But the kind of non-public housing that could be built was still beyond the pocketbook of most of the Wooster Square residents until the Federal Housing Act of 1961 was passed. Then FHA's new Section 221(d)3, with its sub-market interest rates, facilitated production of housing some 20 per cent less expensive than could be privately built, and the Redevelopment Agency was able to schedule construction of new housing within the means of the people in the project area. Sponsored by a local foundation (all 221(d)3 housing requires a nonprofit, limited dividend or cooperative sponsor), Columbus Mall was built on the site of former tenements; it offered three-bedroom apartments for rents at only $91 a month, and required no down-payment, as did cooperatives. Subsequently, thirty-four units of FHA-insured, conventionally financed townhouse-type apartments were built facing the Green on the old Columbus school site; their distinguished design has won them national architectural awards.

There were also non-housing worries engendered by renewal and highway changes. Some merchants with retail produce stores near the Thruway feared that the projected street closings, intended to prevent traffic from going through the neighborhood, would also keep away customers who drove from other parts of the city. They derided the traffic diversions as "crazy." Also, meeting rooms of five social clubs were being cleared and their members were not happy. Only one of the clubs had sufficient means to acquire another building. The other four were unwilling to get together to cut costs. For some, the field office afforded temporary space until the school-community center opened in 1962.

In the summer of 1961, the shirt-sleeved men sitting outside the Green Circle Club on Hamilton Street, in the area across the projected Route 5, were bitter, knowing that their club and their lifetime rented homes were to be razed. "I have a flat that I pay fifty dollars a month for," said a factory maintenance worker. "I've lived here all my life. Sure it's cold water. But if you only make seventy dollars a week and the cheapest you can get is ninety-five to one hundred and twenty dollars, how you gonna pay for it? We'd all like to live in a classy place—but within our means." Said another, referring to University Towers in Oak Street, "The Mayor built two hundred and seventy dollars-a-month apartments. You have to be a banker to rent them. They say they're going to put factories in here, but what factories? They're all moving South." Another asserted, "This is the Mayor's last year!" Six weeks before election, when the state started property acquisition for the new highway, which would cut through the dilapidated eastern section, it cut Lee's margin in those wards.

But the major headache for the city in the Wooster Square project, as it turned out, was the industrial redevelopment. Early in 1957, it became known that Sargent and Company was planning to leave New Haven. Their move would mean a loss of 1,200 local jobs and a payroll of $5,000,000, not to overlook real estate taxes to the city. Lee asked the president, Forbes Sargent, grandson of the founder of the old New Haven hardware firm, to meet with him.

He learned that the company, handicapped by operating in its inefficient eighty-year-old building complex, a rabbit warren of disconnected structures, was also in financial straits and lacked funds to build a new plant. They had acquired an option on land in the suburbs, but meanwhile a number of southern states were making more attractive offers of free sites and plants to the hardware manufacturer. Lee requested an opportunity to present the case for remaining in New Haven to the firm's board.

Through Title I aid, he told them, the government could buy and clear their present plant—assessed at $2,800,000—but with no apparent re-use value or salability, and the company could gain the cash to finance a new plant. Reclamation of land along the harbor and Thruway would make new industrial land available. Lee also provided some compelling fiscal arguments about relocating in an established city whose municipal plant was substantially paid for, rather than in a mushrooming new community where local taxes would become increasingly burdensome.

To some observers it seemed that Forbes Sargent regarded urban renewal as vaguely socialistic. But the opportunity to sell the old factory at assessed value and stay in New Haven appealed to him. The city revised the Wooster Square plan then to accommodate the company.

But the federal renewal program did not yet encourage use of its funds for industrial redevelopment, and the URA did not believe that the costly change met the purposes of the housing act. Fortunately, the state of Connecticut passed industrial redevelopment legislation in 1958. With this new public help Sargent's old plant could be acquired and the company helped to relocate in the new Long Wharf project, stretching between Wooster Square and the Long Island Sound. This project, which went into execution in 1959, was based largely on the reclaimed harbor land, and when it was buildable, in 1963, Sargent's put up a $4,000,000 plant in the area.

There was also room for several more large, and hopefully new, industries in the 348-acre project, which offered a prestige location where plants could be viewed by everyone passing up and down the Connecticut Thruway. No new industry has come in yet, but the privately financed $1,500,000 Regional Food Terminal has opened there, rehousing the city's food wholesalers in a highly desirable site, with excellent transportation access. Another important local firm, Gant Shirts, was planning a new $2,000,000 factory with doubled employment in Long Wharf, too.

In the Wooster Square industrial district, the city also had problems in winning feasible land use appraisals. It took two years to persuade the federal agency to cut the cost from $1 to thirty-five cents a square foot to allow New Haven to compete with the suburbs for the many small concerns that were clustered in the area. During that time, a number moved away. However, forty-one local firms have relocated into the Wooster Square industrial district; eight more plants are under construction or in planning; and a total of $10,000,000 had been invested in new buildings and facilities. Significantly, a number of firms expanded operations in enlarged quarters. The industrial district is also remarkable for its handsome new structures, a striking contrast to the gloomy old factory lofts. (The Redevelopment Agency gave developers a helping hand, providing architectural "guidance.")

ANOTHER SIDE OF THE GREEN

Just northwest of New Haven's nine original squares is the Dixwell neighborhood, named for its main thoroughfare, Dixwell Avenue. This community of 10,000 was next to be designated for urban renewal. Dixwell had an excellent location—practically across the street from Yale. Otherwise, it was a world apart; Dixwell has been described as New Haven's Harlem. In 1958, it was the second predominantly Negro neighborhood in the country to be slated for conservation and rehabilitation rather than clearance for redevelopment.*

Surveys of urban renewal areas are based on the physical condition of the housing and neighborhood; indeed, these are necessary to qualify an area for such federal aid, and the condition of the housing stock is certainly important in determining the feasibility of rehabilitation. But, as cities have slowly come to recognize, one older neighborhood and its residents varies widely from another, and the people—their economic situation, social organization and cultural background—often matter more than the conditions of the buildings or even patterns of tenancy and ownership in estimating a neighborhood's potential for housing rehabilitation.

* The first was Baltimore's Harlem Park.

Aware of these differences, New Haven's development administration had national experts carry out three special surveys—on neighborhood attitudes, the economic feasibility of rehabilitation, and racial factors affecting the potential of renewal. The generally favorable reports encouraged the city to proceed. But not until the execution stage was reached was the full range of problems revealed.

Within the several hundred acres of Dixwell lay many of the underlying obstacles to healthy, slum-free urban centers. But in a small city like New Haven, which has undertaken comprehensive renewal, these matters surface much more rapidly and unavoidably than in a New York, Chicago or Philadelphia where "feasible" neighborhoods are treated and unsolved problems can shift elsewhere.

A comparison of Dixwell and Wooster Square is instructive. Because Wooster Square is predominantly Italian-American and the majority of Dixwell is Negro, many significant differences in what was possible in renewal, as well as what was desired, separated the two. The potential for urban rehabilitation cannot be assessed only from the Wooster Squares of the country.

When some contemporary observers of cities have investigated or written about "healthy" slums and attractive blighted neighborhoods, it seems to be the predominantly Italian neighborhoods from which they have drawn their conclusions. They cite indigenous leaders; satisfactions derived from an apparently substandard yet congenial environment; the ungrading which, purportedly, time alone brings to an ethnic slum.

Indeed, a generation ago many of the negative physical and social indices found in today's Negro slum neighborhoods were apparent in New Haven's Italian districts. Even community attitudes showed some remarkable similarities, as is indicated in studies by Yale social scientists who over the years used New Haven as their laboratory.*

But the differences, some obvious, such as color of skin, others more subtle, are profound. The Italians, though rural, came from

* Landlords exploited them, employers discriminated against them, new neighborhoods were hostile to them. One New Haven real estate agent in the 1930's said of the Italians: "They come here and live like animals . . . eight or ten in a room, and breed like pigs."

villages—villages with ancient traditions and cohesive patterns of social organization which, to a considerable extent, were reconstituted in the new world. Wooster Square became a little old-world city within the new city. Extended family and former villagers lived next door on its streets, bound and sustained by the common foreign language, customs, food, and church. Parochial schools took the overflow of children. Discrimination increased group solidarity; sheer strength of numbers helped them to get ahead. If money was hard to get from Yankee bankers, the Italian community offered the small and budding financier a large-enough base to build a business. And as they prospered, some of the leading men set up agencies to help the others. Even the big family was an economic asset when children left school by ninth grade and found work to help the household. By virtue of its size, the Italian community could also gain the help of politicians, and, in time, political positions for themselves. Labor unions and personnel offices also reflected an ethnic slant. Nor should the fact be minimized that many Italians came to work in the city's factories and railroad—some specifically brought over for that purpose.

Coming from the lowest rung of a static society in a backward region, however, the southern Italian immigrants who comprised 80 per cent of those in New Haven accepted their lower economic position and status in America. They had little innate drive for higher material or social standards, and very limited education. Their children learned through the mass media, as well as school, of the material rewards offered by American life, and the belief that every individual might become wealthy. Some were willing to suffer the emotional and cultural break from their family and group to become Americanized and to advance. And the larger community rewarded them as they became more "American" with jobs of greater status and income. For when the Italian rose from lower to middle class, it was within the general community, not only in his own segment. In two generations, many of New Haven's outstanding doctors, dentists and lawyers were of Italian origin (though many originally came from northern Italy). They were appointed to city boards and succeeded to City Hall in 1946. Some joined new, even Protestant churches, and moved to better neighborhoods and suburbs.

The majority, however, though their economic position had improved, stayed, clinging to familiar institutions and goals and the village tradition. The immigration had long since ceased, and when renewal came, the Italians formed a modest homogeneous neighborhood of working-class people and small businessmen, combining the best of old and new.

Today, of all the "hyphenated Americans" remaining in the city's core, the Italian-American is the ideal rehabilitator. (In Wooster Square, before renewal, it was not uncommon for some tenants to spend hundreds of dollars fixing up their rented apartments.) The cultural differences once separating Italian from American are now an asset. The colorful religious festivals, the bakeries, pizzerias, groceries and restaurants, once established to serve an Italian clientele, draw people from all over. As in other cities, middle-class bohemians in New Haven find the Italian villagers make good neighbors in moderate-rental districts, and they rush to buy Court Street's houses.

But the Italian-American neighborhood, its original sources of supply long since dried up, is dissolving. Its typical resident is becoming middle aged; the newcomers are already changing its special character. Already some Italian-Americans were muttering that the "Yalies" would push them out of Wooster Square by bidding up land values.

NORTHERN DISCRIMINATION

The neighborhood of the Negro is continually being replenished and expanded by newcomers and fast-growing young families. But these latest urbanites bring no village tradition, nor do their institutions adequately compensate for the weakness of family life and culture to help them adjust to the city.

But perhaps most significant of the factors that make the experience of the Italian or other European immigrant strikingly different from that of the urban Negro—at least in New Haven—is that the Negroes as a group have been there for more than a century, arriving several generations before the Italians. Yet they failed to move into the mainstream of the community.

This lack of movement was not, however, due to lack of education and ambition or cultural lag. But as the Negro adopted middle-class values and patterns, he ran up against a caste system in New Haven which, in its own cruel way, was as rigid as that of a southern city. Some doors were open, but those that matter most, shut.

The Negroes who lived in New Haven in abolitionist days seemed on the verge of capturing the American dream. Many were not from the plantation, but from southern households, and were trained as artisans or in services. By virtue of these skills they gained some modest economic success, serving the city's white and non-white community. Building lots were bought, homes completed, money deposited in savings banks. A Negro upper middle class, motivated by the conventional Connecticut morality was vitalized.

After the Civil War, the city's new public school system was desegregated; Negroes lived throughout the city. They developed their own institutions and, when European immigrants invaded some of their earlier districts, many reconsolidated by 1890 around their churches in an area then called, prophetically, Poverty Square. Some houses were jerry-built, thrown together in the rush of industrialization; others were one- or two-family frame houses with yards, typical of New Haven. The stage should have been set for movement into the mainstream.

What took place during the coming decades, as told in Robert A. Warner's study of *New Haven Negroes,* published in 1946, reveals what a city can do to its Negro community when it withholds economic opportunity while allowing educational equality and residential freedom.

The sudden stalemate was, in part, the consequence of numbers and percentages. The small Negro population of New Haven was virtually overwhelmed by the large body of foreigners who suddenly arrived and challenged them at every level. Also, skilled services were becoming commercialized and mechanized. Substantial capital was required to purchase equipment.

The Negro in New Haven was almost systematically driven out of the skilled service occupations which had been his traditional fields. Catering, once a Negro monopoly and source of early affluence, was taken over by the inns of New Haven which, wrote Warner, "would not consider hiring Negro executives." In the nineteenth century, Negroes were chefs and waiters; now no New Haven hotel employed Negroes. The Italians and Greeks took over restaurants and barbershops, helped by developing craft unions. Organized labor displayed ethnic loyalty rather than working-class solidarity; Negroes were excluded. Compared to his European peasant-trained competitors, the Negro was at a multiple disadvantage. Inadequately prepared by slavery for participation in a money economy, his skills now minimized, he was unable to obtain credit from local bankers to buy the new equipment, and lacked a large enough base among his own people.

Within the industrial structure, male Negroes were downgraded to common labor positions; new skilled work went to whites. Ethnic-controlled personnel offices solidified the trend. Certain industrial jobs were designated for Negroes, Warner found. The jobs were "usually unpleasant by reasons of heat, dust, dirt and moisture." And when new machinery eliminated menial tasks, Negroes lost even these industrial jobs. During the great depression, three times as many of them were unemployed as were whites.

As New Haven shifted from a manufacturing community to an institutional and service center, the Negro handicap increased. Stenographic and white-collar jobs were closed to them, Warner said, "in harmony" with "public opinion." Negroes were held unsuitable as clerks or salesmen, even in the white-owned Dixwell stores. They worked as stock boys or janitors. The University substituted white maids in the 1920's and student waiters in the 30's, keeping only some old Negro retainers. The thriving Telephone Company, the city's second-largest employer, hired no Negro women as operators or men as linemen. "The citadel of the white caste system," as Warner called the financial and business community, continued to be unwilling to accept Negro orders or extend loans, thus virtually preventing the establishment of business enterprises by them. Lack of business training, in turn, excluded Negroes from new managerial jobs.

In politics, too, the influence of the Negro community declined, with only 2,000 registered voters in 1934 compared to the Italians' 13,000. The city government was paternalistic; the handpicked ward leader told the Negroes to be quiet and promised to see they got some jobs. The federal post office, which had civil service examinations, was the one place where they could obtain clean work with managerial responsibility, merit advancement and dignity.

Yet the social scientist found "no discrimination" within the schools, from teachers or students. Negroes were cheered in athletics and elected to school offices. "But . . . despite the educational influences of school, press and radio, most youngsters somehow learn from parents and associates to curb their aspirations." Few took business courses or studied stenography; few attended commercial high school. In 1930, nine out of ten employed Negroes, even academy-trained men and college graduates, were menials or laborers.

"In the professions . . . improved educational opportunity has increased Negro participation—but not for practice in New Haven. Doctors, lawyers, technicians, and especially teachers have found they must go south or to northern centers where a larger Negro population provides employment opportunities."

They were free to move to other neighborhoods, but even the upper-class Negro generally lacked the money. Some who tried all their lives could not save enough to buy a house. Warner found most Dixwell homes shabby, as "most are rented by busy [or poor] people." Even their civic and philanthropic institutions had to look outside for financial support. The white community was quite willing to give charity, reluctant to give credit. They eagerly supported Dixwell Community House and served on its board. But since the Negro failed to gain a firm foothold in factory or office employ, "most die penniless."

ALMOST NO MONEY

Dixwell's main rehabilitation problem was not under-investment of total income in property, as in Wooster Square; rather, it appeared, it was the lack of money. In 1950, according to the most recent decennial census available to the city's renewal planners, Dixwell family incomes averaged $3,400—some $2,000 less than the city's families as a whole. Half earned between $2,000 and $3,000 a year. Only 11 per cent of its men held professional or managerial positions—half that for the city as a whole, but many at these earned a precarious living. Thirty-one per cent were service employees or laborers, twice the proportion for the city.

Eighty per cent of the families were renters; the typical residence was over fifty years old and owner-occupied, with several apartments to let. Rents were slightly less in Dixwell than the city average, but this $80 a month was for considerably poorer housing and represented a much greater portion of family income than spent by the average family. And the Dixwell rents were twice the average of those in Wooster Square before renewal. Homeowners had to rent out apartments for as much as the traffic would bear, to earn extra income and pay off the excessive terms of loan sharks and pyramided short-term mortgages which encumbered many properties. That renters were willing to pay so much reflected the limited supply of housing available to them and their unsatisfied demand, according to Chester Rapkin's study on the economic feasibility of rehabilitation of Dixwell.

The core of the old single-family, middle-class houses, many of them owned free and clear, was deteriorating due to age both of structure and owner—the latter typically poor and lacking the means to maintain his property. Even the values of their homes, averaging $6,500, were half those in the city in general; many had spent more in acquiring the property than it was worth—and many felt it was worth more.

Younger families who were able to move got out as soon as possible, their desire for better housing helped by the departure of many white families from close-by neighborhoods into which Negroes now moved. But realtors forced them to pay a substantial premium for the privilege.

Dixwell did not suffer from high vacancy rates as a consequence, however. During the 1950's, as one group moved out, their quarters were quickly occupied by the steadily growing number of still poorer southern Negroes who were moving to New Haven. For the newcomers, Dixwell's slums were a big step up from the rural slum, and New Haven's economic opportunities greater. "You can make somethin' on a day's work up here." But as numbers and family size increased, Dixwell deteriorated still further. Densities and fire rates were the highest in the city; overcrowding common; one quarter of the units were dilapidated and suitable only for clearance. Even 75 per cent of the family units failed to meet the city's housing code standards and needed rehabilitation.

More newcomers increased the distances between the different groups of residents. Some of the variety stores and shoeshine shops along Dixwell Avenue served as fronts for bookies, numbers players, narcotics peddlers and prostitutes. The exuberant street life—brawls and knife-fights among the loafers on the Avenue—attracted policemen, not sightseers. Dixwell was no longer a safe place to live, complained older residents. Roaches and rats were also making inroads; on some blocks, the stench of rotting garbage and dead rats, the odor of the slum, hung heavy.

ONE STRENGTHENING FACTOR

One strengthening factor amidst these tides was Isadore Wexler, who became principal of Dixwell's Winchester elementary school in 1947. Wexler was concerned because the school was not reaching many of the students. An unorthodox educator, he believed that the whole community, not just the school, teaches the child. But the Dixwell community was not an ideal teacher, and the old Winchester building made it extremely difficult for the school to compensate for outside deficiencies.

Soon after Wexler came, he helped the listless community organize a council to discuss the neighborhood's problems; the main issues were housing, jobs and schools. The need for a new school provided them with a tangible cause for working together. Wexler visualized the new building as a school for community use, equipped with a cafeteria, a large gym, an auditorium for after-school meetings and an all-purpose room to be used evenings for adult crafts. But the New Haven School Board was accustomed to traditional methods: give new schools and good teachers to the influential neighborhoods, use discipline to solve problems in the slums, and close down all doors at 3:30. To them, Wexler recalled, "We were disturbers of the peace."

As usual, Dixwell had to go outside for help. Wexler rallied the support of sixty-five citywide agencies; the neighborhood won the building. When it opened in 1952, Winchester was considered the finest elementary school in New Haven. To the neighborhood, it was a great source of pride.

Wexler next convinced the city's Division of Adult Education to put evening classes in neighborhood schools. (Dixwell residents rarely attended the classes in downtown high schools because they felt unwelcome there.) The new program was very successful the first few years. Then attendance began falling off. The education-oriented people of Dixwell were moving out, and the newcomers resisted going to school. "Some were embarrassed to come and admit they didn't read," said Charles Twyman, then a sixth-grade teacher at Winchester School who also headed the Dixwell Renewal Committee. "We had to go to the pool rooms to solicit enrollment for the evening classes." An attempt to organize block groups aborted when its spark plug, a white millionaire with fond memories of his youth in Dixwell, died. The voluntary buisnessman's committee he had headed also fell part. "A neighborhood like this needs paid leadership," Twyman observed.

Then in 1954, two years after the new Winchester School opened, Dixwell received another, unsolicited, improvement. This one was from the New Haven Housing Authority, an autonomous agency with a growing clientele and a shrinking supply of buildable land. The Authority erected a nine-story, 600-unit addition to the 300-unit, low-rise, low-income Elm Haven project which stood next to the school. The new tenants—75 per cent of them non-white—added an unexpectedly large number of children to the neighborhood. "Before we had a chance to build something in the community," recalled Wexler, "the school was cut off from the rest of the neighborhood, street by street." Soon, an estimated 95 per cent of Winchester's students came from the housing project, which had an annual turnover of one third in the 1950's.

To many long-time Dixwell residents, the towering Elm Haven extension, the only high-rise building in the neighborhood, symbolized a growing stigma. With its concentration of social problems, it was a rough and tough place. An estimated 60 per cent of its residents were only recently off farms and plantations in the Carolinas. They had no experience in elevator apartment living, a situation made acute by their many children. Some, relocated from the Oak Street slum, were still problems in their new homes. Most tenants were overwhelmed by the struggle for existence. Mothers could barely cope with their children, much less join the PTA. The average project parent had only reached sixth grade. With the recession and automation, fathers began to lose jobs and desert families. Juvenile delinquency was on the rise. In several years, the families of 40 per cent of the children at Winchester School received Aid to Dependent Children. Sixty per cent of the area's high-school-age students were dropouts.

Dixwell's Community House was unable to reach the river of people flowing through the neighborhood. The one place through which many had to pass—at a rather alarming rate—was Winchester School. Wexler felt the school must help compensate for the people's deficits. But the Board of Education rejected his proposal for a well-staffed after-school program for children and adults. The Housing Authority said it could do nothing; the federal public housing agency did not provide funds for social programs. All that the New Haven Council of Social Agencies could do, apparently, was cooperate with Wexler in making a study.

But Development Administrator Logue, who was by now deeply involved in the renewal of Dixwell, and in the city's social problems, agreed that an after-school program was essential. He brought the matter to the attention of the Mayor. Lee won an annual appropriation of $38,000 for a year-round school-based program financed jointly by the Redevelopment Authority and the New Haven Foundation. Yale student volunteers helped supplement the staff's after-school activities with weekly courses in poetry, science and economics for gifted fourth, fifth and sixth graders. A guidance counselor and social workers were added to the school staff. Dixwell Community House added a job placement office. Teenagers and their parents kept Winchester's gym and meeting rooms busy at night. During the summer, a day camp was run for children.

By 1962, the delinquency rate in Dixwell, although still highest in the city, had actually dropped. But much more needed to be done. The director of the after-school program observed, "One can't find peace of mind to recreate when job opportunities aren't available and the boy or girl has no qualifications for them." To dropouts, the "crime schools" on Dixwell Avenue were more attractive than public school. Because broken families and families without a male head were so numerous, family programs conducted by various agencies in Dixwell were ineffective in reaching fathers or the boys.

DEVELOPING THE PLAN

Still, without the clean modern school and its extended community program, Dixwell would no doubt have disintegrated further. There is "no organized activity unless stimulated," reported Eunice and George Grier in their study of the community. The Redevelopment Agency had to appoint neighborhood leaders to work with its staff member on the renewal plan.

Some residents objected that this Renewal Council only represented the "elite"—teachers, professionals, ministers and businessmen; that it was "handpicked by downtown" in the old New Haven tradition. But there was serious question whether it was possible for a Renewal Council in Dixwell to truly represent the community. While Wooster Square was homogeneous, Dixwell was heterogeneous, its residents running the gamut from upper-class teachers and professionals, to retired domestics, to unemployed, uneducated day laborers. There were differences of opinion and problems of communication in Dixwell between the leaders whom the city recognized and the "man on the street" who might be displaced by renewal as well as the housing project tenants. Few among the latter two groups attended the Renewal Council meetings held at Winchester School, although the sessions were open. Even when their background inclined them to participate, most people had no energy or time for civic activity.

As the survey of community attitudes by Louis Harris Associates found, the dream of many Dixwell renters was to own a home with green grass where they could raise flowers—the suburbs. Only 50 per cent of those surveyed expressed a desire to stay in Dixwell. On the other hand, families living in public housing apartments, some of them relocatees from slums, expressed their desire for "more projects like this here . . . or we would stay in dirty rooming houses all our lives . . . This is real living. . . ."

Developing a renewal plan acceptable to the community was

exceptionally difficult without a stable population, representative leadership and community consensus. As meetings progressed, a split became apparent between the Council majority and some of the elderly owners of substandard residences who would have to spend money on rehabilitation to meet minimum code standards.

The main change proposed in the renewal plan was a limited redevelopment project in the heart of Dixwell. This would clear the six worst blocks around Dixwell Avenue and put there a handsome town center with a landscaped open plaza surrounded by shops and new garden apartments. It was hoped that the center would give the neighborhood the physical focus it lacked before, as well as a new amenity. Present merchants would have priority to relocate in the plaza, but since the proposed clearance would remove a number of small stores along Dixwell Avenue, it was hoped that some of the crime dens that flourished in the back rooms would be permanently eliminated.

The Renewal Council was eager to destroy the Dixwell image, to improve it so that people would not rush away as soon as they could afford to, and so that, in time, white families would move in. They approved a plan to construct in Dixwell only 200 new units of housing, all of them private, around the plaza. Council members were evidently not too concerned that most of the 500 families to be displaced by scheduled slum demolition could not afford the new housing. They were eager to reduce the neighborhood's dense congestion, and, like the city planners, felt that Dixwell, with one third of its present dwelling units public, had enough of these subsidized low-cost dwellings.

Some committee members urged still more demolition, and more new private housing. One man, a lawyer, proposed that all of Dixwell be bulldozed in order to stamp out its name and reputation. The final plan assumed that the 500 units of public housing scheduled to be built in other neighborhoods by the Housing Authority would take care of the Dixwell relocation problem.

Still, many deteriorated dwellings that seemed past salvage were to be saved and rehabilitated. The average Dixwell family's low income and large size made a larger relocation load appear virtually insoluble to the agency. Also, people in other parts of

New Haven were starting to react against the city's growing and spreading Negro population, and some blamed relocation. The existing housing supply in Dixwell would somehow have to serve present residents better.

When the $14,000,000 renewal plan received preliminary federal approval in 1960, a meeting was held to announce it to the residents. A capacity crowd jammed Winchester's auditorium and even cheered the Mayor, although he told them many would be inconvenienced. At last, they apparently felt, something was being done to improve their community. At the public hearings on the plan, some Dixwell church leaders objected that the plan didn't go far enough in "human values." One Renewal Council member subsequently said, "The new plaza is fine, but that's not the renewal we've been looking for. We want changes in people."

IS REHABILITATION FEASIBLE?

To encourage rehabilitation and provide property owners with technical assistance, a field office like that in Wooster Square was established. According to the study Rapkin conducted for New Haven, rehabilitation would be "economically feasible and indeed attractive" for many in Dixwell: FHA mortgage insurance was available to property owners for this purpose in renewal areas, with lower interest rates and a longer period of amortization than conventional loans. Such government-backed rehabilitation would actually lighten the monthly housing expenses of many owners who were burdened by heavy mortgage loans—although they would have to spend more on property improvement. Costly short-term mortgages could be refinanced with the thirty-year loans and lower carrying charges offered in a special FHA renewal section. Moreover, owners could offer tenants much better living accommodations for only a few dollars more a month, he pointed out.

For some Dixwell owners, renewal proved to be a lifesaver. "We no longer have to milk the property to feed ourselves," stated one young father, who had previously been staggering under a series of costly short-term mortgages which encumbered the big three-apartment house in which he lived. Other people were able to buy a home for the first time using the liberal mortgage terms now available.

But the success of the Dixwell rehabilitation program from the start was due to several special situations. The local FHA insuring office was more liberal than many, and was willing to take greater risks in issuing long-term government rehabilitation insurance. Probably even more important was the financial assistance from the Federal National Mortgage Association,* which took the permanent loans on all these FHA-insured mortgages. Fortunately, Congress had foreseen such contingencies in authorizing FNMA to take these loans. The Dixwell project director stated that in the early stages, "Without 'Fanny Mae,' [FNMA] we'd have no rehabilitation program."

New Haven's banks had not yet changed their minds about the Dixwell area, despite renewal. They apparently did not have faith in the promised public improvements to change the area, and most of the people were so marginal that they were still poor credit risks for loans. Indeed, when the Dixwell rehabilitation program began, during the 1961 recession, unemployment was three times as high among Negroes in New Haven as among whites.

But it was difficult for the staff to gain cooperation in the rehabilitation drive even among those who were employed. Communication in the neighborhood was poor, and residents had little money. Many greeted the neighborhood representative with suspicion, and even hostility, although he was a long-time Dixwell resident. Nor was it possible to tell some who had paid more for a property than it was worth that an extra investment would increase their home's net value. For the many poor and aging homeowners whose properties were free and clear, but substandard, the long-range FHA improvement loans would add a burden, as would code inspection. There was also a question whether they could afford maintenance of the property once it was improved due to declining income or no income.

James Mitchell, neighborhood representative and president of the Dixwell Community Council (which had been revived with

* See Chapter 6.

the city's help), openly appealed to racial pride and a better future for Dixwell's children to win cooperation.

By working twice as hard and even more slowly, the Dixwell renewal staff was able to obtain only half as much rehabilitation per structure as in Wooster Square—an average of $2,800—just to bring remaining properties up to code standards. Few in Dixwell could spend extra money on beautifying, nor was there anything of architectural interest to refurbish. As the program advanced, it seemed doubtful that the sympathetic FHA office would issue long-term loans for some of the "junk" scheduled for rehabilitation. Many more structures would have to be cleared. To obtain code compliance on some absentee-owned properties, orders had to be issued by the field inspectors. Within a year after the rehabilitation program started, the Redevelopment Agency expressed concern that the code minimum might never be fully enforced in Dixwell.

By the end of 1965, only half of the Dixwell properties had been rehabilitated. The Redevelopment Agency stated that neighborhood rehabilitation is not a five-year program, as the federal urban renewal agency held it to be. Also, New Haven felt that to encourage rehabilitation with so much demolition and reconstruction going on across the street from homes was not wise. As physical change becomes apparent, people are much more willing to invest in fixing up their homes. (For cases where properties had been over-financed, the agency policy was to wait until owners' equity increased.)

Local bankers were making property improvement loans in Dixwell, some even without FHA mortgage insurance. In part, the same thing that happened in Wooster Square occurred in Dixwell; the bankers had to be shown. As the worst slums were cleared, some private rehabilitation took place, and construction of new housing began, Dixwell's appearance began to improve, and the bankers who had previously written off the area began to reevaluate it. Another favorable and important factor was the altered employment picture in metropolitan New Haven and in incomes in Dixwell. With the war in Vietnam escalating, the area's big aviation plants were so pressed to fill defense orders that they were recruiting in downtown New Haven, and the city was enjoying the lowest unemployment rate in ten years—under 3 per cent. As local positions opened up to lower-skilled workers, and as new federally financed job training programs equipped young men in Dixwell and other inner-city areas to fill these jobs, many families' incomes increased—and with this, they were able to finance home rehabilitation.

More of Dixwell's moderate- and low-income residents could be rehoused in the neighborhood than anticipated when the Dixwell plan was approved because the new federal housing programs had since become available. A number of developments were under way, with FHA's 221 (d)3 providing the financing basis for the first two cooperatives. The larger of them, the Florence Virtue Houses, a handsome 129-unit low-rise development sponsored by the Dixwell Congregational Church and designed by architect John Johansen, was occupied. The other, a group of townhouses undertaken by the Human Relations Council, would soon be open. Two other similar projects with 188 units were in the planning stage.

The Redevelopment Agency has worked with these inexperienced housing sponsors as a "partner"—advising on architectural and building plans, pushing projects through FHA, sometimes suggesting revisions. It makes sure that the housing gets built and that the design of new housing and facilities will be outstanding. The agency also acquired a block of Dixwell slum row houses, had them privately renovated as in Wooster Square's Court Street, and sold apartments to purchasers who availed themselves of (d)3's low-cost mortgages. With the new housing and other improvements, old Dixwell was becoming hard to recognize.

More poor families could also live in Dixwell because of new, more-acceptable low-rent housing programs. The Housing Authority built a sixty-six-unit high-rise building for the elderly, and with the help of the Redevelopment Agency, it also acquired five houses to accommodate nine very large families that could not be fitted into conventional project apartments. For other hard-to-house poor families, the city was anticipating use of rent supplements authorized in the Housing and Urban Development Act of 1965. It had explored the new approach under a federal demonstration grant, and applied for such assistance for 200 families, to be used in Dixwell and elsewhere. A number of low-income Dixwell owners would also be able to afford rehabilitation now with the federal grants of $1,500 authorized for families earning less than $3,000.

Much remained to be constructed—two new churches, a new lodge for the Elks, and the important civic-shopping plaza. But the "new" Dixwell, helped by the changes in its physical environment and many improvements in neighborhood services and community involvement, was already a showcase area for renewal. It had even achieved a considerable degree of integration at Florence Virtue Houses. The white tenants, about 45 per cent of the tenancy, were mostly married graduate students from Yale. The Redevelopment Authority had promoted the excellent housing values of the project among University people.

THE MIDDLE GROUND

In the late 1950's, with Dixwell's renewal about to begin, there still spread out around the core the rest of the city's aging neighborhoods—the Hill (then New Haven's second "Little Italy"), Dwight, Newhallville and Fair Haven.

Forty per cent of the city's dwellings stood in this middle-ground area. Built before the automobile, some in the post-Civil War era, some for affluent owners, they were now dark and uninviting, and their livability was on the wane. Most were more modest frame structures, now two- or three-family houses occupied by lower-middle class and working people; a little over half were lived in by their owners. Shabby exteriors gave evidence of chronic failure to maintain properties; plumbing and wiring were old-fashioned and inadequate. New, low-income tenants were misusing the premises.

Decades of liberal zoning variances, a depression-time mortgage ban and conversion by speculators of some of the old mansions into rooming houses had blighted these areas. Residential streets, dense with bumper-to-bumper parking in front of homes without garages or driveways, were also crowded by through-traffic. Playgrounds and parks were almost nonexistent; the newest school had been constructed before 1910. Juvenile delinquency, a sure sign of weak community life, was on the rise. Health problems were also growing, as were the needs of the increasingly elderly population living there.

For many residents these neighborhoods had distinct advantages. Old-timers had friends and institutions there. Shops were within walking distance; employment nearby; rentals modest. Many newcomers found the best housing there that they had ever had.

These were the unexciting, classic, middle-aged neighborhoods, the "transition" areas which, if ignored, would deteriorate into slums. Federal urban renewal assistance was necessary to improve these neighborhoods adequately. A holding operation would have to be devised until more federal money became available, Logue realized back in 1958.

About that time, Howard Hallman, a political scientist who had just modernized Philadelphia's housing code and enforcement machinery, visited the Development Office. Logue wanted him to work for New Haven, and invented a program for him—"The Middle Ground." In October 1959, the Board of Aldermen adopted Hallman's program and appropriated a budget to staff a new Division of Neighborhood Improvement.

Until more renewal funds became available, the main way the city could help the middle-ground neighborhoods, beyond enforcement of housing code standards, was to improve the performance in those areas of regular departments, agencies and boards, and to make small public investments.

City government is not monolithic, Hallman knew. Usually, old-line agencies go about business—or politics—as usual, their operations often failing to support, or even clashing with, neighborhood improvement efforts. The Buildings Department, for instance, would hand out permits which met its requirements, but these might go against the housing code, which was administered then by the Health Department. To counteract such clashes, and to keep down illegal conversions, the Development Office endeavored to coordinate and use all the city's licensing powers together.

Probably the most flagrant example of neighborhood erosion by local government agencies was New Haven's independent and politically motivated Board of Zoning Appeals. The city's planning staff was revising the old zoning ordinance, but as long as the Board of Appeals continued to grant variances which clashed with renewal, the new code would mean little. Seeds of blight would be sown in still good neighborhoods, as had happened in the past, and middle-ground residents could not be assured that industrial intrusions would end.

Lee had to ask the members of the zoning board to resign. The Mayor then appointed to the board public-spirited citizens whose philosophy was in accord with city improvement, rather than appeasing special interests.

Many regular city departments generally acted only on complaints from political wheels or the more articulate residents. This system worked against older working-class and low-income neighborhoods, despite their greater need. To win better public services for their constituents, political representatives would have to go to city department heads, or directly to the legislative body which voted budgets. But a ward politician's connections in the top administration are usually weak, and legislators are not moved unless residents organize and can exert sufficient pressure.

Lower-class neighborhoods have not been particularly effective at making their collective voice heard, however; usually their residents have personal needs (such as jobs, legal aid and other favors) of more immediate importance. The politician must use his limited time and political leverage to satisfy his constituents' personal needs ahead of their communal desires, which are thus often ignored.

On the other hand, residents of middle- and upper-class neighborhoods have little personal need of political favors and have considerable organizational ability. One of the few ways a local politician can serve them is by seeing that their neighborhoods receive better municipal services and facilities. Thus, as city funds are limited, departments tend to skimp on poorer neighborhoods, a fact which contributes materially to the latter's decline.

Changing this traditional mode of operation was a major aim of the middle-ground efforts. "City agencies need a sense of program instead of complaint," Hallman believed. "Departments must plan with the people in these neighborhoods to make improvements they want."

Field offices were set up in middle-ground neighborhoods, as in Wooster Square and Dixwell. Housing code inspection was administered from these, and staff helped residents organize committees that met with city department representatives. As a result of their complaints, street trees were planted, broken sidewalks mended, benches were provided for mothers and play space for children. In the area to be designated next for Title I, the Hill, the director of traffic and parking met with the resident council and helped devise a plan for off-street parking and traffic diversions to be carried out as part of renewal; this let the neighborhood live with, instead of being eroded by, the automobile.

By demonstrating City Hall's faith in the future of these middle-aged neighborhoods, the administration gave owners sufficient confidence for over $1,000,000 to be spent on property improvements in the first two years before Title I designation.

IV. HUMAN DEVELOPMENT

THE END OF THE LINE

Such municipal action in the middle-ground areas was essential, but not enough. For those areas experienced the big population changes of the 1950's most acutely.

New Haven's population had dropped from 167,000 at the start of the decade to 152,000 in 1960. But this figure did not indicate the full extent and special character of the defection from the city. Some 30,000 whites had left New Haven proper, most of them young families going to the suburbs. White families remaining in middle-ground neighborhoods were older and smaller. An unpublished survey by Yale sociologist August Hollingshead of a large sample of young couples who married between 1948 and 1950 disclosed that only one out of eight interviewed wanted to remain in the city. They wanted single-family detached homes instead of New Haven's two- and three-family structures; they wanted more land; and they wanted better schools.

At the same time, their former residences were being occupied (and overcrowded) more and more by non-white families, frequently of lower class or income, as New Haven's Negro population increased from 9,605 to 22,500 during the decade. Newhallville, for example, was 5 per cent Negro in 1950, most of them middle-class homeowning families. By 1960, as Dixwell burst out into this neighboring district, Newhallville was 50 per cent Negro, many of them low-income renters. Racial change was apparent also in the Dwight area, along State Street and on the Hill.

In these changing neighborhoods the self-fulfilling prophecy of neighborhood deterioration had begun to work. Landlords, more of them absentee, did less. Speculators stepped up activities. New owners, buying on expensive short terms, lacked the means or knowledge to maintain properties.

In spite of the Neighborhood Improvement program, the level of city services was also slipping. The garbage collector and policeman looked down on these racially changing areas. Hallman had difficulty persuading even his housing code inspectors to use the same standards in Newhallville as elsewhere. "They thought because it was Negro, it should be lower." This worked against the basic philosophy that city services should favor such areas, and Hallman had to educate his field representatives.

But there was some truth behind the attitudes expressed by the municipal employees. Many of the newcomers did have lower standards. In spite of a doubled inspection staff, overcrowding continued, as many families were larger or took in boarders. Nor was it possible to persuade some landlords to improve properties after they saw the habits of some new tenants. Even dauntless Relocation Director Al Mermin found it difficult to convince landlords that some families he was trying to place would not wreck the properties.

The changing population was most apparent in the public schools. There, enrollment had actually increased from 20,234 to 21,028 during the decade, in spite of the total drop in the city's population. Negroes comprised only 14 per cent of the city's overall population, but their children made up 20 per cent of the public school population by 1960. Five schools were already 75 to 90 per cent Negro; three others were moving up to 75 per cent. Teachers were concerned with socially unacceptable behavior; lack of response to conventional classroom approaches; poor communication skills; poor attendance; much greater potential than achievement; cultural deprivation. They were worried and often demoralized by the extremely high turnover. The districts of the two new high schools had been quietly divided to bring about racial integration with the same number of Negro students in each, but still 60 per cent of the city's dropouts were non-white. The students also presented new health problems.

The new population's problems and implications for renewal and the future of the city troubled Development Administrator Logue. But no agency appeared ready to improvise and take on new programs to help them.

New Haven has had a history of leadership in social work and philanthropy. But its social agencies were behind the times, fragmented and understaffed due to lack of funds. Relocation had found them shockingly unresponsive. "Put them in public housing" was the solution the private agencies proposed for the misfits of Oak Street. The Community Council, the organization charged by the United Fund with planning for the city's overall health, welfare and recreation needs, had not yet taken cognizance of the newcomers' problems. The political parties were also out of touch with their growing constituency.

At first Logue felt that forming an Urban League, to enroll the city's business community in solving the employment problems of the growing non-white population, would be an answer. But it seemed almost impossible to find responsible leadership. School principal Wexler, as chairman of the CAC's Committee on Human Values, could not arouse civic action. Businessmen seemed uncomfortable and unconcerned when Wexler talked about the Negroes' difficulties, integration or middle-income housing. They expressed skepticism when he explained the multi-faceted causes for the disturbing rise in juvenile delinquency. Many people in New Haven took the "inoculation" approach, proposing curfews and punishment to stop juvenile crime. The attitude of the Board of Education toward the increased number of sixteen-to-twenty-one-year-olds out of school and work was "They had their opportunity; they didn't take advantage of it." The community would not give up its nineteenth-century philanthropic do-goodery and Yankee do-it-yourself attitude to confront the facts.

As was happening more and more in New Haven, new assignments kept devolving to city government. Within two years of his arrival, Hallman found himself deeply involved, at the behest of Development Administrator Logue, in devising a comprehensive plan to cope with the social problems of the middle-ground areas and the unfinished business of Oak Street, Wooster Square and Dixwell.

THE FACTS OF LIFE

Meanwhile, several new functions were introduced into existing departments. The Mayor, at the urging of human relations groups in the city, set up an official "human relations" position, a general euphemism for Negro relations. What was significant is that the new man—appointed to the staff of Development Administrator Logue, who also stood strong on civil rights—recognized the broader dimensions of the job.

Pittsburgher Richard Dowdy was an economist * who had worked for the Pittsburgh Urban League. Dowdy knew that most Negroes were unable to take advantage of Connecticut anti-discrimination laws or local opportunities, in both housing and employment. Some lacked information, others preparation, others were apathetic or cynical. Dowdy was concerned primarily with devising programs to help them help themselves, above all in the employment field.

To awaken New Haven to the growing problem and the need for a local Urban League to help make the new population self-sufficient, Dowdy worked up a fact sheet. It revealed the great incidence of dependency among New Haven's Negroes: they comprised more than 52 per cent of the city's welfare caseload, and received a disproportionate amount of the total spent by public and private social agencies. But this dependency, the sheet also pointed out, was largely a result of discrimination and limited employment opportunities, which were also causing some able Negroes to leave New Haven. The fact sheet also indicated the far-reaching negative effect on occupants of the substandard housing in which so many Negroes had to live. It warned that the past decade's increase in New Haven's Negro population to 14 per cent was only the start; within the foreseeable future, they would comprise 20 per cent or more.

* Dowdy attracted national publicity in the early 1950's when a national corporation headquartered in Chicago planned to hire him for a managerial position, until it learned he was a Negro.

This information was presented to the Community Council by a committee of fifty community leaders whom Dowdy organized. The statistics warranted a prominent story in the *Register*, and stirred up bewildered, socially minded white citizens. "What I would like to know is just what the Urban League can do in a city this size that is not already being done by existing agencies and citizen groups . . ." demanded one in a letter to the editor enumerating the many social, civic, religious and educational agencies in Dixwell. This citizen and others suggested that if more were done for Negroes, their will to solve their own problems would be jeopardized.

The article also angered some of the city's middle- and upper-class Negroes who, said Dowdy, "move out and forget what they left behind." But it provided a springboard for some of his self-help programs. An unpublicized luncheon club for Dixwell leaders, resident and nonresident, began meeting weekly to talk over problems of the Negro community and their solutions. A six-week Leadership Institute for underdeveloped talent was established in Dixwell. The Dixwell Community Council was revived, with renewal neighborhood representative James Mitchell as the city-paid president. The Council sponsored an all-day health clinic at Winchester School and planned other community and school improvement activities. Two Dixwell churches considered sponsorship of nonprofit housing cooperatives to be built as part of the neighborhood renewal. Visits were exchanged with the Hill's renewal council.

Things were starting to move in other parts of the city during 1961. Led by the head of the Yale Divinity School, business and civic leaders formed an Urban League. A Mayor's Committee on Job Opportunities was appointed by Lee to help use new state funds for job retraining. The Council on Social Agencies secured a foundation grant to support a two-pronged program in public housing. Part went for intensive casework with "hopeless" multi-problem families; the rest was to help passive tenants at one project organize to make their wishes felt and change the management's "property custodian" attitude. As a result, shabby tot-lots in that project were restored to usefulness with mothers' help; tenants published a newspaper; deserted community rooms were put back into use for crafts and sewing. "There *is* leadership in the projects," the director of the Social Agencies Council observed, "but it's Negro. The whites are low down on the scale. The Negro has the ability, but he's kept from using it to full advantage due to discrimination."

The city also initiated a Homemaking Service, to reach people who moved from slums to better housing. "Homemakers" were placed in the Dixwell and central relocation offices, in public housing projects, Hallman's Neighborhood Improvement program and the Welfare Department. They offered not only housekeeping advice, but also instruction in child care, nutrition, family budgeting and, if special problems were evident, referred families to the proper social agency.

A STRATEGY EMERGES

Such efforts all helped. But had there not been several more fundamental changes, New Haven might still be applying poultices to new sores which kept erupting, or just be treading water.

A strategy and the means for meeting comprehensively the city's growing social needs began to emerge in 1960, out of the separate responsibilities and thinking of two creative sources that flourished in the Lee administration.

Development Administrator Logue was charged with preparation of the annual capital budget. He kept receiving requests for funds to rehabilitate old schools, most of them located in the inner core, or to put additions onto buildings that should have been torn down. This seemed like throwing good money after bad.

The city's patched-up educational plant was probably even older and more neglected than its housing stock, and more in need of replacement. Nine buildings still in use were described as outmoded in a 1909 report; one of twelve elementary schools built before 1900 was about to celebrate its centennial. Since the late 1920's, when the city's tax base and credit had started to collapse, almost nothing had been done to renew the school plant. Lee's predecessor ran for office on a platform of better schools and higher teachers' salaries, and had ordered a professional survey which tagged the old schools for replacement. But he had acted on only three, one—Winchester—under pressure. Pupils in many schools still studied at broken seats and desks, used outdoor sanitary facilities, studied in dimly lit rooms. Most schools lacked equipment or space for modern science and language instruction.

The majority of people in the inner city, whether long-time residents or newcomers, had never been education-minded. Many had not entered the buildings for decades; some not at all. They were as accustomed to the drab old schools as to their shabby homes. Some had a sentimental attachment to schools they attended as children. Many sent their youngsters to parochial schools.

Their ideas about recreation facilities were also outmoded. The new Conte School in Wooster Square was proposed by the Development Office, and the community service concept—with a library branch, a swimming pool to be used evenings by both youths and adults, as well as attractive meeting rooms for committees or social activities—had evolved with relatively little participation by the renewal committee. (When completed, however, the school proved a major drawing card for middle-class families.)

But as standards in education advanced during the postwar years, and as subject matter and teaching methods changed in wealthier suburbs and required new facilities, the backwardness and inflexibility of the old, ill-equipped New Haven school plant became more and more of a deficit.

"It was obvious as you looked at the city," Logue observed, "that if you were going to be competitive with the suburbs, you had to have stable residential neighborhoods, and these could not be achieved without a good school system, both physically and educationally. But new schools would not be a prudent investment in neighborhoods which had slum housing and whose young families were moving out as they advanced. You had to have renewal and new schools together."

Thus it seemed that creating the best possible schools would vitalize the city's old-fashioned middle-ground neighborhoods—where the oldest schools were located—and make these areas attractive for young families. These schools would be not only places for children to study, but also centers for their communities, serving many different people's needs.

As always, financing was a problem. All the middle-ground neighborhoods required renewal, and eventually all could become eligible for Title I aid. With such federal renewal assistance, the city could build a modern educational plant in its older areas at greatly reduced local costs.* Before a large-scale replacement program was undertaken, Logue believed that a fresh evaluation of school needs was in order. There had been great population shifts since the 1947 survey. Moreover, no building program could be forwarded without the cooperation of the New Haven Board of Education; new educational techniques and philosophy, as well as the larger potential role of the schools in the central city, had to be considered.

BREAKTHROUGH IN THE SCHOOLS

Fortunately, a slow-burning revolution was beginning to ignite within the school board, one which would complement Logue's renewal philosophy and provide the springboard for a major new local undertaking.

The schools' physical decay was a visible symptom of the less obvious but even more debilitating administrative and professional decay that had eroded public education in New Haven. Lee, during his first year as Mayor, visited every classroom and, as ex-officio on the school board, observed its inner workings.

What he saw shocked him deeply. Not only had previous administrations criminally neglected the school plant; they had also played politics with the system, with disastrous results. The city's 1,000 teachers—the largest single body of municipal employees—had come to be regarded primarily as voters and opinion-makers for the party in power, rather than as molders of young minds. Jobs were used as patronage, and appointments controlled

* In Wooster Square, some $1,400,000 was saved by the city in acquiring the built-up six-acre tract for the Conte School: the federal agency absorbed almost the entire high cost of clearing the land—which was some $240,000 an acre—and allowed the city to buy it for re-use value appropriate for a modern one-story school at $10,000 an acre. In turn, the new combined school-community center itself made up a major part of the local non-cash contribution of the total project cost, which the city could split with the state. Thus, one local dollar spent on the school earned another dollar from the state, and these in turn earned four federal dollars for other neighborhood improvements.

by the political machines. Promotions to positions of responsibility in the school system were made on the basis of party loyalty, not ability.

Appointment to the Board of Education, a prerogative of the Mayor's, was a prestige symbol, not an assignment for hard work. Beyond attending board meetings, its conservative members were apparently too busy for school affairs. Generally, their decisions rubber-stamped recommendations of the Superintendent, who built his own empire within the system. Economy was the only apparent principle guiding their decisions. Teachers' salaries, ranging from $2,800 to a $5,000 ceiling, were among the lowest in the state and hardly calculated to attract able people.

To compound matters, as young white families migrated to the suburbs, citizen pressures for good education weakened. Along with the families went good teachers and administrators. Practically the only exceptions were New Haven's two remaining upper-middle-class neighborhoods, whose parents would not tolerate bad teaching. Since they were citywide opinion makers, the Board catered to them. Parochial schools absorbed a steadily larger number of the city's predominantly Roman Catholic pupils. Other remaining middle-class families, if they could afford it, sent their children to the city's excellent private schools, or away to boarding school after the early years. The new migration presented a challenge that the system was not even prepared to recognize.

Lee immediately used his powers as Mayor both to rehabilitate some of the most neglected schools and to alter the school board's composition. The old system was deeply entrenched, and the four-year terms of the seven members of the Board overlapped. The Mayor could make only two appointments for several years. He selected Yale English professor Maynard Mack and Connecticut CIO-AFL Council president Mitchell Sviridoff. Both were strong men with high standards and goals for the system. But they were still in the minority when in 1955, the majority of the Board decided to award a five-year contract to the incumbent Superintendent.

The Lee forces did not gain control until November 1960. The change was signaled by the Board's election then of forty-four-year-old Sviridoff as its chairman. Sviridoff is one of the remarkable products of the depression years, an intellectual who could not afford to attend college but received most of his higher education in the challenging labor movement of the 1930's. He made his mark early as a union leader. A brilliant organizer, an articulate, skilled negotiator and a tireless worker, he organized and then became head of the state's largest union at twenty-four and of the Connecticut CIO at twenty-seven. As a state mediator, Sviridoff was equally popular with management and labor. And when the CIO and AFL merged nationally, his leadership in Connecticut was the key to a relatively peaceful merging in the state of the two bodies, whose head he then became.

The labor leader was one of Lee's principal backers in 1953, and became one of his closest advisors in office. The Mayor, impressed by Sviridoff's unusual abilities and grasp of issues, early drafted him into serving the city, as a member of the CAC executive committee and of the school board. Sviridoff recalls, "Dick Lee got me, as he did others, excited about New Haven and the importance and potential of the city. He started a whole chain reaction of new ideas and projects. Equally important, he opened doors and let you do things."

Like Lee, Sviridoff was appalled by the schools. A far-sighted labor leader, he was more keenly aware than professional educators of the new demands placed on public schools by changing manpower requirements, and by the deficits of the present urban population. "Education is the nerve center of a city," he believed. "The central city school system must dilute the effect of the new migration. But it must also strengthen the college-oriented. That's the way to bring back the middle-class—or to create one."

In many cities, when the programs of two major municipal empires such as the school system and urban renewal converge, they are apt to clash, waste time and energy, and divide the public while they jockey for their respective positions. Fortunately, Logue and Sviridoff went forward together.

Even before becoming president of the school board, Sviridoff had used his growing influence in that body to win support in 1960 for a $40,000 comprehensive study of New Haven's schools to be undertaken by Dr. Cyril Sargent, then director of the Harvard Graduate School of Education. Significantly, the study was done for the Redevelopment Agency *and* Board of Education together. The combined knowledge and plans of both agencies were indispensable to this study, the first in the country to fully consider school building requirements in the light of a central city's new needs. The Development Office could advise Sargent on the major land use changes it had scheduled for neighborhoods where schools requiring replacement were located; it could tell him about the neighborhoods for which he was planning; and, because the agency knew what housing was scheduled for renewal areas and was enforcing occupancy standards, it could also minimize the typical inner-city situation of both underutilized and overcrowded schools. A Citizens' Advisory Committee was appointed to review the evolving program.

THE SARGENT PLAN

"Equalizing educational opportunities for all children" was the basic goal enunciated by the Sargent report. Its proposals, which included abandoning fourteen old schools and spending $20,000,000 for rebuilding the below-high-school system, also opened wide the potential of New Haven's school plant for the community at large.

Sargent proposed that elementary schools go only through fourth grade, and be small and close to home. Ten new intermediate, or community schools, would go through eighth grade, draw on broader neighborhoods and offer special facilities for science, art and foreign language instruction. They would also serve as neighborhood centers, similar to the Conte and Winchester schools, with meeting rooms for adults, athletic and recreation facilities for both school and community use, and classes for vocational and professional improvement for adults. Extra space would be provided in these buildings for decentralized city services such as health, preventive medicine, social services and others required by a neighborhood. Unspoken, but understood, was that these schools would be located to increase racial integration.

The Sargent report also spelled out the savings, about $7,000,000, that the city could realize by coordinating the proposed school building program with federally assisted neighborhood renewal. Without this sharing, or without a substantial tax increase, New Haven might not be able to absorb the $20,000,000 cost in a reasonable time.

The implications of the Sargent proposal for the future of New Haven were so profound that the members of the new Board of Education wanted to gain real public understanding. No public referendum was required for the $13,000,000 school bond issue, but a public hearing was scheduled for the first time in the Board's history.

Between publication of the Sargent report in March and the hearing in May of 1961, the Board members conducted an intensive information campaign, talking with some sixty different community organizations and an estimated 6,000 people.

Sviridoff himself took on the Rotary, the Taxpayers' Association, and the Manufacturers' Division of the Chamber of Commerce. The latter gathering probably marked the first time that a New Haven labor leader had sat down to talk with local businessmen about civic matters. Sviridoff made clear that better education was necessary if high school graduates were to be trainable for new industrial jobs, and thus won the group's interest in the proposal.

At the public hearing, the manufacturers' spokesman testified for the bond issue, bringing out the need to update schools if the city wanted to attract competent management and scientific personnel. A crowd of 1,500 overflowed the auditorium of Hillhouse High that evening, and some had to listen to the proceedings over loudspeakers in adjoining rooms. A hand vote showed that only about fifteen in the entire assemblage opposed the ambitious program. In August, the Board of Aldermen unanimously passed the school bond issue.

The building program broke the educational dam. When people started muttering that new schools alone would not improve instruction, the Board and city administration were delighted. Now, they felt, the public would be receptive to the long overdue rise in teachers' pay. Salaries were scheduled to double by 1963, making the range of $4,800 to $8,000 competitive with suburban systems. These and other significant increases in the school budget under the Lee administration (for supplies, books, repairs, guidance programs, and other across-the-board increases) contributed substantially to a four-mill rise in the local tax rate. Better education required greater expenditures—even more than the current tax rise would permit, it soon became clear.

A countrywide search for a new Superintendent began, and a task force of teachers and citizen leaders conducted an intensive study of curriculum problems and teaching in urban schools. Its report displayed a rare candor in recognizing the changed level of students attending New Haven schools and the differential needs and goals that existed between pupils in different neighborhoods. Its recommendations emphasized new programs both to reduce educational disparities and to encourage excellence. Another citizen-teacher committee studied ways of bringing schools that were not to be replaced up to modern physical standards, and a consultant was retained by the school board to analyze the system's administrative structure.

But many of the task force's proposals could not be implemented for lack of funds. If the community schools were also to be neighborhood centers, as proposed in the Sargent report and accepted in principle by the school board, they, too, would require additional staff.

That such staffed neighborhood centers were badly needed was pointed up by a citywide survey of recreational needs conducted by the CAC. It disclosed that leisure time was a problem for New Haven's youth and for the elderly. The 6,500 youngsters queried expressed a desire for places to get together—for "drop-in" centers, better athletic facilities and more after-school cultural activities. The survey also revealed that for the city's older people—who formed 11.6 per cent of the population by 1960 compared to 9.3 at the start of the 1950's—time hung heavy and failing health was a problem.

New resources were needed, and much better use had to be made of existing ones. Indeed, those in the city who were analyzing unmet needs compared with current efforts saw that while various programs and projects were being carried out under an assortment of public and private auspices, most agencies were viewing the same pathologies from different narrow angles and trying to meet them with special-purpose programs. A more coordinated and comprehensive approach, instead of scattered attacks, was required. The new community schools could provide bases from which such a coordinated effort could be operated in each neighborhood in a close-to-the-people fashion.

The Ford Foundation was then trying to interest a number of cities in developing new programs for human resources in their "gray areas" by offering grants, to be matched locally. New Haven, never shy about approaching potential sources of funds, had been in touch with the Foundation's Public Affairs Program about a leisure-time program, which had not sparked their interest. But the Foundation, impressed by the schools' reorganization, did encourage the imaginative and comprehensive new course that the city was exploring for its gray areas.

This interest stimulated the main organizations and sources in New Haven that could mount such a concerted effort—the Mayor, the Redevelopment Agency, the Board of Education and the Community Council (which had been reorganized after two decades of dormancy)—to get together—at the administration's instigation—and to determine what New Haven needed. The result, by the spring of 1962, was the structuring and funding of a comprehensive human development program to deal with inner-city problems. The program was to be carried out jointly by the New Haven public schools and a new local civic agency created for this purpose, Community Progress Inc.

NEW PATTERNS FOR THE 1960's

Establishment of Community Progress Inc. promised to let New Haven get down to the extra work that central cities of the 1960's must perform for many of their citizens. It would operate in the six crowded inner-city neighborhoods where nearly 80,000 people—some 60 per cent of the New Haven population—lived.* These were also the areas undergoing or slated for federally aided urban renewal. CPI and the new human development program grew out of the city's experience in renewal areas. Officials recognized more and more that the social fabric of the inner city and its physical structure needed strengthening together. For where housing problems existed, a host of other social and economic needs were generally found and were difficult to meet

* This was later expanded to seven neighborhoods with 90,000 people, as the new population and needs spread.

through existing agencies' programs. The city would have to reorient itself and many local institutions to the needs of the present population.

CPI, as the new organization became known, was established as temporary and experimental, with an initial three-year budget of $5,000,000. Half of this was a grant from the Ford Foundation, the major portion being earmarked for education and operation of the new community schools. Requisite matching local funds were ingeniously pooled, primarily from a variety of separate ongoing or potential programs. For example, staff members for youth development programs were available in separate agencies, operating in an uncoordinated manner. Funds for research into juvenile delinquency were available from the U.S. Department of Health, Education and Welfare. The Urban Renewal Administration was already paying neighborhood staff workers whose functions might be given a broader focus. State employment staff and retraining funds were available, but not being used as effectively as they could be. The New Haven Foundation contributed the cash balance of the initial local share.

Community Progress is best known today as New Haven's anti-poverty agency, and it is widely regarded as a national model for the community action instrument required under the federal Economic Opportunity Act of 1964. During 1965, nearly 1,000 government officials, anti-poverty leaders from other cities, representatives of lay and professional organizations and press members visited New Haven to study CPI's operation. In fact, the Ford Foundation's "gray area" programs turned out to be the pilots and proving grounds for much of the subsequent federal anti-poverty legislation. In turn, had the new government funds not come along, the course of CPI would probably have been quite different.

But Community Progress was conceived as, and is, a great deal more than the local instrument to administer and disburse federal anti-poverty funds. The new agency sees itself as a catalyst and coordinator of what might be called "invisible" community renewal—both of people and local institutions. From the start, CPI's avowed goal was to "alter the opportunity structure." It wanted, specifically, to overcome the fragmentation and rigidity of the many local public and private agencies that were narrow in purpose and problem oriented, and to augment their efforts in related opportunity programs to be offered in neighborhoods instead of remote downtown offices.

Jobs, education, housing, use of leisure time and community participation—these were the areas of CPI's particular concern. It hoped to open opportunities in these fields to inner-city residents, and to deal with social problems only as they prevented people from taking advantage of the opportunities. Youth was CPI's chief concern, education the bridge. The community schools were to be the operating base for dealing with local problems, for active recreation and leisure-time activities, for citizen organization meetings, decentralized services and employment programs, as well.

Such an ambitious program required several new kinds of staff jobs. One was that of neighborhood services director, now known as coordinator, who, as a CPI staff person described it, "bridges the gap between people with needs and agencies which are supposed to fill them." Specifically, the coordinator—by 1965 there was one in each of the seven neighborhoods—would be responsible for coordinating social services, encouraging neighborhood organizations and indigenous leadership. A full-time community worker, whose background was similar to the neighborhood, would act as a liaison between residents and programs. He or she would go out and ring doorbells, give assistance to residents in time of trouble, learn their wants and needs, and encourage their use of services and facilities. Another new job category was that of assistant principal for each community school, a twelve-month-a-year job. They would be responsible for developing and supervising the overall program in each of these new kinds of schools, which were to be open and staffed year-round, fourteen hours a day.

Governing Community Progress was a nine-man board, headed by the president of a local bank. It combined both public and private interests. Original members included representatives of the Citizens' Action Commission, Yale University, the Greater New Haven Community Council, the United Fund, the Redevelopment Agency, the Board of Education, plus three appointees of Mayor Lee, who was not a member himself.

The board sought out former school board president Mitchell

Sviridoff to direct the new program. Less than a year before, Sviridoff had left the city and the labor movement to join the Agency of International Development, and he was then based in Washington. But when asked to return to New Haven to head CPI, Sviridoff has recalled, "I couldn't resist it—all the authority and freedom and resources to tackle problems no one has solved, and in the city where you grew up." His right-hand man would be Howard Hallman, who, with city officials, civic leaders and heads of social agencies, had worked out the blueprint for Community Progress, and was now named its deputy director.

CPI started operating in the fall of 1962. As it put program into practice, the organization was and has continued to be pragmatic and evolutionary, expanding as "gaps in service" are demonstrated and new funds become available, or altering its course as original premises prove unsuccessful or impractical. Sviridoff, whose zest and exceptional operational and problem-solving skills set the tone and pace, borrowed a phrase from union days to describe CPI's hard-nosed, building-block approach—"planning on the shop floor."

New Haven's social renewers soon proved themselves as adept as its physical renewers at new program development and execution, and at the closely allied, indispensable, but intricate local art of "federal grantsmanship." (One top CPI staff member calls this "getting the funds from there to here.") At the end of CPI's first three years, nearly $10,000,000, double the original budget, had been expended by or channeled through the new civic agency, and various federal funded acts and agencies * were bearing 67 per cent of the cost. By mid-1965, the Ford Foundation contributed only 17 per cent instead of half—but still a vital sum—allowing Community Progress exceptional flexibility in new program development. Indeed, the Foundation was sufficiently enthusiastic to renew its grant for another three years with $2,500,000 more. The federal bureaucrats, too, appear to like cities that can use their new funds, show results and develop new techniques. As a top official of the Office of Economic Op-

* Labor Department's Manpower Development and Training; Department of Health, Education and Welfare; Juvenile Delinquency Offenses and Control Act; Economic Opportunity Act; special provisions in the 1962 Housing Act.

portunity said, "One of the big problems we have ahead is how to find or produce more Mike Sviridoffs."

By 1965, more than fifty separate programs were under way in New Haven as a consequence of CPI efforts. New Haven had also been made a regional center for training anti-poverty officials. Its neighborhood programs encompassed pre-work remedial instruction for undereducated or illiterate adults; separate, supervised swimming classes for children and mothers; teenage lounges in schools, and a teenage "nightclub" with several hundred dues-paying members, run for and by adolescents; dental, health and x-ray clinics in schools; two store front neighborhood law offices providing free legal aid and counsel; four store front employment centers; a family-centered, eight-agency concerted social services program in the Elm Haven housing project; park maintenance work by unemployed youth in training, one of a series of employment-related programs; "Freddy Fixer" clubs involving 300 young people from ages six to twenty-two in neighborhood fix-up projects; block betterment organizations; adult citizen recreation committees; Golden Age lounges in community schools. Moreover, as these programs proliferated, Community Progress itself became an important local growth industry, employing nearly 200 people, over half of them from the inner city.

TO ACHIEVE RELEVANCE

"Do you know what Community Progress is?" Sviridoff asked a freckle-faced teenager on one of his frequent field visits to the scattered locales of CPI activities. The boy replied, "It's like what you get from heaven. You've got money, and we don't."

In fact, CPI's chief power lies in the foundation and government funds that it has to dispense. It uses these not only to serve inner-city residents directly, but also to encourage meaningful change and greater responsiveness on the part of the established institutions that are supposed to serve them. The phrase Sviridoff used to describe this overall aim is "make the institutions more relevant to the needs of our times."

One way of achieving this goal is to funnel money or extra CPI-paid personnel into institutions or programs. Thus, CPI secured funds to pay the salaries of two extra probation officers who would be attached to the juvenile court but serve where needed, in a field office in the inner city. Similarly, a federal juvenile delinquency grant administered by CPI made it possible to place two special Youth Board members in the Police Department for in-service training. To get employers to modify job requirements in order to hire high school dropouts and youth who may have had a brush with the law, CPI offers federal on-the-job training funds and courses designed cooperatively with the employer by CPI manpower specialists, plus a guarantee of the trainee.

Another tack is to draw personnel from existing institutions into the CPI operation. The Connecticut State Employment Service has placed nine job interviewers from its central New Haven office into CPI's inner-city employment centers. Organized labor participates directly in the manpower effort through the president of the New Haven Central Labor Council, who serves as CPI's labor specialist. Cooperation between separate agencies is encouraged. Full-time liaisons from the Board of Education and the State Employment Service serve in CPI's Manpower Division.

Almost all of CPI's efforts are conducted through or with existing organizations and agencies, so it must use its "club" as diplomatically and realistically as possible, and win support, sooner or later, by performance.

But what particularly distinguishes New Haven's operation from most anti-poverty efforts, and indeed from most community undertakings, is that the various programs are not carried on in isolation. CPI has been working to create a network of inner-city services which strengthen each other. The network concept must be achieved in part at top levels in and with various agencies; but what makes it operational at the base of the pyramid—for the people to be served—are the neighborhood workers. They are the vital links among various Community Progress opportunity programs, on-going services and inner-city residents.

Many of these versatile sub-professional workers—there were nearly fifty in 1965—grew up in the neighborhood where they work, some in the rat-infested, cold-water tenements since eliminated by urban renewal. Many know, either by first-hand experience or association, the rebuffs received because of family background or skin color in the old public school system or employment apparatus. They speak their neighborhood's language, and ignore the clock and weekends, as does Sviridoff. Like him, they are hard-nosed. As one young worker put it, "If we don't buy a program, we won't sell it." Another has described himself and his co-workers as "the trusted souls" of the neighborhoods. "People feel they can talk to us. We aren't government or welfare."

Neighborhood workers do the indispensable job of recruiting for different programs, maintaining personal contacts and conducting follow-ups. They stand on street corners, go to homes, pool halls, grocery stores—wherever people who can take advantage of CPI programs may be found, or where those who have been referred to them might be located. For instance, the schools regularly supply a list of dropouts to their neighborhood employment centers. The workers then go out and contact youngsters in order to interest them in various job training, work-study or employment programs. One result of this cooperative effort during the 1964–65 school year was the registration at neighborhood employment centers of over 70 per cent of the dropouts.

Referrals come from many other bodies in the city. The Relocation Office of the Redevelopment Agency regularly sends each Neighborhood Coordinator a list of people scheduled to move into that area. The workers visit the families, attempt to ascertain which programs would be helpful and try to enroll them. When they come across problems, the workers also refer people to the appropriate agencies.

A big part of their job is listening to people and, in turn, encouraging them. A worker may spend hours at a time and make repeated visits in order to persuade one youngster to sign up for a work-study program, or one reluctant illiterate adult to join a remedial education class. They develop ingenious methods to get people involved. One worker organized a weight-lifting club for the boys in his neighborhood to give him a chance to talk with them about schools and jobs. All workers seem to share the same sense of purpose. As one put it: "We give them the opportunity treatment."

JOBS

Under Sviridoff, the focus of CPI's "opportunity" strategy became, and has remained, fixed on opening up employment opportunities for inner-city residents, especially for the young Negro male. In 1965, employment programs accounted for 36.7 per cent of the CPI budget.

Sviridoff was determined that CPI should be identified in the minds of the people it was serving with success and upward mobility, and believed this meant jobs, especially better jobs. State job training programs, and the federal Manpower Development and Training Act, opened up employment as a major area of activity for CPI. But in order to use the new funds effectively, it was necessary to overcome what Sviridoff called the "flaws in the employment system."

Sviridoff and CPI's top manpower specialist, a former federal labor mediator, early took on the employment situation together. Their approach admirably illustrates the way CPI can cut across old lines and make different needs and various parts of a system, in this case the local economy, more relevant to each other.

Statistics gathered from the Connecticut Department of Labor in 1962 revealed a striking disjuncture in the local job scene. There were 5,500 unemployed in the area, over half of them young, unskilled Negroes; but at the same time 3,500 jobs were open.

Sviridoff looked for ways to wholesale new job openings and dramatically open prestige jobs not previously available to nonwhites, to break through the vicious circle hemming in the young Negro from better employment opportunities. He canvassed several of the growth industries in the metropolitan New Haven–Bridgeport area, major employers and defense contractors like United Aircraft and Avco, to learn their manpower problems. Demand was not for machine operators—blue-collar jobs requiring long apprenticeship and, with rapidly changing technology, promising an uncertain, limited future. Rather the openings were in new middle-skill, white-collar technical jobs, occupations requiring no more than a high school education, basic mathematics and only three to six months' training. Further, these positions were well paid and would continue to expand even if industrial output declined. They would open the way to excellent career opportunities and advancement, if followed up at night school.

Employers, when asked whether they would employ Negroes in these jobs, replied: "You find them and train them; we'll hire them." In fact, they indicated they preferred Negroes. As government defense contractors, they were then feeling the hot breath of the President's Committee on Employment Opportunities. But New Haven's Winchester Division of the Olin Mathieson Chemical Corporation, not a defense contractor, gave the same positive response. The company, which had recently centralized its national research facilities in New Haven, had a number of possible openings. Olin and Avco agreed to participate in three federally financed programs involving fifty trainees.

Community Progress began a pattern of *ad hoc* working committees with employers. The company provided job descriptions; CPI, working with the company, then developed tests to suit particular openings. (In the process a major reason for the State Employment Services locating so few candidates among the unemployed was discovered: many of its evaluation tests were irrelevant.) CPI's neighborhood staff recruited inner-city candidates.

The companies selected seventy-one recruits who passed the new tests with high marks, and soon cooperative eight-week training programs were started at Hillhouse High School and the Eli Whitney Regional Technical School. Two months later, eleven trainees for industrial x-ray technical jobs began work at Avco, with salaries of approximately $100 a week. Three of these trainees had been dropouts; five were Negro; two were former welfare clients. All had been unemployed.

Subsequently, CPI held such meetings with over a dozen major employers in the area—industry, retail, public utilities, colleges and the University and service trades; training programs with job commitments were worked out with each. A Mayor's Working Committee on Employment, which draws together top representatives in the employment system, had already been set up, and it has continued to act as the top-level committee for all manpower programs.

CPI's Manpower Division, which was seventy-strong by late 1965, devotes much of its time to digging out and identifying job opportunities, and then obtaining the necessary preliminary commitments from employers. More and more these opportunities are now found among small manufacturing and service concerns —25 per cent of them companies employing ten people or less, 21 per cent with eleven to twenty-five employees—whose skilled help is being siphoned off by higher-paying major employers in the area. Small firms lack money for training and are usually glad to undertake individual programs hand-crafted and supervised by CPI, with trainees' basic salaries paid by federal manpower funds, even though their hiring criteria must commonly be modified. In fact, the new government-assisted training programs help New Haven's smaller firms to compete for labor in a tight market, and to grow while they help inner-city residents. A 1965 survey showed that 82 per cent of the employers with whom CPI placed individuals spoke well of them; many have come back for more.

The benefits from such on-the-job training opportunities won early grass-roots support for CPI. At first neighborhood workers found that the new agency's efforts were viewed with suspicion and mistrust. But after residents saw tangible results, such as unemployed "hopeless" boys who were trained by and found jobs through CPI, they would defend CPI against critics at neighborhood meetings. Experience has also shown that the manpower programs serve as an opening wedge to interest residents in other activities involving citizen participation.

PREPARING FOR WORK

Equally important, the employment setup has made clear that CPI is not "the Great White Father." A candidate must extend himself, complete a course and do well in order to get a job.

Initially, every job applicant has to go through 'the process" at a neighborhood employment center. These cheerfully decorated, store-front offices bring the state employment machinery close to the people, add to it special counseling and ability-testing services, and demonstrate CPI's special style of "warm bureaucracy."

An applicant talks first with a neighborhood worker, perhaps one who has recruited him out in the neighborhood. The worker prepares him for the process, explaining the chain of steps he must go through, and assures him of the center's interest in his getting a good job. The worker also learns something about the candidate's background and work history. If temporary unemployment is the only problem, the candidate next talks with the State Employment Service placement interviewer.

But for many, such as school dropouts, who lack work experience, the next step will be to talk with a vocational counselor who is part of the employment center. Then the placement interviewer discusses with him what jobs are available and tries to evaluate how the applicant might fit into the job market. Then the candidate goes back to the vocational counselor, who has gathered information from his schools, sometimes the police and previous employers, with the help of the neighborhood worker. The counselor now prepares the candidate for the two-hour general aptitude test which is given by CPI's testing specialist on another day. This preparation is particularly important because many applicants are terrified of tests, having had less than successful experiences with them in school.

When these steps are completed and the aptitude test is scored, the staff that has processed the applicant holds a disposition conference to discuss what the candidate is ready for; this may vary from direct job placement to a combination education-job training program. The vocational counselor discusses the choices with the candidate, and helps prepare him for a job interview—even telling him what to wear, how to look, and how to fill out an application blank. Commonly, the worker follows this up to make sure he goes to the interview and to learn whether the applicant was successful. There are not nearly enough jobs or training opportunities for all candidates, however, and it is not always easy to fit candidates into the available openings. Whatever the disposition, each applicant is followed up at three-month intervals and is assured that if he loses his job he can come back for reevaluation and eventual placement.

The neighborhood workers view themselves as the advocates of the recruits. But even the professionals regard each candidate in CPI's employee-oriented program as an individual, not as a number or case to be fitted into a job slot, or rejected. Emphasis is on bringing the candidate up to his full potential, even if he is already employed. Here, as elsewhere in CPI, concern for people as people is believed to have the single greatest impact.

CPI's job programs proliferated. It became apparent that many inner-city youths were not ready even for on-the-job training. Either they were too young or, if old enough, lacked not only work experience but also essential work attitudes. Many were further handicapped by emotional problems and poor relationships with adult authority figures. Before they could acquire marketable skills, they needed preparation for employment itself: work experience under closer supervision than was provided in existing government-assisted training programs. They had to learn to be punctual, to take orders, to take responsibility for carrying out an assignment and to apply themselves.

A pilot work crew program for such youth was tried out in the summer of 1963, financed by the New Haven Foundation. The experiment proved so successful—30 per cent went on to regular jobs or training programs; 33 per cent back to school—that CPI determined to make the program permanent. Sviridoff was able to convince the Labor Department's Office of Manpower Training that this kind of pre-vocational training should be eligible for government assistance, and by mid-1965, eighteen work crews were in operation, with federal support.

Crews of five to eight boys or girls, receiving a $20-a-week salary, work four hours a day during the week, for various undermanned city agencies such as hospitals and the parks department, for four- to six-month periods. A work crew foreman, another subprofessional job category invented by CPI, supervises the youngsters and gives them special individual counseling and guidance sessions. For many boys on the crews, these foremen serve an extra basic function; they provide the missing father image—manly, tough, but understanding and helpful. "Graduates" of the crews may move up to on-the-job training programs and from there to permanent employment. In CPI's manpower program job applicants often move up through several programs, as in this case.

But many out-of-school youths have no desire to prepare for work, having seen little around them but obstacles and failure. Neighborhood workers must often spend a great deal of time encouraging and persuading them to join a work crew. Some work crew candidates are discouraged by the fact that basic remedial education is a regular part of the program. Although the courses are tailored to the age and needs of each crew member, and no grades or homework are involved, many are antagonistic to returning to school, where they have experienced frustration and failure.

But attitudes change here, too. Seeing a teacher who wants to help them, finding that they are not stupid, some work crew members have even requested homework. The educational component has proved so successful that the original four and a half hours a week of classes were increased to eight. A subsequent elaboration of this program has involved informal meetings of work crew foreman and supervisors with the youngsters' parents. The adults have been very receptive.

For more advanced youth, an intermediate work crew program was established later, allowing them to work without direct supervision by a foreman. Neighborhood Youth Corps funds from the Office of Economic Opportunity finance this program. In the summer of 1965, NYC funds supported special work crews for high school students identified as potential dropouts. A follow-up of the enrollees in the late fall showed no significant change in their school attendance, which suggests that the program played a significant role in preventing their premature withdrawal from school. George Bannett, CPI's director of manpower, observed, "Our manpower programs don't tell them to go back to school, but by showing the importance of education to work, they often have the same effect."

At the Skill Center, set up in a converted warehouse in the fall of 1965, unemployed adults can upgrade their basic education, advance to skill training and then to jobs.

SCHOOLS

Education, child development and community schools, together, use the giant share of CPI's current budget—36.6 per cent, up from 23.5 per cent in 1965, thanks to the new state and federal funds for children in poverty areas.

Classroom programs or teaching-related items financed through CPI include the assistant principals in community schools; remedial reading teachers utilizing new materials and techniques for increasing reading ability—the single biggest inner-city education problem; guidance programs beginning in fifth grade; work-study programs for ninth graders who are potential dropouts; six-week summer school; curriculum assistants to provide special assistance and instruction for regular teachers in new methods and to tailor-make programs for pupils' special needs; the Head Start pre-kindergarten classes for youngsters from culturally deprived homes.

But in education as elsewhere in CPI, it is difficult to draw the line where one program stops and another begins—and this is basic to its approach. Sviridoff has pointed out that CPI does not distinguish between the classroom and after-school activities. Rather, "the whole day is the school day," and neighborhood services are an integral part of a neighborhood's basic educational experience.

The Board of Education in 1962 announced a new policy: that the school buildings should be readily available to the whole community as agencies to strengthen citizen activities and community life. Further, New Haven's Board of Finance appropriated funds for the extra custodial and maintenance services needed to operate the public schools for community use on the new fourteen-hour-a-day, year-round basis.

"People support what they understand and appreciate," noted Lawrence Paquin, who in 1962 became Superintendent of Schools. "Why should they spend millions on buildings that close down at three in the afternoon, on Saturdays and in the summer, especially in a city like New Haven where there is such need for recreation, services and adult programs?"

School principals regard the new relationship between schools and families in the immediate community, as a result of CPI's many school-based adult and student activities, as a major contribution to youngsters' educability.

"One of the big ideas behind the community school is to try to reach kids who don't like school, itself, in other ways," Gerald Barbaresi, principal of the Conte Community School, commented. "To do this, we need to reach the whole family. If they understand what we're trying to do, if they see the schools as a key to a better life, they will encourage their youngsters to study harder."

Many parents had poor experiences in school themselves, and are reluctant to come there. Even if they want their children to learn, often they don't know how to help them or are afraid of appearing ignorant by asking questions. "A very important part of our job is to get them to know we're human," Barbaresi believes. The open-door policy of the community schools and afternoon and evening activities make it possible to reach parents not only on conference days or when their children have misbehaved. Conte's principal likes to have the mothers come in and out for any reason, even just to wheel a baby carriage through the grounds. "It's not enough to have a big beautiful building. Someone has to do a lot of work to get people into the schools." The CPI neighborhood services staff, or "team" (the neighborhood services coordinator, the assistant principal, a group work supervisor, a recreation supervisor and neighborhood workers) which is attached to each community school does this job. They provide after-school activities for youth, furnish services for adults and families at schools, ranging from dental clinics to meeting rooms, and go out in the neighborhoods to recruit. The knowledge they gain of children's homes assists the teaching staff in planning the best kind of educational programs for the pupils.

A new category of neighborhood worker was created in 1965 to help school principals reach homes more directly. The school-community relations workers (first one was assigned to each of the seven community schools, but with new state funds, they have increased to twenty-eight, including elementary schools) are women who live in the school neighborhood, are known to the people and have been active in community affairs. They visit the homes of children with disciplinary, attendance or other school problems, and try to alleviate the family situations that may be responsible. (One family was found to have no food.) They are able to judge what families need and they inform families of services available in schools and elsewhere.

A number of neighborhood services are located outside the schools. Head Start classes, for instance, have spilled over into many kinds of inner-city locations. Schools lack the space, and these classes should be within easy walking distance of homes. Employment services are not based in schools, partly due to the shortage of space, but also because so many of the unemployed dislike school. But all the services offered in a neighborhood are tied together by the coordinator, who works closely with the community school's assistant principal and with the manpower division.

Activities offered or stimulated by CPI's neighborhood teams have caused new life to spring up, even in the most ancient school structures. One outstanding example is the Prince community school, a building long overdue for replacement, but which has been rehabilitated for temporary extended use.

The Prince neighborhood is probably New Haven's toughest and dreariest today, and is scheduled for urban renewal. Before CPI, people were afraid to go out on the streets at night, and the school offered no services or programs. The principal was overwhelmed by neighborhood problems that adversely affected classroom work. He was often blamed for such troubles as youth fights in the streets. But he lacked help to prevent their outbreak, and the Youth Board was in the neighborhood practically every other day to break up fights.

Now the CPI team, led by an exceptionally able coordinator, relieves the principal by reducing many of these former problems. Evenings, the Prince School is brightly lit and full of activity, with youngsters and adults participating in programs that range from the individual tutoring of elementary school pupils by volunteers, to professionally supervised basketball for teenagers and adult literacy classes. Neighborhood people no longer regard the streets as unsafe after dark. They flock to the Prince School eagerly. In fact, the pedestrian traffic created by activities at the school has made the streets more safe. Juvenile disturbances decreased so markedly during 1965 that Youth Board visits dropped to one every other week.

The community school teams also cool off the "long hot summer" for New Haven children. Outings to the beach and nearby places of special interest, an overnight sleep-out in the Conte School courtyard, resident-supervised camping trips and even summer school, keep thousands busy.

But what are the payoffs for students from the new classroom methods and programs? This matter is neither discussed nor documented in the extensive illustrated annual reports published by Community Progress. Elizabeth Wright, director of curriculum for the New Haven public schools, states, "We do not have measurable changes. We feel the things we are doing are good—

reducing the pupil-to-teacher ratio in remedial reading, and that the students benefit from more individual attention. But the children measure exactly the same as before, and no one knows why. This is one of the stickiest parts of the program."

Mrs. Wright, who came to New Haven's schools from suburban Scarsdale two years ago, thinks she has some clues, however. "If you have twenty-five in the class instead of thirty-five, and you have the same teachers, with the same attitudes, teaching the same old things, you get nothing different. We're trying to find new recipes because our experience shows that none of the old ones work."

Relevance of curriculum content is the key, she believes. She has designed some new classroom materials, and is introducing others, such as the Bank Street readers, which are urban centered, and present the information to be learned against a multiethnic background and typical scenes of the inner city. Blow-ups of city scenes, "urban prints," can be used in all classes. In first grade, it can be used to stimulate children to talk in their own vocabulary about what they are familiar with and what interests them; and in twelfth grade, as a background for the discussions of contemporary issues. "Using the old materials of Dick and Jane and suburban scenes is like portraying a bi-plane instead of a jet," Mrs. Wright comments. "Retraining teachers is equally important. But we can't tell the results for a long time."

An outsider is prone to assume, erroneously, that the new school board and new programs caused immediate and sweeping changes throughout the system. But in spite of new programs, most classes are still far too large, and the reform was just a start. The public schools have the largest body of tenure-employed people in the city, and continual efforts must be made by such key officials as Mrs. Wright to change ingrained attitudes, broaden outlooks and win acceptance of new materials.

Each school principal also has enormous autonomy in ordering books and materials. There are showcase principals of the "new" school system, such as the Conte School's Gerald Barbaresi. But many others hold out against new materials or CPI-stimulated efforts to meet with powerless parent bodies, and must be individually sold.

"First you have to change attitudes," Mrs. Wright believes.

One productive effort in the summer of 1966 was an institute financed by the U.S. Office of Education and attended by 110 New Haven teachers. They were taught how to use new materials, and for one week, inner-city neighborhood representatives joined with the institute to let teachers know what parents really want. Through CPI or on her own, Mrs. Wright also encourages parents to write to or talk to the principals, requesting use of the new teaching materials in their children's schools. She also promotes her urban prints in largely white school districts and in New Haven's suburbs.

SIGNS OF SUCCESS

Four years are too short a time to judge how well CPI is achieving its major goals. These, as expressed by Sviridoff, are: "to make people self-sufficient and tie them into opportunity programs; [and] to make local institutions more relevant to the needs of our times." Whether the community at large assumes responsibility for what CPI has begun may be the ultimate test, and this will not be known for years.

There are, nonetheless, many signs of success. Among those that are statistically measurable are the number of people who have participated in and benefited from CPI opportunity programs. For example, pre-kindergarten classes, held year-round, have long waiting lists—even though mothers are required to attend meetings each week to discuss their child's development with the teachers, and also to learn more about nutrition, home management and child behavior. By the end of June 1965, sixteen pre-kindergarten centers were serving 480 three- and four-year-old children. (There were 1,800 children in low-income families in this age range.) Another 620 had already graduated. These children became more confident and educable, as attested by their kindergarten teachers, and even measured by tests. But it is discouraging to see the enormous improvements disappear by second grade. As Mrs. Wright points out, "In Head Start, the children have all that money can buy—a teacher, a teacher's aide and a parent aide. The classes are reduced to fifteen. In kindergarten, there are no extra funds, only one teacher for a class of thirty, and they come up against so much of the old program and institution." Still, New Haven has taken an important step in trying to maintain longer-run gains by continuing counseling of the parents of "Head Start" children through third grade.

Further up the ladder, the increased attendance at summer school of pupils from second grade up is remarkable. In 1965, there were 2,500, compared to 1,864 in 1964—all attending voluntarily, and 5,510 youngsters applied for the summer of 1966. Special tutoring was also being given to 150 children by Yale students. Another 1,500 teenagers worked in paying community jobs in 1965, and thousands enjoyed the various new recreation programs.

A large number of youths and adults have been processed through the neighborhood employment centers since the decentralized manpower program began in October 1963. By September 1965, they numbered 6,502. Over 93 per cent of them were unemployed when they came to the centers, and over 46 per cent were referred by their friends. Thirty-two per cent were under twenty years old.

Of the total, 1,550 were placed on jobs directly; 518 went into on-the-job training; 525 to basic work crews and another 116 into the new intermediate crews; 65 work crew graduates were approved for the Job Corps; 359 were receiving institutional skill training; and 340 had graduated from this program. At the new Skill Center, 170 adults were enrolled in combined basic education-vocation oriented programs during 1965. Of the remaining applicants who were not placed on a job or into a CPI program, about one half found jobs on their own.

The Connecticut State Employment Service found that the neighborhood employment centers helped it to reach more people and place more in jobs. A survey of a sample of those placed revealed that 80 per cent stayed employed. Significantly, another survey undertaken in the fall of 1965 showed that those trained or placed by CPI were receiving average weekly wages 25 per cent higher than they had ever received during their working career.

The volume of CPI job candidates has not dropped. CPI's Manpower Director George Bannett commented, "The job vacancy rate is meaningless for the inner city. There is no true measure of unemployment there. Many people say they are not looking for employment if they do not see the opportunity for jobs or feel themselves unemployable."

Community Progress was dealing more and more with the hard-core cases, such as adults who could not read or write and many who were not measured in the unemployment statistics. In order to determine actual job needs in the inner city, the Manpower Division was planning to conduct a door-to-door survey.

A significant measure of success is the more active participation of adults in community activities. Some are showing considerable initiative in developing programs and agendas for local community improvement and action.

Before CPI, for example, resident participation in the Scranton area had been extremely low. This neighborhood, now comprised largely of Negroes and scheduled for renewal, had many unmet needs. CPI helped eight members of the Scranton School PTA organize a community action committee in October 1964. The group, with expanded membership, charted an attack on neighborhood problems through self-help activities and a program to correct long-overlooked school problems. The group discussed their grievances and goals at separate conferences with Board of Education officials, the Police Chief, the Mayor and the Governor of Connecticut. They won substantial improvements in the school, new recreational programs and increased police services. In January 1965 over 200 neighborhood people turned out to meet the Mayor—the largest gathering in the Scranton area in a generation. Later that year, when the state legislature was considering new educational aid to disadvantaged children, 164 inner-city residents went to Hartford, and representatives testified in favor of aid to help their children. Only three had been to Hartford before.

In the Hill, which is experiencing a heavy outmigration of white families and increase in Negroes, mothers conducted a neighborhood survey to learn what kind of adult programs were desired at the Prince School. One request was that a course in Negro history be given at this integrated school. Serving on the Hill's recreation committee gave many white people their first real opportunity to work with Negroes on matters of common community concern.* The committee chose a dynamic young Negro to represent them at a meeting with city officials.

The "greatest successes" in New Haven's education program have come from adult activities at the community schools, curric-

* The area's original renewal council was not integrated.

ulum director Elizabeth Wright believes. "People who were powerless before are now trying to improve their schools. And the big thing is that curricular changes are being made on the basis of what they say they want." Subjects are even being taught in both Spanish and English in four schools (seventeen teachers were given Spanish instruction in order to do so). Puerto Rican parents did not want their children to be ignorant when they went back to the islands, or to be second-class citizens here.

The advanced curriculum in some schools has also fostered voluntary integration. White families living in the Florence Virtue Houses in Dixwell changed their minds about enrolling children in private schools after they saw the challenging educational program offered at the handsome new Grant elementary school, which is set in the middle of the housing development.

A noteworthy by-product is the large number of volunteer workers from beyond the inner city. They undertake many necessary jobs, from tutoring in the evenings to taking children on field trips. In 1965, such volunteers numbered almost 1,250, which comprised half the total staff from CPI and other city agencies carrying out programs. A local factory owner made his company's premises available to CPI for adult literacy classes to upgrade his undereducated employees.

Ten local and state public agencies and fifteen private agencies are involved in the CPI-stimulated community effort, and many groups are reorganizing along CPI lines. The visiting nurses decentralized their services on the basis of community schools, and the city's Recreation Department placed a full-time supervisor in each of these schools. While the districting of many organizations is not contiguous with CPI's neighborhood centers, some go part of the way. The Family Services Society detached workers to the Hill district. The Department of Libraries proceeded on its own to set up a branch in an empty grocery store in one unserved inner-city neighborhood; it even provided a room in the back where youngsters could sit and talk. This sort of institutional response particularly pleased Sviridoff. "It shows the head librarian is getting infected with the idea." (The Office of Economic Opportunity gave funds to staff three more libraries.) Also as a result the Police Department instituted a course in human relations for its trainees. Another step of particular consequence was the appropriation by the city, in 1965, of some $300,000 to finance special school programs originally supported by CPI.

Not all agencies in the city have been amenable. Some groups are apprehensive, or even hostile to change, and see the new programs as a threat. The neighborhood law offices were delayed for two years by opposition from the local bar association. Apparently, private practitioners feared they would lose business as a result of this new program (pioneered in New Haven with Ford Foundation funds and subsequently taken up by the Office of Economic Opportunity), as free legal services were to be provided for the poor. Also, while heads of agencies or boards may be cooperative, lower-echelon staff people, such as the schoolteachers, tend to resist change. But CPI believes that the many supplementary programs are changing teachers' old negative attitudes, and as assistant principals in community schools are promoted to principals, the changed attitudes percolate down the line even faster.

A new "atmosphere of hope" reported by neighborhood workers in the inner city might be classified as one of the intangible signs of success. But the city's Redevelopment Agency, a close partner of CPI, translates this into more concrete terms. Several key spokesmen for the agency credit the new activities, the growing opportunities, and the greater communication resulting in neighborhoods, as important accelerating influences in home rehabilitation, and in helping neighborhood people to understand urban renewal.

The agency's Executive Director for Operations, Charles Shannon, who served as project director for the Dixwell area during the first few years of renewal, observed late in 1965: "CPI is improving their whole outlook on life. It offers them lots more services—day care centers, health services, employment, tutoring, the Skills Center and Job Corps. And the kids know they have a chance for a job if they stay in school."

Mayor Lee views the stepped-up organization activities, the full-time, paid indigenous workers and staffed community schools as offering one of the best guarantees that high physical standards will be maintained in renewal neighborhoods after official activities are completed. (Indeed, the need for paid staff to keep the citizens' committee going even in Wooster Square was evident after Father Cavicchi left.) Lee hopes that citizen-initiated communication with City Hall will continue, and that there will be more active citizen involvement in local government instead of the former apathy or distrust.

SOME QUESTIONS AND CRITICISMS

One important and informed observer from outside New Haven has suggested that Community Progress did not start early enough to plan programs with the people and develop the talents in neighborhoods. He feels that CPI has been authoritarian and has been imposed on the people from the top. "If you pull Mike [Sviridoff] out, nothing is there, because the people haven't been utilized enough."

A Residents' Advisory Committee to CPI, with three representatives elected from each of the seven inner-city neighborhoods, was not created until the fall of 1965, and only then were neighborhood representatives elected to the Board of Community Progress. More recently, these representatives were given the additional responsibility of conducting "town meetings" to let people speak out.

"The hardest job," according to Sviridoff, 'is to effect permanent institutional change that will count in the long run and keep institutions responsive to changing needs. If not, we could just as well have handed out cash." How effective is participation by the poor in program planning? This question concerns many who are currently re-evaluating the still-young community efforts to fight poverty.

Do pressures from the needy induce meaningful institutional response and social progress? Or is the CPI combination of clout, diplomacy and neighborhood-centered resident activities more effective? And what approach most benefits those in the inner city who are directly affected? In other cities, where "maximum feasible participation" of the poor was sought, as called for in the original Economic Opportunity Act, results commonly have been disappointing. Much time and effort on the part of professional workers is required; first, to help the poor and uneducated organize into groups that have continuity and cohesion, and then to encourage them to speak up and learn the techniques of group action.

It seems doubtful that the top-level inter-agency cooperation and response in New Haven could have been accomplished by a less sophisticated strategy than that of Community Progress, supported by Lee. But how long will it last? And has change perhaps been too "managed," too lacking in controversy here, as in other facets of New Haven's renewal? Does not a certain amount of conflict, of fighting the establishment, also contribute to long-term individual growth and group effectiveness? Still, the rising indigenous leadership in the inner city—both people in CPI and Redevelopment Agency staff jobs, and residents who are starting to speak out and develop programs—appears to be a promising sign for the future of the "new" New Haven.

Community Progress might also be criticized for starting with the "easy" problems, instead of the hard-core cases, and for being too concerned with its public image. But choices must be made, and Sviridoff deliberately decided on a strategy of demonstrable success; he chose to concentrate particularly on opening opportunities for the young Negro male, and in this it made great strides.

The strategy of success led to CPI's major weakness—in the field of housing. Originally this was to be one of the major action areas, along with jobs and education. But it was difficult to find private dwelling units to lease for large, low-income families under New Haven's rent certificate demonstration project. And it was awkward when the Federal Housing Administration insuring office turned down inner-city applicants for government mortgage insurance without an explanation. Not wanting its clientele "to see us as an instrument of their frustration," CPI turned these jobs back to the Redevelopment Agency and Public Housing Authority.

It also seems that any "solution" creates new problems. The Conte Community School, for example, experienced the dilemma of integration of after-school activities. One quarter of the community school's pupils are Negro, and many live in the Farnum Court low-income housing project. But the predominantly Italian adult population of Wooster Square assumed squatters' rights in the Senior Citizens' lounge. On the other hand, Conte's teenage lounge was used almost exclusively by Negro youngsters, and it was difficult to attract whites. Was integration of leisure-time activities a responsibility of the CPI team at community schools? They have let that question ride.

WHERE IS THE STAYING POWER?

New Haven today is an infinitely better, more viable and more livable city than it was a dozen years ago, and it continues to set patterns for other old built-up cities in its planning, its programs and its approach to a wide range of inherited and emerging problems.

But mostly, New Haven has been doing remedial homework —catching up with a half century of decline, and rebuilding, where possible, in terms of modern standards and technology and new human needs. When its renewal is finished, New Haven should once again be the regional distribution and retail center —and for a larger radius. But even with redevelopment, retail sales in the central business district have not yet reached the high of the late 1940's before the postwar suburban migration. Many factory jobs will have been saved, local manufacturers and wholesalers rehoused, and some jobs, as at Macy's, added, compensating in part for those lost since the 1920's. The worst slums will be gone; old houses will be rehabilitated for extended life and owners' pride; some handsome new public facilities and housing built; the tax base will be stronger.*

There remains considerable question, however, whether comprehensive renewal and aggressive administrative and elected leadership can alter the basic style and character of the city. Have these insured urban vitality? Almost everything of consequence that has taken place in New Haven in the past dozen years has been stimulated, put together and forwarded from City Hall, either directly or indirectly. Will someone keep New Haven moving when Lee is no longer Mayor? Or will the city ride along on recent improvements until it sinks once more into decay and

* The loss of land values for the new highways has not been balanced off against increased values in redevelopment areas.

another Lee steps forward? Improvement is not static; steps must continually be taken just to keep a city abreast of the times.

The New Haven business community has shown little initiative. Most of its leaders have had to be dragged into the second half of the twentieth century. New Haven has no privately supported development corporation of the kind other cities find necessary to compete for growth. Aside from Olin Mathieson's research consolidation and the Rockefeller Foundation Virus Laboratories, which moved from New York to the Grace–New Haven Hospital and Yale Medical School complex, New Haven has not been able to attract—though the administration has tried—new research and development laboratories or growth industries.

Some New Haven redevelopment officials have maintained that the Church Street project proves that a city does not require the support and active involvement of its business community in renewal as long as City Hall shows such enterprise. Were it not for the general vitality of the metropolitan area, and for Roger Stevens, things might look quite different inside New Haven proper.

Most of the local politicians, are also behind the times. As one close observer put it: "They were all poor and pulled themselves up by the boot straps. They don't understand what Lee and his bright young men are doing." And Lee has no apparent successor.

Where are the accelerators to gear New Haven into the future as current economic functions fade? Will capable younger people continue to leave such small old cities for suburban homes or for opportunities in the great metropolitan centers? There has been an enormous attrition of top talents in New Haven's physical and social renewal programs, and few of the people mentioned in this study are still there.

That a man of Lee's ability should have stepped forward in a city of New Haven's size and been able to attract such exceptional talent and major outside investors is, in many ways, a fortunate accident that probably would not have occurred without the University. Had it not been for Yale, Stevens would never have looked at New Haven, and even with the University, he has often regretted since that he did.

Yale's position in the New Haven story is ambiguous. Although it makes the city much more than a tired old New England manufacturing town—one attractive to people with intellectual interests and creative talents, and is the second largest employer in the city,* Yale has not really contributed its rich resources and leadership to the community in proportion to its ability and importance. While hundreds of students have tutored in poverty areas, the faculty and various University departments have done little, and the president is regarded with suspicion by the "little people" of New Haven if he tries to use his or the University's prestige. There is also the practical problem that every time Yale grows—and it has grown handsomely in recent years—the city's taxable real estate shrinks.

THE REAL ART OF FEDERAL GRANTSMANSHIP

Is the New Haven experience reproducible? As cities grow, problems seem to increase not mathematically but geometrically, and they are compounded by the remoteness of City Hall and the inertia of sheer mass. Can you wholesale in a city of 8,000,000 what you can retail in one of only 150,000?

In the past, some New York City officials dismissed New Haven's widely heralded renewal achievements as irrelevant for big cities. All of New Haven's 152,000 residents could fit into just one of New York's eighty-seven separate local community districts, the officials have pointed out. And to rehabilitate largely owner-occupied, free-standing homes in no way compares to the seemingly insuperable problems presented by New York's absentee-owned, Old Law tenements and its anonymous new brownstone slums. The problems of poverty, race and slums in New Haven are not nearly as extensive, relatively, as in most big cities.

But New York City's new reform Mayor, John V. Lindsay, soon after his election in November 1965, looked for the top talents in the country to study New York's troubled housing, renewal and anti-poverty programs. He chose the two men most responsible under Lee for New Haven's physical and human development programs: Edward Logue and Mitchell Sviridoff, to

* Olin Mathieson Chemical Corporation, having acquired Winchester Arms, an old New Haven company, is the largest employer.

head task forces of experts to analyze these problems; and he asked each to become head of the new super-administration his group proposed for New York.*

It is said that American cities need an enormous additional infusion of federal funds. The current omnibus figure is one trillion dollars. But top federal officials and Congress worry that most cities do not know how to use even the current funds.

Probably the most important lesson of New Haven's renewal for other cities is its attitude toward the federal and state funds that are becoming available to cities: it not only tries to get as much money as possible by aggressive action and demonstration of need, but also uses the funds wisely and well. More and more, this is the key to the urban future.

How has New Haven been so successful? Certain basic elements emerge from the successive, interlocking phases of the city's physical, municipal and social renewal.

First, New Haven had far-sighted and meaningful plans for its reshaping. These plans and goals, determined before the major grant-in-aid programs were established, provided a framework in which funds could be used.

Lee supported and was identified with city planning long before he was elected Mayor. Coming to office when the funds and powers to eliminate urban decay were becoming available, he brought with him a commitment to improvement of the city, using tools and outside funds where practical, and he publicized the city's plans to give people an understanding of what proposed changes would mean. He displayed executive understanding and enterprise—uniting community leaders behind renewal, seeking out funds,† and attracting innovative staff talents, many from outside New Haven who were not locked in by local tradition, in

* Sviridoff became Administrator of New York's new Human Resources Administration. Logue turned down Lindsay's offer, but his New Haven-trained Boston deputy accepted the number-two job in New York's new Housing and Development Administration.

Some of New Haven's loss of top talents has been caused by other cities' desperate need for able men and women to administer and develop the new programs. But due to remarkable in-depth staffing, New Haven continues to produce "bright young men" for itself. As Lee said to Lindsay, "I don't know what New York is going to do when New Haven runs out of men."

† The city was fortunate in having a local "angel" that provided seed money at many important points. The quiet and continuing contributions of the New Haven Foundation should not be overlooked.

order to use the new tools. But as Mayor he never lost touch with the people, and always remembered that renewal was for *them.*

Lee and his staff viewed the funds and powers as invitations for action to realize local plans and to cure local ills, not as ends in themselves. They fought to adapt public and private aids to solve New Haven's problems and to get new kinds of aid where necessary. They tried to provide for contingencies but they were not afraid to advance projects in spite of apparent problems or for fear of the unknown. Only when you get into project execution, they found, do you learn what the problems actually are. By setting open minds to work in new terrain, the city also developed talents and programs from which many of the nation's cities have since benefited.

A major goal was also to relate different elements of renewal to each other so that both the entire city and its separate parts would benefit. Although Lee at times seemed to worry most about adverse community opinion and the next election, he also accepted the fact that pain for some is the unavoidable price of community renewal; under him, the city did everything it could to minimize the pains of change and help dislocatees.

The Mayor and Logue had an overview of the city in which renewal was not the task of just one agency. Although Lee made renewal and physical development a central function in his administration, both he and his Development Administrator recognized that all city departments, not just those directly involved with renewal, must have high levels of performance if a city is to be renewed. Guided by such perceptions, the Lee administration was the first in the country to make the schools partners of the city in its great new enterprise.

Until the past few years, with the emergence of Community Progress, New Haven was criticized by some for its heavy emphasis on deteriorated urban "hardware" compared to unmet human needs. But experience shows that if the environment of a city is decrepit and physically limiting, achieving social progress will be extraordinarily hard. If, as in New Haven, one is sensitive to the human component, physical renewal readily demonstrates what else the people need, often far better than do social plans. Certainly a decent environment and modern facilities make it much easier to provide adequate services to people.

In the current debate between the merit of welfare or "human" investment versus urban rebuilding, the positive effect of a more attractive community and environment on people's spirit and outlook should not be ignored. As Edward Logue has observed, "The New Haven experience gives me great faith in the utility of bricks and mortar, not only in improving physical conditions, but also in renewing the life of a city."

The Urban Landscape

10

LOOKING BACKWARD AND AHEAD ■ The Demands and Dilemmas of Being Urban in America

The past two decades of activity in American cities have been bewildering.

On the one hand, there has been history-making progess. Century-old slums have been torn down, most of their residents decently rehoused and the cleared sites rebuilt with private funds, according to community plans. Neighborhoods in decline and drab, obsolete business districts have been salvaged and renewed as models for modern urban living and working. Government appropriations and programs to deal with city problems have steadily climbed, and private investment expanded.

Yet at the same time new slums have been born, vast areas

have faded, poverty and crime have grown and racial ghettos have spread out. Some suburbanites have returned to central cities, but even more middle-class white families have left. There are urban highways, center-city arterial by-passes and downtown garages to handle automobile traffic, and new subsidies for mass transportation, yet traffic congestion has worsened. Social programs that hold promise become rapidly outmoded, and new, more encompassing ones must be mounted. Our solutions themselves often create new problems. The available federal billions are a pittance measured against visible needs. It is possible to wonder whether cities must always run to stand still.

Yet a heightened sense of urgency exists at every level. There is an accelerating participation and commitment of individuals, private groups, and public agencies, and a proliferation of new organizations and funded programs. Because the social and racial problems have become so pressing, we forget how far we have come in a few short years.

In less than a generation we have developed and put to work a unique set of tools that is enabling cities to bring about radical changes and remarkable improvements in land and property use, guide private developments, preserve what is worth saving in cities, and face up to social needs. The demands of community and city dwellers are being asserted as never before.

While at the start the tools were crude and often clumsily used or narrowly applied, the cities whose experiences we have followed have learned, as others have, to use them with increasing skill and sensitivity, and to coordinate them with programs designed for a community of people and their businesses and even to minimize the inconvenience during the transition period.

Mayors have changed City Hall's usual role as passive municipal caretaker and stepped forward as leaders and innovators, making city government the co-participant with private enterprise in unprecedented programs. City planning has become more than an academic dream. With new local powers and federal funds, cities have demonstrated that urban improvement is possible; that what has been created, despoiled, or neglected in cities, the community can alter, improve, or rebuild.

There are remarkable new community coalitions; it seems a new era of localism has begun. Old ideological conflicts about public versus private, Republican versus Democrat, and federal intervention versus local autonomy have been buried locally for the cause of bettering our cities. Far from weakening local initiative, federal aid has enabled cities to operate on their own behalf as never before, and an American genius for social inventions has been applied to create new institutional and financial arrangements for bridging the gaps between sectors. The issue of better cities is no longer whether we *can,* but whether we *will,* and how soon and at what cost.

The fact is that we have been engineering an enormous revolution in our ways of doing things in and for cities, a revolution that has only begun. We do not call it a revolution partly because the changes have taken place within the traditional framework of government. But the main reason, I believe, is because good cities are becoming good business and good politics in America.

THE ELEMENTS OF ACTION

Unfortunately, these strikingly altered environments, actions, and viewpoints have not affected all cities nor, certainly, all members of each sector and party. The advances are not uniform even in the exemplary cities we followed, and the outcome is far from certain.

Primarily, these have been years of learning by doing, and in the combined experiences of these cities we have discovered certain fundamentals. One of these is the rudimentary composition of community action: what every city must itself create or marshal in order to carry out sound programs of renewal and community development, and to respond adequately to inherited problems or new challenges.

Leadership Dedicated public and private leadership must work together cooperatively. We know that cities must have the best possible elected leaders—strong, intelligent, resourceful, and responsive. Without them, even a model governmental structure and the millions for new physical and social programs are of little use. Cities also need local business leaders who will use their power, influence, and money on behalf of their community, crossing party lines if need be, backing up government when it must take risks, and carrying local causes to higher levels of influence. Cities need the commitment and influence of their elite.

Community organizations Nonprofit organizations of new kinds are needed at various levels and for many purposes. At the top, organizations can harness the power of the elite and facilitate working relationships between public and private local powers, whether or not the latter live in the central city. In specific areas, new organizations are necessary to encourage or undertake non-economic local developments. On citywide or neighborhood levels, organizations can assist citizens to articulate their needs, opinions, and desires in a more informed, productive fashion.

Plans Various kinds of plans, coordinated at the executive level, are required for physical, human, and economic development, for a transportation system related to land use, for spending related to development goals, and for neighborhood as well as citywide improvement. Foremost among these is needed a persuasive visual image of what the city might be. Without it, the planners and leaders cannot create community consensus for action. A comprehensive, long-range physical development plan provides the framework for acceptable, meaningful change.

Staff Cities should have the best professional staff, both in agencies and new community organizations, that money can buy. Cities are big business, but they are quite different from big business, and the recruitment of the new kinds of talents needed to structure, program, and execute new operations is one of the major innovative challenges that local leaders must tackle. Skilled planner-administrators are relatively few and not waiting for employment; most must be developed on the job.

Information Current facts about local housing conditions and needs, industry and jobs, population, school plants, and other public facilities are required. So is knowledge about emerging national trends: population shifts, new industrial requirements, the changing economic structure, technology, new government aids and programs, and the implications of all these for local development and planning strategies. More information about other cities' experiences would be helpful.

An informed citizenry Cities need an enlightened public that can grasp the nature of its community, perceive current trends, and understand the reason for and the consequences of public actions that must or may be taken. This job of creating an educated public is not just for the schools and news media, although they should do much more than they are doing. It is also the duty of elected officials and politicians, staff heads of agencies and organizations, business leaders, the universities, and citizen organizations.

Money *Much* more money is needed (we do not know how much) from local and state governments; from foundations, nonprofit sponsors, and other private sources; and most of all from the federal government. Without the latter, needed private investment in city renewal will not be forthcoming, nor will slums be eliminated. But it is possible that we now have more federal money and public powers available than we have sound local plans, administrative structures, imagination, and people capable of using them. The talents and initiative recorded in this book are not typical.

THE NATURE OF THE NEW TOOLS

In the process of using the new tools, we have also learned much about their nature and limitations. The most powerful and widely used, the most misunderstood and either unpopular or suspect, is urban renewal. We should be clear about why these attitudes exist.

Many different publics have invested renewal with their particular purposes, and many have become disillusioned because renewal has not, or could not, accomplish all the different things they expected. Hostility is inevitable where the execution has been clumsy or callous. But each advance entails dilemmas, choices, and hardships for some. Where the end product of redevelopment has seemed little better, or perhaps worse, than what existed before, we have been reluctant to admit that the fault lies not with the tool but with our ineptitude in urban design. Urban renewal has revealed how poorly prepared Americans are to create better cities.

Change precipitates opposition. In the case of urban renewal, government has been the handy whipping boy and is blamed because, in trying to remove the mess of the past, it must act where the urban illness is greatest. Some object to the use of renewal for commerce and luxury housing. Probably the single most important reason for public concern and disaffection, however, is that urban renewal has lifted the rug off long-submerged and new slums and forced the community to look at its social and racial problems while it still lacked the means and perhaps the desire to solve them.

Urban renewal is not easy. It is neither a solution nor an end in itself. It is not an economic process. It is not the answer to ending urban slums and, specifically, it is not a housing program, although the federal statute requires localities to rehouse displaced people into standard shelter. One of the most important facts we have learned is that renewal requires a host of supplementary tools and some unusual public and private entrepreneurs for the process to work and benefit those directly affected. For example, we have seen that for renewal to help slum dwellers, or improve housing in lower-income neighborhoods, extensive government assistance and further subsidy is required: low-interest loans or grants for new and rehabilitated housing, municipal tax abatement, government purchase of secondary mortgages, low-rent public housing or rent supplements, and public assistance payments.

What is urban renewal? It is a bundle of powers and funds that afford cities a uniquely versatile tool for bringing about many different kinds of planned changes and improvements in their blighted areas and for carrying out comprehensive development goals. While it is difficult enough to bring about these changes with renewal, such improvements would generally be impossible without it.

Renewal is probably the most complex and demanding local governmental program imaginable. The surprising thing is that it has become so commonplace, and that federally assisted projects have been completed, are being carried out or planned in over 800 cities. Moreover, instead of renewal being an instrument for "no slums in ten years," it seems certain to become a permanent municipal function not only in older central cities, but also in suburbs and developing towns on the fringes of metropolitan areas. Renewal will be the indispensable tool for localities in a continually changing, technically and materially advancing nation to make necessary physical adjustments to keep up with new times.

The practice of renewal has grown more sophisticated, and the urban agenda has broadened as new needs have been demonstrated and improved ways devised. The negative emphasis on slum elimination and prevention of blight has shifted to a positive concern for conserving the past and for the quality of what is built as well as who will use it; the rehabilitation or construction of housing alone has given way to the modernization or creation of complete neighborhoods, from imposing projects on people to making the people indispensable partners in project planning and execution. As the insufficiencies of slum dwellers and the problems of race and poverty have impressed themselves on city renewers, programs have been invented not just to treat symptoms but also to open up economic opportunities, decrease discrimination, and deal with underlying causes.

Our widened vantage now encompasses federal aid for urban open space, recreation, college dormitories, and universities, and we have invented devices for strengthening the local economy and for industrial renewal. In transportation planning we have advanced from the building of urban highways to move vehicles through cities to the development of balanced circulatory systems to move people and goods throughout metropolitan areas.

Education has been increasingly recognized as the indispensable colleague of urban revitalization and investment in people as important as spending on buildings. From a heavy early emphasis on bringing back the white middle class to "save" cities, efforts are now being made to develop new leadership and a new urban middle class among present residents. We have begun to apply advanced systems-analysis techniques for designing urban facilities and answering such questions as what mixture of physical facilities and social and educational services will achieve the most rapid progress in ending city slums and poverty. The new Department of Housing and Urban Development now offers cities congressionally authorized financial incentives to combine physical and social renewal in model city projects.

SOME UNANSWERED QUESTIONS

Yet in most places we have not begun to solve cities' problems. We are still struggling, unsure and falling behind. We think we have put our fingers on answers, but they keep slipping away, and the problems turn out to be quite different from what they seemed. Cities are obviously limited and handicapped in their ability to act. There are too many built-in constraints, too few controls, and too little information. There is too little talent to use what we have. Many problems from the past, such as the character of the local economy, are so deeply embedded that it may take several generations for some cities to emerge into more beneficial patterns. New tools must be investigated, and many other questions and issues raised, faced, and debated.

For instance, we have not begun to grapple fruitfully with one of the most widely recognized problems: how can cities develop and attract the high caliber of elected leaders they require? The level drops off sharply and discouragingly once we get beyond the lucky ten or a dozen cities with shining and headline-making Mayors and the brilliant staff they have attracted or developed.

We have not systematically and thoroughly investigated the application of taxation as an instrument of urban development policies, although there is much talk and some scattered studies. In high-cost metropolitan areas it is apparent that some tax abatement is necessary to reduce shelter costs for the lower-middle-income family, and this device is probably required to effect rehabilitation, as well. What is the result of the real estate tax on slum formation, and can its administration be improved or reformed to induce slum elimination? Should the property tax serve ends other than revenue collection?

While much attention is given to the constraining effect of state and rural legislators, little attention is given to bringing out their potentially constructive role in guiding urban growth and overcoming metropolitan disparities. We have seen some remarkable examples of cities gaining their ends in state capitals when the local leadership formed a consensus and took a determined stand. Could not cities put such pressures on a more systematic basis?

If schools are "the answer," how do we get the money to allow them to perform better, and why haven't they achieved more with the extra funds they have already received? Is education too important to be left to the educators? What, in fact, is the job of education in a nation composed predominantly of city dwellers who will be progressively freed from work?

The businessman is exhorted to recognize his leadership responsibilities, to end employment discrimination, to help improve his city's public education system, to give more than lip service to investment in people. He must speak up and use his power more to achieve these ends. But the primary problem is not the local business leader; he can usually be shown. The crucial impediment is the impersonal corporate management which runs most of the country's business, absorbs many old, locally owned concerns into national complexes, moves plant and office managers from one part of the country to another, and lacks allegiance to any community except, perhaps, its home-office city. This is certainly one of the toughest and most pivotal problems with which urban America must contend. But in this era of accelerating urban growth, our largest metropolitan areas have been growing most quickly, and some are merging into urban regions or megalopoli.

Metropolitan planning of facilities appears to be required—and perhaps metropolitan government is its necessary precursor. Many of our prescriptions are doctrinaire. We are not clear about what size local government unit can be both responsive to people's varying needs and still capable of guiding urban development. Greater New York thought it had solved its governmental problems with the consolidation of 1898. How can we avoid the inertia, the impersonality and mediocrity of the giant bureaucracies that come with big local government? Is there an optimum size for administrative efficiency and economy in the provision of local services?

Neither have we learned to anticipate and deal with the physical and social consequences of new technology. By now we are pretty much agreed that cities are for people—but we are not sure whether they are for people in cars or on foot. We know very little about the effect on man's mental and physical health of noise, fumes, driving in traffic, stress, anonymity, and density, and we are not ready to act on what we know. Laboratory experiments with animals suggest that living in great densities can lead to behavior breakdown—an incapacity of the individual to respond to the world around him—to alienation and withdrawal from social concerns. What does this signify for the citizens of an increasingly urban America, most of whom are now jammed together on one per cent of the land?

THE CURRENT IMPERATIVES

Must city dwellers be so much the victims of blind forces, always acting haltingly after the fact? I think not. We can and should proceed in several areas without further delay to gain a firmer grasp of the urban situation and human condition in cities, as well as a clearer sense of what is coming and which next steps must be taken. The struggles of these renewing cities, and of many others, both decaying and exploding, have persuaded me that there are five current imperatives: development of a real federal urban policy, measures to overcome the fiscal-taxation anomaly, action on a direct cure for poverty, creation of local strategies for desegregation, and acceptance of a new role by urban universities.

The United States has no national policy to guide land use or urban development. The new Department of Housing and Urban Development, while a significant advance over its predecessor, the Housing and Home Finance Agency, is not constituted to serve as the federal urban policy-making body. HUD has little relation to the forces that affect the urban economy, the urban population, or even the construction of housing. It administers only a fraction of the federal programs that bear directly on urbanization and the control of urban development.

What is called for is a centralized executive function—what Wilfred Owen so nicely called "a chief urban worrier"—or a special federal executive agency for urban affairs, comparable to the National Security Council, that can draw together various departments. This need becomes apparent when one runs down just the most obvious federal programs and policies that bear on cities and metropolitan areas but are under the jurisdiction of departments or agencies other than HUD:

Fiscal and tax policies that affect housing production, credit and employment (the Federal Reserve Board, the Bureau of the Budget, the Department of the Treasury); regional economic development, economic aid to depressed areas, industrial location trends (Department of Commerce); highway planning, airport location (the new Department of Transportation, the Civil Aeronautics Board; HUD has urban mass transportation still); research and development contracts in basic science, defense, health, and other behavioral sciences (Department of Defense, Department of Health, Education and Welfare, the National Science Foundation, the Atomic Energy Commission, the National Aeronautics and Space Administration); manpower training, labor statistics, and employment services (Department of Labor); welfare, social security, hospitals, school aid, elementary and secondary teacher training, aids to higher education (HEW); air pollution abatement (HEW); recreation areas, national parks, research into water pollution (Department of the Interior); agricultural mechanization, rural migration trends, use of farm land in urbanizing areas (Department of Agriculture).

And this catalogue does not include a miscellany of special agencies, such as the Office of Economic Opportunity, with its portion of anti-poverty programs, the Small Business Administration, currently an unadopted program; and the General Services Administration, a rather important autonomous agency which determines the location of the federal government's increasing regional offices and employment centers, as well as the design of the buildings.

We have many more federal instruments and more information than we have begun to focus on, much less apply in a systematic manner. Coordination of departmental thinking and use of scattered federal programs in terms of urban development goals could take us a long step in the right direction.

That we have no overall policy body or stated goals is incredible. About 140,000,000 of the present nearly 200,000,000 Americans now live in urban-metropolitan areas, and most of the

65,000,000 more Americans expected by the end of the next two decades will pile in on or close to these congested metropolitan areas.

A great deal could be done to guide future urban development into new regions and to save present metropolitan areas from additional problems by coordinating certain programs now in separate departments and by adding a few new ones: highway construction funds and mass transportation assistance; industrial facility subventions; award of research and defense contracts; job information, relocation expenses, and retraining programs for rural migrants and urban underemployed; 100 per cent mortgage insurance for developers building housing for lower-income groups in specific development areas. If these programs were administered jointly and planning assistance were offered to regional groups in relatively unsettled and suitable areas that wanted to qualify for the combined federal aids and urban growth, future urbanization might turn out to be far more manageable than we suspect. Location of atomic energy power generators could well be the most important single factor in improving urban environments and creating new regions.

Such a focusing of federal programs inevitably suggests a touchy corollary—some form of national resources or land use planning. But the real test of our affluence may be how long we can afford not to bring all the powers we have to bear.

A notable federal step toward program coordination at the local level was recently taken following the prescription of the President's metropolitan study group. This is the new Demonstration Cities (renamed Model Cities) bill, which became law as this book was going to press. The new program specifically encourages a concentrated attack on both physical and social decay in large slum districts of at least seventy cities that will meet stiff federal criteria. The legislation is designed to overcome many of urban renewal's limitations. The act calls for cities to channel into designated districts all appropriate, existing government grants and local agency resources, from health, education, and welfare services to housing loans to small business and the revision of tax codes to stimulate rehabilitation. The hope is that such a concentration will markedly alleviate the problems of the people in slums and also produce visible, adaptable approaches for other cities to follow. Eighty-percent grants * are the main federal bait, but cities must achieve their own local coordination, including winning the cooperation of many intermediary state agencies. The Model Cities pattern is a major advance, but it is no panacea.

Much more can and must be done in Washington itself to rationalize and coordinate federal grants-in-aid and other programs, and to apply new technology to the benefit of cities. Perhaps the first step in this direction should be the appointment by the President of a National Commission to study all federal programs in the light of present and coming urban development and to make proposals. But only the President's leadership can create the needed national commitment.

TO OVERCOME THE FISCAL TAXATION ANOMALY

Such a federal executive agency or function could, I am hopeful, demonstrate to Congress that present grants-in-aid programs for cities, especially for the big cities, are unrealistically low. It could also facilitate the government's next necessary giant step: to provide localities with adequate fiscal resources to deal with local problems instead of spoon-feeding them with inadequate, special-purpose, often indirect grants.

This proposition, which seems radical at first, actually follows the by now well-established tradition of using our remarkably flexible federal fiscal machinery to adapt national resources to local needs and limitations, both in cities and on farms.

Specifically, a fiscal reallocation would be taking cognizance of the current realities of a nation of city dwellers: the centrifugal trends in our economy, the high public costs of dense urban living, the incidence of these costs and the shift in the sources of taxable wealth away from the localities and to the federal government.

The more urban we become, the more local public services we need. We also require new kinds of municipal or metropolitan regulations—from traffic control to control of air and water pol-

* The grants supplement existing federal aid programs.

lution, and perhaps even of ugliness. The fact is that government costs rise not arithmetically but geometrically as city size and density grow. And all these extra local costs do not even include the special welfare and development needs of the urban poor and the high toll of slums in the cities.

As demands on cities' budgets grow, their command of fiscal resources has become relatively more and more limited. There has been a change in the major sources of taxable wealth from real property to personal and corporate income, with localities getting less and less of the total share. Both cities and states are limited in the extent that they can tax incomes, sales, or even property, without driving away tax-paying residents and businesses. Since the federal government can most effectively tax incomes, without regard to their place of origin, it has been chief beneficiary of the remarkable rise in wealth of the past decades. The local disparity between needs and resources had been aggravated in central cities by the outmigration of middle-income families and industries, the obsolescence of plant, and inmigration of a new wave of rural poor.

We have never spent adequately on public services to match our private economic growth and to bring all parts of cities up to decent standards. Paying for all the things that need doing or renewing locally now is clearly beyond local ability. In fact, excessive reliance by cities and suburbs on the property tax has led to some very deleterious and exclusionist development practices within metropolitan areas. Suburbs use "mercantile" zoning with one-, two-, and even four-acre lots to keep out lower-income families and workers with children who make school taxes rise, and they simultaneously provide space for high tax-paying, nonnoxious concerns in industrial parks to which workers who live elsewhere must commute. Cities have distorted the use of urban renewal in a frantic effort to squeeze the highest use and largest return from Title I land for their slipping tax base. Further, meeting the housing needs of their lower-income families is extremely difficult in cities because local government cannot easily afford the tax abatement that is more and more needed to reduce basic shelter costs. Cities will also continue to worry about the expansion of tax-exempt universities and other nonprofit institutions, although their presence is a source of vitality. Tax-conscious groups challenge the non-taxable recreational and open-space areas. Meanwhile, local spending approaches federal levels.

Furthermore, metropolitan consolidation or fiscal federation of separate political and taxing jurisdictions—the "businessman's solution"—is not the answer to the local revenue gap.* The fact is that most of us who live in or use urban areas are subsidized; the freeloading automobile commuter who uses expressways and city-maintained and patrolled streets is a prime example. The poor are only a part of the growing revenue crisis of urban areas. As a matter of fact, suburban taxes are going up proportionately faster than those in central cities and are approaching the latters' high rates.

Several recent proposals for overcoming the governmental fiscal anomaly are now on hand from some of the nation's foremost economists and from special federal commissions and congressional advisory bodies, but they have not yet moved into the arena of legislative proposal. Walter E. Heller, former chairman of the President's Council of Economic Advisors, is the leading exponent of outright grants of federal revenues to the states, since the states bear the major burdens for health, education, and welfare. But cities which have long suffered from being short-changed by the state legislatures worry about this method of sharing federal revenues, and the White House and some federal departments believe that certain criteria should be attached to such state grants.

Another approach which is gaining popularity in some circles is

* The experience of Miami–Dade County, one of the two areas in the United States to establish true metropolitan government in recent decades, furnishes a pertinent guide. (Nashville–Davidson County, the other area, is too new to provide sufficient answers.)

After "Metro" began in Dade County in 1957, some savings were achieved initially through the streamlining of a chaotic congeries of local governments and functions under a professional modern administration. The new government was also able to provide better services at a somewhat lower per-unit cost.

But the longer-run fiscal impact of metropolitan government within just a few years was a rapid rise in public expenditures at a rate faster than that of the burgeoning population. "Metro" federation and good administration made it possible for local government to provide decent services and for previously separate governments to do many necessary things not possible before, such as improve arterial highways and traffic control, and to develop the seaport. Moreover, the ad valorum tax base proved completely inadequate to cope with the accumulated mess of unplanned past growth.

the federally guaranteed minimum family income or a "reverse income tax" for the poor. John Kenneth Galbraith advocates the minimum income because it would relieve cities of a large share of their welfare burden and redistribute rising federal revenues at the points of greatest need. A floor under income for unemployable persons was also proposed in 1966 by the National Commission on Technology, Automation and Economic Development as one means that government should use to offset the negative effects of changed technology on wage earners and to spur economic growth.

If cities are to make a significant dent in urban poverty and slums, much less reach the high level of urban amenity and livability about which there is so much talk, a much larger share of the gross national product must be made available to localities, and to their disadvantaged citizens. Philadelphia's difficulties in realizing its comprehensive plan due to inadequate funds is a case very much to the point.

One happy prospect is that the money may be available by the end of this decade, when federal revenues are expected to exceed federal expenditures. Gardner Ackley, current chairman of the President's Council of Economic Advisors, has stated that by 1970, with the anticipated increase in the national prosperity, the federal treasury should have a surplus of $40,000,000,000. The main question to be considered then, Ackley has said, would be *how* to use the federal surplus. It could be directed to cut taxes, to reduce the national debt, or to increase government spending on public programs.

This forecast suggests that if cities are to get the money they need and want from the anticipated federal surplus before it is eliminated through pressures from groups that are more interested in economy, cities must make persuasive plans for spending the money and also demonstrate their ability to spend it well.

AN ANTIDOTE FOR POVERTY—AND PERHAPS FOR SLUMS

In spite of our brave slogans, we have not even begun to wage a war on poverty. We have only been chipping away at the visible fraction of a vast submerged iceberg, and there is considerable doubt whether even a marked expansion of current anti-poverty, job training and educational programs can rid us of mass poverty or urban slums in a generation. Consider, for example, that a third of the nearly 15,000,000 poor children are in families headed by women who might be better off at home than out at underpaid jobs. Millions more of the poor are ill, physically disabled, or too old to work. Uncounted numbers of working-age men will probably never be retrained for the private job market. Further, the present anti-poverty programs are so complicated and caught up in inter-agency tugs of war, bickering between different levels of government, bureaucratic red tape, and poor local administration that relatively few cities are capable of using them well.

There is a grave injustice in leaving to local initiative the fate of the urban poor, most of whom have migrated to cities from rural areas. During the depths of the depression, the government came to see that piecemeal local programs were insufficient to cure unemployment, and that every battery in the federal arsenal would have to be thrown in to achieve recovery. What we need now is a crash program that is proportionate to the dimensions and special character of current poverty and accompanying social chaos in cities.

And as Galbraith has pointed out, "There is no antidote for poverty that is quite so certain in its effect as the provision of income." He also added that the United States can well afford to bring every family's income up to a minimum decent standard of living. In 1965, he said, provision of this base income for the poor would have used only one third of the amount by which personal incomes rose nationally. From the problems we have seen in cities it seems obvious that they will never clear slums, build or subsidize publicly administered low-rent housing, rehabilitate homes and make the unskilled adult employable as fast as this country could provide the poor with living incomes. Such a minimum income for subsistence farmers and agricultural workers might also ease city problems.

The public welfare system also fails to serve the eligible poor. It requires a drastic overhaul if it is not to continue to be a "major source of poverty," as a citizen committee appointed by Congress to study federal welfare recently reported after a two-year study.

With each state setting its own standards, the Advisory Council on Welfare discovered that half of those now on public assistance receive allowances below the poverty level. An estimated 8,000,000 more—half of those eligible for welfare nationally—did not receive any aid. Most of the latter do not know they are entitled to these benefits. The complete ignorance about public assistance or public housing of so many poor families subsisting in the slums of Southwest Washington when relocation for redevelopment began shows how out of touch and unable to cope even with the welfare world so many poor people in cities are. But we should not have to wait for public dislocation to make such information or rehousing services available.

The federal Advisory Council proposed a federally established minimum income based solely on need (and not all the other humiliating eligibility criteria) as the best way to overcome the present welfare system's shortcomings. More people should be put on rather than pushed off welfare.

An ungrading in rent allowances for families receiving public assistance payments alone would probably do more to get millions out of slums than any reformulation of the public housing program. But local housing codes must be systematically and effectively enforced, and housing information and relocation services provided to help families find decent new homes outside the slum. As long as we continue to treat the housing of the urban poor primarily as a shelter problem, rather than one of inadequate income, we will lag.

Obviously federally aided local programs with long-run promises of ending the poverty cycle must be pursued and expanded; there should be greater appropriations and improved programs for the schooling, health, and training of disadvantaged youth and adults, as well as for their living environments and neighborhood facilities. It would be a serious error to assume that the minimum income can substitute for these programs.

The federal Commission on Automation also proposed a giant WPA as an immediate means for mitigating the social effect of automation. This method would provide the missing ingredient in the Model Cities plan. It would create jobs and income for the underskilled and unemployed by training and paying them to do neglected public work that needs doing, mostly in cities—in hospitals, medical care, public protection, community organization, conservation, sanitation, and the rebuilding and rehabilitation of slum areas.

But retraining and new employment services should not be limited to cities' poverty areas, since as automation advances it will put out of work many people presently employed in cities and farms. Such programs should also be provided at points of migration and be permanent federally aided local functions. At the same time we need a computerized national service to provide information about job vacancies and skill demands, to avoid the disjuncture which caught cities and their new residents in recent years.

STRATEGIES FOR DESEGREGATION

Housing and Urban Development Secretary Robert C. Weaver has pointed out that "The future of the city is inextricably locked to the fate of the urban poor. . . . Until non-whites enter freely and fully into the mainstream of urban life our cities will remain troubled." A minimum living income, an end to poverty, is a prerequisite to reducing both geographical and mental ghettos, but it is only a first step, and non-discrimination is not the only additive required.

What is needed are strategies for desegregation by various local groups to bring Negroes into the mainstream. Many more opportunities are available to Negroes than they are taking advantage of. Ignorance about opportunities and how to take advantage of them, psychological blocks, fear of social rebuff and often rejection serve to perpetuate ghettos just as much as blatant discrimination. The thrust of these strategies need not be housing integration as such (many Negroes, like other ethnic groups, may prefer to live mostly with their own group) but rather freedom of movement and participation.

The great burden will probably fall on non-governmental groups, both voluntary and business, which must staff up to make laws workable and metropolitan areas open. The body that can and must assume leadership in this fundamentally moral issue is the church. The church is a metropolitan institution uniquely able to cut across boundaries of city and suburb, white, and non-white. Some churches have already taken the lead in open-housing drives in the suburbs and sponsorship of integrated middle-income housing. Churches and civic groups must find ways to substitute for the prejudice and fear that come from ignorance and strangeness the natural fellowship that comes with common interests and involvement. We must encourage participation by Negroes in all community institutions, not just those concerned with racial matters.

Business must also recognize that to be color blind in hiring will not end racial discrimination in employment. Companies and business associations have to recruit actively in Negro neighborhoods, establish liaisons with guidance counselors in ghetto schools, even advertise jobs in newspapers that Negroes are most likely to read. Hiring tests and criteria must be revised and modified. Employers will have to stop emphasizing a high school or college diploma when it makes no realistic difference in an applicant's qualifications. And where Negroes lack access to major area employers, a way must be found to provide bus service.

Cities must also face and start acting upon the corollary of dissolving the metropolitan racial schism: getting middle- and upper-middle-income white families with school-age children to move back to or stay in central cities. City budgets and plans, and urban renewal, must be used to make or remake city neighborhoods, facilities, and particularly schools, competitive with the suburbs. It is also important to hold some of those Negroes who can exercise wider choices and who are leaders. Otherwise, when the next boom of family formation comes in the 1970's, the metropolitan economic-racial schism will grow even wider.

NEW WORK FOR URBAN UNIVERSITIES

Urban universities should be more to cities than local growth industries that create jobs and purchasing power; more than brain centers that attract research and development companies; even more than think-machines to formulate social programs and planning techniques.

Universities must also help cities ask and answer the essential question of what all this tooling up is for? We have been so preoccupied with mastering techniques, inventing institutional arrangements, and getting funds, that we have not paused to inquire about urban goals. Robert M. Hutchins has observed about Americans that "The intellectual foundations of the choices we make is messy." This is glaringly evident in our thinking about cities. Once we get beyond welfare minimums and economic motives, we are at sea. We have no vocabulary that describes urban culture, no guiding conception of the city's human functions; we lack philosophy.

It is quite conceivable that in several decades we shall have eliminated the root problems of slums, poverty, racial discrimination, fiscal starvation. We may even achieve metropolitan or regional planning. But we will still not have come to grips with the real problems of people living in vast cities in post-industrial society.

Varied disciplines within the universities can assist cities to prepare an agenda of topics to be explored and studied beyond the obvious technical ones, and to help apply knowledge available in academic studies and the laboratory. They can help particularly in the renewal of certain urban institutions, such as schools. They might have saved us from going so far wrong in public housing.

Universities can also provide local civic forums where continuing dialogues may take place between practitioners and philosophers, political administrators and scholars, planner-architects, psychologists, and environmental biologists, scientists, theologians and civic-business leaders.

But if universities are to realize their great potential for leadership, they will first have to reform themselves. They will have to declare this responsibility to the city (if just in reciprocity for their privileged tax-exempt status) and actively encourage faculty members to focus on the issues and conditions of urban living. Time given in local public service or in leading such seminars must be awarded the credit or status equal to classroom teaching or publication.

The university will also have to reassess the education it offers to undergraduates. It is failing to turn out students equipped to consider the urgent issues. It also forfeits its unique opportunity to encourage students to later become active in public service. Yet, the civil rights and anti-poverty drives have shown that college students are eager for participation and commitment in urban issues. Will we have "educated" men and women who are capable of earning excellent livings, but who cannot control the urban environments in which they live?

THE GOOD BUT COMPLEX LIFE

Will Americans ever realize the ideal of the good life in cities? There are good reasons for pessimism, but also some strong rays of hope.

One encouraging sign is the exceptional men and women who have stepped forward in increasing numbers to meet the urban challenges. Also, Americans are learning that their cities are not temporary habitats that we can use and abuse and then abandon. We are beginning to turn talent, energy, and money to conserve, redevelop, and embellish our urban environments and to make all city neighborhoods livable. We have begun to see the role of cities in a new, positive way, one in which the city not only prevents harm and disease but positively promotes human good.

One reason for optimism is the new awareness on the part of business and government leaders that there is an intimate relationship between local human capital—the education, talents, and well-being of the people who live and work in a community—and the economic vitality and potential for renewal of that community.

In this country, which is dominated by the decisions of commerce and industry, it is particularly encouraging to learn that industry and business are choosing their headquarter locations more and more according to non-economic attractions. The quality of life and the standard of services and amenities offered by an area—its schools, housing, transportation, general environment, accessible recreation facilities, universities, and cultural activities—now determine where the foot-loose growth industries and research and development laboratories go. And these are conditions over which community decisions and plans can have a decisive influence.

Thus it appears likely that the new requirements of industries which must compete for top talents will in effect force cities and their metropolitan environs to achieve and maintain high standards. For in the coming era, competition will not be as much between central cities and their suburbs, as in recent past decades, but rather among metropolitan regions.

Perhaps it is naïvely optimistic, though I hope not, to expect a change in attitude among practical men of achievement and responsibility in industry about their products, as they recognize the importance of a good urban environment in protecting and developing to the maximum vital human resources.

Yet the prospect before us and our cities will always be ambiguous and paradoxical. As Americans gain greater discretionary income, as technology offers extraordinary new conveniences, options, and mobility, the conditions of living in a predominantly urban society by necessity will reduce individual freedom. New community restrictions must be imposed on people's use of products, as well as real property. There is, for example, the growing threat of noise pollution in cities. Where should use of transistor radios be allowed? How many decibels may a construction drill rise? Should use of automobile horns in cities be banned?

We should begin to concern ourselves, too, with the human effects of information technology—the use of machines and automatic signals to order human movements, to facilitate communication, to store knowledge, provide information, guide decisions at a rate exceeding population growth. The syndrome that threatens from this reliance on thinking machines is as yet a mere cloud on the horizon for most people, but it hovers over the urban scene. It has been described by Richard Meier as "the special form of harassment which results from man's being the target of too many 'messages'—too much communication from too many sources." An information overload that exceeds human capacity to absorb and handle it causes mounting disorder and confusion, and finally a desire of the individual to cut all connections with society, to escape.

The ambiguity of progress in a technically advanced urban society makes it essential for Americans to cultivate new ways of looking at things and to reinforce certain qualities of mind and spirit. An urban people must be sophisticated. We must give up a certain naïvete and the search for panaceas. We must learn to live with what Stephen K. Bailey has called "the politics of conflict"; to accept the fact that any solution or advance carries with it both gains and losses. We shall have to recognize that even with the best leaders, talents, information, and plans, we will never have all the answers, and many forces will always be beyond our control. Accidents of timing, fortuitous events, changes in corporate policies, social unrest, wars, and inventions will always complicate our advances. Yet we must act if we are to try to master our urban environment. We must have the courage to move ahead aware that our information will always be insufficient, and to move toward solutions which will always be partial and imperfect.

This means that individual commitment, moral concern, openness to experience, and willingness to act and take risks based on one's beliefs are essential. In spite of the plethora of organizations, increasing information, and numerous tools, the significant breakthroughs have been made not by committees or as the result of market studies but by individuals.

Even with man central to our urban plans, we shall have to recognize that "man" is not a statistical average, but many different people with many different open-ended tastes, desires, needs, and goals. Nor is man rational. He does not flock to the good but dull small cities like New Haven that have "solved" their problems, nor even to the center of a beautifully planned city like Philadelphia. He wants to go where the action is—the bright lights, the jobs, the good times, the great experiences—the nerve-wracking, anonymous, but exciting hub of mid-Manhattan. Or else he chooses the non-city city of Los Angeles. Perhaps we must accept discomfort, stress, and anomie as the price of exciting diversity and the variety of opportunities that only the big cities can afford, and seek for ways to balance this stress by creating oases and retreats where the individual can go on occasion to seek inner renewal.

Perhaps we must also redefine the good life to be sought in cities. As John W. Gardner noted in *Self-Renewal*, physical comfort, diversion, gratification, the state of having realized one's goals, do not constitute happiness for man. Americans have achieved the comforts and pleasures to which poor nations aspire and have learned that these are not enough. "The truer version involves striving towards meaningful goals—goals that relate the individual to a larger context."

Will our cities always be in a race with time? "The really important tasks are never finished," Gardner wrote.

If well run, the race itself will constitute the good life.

Bibliography

To gain an understanding of how American cities developed and of what is happening in them today, it is necessary to dig into diverse sources from both past and present, and to piece together many bits of information and separate strands of thought.

The primary and major sources for this study were not in libraries, but in the undocumented words, experiences and plans of the people and cities about which I have written. My basic material was garnered from hundreds of interviews, supplemented by correspondence, and from dozens upon dozens of reports issued by local public bodies, civic organizations and federal agencies. Various congressional committee hearings and articles published in professional journals, general periodicals and daily newspapers over the past few decades also provided much useful information. To list all these, however, would be beyond the scope of a bibliography that is intended, as is the book itself, for the interested citizen, official or general student, not the specialist. In fact, many important printed sources are not available in libraries, and thus cannot be readily obtained.

Nonetheless, I found many books indispensable as I sought to understand and interpret the complex of past and present forces that are at work in our cities. I have listed these books, plus some special landmark publications in the field of housing, urban renewal and development, that I found pertinent. The list is intended to be supplemental and suggestive—of possible interest to the reader who may wish to explore further topics discussed in the book. It is not a comprehensive survey of the vast literature in the field. In order to facilitate the reader's pursuit of the subject of American cities, I have grouped the books under certain broad topic headings, although it should be understood that there is considerable overlapping from one area to another. These groupings may also indicate the author's general approach.

AMERICAN URBAN DEVELOPMENT

1. The Political, Cultural and Economic Framework

Adams, James Truslow, *The Epic of America,* Little, Brown and Company, Boston, 1932.

Adrian, Charles, *Governing Urban America,* McGraw-Hill, New York, 1933.

Andrews, Wayne, *Architecture, Ambition and Americans,* Harper and Brothers, New York, 1947.

Arnold, Thurman, *The Folklore of Capitalism,* Yale University Press, New Haven, 1937. (Yale paperbound, 1959)

Banfield, Edward C. (ed.), *Urban Government,* The Free Press of Glencoe, New York, 1961.

Beard, Charles A., *Public Policy and the General Welfare,* Farrar and Rinehart, New York, 1941.

Beard, Charles A. and Mary R., *The Rise of American Civilization,* 2 vols., The Macmillan Company, New York, 1927.

Beard, Miriam, *A History of the Business Man,* The Macmillan Company, New York, 1938.

Brogan, Dennis W., *Politics in America,* Harper and Brothers, New York, 1954.

Bruckberger, R. L., *Image of America,* Viking Press, New York, 1939.

Butts, R. Freeman and Lawrence Cremin, *A History of Education in American Culture,* Henry Holt and Company, 1953.

Dearing, Charles L. and Wilfred Owen, *National Transportation Policy,* Brookings Institution, Washington, D.C., 1949.

Gaus, John M., Leonard D. White and Marshall E. Dimock, *The Frontiers of Public Administration,* University of Chicago Press, Chicago, 1936.

Gilmore, Harlan, *Transportation and the Growth of Cities,* The Free Press of Glencoe, Glencoe, Ill., 1953.

Good, H. G., *A History of American Capitalism,* The Macmillan Company, New York, 1956.

Hacker, Louis, *The Triumph of American Capitalism,* Simon and Schuster, New York, 1940.

Hillhouse, A. M., *Municipal Bonds; a Century of Experience,* Prentice-Hall, Inc., New York, 1936.

Hofstadter, Richard, *The American Political Tradition,* Alfred A. Knopf, Inc., New York, 1948.

Hunter, Floyd, *Community Power Structure,* University of North Carolina Press, Chapel Hill, 1953.

Kimball, Fiske, *American Architecture,* The Bobbs-Merrill Company, New York, 1928.

Mason, Edward S. (ed.), *The Corporation in Modern Society,* Harvard University Press, Cambridge, 1960.

Morison, Samuel Eliot and Henry Steele Commager, *The Growth of the American Republic,* 2 vols., Oxford University Press, New York, 1940.

Moses, Robert, *Theory and Practice in Politics,* Harvard University Press, Cambridge, 1939.

Mumford, Lewis, *The Culture of Cities,* Harcourt, Brace and Company, New York, 1938.

Neff, Frank A., *Municipal Finance,* The McGuin Publishing Company, Wichita, Kansas, 1939.

Parkes, Henry Bamford, *The American Experience,* Alfred A. Knopf, Inc., New York, 1947; Vintage Books, New York, 1959.

Parrington, Vernon L., *Main Currents in American Thought,* 2 vols., Harcourt, Brace and Company, New York, 1927. (Harvest paperback)

Phillips, Jewell Cass, *Municipal Government and Administration in America,* The Macmillan Company, New York, 1960.

Queen, Stuart A. and David B. Carpenter, *The American City,* McGraw-Hill, New York, 1953.

Report of the Urbanism Committee to the National Resources Committee, *Our Cities, Their Role in the National Economy,* U.S.G.P.O., Washington, D.C., 1937.

Soule, George, *Economic Forces in American History,* William Sloane Associates, Inc., New York, 1952.

Tunnard, Christopher and Henry Hope Reed, *American Skyline; the Growth and Form of Our Cities and Towns,* Houghton Mifflin Company, Boston, 1955.

Weber, Max, *The City* (trans. by Don Martindale and Gartrud Neuwirth), The Free Press of Glencoe, Glencoe, Ill., 1958; Colliers Books, New York, 1962.

2. *Historic Periods in the Development of American Cities From Constitutional Convention to Reform*

Bryce, Lord James, *The American Commonwealth,* 2 vols., G. P. Putnam's Sons, New York, 1959. (1st ed., 1888)

Commager, Henry Steele (ed.), *America in Perspective: The United States Through Foreign Eyes,* Random House, New York, 1947.

Davis, Rich Dewey, *National Problems, 1885–1897,* Harper and Brothers, New York, 1907.

De Tocqueville, Alexis, *Democracy in America,* 2 vols., Alfred A. Knopf, Inc., New York, 1945. (1st American ed., 1838)

Dickens, Charles, *American Notes,* Oxford University Press, London and New York, 1957. (1st ed., 1842)

Dos Passos, John, *The Head and Heart of Thomas Jefferson*, Doubleday and Company, New York, 1954.

Dunbar, Seymour, *A History of Travel in America*, The Bobbs-Merrill Company, Indianapolis, 1915.

Hadley, Arthur Twining, *Railroad Transportation*, G. P. Putnam's Sons, New York, 1886.

Hendrick, Burton Jr., *The Age of Big Business*, Yale University Press, New Haven, 1920.

Hibbard, Benjamin, *A History of the Public Land Policies*, The Macmillan Company, New York, 1924.

Holbrook, Stewart, *The Story of American Railroads*, Crown Publishing Company, New York, 1934.

Horwich, Isaac A., *Immigration and Labor*, G. P. Putnam's Sons, New York, 1912.

Josephson, Matthew, *The Robber Barons*, Harcourt, Brace and Company, New York, 1934.

Kirkland, Edward Chase, *Men, Cities and Transportation*, (*New England, 1820–1900*), Harvard University Press, Cambridge, 1948.

Muirhead, James F., *The Land of Contrasts*, Lawson, Walte and Company, Boston, New York and London, 1898.

Quiett, Glenn Chesney, *They Built the West: An Epic of Rails and Cities*, D. Appleton-Century Company, New York, 1934.

Robbins, Roy M., *Our Landed Heritage*, Princeton University Press, Princeton, N.J., 1942.

Schlesinger, Arthur Meier, *The Rise of the City, 1878–1898*, The Macmillan Company, New York, 1938.

Spearman, Frank H., *The Strategy of the Great Railroads*, Charles Scribner's Sons, New York, 1904.

Trollope, Anthony, *North America*, Harper and Brothers, New York, 1862.

United States Bureau of the Census, *A Century of Population Growth, 1790–1900*, Washington, D.C., 1909.

Weber, Adna F., *The Growth of Cities in the 19th Century, a Study in Statistics*, Columbia University Press, New York, 1899.

Wortley, Lady Emmeline S., *Travels in the United States during 1849 and 1850*, Harper and Brothers, New York, 1851.

The Era of Reform

Addams, Jane, *Twenty Years at Hull House*, The Macmillan Company, New York, 1911.

Beard, Charles A., *American City Government*, Century Company, New York, 1911.

Goldman, Eric F., *Rendezvous With Destiny*, Alfred A. Knopf, Inc., New York, 1955.

Hofstadter, Richard, *The Age of Reform*, Alfred A. Knopf, Inc., New York, 1955.

Howe, Frederic C., *The Confessions of a Reformer*, Charles Scribner's Sons, New York, 1925.

Howe, Frederic C., *European Cities at Work*, Charles Scribner's Sons, New York, 1914.

Howe, Frederic C., *The Modern City and Its Problems*, Charles Scribner's Sons, New York, 1915.

Riis, Jacob A., *How the Other Half Lives; Studies among the Tenements of New York*, Charles Scribner's Sons, New York, 1914.

Steffens, Lincoln, *The Autobiography of Lincoln Steffens*, Harcourt, Brace and Company, New York, 1931.

Steffens, Lincoln, *The Shame of the Cities*, McClure, Phillips and Company, 1904; Hill and Wang, New York, 1957.

Steward, Frank Mann, *A Half Century of Municipal Reform*, University of California Press, Los Angeles and Berkeley, 1950.

Ware, Louise, *Jacob A. Riis*, D. Appleton-Century Company, New York, 1930.

Wilcox, Delos F., *Great Cities in America*, The Macmillan Company, New York, 1910.

From Reform to Depression

Allen, Frederick Lewis, *Only Yesterday*, Harper and Brothers, New York, 1931.

Lewis, Sinclair, *Babbitt*, Harcourt, Brace and Company, New York, 1922.

MacMichael, Stanley L. and Robert F. Bingham, *City Growth and Values*, MacMichael Publishing Company, Cleveland, 1923.

Sparks, Frank M., *The Business of Government*, Rand McNally and Company, Chicago, 1916.

Sullivan, Mark, *Our Times*, vols. 1–3, Charles Scribner's Sons, New York, 1929.

Wilcox, Delos F., *Analysis of the Electric Railway Problem*, the author, New York, 1921.

Depression, Post-War and Beyond

Allen, Frederick Lewis, *The Big Change*, Harper and Brothers, New York, 1952.

Einaudi, Mario, *The Roosevelt Revolution*, Harcourt, Brace and Company, New York, 1959.

Futterman, Robert A., *The Future of Our Cities*, Doubleday and Company, Inc., Garden City, New York, 1961.

Galbraith, John Kenneth, *The Affluent Society*, Houghton Mifflin Company, Boston, 1958.

Gardner, John W., *Self-Renewal*, Harper and Row, New York, 1963.

Geen, Elizabeth, Jeanne R. Lowe and Kenneth Walker (eds.), *Man and the Modern City*, University of Pittsburgh Press, Pittsburgh, 1963.

Gottman, Jean, *Megalopolis*, The Twentieth Century Fund, New York, 1961.

Ickes, Harold L., *The Secret Diary of Harold L. Ickes*, Simon and Schuster, New York, 1953.

Lerner, Max, *America as a Civilization*, Simon and Schuster, New York, 1957.

Lubell, Samuel, *The Future of American Politics*, Harper and Brothers, New York, 1951.

Owen, Wilfred, *Cities in the Motor Age*, Viking Press, New York, 1959.

Schlesinger, Arthur M. Jr., *The Coming of the New Deal*, Houghton Mifflin Company, Boston, 1959.

Schlesinger, Arthur M. Jr., *The Crisis of the Old Order*, Houghton Mifflin Company, Boston, 1957.

Schlesinger, Arthur M. Jr., *The Politics of Upheaval,* Houghton Mifflin Company, Boston, 1960.
Vernon, Raymond, *The Changing Economic Function of the Central City,* Committee for Economic Development, New York, 1959.
Wecter, Dixon, *The Age of the Great Depression,* The Macmillan Company, New York, 1948.

3. Development and Government of Specific Cities

Chicago

Hayes, D. B., *Chicago, Crossroads of American Enterprise,* Julian Messner, Inc., New York, 1944.
Hoyt, Homer, *One Hundred Years of Land Values in Chicago, 1830–1933,* The University of Chicago Press, Chicago, 1933.
Merriam, Charles, *Chicago, A More Intimate View of Urban Politics,* The Macmillan Company, New York, 1929.

New Haven

Dahl, Robert A., *Who Governs? Democracy and Power in an American City,* Yale University Press, New Haven, 1961.
Dana, Arnold Guyot, *New Haven's Problems,* The Tuttle, Morehouse and Taylor Company, New Haven, 1937.
Osterweiss, Rollin G., *Three Centuries of New Haven, 1638–1938,* Yale University Press, New Haven, 1953.
Van Dusen, Albert E., *Connecticut,* Random House, New York, 1961.
Wolfinger, Raymond E., *The Politics of Progress,* Center for Advanced Study in Behavioral Sciences, Stanford, California, April, 1961. (unpublished)

New York

Hoover, Edgar M. and Raymond Vernon, *Anatomy of a Metropolis,* vol. 1, New York Metropolitan Region Study, Harvard University Press, Cambridge, 1959.
Lichtenberg, Robert M., *One-Tenth of a Nation,* vol. 7, New York Metropolitan Region Study, Harvard University Press, Cambridge, 1960.
Low, Frances, *The History of New York City Housing,* New York, 1965. (unpublished)
Moses, Robert, *Working for the People: Promise and Performance in Public Service,* Harper and Brothers, New York, 1956.
Rodgers, Cleveland, *Robert Moses: Builder for Democracy,* Henry Holt and Company, New York, 1952.
Roosevelt, Franklin D., *The Happy Warrior,* Houghton Mifflin Company, New York, 1928.
Sayre, Wallace and Herbert Kaufman, *Governing New York City,* Russell Sage Foundation, New York, 1960.
Tugwell, Rexford Guy, "New York," in William A. Robson (ed.), *Great Cities of the World,* George Allen and Unwin, Ltd., London, 1954, pp. 413–48.
Tugwell, Rexford Guy, *The Art of Politics,* Doubleday and Company, New York, 1958. (chapter on Fiorello LaGuardia)

Vernon, Raymond, *Metropolis 1985*, vol. 9, New York Metropolitan Region Study, Harvard University Press, Cambridge, 1960.

Philadelphia

Burt, Struthers, *Holy Experiment*, Doubleday, Doran and Company, New York, 1945.

Deutermann, Elizabeth P., *Economic Development*, Technical Report #13, Community Renewal Program, Philadelphia, December, 1964.

Lafore, Lawrence and Sarah Lee Lippincott, *Philadelphia: The Unexpected City* (Philadelphia ed.), Doubleday and Company, Inc., Garden City, New York, 1965.

Reichley, James, *The Art of Government, Reform and Organization Politics in Philadelphia*, A Report to The Fund for the Republic, New York, 1959.

Scharf, J. Thomas and Westcott Thompson, *History of Philadelphia, 1609–1884*, 3 vols., L. H. Everts and Company, Philadelphia, 1884.

Pittsburgh

Chinitz, Benjamin and Edgar M. Hoover (eds.), *Region in Transition*, vol. 1, Economic Study of the Pittsburgh Region, University of Pittsburgh Press, Pittsburgh, 1963.

Harper, Frank C., *Pittsburgh: Forge of the Universe*, Comet Press Books, New York, 1957.

Klein, Philip, *A Social Study of Pittsburgh*, New York School of Social Work, New York, 1938.

Lorant, Stefan, *Pittsburgh, The Story of an American City*, Doubleday and Company, Inc., Garden City, New York, 1964.

The Pittsburgh Survey, 6 vols., Russell Sage Foundation, New York, 1914.

O'Connor, Harvey, *Mellon's Millions, The Biography of a Fortune*, John Day Company, Philadelphia, 1933.

Patman, Wright, *Bankerteering, Bonuseering, Melloneering*, Peerless Printing Company, Paris, Texas, 1934.

Other Cities

Fowler, Richard B. and Henry C. Haskell, *City of the Future, A Narrative History of Kansas City, 1850–1950*, F. Glenn Publishing Company, Kansas City, Missouri, 1950.

Rose, William G., *Cleveland, The Making of a City*, World Publishing Company, Cleveland and New York, 1936, 1950.

Still, Bayrd, *Milwaukee, The History of A City*, State Historical Society of Wisconsin, Madison, Wisconsin, 1948.

THE NEW TOOLS: HOUSING, CITY PLANNING AND URBAN RENEWAL

Abrahamson, Julia, *A Neighborhood Finds Itself*, Harper and Brothers, New York, 1959.

Abrams, Charles, *The Future of Housing*, Harper and Brothers, New York, 1946.

Banfield, Edward C. and Morton Grodzins, *Government and Housing in Metropolitan Areas,* McGraw-Hill, 1958.

Bauer, Catherine, *Modern Housing,* Houghton Mifflin Company, Boston, 1934.

Colean, Miles, *Renewing Our Cities,* The Twentieth Century Fund, New York, 1953.

"Current Developments in Housing," *The Annals of the American Academy of Political and Social Science,* vol. 190, Philadelphia, March, 1937.

Dyckman, John W. and Reginald R. Isaacs, *Capital Requirements for Urban Development and Renewal,* McGraw-Hill, New York, 1961.

The Editors of *Fortune* magazine, *The Exploding Metropolis,* Doubleday and Company, Inc., New York, 1958.

Eskew, Garnett L., *Of Land and Men,* Urban Land Institute, Washington, D.C., 1959.

Fisher, Robert Moore, *Twenty Years of Public Housing,* Harper and Brothers, New York, 1959.

Ford, James *et al., Slums and Housing,* 2 vols., Harvard University Press, Cambridge, 1936.

Greer, Guy, *Your City Tomorrow,* The Macmillan Company, New York, 1947.

Greer, Guy and Alvin W. Hansen, *Urban Redevelopment and Housing: A Program for Post-War,* National Planning Association, Planning Pamphlet #10, December, 1941.

Haar, Charles M., *Federal Credit and Private Housing,* McGraw-Hill, New York, 1960.

Haar, Charles M., *Land-Use Planning: A Casebook of the Use, Mis-use and Re-use of Urban Land,* Little, Brown and Company, Boston, 1959.

Jacobs, Jane, *The Death and Life of Great American Cities,* Random House, New York, 1961.

McDonnell, T. L., *The Wagner Housing Act,* Loyola University Press, Chicago, 1957.

"Metropolis in Ferment," *The Annals of the American Academy of Political and Social Science,* vol. 314, Philadelphia, November, 1957.

Meyerson, Martin and Edward C. Banfield, *Politics, Planning and the Public Interest: The Case of Public Housing in Chicago,* The Free Press of Glencoe, Glencoe, Ill., 1955.

Millspaugh, Martin and Gurney Breckenfield, *The Human Side of Urban Renewal,* Fight-Blight, Inc., Baltimore, 1958.

Mitchell, Robert B. and Chester Rapkin, *Urban Traffic, a Function of Land Use,* Columbia University Press, New York, 1954.

Nash, William, *Residential Rehabilitation,* McGraw-Hill, New York, 1959.

Post-War Economic Policy and Planning, Part II: Housing and Urban Redevelopment, Hearings before the Subcommittee on Housing and Redevelopment of the Special Committee on Post-War Economic Planning, U.S. Senate, 79th Congress, 1st session, 1945.

The President's Advisory Committee on Government Housing Policies and Programs, A *Report to the President of the United States,* U.S.G.P.O., Washington, D.C., December, 1953.

Rannalls, John, *The Core of the City,* Columbia University Press, New York, 1956.

Rapkin, Chester, *The Real Estate Market in an Urban Renewal Area,* The New York City Planning Commission, New York, February, 1959.

Rapkin, Chester and William G. Grigsby, *Residential Renewal in the Urban Core,* University of Pennsylvania Press, Philadelphia, 1963.

Rossi, Peter H. and Robert A. Dentler, *The Politics of Urban Renewal: The Chicago Findings,* The Free Press of Glencoe, Glencoe, Ill., 1961.

Segal, Jack M. and William C. Brooks, *Slum Prevention Through Conservation and Rehabilitation,* Advisory Committee on Government Housing Policies and Programs, U.S.G.P.O., Washington, D.C., November 15, 1953.

Sogg, Wilton S. and Warren Wertheimer, "Urban Renewal: Problems of Eliminating and Preventing Urban Deterioration," *Harvard Law Review, January,* 1959, vol. 72, no. 3, pp. 504–52.

Straus, Michael W. and Talbot Wegg, *Housing Comes of Age,* Oxford University Press, New York, 1938.

Straus, Nathan Jr., *The Seven Myths of Housing,* Alfred A. Knopf, Inc., New York, 1945. (2nd ed.)

"Urban Housing and Planning," *Law and Contemporary Problems,* School of Law, Duke University, vol. XX, no. 3, Summer, 1955.

Walker, Mabel L. *et. al., Urban Blight and Slums,* Harvard City Planning Study XII, Harvard University Press, Cambridge, 1938.

Walker, Robert A., *The Planning Function in Urban Government,* University of Chicago Press, Chicago, 1950. (2nd ed.)

Wheaton, William L. C., *The Evolution of Federal Housing Programs,* University of Chicago, August, 1953. (unpublished dissertation)

Winnick, Louis, *Rental Housing: Opportunities for Private Investment,* McGraw-Hill, New York, 1958.

Wood, Edith Elmer, *Introduction to Housing,* United States Housing Authority, Federal Works Agency, Washington, D.C., 1940.

Woodbury, Coleman (ed.), *The Future of Cities and Urban Redevelopment,* The University of Chicago Press, Chicago, 1953.

Woodbury, Coleman (ed.), *Urban Redevelopment: Problems and Practices,* The University of Chicago Press, Chicago, 1953.

Journals and Periodicals

Architectural Forum

Architectural Record

House and Home

The Journal of the American Institute of Planners

The Journal of Housing

National Civic Review

SOCIAL ISSUES

Abrams, Charles, *Forbidden Neighbors,* Harper and Brothers, New York, 1955.

Allport, Gordon, *The Nature of Prejudice,* Doubleday and Company, Inc., Garden City, New York, 1954, 1958.

Bendix, Richard and Seymour Lipset (eds.), *Class, Status and Power,* The Free Press of Glencoe, Glencoe, Ill., 1953.

Buell, Bradley and Associates, *Community Planning for Human Services,* Columbia University Press, New York, 1952.

Child, Irwin L., *Italian or American*, Yale University Press, New Haven, 1943.

Cloward, Richard and Lloyd E. Ohlin, *Delinquency and Opportunity*, The Free Press of Glencoe, Glencoe, Ill., 1960.

Conant, James Bryant, *Slums and Suburbs*, McGraw-Hill, New York, 1961.

Drake, St. Clair and Horace R. Clayton, *Black Metropolis*, 2 vols., Harcourt, Brace and Company, New York, 1945. (Harper Torchbook, 1962)

Frazier, E. Franklin, *Black Bourgeoisie*, The Free Press of Glencoe, Glencoe, Ill., 1957.

Frazier, E. Franklin, *The Negro Family in the United States*, University of Chicago Press, Chicago, 1946.

Frazier, E. Franklin, *The Negro in America* (rev. ed.), The Macmillan Company, New York, 1957.

Ginzberg, Eli, *The Negro Potential*, Columbia University Press, New York, 1956.

Ginzberg, Eli, *The Uneducated*, Columbia University Press, New York, 1953.

Glazer, Nathan and Daniel P. Moynihan, *Beyond the Melting Pot*, The M.I.T. Press, Cambridge, 1963.

Glazer, Nathan and Davis McEntire, *Studies in Housing and Minority Groups*, University of California Press, Berkeley, 1960.

Grier, Eunice and George, *Privately Developed Interracial Housing*, University of California Press, Berkeley, 1960.

Grodzins, Morton, *The Metropolitan Area as a Racial Problem*, University of Pittsburgh Press, Pittsburgh, 1956.

Handlin, Oscar, *The Newcomers*, Harvard University Press, Cambridge, 1959.

Handlin, Oscar, *The Uprooted*, Little, Brown and Company, Boston, 1951.

Hansen, Carl F., *The Amidon Elementary School*, Prentice-Hall Inc., Englewood Cliffs, N.J., 1962.

Laurenti, Luigi, *Property Values and Race: Studies in Seven Cities*, University of California Press, Berkeley, 1960.

McConnell, John W., *The Evolution of Social Classes*, American Council on Public Affairs, Washington, D.C., 1942.

McEntire, Davis, *Residence and Race*, University of California Press, Berkeley, 1960.

Myrdal, Gunnar, *An American Dilemma*, Harper and Brothers, New York, 1944.

Pisani, Lawrence F., *The Italian in America*, Exposition Press, New York, 1957.

Reissman, D., *Class in American Society*, The Free Press of Glencoe, Glencoe, Ill., 1959.

Riessman, Frank R., *The Culturally Deprived Child*, Harper and Row, New York, 1962.

Salisbury, Harrison E., *The Shook-Up Generation*, Harper and Brothers, New York, 1958.

Sexton, Patricia C., *Education and Income*, Viking Press, New York, 1961.

Taeuber, Karl E. and Alma F., *Negroes in Cities*, Aldine Publishing Company, Chicago, 1965.

United States Commission on Civil Rights Reports, Book 2, *Education*, U.S.G.P.O., Washington, D.C., 1961.

United States Commission on Civil Rights Reports, Book 3, *Employment*, U.S.G.P.O., Washington, D.C., 1961.

United States Commission on Civil Rights Reports, Book 4, *Housing*, U.S.G.P.O., Washington, D.C., 1961.

Warner, Robert A., *New Haven Negroes: A Social History*, Yale University Press, New Haven, 1940.

Williams, John A. (ed.), *The Angry Black*, Lancer Books, New York, 1962.

Wilner, Daniel, Rosabelle A. Walkley and Stuart W. Cook, *Human Relations in Interracial Housing*, University of Minnesota Press, Minneapolis, 1953.

Wilson, James Q., *Negro Politics*, The Free Press of Glencoe, Glencoe, Ill., 1960.

Whyte, William Foote, *Street Corner Society*, University of Chicago Press, Chicago, 1955. (2nd ed.)

Journals and Periodicals

American Sociological Review
Commentary
The Journal of Social Issues
Public Opinion Quarterly

Special mention should also be made of the occasional papers on current issues in government and American society published by the Center for the Study of Democratic Institutions, Santa Barbara, California.

Index

Abrams, Frank: 85, 86
Ackley, Gardner: 570
ACTION, Inc.: 40, 152
ADC, *see* Aid to Dependent Children
Advisory Council on Welfare: 572
Aid to Dependent Children: 280–283, 499
Aluminum Company of America: 113, 142, 198
American Civic and Planning Association: 40n.
American Friends Service Committee: Philadelphia housing renewal project, 334–335
An American Dilemma (Myrdal): 293
Andrews, Norris: 468
Anti-poverty program: New Haven's Community Progress Inc. and, 523, 527
Aron, Ely M.: 288
Avalon Foundation: 41
N. W. Ayer and Son: 324, 339

Bacon, Edmund N.: 321, 323, 331, 333
Bahr Corporation: 436
Bailey, John A.: 389
Bailey, Stephen K.: 577
"Baltimore plan": 35
Banks, James G.: 205; and Southwest Washington project, 210–231
Barbaresi, Gerald: 535
Barr, Joseph: 137
Batten, Harry A.: 324, 339
Bauer, Catherine: 254
Bannett, George: 534, 540
Berman v. Parker: 199–200, 476
Bonan, Seon Pierre: 349
Boston, Mass.: Washington Park project, 267–269; West End neighborhood, 209
Bowles, Chester: 423
Brookings Institution: 108
Brooklyn, N.Y.: 67, 107
Bureau of the Census: 209n.
Bush, Prescott: 425, 433

Capehart, Homer: investigation by, 171
Carnegie, Andrew: 120
Caspert, Samuel: and Manhattantown project (N.Y.C.), 75–76
Cavicchi, Fr. Ugo: 465, 467, 468, 479, 544
Celentano, William: 467
Changing Economic Function of the Central City (Vernon): 314
Chase Manhattan Bank: 88
Chicago, Ill.: 10, 11, 39; Aid to Dependent Children, 281–282; Chicago Planning Commission, 37; and city planning, 16; Committee on New Residents, 287–288; Hyde Park-Kenwood renewal program, 269–271; interracial hous-

ing, 261; job-training, 288; Lake Meadows project, 37, 166, 245–246; land speculation, 20; neighborhood renewal, 37; open-housing demonstrations, 242; Prairie Shores, 245–246; West Side, 294n.
City Growth and Values: 19
City of New York, *see* New York City
City Record, The (N.Y.C.): 71
Civil rights: and housing renewal, 512; New York City open-occupancy housing, 65; *see also* United States Commission on Civil Rights
Civil Rights Law (1964): 241
Clark, Joseph S., Jr.: and Philadelphia renewal, 328–337; and Philadelphia transportation problems, 384–385; 390, 391
Clark, Kenneth: 298, 309
Cleveland, Ohio: 11
Cloward, Richard: 285, 292
Cole, Albert M.: 90, 91, 407
Colean, Miles: 477
Columbian Exposition (1893): 16
Committee for Economic Development: 303
Conant, James: 294, 299, 309, 310
Congress of Racial Equality: 286
Connecticut General Life Insurance Company: 452
CORE, *see* Congress of Racial Equality
Courant (Hartford): 407, 436

Dahl, Robert A.: 419
Daily News (New York): 89
Daily News (Washington, D.C.): 218
Daily Worker: 79
Daley, Richard: 287
Dark Ghetto (Clark): 298
Davenport, John: 416
Davies, J. Clarence, Jr.: 97, 98, 99, 100, 102, 103
Day, William: 345
Death and Life of Great American Cities, The (Jacobs): 102n.
DeLauro, Theodore: 479 *passim*
Delinquency and Opportunity (Cloward and Ohlin): 285, 292–293
Demonstration Cities bill: 566; *see also* Model Cities
Department of Housing and Urban Development: 101n., 199, 564
Des Moines, Iowa: 39
Deutsch, Martin: 308
Dilworth, Richardson: 320, 324; and Philadelphia renewal, 328–329, 336, 343, 350–351, 387, 390, 391, 400
Discrimination in housing, *see* Housing; Open-occupancy housing; Segregation in housing
District of Columbia: National Capital Housing Authority, 223, 230–231; Redevelopment Land Agency, 173, 175, 205, 224; United Planning Organization, 231; *see also* Southwest Washington; Washington, D.C.
Division of Slum Clearance and Urban Redevelopment, 32
Douglas, Paul: 204
Dowdy, Richard: study of New Haven Negroes, 512–514
Dowling, Robert: 140, 141
Duffus, R. L.: 124

Education: 292–310; big business and, 302–304; big-city school systems, 299–302; "dropouts," 292, 298–299; educability of "culturally disadvantaged," 296–299, 304–310, 356–357; expanded program, 534–543; and job opportunities, 292–296; "multi-institutional laboratories" program, 309; New Haven, 514–528; Philadelphia, 401–403; "Sargent plan," 519–522; schools, and population changes, 510–512; Skill Center, 534, 540; universities and urban problems, 574–576; Universities-Related Public Schools program, 376–377
Edwards, G. Franklin: 229
Edwards, Richard: 443
Eisenhower, Dwight D.: 91; appoints advisory committee on housing, 35

Elementary and Secondary Education Act (1965): 305
Employment: anti-discrimination laws, 295n.; Community Progress Inc., 528–534; Negro unemployment rate, 294n.; opportunities for slum dwellers, 288–292
Equitable Life Assurance Society: Gateway Center (Pittsburgh) project, 140–142, 145, 147

Fair Housing Conference (1965): 248, 249
Fantini, Mario: 306, 310
Federal Housing Administration: 33, 74–75, 234, 476, 477; continued usefulness of, 198–200; debt service, 184; middle-income housing, 235; and New York City, 90–92; original function of, 168; Philadelphia Society Hill project, 349–350; refinancing, 245n.; rent supplements, 265; Robert Moses and, 76–77; role in residential redevelopment, 167–172; Section 220 legislation, 170, 177; Section 221 (d)3 program, 249–253; Section 608 legislation, 171; segregated housing, 239; special assistance legislation for (1954), 170; "test of feasibility," 180–185
Federal National Mortgage Association: 250, 503
Federal Urban Renewal Program: 38; *see also* Housing Act of 1954
Federation Bank of New York City: 97, 98
Felt, James: 96, 97, 98, 102
Ferguson, Homer: 204, 205
FHA, *see* Federal Housing Administration
Filter process: housing market and, 235–236
Finnegan, James: 330
Follin, James: 90
Ford Foundation: 236, 522, 523, 525; "gray area" programs, 522–523; school improvement program, 303–304
Fordham University: 91
Fort Worth, Texas plan: 383
Fortune: 59, 288
G. Fox and Company: 452–453
Frazier, E. Franklin: 223
Freedman, Abraham: 333
Freese, Carl: 430
Fresno, Calif.: 383n.
Frick, Henry: 122, 123n.
Fried, Walter: 85
Fuchs, Victor: 291

Galbraith, John Kenneth: 570, 571
Gans, Herbert: 209
Gardner, John W.: 306, 578
General Electric Company: 198
General Services Administration: 565
Gerosa, Lawrence: 95–96
Ghetto life: 283–288
Gilbane Building Company: 438, 459
Gimbel, Bernard: 86
Good Will Industries: 218
John Graham Associates: 438
Great Cities program: 306, 307
Green, Thomas M.: 440
Green, William: 321
Greenfield, Albert M.: Philadelphia renewal and, 341–347
Greenleigh Associates: Aid to Dependent children study by, 281–283
Greer, Guy: 29–30
Grier, Eunice and George: 246, 247
Grigsby, William: 238
Victor Gruen Associates: 383
Gulf Oil Corporation: 122, 198

Hadley, Arthur Twining: 416
Hallman, Howard: 507, 511
Hansen, Alvin: 29–30
Harlan, Senator: 15
Harper's: 124, 329
Harriman, Averell: 262
Harris, Louis: 241
Hartford, Conn.: Constitution Plaza, 453; downtown redevelopment, 452–453
Haryou-Act: 301
Hauser, Philip: 293
Haussmann, Baron Eugene: 79
Hazlett, Theodore, Jr.: 152, 153

Head Start program: 305, 307–308, 536
Hechinger, Fred: 307
Heller, Walter E.: 569
Herald (New Britain): 436
Herald Tribune (New York): 78n., 89
Higgenbotham, A. Leon, Jr.: 353
Hill, G. Albert: 422
Hollingshead, August: 509
Hommann, Mary: 479
Hopkinson, Edward: 330
Horne, Joseph: 142
Housing: discriminatory practices, 65, 236–245; early legislation, 16–17; filter process of housing market, 235–236; New Deal and, 22–27; New York City shortage of, 93–96; Philadelphia's pioneering program, 332–337; "problem" families, 275–276; slum profiteering, 16–17; special assistance, 234; suburban, 238–241; units demolished annually, 233; *see also* Housing Acts; Low-income housing; Middle-income housing; Open-occupancy housing; Public housing; Segregation in housing
Housing Act of 1937: 26–27, 33
Housing Act of 1949: 66, 253, 340; amendment concerning real estate taxes, 69n.; National Housing Policy, 33; Title I, 30–34, 165–166 (*see also* Title I entry)
Housing Act of 1954: 94, 341; urban renewal, 34–36
Housing Act of 1961: middle-income units, 234–23[illegible]
Housing and Home Finance Agency: 32, 33, 209, 409, 485, 564; Community Renewal Program, 336; Demonstration Project, 225–229; Division of Slum Clearance and Urban Redevelopment, 32; housing report, 237; New York City and, 82, 85
Housing and Urban Development Act of 1965: 265
Howe, Louis: 55

Ickes, Harold: 56, 57n.
Ihlder, John: 223
ILGWU, *see* International Ladies' Garment Workers' Union
Impellitteri, Vincent: 84
Income: and non-white housing market, 246–249
Industrial revolution: 10–12
International Ladies Garment Workers Union: 82, 88
Interstate Highway Bill (1956): 39
Isaacs, Stanley: 83

Jack, Hulan: 97, 98
Jackson, John Day: 412, 455
Jacobs, Jane: 102, 254
Jefferson, Thomas: 8, 9, 10
Job Corps: 292
Jones and Laughlin Co.: 145
Justement, Louis: 173

Kansas City, Kan.: integration in, 242
Kansas City Star: 242
Kaufmann, Edgar J. (Kaufmann's Department Store): 134 *passim*
Kennedy, John F.: 3
King, Martin Luther: 242
Koppers Corp.: 122
Kramer, Fred: 245, 246

La Guardia, Fiorello: 47, 55, 56, 57, 64, 84, 131n., 320; and city planning, 60, 62–63
Lamberton, Robert: 321–322
Laurenti, Luigi: 240
Lawrence, David: and Pittsburgh program, 115, 130–133, 137, 140, 144, 148, 149, 345
Leach, Ed: 138
Lee, Richard C.: and New Haven renewal, 405–415, 417–452, 474, 482–551 *passim*
Lefkowitz, Louis J.: 281
L'Enfant: 173
Lerner, Max: 257
Lewis, Edwin O.: 338
Ligonier, Penna.: 124, 153
Lindsay, John V.: 70, 105, 548, 549n.
Logue, Edward C.: 423, 434, 451, 453, 464, 474, 548, 549n.; "Middle Ground" program, 507; on

New Haven program, 551; and New Haven school system, 515–516
Lohmann, Carl: 418
Los Angeles, Calif.: 15; interracial housing problems, 261; Watts area, 267, 286
Low-income housing: FHA program for private construction, 249–253

Mack, Maynard: 517
R. H. Macy Co.: and New Haven renewal program, 435, 440–445, 458
Malley, Edward W.: 441
Malley Company: 441 *passim*
Malley, W. Ward, Jr.: 445
Manpower Development and Training Act: 529
Martin, Edward: 130, 138
Martin, Park: 127, 128, 129, 132, 156, 159, 325
Mass Transit Act (1964): 391, 392
Olin Mathiesen Chemical Corporation: 530, 547, 548n.
McEntire, David: 275
McGinnis, Patrick: 421
F. H. McGraw Company: 452
McGuire, Mrs. Marie: 255, 263
Mellon, Andrew: 122–123
Mellon, Richard K.: 115, 125, 126, 129, 136, 138, 143; Pittsburgh housing, 152–156
Mellon, Thomas: 122
T. Mellon and Sons (bank): 122
Mermin, Al: 510
Metropolitan Life Insurance Company; and Stuyvesant Town project (New York City): 64, 65, 66, 77n., 139, 166, 167
Miami-Dade County: metropolitan government and, 569n.
Middle-income housing: 234–235; FHA program for private construction, 249–253
Midwestern Minority Housing Market: 241, 247
Milwaukee, Wis.: 11
Minchiatti, Fr.: 472
Mitchell, James: 503, 513
Mitchell, Robert B.: 322, 323
Mitchell-Lama housing cooperatives (New York City): 96, 99, 107n., 251–253
Model Cities bill: 566–567, 572; *see also* Demonstration Cities
Montgomery, Dorothy S.: 333
Moses, Robert: 47–98, 116, 132, 263, 334; bargaining position of, 80; bridge-building program for New York City, 57–59; career summarized, 51–59; evaluation of, 106–108; Manhattantown project, 74–77; Mayor's Committee for Slum Clearance, 48, 52, 66; and New York City charter of 1938, 61–62; "New York method," 69–72; New York State Power Authority, 96; New York State projects, 54; Parks Commissioner, importance of, 55–56; and Planning Commission, 60–63; political value of, 50; on rehabilitating property, 92; relations with Mayor Wagner, 85; Stuyvesant Town, 64–65; and Title I program, 54, 63, 65–96, 96–98; World's Fair (1964), 98
Moynihan, Daniel P.: 293
Muller, John H.: 147n.
Municipal reform movement: 15–19
Myrdal, Gunnar: 293

NAACP, *see* National Association for the Advancement of Colored People
Nashville-Davidson County: metropolitan government and, 569n.
National Association for the Advancement of Colored People: 286
National Commission on Technology, Automation and Economic Development: 570
National Committee Against Discrimination in Housing, 244, 249
National Resources Planning Committee: 28
Negro Politics (Wilson): 286
Negroes: desegregation strategies,

573–574; discrimination against, in housing, 236–245; ghetto life and, 283–288; migration of, 39; in New York City, 93; Philadelphia program and, 352–357; social problems and (New Haven), 512–514
Negroes in Cities (Taeuber): 248
New Deal: 18, 61; Pittsburgh and, 124; slum-clearance programs, 22–27
New Haven, Conn.: 39, 53, 405–551; Church Street project, 408, 409, 429–440, 445–447, 447–452, 454, 457–463; Citizens' Action Commission formed, 420, 454; Community Progress Inc., 522–546, 550, and evaluation of, 539–546; Court Street rehabilitation, 483–484; Dixwell neighborhood, 489–506, 513, 542, 543; expanded educational program, 534–543; Farnum Court, 545; growth of blight in, 410–415; Head Start, 307; industrial-redevelopment problems, 487–489; "Middle Ground" program, 506–509; as model for renewal programs, 548–551; Negro population, 489–506; Neighborhood Improvement program, concept of, 510; Newhallville, 510; Oak Street project, 422, 424–429, 464; Prince neighborhood, 537; redevelopment programs evaluated, 546–548; "Sargent plan" for education, 519–522; schools, and population changes, 510–512; school system reforms, 514–528, 537–539; Scranton area, 541; Skill Center, 534, 540; social renewal, 525–526; Urban League formed, 511–514; Wooster Square project, 464–474, 478–485, 490, 516n., 545; Yale University, 415–417, 456–457; zoning, 507–508
New Haven Foundation: 421, 549n.
New Haven Negroes (Warner): 493
New Orleans, La.: 267
New York City: 39, 45–109; Bedford-Stuyvesant area, 106, 294n.; Board of Estimate, 62–63, 79–80, 167; bridge-building program in, 57–59; Brooklyn, 67, 107; budget allocations, 280; Central Park, 51; charter of 1938, 60; Citizens' Advisory Committee, 104, 105; Citizens' Housing and Planning Council, 86; Citizens' Union, 63n., 76, and Title I investigation by, 97–98; City Planning Commission, 60, 67, 71n., 73, 82–83, 84, 92, 96; City-Wide Council for Better Housing, 82; Columbus Circle (Coliseum) project, 77, 86, 90, 94, 108; Community Service Society, 82; Corlears Hook project, 81–82; effect of Robert Moses on local leadership, 84; Godfrey Nurse-North Harlem project, 83; Greater New York Planning Council, 98; Greenwich Village, 101; Harlem, 67, 106; Higher Horizons program, 305, 306, 307; Housing and Development Administration, 549n.; Housing and Redevelopment Board, 98, 99, 100, 101, 104; housing shortage, 93–96; interracial housing problem, 262–263; Jones Beach, 51, 52, 78n.; Kips Bay project, 89; Lincoln Center for the Performing Arts, 49, 87, 108; Lincoln Square project, 49, 87, 88; luxury housing, 94–95; Manhattantown project, 74–77, 83, 89, 273; Mayor's Advisory Council, 85–86; Mayor's Committee on Housing, 82, 86; Mayor's Committee on Slum Clearance, 66, 68–69, 70, 71, 72–74, 84, 88, 97, and critics of, 76, 90; Mitchell-Lama housing program, 96, 99, 107n., 251–253; moderate-cost housing, 95; Morningside Heights, Inc., 81; New Haven program and, 548; "New Law" tenements, 49n.; New York Citizens Housing and Planning Council, 175; New York Convention and Visitors' Bureau, 86; New York Public Housing Authority, 65, 82; New York Uni-

versity "adoption" of a public school, 309; New York University-Bellevue redevelopment project, 87, 89; "Old Law" tenements, 49n.; open-housing law (1957), 93n.; Park West Village, 89; public-housing design, 263–264; public school system, 299–302, 304n., 305; Queens, 107; rehabilitation concept, 94–96; relocation of tenants, 69–70; rent control, 94; Rockefeller Center, 141n.; South Bronx area, 106, 107; standards for tenants in public housing, 258n.; Stuyvesant Town project, 64–65, 66, 77n., 139, 166; Title I projects in, 48–51, 65–108; Triborough Bridge Authority, 51, 56, 58n., 62n., 76, 84, 86, 90; United Housing Foundation, 81; Washington Square South project, 77, 81, 95; West Side Urban Renewal project, 271–275; West Village project, 101–103; Women's City Club, 82, 83; and "Workable Program," 85; World's Fair (1939) site, 51; World's Fair (1964), 98; zoning, 21, 59n., 60, 141n.; *see also* Haryou-Act; Moses, Robert
New York Life Insurance Company: 166
"New York method": 69–72
New York Regional Plan Association: 85n.
New York State: parks for, 54; parkways in, 54; Redevelopment Companies Act (1943), 64, 77, 95; Title I funds, 406n.
New York State Power Authority: 96
New York Times: 58, 255; on Higher Horizons program, 307; Robert Moses and, 89–90, 98
New York University: 87, 89, 309
Newburgh, N.Y.: public welfare, 281
Newsweek: 241
Noise pollution: 577
Nolen, John: 173
Norman, Dorothy K.: 287
O'Brion, Frank: 430, 434, 456
O'Dwyer, William: 57, 58, 64, 84, 97
Office of Economic Opportunity: 267, 286, 525–526, 534, 542, 543, 565
Ohlin, Lloyd: 285, 292
O'Keefe, Paul: 98
Omaha, Neb.: 14
Open-occupancy housing: California, 244, 261; Capitol Park Apartments, Washington, D.C., 189–190; Chicago, 242, 245–246, 261; effectiveness of legislation for, 243–245; executive order (1962), 242; in Kansas City, Kan., 242; open-housing law in New York City, 93n., 189; state legislation, 243; *see also* Housing; Segregation in housing
Our Cities—Their Role in the National Economy: 29, 30
Owen, Wilfred: 564

PACE (Projects to Advance Creativity in Education): 308–309
Paquin, Lawrence: 535
Parkinson, Thomas J.: 139, 140
Pei, Ioeh Ming: 349
Penn, William: 316, 323
Pennsylvania Manufacturing Association: 124
Pennsylvania Railroad: 137–138, 331, 372
Perkins, Holmes: 347
Perry, Lester: 142
Philadelphia, Penna.: 313–404; attracting business to, 370–373; "Better Philadelphia Exhibition," 323; center city renewal, 337–343, 367–373; Chamber of Commerce, 362, 402; Citizens' Council on City Planning established, 322; City Planning Commission established, 322; City Policy Committee, 321–322; Civilian Police Review Board, 353; Commission on Human Relations, 354–357; Community Renewal Program, 394–401; cultural facilities, expansion of, 379; design in urban renewal, 347–351; East

Poplar project, 334–335; education program, 373–379, 401–403; and for culturally deprived, 356–357; employment situation, 356, 360–367; Food Distribution Center, 339; Greater Philadelphia Movement formed, 325; housing program, 332–337, for non-whites, 353–360; Independence Hall, 339; Independence Mall, 371; Market Street East project, 380–382; new charter, 326–328; Old Philadelphia Development Corporation formed, 345; Opportunities Industrialization Center, 401; Penn Center, 331–332, 346; Philadelphia Housing Association, 321, 359, 397–398; Philadelphia Industrial Development Corporation, 362–365; philosophy of redevelopment, 313–322; population changes in, 351–357; public housing, 264, 333, 335, 358–359; Redevelopment Authority, 333–336, 340, 348–352; renewal potentials, 367–377, and program evaluated, 393–404; shopping facilities, 379–382; Society Hill project, 343–351, 368; Southwest Temple project, 356–357; Temple University, 375–376; Title I aid, 340–341; transportation program, 382–393; Universities-Related Public Schools program, 376–377; University City Science Center, 377–378, 379; Washington Square East, 339, 343, 351; West Philadelphia Corporation established, 375; "Young Turk" reformers, 320–321

Phillips, Walter: 321, 322, 336

Pittsburgh, Penna.: 110–163; ACTION-Housing, Inc., 154–155, 160–162; Allegheny Conference on Community Development, 115; Allegheny Conference on Post-war Planning, 127, 130, 136, 140, 150, 325; Allegheny County Planning Commission, 127; depression and, 124; education program, 162, 307; Gateway Center project, 140–144, 147, 163, 345, 347; industrialization, 117–121; Jones and Laughlin industrial redevelopment project, 146; Lower Hill redevelopment, 150–151; Mellon family and, 122–126; Mellon Square development, 143, 147, 148, 163; New Deal and, 124; "Pittsburgh formula," 115; Pittsburgh Housing Association, 123, 152; Pittsburgh Regional Planning Association, 125; Point State Park, 130, 138–140, 148; public-housing design, 264; Public Parking Authority, 136, 144; Redevelopment Authority, 140, 141, 142, 143, 145; redevelopment program summarized and evaluated, 110–114, 156–163; Regional Industrial Development Corporation, 152; "Renaissance" of, 114, 117; revenue through redevelopment, 114n.; Schenley Park, 120; smoke abatement, 145; Title I, 149, 151

Pittsburgh Consolidation Coal: 122

"Pittsburgh formula": 115

Pittsburgh Plate Glass Co.: 122, 142, 145

Pittsburgh Survey: 120

Planned Parenthood: 219, 221

Post (Washington, D.C.): 189, 211

Powell, Adam Clayton: 261–262

President's Advisory Committee on Housing Policies: establishment of, 35–36

President's Committee on Employment Opportunities: 530

President's Council of Economic Advisers: 569–570

Press (Pittsburgh): 138

Privately Developed Interracial Housing (Grier): 246

Property Values and Race: 240

Public housing: 234; architecture of, 263–264; cutback of program for, 253–256; costs absorbed by, 262; federal aid to, 24–27; financing formula, 276–277; new approaches (1965 legislation), 265–

269; sites for, 259–262; social factors, 262–263; tenants in, 256–259; *see also* Relocation: Southwest Washington
Puerto Ricans: in New York City, 63, 93

Rafsky, William: 333, 336, 344
Rauh, Joseph L.: 189–190
Real estate agents: and discrimination against non-whites, 236–245
Redevelopment: downtown, 440–459; financing of, 27–37, 194–198, 447–452; property rights, problems of, 445–447; redevelopment formula, 165; residential, and FHA's role in, 167–172; *see also* Rehabilitation; Urban renewal
Register (New Haven): 412, 416, 436, 456
Rehabilitation of property: keys to, 474–485; New York City and, 94, 96; Robert Moses on, 92; and tenant dissatisfaction, 485–489
Relocation of families: 203–231; business, 426; education for, 224–229; in New Haven, 426, 489, 505; in New York City, 69–70; Philadelphia, 335–336, 359; public housing and, 206–207; Southwest Washington program, 210–231; tenant resistance to, 214–217; Title I provisions for, 207; unsolved problems, 224–231
Rent control: in New York City, 94
Rent supplement program: 265
Rental Housing (Winnick): 168
Reynolds Metals Development Corporation: 197
Richards, Wallace K.: 126, 127, 128, 132, 143, 149, 156
Ring, James: 259
Robin, John P.: 140; and Philadelphia renewal, 345–347
Rochester, N.Y.: 39
Rockefeller, David: 85
Rockefeller, John D. III: 87, 88
Rockefeller Foundation Virus Laboratories: 547
Rohm and Haas: 371
Roosevelt, Franklin D.: 55, 56, 57, 61, 92, 131, 320
Roosevelt, Franklin D., Jr.: 76
Roosevelt, Theodore: 53
Rosenman, Samuel: 76
Rotival, Maurice E. H.: 417, 418, 420, 421, 422, 423
Rowe, Lucius: 430, 434
Rubin, Max: 299

Russell Sage Foundation: 120
St. Louis, Mo.: Banneker Schools' program, 306n.
Salisbury, Harrison: 255
Salvation Army: 218, 224
Samuels, Bernard: 322, 323–324, 326
San Francisco, Calif.: 15, 143; Hunters Point, 267
San Jose, Calif.: 39
Sargent, Cyril: 518–522
"Sargent plan" for education: 519–522
Saturday Evening Post: 102
Savitt, Robert: 436
Scheuer, James H.: and Southwest Washington project, 172, 175–180, 188, 189, 191–193
Schultz, Theodore W.: 303
Scully, Cornelius: 129, 131
Searles, John R., Jr.: 175, 176, 178, 191, 210, 212, 213
Segregation in housing: factors promoting, 235–241; and property values, 240–241; racial, 236–245; *see also* Housing; Open-occupancy housing
Self-Renewal (Gardner): 578
Shanahan, Thomas J.: 88, 97, 98
Shannon, Charles: 543
Sheraton Corporation: 435, 450
Shopping centers: redevelopment and, 440–445
Skerritt, James: 480, 484
Slums: definition of, 26n.; first publicly assisted, privately financed clearance project, 64; government "write-down" concept, 29; profit from, 12; relocation practices and, 207–208
Slums and Suburbs (Conant): 309, 310

Small, Mary R.: 471, 472, 474
Small Business Administration: 565
Smith, Alfred E.: 52n., 53, 54, 55, 131
Smith, Mrs. Chloethiel Woodard: 173, 180, 185, 186
Smoke abatement: 145
Social renewal, *see* New Haven: Community Progress Inc.
Southwest Washington, D.C., project: 172–200, 572; Amidon School, 195–196; *Berman* v. *Parker* ruling, 199–200, 476; Capitol Park Apartments, 180, 182, 185, 186, and racial integration, 189–190; redevelopment of property, 172–200; relocation of tenants, 203–231; Smith-Justement plan, 173–174; Zeckendorf plan, 174–175; *see also* District of Columbia
Spellman, Cardinal: 88
Steffens, Lincoln: 121
Stevens, Roger L.: 178, 188, 547; and New Haven renewal, 405–551 *passim;* and Southwest Washington program, 192–193
Stonorov, Oskar: 322
Straus, Nathan, Jr.: 27, 85, 86
Strayer, Martha: 218
Sviridoff, Mitchell: 464, 544, 548; heads N.Y.C. Human Resources Administration, 549n.; and job-opportunities program in New Haven, 528–534; and New Haven school system, 517–520

Taeuber, Alma and Karl: 248
Taft, Robert A.: 65; and Title I, 31
Tate, James H. J.: 400, 401
Taylor, Ralph: 432
Temple University: 375–376
Times (Hartford): 436
Title I (Housing Act of 1949): commercial redevelopment, 432n.; "fair value" clause, 91; and financing renewal, 568; housing units, 232; New Haven programs, 406; New York City program under, 48–51, 65–108; and "New York method," 69–72; non-residential projects, 232; original objective of, 169; Philadelphia projects, 340–341; Pittsburgh, 149, 151; relocation statute, 206–207; Southwest Washington, 164–200; sponsorship problem, 178–180; *see also* Housing Act of 1949
Toledo, Ohio: depression and, 23
Transportation: cities and, 38–39; federal aid to, 390–391; Philadelphia program, 382–393
Travelers Insurance Company, The: 453
Tugwell, Rexford: 61–63
Twyman, Charles: 498

Ungar, Sidney: 97
United States Commission on Civil Rights: discriminatory policies of lending institutions, 238; report by, 236
United States Commission on Race and Housing: 236, 240, 275
United States Department of Labor: 294n.; on-the-job market, 289, 291–292
United States Housing Agency: 27, 254
United States Office of Education: 539
United States Senate: FHA insurance-program hearings in New York City (1954), 74–76
United States Steel Corporation: 119, 142
United States Supreme Court: *Berman v. Parker,* 199–200; on eminent domain, 78
Universities, urban: and urban problems, 574–576
University of Pennsylvania Institute for Urban Studies: 238
Urban America, Inc.: 40n., 152n.
Urban League: 286
Urban renewal: city planning role in, 313–316; community organizations and, 558; design excellence and, in Philadelphia, 347–351; employment and, 314; evaluation of, 555–578 expansion of Title I, 34; FHA terms for, 170; fi-

nancing, 559, 562, 567–570; "human side" of, 204; leadership, 557–558, 562; New Haven as model, 405–407; professional staff and, 558; "Workable Program" concept, 36, 85, 90; *see also* Housing Act of 1954
Urban Renewal Administration: 209n., 225, 244, 432, 433, 472, 523
Urbanism Committee: 29, 30

Van Buskirk, Arthur: 129, 130, 132, 136, 139, 142, 156, 159
Vernon, Raymond: 314, 315, 370n.
Veterans Administration: 169

Wagner, Robert F., Jr.: 84, 91–92, 98, 103, 273; Mayor's Advisory Council, 85–86
Wall Street Journal, The: 71
Warner, Robert A.: 493
Washington, George: 173
Washington, D.C.: 39; Aid to Dependent Children, 280; municipal government, aid to, 23–24; non-white–white population ratio, 248; and urban growth, 13–15; *see also* District of Columbia; Southwest Washington
Weaver, Robert C.: 101n., 276, 409, 573
Webb and Knapp: 175, 177, 180, 346, 349; Southwest Washington, 187–188
Welch, G. Harold: 427, 428, 438, 455
Welfare system: 570–573
Westinghouse Electric Corporation: 113, 122, 145
Wexler, Isadore: 497, 498, 511
Wheaton, William L. C.: 393
Wilcox, Preston: 300
Wilkins, Roger C.: 453
Wilson, James Q.: 261, 286
Winchester Repeating Arms: 412
Wingate, Livingston L.: 301
Winnick, Louis: 168
Wood, Elizabeth: 254
Wooster, Catherine Bauer, *see* Bauer, Catherine
Works Progress Administration: 24
WPA, *see* Works Progress Administration
Wright, Elizabeth: 537–539, 542
Wright, Frank Lloyd: 52

Yale University: 415–417, 456–457
Yunich, David: 458

Zeckendorf, William: 88, 89, 174–175, 346, 348, 349; method of financing, 174n.
Zoning: 20–22; negative character of, 21–22; in New Haven, 507–508; in New York City, 21, 59n., 60, 141n.; over-zoning, 21

✦ ABOUT THE AUTHOR

JEANNE R. LOWE has traveled to cities all over the United States, and has visited certain cities numerous times to study their problems, to follow the progress of their renewal, and to interview the leaders as well as many citizens who have been involved in the far-reaching efforts to restore and adapt cities to the present and the future. Jeanne Lowe is the author of *Urban Renewal in Flux: The New York City View* and is co-editor of *Man and the Modern City*.

Miss Lowe was on the staff of *Time* and *The Reporter* and has written for *Harper's Magazine, Architectural Forum, The Saturday Evening Post*, and other nationally known magazines. Jeanne Lowe has specialized in urban affairs for the last dozen years. Miss Lowe was assistant public information manager for Action, Inc., (now merged with Urban America, Inc.). She directed Goucher College's 75th Anniversary Program on "Human Values in the Emerging American City," and has been a consultant to the Ford Foundation. In addition, she has done research study on metropolitan leadership for the Committee for Economic Development.

Jeanne Lowe was graduated from Vassar College and is a resident of New York City.